Ancient Letters and
the New Testament

Ancient Letters and the New Testament

A Guide to Context and Exegesis

Hans-Josef Klauck

With the collaboration of Daniel P. Bailey

B

Baylor University Press
Waco, Texas

Translated from *Die antike Briefliteratur und das Neue Testament: Ein Lehr-
und Arbeitsbuch* / Hans-Josef Klauck © 1998 Verlag Ferdinand Schöningh,
Paderborn, Germany, with revisions and additions for the English edition.
Translated and edited by Daniel P. Bailey.

Book Design: Diane Smith
Cover Design: Pamela Poll
Cover Image: "Letter from Apion" from an Egyptian soldier in the Roman
   navy to his father. Staatliche Museen zu Berlin, Berlin, Germany. Photo
   Credit: Bildarchiv Preussischer Kulturbesitz/Art Resource, NY
Back Cover Image: Codex Sinaiticus. Used by permission of the British
   Library (Add. 43725 f. 323).
Figure 1: "The Manufacture of Papyrus" from *Der Neue Pauly*, vol. 9
   (2000). Used by permsission.
Figure 2: E. G. Turner, *The Typology of the Early Codex* (Philadelphia:
   University of Pennsylvania Press, 1977) 45. Reprinted by permission of
   the University of Pennsylvania Press.

Library of Congress Cataloging-in-Publication Data

Klauck, Hans-Josef.
 [Antike Briefliteratur und das Neue Testament. English]
 Ancient letters and the New Testament : a guide to context and exegesis /
Hans-Josef Klauck with the collaboration of Daniel P. Bailey.
   p. cm.
 Includes bibliographical references and indexes.
 ISBN-13: 978-1-932792-40-9 (pbk. : alk. paper)
 1. Bible. N.T. Epistles--Language, style--Textbooks. 2. Classical letters--
History and criticism--Textbooks. 3. Letter writing, Classical--Textbooks.
I. Bailey, Daniel P. II. Title.

 BS2635.6.L3K5313 2006
 227'.06--dc22

                      2006020603

Printed in the United States of America on acid-free paper with a
minimum of 30% pcw recycled content.

Contents

Preface

"I think I should understand that better," Alice said very politely, "if I had it written down: but I can't quite follow it as you say it."

– Lewis Carroll, *Alice in Wonderland*, chap. 9

Picking up on an incomplete ancient definition that requires some supplementation, we have grown accustomed to regarding a letter as "half of a dialogue" or as a continuation of a conversation by other means. Recently we have also learned to understand the letter as a speech or sermon, which has been put down in writing only of necessity under the pressure of circumstances. But does the inalienable writtenness of a letter not also have its positive side? The same written form that forces the author to more intense reflection also provides the addressee with opportunities for unhurried reading and interpretive rereading. Just as in Alice's experience, some things that pass us by when we only hear them become easier to understand when we have them before our eyes in writing.

Not only in their main theme but also in their genesis, the following reflections are inextricably bound up in the dialectical relationship of hearing and reading, lecturing, conversing, writing and—hopefully—being read. They have grown out of courses and seminars designed to provide an introduction to the New Testament letters and their ancient literary environment. I can only hope that some spark of the excitement that was not infrequently experienced by those who worked together with me on these materials also comes across to the reader.

The ancient letter-writing handbooks acknowledged among others the epistolary type known as the letter of thanks, and an expression of thanks is one of the stock formulas of the papyrus letters and the letters of Paul; it is therefore all the more fitting at the beginning of a book about letters. This is the English edition of a book that appeared 1998 in German under the title *Die antike Briefliteratur und das Neue Testament: Ein Lehr- und Arbeitsbuch*. It is not a simple translation, but the text of the German edition has been thoroughly revised, updated, and also enlarged. For this I am especially grateful to three persons. Carey C. Newman of Baylor University Press was very enthusiastic about this project from the very beginning and has been instrumental in the realization of this English edition. My research assistant Trevor W. Thompson has transformed and updated the bibliographies. Daniel P. Bailey has done much more than just translating and editing the German text. He has also added explanatory notes on philological and other subjects to the text and the footnotes (which I have approved), and through his careful questioning he has forced me to rethink quite a few points and to improve my argument. It is to be hoped that this makes the book not only better, but especially also more user-friendly for the English-speaking student. To all three of them I extend a deeply felt word of thanks.

Hans-Josef Klauck
The University of Chicago
Divinity School

Abbreviations

Abbreviations for both primary and secondary sources have been taken in the first instance from *The SBL Handbook of Style: For Ancient Near Eastern, Biblical, and Early Christian Studies*, ed. by P. H. Alexander, et al. (Peabody, Mass. 1999). Additional abbreviations have been taken from the *Internationales Abkürzungsverzeichnis für Theologie und Grenzgebiete*, ed. by S. M. Schwertner (Berlin ²1992) or from its equivalent, the *Theologische Realenzyklopädie: Abkürzungsverzeichnis*, ed. by S. M. Schwertner (Berlin ²1994). A few abbreviations have been coined (e.g., *DSSSE*).

Papyrus Citations and Quotations

Quotations from the papyri are taken from the translations in the most accessible text collections as indicated, e.g., Deissmann, *Light from the Ancient East*, Hunt and Edgar, *Select Papyri* (Sel.Pap.), and White, *Light from Ancient Letters* (see Bib. 1 in the General Bibliographies). But modifications have also been introduced, and the absence of a cited source for a papyrus translation often means it has been translated independently (e.g., P.Enteuxis 87 in Exercise 11). The papyri are cited according to the abbreviations in the *Checklist of Editions of Greek, Latin, Demotic, and Coptic Papyri, Ostraca, and Tablets*, ed. by J. F. Oates, et al. (Oakville, Conn. ⁵2001). This list is also available on the Web at http://scriptorium.lib.duke.edu/papyrus/texts/clist.html.

Greek and Latin Writers

Greek and Latin writers of classical antiquity are cited according to the standard abbreviations of their work titles, although the less obvious titles are often written out (see *The SBL Handbook of Style*,

237–63). The quotations follow the LCL, where available, or other translations, as indicated.

General

Aram.	Aramaic
Bib.	Bibliography
col(s).	column(s)
Ep.	*Epistula(e)*, *Epistle(s)*
ET	English translation
FS	Festschrift
Gk.	Greek
Heb.	Hebrew
l., ll.	line(s) in ancient papyrus texts and inscriptions
lit.	literally; literature
MS(S)	manuscript(s)
NF	Neue Folge
no(s).	number(s)
NS	new series
Or.	*Oration(es)*, *Oration(s)*
sec.	section

Bible Texts and Translations

Brenton	L. C. L. Brenton, *The Septuagint Version of the Old Testament, according to the Vatican Text*, Translated into English. London, 1844. Reprinted: *The Septuagint with Apocrypha: Greek and English*. Grand Rapids, 1972
KJV	King James Version
LXX	Septuagint
MT	Masoretic Text
NIV	New International Version
NJB	New Jerusalem Bible
NJPS	*Tanakh: The Holy Scriptures: The New JPS Translation according to the Traditional Hebrew Text*
NRSV	New Revised Standard Version
Rahlfs	A. Rahlfs, *Septuaginta: Id est Vetus Testamentum graece iuxta LXX interpretes*. 2 vols. Stuttgart, 1935
REB	Revised English Bible
RSV	Revised Standard Version

Journals, Monograph Series, and Other Reference Works

AB	Anchor Bible
ABD	*Anchor Bible Dictionary.* Ed. by D. N. Freedman. 6 vols. New York, 1992
ABRL	Anchor Bible Reference Library
AGJU	Arbeiten zur Geschichte des antiken Judentums und des Urchristentums
AJP	*American Journal of Philology*
AnBib	Analecta biblica
ANRW	*Aufstieg und Niedergang der römischen Welt: Geschichte und Kultur Roms im Spiegel der neueren Forschung.* Edited by H. Temporini and W. Haase. Berlin, 1972–
ANTC	Abingdon New Testament Commentaries
APAT	*Die Apokryphen und Pseudepigraphen des Alten Testaments.* Translated and edited by E. Kautzsch. 2 vols. Tübingen, 1900
ATANT	Abhandlungen zur Theologie des Alten und Neuen Testaments
AuA	*Antike und Abendland*
BAW	Die Bibliothek der Alten Welt
BBB	Bonner biblische Beiträge
BBET	Beiträge zur biblischen Exegese und Theologie
BBR	*Bulletin for Biblical Research*
BECNT	Baker Exegetical Commentary on the New Testament
BETL	Bibliotheca ephemeridum theologicarum lovaniensium
BGU	*Aegyptische Urkunden aus den Königlichen Staatlichen Museen zu Berlin, Griechische Urkunden.* 15 vols. Berlin, 1895–1983
BibOr	Biblica et orientalia
BKAT	*Biblischer Kommentar, Altes Testament.* Edited by M. Noth and H. W. Wolff
BKAW	Bibliothek der klassischen Altertumswissenschaften
BKP	Beiträge zur klassischen Philologie
BNP	*Brill's New Pauly: Encyclopedia of the Ancient World.* Edited by H. Cancik, H. Schneider, C. F. Salazar, and D. E. Orton. Leiden, 2002–

BNTC	Black's New Testament Commentary
BSA	Biblioteca di studi antichi
Budé	Collection des universités de France
BWANT	Beiträge zur Wissenschaft vom Alten und Neuen Testament
ByzZ	*Byzantinische Zeitschrift*
BZ	*Biblische Zeitschrift*
BZAW	Beihefte zur Zeitschrift für die alttestamentliche Wissenschaft
BZNW	Beihefte zur Zeitschrift für die neutestamentliche Wissenschaft
CBQ	*Catholic Biblical Quarterly*
CBQMS	Catholic Biblical Quarterly Monograph Series
CGLC	Cambridge Greek and Latin Classics
CJ	*Classical Journal*
ConBNT	Coniectanea neotestamentica or Coniectanea biblica: New Testament Series
CP	*Classical Philology*
CPJ	*Corpus papyrorum Judaicarum*. Edited by V. Tcherikover. 3 vols. Cambridge, Mass. 1957–1964
CQ	*Classical Quarterly*
CSG	Collana di studi greci
CTJ	*Calvin Theological Journal*
CurBS	*Currents in Research: Biblical Studies*
DDBDP	Duke Databank of Documentary Papyri (available at www.perseus.tufts.edu)
DJD	Discoveries in the Judaean Desert
DNP	*Der neue Pauly: Enzyklopädie der Antike*. Edited by H. Cancik and H. Schneider. Stuttgart, 1996–2003
DSSSE	*The Dead Sea Scrolls Study Edition*. By F. García Martínez and E. J. C. Tigchelaar. 2 vols. Leiden and New York, 1997–1998; revised, 2000
dtv	Deutscher Taschenbuch-Verlag
EBib	Études bibliques
ECC	Eerdmans Critical Commentary
EdF	Erträge der Forschung
EKKNT	Evangelisch-katholischer Kommentar zum Neuen Testament

ETS	Erfurter theologische Studien
EvQ	*Evangelical Quarterly*
FB	Forschung zur Bibel
FC	Fathers of the Church
FF	Foundations and Facets
FRLANT	Forschungen zur Religion und Literatur des Alten und Neuen Testament
GBS	Guides to Biblical Scholarship
GCS	Die griechische christliche Schriftsteller der ersten [drei] Jahrhunderte
GNS	Good News Studies
GRBS	*Greek, Roman, and Byzantine Studies*
GTA	Göttinger theologische Arbeiten
HBS	Herders Biblische Studien
HNT	Handbuch zum Neuen Testament
HNTC	Harper's New Testament Commentaries
HTKNT	Herders theologischer Kommentar zum Neuen Testament
HTR	*Harvard Theological Review*
HTS	Harvard Theological Studies
HUCA	*Hebrew Union College Annual*
HUT	Hermeneutische Untersuchungen zur Theologie
HvTSt	*Hervormde teologiese studies*
ICC	International Critical Commentary
IEJ	*Israeli Exploration Journal*
Int	*Interpretation*
JAC	Jahrbuch für Antike und Christentum
JAOS	*Journal of the American Oriental Society*
JBL	*Journal of Biblical Literature*
JDS	Judean Desert Studies
JETS	*Journal of the Evangelical Theological Society*
JHS	*Journal of Hellenic Studies*
JJS	*Journal of Jewish Studies*
JQR	*Jewish Quarterly Review*
JR	*The Journal of Religion*
JRS	*Journal of Roman Studies*
JSRHZ	Jüdische Schriften aus hellenistisch-römischer Zeit
JSJ	*Journal for the Study of Judaism in the Persian, Hellenistic, and Roman Periods*

JSJSup	Supplements to the Journal for the Study of Judaism
JSNT	*Journal for the Study of the New Testament*
JSNTSup	Journal for the Study of the New Testament: Supplement Series
JSP	*Journal for the Study of the Pseudepigrapha*
JSPSup	Journal for the Study of the Pseudepigrapha: Supplement Series
JTS	*Journal of Theological Studies*
JTSA	*Journal of Theology of South Africa*
KEK	Kritisch-exegetischer Kommentar über das Neue Testament
KlPauly	*Der kleine Pauly*
LAW	*Lexikon der Alten Welt*
LB	*Linguistica Biblica*
LCL	Loeb Classical Library
LD	Lectio divina
LEC	Library of Early Chrsistianity
LEH	J. Lust, E. Eynikel, K. Hauspie, *Greek-English Lexicon of the Septuagint*. Rev. ed. Stuttgart, 2003
LSJ	Liddell, H. G., R. Scott, H. S. Jones, *A Greek-English Lexicon*. 9th ed. with revised supplement. Oxford, 1996
MdB	Le Monde de la Bible
MGWJ	*Monatschrift für Geschichte und Wissenschaft des Judentums*
MH	*Museum Helveticum*
MThSt	Marburger theologische Studien
NEchtB	Neue Echter Bibel
Neot	*Neotestamentica*
NewDocs	*New Documents Illustrating Early Christianity*. Edited by G. H. R. Horsley and S. Llewelyn. North Ryde, N.S.W., 1981–
NHC	Nag Hammadi Codex
NIB	*The New Interpreter's Bible*
NICNT	New International Commentary on the New Testament
NIGTC	New International Greek Testament Commentary
NJPP	*Neue Jahrbücher für Philologie und Pädagogik*

NovT	*Novum Testamentum*
NovTSup	Novum Testamentum Supplements
NPNF[1]	Nicene and Post-Nicene Fathers, Series 1
NPNF[2]	Nicene and Post-Nicene Fathers, Series 2
NTA	Neutestamentliche Abhandlungen
NTG	New Testament Guides
NTL	The New Testament Library
NTOA	Novum Testamentum et Orbis Antiquus
NTR	New Testament Readings
NTS	*New Testament Studies*
OCD[3]	*Oxford Classical Dictionary.* Edited by S. Hornblower and A. Spawforth. 3d ed. Oxford, 1996; rev. 2003
OCT	Oxford Classical Texts/Scriptorum classicorum bibliotheca oxoniensis
OGIS	*Orientis graecae inscriptiones selectae.* Edited by W. Dittenberger. 2 vols. Leipzig, 1903–1905
ÖTBK	Ökumenischer Taschenbuch-Kommentar
OTP	*Old Testament Pseudepigrapha.* Edited by J. H. Charlesworth. 2 vols. New York, 1983
PG	*Patrologia Graeca.* Edited by J.-P. Migne. 162 vols. Paris, 1857–1886
PGM	*Papyri graecae magicae: Die griechischen Zauberpapyri.* Edited by K. Preisendanz. Berlin, 1928
PSI	*Papiri greci e latini (Pubblicazioni della Società Italiana par la ricerca dei papiri greci e latini in Egitto).* 14 vols. Firenze 1912–1957
PTMS	Pittsburgh Theological Monograph Series
PVTG	Pseudepigrapha Veteris Testamenti Graece
RAC	*Reallexikon für Antike und Christentum*
RB	*Revue biblique*
RMP	*Rheinisches Museum für Philologie*
RNT	Regensburger Neues Testament
RevQ	*Revue de Qumran*
SAQ	Sammlung ausgewählter kirchen- und dogmengeschichtlicher Quellenschriften
SBB	Stuttgarter biblische Beiträge
SBLDS	Society of Biblical Literature Dissertation Series
SBLMS	Society of Biblical Literature Monograph Series

SBLSBS	Society of Biblical Literature Sources for Biblical Study
SBLSP	*Society of Biblical Literature Seminar Papers*
SBLTT	Society of Biblical Literature Texts and Translations
SBLWAW	Society of Biblical Literature Writings from the Ancient World
SBS	Stuttgarter Bibelstudien
SC	Sources chrétiennes. Paris: Cerf, 1943–
SD	Studies and Documents
Sel.Pap.	*Select Papyri*. Edited by A. S. Hunt and C. C. Edgar. 2 vols. LCL. London and New York, 1932–1934
SIG[3]	*Sylloge inscriptionum graecarum*. Edited by W. Dittenberger. 4 vols. 3d ed. Leipzig, 1915–1924
SKK.AT	Stuttgarter kleiner Kommentar: Altes Testament
SKP	Studien zur klassischen Philologie
SNTSMS	Society for New Testament Studies Monograph Series
SNTU	*Studien zum Neuen Testament und seiner Umwelt*
SNTW	Studies of the New Testament and Its World
SP	Sacra Pagina
SQAW	Schriften und Quellen der Alten Welt
StPB	Studia post-biblica
SubBi	*Subsidia biblica*
SUNT	Studien zur Umwelt des Neuen Testaments
TANZ	Texte und Arbeiten zum neutestamentlichen Zeitalter
TB	Theologische Bücherei: Neudrucke und Berichte aus dem 20. Jahrhundert
Teubner	Bibliotheca scriptorum graecorum et romanorum teubneriana
THKNT	Theologischer Handkommentar zum Neuen Testament
TLG	*Thesaurus Linguae Graecae*
TLZ	*Theologische Literaturzeitung*
TRE	*Theologische Realenzyklopädie*. Edited by G. Krause and G. Müller. Berlin, 1977–
TRu	*Theologische Rundschau*

TSAJ	Texte und Studien zum antiken Judentum
TU	Texte und Untersuchungen
TuscBü	Tusculum-Bücherei
TynBul	*Tyndale Bulletin*
UNT	Untersuchungen zum Neuen Testament
UPZ	*Urkunden der Ptolemäerzeit (ältere Funde)*. Edited by U. Wilcken. 2 vols. in 4. Berlin, 1927–1957
UTB	Uni-Taschenbücher
WBC	Word Biblical Commentary
WdF	Wege der Forschung
WUNT	Wissenschaftliche Untersuchungen zum Neuen Testament
ZAC	*Zeitschrift für Antikes Christentum*
ZBK	Zürcher Bibelkommentare
ZNW	*Zeitschrift für die neutestamentliche Wissenschaft und die Kunde der älteren Kirche*

General Bibliographies

1. Text Collections

Bardt, C. *Römische Charakterköpfe in Briefen, vornehmlich aus caesarischer und trajanischer Zeit.* Leipzig 1913.

Brooke, D. *Private Letters, Pagan and Christian: An Anthology of Greek and Roman Private Letters from the Fifth Century before Christ to the Fifth Century of Our Era.* London 1929.

Burnet, R. *L'Égypte ancienne à travers le papyrus.* Paris 2003.

Büttner, H. *Griechische Privatbriefe.* Mitteilungen aus der Papyrussammlung der Giessener Universitätsbibliothek 3. Giessen 1931.

Chapa, J. *Letters of Condolence in Greek Papyri.* Papyrologica Florentina 29. Florence 1998.

Costa, C. D. N. *Greek Fictional Letters: A Selection with Introduction, Translation, and Commentary.* Oxford 2001.

Cugusi, P. *Corpus epistularum Latinarum: Papyris Tabulis Ostracis servatarum.* 2 vols. Papyrologica Florentina 23. Florence 1992.

Daum, G. *Griechische Papyrus-Briefe aus einem Jahrtausend antiker Kultur.* Schöninghs Griechische Lesehefte 2. Paderborn 1959.

Deissmann, A. *Bibelstudien: Beiträge, zumeist aus den Papyri und Inschriften, zur Geschichte der Sprache, des Schrifttums und der Religion des hellenistischen Judentums und des Urchristentums.* Marburg 1895; repr. Hildesheim 1977. Esp. 187–252: "Prolegomena zu den biblischen Briefen und Episteln."

———. *Licht vom Osten: Das Neue Testament und die neuentdeckten Texte der hellenistisch-römischen Welt.* Tübingen ⁴1923 (¹1908). Esp. 116–213.

———. *Bible Studies: Contributions Chiefly from Papyri and Inscriptions to the History of the Language, the Literature, and the*

Religion of Hellenistic Judaism and Primitive Christianity. Translated by Alexander Grieve. Edinburgh 1901; repr. Peabody, Mass. 1988. Esp. 1–60.

_____. *Light from the Ancient East: The New Testament Illustrated by Recently Discovered Texts of the Graeco-Roman World*. Translated by Lionel R. M. Strachan. Revised ed. New York ²1927 (¹1910). Esp. 149–227: "A Series of Twenty-Six Ancient Letters (from Originals), representative of Non-Literary Writing."

Helbing, R. *Auswahl aus griechischen Papyri*. Sammlung Göschen 625. Berlin and Leipzig 1912.

Hengstl, J. *Griechische Papyri aus Ägypten als Zeugnisse des öffentlichen und privaten Lebens*. TuscBü. Munich 1978.

Hercher, R. *Epistolographi graeci*. Paris 1873; repr. Amsterdam 1965.

Hofmann, M. *Antike Briefe*. TuscBü. Munich 1935.

Hunt, A. S. and C. C. Edgar. *Select Papyri I–II*. LCL. 1932–1934.

Malherbe, A. J. *The Cynic Epistles: A Study Edition*. SBLSBS 12. Missoula 1977.

Milligan, G. *Selections from the Greek Papyri*. Cambridge 1910.

Naldini, M. *Il Cristianesimo in Egitto: Lettere private nei papiri di secoli II–IV*. New expanded edition. Biblioteca Patristica 32. Fiesole 1998.

Rosenmeyer, P. A. *Ancient Greek Literary Letters: Selections in Translations*. Routledge Classical Translations. London and New York 2006.

Rüdiger, H. *Briefe des Altertums*. BAW. Zürich ²1965.

Schubart, W. *Ein Jahrtausend am Nil: Briefe aus dem Altertum*. Berlin ²1923.

Trapp, M. *Greek and Latin Letters: An Anthology with Translation*. CGLC. Cambridge 2003.

White, J. L. *Light from Ancient Letters*. FF. Philadelphia 1986.

Wilcken, U. *Grundzüge und Chrestomathie der Papyruskunde*. Vol. I: *Historischer Teil. II. Hälfte: Chrestomathie*. Leipzig 1912; repr. Hildesheim 1963.

Witkowski, S. *Epistulae privatae graecae quae in papyris aetatis Lagidarum servantur*. Teubner. Leipzig ²1911.

2. The Greco-Roman Letter

Buzón, R. "Die Briefe der Ptolemäerzeit: Ihre Struktur und ihre Formeln." Diss. Heidelberg 1984.

Cavarzere, A. "Caro amico ti scrivo. 'Privato' e 'pubblico' nella letteratura epistolare di Roma." In A. Chemello, ed., *Alla Lettera: Teorie e pratiche epistolari dai Greci al Novecento*. Milan 1998. 11–31.

Cribiore, R. "Windows on a Woman's World: Some Letters from Roman Egypt." In A. Lardinois and L. McClure, eds., *Making Silence Speak: Women's Voices in Greek Literature and Society*. Princeton 2001. 223–39.

Cugusi, P. *Evoluzione e forme dell'epistolografia latina nella tarda repubblica e nei primi due secoli dell'impero con cenni sull'epistolografia preciceroniana*. Rome 1983.

————. "L'epistolografia: Modelli e tipologie di communicazione." In G. Cavallo, P. Fedeli, and A. Giardina, eds., *Lo spazio letterario di Roma antica*, vol. 2: *La circolazione del testo*. Rome 1989. 379–419.

Döllstädt, W. "Griechische Papyrusprivatbriefe in gebildeter Sprache aus den ersten vier Jahrhunderten nach Christus." Diss. Borna-Leipzig 1934.

Dziatzko, K. "Brief." *Paulys Realencyclopädie der classischen Altertumswissenschaft* 3 (1897) 836–43.

Exler, F. X. J. *The Form of the Ancient Greek Letter: A Study in Greek Epistolography*. Washington 1923; repr. Eugene, Ore. 2003.

Gauger, J.-D. *Authentizität und Methode: Untersuchungen zum historischen Wert des persisch-griechischen Herrscherbriefs in literarischer Tradition*. Studien zur Geschichtsforschung des Altertums 6. Hamburg 2000.

Goldstein, J. A. *The Letters of Demosthenes*. New York and London 1968.

Hout, M. J. P. van den. "Studies in Early Greek Letter Writing." *Mnemosyne* 4 ser., vol. 2 (1949) 18–41, 138–53.

Koskenniemi, H. *Studien zur Idee und Phraseologie des griechischen Briefes bis 400 n.Chr.* Suomalaisen Tiedeakatemian toimituksia. Sarja B 102.2. Helsinki 1956.

Luschnig, C. A. E. *Latin Letters: Reading Roman Correspondence*. Newburyport, Mass. 2005.

Malherbe, A. J. *Ancient Epistolary Theorists.* SBLSBS 19. Atlanta 1988.

Monaco, G. "L'epistola nel teatro antico." *Dioniso* 39 (1965) 334–51.

Olsson, B. *Papyrusbriefe aus der frühesten Römerzeit.* Uppsala 1925.

Roberts, W. *History of Letter-Writing from the Earliest Period to the Fifth Century.* London 1843.

Rosenmeyer, P. A. *Ancient Epistolary Fictions: The Letter in Greek Literature.* Cambridge 2001. See also the review by H. J. Klauck in *BZ* 46 (2002) 274–75.

Salles, C. "L'épistolographie hellénistique et romaine." In J. Schlosser, ed., *Paul de Tarse: Congrès de L'ACFEB (Strasbourg, 1995).* LD 165. Paris 1996. 79–97.

Schmidt, P. L. "Epistolographie." *KlPauly* 2 (1967) 324–27.

Schneider, J. "Brief." *RAC* 2 (1954) 564–85.

Sebaste, B. *Lettere e Filosofia: Poetica dell'epistolarità.* Materiali per la storia dell'estetica 43. Florence 1998.

Seeck, O. "Der antike Briefe." *Deutsche Rundschau* 133 (1907) 55–70.

Stirewalt, M. L., Jr. *Studies in Ancient Greek Epistolography.* SBL Resources for Biblical Study 27. Atlanta 1993.

Stowers, S. K. *Letter Writing in Greco-Roman Antiquity.* LEC 5. Philadelphia 1986.

Suárez de la Torre, E. "La epistolografía griega." *Estudios clásicos* 23 (1979) 19–46.

Sykutris, J. "Epistolographie." *Paulys Realencyclopädie der classischen Altertumswissenschaft,* Supplementband 5 (1931) 185–220.

Thraede, K. *Grundzüge griechisch-römischer Brieftopik.* Zetemata 48. Munich 1970.

Tibiletti, G. *Le lettere private nei papiri greci del III e IV secolo d.C.: Tra paganesimo e cristianesimo.* Scienze filologiche e letteratura 15. Milan 1979.

White, J. L. *The Form and Function of the Body of the Greek Letter: A Study of the Letter-Body in the Non-Literary Papyri and in Paul the Apostle.* SBLDS 2. Missoula 1972.

———. *The Form and Structure of the Official Petition: A Study in Greek Epistolography.* SBLDS 5. Missoula 1972.

———. "The Greek Documentary Letter Tradition Third Century B.C.E. to Third Century C.E." *Semeia* 22 (1981–1982) 89–106.

_____. "Ancient Greek Letters." In D. E. Aune, ed., *Greco-Roman Literature and the New Testament: Selected Forms and Genres*. SBLSBS 21. Atlanta 1988. 85–105.

White, J. L., ed. *Studies in Ancient Letter Writing*. Semeia 22. Chico, Calif. 1982.

Winter, J. G. *Life and Letters in the Papyri*. University of Michigan Studies: The Jerome Lectures. Ann Arbor 1933.

Zelzer, M. "Die Briefliteratur." In L. J. Engels and H. Hofmann, eds., *Spätantike*. Neues Handbuch der Literaturwissenschaft 4. Wiesbaden 1997. 321–53.

Zilliacus, H. *Zur Sprache griechischer Familienbriefe des III. Jahrhunderts n.Chr. (P. Michigan 214–221)*. Commentationes Humanarum Litterarum XIII/3. Helsingfors 1943.

3. The Early Jewish Letter

Alexander, P. S. "Epistolary Literature." In M. E. Stone, ed., *Jewish Writings of the Second Temple Period*. Compendia rerum Iudaicarum ad Novum Testamentum 2.2. Assen and Philadelphia 1984. 579–96.

Fitzmyer, J. A. "Some Notes on Aramaic Epistolography." *JBL* 93 (1974) 201–25.

_____. "Aramaic Epistolography." *Semeia* 22 (1981) 25–57.

Pardee, D. *Handbook of Ancient Hebrew Letters*. SBLSBS 15. Chico, Calif. 1982.

Schwiderski, D. *Handbuch des nordwestsemitischen Briefformulars: Ein Beitrag zur Echtheitsfrage der aramäischen Briefe des Esrabuches*. BZAW 195. Berlin 2000.

Taatz, I. *Frühjüdische Briefe: Die paulinischen Briefe im Rahmen der offiziellen religiösen Briefe des Frühjudentums*. NTOA 16. Göttingen 1991.

4. The Early Christian Letter

Andresen, C. "Zum Formular frühchristlicher Gemeindebriefe." *ZNW* 56 (1965) 233–59.

Arzt-Grabner, P. *Philemon*. Papyrologische Kommentare zum Neuen Testament 1. Göttingen 2003.

Aune, D. E. *The New Testament and Its Literary Environment*. LEC 8. Philadelphia 1987. 158–225.

_____. *The Westminster Dictionary of New Testament and Early Christian Literature and Rhetoric*. Louisville and London 2003.

Bahr, G. J. "Paul and Letter Writing in the First Century." *CBQ* 28 (1966) 465–77.

_____. "The Subscriptions in the Pauline Letters." *JBL* 87 (1968) 27–41.

Berger, K. "Apostelbrief und apostolische Rede: Zum Formular frühchristlicher Briefe." *ZNW* 65 (1974) 190–231.

Bjerkelund, C. J. *PARAKALÔ: Form, Funktion und Sinn der parakalô-Sätze in den paulinischen Briefen*. Bibliotheca theologica Norvegica 1. Oslo 1967.

Burnet, R. *Épîtres et lettres, Iʳ–IIᵉ siècle: De Paul de Tarse à Polycarpe de Smyrne*. LD 192. Paris 2003.

Delorme, J. "Une pratique de lecture et d'analyse des lettres du Nouveau Testament. " In L. Panier, ed., *Les lettres dans la Bible* (Bib. 4) 15–44.

Del Verme, M. *Le formule di ringraziamento post-protocollari nell'epistolario paolino*. Presenza 5. Rome 1971.

Doty, W. G. *Letters in Primitive Christianity*. GBS. New Testament Series. Philadelphia ³1979.

Funk, R. W. *Language, Hermeneutic, and Word of God: The Problem of Language in the New Testament and Contemporary Theology*. New York 1966. 224–305.

_____. *Parables and Presence: Forms of the New Testament Tradition*. Philadelphia 1982. 81–110.

Gamble, H. J. "Letters in the New Testament and in the Greco-Roman World." In J. Barton, ed., *The Biblical World*. Vol. 1. London and New York 2002. 188–204.

Karrer, M. *Die Johannesoffenbarung als Brief: Studien zu ihrem literarischen, historischen und theologischen Ort*. FRLANT 140. Göttingen 1986.

Lohmeyer, E. "Briefliche Grußüberschriften." *ZNW* 26 (1927) 158–73. Reprinted in idem, *Probleme paulinischer Theologie*. Stuttgart 1955. 7–29.

Müller, M. *Vom Schluß zum Ganzen: Zur Bedeutung des paulinischen Briefkorpusabschlusses*. FRLANT 172. Göttingen 1997.

Mullins, T. Y. "Petition as a Literary Form." *NovT* 5 (1962) 46–54.

_____. "Disclosure: A Literary Form in the New Testament." *NovT* 7 (1964–1965) 44–50.

_____. "Greeting as a New Testament Form." *JBL* 87 (1968) 418–26.

_____. "Formulas in New Testament Epistles." *JBL* 91 (1972) 380–90.

_____. "Visit Talk in New Testament Letters." *CBQ* 35 (1973) 350–58.

_____. "Benediction as a Form." *Andrews University Seminary Studies* 15 (1977) 59–64.

Murphy-O'Connor, J. *Paul the Letter-Writer: His World, His Options, His Skills.* GNS 41. Collegeville 1995.

O'Brien, P. T. *Introductory Thanksgivings in the Letters of Paul.* NovTSup 49. Leiden 1977.

Olson, S. N. "Epistolary Uses of Expressions of Self-Confidence." *JBL* 103 (1984) 585–97.

_____. "Pauline Expressions of Confidence in His Addresses." *CBQ* 47 (1985) 282–95.

Panier, L., ed. *Les lettres dans la Bible et dans la littérature: Actes du colloque du Lyon, 3–5 juillet 1996.* LD 181. Paris 1999.

Peterson, E. "Das Praescriptum des 1. Clemens-Briefes." In idem, *Frühkirche, Judentum und Gnosis: Studien und Untersuchungen.* Freiburg 1959; repr. Darmstadt 1982. 129–36.

Richards, E. R. *The Secretary in the Letters of Paul.* WUNT 2/42. Tübingen 1991.

_____. *Paul and First-Century Letter Writing: Secretaries, Composition and Collection.* Downers Grove, Ill. 2004.

Roller, O. *Das Formular der paulinischen Briefe: Ein Beitrag zur Lehre vom antiken Briefe.* BWANT 58. Stuttgart 1933.

Sanders, J. T. "The Transition from Opening Epistolary Thanksgiving to Body in the Letters of the Pauline Corpus." *JBL* 81 (1962) 348–62.

Schnider, F. and W. Stenger. *Studien zum neutestamentlichen Briefformular.* New Testament Tools and Studies 11. Leiden 1987.

Schoon-Janssen, J. *Umstrittene "Apologien" in den Paulusbriefen: Studien zur rhetorischen Situation des 1. Thessalonicherbriefes, des Galaterbriefes und des Philipperbriefes.* GTA 45. Göttingen 1991.

Schubert, P. *Form and Function of the Pauline Thanksgivings.* BZNW 20. Berlin 1939.

Stirewalt, M. L., Jr. *Paul, the Letter Writer.* Grand Rapids 2003.

Vouga, F. "Der Brief als Form der apostolischen Autorität." In K. Berger, F. Vouga, M. Wolter, and D. Zeller, eds., *Studien und Texte zur Formgeschichte*. TANZ 7. Tübingen 1992. 7–58.

Weima, J. A. D. *Neglected Endings: The Significance of the Pauline Letter Closings*. JSNTSup 101. Sheffield 1994.

Wendland, P. *Die urchristlichen Literaturformen*. HNT I/3. Tübingen ³1912. 342–81.

White, J. L. "Introductory Formulae in the Body of the Pauline Letter." *JBL* 90 (1971) 91–97.

_____. "Saint Paul and the Apostolic Letter Tradition." *CBQ* 45 (1983) 433–44.

_____. "New Testament Epistolary Literature in the Framework of Ancient Epistolography." *ANRW* II.25.2 (1984) 1730–56.

Wiles, G. P. *Paul's Intercessory Prayers: The Significance of the Intercessory Prayer Passages in the Letters of St Paul*. SNTSMS 24. Cambridge 1974.

5. Ancient Rhetoric

Anderson, R. D., Jr. *Ancient Rhetorical Theory and Paul*. Contributions to Biblical Exegesis and Theology 18. Rev. edn. Kampen 1999.

Eisenhut, W. *Einführung in die antike Rhetorik und ihre Geschichte*. Altertumswissenschaft. Darmstadt ⁵1994.

Fuhrmann, M. *Die antike Rhetorik: Eine Einführung*. Munich ⁴1995.

Göttert, K. H. *Einführung in die Rhetorik: Grundbegriffe, Geschichte, Rezeption*. UTB 1599. Munich 1991.

Habinek, T. *Ancient Rhetoric and Oratory*. Malden, Mass. 2005.

Hommel, H. "Griechische Rhetorik und Beredsamkeit." In E. Vogt, ed., *Griechische Literatur*. Neues Handbuch der Literaturwissenschaft 2. Wiesbaden 1981. 337–76.

Kennedy, G. A. *The Art of Rhetoric in the Roman World: 300 B.C.–A.D. 300*. Princeton 1972.

Lausberg, H. *Handbook of Literary Rhetoric: A Foundation for Literary Study*. Translated by M. T. Bliss, A. Jansen, and D. E. Orton. Edited by D. E. Orton and R. D. Anderson. Leiden 1998.

Martin, J. *Antike Rhetorik: Technik und Methode*. Handbuch der Altertumswissenschaft II/3. Munich 1974.

Ottmers, C. *Rhetorik*. Sammlung Metzler 283. Stuttgart 1996.

Plett, H. F. *Einführung in die rhetorische Textanalyse*. Hamburg ⁹2001.

Porter, S. E., ed. *Handbook of Classical Rhetoric in the Hellenistic Period, 330 B.C.–A.D. 400*. Leiden 1997.

Porter, S. E. and T. H. Olbricht, eds. *Rhetoric and the New Testament: Essays from the 1992 Heidelberg Conference*. JSNTSup 90. Sheffield 1993.

————. *Rhetoric, Scripture and Theology: Essays from the 1994 Pretoria Conference*. JSNTSup 131. Sheffield 1996.

Ueding, G. and B. Steinbrink. *Grundriß der Rhetorik: Geschichte – Technik – Methode*. Stuttgart 1986.

Volkmann, R. *Die Rhetorik der Griechen und Römer in systematischer Übersicht*. Leipzig ²1885; repr. Hildesheim 1963.

Watson, D. F., ed. *Persuasive Artistry: Studies in New Testament Rhetoric in Honor of George A. Kennedy*. JSNTSup 50. Sheffield 1991.

Watson, D. F. and A. J. Hauser. *Rhetorical Criticism of the Bible: A Comprehensive Bibliography with Notes on History and Method*. Biblical Interpretation Series 4. Leiden 1994.

6. Papyrology

Montevecchi, O. *La papirologia*. Manuali universitari. Turin 1973; Milan ²1988.

Oates, J. F., R. S. Bagnall, W. H. Willis, and A. Worp, eds. *Checklist of Editions of Greek, Latin, Demotic, and Coptic Papyri, Ostraca, and Tablets*. Bulletin of the American Society of Papyrologists Supplement 9. Oakville, Conn. ⁵2001.

Pestman, P. W. *The New Papyrological Primer*. Leiden 1990.

Rupprecht, H. A. *Kleine Einführung in die Papyruskunde*. Die Altertumswissenschaft. Darmstadt 1994.

Schubart, W. *Einführung in die Papyruskunde*. Berlin 1918; repr. 1980.

Turner, E. G. *Greek Papyri: An Introduction*. Princeton 1968.

7. Other Literature

Berger, K. "Hellenistische Gattungen im Neuen Testament."
ANRW II.25.2 (1984) 1031–1432, 1831–85, esp. 1326–63.

Bieringer, R., ed. *The Corinthian Correspondence.* BETL 125.
Löwen 1996.

Dormeyer, D. *Das Neue Testament im Rahmen der antiken
Literaturgeschichte. Eine Einführung.* Die Altertumswissenschaft. Darmstadt 1993. 190–98.

_____. *The New Testament among the Writings of Antiquity.* (ET
of Dormeyer, *Das Neue Testament.*) Translated by R. Kossou.
Sheffield 1998. 205–13.

Kertelge, K., ed. *Paulus in den neutestamentlichen Spätschriften: Zur
Paulusrezeption im Neuen Testament.* Quaestiones disputatae 89.
Freiburg 1981.

Klauck, H. J. *The Religious Context of Early Christianity: A Guide to
Graeco-Roman Religion.* Translated by B. McNeil. Edinburgh
2000; paperback ed. Minneapolis 2003.

Reck, R. *Kommunikation und Gemeindeaufbau: Eine Studie zu
Entstehung, Leben und Wachstum paulinischer Gemeinden in den
Kommunikationsstrukturen der Antike.* SBB 22. Stuttgart 1991.

Schnelle, U. *Einleitung in das Neue Testament.* UTB 1830.
Göttingen ⁵2005.

_____. *The History and Theology of the New Testament.* (ET of
Schnelle, *Einleitung.*) Translated by M. Eugene Boring.
Minneapolis, Minn. 1998.

Strecker, G. *Literaturgeschichte des Neuen Testaments.* UTB 1682.
Göttingen 1992. 56–121.

List of Bibliographies

List of Exercises

Introduction

Bibliography 8: **J. G. Altman**, *Epistolarity: Approaches to a Form* (Columbus 1982). – **J. Anderegg**, *Schreibe mir oft! Zum Medium Brief zwischen 1750 und 1830* (Göttingen 2001). – **T. O. Beebee**, *Epistolary Fiction in Europe, 1500–1850* (Cambridge 1999). – **H. Belke**, "Die Multi-funktionalität einer literarischen Gebrauchsform am Beispiel des Briefes," in idem, *Literarische Gebrauchsformen*, Grundstudium Literaturwissenschaft 9 (Düsseldorf 1973) 142–57. – **P. Bürgel**, "Der Privatbrief: Entwurf eines heuristischen Modells," *Deutsche Vierteljahresschrift für Literaturwissenschaft und Geistesgeschichte* 50 (1976) 281–97. – **K. Ermert**, *Briefsorten: Untersuchungen zu Theorie und Empirie der Textklassifikation*, Germanistische Linguistik 20 (Tübingen 1979). – **R. B. Essig**, *Der offene Brief: Geschichte und Funktion einer publizistischen Form von Isokrates bis Günther Grass* (Würzburg 2000). – **J. How**, *Epistolary Spaces: English Letter Writing from the Foundation of the Post Office to Richardson's Clarissa*, Studies in Early Modern English Literature (Aldershot, Hants, England and Burlington, Vt. 2003). – **P. von Matt**, "Wer hat Robert Walsers Briefe geschrieben?" in idem, *Das Schicksal der Phantasie: Studien zur deutschen Literatur* (Munich 1994) 313–20. – **R. M. G. Nickisch**, *Brief*, Sammlung Metzler 260 (Stuttgart 1991). – **E. Pankow**, *Brieflichkeit: Revolutionen eines Sprachbildes* (Munich 2002). – **O. Seidlin**, "Schillers 'Trügerische Zeichen': Die Funktion der Briefe in seinen frühen Dramen," in idem, *Von Goethe zu Thomas Mann: Zwölf Versuche*, Kleine Vandenhoeck-Reihe 170S (Göttingen ²1969) 94–119. – idem, "Coda: Eine Brief-Interpretation," in idem, *Klassische und moderne Klassiker: Goethe – Brentano – Eichendorff – Gerhart Hauptmann – Thomas Mann*, Kleine Vandenhoeck-Reihe 355S (Göttingen 1972) 127–37. – **T. Van Houdt**, et al., eds., *Self-Presentation and Social Identification: The Rhetoric and Pragmatics of Letter Writing in Early Modern Times*, Supplementa Humanistica Lovaniensia 18 (Leuven 2002). – **F. J. Worstbrock**, ed., *Der Brief im Zeitalter der Renaissance*, Mitteilung IX der Kommission für Humanismusforschung, Acta humaniora (Weinheim 1983).

1

Charles Dickens's first novel, which immediately made him a literary sensation, was *The Pickwick Papers*, first published serially from 1836 to 1837 under the pseudonym Boz[1] and in book form in 1837. At the beginning of chapter 37 we find the following scene:[2]

> "Mr. Weller," said Mrs. Craddock, upon the morning of this very eventful day, "here's a letter for you."
> "Wery odd that," said Sam, "I'm afeerd there must be somethin' the matter, for I don't recollect any gen'lm'n in my circle of acquaintance as is capable o' writin' one."
> "Perhaps something uncommon has taken place," observed Mrs. Craddock.
> "It must be somethin' wery uncommon indeed, as could perduce a letter out o' any friend o' mine," replied Sam, shaking his head dubiously; "nothin' less than a nat'ral conwulsion, as the young gen'lm'n observed ven he wos took with fits. It can't be from the gov-'ner," said Sam, looking at the direction. "He always prints, I know, 'os he learnt writin' from the large bills in the bookin' offices. It's a wery strange thing now, where this here letter can ha' come from." As Sam said this, he did what a great many people do when they are uncertain about the writer of a note,—looked at the seal, and then at the front, and then at the back, and then at the sides, and then at the superscription; and, as a last resource, thought perhaps he might as well look at the inside, and try to find out from that.
> "It's wrote on gilt-edged paper," said Sam, as he unfolded it, "and sealed in bronze vax vith the top of a door-key. Now for it." And, with a very grave face, Mr. Weller slowly read as follows:
>> "A select company of the Bath footmen presents their compliments to Mr. Weller, and requests the pleasure of his company this evening, to a friendly swarry, consisting of a boiled leg of mutton with the usual trimmings. The swarry to be on table at half past nine o'clock punctually."

After such a suspenseful buildup we might be tempted to think the contents of this letter rather disappointing—nothing more than an invitation to dinner with a group of colleagues. But this scene actually portrays very vividly the high value people in the ordinary classes placed on the letter in the early nineteenth century and

---

[1] On the phenomenon of publication and letter writing under a pseudonym see below, chap. 8, sec. B.3.

[2] C. Dickens, *The Pickwick Papers*, ed. J. Kinsley, The World's Classics (Oxford 1988) 464.

what fears and expectations it could occasion. As far as the contents are concerned we see only how little things have changed over the centuries, for the short invitation letter to a festive meal is well known from numerous texts from the second and third centuries CE, as the following two examples show:[3]

P.Oxy. I 110	**P.Oxy. I 111**
Ἐρωτᾷ σε Χαιρήμων δειπνῆ-σαι εἰς κλείνην τοῦ κυρίου Σαρά-πιδος ἐν τῷ Σεραπείῳ αὔριον, ἥτις ἐστὶν ιε', ἀπὸ ὥρας ϑ'.	Ἐρωτᾷ σε Ἡραὶς δειπνῆσαι εἰς γάμους τέκνων αὐτῆς ἐν τῇ οἰκίᾳ αὔριον, ἥτις ἐστὶν πέμπτη, ἀπὸ ὥρας ϑ'.
Chaeremon requests your company at dinner at the table of the lord Sarapis in the Serapaeum tomorrow, the 15th, at 9 o'clock.	Herais requests your company at dinner in celebration of the marriage of her children at her house tomorrow, the 5th, at 9 o'clock.

In an entirely different vein from Dickens that is not at all humorous, Franz Kafka expresses his feelings about letter writing in one of his letters to his girlfriend Milena:[4]

> [Y]ou know after all how I hate letters. All the misfortune of my life . . . derives, one could say, from letters or from the possibility of writing letters. People have hardly ever deceived me, but letters always. . . . The easy possibility of letter-writing must—seen merely theoretically—have brought into the world a terrible disintegration of souls. It is, in fact, an intercourse with ghosts, and not only with the ghost of the recipient but also with one's own ghost which develops between the lines of the letter one is writing and even more so in a series of letters where one letter corroborates the other and can refer to it as a witness. How on earth did anyone get the idea that people can communicate with one another by letter! Of a distant person one can think, and of a person who is near one can catch hold—all else goes beyond human strength. Writing letters, however, means to denude oneself before the ghosts, something for which they greedily wait. Written kisses don't reach their destination, rather they are

---

[3] For additional comparative material and secondary literature see H. J. Klauck, *Religious Context* (Bib. 7) 138–39; cf. further C. H. Kim, "The Papyrus Invitation," *JBL* 94 (1975) 391–402.

[4] F. Kafka, *Briefe an Milena*, ed. W. Haas (New York 1952) 259–60 = ET, *Letters to Milena*, ed. W. Haas, trans. T. and J. Stern (New York 1953) 229.

drunk on the way by the ghosts. It is on this ample nourishment that they multiply so enormously.

Here the basic purpose of letter writing—to facilitate communication between persons separated by distance—is turned on its head. It is no longer persons who experience an exchange with one another through letters, but ghosts, *their* ghosts. For Kafka letters seem to awaken the demons in one's own breast that had better be left asleep.

These examples also show that letters are a theme of literary scholarship (cf. Nickisch). This is not true only for epistolary novels (cf. Altman) such as Samuel Richardson's *Pamela* (1740) and *Clarissa* (1748) or Goethe's *The Sorrows of Young Werther* (1774), nor only for letters interspersed in other narrative works. Nor does it apply only to the correspondence of poets and writers, from which something can naturally be gleaned for their biography or the biographical placement of their works. Even completely ordinary private and business letters have attracted the attention of literary critics as literary forms (cf. Belke). New genres have developed that were not known as such before, such as the letter to the editor or the open letter. The German language also knows for example of a so-called "blue letter" (*Blauer Brief*).[5] This can cover the same range as our English term "pink slip" in that a blue letter can also communicate termination of employment, but usually a blue letter is sent to the parents of school age children, warning that their child might not pass on to the next grade.

Letters can also be useful in the study of social history. Very instructive in this regard are the many letters sent back home to Germany or Switzerland from emigrants to North America in the nineteenth century. These also provide something relevant for our purposes, because here we unexpectedly encounter the New Testament letters. I quote from Nickisch's monograph (209–10):[6]

---

[5] According to the German version of the Wikipedia online encyclopedia, "The designation [sc. *Blauer Brief*] comes from the eighteenth century, when officials in Prussia used envelopes made of cheap paper. This paper was made mainly of rags, often from uniforms, which were Prussian blue at the time." The American English term "pink slip" is of more recent origin, from about 1915.

[6] Cf. also the text collection by W. Helbich, W. D. Kamphoefner, and U. Sommer, eds., *Briefe aus Amerika: Deutsche Auswanderer schreiben aus der Neuen Welt 1830–1930* (Munich 1988).

The bulk of the emigrants were tradesmen, small farmers, day laborers, land and industry workers—people who just a few years earlier had still been in school and whose previous contacts with literature were mainly in the form of the Bible, the catechism, the local paper, and the illustrated family calendar with proverbs and sayings. It was their moving new experiences as emigrants that made them into letter writers. . . . Obviously these linguistic productions so laboriously put to paper were not meant for publication; they are anything but "literary." And the helplessness of these untrained Lutheran or Reformed letter writers as they naively took the apostolic letters as their models thanks to their Bible knowledge is almost touching. Nevertheless, these ponderously naive letters of the emigrants had an amazing effect. Their contents and portions of their actual wording caused a great sensation in the village community of the individual who received them privately, and often the whole letter was then circulated, read, and discussed. In this way the letter developed a promotional effect that the writer could scarcely have envisaged.

The last two sentences could almost be applied to the letters of the Apostle Paul. Nickisch moreover points out that the daily newspaper and the scholarly journal also developed from the letter. Newsletters sent home from merchants and diplomats and the correspondence of scholars among themselves that seemed worthy of publication form their nucleus. Nickisch defines the letter as "a substitute for a conversation with the purpose of a dialogical exchange" (12). The characteristic "time lag" of a letter (Nickisch 11; so also Altman 118) is to be seen as that which distinguishes it from other forms of speech. The conversational character is slowed down and mediated by the spatial and temporal distance between the writing of the letter and the act of reading it. This involves a loss of immediacy over against oral communication, but it brings with it a possible gain of deepened reflection on both sides. This is not far from the ancient definition of a letter as "half of a dialogue" (see below chap. 5, sec. A.1).

What the future might hold for the letter in an age of cell phones, fax machines, and email or how its character might be forced to change are questions that can safely be left to others. Instead we turn here to the distant past, to which we have already referred in our present-day reflections. Our attention is devoted to the early Christian epistolary literature in its ancient literary and socio-cultural context, and it is this that will especially occupy our first steps.

As a foundation we will read two short private letters of the Roman soldier Apion to his family in Egypt from the second century CE—letters that not coincidentally have often served as textbook examples. We will analyze their structure and compare it with that of two similarly short letters from the New Testament, namely 2 and 3 John. All the other questions will arise naturally from here. Hence we must go into the practical realities of letter writing (chap. 2) and then study the different manifestations of letter writing in the ancient world. These include recommendation letters, royal letters, and imperial letters (chap. 3), literary letters by Greek and Latin poets and philosophers (chap. 4), and epistolary theory (chap. 5). Unquestionably important for the New Testament is everything we can discern about letters in early Jewish writings (chap. 6). Our overall goal is to arrive at a better understanding of New Testament letter production, to which we devote chapters 7 and 8.

Exercises

1. What conclusion would you draw from the application of the English word "brief" to certain documents, as in the expressions "legal *brief*" or "a *brief* of the proceedings," combined with the fact that the normal German word for a letter (not just a legal letter) is *Brief*, although it should also be noted that German uses a different word for "brief" or "short" (*kurz*)? What is the origin of these words? Make up as many expressions as you can of the form "letter of ____" or "____ letter."

2. Do you think that the historical advancement of the postal service to daily postal delivery has helped letter writing or hurt it? What grounds could there be for the claim that the letter in today's culture has regressed as a literary art form? What do you think of the following statement about the letter form from the year 1962: "It is outmoded; whoever is still capable of it possesses an archaic skill; actually no letters can be written any more. . . . Those that are written have something false about them, because through their gesture of an immediate report letters make a devious claim to naivety"?

3. Attempt to analyze and place the following letter:

Dear Parents,

... The last two years have taught me how little we can get along with. ... When we think how many people every day now lose everything, we really have no right to call anything our own.

Is H.W. actually flying in the East now? And R[enate]'s husband? Thank you very much for your letter. ... I read my letters here till I know them by heart. —Now for a few more requests: unfortunately there were no books handed in here for me today; Commissar Sonderegger would be willing to accept them every now and then. ... I should be very grateful for them. There were no matches, face-cloths, or towel this time. Excuse my mentioning that; everything else was splendid. Could I please have some tooth-paste and a few coffee beans? Dear Father, could you get me from the library *Lienhard* and *Abendstunden eines Einsiedlers* by H. Pestalozzi, *Sozialpädagogik* by P. Natorp, and Plutarch's *Lives of Great Men*?

I am getting on all right. Do keep well. Many thanks for everything.

With fondest love, Your grateful _____.

1

Foundations—Two Letters of Apion and Two Letters of the "Elder"

A. The Text of the Two Letters of Apion

Bibliography 9: Editions and translations (sometimes including commentary): BGU 2 (1898) 84–85 (ed. **P. Viereck**) 297 (ed. **F. Krebs**). – **D. Brooke**, *Letters* (Bib. 1) 93 (only no. 1; reprint of G. Milligan). – **G. Daum**, *Papyrus-Briefe* (Bib. 1) 27–28 (only no. 1). – **A. Deissmann**, *Light from the Ancient East* (Bib. 1) 179–86 (with photograph). – **R. Helbing**, *Auswahl* (Bib. 1) 100–105 (only no. 1). – **J. Hengstl**, *Griechische Papyri* (Bib. 1) 213–15 (only no. 1). – **A. S. Hunt** and **C. C. Edgar**, *Select Papyri* (Bib. 1) 1:304–7 (only no. 1). – **H. Lietzmann**, *Griechische Papyri*, Kleine Texte 14 (Bonn ²1910) 4–5 (only no. 1). – **G. Milligan**, *Selections* (Bib. 1) 90–92 (only no. 1). – **F. Preisigke**, "Familienbriefe aus alter Zeit," *Preußische Jahrbücher* 108 (1902) 88–111, esp. 101–3. – **W. Schubart**, *Jahrtausend* (Bib. 1) 97–99 (only no. 1). – **J. L. White**, *Light from Ancient Letters* (Bib. 1) 159–61. – **U. Wilcken**, *Grundzüge* I/2 (Bib. 1) 565–66 (only no. 1). – **J. G. Winter**, "In the Service of Rome: Letters from the Michigan Collection of Papyri," *CP* 22 (1927) 237–56.

1. The First Letter of Apion (BGU II 423)

> Ἀπίων Ἐπιμάχῳ τῶι πατρὶ καὶ
> κυρίῳ πλεῖστα χαίρειν. Πρὸ μὲν πάν-
> των εὔχομαί σε ὑγιαίνειν καὶ διὰ παντὸς
> ἐρωμένον εὐτυχεῖν μετὰ τῆς ἀδελφῆς
> 5 μου καὶ τῆς θυγατρὸς αὐτῆς καὶ τοῦ ἀδελφοῦ
> μου. Εὐχαριστῶ τῷ κυρίῳ Σεράπιδι,
> ὅτι μου κινδυνεύσαντος εἰς θάλασσαν
> ἔσωσε εὐθέως. Ὅτε εἰσῆλθον εἰς Μη-
> σήνους, ἔλαβα βιατικὸν παρὰ Καίσαρος

10   χρυσοῦς τρεῖς καὶ καλῶς μοί ἐστιν.
       Ἐρωτῶ σε οὖν, κύριέ μου πατήρ,
       γράψον μοι ἐπιστόλιον πρῶτον
       μὲν περὶ τῆς σωτηρίας σου, δεύ-
       τερον περὶ τῆς τῶν ἀδελφῶν μου,

15   τρ[ί]τον, ἵνα σου προσκυνήσω τὴν
       χέραν, ὅτι με ἐπαίδευσας καλῶς
       καὶ ἐκ τούτου ἐλπίζω ταχὺ προκό(μι-)
       σαι τῶν θε[ῶ]ν θελόντων. Ἄσπασαι
       Καιπίτων[α πο]λλὰ καὶ το[ὺς] ἀδελφούς

20   [μ]ου καὶ Σε[ρηνί]λλαν καὶ το[ὺς] φίλους μο[υ].
       Ἔπεμψά σο[ι εἰ]κόνιν μ[ου] διὰ Εὐκτή-
       μονος. Ἔσ[τ]ι [δέ] μου ὄνομα Ἀντῶνις Μά-
       ξιμος   Ἐρρῶσθαί σε εὔχομαι.
            Κεντυρί(α) Ἀθηνονίκη.

In the left margin, perpendicular to the main text (as addendum):

25   Ἀσπάζεταί σε Σερῆνος ὁ τοῦ Ἀγαθοῦ [Δα]ίμονος [καὶ ....]ς
       ὁ τοῦ [...]
       ρος καὶ Τούρβων ὁ τοῦ Γαλλωνίου καὶ Δ[....]νᾶς ὁ τ[οῦ .....]σεν
       [. . .]
       [....]. [...]. [   ]

Verso (outside address):

       ε[ἰς] Φ[ιλ]αδελφίαν Ἐπιμ **X** άχῳ ἀπὸ Ἀπίωνος υἱοῦ.

In the opposite direction (additional address):

       Ἀπόδος εἰς χώρτην πρίμαν **X** Ἀπαμηνῶν Ἰο[υλι]ά[ν]ου Ἀν.[..]
30   λιβλαρίῳ ἀπὸ Ἀπίωνος ὥσ **X** τε Ἐπιμάχῳ πατρὶ αὐτοῦ.

Translation (cf. J. L. White [modified]):

Apion to Epimachos, his father and | lord, very many greetings.

    Before | all else I pray that you are well and that | you may prosper in continual health, together with my sister | [5] and her daughter and my brother. |

    I give thanks to the lord Serapis, | because when I was endangered at sea, | he rescued (me) immediately.

    When I arrived at Mi- | senum, I received as traveling money (*viaticum*) from Caesar | [10] three gold pieces, and I am well.

Therefore, I request you, my lord father, | write me a letter, first | about your welfare, se- | condly about the welfare of my siblings, | [15] thirdly, in order that I may make obeisance before your | hand(writing), because you trained me well, | and I hope by this means quickly to ad- | vance, the gods willing.

Salute | Kapiton very much and my siblings | [20] and Serenilla and my friends. | I sent my portrait to you through Eukte- | monos. My name is Antonius Ma- | ximus.

I pray that you are well. |

Company Athenonike. |

In the left margin (addendum):

[25] Serenos, the (son) of Agathodaimon, salutes you …, and …, the (son) of | …ros, and Tourbon, the son of Gallonios, and D…nas, the (son) of ….

On the reverse (outside address):

To Philadelphia, to Epimachos from (his) son, Apion.

In the opposite direction (additional address):

Deliver at the camp of the first cohort of the Apameni (*cohors prima Apamenorum*) to Julianus, vice-secretary (Gk. λιβλάριος; Lat. *libellarius*), (this letter) from Apion so that (it might be forwarded) to his father, Epimachos.

The letter, which is dated to the second century CE on the basis of paleography, consists of only a single papyrus sheet. It was found where its recipient lived, in the Fayum, a region of Egypt west of the Lower Nile on one of its branches. This was also the home of the letter's author, a young man with the Egyptian name Apion, who writes to his father Epimachos, addressing him respectfully as "lord." Apion also has a sister, who in turn is the mother of a daughter, and a brother, and he wishes his entire family health and well-being. In crossing the Mediterranean he fell into danger at sea and now thanks the Greco-Egyptian god Serapis, whom he refers to as *kyrios* or "lord" in keeping with the custom of the time, to whom he presumably cried for help.

Why did Apion take to the sea in the first place? While at home in Egypt he had let himself be recruited by Roman troops for the imperial fleet and was subsequently shipped off to Misenum, a Roman military harbor on the Gulf of Naples. Having arrived there he immediately received a *viaticum* of three gold pieces—a Latin term more or less appropriately transliterated into Greek as βιατικόν in line 9 (Greek β was already beginning to be pronounced like the English letter "v" in the second century CE, as in Modern Greek). This refers to Apion's money for travel and maintenance, which he obviously did not receive directly from the Roman emperor but from the bursar of the imperial regiment. Three gold pieces correspond to 75 drachmas, equivalent to two or three months of ordinary wages—no wonder Apion expresses contentment with his situation.

Apion now asks his "lord father" for a short letter (ἐπισ-τόλιον) from home with news of his father's health (σωτηρία) and that of his siblings (the generic plural τῶν ἀδελφῶν in line 14 refers to both the sister and brother of *ll.* 4–5). Furthermore, he wants the opportunity of "making obeisance" to his father's hand-writing, which he could do, for example, by drawing the letter to his lips for a kiss (the verb in *l.* 15, προσκυνέω, can mean either to make obeisance or to kiss). He thereby expresses his thanks once again that his father has raised him so well and that he can, for example, read and write (even though he need not have written this letter with his own hand: see the text below, with n. 3). This will stand him in good stead in his future career in the Roman navy, subject to the gracious approval of the gods (the phrase "if the Lord wills" also occurs in James 4:15 and is there-fore designated the *conditio Jacobea*). The father is also asked to pass on further greetings, first to a man by the name of Kapiton, secondly to the ἀδελφούς, which probably refers here in line 19 as in line 14 to the sister and brother of lines 4–5—thus designat-ing not "brothers" but more precisely "siblings." This also implies that the next person to be greeted, Serenilla, cannot be the sister of the writer, who happens to have the name Sabina as we learn from the second letter, but is rather one of the "friends" mentioned in summary at the end.

Before his concluding wish for his father's well-being, Apion quickly adds two further pieces of information. Depending on the interpretation of the verb ἔπεμψα, he either informs his father that he has previously "sent" him something through his countryman Euktemonos or, if ἔπεμψα is an epistolary aorist (i.e., representing past time only for the letter recipient, but present time for the writer), that he is now sending his father something extra, but separately from this letter, namely through Euktemonos. The item that Euktemonos is to deliver personally (which is too private to be conveyed by the military post) is a portrait, quickly sketched by a professional painter on a sheet of papyrus, that in all probability portrays Apion in his military uniform. Apion has also taken on a Roman name, Antonius Maximus. This had no legal force, since Roman citizenship was not granted to soldiers of the fleet until the end of their service at the earliest. But it was very useful for Apion's father to know his new name so that he could correctly address his response letter, and for this purpose Apion also includes his military unit, Κεντυρία ᾿Αθηνονίκη or Company Athenonike (*l.* 24). Analogously to the land forces, where a company or "century" means a hundred men as a military unit, the term κεντυρία is used in this case to designate the warship, which bears the proud name Athenonike, "Athena as Victor" or "Victory in the Name of Athena," the Greek goddess.

Nor is this enough. In the left margin several other young men send their greetings, only two of whose names, Serenos and Tourbon, we can decipher with certainty. It is striking that the fathers' names are always given together with those of their sons. This has the following background: Along with Apion, other comrades and members of his age group from his area reported to the military and now find themselves in Apion's proximity. Their fathers are named so that there will be no confusion when their greetings are forwarded in their home area.

All this is found on the front of the papyrus sheet. On the back, which is turned to the outside when the papyrus is folded, stands the first outside address, included when the letter was written: to the little village of Philadelphia in the Fayum (also known as the district of Arsinoe or the Arsinoite nome) from Apion, the son, to Epimachos, his father. The letter **X** as printed above in the Greek text of the outside address is an academic convention to mark the place where the string of papyrus fibers used to tie the folded papyrus cuts through the letters. Also on the outside, but written in the opposite direction, is an additional address, presumably added not by Apion but by the secretarial office of the garrison in

Misenum. The letter is to be carried by military post to the first cohort of the Apameni (*cohors prima Apamenorum*), which was in fact stationed in Egypt at this time, where it is to be received by a certain Julianus,[1] whose Greek title as a λιβλάριος is perhaps a transliteration not of the Latin *librarius*, as often maintained, but of *libellarius* (or *pro libellario* if we read ἀντί instead of 'Αν[…]).[2] Either way it designates Julianus as a secretary or military archivist.

---

[1] The case-ending -ου of Julianus's name in the second outside address, 'Απόδος … 'Ιουλιάνου λιβλαρίῳ, requires comment. If taken as genitive, as it first appears, the text would mention two people, one named, the other not: "the λιβλάριος of Julianus." Julianus would then be the commander of the cohort of the Apameni, and Apion's letter would be delivered to Julianus's secretary to be forwarded to Epimachos. But none of the scholars in Bib. 9 unequivocally favors this reading; Daum (72) mentions it only as a possibility. Most translators, including Deissmann, Hengstl, Hunt and Edgar, Milligan, and White, believe that Julianus himself is the λιβλάριος and that the construction is an apposition, more regularly written as 'Ιουλιάνῳ λιβλαρίῳ (for the form 'Ιουλιάνῳ, cf. P.Oxy. III 488.1 [II or III CE]). Here 'Ιουλιάνου serves as the dative instead of 'Ιουλιάνῳ, but the difference of form implies no difference of meaning. For as F. T. Gignac writes about the case-endings of second declension nouns in the papyri of this period, "Fluctuation between -ου and -ω(ι) in the gen. and dat. sg. cannot be considered significant for morphology. It is caused partly by the confusion of -ου for -ω(ι) in the speech of some writers and partly by a syntactic confusion of the gen. and dat. cases" (*Grammar of the Greek Papyri of the Roman and Byzantine Periods*, vol. 2: *Morphology* [Milan 1981] 22).

[2] For the opposite view, preferring *librarius* over *libellarius*, see Deissmann, *Light*, 182 n. 26. The linguistic data can be argued either way. In favor of λιβλάριος = *libellarius* is the fact that *librarius* is elsewhere transliterated more straightforwardly as λιβράριος, e.g., *Bulletin de Correspondence Hellénique* 7.275 (II CE) (cited by both Barber and Glare), leaving λιβλάριος to be traced to a different Latin term. This seems to be the opinion of the revised LSJ supplement, for the equation or cross-reference of λιβράριος with "cf. λιβλάριος" in the original *Supplement* by E. A. Barber (1968) 93, s.v. λιβράριος has since been removed in the *Greek-English Lexicon: Revised Supplement* by P. G. W. Glare (Oxford 1996) 196, s.v. λιβράριος. On the other hand, the same -βλ- instead of -βρ- spelling that might otherwise be thought to favor *libellarius* is taken by Gignac as evidence of the opposite in his analysis of λειβλάρεις = *librarius* in P.Oxy. I 43 R v. 19 (295 CE) (Gignac, *Grammar* 2:27).

2. The Second Letter of Apion (BGU II 632)

Ἀν[τώνι]ος Μάξιμος Σαβίνῃ
τῇ ἀδελφῇ πλεῖστα χαίρειν.
Πρὸ μὲν πάντων εὔχομαί
σε ὑγιαίνειν, καὶ ᾿γω γὰρ αὐτὸς
5 ὑγιαίν[ω]. Μνίαν σοι ποιούμε-
νος παρὰ τοῖς [ἐν]θάδε θεοῖς
ἐκομισάμην [ἓ]ν ἐπι[σ]τόλιον
παρὰ Ἀντωνε[ί]νου τοῦ συν-
πολ[ε]ίτου ἡμῶν. Καὶ ἐπιγνούς
10 σε ἐρρωμένην λίαν ἐχάρην.
Καὶ ᾿γω διὰ πᾶσαν ἀφορμὴν
ο[ὐ]χ ὀκνῶ σοι γράψαι περὶ
τῆ[ς] σωτηρίας μου καὶ τῶν
ἐμῶν. Ἄσπασαι Μάξιμον
15 πολλὰ καὶ Κοπρὴν τὸν κύριν
μ[ου. Ἀ]σπάζεταί σε ἡ σύμβι-
ός [μου Α]ὐφιδία καὶ Μάξιμος
[ὁ υἱός μ]ου, [οὗ] ἐστι[ν] τὰ γενέ-
[σια Ἐ]πειπ τριακὰς καθ᾿ Ἑλ-
20 [ληνα]ς, καὶ Ἐλπὶς καὶ Φορτου-
[νᾶτα]. Ἄσπ[α]σαι τὸν κύριον
– Six further lines are destroyed –

28 [ἐρρῶσθαί σε εὔχο]μαι.

Verso:

[Σαβίνῃ] ἀ[δε]λφ[ῇ] ἀπ[ὸ] Ἀντ[ω]νίου Μαξίμ[ο]υ ἀδελ[φοῦ.]

Translation:

Antonius Maximus to Sabina, | his sister, very many greetings.

Before all else I pray | that you are well, for I myself | [5] am well.

While making mention of you | before the gods here, | I received a letter from Antonius our fellow- | citizen. And when I learned that | [10] you are well, I rejoiced exceedingly. | And I, at every opportunity, | do not hesitate to write to you about | my welfare and (that) of | my family.

Greet Maximus | [15] much and Kopres, my lord. | My wife (life partner: ἡ σύμβιος), | Aufidia, greets you and so does Maximus, | my son, whose birth- | day is the thirtieth of Epeiph according to the Greek (calendar), | [20] as well as Elpis and Fortu- | nata. Greet my lord

[six mutilated lines, 22–27, probably containing additional greetings]

[28] I pray that you may be well.

Verso (outside address):

To Sabina, (his) sister, from (her) brother Antonius Maximus.

The handwriting of the second letter looks different from that of the first,[3] which could point to the use of a paid scribe in at least one of the two instances. Nevertheless, the names and content allow us to assume one and the same sender for both letters. The father and niece from the first letter seem to have died in the meantime, since they are no longer mentioned. Apion now introduces himself from the beginning with his Roman name Antonius Maximus and addresses himself directly to his sister Sabina. He undergirds his health wish to her with a report of his own health. Without hesitation he can turn to οἱ ἐνθάδε θεοί, "the gods here" (i.e., the favorite local gods of his current post), when he wants to remember his sister in prayer. A brief letter that Antonius Maximus has received from another Egyptian named Antonius reporting that all is well at home gives him an occasion for joy and an opportunity once again to report home with a few lines.

Beyond this the letter lacks any real content, so that it serves in the first instance to maintain communication and give Antonius Maximus reassurance, since the greetings begin already in line 14. Maximus will be a nephew named after Antonius Maximus and the "lord" Kopres will be his father, Sabina's husband. Apion—or rather, Antonius Maximus—now has a wife or consort (σύμβιος in *ll.* 16–17) by the name of Aufidia, a son, also named Maximus, who was both on June 24 (i.e., Epeiph 30 on the Greek calendar), and two daughters with the expressive names Elpis ("Hope") and Fortunata ("Fortunate").

The rest of the greetings, which once filled six lines, are unreadable, and the wish for well-being at the end in line 28 is easier to guess than to recognize. This time an uncomplicated address on the verso suffices, which could speak for the conjecture that Antonius Maximus is currently stationed with his regiment in

---

[3] F. Krebs's comment on this letter in the original publication, BGU 2:297, "by the same hand as no. 423" (i.e., the first letter), does not seem to me to be above all suspicion; cf. also Winter 239 on the first letter: "Whether Apion wrote his own letter or not is not known, but the probability is that he dictated it to a letter-writer."

Alexandria and therefore has more opportunity to write and receive letters.

It is not without good reason that A. Deissmann commented on this second letter:

> Written in a perfectly familiar strain, simply to impart family news and to convey all sorts of greetings, it nevertheless, like that other letter of richer content to the father, gives us a glimpse of the close net of human relationships, otherwise invisible, which the giant hands of the Roman army and navy had woven with thousands of fine, strong threads and spread from coast to coast and from land to land over the enormous extent of the Mediterranean world at the time of the infancy of Christianity. (*Light from the Ancient East*, 186)

B. Standard Letter Components

Bibliography 10: P. Arzt, "'Ich danke meinem Gott allezeit . . .': Zur sogenannten 'Danksagung' bei Paulus auf dem Hintergrund griechischer Papyrusbriefe," in F. V. Reiterer, ed., *Ein Gott—eine Offenbarung: Beiträge zur biblischen Exegese und Spiritualität*, FS N. Füglister (Würzburg 1991) 417–37. – idem, "The 'Epistolary Introductory Thanksgiving' in the Papyri and in Paul," *NovT* 36 (1994) 29–46. – idem, *Philemon* (Bib. 4). – **D. E. Aune**, *Dictionary* (Bib. 4), s.v. "Epistolography," 162–68, esp. 166–67; "Letters, literary genre of," 268–72; "Prescriptions, epistolary," 372. – **P. Cugusi**, *Evoluzione* (Bib. 2) 43–72. – **F. X. J. Exler**, *The Form of the Ancient Greek Letter* (Bib. 2). – **G. Geraci**, "Ricerche sul Proskynema," *Aegyptus* 51 (1971) 3–211. – **G. A. Gerhard**, "Untersuchungen zur Geschichte des griechischen Briefes I. Die Formel ὁ δεῖνα τῷ δεῖνι χαίρειν," *Philologus* 64 (1905) 27–65. – **M. J. P. van den Hout**, "Studies" (Bib. 2). – **T. Y. Mullins** (all titles from Bib. 4). – **B. Olsson**, *Papyrusbriefe* (Bib. 2). – **J. T. Reed**, "Are Paul's Thanksgivings 'Epistolary'?" *JSNT* 61 (1996) 87–99. – **G. Tibiletti**, *Le lettere private* (Bib. 2) 28–74. – **J. A. D. Weima**, *Neglected Endings* (Bib. 4) 28–56. – **J. L. White**, *The Form and Function of the Body of the Greek Letter* (Bib. 2). – idem, *The Greek Documentary Letter Tradition* (Bib. 2). – idem, *Ancient Greek Letters* (Bib. 2).

1. Letter Opening

a) Letter Prescript

The clearest sign that we have a letter before us is its so-called pre-script, which—not to be confused with the outside address—opens the letter text on the inside. Its basic tripartite format is easy to recognize in the two Apion letters:

(1) Apion   *superscriptio* or superscription, sender's
    or Antonius Maximus   name in the nominative

(2) to Epimachos   *adscriptio* or adscription, addressee's
    or Sabina   name in the dative

(3) Greetings!   *salutatio* or salutation, greeting in the
                           infinitive (χαίρειν)

Syntactically these three elements form a single sentence. However, while typical of letters, it is unusual for Greek sentences at large to have the initial nominative followed not by a finite verb form such as the imperative χαῖρε ("Greetings!" or "Be greeted!"), but rather by a greeting expressed in the *infinitive*, here χαίρειν. Even the ancient grammarians racked their brains over this (cf. Gerhard). Fortunately, there is a solution to the infinitive problem that also explains the use of the third person for both sender and recipient as well as the sense of the verb χαίρω in the light of its standard meaning "to rejoice." This solution presupposes an older oral messenger formula (so also Gerhard 55, who draws on the messenger formulas of the Old Testament for comparison). The messenger arrives on the scene and says: τάδε λέγει, "Thus says A to B, etc." In direct discourse the end of this formula can indeed be completed by the imperative χαῖρε, "rejoice!" But in indirect discourse the infinitive χαίρειν is used, which leads to the statement, "A tells (λέγει) B to rejoice (χαίρειν)"[4] or also "to feel greeted." The verb λέγει falls away when the oral usage is reduced to writing, and the resulting letter opening is left with an ellipse with merely χαίρειν. For the outside address writers used another formula, which can also open official petitions on the inside of the letter, where it expresses the sender's subordination to the recipient: "To B (dat.) from (ἀπό, παρά) A." The missing verb in this

---

[4] Plato, or the pseudonymous author writing in his name, understands the standard greeting χαίρειν in this original sense "to rejoice" and therefore rejects it as a proper greeting for either God or humans; cf. *Ep.* 3 at 315b–c and below, n. 8. See now also P. Arzt-Grabner, *Philemon* (Bib. 4) 109–11 and R. Wachter, "Griechisch χαῖρε: Vorgeschichte eines Grusswortes," *MH* 55 (1998) 65–75.

formula can be supplied mentally or, as in the case of the additional address of Apion's first letter, the verb ἀπόδος can be supplied directly, "*Give* [this] to B" (e.g., Ἐπιμάχῳ).

This derivation of the infinitive χαίρειν (and ὑγιαίνειν) can still be readily retraced in a text from the fourth century BCE engraved on both sides of a lead tablet that is considered one of the oldest preserved Greek private letters. Unlike the later elliptical formula the driving verb (here ἐπέστειλε) has not yet disappeared (*SIG*³ III 1259):[5]

Outside Address:

> Take (φέρειν) to the earthenware
> pottery and give (ἀποδοῦναι) to Nausias
> or Thrasykles or his son.

Inside Text:

> Mnesiergos
> sends (ἐπέστειλε)[6] to the people at home (his instructions for them)
> to rejoice (χαίρειν) and to be healthy (ὑγιαίνειν),
> and says it to be (ἔχειν) so also with him.
> Dispatch a covering, if you please,
> sheepskins or goatskins,
> the cheapest possible and not shaped into cloaks,
> and shoe-soles; I will make a return when I get the chance.

Yet the health wish ὑγιαίνειν that follows Mnesiergos's greeting (χαίρειν) already takes us beyond the prescript to the next part of

---

[5] This letter is available among other places in M. Trapp, *Greek and Latin Letters* (Bib. 1) 50–51 §2, 198–99 (translation modified above); A. Deissmann, *Light from the Ancient East* (Bib. 1) 150–52; S. Witkowski, *Epistulae* (Bib. 1) 135–36. Cf. W. Crönert, "Die beiden ältesten griechischen Briefe," *RMP* 65 (1910) 157–60. A still older artifact, also engraved on lead and originating around 500 BCE, is the letter of Achillodoros from Berezan on the Black Sea. Cf. M. Trapp, *Letters*, 50–51 §1, 195–98; J. Chadwick, "The Berezan Lead Letter," *Proceedings of the Cambridge Philological Society* 19 (1973) 35–37; J. P. Wilson, "The 'Illiterate Trader'?" *Bulletin of the Institute of Classical Studies* 42 (1998) 29–53; P. A. Rosenmeyer, *Ancient Epistolary Fictions* (Bib. 2) 29–30.

[6] Literally "sent," the epistolary aorist.

the letter formula. In and of itself, the tripartite letter prescript "A to B, greetings" remains relatively inflexible in the Greek and Roman letter formula and shows itself capable of expansion only to a very limited extent—a fact that makes the long expansion of the superscription in Romans 1:1-6 (cf. the adscription and salutation in v. 7) all the more remarkable: it is said to be the longest epistolary prescript from Greek antiquity.[7] Familial designations of the recipients are among the most readily added elements, as in "Epimachos, *his father and lord*" or "Sabina, *his sister*," whereas χαίρειν can be intensified by the addition of πλεῖστα, πολλά, etc. to mean "*very many* greetings." Therefore it must be counted as an intentional innovation when Plato in his letters chooses the greeting εὖ πράττειν, "welfare," "prosperity," "well-doing,"[8] instead of χαίρειν and when Epicurus, who sometimes uses Plato's εὖ πράττειν, also composes his own greetings εὖ διάγειν, "a good life" and σπουδαίως ζῆν, "live well";[9] it is no accident that the infinitive is retained in each case. A letter of consolation for the death of a child begins as befits the occasion with εὐψυχεῖν, "be of good courage" or "take heart,"[10] instead of the usual χαίρειν. Incom-

---

[7] "This is the longest opening of all known Greco-Roman letters," writes D. E. Aune, *Dictionary* (Bib. 4), s.v. "Romans, Paul's Letter to the," 429, citing F. Schnider and W. Stenger, *Studien zum neutestamentlichen Briefformular* (Bib. 4) 12–13.

[8] According R. G. Bury (*Plato*, LCL 9:394 n. 1), Plato's εὖ πράττειν "is purposely ambiguous, meaning either 'act well' or 'fare well' (i.e., 'prosper'); cf. *Gorg.* 495e, *Rep.* 353e." While Epistles 6–8 probably count as genuine, this greeting also occurs in the ten other epistles attributed to Plato. The preference of εὖ πράττειν over χαίρειν is explicitly discussed at the start of Epistle 3.

[9] So according to Diogenes Laertius, who reports Epicurus's special greetings in *Lives* 3.61; 10.14. Text in R. D. Hicks, *Diogenes Laertius: Lives of the Eminent Philosophers*, LCL, 2 vols. (1925) 1:330–31; 2:542–43. These two passages offer only second-hand (but doubtless reliable) attestation for Epicurus's alternative greetings, since these are not actually found in Epicurus's preserved letters to Herodotus, Pythocles, and Menoeceus beginning in *Lives* 10.34–35, 83–84, and 121a–122 respectively, where the greeting is the standard χαίρειν. See further on Epicurus below, chap. 4, sec. B.1.

[10] P.Oxy. I 115 (pp. 181–82, with translation), letter from Eirene to Taonnophris and Philo (II CE). Text and translation also in A.

plete prescripts, when and where they occur, can be a sign that the document is a draft or a copy.

b) Letter Proem

Between the letter prescript and the main body of the letter containing the actual content for which it was written, we frequently find stereotypical, longer or shorter transitional expressions which we can classify as the letter proem, even though this cannot always be delineated clearly. In the two letters of Apion we would have to include the wish for health or well-being that follows the prescript and involves the verb ὑγιαίνειν. In the first example this wish applies to the father and the whole family in lines 2b–6a, and in the second it includes Apion's own health together with that of his sister in lines 3–5. A preliminary stage in the development of such expressions was the so-called *formula valetudinis*, which we still find described in Seneca: "The old Romans had a custom which survived even into my lifetime. They would add to the opening words of a letter, 'If you are well, it is well; I also am well'" (*Ep.* 15.1). The Latin wording *si vales, bene est, ego valeo* became so well known that it could even be abbreviated in private letters as S V B E E V (much as authors of emails today use IMHO for the common disclaimer "in my humble opinion"), but the formula is also common in Greek letters from the early and middle Hellenistic period, though apparently not much later.[11] In the letter of

---

Deissmann, *Light from the Ancient East* (Bib. 1) 176–78; J. L. White, *Light from Ancient Letters* (Bib. 1) 184–85; M. Trapp, *Greek and Latin Letters* (Bib. 1) 118–19; see below Exercise 46.

[11] Immediately after the opening greeting χαίρειν in a letter from Artemidorus to Zenon from 252 BCE (Sel.Pap. I 93), we read: εἰ ἔρρωσαι, εὖ ἂν ἔχοι· ἔρρωμαι δὲ καὶ ἐγώ, "If you are well, it would be excellent; I too am well"—the exact equivalent of the Latin. A hundred years later we find the formula abbreviated in a greeting to two brothers: εἰ ἔρρωσθαι [read: ἔρρωσθε], ἔρρωμαι δὲ καὐτοί [read: καὐτός], "If you are well, (it would be excellent); I myself am well" (Sel.Pap. I 99 [154 BCE]; cf. White, *Light from Ancient Letters*, 73). In a variation, the parallelism is broken by replacing the verb ἔρρωμαι by ὑγιαίνω: εἰ ἔρρωσαι, ἔχοι ἂν καλῶς· ὑγιαίνομεν δὲ καὶ ἡμεῖς, which moreover is an example of the epistolary plural, "*I* (not *we*) too am in good health" (Sel.Pap. I 88 [257 BCE]). Almost identical is 2 Maccabees 11:27, where the plural represents

Mnesiergos above, as often elsewhere, the infinitive ὑγιαίνειν in the proem is combined with the χαίρειν in the prescript, yet it differs in not being a required element of a letter.[12] But ὑγιαίνειν also occurs at the conclusion of letters, and begins precisely from the first century CE onward to move more frequently into the letter opening. One sees by this how such formulas can migrate.

This phenomenon of the migration of formulas is also significant for another problem. It is debatable whether further elements can be included in the proem beyond the health wish. Possible elements of the proem would include in Apion's first letter his thanksgiving to the lord Serapis in lines 6–8, and in his second letter his assurance of his prayers for his sister in lines 5b–6, as well as his expression of joy over the report of her welfare in a letter from Egypt in lines 7–10. The alternative would be to allocate these parts not to the proem but to the letter's body, which once again has its own subdivisions. There they would function as the "body opening" (cf. White). It is possible that the allocation of elements to the proem or to the body varies from letter to letter. But since Apion's two letters already have a proem with their health wish and since the second letter would be reduced almost to nothing if it had a six-line proem (5b–10) but little more than a three-line body text (11–14a), it is advisable to include the above mentioned lines in the body.

---

the royal "we" of Antiochus V: εἰ ἔρρωσθε, εἴη ἂν ὡς βουλόμεθα· καὶ αὐτοὶ δὲ ὑγιαίνομεν, "If you are well, it is as we desire. We also are in good health." For a more complicated variation (also with ὑγιαίνομεν), see UPZ I 64 (White, *Light*, 72–73). Shortly after the third and second century BCE dates of these examples, around 90 BCE, the *formula valetudinis* begins to pass out of style in Greek letters according to J. A. Goldstein, whereas it survives much longer in Latin letters. Goldstein appeals to this in his textual criticism of the formula in 2 Maccabees 9:20-21a, where it is part of a letter from Antiochus IV Epiphanes. See J. A. Goldstein, *II Maccabees*, AB 41A (New York 1983) 364 and below chap. 6, Exercise 32 on 2 Macc 9:19-27, together with its Answer Key. This does not however affect the letters of Romans writing in Greek, where the formula can indeed be found later than 90 BCE, as for example in the letter of Octavius (later Augustus) Caesar Imperator to the city of Ephesus in 39/38 BCE, in Trapp, *Greek and Latin Letters* (Bib. 1) 150–53 (§64).

[12] Hence a boy named Theon threatens to stop sending the greeting of health to his father in P.Oxy. I 119.5 and includes none in his letter (see below Exercise 4).

Matters are different in letters where the assurance of the writer's prayers immediately follows the health wish and forms a syntactical unit with it so that it must be counted part of the proem. An example would be a letter from a husband (Serenos) to his wife, P.Oxy. III 528.3–6: "Before all else I pray for your health, and every day and evening I perform an act of veneration (προσκύνημα) on your behalf to Thoeris (the goddess) who loves you." The assurance of prayers in the second part of this sentence, frequently found in letters, is commonly designated by the Greek word προσκύνημα as a "proskynema formula" (cf. Geraci).

2. Letter Body

The body of a letter is normally the longest of all its parts and can occasionally extend to several pages (even filling a whole book-roll in the case of Paul's letters). This requires an internal structure that identifies the body's opening and closing and further typical letter formulas in between. As already indicated, in Apion's first letter it is best to consider his thanksgiving to the lord Serapis for rescuing him from danger at sea in lines 6–8 as the actual body opening rather than the proem, whereas in the second letter the same role is fulfilled by Apion's remembrance of his sister before the gods and his related expression of joy over her welfare in lines 5b–10. Assurances of prayer and expressions of joy are frequently attested in other letters, usually in the proem or body opening. But this does not apply to the thanksgiving, which is less frequent and counts as one of the special features of Apion's first letter (cf. Arzt; also Reed).

Beyond Apion's assurance of prayer and expression of joy in his second letter, the only non-formulaic element that remains as the main part of the body is his single-sentence reflection about his letter-writing plans in lines 11–14a. In this case the letter body lacks any formal closing. The essential content that fills the body of Apion's first letter is his announcement of his safe arrival in Misenum and his receiving his *viaticum* in lines 8–10. This letter also continues with Apion's request of a letter from his father in lines 11–18, which simultaneously serves as the formal body closing. Such requests can also appear elsewhere in the body, but regardless of placement they usually follow a certain structure: a verb of request (here ἐρωτάω), an address in the vocative, a polite set phrase, and the naming of the action sought by way of response (cf. Mullins, "Petition").

3. Letter Closing

Beyond the body closing (if there is one) the actual letter closing in the two Apion letters consists of the closing greeting or wish "I pray you are well," found in line 23 of the first letter and line 28 of the second. The Greek wording, ἐρρῶσθαί σε εὔχομαι, once again uses the infinitive of indirect discourse, only unlike the case with the infinitive χαίρειν in the letter opening, its driving verb, εὔχομαι, is not elided (ἐρρῶσθαι is the perfect passive infinitive of ῥώννυμι). This is already an expansion of the older and more common closing imperative ἔρρωσο, plural ἔρρωσθε, literally "Be strong," but often translated in epistolary closings as "Farewell," equivalent to Latin *vale* or plural *valete* (cf. Acts 15:29).[13] Instead of this writers could also use a less common formula preferred in letters of petition or request, εὐτύχει (imperative of εὐτυχέω), literally "Fare well," "Prosper," or "Have success." Other greetings, which can also double as epistolary closings in their own right, are placed before the actual closing greeting in lines 18–20 of the first Apion letter and lines 14–27 of the second, and also in the margin of the first letter as an addendum beginning in line 25. Nevertheless, it is important to differentiate the various types of greetings. They can be differentiated and classified simply by noticing the implicit subject of the verb of greeting, typically ἀσπάζομαι (cf. Mullins, "Greeting"). We then arrive at the following three types:

(1) Direct greeting of the sender to the addressee, using a first-person indicative: "I greet you" (ἀσπάζομαι).
(2) Request from the sender to the addressee to greet a third person, using a second-person imperative: "Greet X for me" (ἀσπάζου, ἀσπάσαι).
(3) Forwarded greetings from a third person (or group) to the addressee, using a third-person indicative: "X also greets you" (ἀσπάζεται [ἀσπάζονται]).

---

[13] The form ἔρρωσθε in Acts 15:29 in the letter of the apostolic council is one of only two perfect imperatives in the New Testament outside the verb οἶδα, another perfect tense with present sense.

The direct greeting of the "first person type" is relatively rare and is lacking in the two letters of Apion, but it does occur elsewhere.[14] Greeting requests of the "second person type" occur in lines 18–20 of the first Apion letter and lines 14–16a and 21–27 (largely mutilated) of the second letter. Forwarded greetings of the "third person type" are found in the margin of the first letter and lines 16–21 of the second, where Antonius Maximus's wife, son, and daughters send their greetings.

With this a typical letter is concluded, unless the date is also appended at the end, although this is often lacking in private letters, as in Apion's examples. Signing one's name at the end, as we are used to doing, is not part of the ancient letter formula, and the outside address (also designated by the Latin term *inscriptio*) stands on the back of the papyrus sheet and therefore no longer belongs to the letter formula in the narrower sense. (Hence none of the original outside addresses of the New Testament letters remain.) Although we are already in a position to begin to summarize in a schematic presentation the epistolary building blocks we have discovered, we will postpone this until the end of the chapter. First, after the exercise below, which is intended for independent work, we will turn to two sample letters from the New Testament, 2 and 3 John. This will enable us to show concretely why it makes sense to engage with the Greco-Roman letters for the sake of the New Testament. It will also expand the repertoire of letter components that will feed into our final schematic presentation.

[14] A search of the Duke Databank of Documentary Papyri (DDBDP) on the Packard Humanities Institute disk 7 (now available in the public domain at www.perseus.tufts.edu) found 56 occurrences of the first person ἀσπάζομαι in vols. 1–68 (documents 1–4707) of *The Oxyrhynchus Papyri*. Cf., e.g., the letter of Ophelia to her mother in P.Oxy. VI 963, which begins after the χαίρειν with ἀσπάζομαί σε, μῆτηρ, etc.

Exercise

4. Try to discern the structure of the following letter from the second or third century CE according to the conventions of an ancient Greek letter. Then reconstruct its situation: Who is writing? Who is the recipient? What is the occasion? etc. (P.Oxy. I 119.)

Note: The letter uses many non-standard Greek spellings. Nevertheless, to simplify the reading, corrections have been made to the spellings as well as the grammar—e.g., the dative σοι as the indirect object in *ll.* 4–5 (instead of the accusative σε)— in the light of the corrected text in the DDBDP (cf. also *l.* 7 πάλιν = Duke πάλι; 10 με = Duke μή).

Θέων Θέωνι τῷ πατρὶ χαίρειν.
καλῶς ἐποίησας οὐκ ἀπήνεγκές με μετ᾽ ἐ-
σοῦ εἰς πόλιν. εἰ οὐ θέλεις ἀπενεγκεῖν μετὰ σοῦ εἰς Ἀλεξάνδριαν οὐ μὴ γράψω σοι ἐ-
5 πιστολὴν οὔτε λαλῶ σοι οὔτε ὑγιαίνω σε,
εἶτα ἂν δὲ ἔλθῃς εἰς Ἀλεξάνδριαν οὐ
μὴ λάβω χεῖρα παρὰ [σ]οῦ οὔτε πάλιν χαίρω
σε λοιπόν. ἂν μὴ θέλῃς ἀπενέγκαι μ[ε]
ταῦτα γίνεται. καὶ ἡ μήτηρ μου εἶπε Ἀρ-
10 χελάῳ ὅτι ἀναστατοῖ με· ἆρον αὐτόν.
καλῶς δὲ ἐποίησας δῶρά μοι ἔπεμψας
μεγάλα ἀράκια. πεπλάνηκαν ἡμᾶς ἐκε[ῖ]
τῇ ἡμέρᾳ ιβ (= 12) ὅτι ἔπλευσας. λοιπὸν πέμψον εἴ[ς]
με παρακαλῶ σε. ἂν μὴ πέμψῃς οὐ μὴ φά-
15 γω, οὐ μὴ πίνω· ταῦτα.
ἐρρῶσθαί σε εὔχ(ομαι).
Τῦβι ιη (= 18).

Verso:

ἀπόδος Θέωνι [ἀ]πὸ Θεωνᾶτος υἱοῦ.

Theon to his father Theon, greetings.
You did a fine thing. You didn't take me with y-
ou into town. If you don't want to take [me] with you to Alexandria, then I won't write you a letter, and I won't speak one word to you or wish you good health.

And if you go to Alexandria [without me], from now on I won't
take your hand and I won't greet
you. So if you won't take me along,
these things [will] happen. Even my mother said to Archelaus [my brother] "he is driving me mad—take him away."
You did a fine thing. You sent me
fine presents: locust beans! They deceived us there
on the twelfth day, when you sailed. Finally, send for
me, please, please. If you don't send [for me], I won't eat
and I won't drink. So there.
Farewell, I pray you.
[dated] the 18th of Tybi [January]

Address:

Deliver to Theon from Theonas his son.

C. The Two Letters of the "Elder"

Bibliography 11: D. E. Aune, *Dictionary* (Bib. 4), s.v. "*Captatio benevo-
lentiae*," 89. – **J. A. du Rand**, "Structure and Message of 2 John," *Neot* 13
(1979) 101–20, repr. in idem, et al., *Studies in the Johannine Letters*
(Bloemfontein, South Africa 1981) 101–20 – idem, "The Structure of 3
John," ibid., 121–31. – **R. W. Funk**, "The Apostolic Presence: John the
Elder," in idem, *Parables and Presence* (Bib. 4) 103–10 = "The Form and
Structure of II and III John," *JBL* 86 (1967) 424–30. – **H. J. Klauck**, *Der
zweite und dritte Johannesbrief*, EKKNT 13/2 (Zürich and Neukirchen-
Vluyn 1992). – **M. Leutzsch**, *Die Bewährung der Wahrheit: Der dritte
Johannesbrief als Dokument urchristlichen Alltags*, Bochumer Altertums-
wissenschaftliche Studien 16 (Trier 1994). – **J. M. Lieu**, *The Second and
Third Epistles of John*, SNTW (Edinburgh 1986), esp. 37–51. – **G.
Strecker**, *The Johannine Letters: A Commentary on 1, 2, and 3 John*,
Hermeneia (Minneapolis 1996). – **M. Trapp**, *Greek and Latin Letters*
(Bib. 1) 104–7, 257–59 (2 John). – **D. F. Watson**, "A Rhetorical Analysis
of 2 John according to Graeco-Roman Convention," *NTS* 35 (1989)
104–30. – idem, "A Rhetorical Analysis of 3 John: A Study in Epistolary
Rhetoric," *CBQ* 51 (1989) 479–501.

With only 245 and 219 Greek words, respectively, the Second and
Third Letters of John are the two shortest texts in the canon of

the New Testament. This makes them especially well suited to a formal analysis that needs clear and transparent examples. These two letters have long been considered paradigmatic examples of early Christianity's adaptation of the Hellenistic and Roman imperial letter formula. The following analysis will concentrate on the epistolary structural elements of these two writings, which we will read in parallel, referring detailed questions of content to the commentaries (cf. Klauck; Strecker). The opening and closing conventions and their relationship to the Greco-Roman parallels are further illuminated by the printing of the Greek for these sections.

1. Letter Opening

a) Letter Prescript

2 John 1-3

1 a Ὁ πρεσβύτερος ἐκλεκτῇ
   κυρίᾳ καὶ τοῖς τέκνοις
   αὐτῆς,
  b οὓς ἐγὼ ἀγαπῶ ἐν ἀληθείᾳ,
  c καὶ οὐκ ἐγὼ μόνος ἀλλὰ
   καὶ πάντες οἱ ἐγνωκότες
   τὴν ἀλήθειαν,
2 a διὰ τὴν ἀλήθειαν τὴν
   μένουσαν ἐν ἡμῖν
  b καὶ μεθ' ἡμῶν ἔσται εἰς τὸν
   αἰῶνα.
3 a ἔσται μεθ' ἡμῶν χάρις
   ἔλεος εἰρήνη
  b παρὰ θεοῦ πατρὸς
  c καὶ παρὰ Ἰησοῦ Χριστοῦ
   τοῦ υἱοῦ τοῦ πατρὸς
  d ἐν ἀληθείᾳ καὶ ἀγάπῃ.

3 John 1

1 a Ὁ πρεσβύτερος Γαΐῳ τῷ
   ἀγαπητῷ,
  b ὃν ἐγὼ ἀγαπῶ ἐν ἀληθείᾳ.

1 a The elder to an elect lady
   and her children,
  b whom I love in truth,
  c and not only I but also all
   who know the truth,
2 a because of the truth that
   abides in us
  b and will be with us forever:
3 a Grace, mercy, and peace will
   be with us
  b from God the Father

1 a The elder to the beloved
   Gaius,
  b whom I love in truth.

c and from Jesus Christ,
   the Father's Son,
d in truth and love.

The three components of a properly formed Greek letter prescript also provide the framework for 2 John 1-3 and 3 John 1. Nevertheless, some peculiarities and variations are immediately noticeable, and the tripartite structure is broken off and overlaid with other schemes. We now investigate this in more detail.

i) Identification of the Sender (*superscriptio*)

The sender is given in the nominative as usual at the beginning of both letters. An anomaly is that the author introduces himself not with a personal name but with a title, ὁ πρεσβύτερος, "the elder." Here this is less an indication of an office or function than of the high respect the author enjoys both in the churches he addresses and his own church because of his long experience of faith and life. According to the findings of recent research, the elder may have been an esteemed spiritual-theological teacher in the Johannine circle of churches. He possesses a charismatic authority grounded in his character and in the common history he shares with other believers. Because of certain events he sees himself compelled to intervene in other churches in his region through his letters and emissaries.

ii) Identification of the Addressee (*adscriptio*)

Only 3 John gives the addressee a personal name, complete with an attribute: "to the *beloved* Gaius."[15] Gaius is a common Roman forename that appears several times in the New Testament for different persons. Second John by contrast is addressed to "an elect lady (ἐκλεκτῇ κυρίᾳ) and her children." One need not look long for the individual person behind the designation "lady," since the author attaches this title, as the whole letter confirms, to a

---

[15] Similar formulations, although using the adjective as superlative rather than positive, include, e.g., P.Tebt. II 408.1–3 (III CE): "Hippolytos to his *dearest* (φιλτάτῳ) Akousilaos many greetings" (cf. P.Tebt. II 410.1–2); P.Oxy. II 292.1–2 (ca. 25 CE): "Theon to his *most esteemed* (τιμιωτάτωι) Tyrannos many greetings"; in J. L. White, *Light from Ancient Letters*, §§73, 75, 79.

particular local church. He thereby avails himself of the rhetorical device of *fictio personae*, which in this case personifies a group as an individual. According to ancient rhetoric this figure was frequently used for collectives (fatherland, cities, etc.), but the author also has ready examples in the metaphorical language of the Old Testament and early Jewish writings. Hence we encounter "virgin Israel" (Jer 31:21), "daughter Zion" (Jer 4:31), and "daughter Jerusalem" (Isa 37:22), as well as the promise to the members of the people of Israel: "All your (sg.) children shall be taught by the Lord, and great shall be the prosperity of your (sg.) children" (Isa 54:13).

iii) Greeting (*salutatio*)

The opening greetings in 2 and 3 John are more difficult to analyze from purely Greco-Roman parallels. A side-glance at Paul helps us move forward. In his letters the *salutatio* has taken on the form "Grace to you and peace" (1 Thess 1:1) or more fully "Grace to you and peace from God our Father and the Lord Jesus Christ" (1 Cor 1:3). The profane χαίρειν is superseded by the biblically and theologically loaded pair "grace and peace" (χάρις καὶ εἰρήνη), which resonates with the promise of the great shalom. This replacement is made easier by the fact that χαίρειν and χάρις not only sound similar but are from related roots. Syntactically the typical Pauline opening consists of two parts or two noun clauses: one with the sender and addressee, the other with the wish for grace and peace. Scholars commonly trace this new development to the superimposing of the two-part oriental letter opening over the one-part Greek prescript, but the evidence for this is not as clear as often suggested (see below chap. 6 on Jewish letters).

The "grace and peace" form of greeting is still easy to recognize in 2 John 3, except that at the beginning the verbal paraphrase "there *will be* (ἔσται) with us grace, mercy, and peace," already anticipated by the ἔσται in v. 2b, is added to supplement the Pauline verbless clause. But this does not yet explain everything, because the whole prescript is further overlaid with yet another concrete scheme revolving around the terms truth and love. The concentricity becomes clear as soon as one discovers the *inclusio* of "whom I love in truth" in v. 1b with "in truth and love" in v. 3d. At the center of the *inclusio* are the semantically related expressions in vv. 2a–b and 3a, ordered partly in parallel and partly chiastically (e.g., μεθ' ἡμῶν ἔσται . . . ἔσται μεθ' ἡμῶν). Truth and love are leitmotifs of Johannine theology, introduced almost imperceptibly, which in the context of the prescript could already serve as a badge of group identity. Therefore we already observe here what holds true of the bulk of New Testament epistolary literature: the prescript is considerably expanded in certain places, and the expansions occur in view of the central content and purpose of the following document.

By contrast there are no real expansions in 3 John 1. Here the *salutatio* is completely lacking even in modified form. This is very unusual, because otherwise the greeting can be dropped only in business letters and more rarely in official correspondence, in addition to philosophical letters, which have a very different instructional content. Neither can the health wish in 3 John 2 (which belongs to the proem, not the prescript) or the far removed peace wish in 3 John 15 be seen as a substitute for the lacking greeting. What we are offered in compensation is the relative clause in v. 1b, "whom I love in truth." This introduces in the shortest possible form those key terms developed more fully in 2 John 1–3, although there the Christian opening greeting of "grace, mercy, and peace" is also included.

b) Letter Proem

i) Health Wish

3 John 2

1 a Ἀγαπητέ, περὶ πάντων
     εὔχομαί
  b σε εὐοδοῦσθαι
  c καὶ ὑγιαίνειν,
  d καθὼς εὐοδοῦταί σου ἡ ψυχή.

1 a Beloved, I pray that in all
     respects
  b you may prosper
  c and be in good health,
  d just as your soul prospers.

The health wish well known from the two letters of Apion (once again εὔχομαί σε ὑγιαίνειν) also forms the proem or rather the first part of the proem in 3 John 2 (cf. Funk 109: "The conventional health wish in 3 John 2 marks this letter as the most secularized in the New Testament"). The mention of the "soul" in v.

2d results from the attempt to reach greater spiritual depth: The elder shows himself concerned for the physical and spiritual salvation of Gaius. Only the reader unfamiliar with this formula from the stock of epistolary topoi would fall prey to the mistake some interpreters make when they conclude from the health wish that Gaius was or recently had been sick, or that he had destroyed his health in his quarrel with Diotrephes (see below).

ii) Expression of Joy

2 John 4	**3 John 3-4**

4 a Ἐχάρην λίαν
  b ὅτι εὕρηκα ἐκ τῶν τέκνων
    σου
  c περιπατοῦντας ἐν ἀληθείᾳ,
  d καθὼς ἐντολὴν ἐλάβομεν
    παρὰ τοῦ πατρός.
	3 a Ἐχάρην γὰρ λίαν
	  b ἐρχομένων ἀδελφῶν
	  c καὶ μαρτυρούντων σου τῇ
	    ἀληθείᾳ,
	  d καθὼς σὺ ἐν ἀληθείᾳ
	    περιπατεῖς.
	4 a μειζοτέραν τούτων οὐκ
	    ἔχω χαράν,
	  b ἵνα ἀκούω
	  c τὰ ἐμὰ τέκνα ἐν τῇ
	    ἀληθείᾳ περιπατοῦντα.

4 a I was overjoyed
  b to find some of your children
  c walking in the truth,
  d just as we have been
    commanded by the Father.
	3 a For I was overjoyed
	  b when the brothers arrived
	  c and testified to your truth,
	  d namely how you walk in the truth.
	4 a I have no greater joy than this,
	  b to hear
	  c that my children are walking in the truth.

Here once again one can debate whether the expression of joy by means of χαρά and especially ἐχάρην λίαν (cf. λίαν ἐχάρην in the second Apion letter [*l.* 10]) should be regarded as the proem, or should rather be allocated to the body opening, at least in the case of 3 John. But because in 2 John (which also lacks the health wish) we must count the expression of joy as the only element of the proem, the close parallels between the two letters that are becoming ever more apparent argue in favor of leaving the expression of joy in the proem for 3 John as well.

Beyond this set phrase, important content is also included in each letter. The children, including Gaius, who are mentioned in the expression of joy in each proem are Christian believers in the churches being addressed. To the author's great joy they show, at least partly through their conduct, that they have made room in their hearts for God's truth and are following his love commandment. At the same time this is not just the author's simple, unmotivated observation, for it also fulfills the function of a *captatio benevolentiae*, another element typically located in the letter proem. This Latin phrase for a well-known figure of ancient rhetoric signifies the speaker's or writer's "fishing for goodwill" with his audience. By praising the addressees—or even, when necessary, by flattering them—this rhetorical figure seeks to put them in a good mood that will make them receptive to the message (cf. Aune).

2. Letter Body

a) *Body Opening: Request*

2 John 5-6	**3 John 5-8**
5 a But now I ask (ἐρωτῶ) you, dear lady,	5 a Beloved, you do faithfully (πιστὸν ποιεῖς)
b not as though I were writing you a new commandment,	b whatever you do for the brothers,
c but one we have had from the beginning,	c even though they are strangers to you;
d let us love one another.	
	6 a they have testified to your love before the church.
6 a And this is love,	b You will do well (καλῶς ποιήσεις)
b that we walk according to his commandments;	c to send them on (in a manner) worthy of God;
	7 a for they began their journey for the sake of "the Name,"
	b accepting no support from the Gentiles.
c this is the commandment	8 a Therefore we ought
d just as you have heard it from the beginning	b to support such people,
e —you must walk in it (= in love).	c so that we may become co-workers with the truth.

The body opening in each of these shorter letters begins with an address to the addressee ("lady") or addressees ("beloved") and an epistolary request. In 2 John 5 this request is clearly designated as such by the verb ἐρωτάω, exactly as in the first Apion letter (*l.* 11). Here the request is that the addressees keep the love commandment.

While perhaps not immediately apparent, there is also a request in 3 John 5-8 that uses another typical letter formula, which moreover occurs exceptionally frequently in the papyrus letters, namely καλῶς ποιήσεις, "you will do well," addressed to Gaius. This serves as a polite circumlocution for the more direct request by ἐρωτῶ. As a parallel we may cite P.Oxy. II 299.3–4: καλῶς ποιήσεις πέμψεις μοι αὐτάς (referring to the sending of eight δραχμάς as repayment). Yet this expression can also be simplified in translation as an equally polite request using "please," here: "*Please* send our dear brothers on their way in a manner worthy of God." Formed by analogy to this is the parallel expression πιστὸν ποιεῖς, "you do faithfully," in 3 John 5a (cf. Funk 106: "It is undoubtedly a Christian counterpart of that idiom"). In P.Oxy. I 119 (see Exercise 4) the young Theon used this widespread idiom sarcastically in his complaint (καλῶς ἐποίησας, *ll.* 2, 11), which may be captured idiomatically by English expressions such as "that's just swell" or "great!" Despite his standing in the churches, the elder formulates his request in 3 John 5-8 with this reserved indirect expression, because he wants Gaius to continue showing hospitality to missionaries in his home and preparing them for their ongoing journey. The request is conspicuous for its cautiousness, which is miles away from an imperious command or even an urgent plea.

b) Body Middle: Information

2 John 7		3 John 9-10	
7 a	For many deceivers have gone out into the world,	9 a	I have written something to the church;
b	those who do not confess	b	but Diotrephes, who likes to put himself first among them,
c	that Jesus Christ has come in the flesh;	c	does not acknowledge our authority (lit. receive us).
d	any such person is the deceiver and the antichrist!	10 a	So if I come,
		b	I will call attention to the works

c that he is doing
d in spreading false charges
  against us.
e And not content with those
  charges,
f he refuses to welcome the
  brothers himself,
g and even those who want to
  do so
h he prevents
i and expels from the church.

In its informative section 2 John addresses the appearance of false teachers whom the elder suspects of holding an erroneous Christology (v. 7). A more concrete situation is addressed in 3 John 9-10, a passage that is once again enlightening because it exposes the entire virtually destroyed communication network in which our letter is embedded. A church leader named Diotrephes has completely broken off communications with the elder. Diotrephes did not allow a letter that the elder had written to the church Diotrephes controls to be read openly (v. 9). In contrast to Gaius, Diotrephes does not welcome traveling missionaries himself (v. 10f), and he also prevents other church members from doing so by his massive threats (vv. 10g–i). The presbyter now puts forward a proposed visit of his own, which he will use to call Diotrephes to account (vv. 10a–d), but he conspicuously restrains his tone in this announcement as well. Perhaps he did not actually hold enough power to make Diotrephes particularly frightened by this prospect.

c) Body Middle II: Exhortation

2 John 8-9

8 a Be on your guard,
  b so that you do not lose
  c what we have worked for,
  d but may receive a full
    reward.
9 a Everyone who runs ahead
  b and does not abide in the
    teaching of Christ
  c does not have God;

3 John 11

11 a Beloved, do not imitate what
     is evil
   b but what is good.

   c Whoever does good

   d is from God;

d whoever abides in the teaching	e whoever does evil
e has both the Father and the Son.	f has not seen God.

In 2 John 8-9 the information about the appearance of false teachers in v. 7 leads to an exhortation to the congregation to remain in the teaching of Christ and avoid being deceived by those who claim false progress. The exhortation to Gaius in 3 John 11 has a more precise aim, to encourage him not to measure himself by the bad example of Diotrephes but to continue his own exemplary behavior. Yet it achieves this aim with a very general proverbial sentence. The author thereby conforms to the recommendation of an ancient handbook of style that advises letter writers to adorn their letters with proven proverbs, because a proverb is common property that unites the author and the addressee.[16]

d) Body Closing: Instructions / Recommendation

2 John 10-11	**3 John 12**
10a If any one comes to you	12a For Demetrius (favorable) testimony has been given by everyone
b and does not bring this teaching,	
c do not receive him into the house	b and by the truth itself;
d and do not speak a greeting to him,	c and we too testify,
11a for the one who speaks a greeting to him	d and you know
b participates in his evil deeds.	e that our testimony is true.

The two shorter letters of John depart from each other most radically in this passage. The command in 2 John 10, with its support in v. 11, converts the information about the false teachers in v. 7 and the intervening warning in vv. 8-9 into instructions for behavior: traveling missionaries of the opposing party with the wrong message should be denied access to the house church so that they do not come to speak in the church meetings and cause damage (the problem as such is also well known elsewhere in early Christianity). The imperative "do not speak a greeting to him" in v. 10d reads καὶ χαίρειν αὐτῷ μὴ λέγετε in Greek, thus present-

---

[16] Demetrius, *De elocutione* 232 (see below chap. 5, sec. A.1).

ing us again with the same infinitive χαίρειν that we have already come to know as the classical greeting formula in the ancient letter prescript. Through its initial request, its information, its exhortation, and its final instructions at the conclusion of the letter body, the whole of 2 John gains an unmistakable paraenetic-hortatory character.

In 3 John 12, by contrast, a threefold testimony is given for Demetrius (cf. Deut 19:15). Apparently Demetrius is going to be introduced to Gaius (either now as the possible carrier of this letter, or on a later occasion) as an emissary or a leader of a small delegation, and he accordingly needs this explicit certification and recommendation. Therefore the letter as a whole, although set against the background of an acute conflict, nevertheless has a dominant tone of recommendation and seeking good will. The letter of recommendation, which has a firm place in early Christianity, will become a subject in its own right as we proceed (see below, chap. 3, sec. B).

3. Letter Closing

a) Epilogue: Prospective Visit

2 John 12	3 John 13-14
12a Although I have much to write to you (pl.),	13a I have much to write to you (sg.),
b I did not want (to do so)	b but I do not want to write to you
c with paper and ink;	c with ink and pen;
d instead I hope	14a instead I hope
e to come to you	b to see you soon,
f and to talk mouth to mouth [i.e., face to face],	c and we will talk mouth to mouth.
g so that our joy may be complete.	

The letters once again run in surprisingly close parallel at their conclusion, where the elder reveals his intention to make a visit. A writer's wish for a visit with its various emotional overtones, whether more friendly and longing or more warning and threatening, is a figure well known from numerous examples in the papyrus letters, where we read for example: "If the gods will, I will therefore try to come to you for the feast of Amesysia" (P.Oxy. XIV 1666.15–17 [III CE]); "So soon as I arrive from the delivery of the copper I will have a conversation with you" (P.Hib. I 66.4 [228 BCE]), "For I myself also hope to come to you soon" (P.Mich. VIII 481.14–15). But first our author reflects upon the act of writing and realizes that much must remain unsaid, not simply because the short papyrus sheet has come to an end or because of time pressure, but because everything essential has basically already been said. Letter-based communication has its natural limits. A "face-to-face" situation is to be preferred, which enables a direct exchange from person to person. The formulation that the presbyter chooses for this communication, "mouth to mouth" (2 John 12f; 3 John 14c), which essentially means "face to face," is adopted from the Old Testament: only with Moses will God speak "mouth to mouth" (Num 12:8 RSV). The letter writer also gives us an incidental insight into his working conditions, for by combining 2 John 12c and 3 John 13c, we get the triad of paper, ink, and pen—everything needed for writing (see below chap. 2).

As far as the structure of these letters is concerned, it seems advisable to allocate the announcement of the elder's planned visit in each case to the letter closing rather than the body closing, but to differentiate it there from the closing greetings. This enables us to go beyond our analysis of the letter closings of the two Apion letters and subdivide the letter closing by analogy to the letter opening. We therefore differentiate between the "epilogue," which runs parallel to the proem, and a final element that corresponds with the prescript and that we therefore designate as the "postscript" (for a P.S. in our modern sense we reserve the term "addendum"). The letter as a whole therefore acquires a concentric structure, with several frames around the body middle, which does not, however, mean that the most important statements necessarily stand in the middle (they are often more appropriately placed at the end or also the beginning of the letter body).

The postscript is realized by the closing greeting and, where given, the date. Further greetings can also be included, but here there are possible variations. The epilogue can also be formulated in various ways. In our case this occurs through the reflection on the act of writing and the wish for a visit, which elsewhere can also function where necessary as the body closing.

b) Postscript: Closing Greetings

2 John 13	3 John 15
13a The children of your elect sister greet you (ἀσπάζεται).	15a Peace to you. b The friends greet you (ἀσπάζονται). c Greet (ἀσπάζου) the friends (there), each by name.

In 2 John 13 the presbyter does not send greetings himself but forwards them from a third party, namely the members of his home church; this is therefore a greeting of the "third person" type (see above, pp. 24–25). The application of the opening metaphor from 2 John 1 of the "elect lady and her children," representing the receiving church, also to the "children of your elect sister," signifying the sending church here in 2 John 13, gives this closing greeting its special Johannine stamp. In the metaphorical word-play that the author here executes with a perfect *inclusio*, the receiving church and the elder's home church are sisters, and their children, the local believers in each place, are not just cousins but siblings. The author therefore reconfigures the otherwise dry letter formalities in order to raise the entire text to a symbolic theological level. It is a piece of family correspondence, perfectly comparable with the Apion letters, only here the family must be understood as the *familia Dei*.

In 3 John 15 the closing greeting consists of three parts. It begins with a peace wish. This can appear either in the *salutatio* of the prescript, as in 2 John 3 or, as here, in the letter closing (cf. also Gal 6:16). Because 3 John as a whole is otherwise in conspicuous alignment with the Hellenistic letter formula, the peace wish in v. 15a may have been conceived as a replacement for the common closing formula ἔρρωσο or ἔρρωσθε (see above). The second element is the forwarding of greetings from a third party, once again the members of the author's home church (here called the "friends" rather than the "children"), while in the final component the author uses the second person greeting request (ἀσπάζου) to ask Gaius to greet other Christians in that area on his behalf. That Gaius is asked to greet the friends by name belongs to the standard letter repertoire: "Greet all your friends, each by name" (P.Mich. VIII 472.20–21); "Greet Tasokmenis, my lady sister, and Sambas and Soueris and her children and Sambous and all the relations

and friends, each by name" (P.Mich. III 203.33–35). As already
indicated, the title "friends" in 3 John 15 accomplishes what would
otherwise be conveyed by the designations "children," "brothers,"
and "sisters."[17] Such titles imply the vision of a community in
which all members may understand each other as siblings and
friends. This once again fits well with the tone of recommendation
and good will in the letter.

Finally, we turn our attention to the conspicuous points of
contact both in structure and partly in wording between the two
shorter letters of John, which are closer than those in the two
Apion letters. The simplest explanation may still be the one that
holds that at least 2 and 3 John were written by the same author,
yet without this necessarily having any far-reaching implications
for the authorship of 1 John, let alone the Gospel of John. Access
to common traditions and knowledge of set formulas by two different authors would not suffice on their own to explain these
points of contact. If one wished to depart from the thesis of a common author, one would have to assume conscious imitation of one
of the writings by the author of the other.

D. From Model Letter to Letter Model

We have read four letters, presented another in Exercise 4, and
cited from additional ones. In practice there are no model letters,
nor were the ones chosen here intended as such. Rather each letter draws from the stock of formulas, adapts the existing letter
template for its own purposes, and also includes distinctive material depending on the specific situation and the individuality of
each author. Nevertheless, our study of these letters has uncovered
a repertoire of components that can be systematized to a certain
extent. The following overview attempts to incorporate what we

[17] But the NRSV is different. In order to avoid the gender specificity
of the term ἀδελφοί, "brothers," which it translates elsewhere in the
New Testament by "brothers and sisters," the NRSV of 3 John has
instead taken the term "friends" from 3 John 15 and has consistently
inserted it in place of "brothers" in vv. 3, 5, 10, thus erasing the distinction between ἀδελφοί and φίλοι. Yet the language here is truly distinctive, for while Jesus calls his disciples his "friends" (John 15:15), 3 John
15 is the only place in the New Testament where the members of a
Christian congregation are referred to collectively as "the friends."

have already learned while supplementing with discoveries yet to come. That it is not intended to be understood rigidly should be clear from the fact that some components receive multiple mention in different positions of the letter (e.g., remembrances, requests, recommendations, exhortations, and travel plans). We are thus equipped with a basic conceptual grid that we can consult and apply flexibly when analyzing further letters (see the outline on the next page).

Exercise

5. Structure the brief 25-verse letter of Philemon according to the principles of epistolary analysis learned in this chapter.

Overview of Typical Letter Components

I. **Letter Opening**
   A. Prescript
      1. sender: *superscriptio* / superscription (nominative)
      2. addressee: *adscriptio* / adscription (dative)
      3. greeting: *salutatio* / salutation (infinitive) (χαίρειν)
   B. Proem
      – prayer-wish (εὔχομαι) for health or well-being (ὑγιαίνειν)
      – thanksgiving (εὐχαριστῶ)
      – remembrance (μνείαν ποιούμενος) before the gods (God), intercession
      – expression of joy (χαρά, ἐχάρην)

II. **Letter Body**
   A. Body Opening
      – remembrance or intercession, expression of joy, etc.
      – disclosure formula (θέλω σε γινώσκειν, εἰδέναι), request formula (ἐρωτῶ), etc.
      – recommendation of self or others (συνίστημι, ἐπαινῶ)
   B. Body Middle
      – information
      – appeal, instructions
      – exhortation (παρακαλῶ), recommendation
      – request (ἐρωτῶ) (placed in various locations)
      – diverse clichés (set phrases)
   C. Body Closing
      – possible request, exhortation
      – travel and visitation plans

III. **Letter Closing**
   A. Epilogue
      – concluding exhortations
      – reflection on the act of writing
      – plans for a possible visit
   B. Postscript
      – greetings:
         • direct greeting, ἀσπάζομαι (1st person)
         • request to send greetings, ἀσπάζου, ἀσπάσαι (2nd impv.)
         • forwarded greeting, ἀσπάζεται (-ονται) (3rd person)
      – wishes: "farewell"; "I pray you are well" (ἐρρῶσθαι)
      – endorsement of the letter in the author's own hand
      – date

2

Practical Realities—
Paper and Postal Systems

A. Writing Materials and Procedures

Bibliography 12: H. Blanck, *Das Buch in der Antike*, Beck's Archäologische Bibliothek (Munich 1992). – **T. Dorandi** and **J. Quack,** "Papyrus I. Material," *DNP* 9 (2000) 298–99 (English version forthcoming in *BNP*). – **H. Hunger,** "Antikes und mittelalterliches Buch- und Schriftwesen," in idem, et al., *Die Textüberlieferung der antiken Literatur und der Bibel*, dtv Wissenschaftliche Reihe 4176 (Munich ²1975) 25–147. – **A. Lemaire,** "Writing and Writing Materials," *ABD* 6 (1992) 999–1008, esp. 1001–4. – **N. Lewis,** *Papyrus in Classical Antiquity* (Oxford 1974). – idem, *Papyrus in Classical Antiquity: A Supplement*, Papyrologica Bruxellensia 23 (Brussels 1989). – **H. Maehler,** "Books, Greek and Roman" and "Papyrology, Greek," *OCD³* (2003) 249–52; 1109–11. – **J. Murphy-O'Connor,** *Paul* (Bib. 4) 1–37. – **R. Parkinson** and **S. Quirke,** *Papyrus*, Egyptian Bookshelf (Austin, Tex. 1995). – **P. J. Parsons,** "Background: The Papyrus Letter," *Didactica Classica Gandensia* 20 (1980) 3–19. – **H. Ragab,** *Le Papyrus* (Cairo: Dr. Ragab Papyrus Institute, 1980). – **E. R. Richards,** *Secretary* (Bib. 4) 15–127. – **W. Roberts,** *History* (Bib. 2) 9–34. – **O. Roller,** *Formular* (Bib. 4) 4–46. – **J. L. White,** *Light from Ancient Letters* (Bib. 1) 213–17. – **K. Ziegler,** "Kalamos 2," *KlPauly* 3:53. – Literature on papyrology in Bib. 6.

With the Apion letters we have already spoken of the front and back sides of a papyrus sheet, of the string of papyrus fibers that cuts through the letters of the outside address, and of the instructions for the delivery of the letter. The letters of the elder add a further reference to paper, ink, and pen. We therefore take this opportunity to investigate more thoroughly the production of letters in antiquity and the possibilities for conveying them.

1. Ancient Letter Materials

There is hardly any limit to the ideas people have come up with for letter writing materials.[1] The Romans, at least according to Pliny the Elder, at first wrote on bast fibers from the inner bark of certain trees (*Nat. hist.* 13.20.69), although this remains unproven (but see the illustration of a Singhalese book of palm leaves and a book of bast from Sumatra in Blanck 53). As recently as the 1970s, archeologists discovered paper-thin wooden tablets in a Roman military fortress at Vindolanda on Hadrian's Wall in Britain that were still being used for letters around 100 CE (this is also the earliest documentary source of Latin handwriting by women).[2] One would write on one side in two columns, score the tablet in the middle with a sharp knife, and fold it together (Blanck 48–49). Scholars have known for a longer time of somewhat thicker wooden tablets, bound together two or more at a time, with writing surfaces whitened by chalk or plaster to allow the writing to appear more clearly. Another possibility was to attach a raised border to a wooden panel and fill it with wax. This produced a wax tablet on which one could inscribe a text into the wax with the pointed end of a stylus and erase it by smoothing the wax with the blunt end. The Roman historian Livy speaks of old linen books (10.38.6: *liber linteus*), and an Estrucian festival calendar was found recorded on linen, used secondarily as mummy wrappings (Blanck 54–55). The letter of Mnesiergos (see above chap. 1, sec. B.1.a) was engraved on a lead tablet. The deceased were buried with small gold plates bearing instructions for life in the afterworld.[3] The Qumran Copper Scroll (3Q 15) with its incised letters is well known. At Qumran we also find texts on leather, though not unexpectedly, since this is used even today as a writing material for Torah scrolls. In 1 Maccabees a letter from the Romans to the Jewish people was written on bronze tablets (1 Macc 14:16-19).

---

[1] The most unusual material of all might well be the *apple* used for a letter in Hellenistic erotic poetry; cf. P. A. Rosenmeyer, *Ancient Epistolary Fictions* (Bib. 2) 108–30.

[2] An example is the letter of Claudia Severa, Vindolanda tablet II 291, in which she writes the concluding greeting in her own hand, clearly distinguishable from that of the scribe. See below chap. 4, p. 107.

[3] Further information in H. J. Klauck, *Religious Context* (Bib. 7) 119–20.

Important royal letters were subsequently engraved in stone and thus remain for posterity as inscriptions.

Among all these ancient writing materials that now seem "exotic" by our standards, the only one that still plays a significant role in personal and business correspondence in the Greco-Roman period is the potsherds, so-called *ostraca*, on which people scribbled messages or wrote them in ink. For example we possess such an ostracon, written on 2 June 72 CE (fourth year of Vespasian), that certifies that a certain Egyptian Jew has paid the special imperial tax that became obligatory for Jews after the destruction of the temple in 70 CE (O.Edfou 120):[4]

> Josepos, son of Jason,
> in respect of the two-denar tax
> on the Jews for the 4th year, 8 drachmai 2 obols.
> Year 4 of Vespasian, Payni 8.

As discarded material such shards of clay or also limestone were inexpensive and readily available. However, because of their restricted writing surfaces they were suitable only for receipts, notices, exercises, and short messages, but not for longer letters. Outstripping all competition among the writing media was another material of organic origin, *papyrus* (πάπυρος), which lies behind our word "paper." The finished papyrus, especially in roll form, is more commonly referred to in Greek as (ὁ) χάρτης,[5] Latin *charta* (source also of English "card"; cf. "card stock"). Χάρτης refers to a roll of papyrus when designating quantity, but generically also denotes the "paper" made from the papyrus plant; the only two biblical occurrences conveniently illustrate both senses, πᾶς ὁ χάρτης meaning "the entire *scroll*" (Jer 43:23 LXX = 36:23 MT: כָּל־הַמְּגִלָּה),[6] and χάρτης καὶ μέλαν meaning "*paper* and ink" (2 John 12). The diminutive form τὸ χαρτίον likewise refers to a roll of papyrus, hence a χαρτίον βιβλίου is a "roll of a book"

---

[4] Text and translation also in *CPJ* II 165.

[5] First-declension masc. noun, gen. χάρτου, on the analogy of προφήτης, -ου.

[6] The translation of Heb. מְגִלָּה, "roll" or "scroll," by χάρτης (and also χαρτίον) is one of the factors that has led classicists to conclude that χάρτης generally designates a whole roll of papyrus and not an individual sheet. Cf. Lewis 70–78, esp. 71–72.

(מְגִלַּת־סֵפֶר, Jer 43:2, 4).[7] An unwritten papyrus roll—and especially a written one—could also be designated by βύβλος or βίβλος alone ("book"; origin of the word "Bible").[8]

Papyrus as a writing material is obtained from the papyrus plant, a marsh reed[9] that thrived especially in Egypt in the Nile delta and Nile valley and had many different uses. One could chew the stalks, use the fibers to make rope, sails, boats, and clothing, or use the woody roots as firewood, the blossoms as garlands, and the ashes to make medications (Blanck 57). Paper manufacture used the pith from the inside of the triangular stalk. How this was done concretely is presented on the whole with admirable clarity by Pliny the Elder in his *Natural History*, though a few of his details seem unclear or contradictory:[10]

> **71** Papyrus grows in the swamps of Egypt or else in the sluggish waters of the Nile where they have overflowed and lie stagnant in pools . . .; it tapers gracefully up with triangular sides to a length of not more than about 15 feet. . . . **74** Paper is made from the papyrus plant by separating it with a needle point into very thin strips as broad as possible. The choice quality comes from the centre, and thence in the order of slicing . . . [various grades of paper are here discussed]. **77** Paper of whatever grade is fabricated on a board moistened with water from the Nile: the muddy liquid serves as the bonding force.[11] First there is spread flat on the board a layer consisting

---

[7] Χαρτίον on its own designates a book-roll (again מְגִלָּה) in ten further instances in Jeremiah 43.

[8] The envisioned "book" (βίβλος) of papyrus in Job 37:20 is not the written book, but only a fresh roll waiting for a scribe: "Have I a book (βίβλος) or a scribe by me, that I may stand and put man to silence?" Further (classical) examples of both written and unwritten βίβλοι in Lewis 78 with n. 15 (cf. 79 n. 16).

[9] Cf. Job 8:11: "Can papyrus grow where there is no marsh? Can reeds flourish where there is no water?"

[10] *Nat. hist.* 13.21.68–13.27.89. Translation of §§74–82 from Lewis 36–41; otherwise from H. Rackham, *Pliny: Natural History*, LCL 4 (1945) 138–53.

[11] Modern studies have shown this to be inaccurate. It is not anything special in the Nile water, nor even the "intervening paste" (*glutinum*) mentioned in §82, that binds together the cross-laid strips of papyrus during pressing; no such paste has yet been detected in chemical analyses of ancient papyri. Pliny's "bonding force" is in fact only "the

of strips of papyrus running vertically, as long as possible, with their
ends squared off. After that a cross layer completes the construction.
Then it is pressed in presses, and the sheets thus formed are dried in
the sun and joined to one another, (working) in declining order of
excellence down to the poorest.[12] There are never more than twenty
sheets in a roll. **78** There is a great variation in their breadth [i.e.,
from thirteen digits down to six]. . . . **81** Rough spots are rubbed
smooth with ivory or shell. . . . **82** Common paste made from finest
flour is dissolved in boiling water with the merest sprinkle of vine-
gar[13]. . . . A more painstaking process percolates boiling water
through the crumb of leavened bread; by this method the substance
of the intervening paste is so minimal that even the suppleness of
linen is surpassed. Whatever paste is used ought to be no more or
less than a day old. Afterwards it is flattened with the mallet and
lightly washed with paste, and the resulting wrinkles are again
removed and smoothed out with the mallet.[14] **83** This process may
enable records to last a long time. . . . **89** This commodity is also
liable to dearth, and as early as the principate of Tiberius a shortage
of paper led to the appointment from the senate of umpires to super-
vise its distribution, as otherwise life was completely upset.

---

natural gummy substance contained in the cell sap of the papyrus pith"
(Lewis 47 with literature in 47–48 n. 16). The resulting bond is perma-
nent: "Ancient papyri have been torn, crumpled, and otherwise damaged
in their centuries of internment, but only rarely have the two layers come
apart" (ibid. 50).

[12] This too is misleading. The various qualities of papyrus sheet were
not combined into a single roll to form a mixed grade, but rather separated by grade to form several different rolls, each with a consistent grade
of paper (cf. Lewis 53–54).

[13] As already indicated (cf. n. 11), this artificial paste was neither
applied between the vertical and horizontal layers of papyrus strips to
bind them into a papyrus sheet, nor spread over the surface of the sheet
in the process of finishing. However, a paste *was* used to glue together the
dry, finished sheets at their overlapping edges to produce a roll (cf. Lewis
51–52, 64).

[14] This pounding or tapping procedure was probably only used at the
seams that resulted when the finished sheets were glued together into a
roll. These seams were so skillfully "ironed out" that one could easily
write over them with a reed pen and did not notice the seams upon
inspection; cf. E. G. Turner, *Greek Papyri* (Bib. 6) 5, quoted in Lewis 51
n. 24.

In between these statements Pliny also expounds upon six or eight different grades of paper (§§74b–76, 78–80), which also affected the price. The cheapest (called "emporitic" after its use by merchants, ἔμποροι) could only be used as wrapping paper (§76), while the most expensive was of a yellowish-white color, very pliable, and known for its durability (§83). Yet as an organic material papyrus was also at risk: when exposed to moisture it began to disintegrate and decay. This is also the reason why the papyri that have been preserved until today are found almost exclusively in the dry desert climate of Egypt. It is here that the great modern discoveries of papyri were made, beginning in the nineteenth century. Particularly productive were the rubbish heaps of ancient cities and small towns, the ruins of buildings and—because of the secondary use of papyrus as cartonnage to wrap mummies—burial sites. The number of papyri discovered in this way, not nearly all of which have been published, reaches literally into the hundreds of thousands (one estimate claims 400,000). In evaluating their importance for the social and literary history of this time, we must remember that although these papyri at first give only the particulars of their setting in Egypt and its society, many of these finding are also more widely applicable to the Mediterranean world in the Greco-Roman period.

Papyrus received competition as the universal writing material only relatively late from parchment or vellum. Although the product of animal skins, parchment was prepared differently from leather—not by tanning but by scraping, stretching, drying, and smoothing the skins. Although parchment is less sensitive to external conditions, it did not begin to replace papyrus until the second century CE, and then at first only gradually and for literary works. There are next to no letters on parchment;[15] for letters and other documents papyrus was preferred until the tenth or eleventh century, when paper as we know it, which originated in China and was brought to the West by Arabs, established itself.[16]

[15] As of 1923, A. Deissmann knew of only a single example of an ancient parchment letter: cf. *Licht vom Osten* (Bib. 1) 118 n. 1 = *Light from the Ancient East* (Bib. 1) 149 n. 1.

[16] Papyrus continues to be produced today in small quantities for the art and tourist market. Its cultivation and manufacture had to be reintroduced to Egypt in the 1960s, where it had since died out. Chiefly respon-

2. Scrolls, Ink, Pen, and Handwriting

As Pliny informs us, individual papyrus sheets were produced by placing the two layers of papyrus strips on the board in the same configuration in which the papyrus would be used, i.e., with the primary writing surface facing up. One first arranged vertically on the board the generally longer strips of papyrus that would become the back (*verso*) of the papyrus and form the height dimension, then overlaid horizontally another layer of generally shorter strips that would become the front (*recto*) for writing and would form the width dimension, as in the illustration in Figure 1 on the next page. This layout was essential so that the scribes could write with the grain of the horizontal layer, although writing against the grain, on the back, is not unknown (see below on the "opistograph").

Like modern standard paper sizes (e.g., 8.5 by 11 inches), Pliny describes the ancient grades beginning with the width dimension, but he does not mention the heights, which were even more important to control when forming a roll (the widths of sheets within a roll could vary; cf. Lewis 56 n. 31). According to Pliny the standard widths ranged from 6 to 13 Roman "digits" (*digiti*) or 4.4 to 9.5 inches (11 to 24 cm),[17] the broadest being of the best quality. The heights of the sheets were generally somewhat greater and varied between 8 and 16 inches, excluding "custom orders" (Pliny also mentions a custom order for the width, called the "macrocolum," a cubit wide, cf. §80).

---

sible for this development is the Egyptian engineer Hassan Ragab and his Papyrus Institute in Cairo, also known as the Papyrus Museum (for further information see the Internet). Technical aspects are described in Ragab's dissertation, published as *Le Papyrus* (Cairo 1980). Ragab's Figure 82 on p. 136 has an actual sample of modern handmade papyrus pasted into the book. For a color photograph of papyrus preparation see H. Reimer-Epp and M. Reimer, *The Encyclopedia of Papermaking and Bookbinding* (London and Philadelphia 2002) 8. A modern method for making papyrus, somewhat different from Pliny's ancient account, is described in L. A. Bell, *Papyrus, Tapa, Amate, and Rice Paper* (McMinnville, Ore. 1983) 14–38, esp. 23–28.

[17] One Roman *digitus* = 0.73 inches or 1.85 cm (Lewis 56).

Figure 1. *Stages of papyrus manufacture: (left) removing the outer husk from the papyrus stalk and cutting strips from the inner pulp. Overlaying of horizontal* (recto) *strips over vertical* (verso) *strips, hammering to bring out the natural adhesive (Pliny mentions an artificial paste), and surface finishing. Image from "Papyrus,"* DNP *9 (2000) 299.*

A papyrus roll was produced by joining these upright rectangular sheets at their sides. This involved slightly overlapping the right edge of one sheet over the left of the next and gluing them together. The surface was then polished, particularly at the joins between sheets (however, the illustration in Figure 1 represents the entire surface being polished). The joins could be written over if necessary, since the overlap of right edge over the left allowed the pen to run "downhill" over the join. A completed papyrus roll with the joined sheets and columns written over the joins is shown below in Figure 2:

Figure 2. *Illustration of an open papyrus roll, showing the overlapping of the right edge of a sheet over the left to form a join, and the writing of the columns over these joins. Image drawn by W. E. H. Conkle, from E. G. Turner,* The Typology of the Early Codex *(Philadelphia: University of Pennsylvania Press, 1977) 45.*

The completed rolls measured approximately 5 to 15 feet, with some as long as 30 feet, although the "world record" is currently held by a papyrus roll of 132 feet in the British Museum (Lewis 55 n. 29). A roll of about 20 feet could accommodate, for example, an entire work such as Plato's *Symposium* (Blanck 85). For letters one simply cut off a piece of the desired length from the roll, often only a single sheet, and then fitted the message into that space. Seneca once said that a letter "ought not fill the reader's left hand" (*Ep.* 45.13)—in other words, ought not become a scroll needing the left hand to roll it up—while Cicero, who could also write longer letters, simply stopped when he approached a second page in one of his letters to his friends (*Fam.* 11.25.2: *altera iam pagella procedit*). The two letters of Apion and the two of the "elder" of 2–3 John fit within this limit.

The ink essentially consisted of lamp black or soot, which was mixed with water and a rubbery gum adhesive. In Greek it is therefore called τὸ μέλαν, the "black," but red ink was also produced. Vendors sold the ink in the dried condition; for writing it was blended again with water. As a writing instrument the Egyptians first selected the rush, whose point, when chewed up, works like a fine brush. But the standard writing instrument over the long term became the reed pen. The word for it, κάλαμος, has a wide semantic range and signifies many practical uses of the reed. It covers "all kinds of pipe and reed . . . for the production of arrows, flutes, shawms [a woodwind with a double reed], and pens, for thatching houses, building arches, sealing joints, making ropes, and also as fuel and for all kinds of domestic and medical purposes" (Ziegler). For writing the pen was given a diagonal point with a knife and pumice stone and resharpened if necessary. By a fine incision though this point one obtained two points, as with a modern metal fountain pen, that made writing more reliable.

Scribes of multi-page documents wrote line by line in broader or narrower columns, placing the columns side by side down the length of the scroll, just as the papyrus sheets are joined side to side. Yet these columns did not need to stay within the artificial limits of the papyrus sheets, since it was easy to write over the joins, as we have seen (Figure 2). The character style of literary texts on papyrus resembles that of the inscriptions: capital letters are set carefully next to each other, without ligatures and without long ascenders and descenders. But private, business, and official correspondence was different. Here a cursive develops in our period (not to be confused with the later Byzantine miniscule) in which the individual letters are written more roundly and are connected by a single stroke in groups that could also cross word boundaries (Hunger 72–107). For a document to be continued on the back of the piece of papyrus as a so-called "opistograph" was a rarity—hence the pregnancy of the mention of the "scroll written on the inside and on the back" in Revelation 5:1. But the back could be used later for other notes, if the owner of the papyrus no longer felt a need for the text on the front.

Shorter letters were either rolled or folded together. One then wound them with a cord and sealed them if necessary over the knot. The back of the papyrus thus became the exterior of the letter, which serves as the place for the outside address or, for other documents, a brief summary of the contents.

We know of papyrus letters and other texts in which the external circumstances of letter writing itself became the topic. Thus one letter writer complains that although he even sent his would-be correspondent "letter-writing papyri" or χάρτας ἐπιστολικούς, he did not consider it necessary to respond (P.Flor. III 367.7–10).[18] In another letter from the first century CE (P.Grenf.

---

[18] However, this "writing paper" is not necessarily a special grade of stationery for letters. Hence Lewis writes: "In these humble contexts the expression no doubt means 'paper good enough to write on,' that is, in

II 38.5–9),[19] the writer apparently places ten orders of "eight-tome" papyrus roll (ὀκτατόμου χάρτου δέκα), five orders of "four-tome" papyrus roll (τετρατόμου χάρτου πέντε)—the exact quantities thereby designated are uncertain[20]—and fifteen orders of reed pens (καλάμων γραφικῶν δεκάπεντε);[21] he also requests eight staters of ink (μέλανος στατῆρας ὀκτώ).[22] Cicero writes his brother Quintus: "This time it will be quality pen (*calamo*) and well-mixed ink (*atramento*) and ivory-finished paper (*charta*), since

---

the middle range of quality—superior to the 'emporitic' [= wrapping paper], obviously, but not one of the top grades" (46; cf. 91 n. 8, 131 n. 19 on P.Flor. III 367).

[19] P.Grenf. II 38.5–9 is reprinted in S. Witkowski, *Epistulae* (Bib. 1) 122, but we have used a different transcription of the text. See the next note.

[20] This presentation is based in part on the corrected Duke version of this papyrus (DDBDP). The Duke version of the order of ten reads (here with the P.Grenf. original in curly brackets): [ὀκ]τατόμου {[χαρ]τία δομοῦ} χάρ[του] δέκα, while the order of five reads: καὶ [τετ]ρατόμου {[...]ρα δομοῦ} χάρτου πέντε. These readings ὀκτατόμου and τετρατόμου χάρτου are also accepted by Lewis 77 n. 9; cf. similarly Sel.Pap. 1:285 note *c*. The LSJ *Greek-English Lexicon: Revised Supplement* (ed. P. G. W. Glare, 1996) defines τετράτομος as: "of a papyrus roll, *consisting of four* τόμοι, χάρτας τετρατόμους PLond.ined. 2134 (*JHS* 55.95, ii AD)." Obviously if this were taken here to refer to five quadruple rolls (i.e., 20 rolls), then an order of ten eightfold rolls (80 rolls) would be unrealistic. But if this means rolls consisting of (cut into? cf. τόμος with τέμνω) four and eight τόμοι, respectively, then the figures need to be inverted: five quarter-rolls and ten eighth-rolls would constitute the same amount of papyrus (one roll and a quarter). Lewis cites P.Grenf. II 38 as an example of the customer's opportunity "to buy smaller quantities than a roll at retail" (55 n. 29, with further papyrus citations). He adds that "where the two terms [sc. χάρτης and τόμος] differed it was χάρτης that designated the larger unit, a single χάρτης sometimes encompassing . . . three, four, and even eight τόμοι" (76–77, again with reference to P.Grenf. II 38 in 77 n. 9, already cited above).

[21] A γραφικὸς κάλαμος (see also 3 Macc 4:20) is literally a "writing reed" and therefore a "reed pen," but the single term κάλαμος is also sufficient to designate the reed pen, as in 3 John 13.

[22] The Duke text, printed above, corrects the faulty grammar of P.Grenf. II 38 by reading the gen. μέλανος for the acc. μέλαν and the acc. pl. στατῆρας for the gen. sg. στατηροῦ.

you say you could hardly read my last letter" (*Quint. fratr.* 2.15.1
[LCL 28:135]). In 3 Maccabees the Egyptian scribes are ordered
by their king, Ptolemy IV Philopator, to register all the Jews in the
country for the purpose of extermination. When they failed to
complete this task and were accused by the king of taking bribes
to help the Jews, the scribes defended themselves by proving that
"both the stock of papyrus (χαρτηρίαν)[23] and the reed pens
(γραφικοὺς καλάμους) they were using had already given out" (3
Macc 4:20)—a saving event that the Jewish author attributes to
divine providence (cf. 4:17-21). Finally, a judgment scene from the
Testament of Abraham brings together all the writing materials and
implements: "On the table lay a book whose thickness was six
cubits, while its breadth was ten cubits. On its right and on its left
stood two angels holding papyrus and ink and pen" (*T. Ab.* 12:7-8;
OTP 1:889).

[23] Since χαρτηρία occurs only here in 3 Maccabees 4:19 in surviving
ancient Greek literature (cf. TLG), its precise nuance and distinction
over against χάρτης is unclear. The above translation "stock of papyrus"
is from the LXX lexicon of LEH. Although LSJ considers χαρτηρία an
exact synonym of χάρτης, thus justifying the NRSV translation by "the
paper . . . had already given out," this is hardly different from saying that
the Egyptian scribes' papyrus stocks ran out. More serious however from
the perspective of the scribes is the possibility that not only their stock of
paper but the "paper mill" (*OTP*) or "Papierfabrik" (*APAT*) itself had
failed to keep up production. Although the story is fantastic there is a
certain logic to this last suggestion, since this persecution of the Jews is
set in Ptolemaic Egypt and particularly Alexandria, where many papyrus
"factories" would indeed be located owing to the nearness both of
papyrus plants in the surrounding marshes and of the seaports for export
shipping. However, lexically this local sense of a paper *mill* or *factory*
would be more certain had the form been not the feminine χαρτηρία but
the (unattested) neuter χαρτήριον, cf. e.g. ἐργαστήριον, "workshop."

Exercise

6. The following text is from the *Paraleipomena Jeremiou* 6:19-
    20. What does it say about the writing procedure? What
    else is significant for our topic? Judging from this excerpt,
    when do you think the *Paraleipomena Jeremiou* was written,
    and what are its general contents? Where would one find
    an edition or translation? The text runs:

    And Baruch sent to the marketplace of the gentiles and got
    papyrus (χάρτην) and ink (μέλανα), and he wrote the following
    letter: "Baruch, the servant of God, writes to Jeremiah in the cap-
    tivity of Babylon: Hail and rejoice (χαῖρε καὶ ἀγγαλλιῶ)! For
    God has not left us to pass out of this body grieving over the city
    which was desolated and outraged.

---

3. Scribes and Secretaries

Our first question is: Who actually took pen in hand and wrote
down the letter on papyrus? To this we want to answer spontaneously: in our two model examples from chapter 1, it must have
been Apion and the elder. We would thereby be following the old
thesis of O. Roller, who thought that "a person trained to write
might occasionally write down a brief letter of only a few words or
lines in their own hand, and many, but by no means all, original
papyrus letters might have been written in the author's own hand"
(4). But that is not so certain, as the possibility of different hands in
the two Apion letters suggests, and even Roller finds it necessary to
qualify his thesis substantially. We would also have to know among
other things to what extent we could presuppose a knowledge of
reading and writing among those who took part in the communication process. The two questions are not identical, however,
because it is not only conceivable but also occurred in practice (as
we shall see) that even very educated authors sometimes availed
themselves of outside help for writing down their letters.

We can begin in very broad terms by assuming that "in Greco-
Roman antiquity, at least up to the end of the third century CE,
reading and writing was a skill accessible to everybody" (Blanck
39). It was taught in elementary schools, which were open to the

wider public, through writing exercises, reading exercises, and dictation. This also applies to Egypt,[24] although there the problem of
different regional languages also enters in, for someone could be
regarded as ἀγράμματος, i.e., unable to read or write, simply for
failing to master Greek. What someone made or could make of
the opportunities that were in principle available varied greatly
from case to case, and there remains a wide range over which complete illiteracy and perfect reading and writing ability form only
the two endpoints. We must reckon with the fact that a part of the
population could read and write only hesitantly and with great
effort,[25] and that they sometimes had to piece together words syllable by syllable. Moreover, the capabilities of reading and writing
did not always go hand in hand, so that someone able to read a letter would not necessarily also be able answer it, but might need the
help of a friend or a professional scribe, as we shall see.

Official letters and legal documents in particular allow us to
determine the situations in which people needed help with their
letters, for near the conclusion of such letters we often find the so-
called "illiteracy formula." Here the scribe states his name and
certifies, apparently as required by law, that he wrote the letter for
someone else who was not in a position to do so. Scribes commu-
nicated the letter-senders' inability to write for themselves by several formulas, using a participle, an infinitive, or both. Hence in a
contract of apprenticeship from 66 CE between the father of a boy
and the weaver to whom the boy is to be apprenticed, the scribe
states the weaver's illiteracy by means of a causal participle: "I,
Zoilus, son of Horos . . . have written for him [the weaver],
because *he does not know* (μὴ ἰδότος = εἰδότος) letters (i.e., is illit-

---

[24] Cf. White 215: "The extensive amount of papyrus correspondence
at all levels of Egyptian society suggests that illiteracy was not as great in
the ancient world, even in smaller towns and villages of Egypt, as we
thought only a century ago." It nevertheless remains very difficult to estimate the level of ancient literacy, and one more skeptical proposal which
has won some approval estimates it only at ten percent of the population,
with up to thirty or even forty percent (but only of the freeborn men) in
a few cities and only five percent in the Latin West. So W. V. Harris,
Ancient Literacy (Cambridge, Mass. 1989) 328–30.

[25] Cf. H. C. Youtie, "Βραδέως γράφων: Between Literacy and Illiteracy," *GRBS* 12 (1971) 239–61.

erate)."[26] The older formula with the infinitive is also found: "I, the aforesaid Aphrodisios specified before, have written [as γραμματεύς of the local weaver's guild] for him, Herakles [chairman of the guild], because *he does not know* (μὴ εἰδέναι) letters (i.e., is illiterate)."[27] Another formula combines a participle and infinitive for the sender's illiteracy, with the scribe speaking in the third person rather than the first: "Isidoros, public scribe (νομογράφος), has written for him, because he *professes not to know* (φαμένου μὴ εἰδέναι) letters (i.e., to be illiterate)."[28] Although the illiteracy formula is usually stated from the scribe's perspective, in other instances the sender's own mention of his difficulty in writing is enough to justify his employment of a scribe:[29]

> Asklepiades, son of Charmagon,
> to Portis, son of Permamis, greeting.
> I have received from you the fruit
> that falls to me . . .
> and I lay nothing more to your charge.
> Eumulos son of Herma has written for him,
> having been asked to do so because
> he writes somewhat slowly.

However, business partners who knew how to write nevertheless often had others draw up contracts for them. An agreement to divide the ownership of slaves and their descendants among three brothers has three additions at the end that contrast with each other and with the main text. These are introduced by ὑπογραφὴ ἰδία τῶν τριῶ(ν) γεγραμ(μένων), "autograph subscription of the three persons mentioned."[30] Three names do in fact follow, but unlike our signature today, these alone are never sufficient in

---

[26] P.Oxy. II 275.41–43: ὑπὲρ αὐτοῦ μὴ ἰδιότος γράμματα (Sel.Pap. 1:38–41). Cf. similar examples in F. X. J. Exler, *Ancient Greek Letter* (Bib. 2) 124–27.

[27] P.Ryl. 94.14–16 (14–37 CE): διὰ τὸ μὴ εἰδέναι αὐτὸν γράμματα (Sel.Pap. 2:188–89).

[28] P.Hamb. 4.14–15 (87 CE): ἔγραψεν ὑπὲρ αὐτοῦ φαμένου μὴ εἰδέναι γράμματα (Sel.Pap. 2:174–77).

[29] O.Wilck. 1027 (another ostracon, this time from the Ptolemaic period); cf. A. Deissmann, *Light from the Ancient East* (Bib. 1) 166.

[30] *PSI* VIII 903 (47 CE); also in Sel.Pap. 1:152–55.

antiquity for the authentication of a text. Instead the substantial content of the agreement must also be repeated and confirmed in abbreviated form, as happens here.

In private correspondence this express mention of one's name at the end is missing because it was considered unnecessary. However, if private letters from the same sender exhibit different handwriting, or if letters of completely different senders are drawn up in the same handwriting, then the use of paid scribes or literate friends and relatives becomes clear. There are further indications of outside help if parts of the letter show the marks of the actual sender, for example, if the concluding health wish is entered later in a second hand (that of the actual sender), or the sender mentions his name and the reason for the letter, or other smaller changes are made (Richards 21–22). However, the formula in the prescript indicating that the author is writing to the addressee *"through* (διά) person X" (as below in P.Oxy. IV 724, where X = Gemellus) need not be an indication of the intervention of a scribe, since the letter carrier can also be meant (Richards 69–73). Moreover, when a scribe was involved, the sender could always refer to him as the "letter writer" or ἐπιστολόγραφος (Richards 16).

For texts of the caliber of the Apion letters, professional scribes were available who offered their services in the market and on the road. From here is a long way up to the private secretary of a distinguished, rich Roman, and the speed at which scribes could take dictation also varied widely. In a famous passage Cicero contrasts his secretary Tiro, his right-hand man, with another slave he retained for writing: "For that reason I did not dictate it even to Tiro, who is by way of taking down whole periods together, but syllable by syllable to Spintharus" (*Letters to Atticus* 13.25.3). Dictating *syllabatim*, syllable by syllable, seems to have been the rule, about which employers of scribes frequently complained. Writers were therefore all the more pleased when then could dictate *viva voce*, at a normal rate of speech, to a speedy stenographer. Cicero's secretary Tiro is regarded as the inventor of the "Tironian notes," a system of shorthand for the purpose of high-speed transcription which, however, was specific to the Latin language. For Greek tachygraphy reliable details are even more difficult to come by than for Latin; what we do have is, for example, a contract in letter form from 155 CE about training a slave to write shorthand (P.Oxy. IV 724):[31]

> Panechotes also called Panares, ex-cosmetes of Oxyrhynchus, *through his friend Gemellus* [perhaps the letter carrier rather than the scribe: see above], to Apollonius, writer of shorthand (σημιογράφῳ, lit. "sign writer"), greeting. I have placed with you my slave Chaerammon to learn the signs (σημείων) which your son Dionysius knows, for a period of two years . . . for the fee agreed upon between us of 120 silver drachmae, with exception of feast days; and of this sum you have had a first instalment of 40 drachmae, and you will receive a second instalment of 40 drachmae when the boy has learned all the commentary [a collection of tachygraphic signs] by heart, and the third instalment, the remaining 40 drachmae, you will receive at the end of the period when the boy can write and read from prose of all kinds without fault. . . . The 18th year of the Emperor Caesar Titus Aelius Hadrianus Antoninus Augustus Pius, Phamenoth 5.

In order to help determine more accurately the possible cooperation of a secretary of whatever category in the emergence of a letter, E. R. Richards has produced a useful typology of four categories (97–111). We therefore differentiate:

- the secretary as a mere "recorder" who writes down the text strictly by dictation, either *syllabatim* or *viva voce* as his skills allow;
- the secretary as an "editor," which suggests that the author speaks and the secretary meanwhile takes detailed notes, which he uses as a draft for the letter;
- the secretary as a "co-author" to whom the author gives only some content catchwords and the main line of argument, while the secretary's task is to convert this into a properly styled letter;
- the secretary as a "composer" who is simply told by his client that this or that letter has to be answered in his name or written to a certain person; all the rest is left to the experience and skill of the secretary.

---

[31] Translation from Sel.Pap. 1:44–51. Text also in J. Hengstl, *Griechische Papyri* (Bib. 1) 244–46 and P. W. Pestman, *Papyrological Primer* (Bib. 6) 186–87.

This results in a scale for the secretarial role that runs from a letter that the author who lends his name to it entirely controls ("author-controlled") to a letter for which the secretary alone is basically responsible ("secretary-controlled").

Against this background, a letter written in the author's own hand acquires a special significance. It is not born of necessity or stinginess, as if the author did not want to pay a professional scribe, but rather appears "as something special, almost as a demonstration of the most intimate friendship, or of great honor, respect, or condescension, or of great emotion—in short always as something extraordinary" (Roller 15).

Exercise

7. Compare Romans 16:22; Galatians 6:11; 1 Corinthians 1:1 and their context to what has been said in this section. What conclusions can be drawn about the Apostle Paul's letter-writing practice? How far does the range of Galatians 6:11 extend in the text? What is the function of Sosthenes?

B. Possibilities for the Conveyance of Letters

Bibliography 13: F. F. Bruce, "Travel and Communication (NT World)," *ABD* 6 (1992) 648–53. – **E. J. Epp**, "New Testament Papyrus Manuscripts and Letter Carrying in Greco-Roman Times," in B. A. Pearson, et al., eds., *The Future of Early Christianity*, FS H. Koester (Minneapolis 1991) 35–56. – **A. Kolb**, *Transport und Nachrichtentransfer im Römischen Reich*, Klio Beihefte NF 2 (Berlin 2000). – **S. R. Llewelyn**, "The Conveyance of Letters," *NewDocs* 7 (1994) 1–57. – **M. M. Mitchell**, "New Testament Envoys in the Context of Greco-Roman Diplomatic and Epistolary Conventions: The Example of Timothy and Titus," *JBL* 111 (1992) 641–62. – **J. Murphy-O'Connor**, *Paul* (Bib. 4) 37–41. – **F. Preisigke**, "Die ptolemäische Staatspost," *Klio* 8 (1907) 241–77. – **R. Reck**, *Kommunikation* (Bib. 7) 106–12 (with further literature). – **W. Riepl**, *Das Nachrichtenwesen des Altertums mit besonderer Rücksicht auf die Römer* (Leipzig 1913; repr. Hildesheim 1972). – **M. L. Stirewalt, Jr.**, "Paul's Evaluation of Letter Writing," in J. M. Myers, O. Reimherr, and H. N. Bream, eds., *Search the Scriptures*, FS R. T. Stamm,

Gettysburg Theological Studies 3 (Leiden 1969) 179–96. – **P. Stoffel**, *Über die Staatspost, die Ochsengespanne und die requirierten Ochsengespanne: Eine Darstellung des römischen Postwesens auf Grund der Gesetze des Codex Theodosianus und des Codex Iustinianus*, Europäische Hochschulschriften III/595 (Frankfurt a.M. 1994). – **W. L. Westermann**, "On Inland Transportation and Communication in Antiquity," *Political Science Quarterly* 43 (1928) 364–87. – **J. L. White**, *Light from Ancient Letters* (Bib. 1) 214–16.

A well-organized, relatively safe system for the transmission of messages through letters and other means existed in the ancient world only where national interests were at stake. The earliest reports about this concern the Persian empire, about whose messenger system Herodotus writes with obvious admiration (*Hist.* 8.98.1–2):

> Now there is nothing mortal that accomplishes a course more swiftly than do these messengers, by the Persians' skillful contrivance. It is said that as many days as there are in the whole journey, so many are the men and horses that stand along the road, each horse and each man at the interval of a day's journey; and *these are stayed neither by snow nor rain nor heat nor darkness from accomplishing their appointed course with all speed.*[32] The first rider delivers his charge to the second, the second to the third, and thence it passes on from hand to hand, even as in the Greek torch-bearer's race in honour of Hephaestus. This riding-post is called in Persia, *angereïon* (ἀγγαρήιον).[33]

[32] A slightly more poetic version of this line from Herodotus effectively serves as the *unofficial* "motto" of the U.S. Postal Service. As the Postal Service explains: "Contrary to popular belief, the United States Postal Service has no official motto. However, a number of postal buildings contain inscriptions." The most familiar of these is the unattributed Herodotus quotation on the General Post Office building in New York City: "*Neither snow nor rain nor heat nor gloom of night stays these couriers from the swift completion of their appointed rounds.*" Professor George H. Palmer of Harvard University selected this translation of Herodotus from among several others. (Source: www.usps.com/history/his8.htm.)

[33] Trans. A. D. Godley, *Herodotus*, LCL 4 (1925) 97. As Godley explains (97 n. 2), "ἄγγαρος is apparently a Babylonian word, the Persian word for a post-rider being in Greek ἀστάνδης . . . ἄγγαρος passed into Greek usage; *cp.* Aesch. Ag. 282." According to LSJ, ἀγγαρήιος is the Ionic form of ἄγγαρος, as in Herodotus 3.126, while ἀγγαρήιον, used here in 8.98, is the neuter substantive.

Xenophon adds that this goes back to an edict of Cyrus (*Cyropaedia* 8.6.17–18). His version of the story includes the claim of some who say that the Persian relay system "gets over ground faster than the cranes." While Xenophon regards this as slightly exaggerated, he still has to admit that "it is at all events undeniable that this is the fastest overland travelling on earth" (§18). In the book of Esther the Jews in Persia are affected by this system: Special couriers are sent into all the provinces with letters ordering a pogrom, instigated by Haman (Esth 3:12-13). Later the edict protecting the Jews brought about by Esther and Mordechai travels the same way: "He (sc. Mordecai) wrote letters [through secretaries] in the name of King Ahasuerus, sealed them with the king's ring, and sent them by mounted couriers riding on fast steeds bred from the royal herd" (8:10).

Alexander the Great became acquainted with the Persian postal system during his conquests, and his successors—the Seleucids in Syria, the Antigonids in Asia Minor and Greece, and the Ptolemies in Egypt—tried to develop a comparable system in the areas under their control (cf. Preisigke). From there the system developed into to the extremely efficient Roman *cursus publicus*, which began under Caesar and was established under Augustus. Thus Suetonius reports in his biography of Augustus (49.3):

> To enable what was going on in each of the provinces to be reported and known more speedily and promptly, he at first stationed young men at short intervals along the military roads, and afterwards vehicles (*vehicula*). The latter has seemed the more convenient arrangement, since the same men who bring the dispatches from any place can, if occasion demands, be questioned as well. (*Suetonius* LCL 1:229)

We can still make out two phases in this text. In the earlier model, a relay system on the Persian pattern, the first of the "young men" passed the message on to the second and then stayed behind, etc. But eventually the other practice became established, allowing a single messenger who was provided with a "vehicle" (probably a cart)[34] and fresh horses at each relay station to cover the whole dis-

---

[34] White, *Light from Ancient Letters*, 214, writes of the Augustan postal service: "Later, couriers thundered down highways in *chariots* and all other travelers had to give up the right of way" (italics added). But despite the cinematic image of the chariot race in Ben Hur that this may

tance. The advantage of this was that the courier could supplement the letter with oral information. In order to carry out his assignment, the courier received a special "passport," Latin *diploma* (cf. Suetonius, *Aug.* 50; Cicero, *Fam.* 6.12), that granted him numerous privileges. The general population of the province had to maintain the stations, supply drawing and load-bearing animals free of charge, and provide further support services (apparently only the provisions had to be paid for). Only in a genuine emergency did Pliny the Younger dare to issue one of these coveted passports to his wife for private reasons, and even then he felt he had to explain it to the emperor Trajan (*Ep.* 10.120.1–3). It may have been easier to operate on the fringe of legality by giving personal messages to official couriers who were already on their way. Our word "post" has its origin in the Roman *cursus publicus*. As White explains, "'post' is derived from the Latin *positus*, which means 'fixed' or 'placed' and refers to the fixed posts or stations in the relay system" (214). Nevertheless, it must be noted that this was still a state postal service in the strict sense, intended only for the purposes of the government, administration, and military.

Private citizens had to look for other possibilities for the delivery of letters. The wealthy could send their own slaves or avail themselves of independent couriers, the so-called *tabellarii*. Usually they were paid by the sender, but for a message that he urgently awaited, Pliny the Younger offered to remunerate the courier (*tabellario*) himself and even promised a bonus (*Ep.* 3.17.2). There were also private tax collectors or so-called "tax farmers" who bought the taxation rights of larger regions from the government and kept a surtax for themselves while returning the rest to the government. They too maintained their own courier service, which they shared with others for a price. Family members, friends, merchants, soldiers—all could be given letters when they went on journeys. That there actually was a "culture of letter writing" (P. A. Rosenmeyer) depends not least on the fact that "each traveler was also (at least potentially) a postman at the same time" (Reck 109).

Some uncertainties were certainly associated with these chance deliveries by incidental couriers, a fact about which Cicero,

---

conjure up for many readers, a more utilitarian horse-drawn cart or carriage may be closer to the reality, especially if the courier also had a driver and was forced to travel through the night.

to whose extensive correspondence we owe our most animated view of the ancient letter system (Riepl 243–44), not infrequently complained. A letter to his friend Atticus that he gave to the first man he met (*Att.* 2.12.4) does not reach its destination on the first try but is returned to Cicero to be sent again (2.13.1). On another occasion a slave dawdles around for more than 40 days before he thinks of delivering the letter (*Letters to Friends* 8.12.4). There is always the question of how trustworthy the messengers are, whether they will leave the letter untouched and handle its delicate contents with care. Thus Cicero writes: "I have been rather slow about making [a reply] because I can't find a trustworthy carrier. There are so few who can carry a letter of any substance without lightening the weight by perusal" (*Att.* 1.13.1).

Members of a lower social class than the wealthy Romans were surely even more severely affected by such perils. One therefore understands all the better the request for delivery confirmation in some papyrus letters, with side-blows against unreliable carriers, who are held in general suspicion:[35]

> **P.Oxy. II 300.3–6**: I sent the breadbasket to you by Taurinos, the camel driver; regarding which, please send word to me that you received it.

> **P.Mich. VIII 481.5–8**: Receive from the one who brings this letter to you a basket and write back to me what you find in it.

> **P.Mich. VIII 499.12–14**: I wrote to you often, and the negligence of those who carry (the letters) has accused us falsely as negligent.

---

[35] Texts and translations of the following six letters in White, *Light from Ancient Letters*. See, in order, White's nos. 94 (Indike to Thaisous), 112 (Terentianus to Tasoucharion), 115b (to Apollinarius the veteran from his brother Sabinianus), 104a, 104b (Apollinarios the recruit to his mother), and 10 (Simale to Zenon), pp. 146, 177, 183–84, 161–62, 164, 33–34, respectively. Although White does not link Apollinarios the recruit to Apollinarius the veteran in his commentary (and offers no rationale for the Greek -ος ending here and the Latinized -*us* there), his index s.v. *Apollinarios* suggests that they may be the same person and lists all four letters 104a–b and 115a–b together: "Apollinarios, recruit (and veteran?) [pp.] 161–62, 164, 182–84."

When people are wringing their hands looking for letter carriers, they will gladly take every opportunity to convey a written message through an acquaintance or a stranger who is traveling in the right direction. This was done by Apion in his second letter, and by another Egyptian recruit, Apollinarios, who communicates to his mother: "When I found someone who was journeying to you from Cyrene, I thought it a necessity to inform you about my welfare" (P.Mich. VIII 490.5–7), and who apparently reacts in another letter to her implicit reproach: "And, for my part, if I ever find someone (to carry the letter), I will write to you; I certainly will not hesitate to write to you" (P.Mich. VIII 491.13–14). The fact that these letters often had to be delivered by someone the sender knew personally also had its advantages. The deliverer is then available to transmit oral information and answer further inquiries that go beyond what was written in the letter. Sometimes this was even planned into the letter from the start, as in P.Col. III 6.14–16: "The rest (i.e., anything else that remains) learn from the one who carries the letter to you. For he is no stranger to us."

All these factors also carry substantial implications for the Apostle Paul's activity as a letter writer. The mere existence of his correspondence is already a sign of the close network of relationships that had developed between the individual churches, which also made a sufficient number of letter carriers available. It is probably no accident that Paul preferred to stay in urban centers such as Corinth and Ephesus, which had heavy tourist traffic and good travel connections with all provinces of the empire. Paul also knew how to ensure the safe transmission of his letters by security measures, as when he sends off a close co-worker such as Titus with a letter and leaves the oral explanation to him. But we should not regard these envoys as simply a stopgap measure or an imperfect substitute for the desired personal presence of the apostle. There were situations that could be dealt with better by envoys and tasks that could be accomplished only by envoys (cf. Mitchell).

Exercises

8. In our introduction we became familiar with two ancient dinner invitations (P.Oxy. I 110 and 111); a third example follows. Pay attention to the particulars of content, but try above all to reconstruct the social setting in which such an extremely short message could have been delivered.

   P.Köln I 57 (Oxyrhynchus, 3rd cent. BCE)

καλεῖ σε ὁ θεὸς	The god calls you
εἰς κλείνην γεινο(μένην)	to a banquet being held
ἐν τῷ Θοηρείῳ	in the Thoereion
αὔριον ἀπὸ ὥρ(ας) θ'.	tomorrow from the 9th hour.

9. What does the following passage from Flavius Josephus say about the delivery of letters? The text, whose historical context must first be determined, is found in *War* 2.203 and runs:

   To this dispatch [lit., epistle] [sc. from Petronius] Gaius replied in no measured terms, threatening to put Petronius to death for his tardiness in executing his orders. However, it so happened that the bearers of this message were weather-bound for three months at sea, while others, who brought the news of the death of Gaius, had a fortunate passage. So Petronius received this last information twenty-seven days earlier than the letter conveying his own death warrant.

10. Read the following text from Paul in 2 Corinthians 3:1-3, paying attention to such questions as: What situation is Paul referring to? How does he translate it into picture language? How are the roles divided up in connection with the "letter" he talks about in v. 2? Who is the sender, who are the addresses, what is the content, and what part does Paul play in this?

    2 Cor. 3:1 Are we beginning to commend (συνιστάνειν) ourselves again? Surely we do not need, as some do, letters of recommendation (συστατικῶν ἐπιστολῶν) to you or from you, do we? **2** You yourselves are our letter (ἐπιστολή), written on our hearts, to be known and read by all; **3** and you show that you are a letter of Christ, prepared by us, written not with ink but with the Spirit of the living God, not on tablets of stone but on tablets of human hearts.

3

Nonliterary and Diplomatic Correspondence

A. Questions of Classification

Bibliography 14: M. Buss, "Principles for Morphological Criticism: With Special Reference to Letter Form," in R. A. Spencer, ed., *Orientation by Disorientation: Studies in Literary Criticism and Biblical Literary Criticism*, FS W. A. Beardslee, PTMS 35 (Pittsburgh, Pa. 1980) 71–86. – **P. Cugusi**, *Evoluzione* (Bib. 2) 105–36. – **A. Deissmann**, *Light from the Ancient East* (Bib. 1) 227–51. – **W. G. Doty**, "The Classification of Epistolary Literature," *CBQ* 31 (1969) 183–99. – **H. Koskenniemi**, "Cicero über die Briefarten (Genera Epistularum)," *Arctos* NF 1 (1954) 97–102 (= FS E. Linkomies). – **H. Hunger**, *Buch- und Schriftwesen* (Bib. 12). – **E. R. Richards**, *Secretary* (Bib. 4) 14–23. – **K. Thraede**, "Zwischen Gebrauchstext und Poesie: Zur Spannweite der antiken Gattung Brief," *Didactica Classica Gandensia* 20 (1980) 179–218. – **J. L. White** and **K. A. Kensinger**, "Categories of Greek Papyrus Letters," *SBLSP* 1 (1976) 79–91.

The multitude of letters that have come down to us from antiquity presents us with considerable problems of classification that have not found a single simple or widely accepted solution. If we focus for the moment only on the types of writing materials, then papyrus could be used for recording any number of different kinds of writings. In the words of one specialist, papyrus was used for "all works of literature from first draft to final copy, but also all types of documents, including official and private letters, petitions and complaints, records of various authorities, minutes of municipal councils, accounts and lists of bank and tax officials, journal entries, contracts of sale, lease, and marriage, wills, birth and death announcements, etc." (Hunger 32)—and significantly a letter frame is used for many of these types of texts, beyond the letter in the narrower sense. Even the letter-edict of the emperor Claudius to the Alexandrians is preserved on papyrus, although in this case only accidentally (see below), since otherwise royal letters are mainly known from their subsequent engraving on stone or quotation by ancient historians. For the bulk of papyrus letters the category that immediately suggests itself is that of the private letter, and for the Apion letters, for example, which belong to the subset of family letters, this is certainly appropriate. But the category "private letters" has the disadvantage of not covering papyrus texts with a letter frame but a legal, official, or commercial character. On the other hand, famous writers and philosophers, whose letters scholars usually classify separately from those in the papyrus corpus because they came down to us differently, through a literary process, have also written letters of purely private character. Collections of Cicero's letters occupy a special place because they highlight the transition from the private to the literary letter.

In this situation we have little choice but to opt for a pragmatic solution that allows us to organize the material into suitable groupings for further work. We therefore differentiate between (1) nonliterary letters, also called "documentary" letters (so, e.g., J. L. White), (2) diplomatic letters or royal and imperial letters, and (3) literary letters.

(1) *Nonliterary letters* are purely occasional documents, written without a sideward glance to the broader public or posterity and therefore preserved mostly on papyrus in the original rather than in copies. In point of detail this category is open to further subdivision. Hence we find private letters, official letters—a distinction we see Cicero making in court (*Flacc.* 37: *in publicis sed etiam in privatis litteris*, "on both public and private letters" [LCL 10:483])—and business letters. With the help of epistolary theory (see below chap. 5) we can further distinguish various types (mainly within the genre of the private letter) such as the family letter, the friendly letter, the letter of recommendation, the letter of exhortation, the letter of praise or blame or, to single out one particular type, the letter of consolation. We have already become familiar with family letters through Apion's correspondence. But from among the other categories, we will discuss in the next section only the letter of recommendation because of its affinities to certain New Testament passages, such as 2 Corinthians 3:1 (see above Exercise 10).

The sphere into which the ancient letter radiates is exceptionally broad particularly in the nonliterary realm, and ultimately resists almost all attempts at classification. One repeatedly stumbles on surprising finds where one least expects them—for example, in magical papyri and similar texts in other media. Some of the lead curse tablets that are inscribed with imprecations and plunged into pits or wells take the form of letters to a dead person who is pressed into service as a letter carrier in the afterworld.[1] The letter form is occasionally used as a framework in the *Greek Magical Papyri*. Letters are used to pass rituals and secret formulas from a father to a son or daughter (cf. the closing formula in *PGM* XIII 343: ἔρρωσο, τέκνον) or from magicians to a king, as the prescript in *PGM* IV 154–55: "Nephotes to Psammetichos, immortal king of Egypt. Greetings."[2]

(2) Although the category of the nonliterary *official letter* is fluid, it is useful to set apart from this practical, everyday use of official correspondence, mostly by people who would otherwise remain unknown to us, another textual group: the *diplomatic letters*, which usually means royal or imperial letters that carry some political weight. A criterion for their identification can be their secondary conservation in inscriptions or quotation by historians. Unfortunately, these texts are seldom used for comparison with the New Testament. Below we discuss two examples, a letter of the Seleucid ruler Antiochus III the Great and one of the emperor Claudius, because both introduce us to eventful periods of Jewish history.

(3) *The literary letters* with few exceptions have come down to us only in copies and collections, which already indirectly documents their claim to permanence. Once again this category exhibits great breadth. Rhetorical school exercises and forgeries for propaganda purposes are covered, as well as poetic verses of writers like Ovid or Horace and the letters embedded in ancient novels. Philosophical doctrinal treatises in letter form are also included, although it is sometimes not entirely clear whether these were intended for real addressees or simply used the letter form as a transparent exercise of fiction. The literary letters are given a

---

[1] Cf. F. Graf, *Gottesnähe und Schadenszauber: Die Magie in der griechisch-römischen Antike* (Munich 1996) 118–19; cf. also 94 for what follows.

[2] H. D. Betz, ed., *The Greek Magical Papyri in Translation* (Chicago ²1992) 40.

chapter of their own because of their importance (chap. 4), although we should always remember that we are working only with pragmatic categories that help us cope with the overwhelming amount of material.

At this point a note on the history of interpretation is necessary. In his day (cf. *Licht vom Osten* [¹1907]), A. Deissmann sought to cut through the knot involved in letter classification by positing a simple dichotomy between a letter and an epistle: "The letter is a piece of life, the epistle is a product of literary art" (*Light from the Ancient East*, 230).[3] His main aim in this was to present the letters of Paul as nonliterary texts that one could best compare with private papyrus letters, in order then to set apart Paul's (real) "letters" from the less occasional and more formal, homiletic, or treatise-like (catholic) "epistles" such as James and Hebrews. An essential part of Deissmann's categorization lives on the distinction between non-literary and literary letters, which nobody denies today, and therefore Deissmann hardly deserves the sharp censure he gets in some of the more recent literature. That Deissmann's simple bifurcation of letter types is insufficient in the long run and that he made too little use of transitional categories goes without saying. Nevertheless, more sympathetic recent scholarship has demonstrated a simple way of making Deissmann's two categories of the "letter" and "epistle" more flexible, namely by combining them to make four categories.[4] But the real difficulty lies in the appli-

---

[3] For a good summary of Deissmann see Doty 183–92.

[4] So R. E. Brown. In his standard work *An Introduction to the New Testament*, ABRL (New York 1997), Brown labels each of the 21 freestanding New Testament letters as either a Letter, a Letter (Epistle), an Epistle (Letter), or an Epistle (actually a non-category: see below), thus providing two "transitional" categories with an explicit nod to Deissmann. Compare the book designations in Brown's table of contents for chapters 12–14 (1–3 John), 18–24 (undisputed Paulines), 26–31 (disputed Paulines and Pastorals), and 32–36 (Catholic Letters/Epistles) with Brown's explanation and application of Deissmann's categories on pp. 410–11. Moreover, Brown's application of these categories remains largely "Deissmannes-que." Hence each of the undisputed Paulines is a "Letter," as are 2 Thessalonians, Colossians, and the Pastorals; only Ephesians within the Pauline corpus is designated the "Epistle (Letter) to the Ephesians." The other writings in Brown's more literary category of the Epistle (Letter) include—with Deissmann—1 John, James, and 2 Peter, while in a slight retreat from Deissmann, Hebrews and Jude are each designated primarily as a "Letter" and secondarily as an "Epistle," while 1 Peter is even further from Deissmann's analysis as simply a Letter (cf. the undisputed Paulines), like 2 and 3 John. Most telling in this presentation is the fact that Brown

cation: Are the "letters" of Paul really so unliterary and so little comparable with the literary letters or "epistles" as Deissmann would have it? Here
further discussion is necessary.

Exercise

11. To which of the above letter types would you assign the fol-
    lowing document? How would you characterize it in gen-
    eral? (P.Enteuxeis 87)

To king Ptolemy greetings from Apollodotos, (one) of the inhabitants
    in Alabanthis. I am being wronged by Mnaseas,
the administrator of the outer regions. Though I owe nothing to
    the king and am also not
registered by him (in a list of debtors), he takes a pledge from me
    and vexes my gooseherd. I therefore ask you,
king, if it seems good to you, to give an order to the governor
    Diophanes to write to the overseer Herodotos that he, if I
am shown as owing nothing nor having been registered (as a
    debtor) by Mnaseas, does not allow Mnaseas to
take a pledge from me nor to vex my people. Once this has happened,
    I will be (someone who) through you, king,
has attained justice.
Farewell.

Second hand:

To Herodotos . . . 25th year, 26th Loios, 13th Choiak.

Verso:

25th (year), 26th Loios, 13th Choiak.
Apollodotos against Mnaseas,
because of a pledge.

---

nowhere uses his implicit fourth category of the (purely literary)
"Epistle." For no New Testament composition with letter features was
ever written primarily for publication as a literary work in which the
addressees served as little more than a convenient foil.

B. Letters of Recommendation

Bibliography 15: R. Buzón, *Briefe* (Bib. 2) 46–86. – **H. Cotton**, *Documentary Letters of Recommendation in Latin from the Roman Empire*, BKP 132 (Königstein im Taunus 1981). – eadem, "Greek and Latin Epistolary Formulae: Some Light on Cicero's Letter Writing," *AJP* 105 (1984) 409–25. – **A. von Dobbeler**, "Die Macht der Briefe und die Kraft des Geistes: Eine Antithese in Apg 9 und 2 Kor 3 und ihr religions-geschichtlicher Hintergrund," in A. von Dobbeler, K. Erlemann, and R. Heiligenthal, eds., *Religionsgeschichte des Neuen Testaments*, FS K. Berger (Tübingen and Basel 2000) 49–65. – **C. W. Keyes**, "The Greek Letter of Introduction," *AJP* 56 (1935) 28–44. – **C. H. Kim**, *Form and Structure of the Familiar Greek Letter of Recommendation*, SBLDS 4 (Missoula 1972). – **M. Leutzsch**, *Bewährung* (Bib. 11) 18–30, 185–88. – **P. Marshall**, *Enmity in Corinth: Social Conventions in Paul's Relations with the Corinthians*, WUNT 2/23 (Tübingen 1987) 91–129. – **R. Reck**, *Kommunikation* (Bib. 7) 112–16. – **S. K. Stowers**, *Letter Writing* (Bib. 2) 153–65: Letters of Mediation. – **G. Tibiletti**, *Le lettre private* (Bib. 2) 102–4: Lettere di presentazione.

In 3 John we encountered epistolary recommendations of Demetrius (v. 12) and other traveling brothers (vv. 5-8), and in 2 Cor 3:1, Paul mentions the kinds of "letters of recommendation" (συστατικαὶ ἐπιστολαί) that his opponents could produce but which he refused to rely on in his own ministry (see Exercise 10). This provides an opportunity for us to investigate the type of letter that scholarship knows as the "letter of recommendation" or, with a slightly different emphasis, as the "letter of introduction" or the "letter of mediation." But in this case we can also start with an ancient letter writing handbook of the second or first century BCE by a certain Demetrius, who lists as second among his twenty-one letter types the συστατικός (sc. τύπος) or "commendatory type," which he defines by the following example (*Epistolary Types* 2):[5]

> So-and-so, who is conveying this letter to you, has been tested by us and is loved on account of his trustworthiness (πίστιν). You will do well (καλῶς ποιήσεις) if you deem him worthy of hospitality both for my sake and his, and indeed for your own. For you will not be sorry

[5] Pseudo-Demetrius, *Typoi epistolikoi* 2. Text and translation in A. J. Malherbe, *Ancient Epistolary Theorists* (Bib. 2) 32–33; cf. there also pp. 74–75 and below, chap. 5, sec. B.

if you entrust to him, in any matter you wish, either words or deeds of a confidential nature. Indeed, you, too, will praise him to others when you see how useful he can be in everything.

What is here formulated as "theory" is in reality oriented to existing practice. This is confirmed by an actual letter of recommendation in Latin from the second century CE, which runs (in part) as follows:[6]

> To Julius Domitius, military tribune of the legion, from Aurelius Archelaus, his *benificiarius*, greeting. I have once previously recommended to you my friend Theon, and now again, Sir, I beg you to look upon him as if he were myself.[7] He is indeed a man worthy of your affection. He has left his family, his property and business and followed me, and through all he has shielded me from care. I beg you therefore to grant him admittance to your presence (*ut habeat introitum at te*).

The letter is addressed to a certain Roman military tribune from Aurelius Archelaus, his *benificiarius*, that is, a soldier who has been released from his other duties for special assignments, such as guarding his commander, and who now intercedes with his "boss" for his own former assistant or errand boy, Theon. The military context also helps us to understand such surprising formulations as "he has left his family" and has "followed me," without necessarily postulating Christian influence.

If one works through the numerous examples of letters of recommendation—Kim has collected 83 of these, while Leutzsch lists 120—and then compares them with the theory, one arrives at the standard components of an ancient letter of recommendation. The basic structure involves a triangular relationship between the letter writer (A), the recipient (B), and the person being recommended, the "recommendee" (C). The individual elements include the following:

---

[6] P.Oxy. I 32.4–15. Text and translation in A. S. Hunt and C. C. Edgar, *Select Papyri* (Bib. 1) 1:320–23. Also available in Cotton (1981) 15–23; in Kim as no. 57; and in P. Cugusi, *Corpus epistolarum Latinarum* (Bib. 1) 1:179 (with commentary 2:214–19).

[7] Which is to say, consider him to be me; treat him like you treat me; cf. Phlm 17.

- Establishment of the personal integrity of the recommendee (C), who often delivers the letter.
- Explanation of the special relationship that exists between the recommendee (C) and the letter writer (A), whether that relationship exists because of family ties, friendship, business dealings, or other activities.
- Reminder of the existing bond of friendship and trust between the letter writer (A) and the recipient (B).
- Request to the recipient (B), for the sake of his friendship with the writer (A), to receive the recommendee (C) graciously and to extend to him the same warm feelings that are felt toward the writer (A).

The letter of recommendation is therefore supported by the two relationships in which the *sender* (A) is already involved, that is, between A and B and A and C. The letter's aim is to complete this triangle by creating a relationship in the still open situation between B and C, which was always necessary when B and C did not yet know one another. The mediating and introducing services of A were then in high demand. The verb συνίστημι, which is to be translated by "commend" or "recommend" in these letters (cf. Paul and Phoebe in Rom 16:1), has the basic meaning of "bringing together" and hence by extension of "presenting" or "introducing unacquainted people to one another." Yet the possibility that B and C already knew each other cannot be excluded in every case. Therefore there was sometimes a need for A to restore or strengthen an existing relationship between B and C that had been strained for some reason. The immediate purpose of many letters of recommendation was to request hospitality for C in order to ease the journey, for which we need compare only P.Oslo II 55.7–9: καλῶς οὖν ποιήσεις, ἄδελφε, τοῦτον ὑποδεξάμενος ὡς ἂν ἐμέ, "you will do well, brother, to welcome this person (Theon) as you would welcome me." But such letters could also accomplish other aims such as securing the recommendee a position or acceptance into an apprenticeship, or getting further recommendations.

At the center of this type of letter, which in this respect resembles the *enteuxis* or petition (see Exercise 11), stands the epistolary request. Its Greek form in a letter of recommendation from 25 CE runs: διὸ παρακαλῶ σε μετὰ πάσης δυνάμεως ἔχειν αὐτὸν συνεσταμένον, "Wherefore, I entreat you with all my power to *regard* him *recommended*" (P.Oxy. II 292.5–7 [White, *Light* §79]), or similarly in an oft-cited example from the year 6 CE: ἐρωτηθεὶς ἔχε αὐτὸν συνεσταμένον, "Please *regard* him as *recommended*" (P.Mert. II 62.6–7 [White §77]). This use of *regarding* someone as recommended displays an undeniable relationship to a Latin formula that is very common in Cicero's *Letters to Friends*, whose thirteenth book consists almost entirely of letters of recommendation. It is especially conspicuous in one instance where in a metaphorical play, the *dignitas* of the writer, Cassius, is commended to the high regard and care of the recipient, Cicero: *a te peto, ut dignitatem meam commendatam tibi habeas*, "May I ask you to *regard* my *public standing* as entrusted to your care?" (Cicero, *Fam.* 12.12.2). Because Cicero's correspondence is older than almost all papyrus letters, it seems that the Latin expression has influenced the Greek formula, rather than the other way around (see Cotton). The body of such letters occasionally closed with a reminder that the addressee would once again earn the personal thanks of the sender and could therefore hope—the implication is overhead—to receive a return of the favor when opportunity arose. One need only compare P.Mert. II 62, cited above, here lines 9–12, "By (your) doing this, I shall be favored by you. Moreover, in turn, you indicate whatever you should choose, and I shall act accordingly without hesitation," or also Cicero, *Fam.* 13.2.1: *mihi certe gratissimum feceris*, "I shall certainly be most grateful."

The danger that letters of recommendation could become mere obligations that the author fulfills without much enthusiasm at the urging of the one seeking the recommendation cannot be excluded. Cicero therefore assigns his recommendations various levels of priority and develops devices for signaling this to his addressees (cf. Marshall 94–95). Epictetus criticizes the practice of recommendation letters by approvingly quoting Diogenes the Cynic (see below, chap. 4, sec. B.4), who answered a request for a recommendation as follows:

> That you are a man he will know at a glance; but whether you are a good or a bad man he will discover if he has the skill to distinguish between good and bad, and if he is without that skill he will not discover the facts, even though I write him thousands of times. (Epictetus, *Diss.* 2.3.1)

In other words, one's own character must suffice as a recommendation without corroboration from another source. On another occasion one of Epictetus's recommendation letters fails because it was too faithful to the truth (*Diss.* 1.9.27–28).

Recommendations need not dominate the whole letter, which would then be a pure recommendation letter, for they can also be interspersed in letters with different purposes, as in the second half of the text of P.Oxy. IV 743, particularly lines 33–35 (II BCE): "Whatever he may stand in need of from you, assist him in that, as he will be as agreeable for you as he is for me" (White, *Light* §71). This is especially important for the New Testament, where pure letters of recommendation do not occur. Yet the existence of such letters is certainly mentioned, and some passages embedded in the New Testament letters have the character of recommendations. In his pre-Christian days Paul seems to have been less averse to the practice of recommendation letters than he is later in 2 Corinthians 3:1-3. As a persecutor of Christians Paul carried letters with him to gain admittance into the synagogues in Damascus as an otherwise unknown representative of the high priest and the Jewish elders (Acts 9:1-2; 22:5). Matters are similar with the Jewish Christian missionary Apollos. When he wants to cross the Aegean from Ephesus to Corinth to visit the church there that does not yet know him, "the brothers" in Ephesus write to "the disciples" in Achaia asking them to welcome him (Acts 18:27). Paul formally "commends" (συνίστημι) the deaconess Phoebe from Cenchrae near Corinth in Romans 16:1-2 when she wants to go to Rome, presumably carrying Paul's Letter to the Romans, and he also writes recommendations in his other letters for Timothy (1 Cor 16:10-11), Titus (2 Cor 8:23-24), and Epaphroditus (Phil 2:25-30); the same practice is carried on in letters by Paul's pupils, including Colossians with its recommendation of Epaphras (Col 1:7-8). Paul also promises to write letters for the members of the Corinthian church who are to deliver the contribution to the believers in Jerusalem (1 Cor 16:3). The Letter to Philemon bears the character of a letter of recommendation for the runaway slave Onesimus.

Communication science acknowledges the general rule that "proven methods of communication are not replaced by new techniques" (Reck 112), and the letter of recommendation provides a striking case in point: "Even today letters of recommendation, references, etc. play an important role in establishing relationships between previously unknown partners" (ibid.)

Exercise

12. Analyze the following letter for its elements of recommendation and its basic constellation of the writer, addressee,
and recommendee. In what points does it differ from the
examples cited above? (Pliny the Younger, *Ep.* 9.21; trans.
B. Radice: *Pliny: Letters and Panegyricus*, LCL, vol. 2 [1969]
119, 121.)

The freedman of yours with whom you said you were angry
has been to me, flung himself at my feet, and clung to me as if I
were you. He begged my help with many tears, though he left a
good deal unsaid; in short, he convinced me of his genuine peni-
tence. I believe he has reformed, because he realizes he did
wrong. You are angry, I know, and I know too that your anger was
deserved, but mercy wins most praise when there was just cause
for anger. You loved the man once, and I hope you will love him
again, but it is sufficient for the moment if you allow yourself to
be appeased. You can always be angry again if he deserves it, and
will have more excuse if you were once placated. Make some con-
cession to his youth, his tears, and your own kind heart, and do
not torment him or yourself any longer—anger can only be a torment to your gentle self.

I'm afraid you will think I am using pressure, not persuasion,
if I add my prayers to his—but this is what I shall do, and all the
more freely and fully because I have given the man a very severe
scolding and warned him firmly that I will never make such a
request again. This was because he deserved a fright, and is not
intended for your ears; for maybe I *shall* make another request
and obtain it, as long as it is nothing unsuitable for me to ask and
you to grant. Farewell.

C. Hellenistic Royal Letters

Bibliography 16: L. Boffo, *Iscrizioni greche e latine per lo studio della Bibbia*,
Biblioteca di storia e storiografia dei tempi biblici 9 (Brescia 1994) 66–79.
– **J. D. Gauger**, *Beiträge zur jüdischen Apologetik: Untersuchungen zur
Authentizität von Urkunden bei Flavius Josephus und im I. Makkabäerbuch*,
BBB 49 (Cologne and Bonn 1977) 1–151 (on the Zeuxis inscription). –
idem, *Authentizität* (Bib. 2) (with comprehensive coverage of the literary

tradition, but also with many supplemental references to the inscriptions). – **R. Herzog**, "Griechische Königsbriefe," *Hermes* 65 (1930) 455–71. – **F. Millar**, "Emperors at Work," *JRS* 57 (1967) 9–19. – **J. H. Oliver**, *Greek Constitutions of Early Roman Emperors from Inscriptions and Papyri*, Memoirs of the American Philosophical Society 178 (Philadelphia 1989). – **A. Schalit**, "The Letter of Antiochos III to Zeuxis Regarding the Establishment of Jewish Military Colonies in Phrygia and Lydia," *JQR* 50 (1959–1960) 289–318. – **W. Schubart**, "Bemerkungen zum Stile hel- lenistischer Königsbriefe," *Archiv für Papyrusforschung* 6 (1920) 324–47. – **R. K. Sherk**, *Roman Documents from the Greek East: Senatus consulta and Epistulae to the Age of Augustus* (Baltimore 1969). – **C. B. Welles**, *Royal Correspondence in the Hellenistic Period: A Study in Greek Epigraphy* (New Haven 1934; repr. Chicago 1974) (the standard work). – **A. Wilhelm**, *Griechische Königsbriefe*, Klio Beiheft 48 (Leipzig 1943; repr. Aalen 1969).

Hellenistic royal letters have received too little attention in New Testament exegesis.[8] After their beginnings with Philip II of Macedonia and his son Alexander the Great, they have their hey- day in the period of the Diadochi between 300 BCE and the beginning of Roman rule in the East. In the secretarial offices of the individual kingdoms a particular style of letter is developed and cultivated that has two roots according to Charles Bradford Welles in his standard monograph on the subject: the private let- ter and the city decree, which makes its influence felt even in the sentence structure of royal letters (Welles xli–xliv). Sometimes rhetorical characteristics also shine through (cf. Welles xliv on his no. 1 = *OGIS* 5: "almost more of a speech than a letter").

Royal letters were addressed principally to cities, then also to civic organizations, troops, administrators, and priests. They have come down to us in two rather unusual ways, in quotations by his- torians and above all in inscriptions on stelae or building walls. The letters were usually copied on stone soon after receipt at the wishes of the recipients, who wanted to honor the king and had a

---

[8] One notable exception is C. J. Bjerkelund, *PARAKALÔ* (Bib. 4) 59–74. See now also M. L. Stirewalt, Jr., *Paul the Letter Writer* (Bib. 4), who argues for a greater similarity between the Pauline letters and the official letters of kings, emperors, governors, and other rulers already on formal grounds, cf. 54: "In these five units—identification of primary sender, naming of cosenders, multiple address, dual structure of the body, and subscriptions—Paul adapted the conventions of official corre- spondence."

vested interest in recording and displaying the privileges they had been granted. However, in one case letters written in 163–156 BCE by Eumenes II and Attalus II, kings of Pergamum, to Attis, priest of the temple of Cybele at Pessinus, were not copied until some 150 years later (end of the first century BCE), when they were inscribed on the temple walls to revive the memory of the past glory of the temple and its priest (Welles no. 55–61 = *OGIS* 315). Instructions for the production of an inscription can even be contained in the letter itself. Such is the case in a letter from the Seleucid ruler Antiochus III the Great about the appointment of a chief priest at Daphne in 189 BCE (Welles no. 44 = *OGIS* 244). This closes with the following instructions from the king: "Give orders, also, *to inscribe a copy of the letter on stelae* (ἀναγραφῆναι δὲ καὶ τῆς ἐπιστολῆς τὸ ἀντίγραφον εἰς στήλας) and to set them up where they may best be seen" (*ll.* 41–43). This letter—or rather, inscription—is dated to 189 BCE in its final line (*l.* 44), which is a great help for historical reconstruction, as it is in similar letters, such as those of the Pergamene kings Attalus II and Attalus III between 142 and 135 BCE (see Welles nos. 65–67, final lines).

A Hellenistic king's letter might also include attachments, such as a city's resolution to honor and thank him for his benefactions or cover letters from middle ranking officials. Thus a letter found on a newly discovered inscription (see Boffo) from Antiochus III to his governor Zeuxis in Lydia concerning Antiochus's chief priest (who remains anonymous) is preceded by two prefixed documents: the second is a letter from Zeuxis to Philotas in which he forwards the king's letter to Philotas, who is to see that its instructions are carried out; and the first is Philotas's letter to Bithys, who apparently stood at the end of the chain of command. This also gives us an opportunity to cast a side glance at the literary tradition, for a letter from Antiochus III to the same Zeuxis is summarized by Josephus in *Ant.* 12.148–53. Its topic is the settling of 2000 Jewish families from Mesopotamia and Babylonia as a loyal military colony of the Seleucid empire in the turbulent regions of Lydia and Phrygia. One must proceed cautiously in view of the suspicion of inauthenticity that is often raised against this document in Josephus (see Schalit). Stylistically the two letters of Antiochus III to Zeuxis unwittingly betray their different means of transmission. As a final example of letter attachments, a letter from Seleucus I Nicator to Miletus preserved in an inscription (Welles no. 5 = *OGIS* 214) attaches a detailed list of the golden vessels that the king sent by messengers to be deposited in the temple of Apollo. The list served as a check on those carrying the vessels and protected the king's property once it was inscribed at the temple.

Despite the great gap in power between the sender and the recipients, royal letters sometimes appeal to friendship as the basis for mutual good relations. Around the year 240 BCE, when the residents of the island of Cos ask Ziaelas king of Bithynia to befriend their city (φιλανθρωπεῖν) (see Welles no. 25.8), the king gives the following assurances:

> Especially do we continue to make much of our father's (other) friends and of you, because of his personal acquaintance with your people and because king Ptolemy, our friend and ally, is friendly toward you, and still further because your envoys expressed with great enthusiasm the good-will which you have for us. (Welles no. 25 = *SIG*³ 456.17–29)

By contrast, the health wish typical of the proem of private letters "is rare in the royal letters" (Welles 248) because it is more fitting in an exchange between individuals. Yet it does occasionally occur in royal letters to particular individuals, as in a letter from Attalus II to a priest (Welles no. 61.1–2), or with elaboration in a letter exchange between two kings (Welles no. 71 = *OGIS* 257):

> King Antiochus (VIII or IX) to king Ptolemy (IX), also
> called Alexander, his brother, greeting. If you were well it would be as
> we wish; we ourselves were well and were remembering you
> with love.

Further noteworthy peculiarities of the royal letters occur in the epistolary prescript. Here we find the otherwise rare phenomenon of letters addressed not to a single addressee but to a collective such as a city, a council, or another political entity, and sometimes naming not one but two senders. Since this also applies in a modified form to the letters of Paul, we have collected a few examples of this characteristic feature:

> King Seleucus (I) to the council and the people of Miletus, greeting. (Welles no. 5 = *OGIS* 214; 288–87 BCE).

> King Lysimachos to the council and the people of Samos, greeting. (Welles no. 7 = *OGIS* 13; 283–82 BCE).

King Seleucus (I) and Antiochus (his son) to Sopatros, greeting.
(Welles no. 9; 281 BCE).

King Antiochus (III) to the council and the people of Magnesia,
greeting.
(Welles no. 31 = *OGIS* 231; ca. 205 BCE).

King Theodoros and Amynander to the council and the people of
Teos, greeting.
(Welles no. 35; 205–201 BCE).

King Antiochus (III) to generals, cavalry, and infantry officers, soldiers,
and the rest, greeting.
(Welles no. 39 = *OGIS* 217; 203 BCE).

King Seleucus (IV) to Theophilus and the magistrates and the city of
Seleucia in Pieria, greeting.
(Welles no. 45; 186 BCE).

Queen Laodike to the council and the people of Sardis, greeting.[9]

After the Hellenistic royal letters had run their course, their function is taken over by the correspondence first of the Roman magistrates (see Sherk)[10] and then of the Roman emperors, which we
also know of partly through inscriptions. Below is a formal letter
of thanks from the emperor Hadrian to an association of young
men in Pergamum who had sent him a letter of congratulations on
his accession to the throne and who preserved his letter of reply
on white marble in their gymnasium. The most striking feature is
Hadrian's extensive self-introduction, which would be unusual in a

---

[9] This is the beginning of the oldest letter of a queen, the wife of
Antiochus III, which was written and copied on marble in 213 BCE. In
it the queen accepts the sacral honors given to her. This recently discovered text is available in P. Gauthier, *Nouvelles inscriptions de Sardes II*,
Hautes études du monde gréco-romain 15 (Geneva 1989) 48–49.

[10] See also the letter of Octavian (later Augustus) of 39/38 BCE to the
city of Ephesus that was found in the city of Aphrodisias, in M. Trapp,
Greek and Latin Letters (Bib. 1) 150–53 §64, 300–302. This letter to
Ephesus, whose content involves Aphrodisias, was first inscribed on the
wall of the theater in Aphrodisias at the beginning of the third century CE
out of the need to illustrate the city's history more publicly; it must therefore have been preserved and available in another form in the archives.

private letter but has certain analogies in the Pauline epistolary prescripts (*SIG*³ 831):

> To good fortune.
> The Emperor and Caesar, of the god
> Trajan Parthicus a son,
> of the god Nerva a grandson,
> Trajan Hadrian Augustus,
> of tribunician power,
> to the association of young men
> (living) in Pergamum, greetings.
> Since I have learned—by your letter
> and by the fact that you have sent
> Claudius Kyros—the amount of joy
> that you, as you (correctly) declared,
> have shared with me, I decided
> that this (attitude) demonstrates
> your character as excellent men.
> Be well (εὐτυχεῖτε).
> On the 3rd, before the Ides of November,
> from Juliopolis.

The royal and imperial letters are a very important source of our knowledge of ancient history because of their contents. Yet this aspect has not been given the attention it deserves in our survey, which is more oriented to letter forms and structures. To begin to redress this imbalance we have selected for a closer reading in the next section an imperial letter that directly touches upon the history of Diaspora Judaism in Egypt and takes us into the New Testament period.

Exercise

13. Read the following royal letter. Determine its structure and content and attempt to place it, as far as possible, in its historical and cultural setting (Welles no. 67 = *OGIS* 331/IV):

> King Attalus to the council and the people of Pergamum, greeting. Since
> queen Stratonice my mother, the most pious of all women
> and exceeding in love for my father and for me,
> was reverently inclined toward all the gods and especially
> toward Zeus Sabazius, whom she brought as an ancestral divinity into
> our native city, and whom, as he was our comrade and helper in
> many deeds and many dangers, we decided because of his
> manifestations of divine power to enshrine in the temple of
> Athena Nicephorus.
> This we thought would be a place suitable and worthy of him,
> and we gave orders accordingly about the sacrifices and proces-
> sions and mysteries
> which are to be held for him before the city at the proper times
> and places.
> We have also created for him a hereditary priest, my Athenaeus,
> who exceeds in piety and
> excellence and in constant faith toward us. In order, therefore,
> that the honors of the god and the grants made to Athenaeus may
> remain immovable and unchanged forever,
> we decided that the ordinances written by us
> be entered in your sacred laws.
> Year 4, Dius 4. Lytus (delivered the letter) from Pergamum.

D. An Imperial Letter: Claudius to the Alexandrians

Bibliography 17: H. I. Bell, *Jews and Christians in Egypt: The Jewish Troubles in Alexandria and the Athanasian Controversy, Illustrated by Texts from Greek Papyri in the British Museum* (London 1924) 1–37 = the *editio princeps* of Claudius's letter to the Alexandrians, P.Lond. VI 1912. (**Note**: P.London is a seven-volume work under the general title *Greek Papyri in the British Museum*, by the British Museum Dept. of Manuscripts, ed. by F. G. Kenyon, et al. According to vol. 7 of that work, Bell's *Jews and*

Christians is to be considered vol. 6 of the series, as implied also by Bell's subtitle. However, American libraries following the Library of Congress generally catalog Bell's volume as a freestanding work, BR190.B4 [or 45] 1924 [repr. 1972, 1977], separately from *Greek Papyri in the British Museum*, PA3304.B8 [or 85] 1893.) – **W. Bergmann** and **C. Hoffmann**, "Kalkül oder 'Massenwahn'? Eine soziologische Interpretation der anti-jüdischen Unruhen in Alexandria 38 n.Chr.," in R. Erb and M. Schmidt, eds., *Antisemitismus und jüdische Geschichte*, FS H. A. Strauss (Berlin 1987) 15–46. – **H. Hegermann**, in J. Leipoldt and W. Grundmann, eds., *Umwelt des Urchristentums*, vol. 2 (Berlin ³1971) 250–53 (German translation). – **A. S. Hunt** and **C. C. Edgar**, *Select Papyri*, LCL (Bib. 1) 2:78–89. – **A. Kasher**, *The Jews in Hellenistic and Roman Egypt: The Struggle for Equal Rights*, TSAJ 7 (Tübingen 1985) 310–26. – **S. Lösch**, *Epistula Claudiana: Der neuentdeckte Brief des Kaisers Claudius vom Jahre 41 n.Chr. und das Urchristentum. Eine exegetisch-historische Untersuchung* (Rottenburg 1930). – **J. H. Oliver**, *Constitutions* (Bib. 16) 77–88. – **P. W. Pestman**, *Papyrological Primer* (Bib. 6) 105–9 (only partly). – **V. A. Tcherikover** and **A. Fuks**, *Corpus Papyrorum Judaicarum*, vol. 1 (Cambridge, Mass. 1957), esp. 69–74 (from the Prolegomena); vol. 2 (1960) 36–55 (as *CPJ* II 153, with text, translation, and commentary). – **J. L. White**, *Light from Ancient Letters* (Bib. 1) 125–37 (with additional texts and translation). – There is a valuable overview of "Imperial Letters on Papyrus" with 33 items from Augustus to Diocletian in **F. J. A. Hoogendijk** and **P. van Minnen**, "Drei Kaiserbriefe Gordians III. an die Bürger von Antinoopolis," *Tyche* 2 (1987) 41–74, esp. 68–69.

In 1920–1921 in the city of Philadelphia in the Fayum, Apion's hometown (see chap. 1), archeologists discovered the archives of a tax collector containing documents from the period from Tiberius to Nero. On the back of a papyrus that included tax records on the front and also on part of the back stands a copy in the same hand of the letter that the emperor Claudius addressed to the Alexandrians in 41 CE, which the Roman prefect in Alexandria immediately ordered to be published. Why this letter should have attracted special interest in the office of a tax collector we can only guess; perhaps it played a role in tax assessments of non-native Alexandrians. The text is written very carelessly and requires many corrections. Some of the phenomena, especially the frequent itacisms (including the mistaking of different Greek vowels sharing the same "ee" sound and other errors of hearing), suggest that the first transcript may have been taken down by dictation. (There are 166 itacisms and other errors within the 105 lines of the letter according to the Duke Databank,[11] and White also notes some 60 corrections.) Possibly a secondary copy was made from this *Vorlage*, which could also explain some of the gaps of content. Despite these difficulties, this much-discussed text, first published as P.Lond. VI 1912 and again as *CPJ* II 153, is a first-class document of ancient history.

The following minimal historical background is necessary for understanding our letter. After Gaius Caligula became emperor in 37 CE, severe tensions built up between the Greek and Jewish populations in Alexandria that finally erupted in a dreadful anti-Jewish pogrom. Philo presents the events in detail in his work *Against Flaccus*, the Roman prefect. Philo then led the Jewish delegation from Alexandria to Rome, which pressed for redress of grievances without success, and wrote of his experiences in his *Embassy to Gaius*. After the murder of Gaius Caligula in 41 CE the tide appears to turn. The Jews offer spirited resistance and go on the counter attack (cf. Josephus, *Ant.* 19.278: they "took heart again and at once armed themselves"). In the same year of 41, Caligula's successor Claudius orders the two instigators of the anti-Jewish intrigues, Isidoros and Lampon, to be executed, though for a different reason (i.e., their false accusation of Agrippa I), which in turn gives rise to the so-called *Acts of the Alexandrian (Pagan) Martyrs*.[12] An embassy of the Greeks in Alexandria comes to Claudius to

---

[11] The first few corrections of P.Lond. VI 1912 in the DDBDP call attention to the itacisms and other phonetic but non-standard spellings typical of many papyri, as well as the (genuine or perceived) mistakes of grammar. We give the corrections first, followed by the original in parentheses: line 2 ἱερωτάτης (ἱεροτάτης, phonetic o = ω), 3 εἰς (ἰς, itacism), 3 πόλιν (πόλειν), 4 πόλις (πόλεις), 5 ἠδυνήθη (ἠδυνήθην, mistaken 1st pers. for 3rd), 6 ἀναγκαῖον (ἀνανκαῖον, phonetic, γ before κ = ν), 8 ἀναγινώσκοντες plur. (ἀναγεινόσκων sing.). The last example is more a perceived than a real grammatical error, since κατ᾽ ἄνδρα ἕκαστον ἀναγινώσκων αὐτήν, "each person upon reading it [the epistle]," is a proper construction according to the grammar (cf. sing. κατ᾽ ἄνδρα). It is rather the DDBDP editors who have attempted a construction according to sense, similar to the British sense-construction of the corporate singular as a plural, against the American grammatical singular, e.g.: "Now IBM *are* beating the competition" (American: "IBM *is* beating").

[12] For a selection see *CPJ* II 154–59; cf. H. A. Musurillo, *The Acts of the Pagan Martyrs: Acta Alexandrinorum* (Oxford 1954).

congratulate him on his accession to the throne and to offer him various honors, but also to advance its own interests and to incriminate the Jewish side, which for its part reacts with a counter embassy (or perhaps two embassies: see *l.* 91 with its commentary). Claudius mentions both the Greek and the Jewish embassies in his letter, which was produced in the imperial secretarial office. The letter was either written in Latin and then translated into Greek, or written in Greek with traces of Latin influence.

Below we reproduce with slight variations the translation of White (133–36) with a side-glance to Tcherikover's translation in *CPJ* II 153, occasionally modifying the word order to align the English with the Greek (although this can be done only imperfectly). This is followed by a more detailed outline and comments on the most important questions of content.

P.London VI 1912

Column I

I. THE PREFECT'S PROCLAMATION

Lucius Aemilius Rectus says:
since at the reading of the most sacred
and beneficent letter to the city
not all the population
5 was able to be present because of its size,
I considered it necessary to display
the letter (publicly) in order that each person
upon reading it individually
may marvel at the greatness of our deified Caesar
10 and be grateful for his good will towards the city.
(Year) 2 of Tiberius Claudius
Caesar Augustus Germanicus, the Emperor, the fourteenth day of
the month Neos
Sebastos.

Column II

II. CLAUDIUS'S LETTER

A. Letter Opening

1. Prescript

14 Tiberius Claudius Caesar Augustus Germanicus the Emperor,
Pontifex Maximus,

15 holder of the tribunician power, consul designate,
16a to the city of the Alexandrians greeting (χαίρειν).

2. Proem

16b Tiberius Claudius Barbillus, Apollonios son of Artemidoros,
    Chairemon son of Leonidas, Marcus Julius Asklepiades, Gaius
        Julius Dionysios,
    Tiberius Claudius Phanias, Pasion son of Potamon, Dionysios son
        of Sabbion,
    Tiberius Claudius ‹Archibios›, Apollonios son of Ariston, Gaius
        Julius Apollonios, Hermaiskos
20 son of Apollonios, your ambassadors (πρέσβεις), having delivered
    to me your decree, spoke at length about
    the city, directing my attention to your good will towards us,
    which, you may be sure, has been stored up by me (in my memory)
        for a long time.
    For it arises because you are reverent by nature regarding the
        Augusti, as
    has become well known to me through many examples, and
        specifically through (your) being
25 zealously disposed toward, and zealously reciprocated by, my own
        family, concerning which,
    to speak only about the most recent example, and to pass by the
        others, the best witness is my brother,
    Germanicus Caesar, who addressed you with the most genuine
        words of mouth.
    Wherefore, I willingly accepted the honors given by you to me,
29a even though I have no taste for such things.

B. Letter Body

1. Cultic Honors to Claudius

29b In the first place, then,
30 I permit you to observe my birthday as a deified Augustus in the
        manner that you yourselves have
    proposed. To the erection in their various places of the statues
    of me and my family I agree; for I see
    ‹that› you are zealous to set upon every side memorials of your
        reverence
    for my family. [34b] Concerning the two golden statues,
35 the one representative of the Pax Augusta Claudiana shall be set up
        at Rome,
    as my most honored Barbillus proposed and entreated,
    though I preferred to deny (the request) because it seemed too
        offensive

Column III

and the other (statue), in the manner you requested, shall take part
    in the procession on my name
days with you, and let a throne accompany it too,
40 adorned with whatever ornamentation you desire. [40b] It would
    probably be foolish,
while allowing such honors, to refuse to establish a Claudian tribe
and to sanction groves according to the custom of Egypt.
    Wherefore,
I also grant these things to you. [43b] If you wish, you may also set
    up
the equestrian statues of Vitrasius Polio my procurator. [44b] As for
    the
45 erection of the four-horse chariots which you wish to set up to me
    ‹at the en›trances of the country,
I accede, for one to be set up at Taposiris, the Libyan town of that
    name,
one at Pharos in Alexandria, a third at Pelusium
in Egypt. [48b] But the (appointment of a) high priest to me, and the
    construction of temples,
I deprecate, not wishing to be offensive to my contemporaries
50 and because I consider temples and the like
to be set apart in all ages for the gods alone.

2. Favors Asked by the Greek Embassy

52 (περὶ δὲ τῶν αἰτημάτων . . .) Concerning the requests which you
    have been anxious to receive from me,
I decide as follows. To all *those who have been registered as*
    epheboi (τοῖς ἐφηβευκώσει [read: -κόσι]) up to the time of
my principate I preserve as certain their Alexandrian
55 citizenship, with all the privileges and indulgences of the city,
except some who secretly entered among you, though born of slave
    parents,
having contrived *to become epheboi* (ἐφηβεῦσαι), and I decide no
    less that the other things
be confirmed which were granted to you by the emperors before
    me,
and by the kings and the prefects, in the same way as the deified
    Augustus confirmed them.

Column IV

60 It is my will that the *neokoroi* [temple wardens] of the Alexandrian
    temple of the deified

Augustus be chosen by lot, just as they are chosen by lot in
   Kanopos
for the same deified Augustus. [62b] Concerning (your suggestion
   that) the municipal
magistrates be triennial, it seems to me you have decided well,
for magistrates will behave more moderately through fear of the
   account
65 they will have to render for what was done badly during their
   term of office. [66b] Regarding the senate (περὶ δὲ τῆς βουλῆς),
   what indeed your custom was
under ancient kings, I have no means of saying, but that
you did not have one under the Augusti before me you are well
   aware. Because this is now a new
matter, being formulated for the first time, and it is uncertain
   whether it will be advantageous
70 to the city and to my own interests, I wrote to Aemilius Rectus
   to examine the matter and to inform me whether it is necessary that
   the senate be constituted
and the manner, if then it should be appropriate to so assemble,
   according to which it will be constituted.

3. The Jewish Question

73 Regarding the disorder and sedition against the Jews—or, rather, if
   the truth
be told, the war—and the question of who should be held
   responsible, although
75 at the disputation your ambassadors
   argued vigorously and at length, especially Dionysios son of Theon,
   notwithstanding
I have not desired to make a detailed examination (of the hostility),
   but I have stored up within me
an immutable hostility against those who renewed the conflict.
Simply stated, if you do not lay to rest this
80 destructive and obstinate hostility against one another, I shall be
   forced
to show what a benevolent ruler can become when turned to (inflict)
   a justified wrath.
Wherefore, still even now, I entreat you that, on the one hand, the
   Alexandrians
behave gently and kindly towards the Jews,
who have inhabited the same city for many years,

Column V

85 and that they not be destructive of any customs observed by them in
        the worship
    of their god, but that they be allowed to observe their customs
    as during the time of the deified Augustus, which I too
    have confirmed, having heard both sides. [88b] On the other hand, I
        order the Jews,
    unreservedly, not to waste effort seeking more than what they
        formerly
90 had nor, as if they lived in two (separate) cities,
    to send two embassies in the future,
    a thing which was never done before, nor to force their way
        (ἐπισπαίειν [corr. ἐπεισπαίειν])[13] into
    contests (presided over by) the *gymnasiarchoi* and the *kosmetai*.
    Rather, they must enjoy the advantages which derive from their
        own status
95 and, indeed, they have a plentiful abundance of good things in an
        alien city.
    Nor are they to bring in or to admit Jews who are sailing down from
        Syria or Egypt,
    by means of which
    I will be forced to conceive an even more serious suspicion.
        Otherwise,
    I will take vengeance against them in every respect, just as though
100 they were a widespread plague infecting the whole inhabited world.
        [100b] (But) if
    you both (Alexandrians and Jews) forsake such things and are
        willing to live with gentleness

[13] White, 88 n. 92, corrects ἐπισπαίειν το ἐπ-εισ-παίειν, taking
the -ισ- of the former as an itacism for -εισ-, following Hunt and Edgar,
Tcherikover, and others in what has now become the "received" reading.
However, ἐπισπαίειν itself represents a correction of Bell's *editio princeps*
of 1924, which reads ἐπισπαίρειν, retaining the *rho* (marked as uncertain) but without the assumption that -ισ- is an itacism—a reading not
mentioned by White or Hunt and Edgar. Kasher goes back to Bell's ἐπισπαίρειν to get a different sense: the Jews in Alexandria were not seeking to "force their way in to" (ἐπεισπαίειν) the sports contests in the
gymnasium in order to gain citizen rights. Rather, they were violently
disrupting or "harassing" (ἐπισπαίρειν) the more public spectacles
sponsored by the *gymnasiarchoi* and *kosmetai*, because Jews had previously
been mocked, tortured, and executed in such settings. See the
Commentary below.

and kindness toward one another,
I, for my part, will have the greatest consideration for the city,
just as one which has a long-standing familial status with us.

C. Letter Closing

105 I bear witness to my friend, Barbillus, who has always had
    consideration
for you before me and who, on this occasion,
has fully advocated your case,
as well as to my friend, Tiberius Claudius Archibios.
    Good-bye (ἔρρωσθαι).

OUTLINE

I. The Prefect's Proclamation (1–13)
II. Claudius's Letter (14–109)
   A. Letter Opening (14–29a)
      1. Prescript (14–16a)
      2. Proem (16b–29a)
         a) The Greek Embassy from Alexandria (16b–22)
         b) *Captatio benevolentiae* (23–29a)
   B. Letter Body (29b–104)
      1. First Issue: Cultic Honors to Claudius (29b–51)
         a) Birthday Festival and Statues (29b–34a)
         b) Two Golden Statues, Procession, and Throne (34b–40a)
         c) Claudian Tribe and Sacred Groves (40b–43a)
         d) Equestrian Statues (43b–44a)
         e) Four-Horse Chariots (44b–48a)
         f) High Priest and Temples (48b–51)
      2. Second Issue: Favors Asked by the Greek Embassy (52–73)
         a) Citizenship and Ephebes (52–59)
         b) Temple Wardens (60–62a)
         c) Three-Year Term of Office for Magistrates (62b–66a)
         d) City Senate (66b–72)
      3. Third Issue: The Jewish Question (73–104)
         a) Earlier Unrest (73–78)
         b) Threat (79–81)
         c) Advice to the Alexandrians (82–88a)
         d) Advice to the Jews, Including the Issue of the Two
           Jewish Embassies (88b–100a)
         e) Advice to Both (100b–104)

C. Letter Closing (105–109)

    1. Commendation of Two of the Greek Ambassadors (105–108)

    2. Closing Greeting, ἔρρωσθαι (109)

COMMENTARY

1–13 (*ll*). The text of Claudius's letter is prefaced by an edict in which Lucius Aemilius Rectus, the Roman prefect of Egypt appointed shortly before Caligula's murder (also known from other sources, including inscriptions and papyri), orders the publication of the letter, probably as an inscription and possibly supplemented by papyrus copies.

9. Because White's translation "of our *deified* Caesar" uses an attributive modifier (English past participle), readers might at first assume that he has read the emended text with the added iota that yields the attributive adjective as proposed by Wilcken: τοῦ θείου ἡμῶν Καίσαρος, "of our *divine* Caesar" (cf. the Latin *divus*, gen. *divi*). But as White makes clear (137 n. 9), he actually rejects Wilcken's emendation and reads the noun, τοῦ θεοῦ ἡμῶν Καίσαρος, which Tcherikover translates more straightforwardly: "of our *god* Caesar" (42). There is no need to alter this noun, because in Roman Egypt rulers from Julius Caesar onward could be referred to as θεός without further ado; the prefect L. Aemilius Rectus has simply adopted this usage. See below on *ll*. 59–62.

11–13. The date: "(Year) 2 of Tiberius Claudius . . . , the fourteenth day of the month Neos Sebastos" is equivalent to 10 November 41 CE.

17. Chairemon son of Leonidas, a member of the Greek embassy to Claudius, is probably the same Alexandrian who emerged as an anti-Semitic writer according to Josephus, *Apion* 1.288–92. On the names of the rest of the Alexandrian Greek ambassadors in *ll*. 16b–20a, see the commentaries by Bell and Tcherikover.

23–25. Claudius's mention of the Alexandrians' reverence for the Augusti and zeal for his own family (cf. also the "good will," εὔνοια, of *l*. 22 [English *l*. 21]) sounds a little exaggerated given the frequent resistance to Rome by the Alexandrians, but it fulfills the rhetorical function of the *captatio benevolentiae* to gain the audience's favor.

26–27. Claudius's brother Germanicus was in Egypt in 19 CE, where he also visited Alexandria, campaigned for his cause, and was welcomed as a potential contender for the throne over against Tiberius, who had ruled since 14 CE (cf. Tacitus, *Ann.* 2.59). Whether the statement that Germanicus "addressed you [Alexandrians] with the most genuine words of mouth" implies that Germanicus spoke in Greek is not certain.

34b–37. A golden statue of Claudius himself (the term ἀν-δριάς, ἀνδριάντος suggests a statue of an ἀνήρ) as the personification of the *Pax Romana* or "Roman peace" that Augustus restored and that subsequent emperors had to maintain is apparently something that Claudius considers a bit over the top. Yet against his natural inclination, Claudius is persuaded by the leading Alexandrian ambassador, bearing the Roman name Tiberius Claudius Barbillus (listed first in among the ambassadors in *l.* 16b and mentioned again in the closing greeting in *l.* 105), to allow such a statue of *himself* to be erected in Rome. The alternative explanation, according to which Claudius is supposed to have been persuaded by Barbillus to allow a statue of the *goddess Rome* to be erected in *Alexandria*, is less convincing.

38. Who is to be represented by the second of the two golden statues (*l.* 34b) is not stated; that it was Claudius's wife Messalina must remain a matter of conjecture.

41. Claudius permits the establishment of his own φυλή in Alexandria, and while both Tcherikover and White translate this appropriately in its basic meaning as the "Claudian *tribe*," the term can also refer to a district or civic body.

42. Picking up on the possibility of the Claudian φυλή as certain district or nome in *l.* 41, Bell understands the expression κατὰ νόμον Αἰγύπτου, normally translated "according to the *custom* of Egypt," to indicate that Claudius permitted sacred groves to be planted "in that *nome* of Egypt" that would also be known as the Claudian φυλή. However, I know of no other scholar who has followed him in this. Moreover, for Bell's meaning we should really reaccent on the ultima, κατὰ νομὸν Αἰγύπτου (cf. LSJ s.v. νομός II.2, of the districts of Egypt).

43–44. C. Vitrasius Pollio was the predecessor of L. Aemilius Rectus as the prefect of Egypt. According to the text the equestrian statues most probably represented Vitrasius Pollio himself (similar cases are attested), and Claudius permits the Alexandrians to erect them. The alternative is that these are not statues of Vitrasius Pollio, but ones paid for by him and given to the city, representing Claudius.

48–51. Claudius's reticence to accept all the honors of the imperial cult (cf. *l.* 29a: "I have no taste for such things") is a characteristic he appears to have expressed on more than one occasion. Here he forbids the Alexandrians to found an imperial priesthood in his name or to build temples for him, because he is still a living, human ruler. His support for the Alexandrian temple of the deified Augustus in *ll.* 60–63 does not contradict this (see below).

49–50. Claudius declines the honor of having his own high priest and temples with the reasoning: "because I do not wish to be offensive to my *contemporaries*," οὔτε φορτικὸς τοῖς κατ' ἐμαυτὸν ἀνθρώποις βουλόμενος (so White). But the expression τοῖς κατ' ἐμαυτὸν ἀνθρώποις here could be understood in a more pregnant sense to mean "to (other) humans like myself," who are not deified figures.

53. The ἐφηβευκότες are those who have become ἔφηβοι or joined the ἐφηβεία (cf. also *l.* 57, ἐφηβεῦσαι). They are not the graduates of the gymnasium who have already become full citizens, but rather the boys or adolescents who by virtue of having a father who is a citizen (but see below on *ll.* 56–57) have had their names entered into the list of those entitled to a gymnasium education (though this was more like a training camp than a modern high school). This social rank was a prerequisite for the rights of citizenship in Alexandria and other Greek cities, and the adolescence of elite boys, the custom or institution governing this period of their lives, the training they receive, and their group of fellow *epheboi* can all be called their ἐφηβεία. See in addition to Tcherikover 46–47 the article by H.-J. Gehrke, "Ephebeia," *DNP* 3 (1997) 1071–75 = *BNP* 4 (2004) 1018–21.

56–57. Although the fathers of these boys are apparently Alexandrian citizens, the boys, since born of slave mothers (ὡς ἐγ [ἐκ] δούλων γεγονότες probably means this rather than White's generic "slave parents"), are treated as if their fathers had not been citizens at all, and this "legal fiction" effectively excludes them from being registered as *epheboi* and becoming citizens. As Kasher puts it (313):

> Beyond a doubt he [Claudius] meant the offspring of Alexandrian fathers and slave women, people "born of servile mothers" . . . .

Already in the Ptolemaic period (. . .) such people were required on all official documents to append only their mother's name to theirs, to show their illegitimate birth, for according to law (though not perhaps in practice) the fathers were considered to be unknown. It was natural for such men to deceive the authorities either by concealing the names of their mothers or by failing to register in the specified manner, so that they could attain the status of citizens. Since during the Roman period the criterion for citizenship of a "citizen son of citizens" no longer had legal validity, having been replaced by a gymnasium education, the wall of exclusivity of Alexandrian citizenship developed cracks . . . , and many people were able to enter the ranks of the *epheboi* in explicit violation of the law.

59–62. "The god Augustus," ὁ θεὸς Σεβαστός (White: "the deified Augustus"; see above on *l.* 9). The practice of referring to the *divus Augustus* or "divine Augustus," who after his death and apotheosis became a part of the Roman pantheon, by the term θεός is not a problem in Eastern usage, nor is the existence of an Augustan temple and priesthood or the coveted office of a νεωκόρος (temple warden), which is also known from the imperial cult in Asia Minor.

66–68. The "ancient kings" Claudius refers to are the Ptolemies. Although he feigns ignorance about the Alexandrians' claim to have had a βουλή (council or senate) in those pre-Roman times, in fact there was an Alexandrian βουλή under the Ptolemies, which was first done away with by Augustus. Claudius knows this already, but he is playing for time.

70–72. Claudius's delay tactic of writing the Egyptian prefect Aemilius Rectus about the matter of a senate apparently paid off, for the Alexandrians did not regain the βουλή they had under the Ptolemies until 200 CE under the emperor Severus.

73–74. Because Philo's description in his *Against Flaccus* of the pogrom in Alexandria in 38 CE resembles the circumstances of civil war, Claudius is not exaggerating when he says that the "sedition against the Jews" might just as well be called a "war."

74–78. Because Claudius is primarily concerned with the restoration of peace and order, he does not allow himself to be drawn into assigning blame in the conflict between Jews and Greeks in Alexandria, although the Greek embassy, including Dionysios son of Theon, pressed him to do so. Nor would this necessarily have been to their advantage, for Claudius would have to remind the Alexandrians that they began the conflict under Gaius Caligula in 38 CE. But he also knows that the Jews have since played their own part in heating up the exchange through their counter-measures, as he indicates in *ll.* 77b–78. It is they who have "renewed the conflict," and therefore they will be the targets of Claudius's "justified wrath" (ὀργή, *ll.* 78, 81) if the conflict does not cease.

76. Dionysios son of Theon is identical with Gaius Julius Dionysios in *l.* 17.

85–87. The Alexandrians are "not to be destructive of any customs observed by [the Jews] in the worship of their god." This is formulated in the light past experience. In 38 CE the Alexandrians had among other things besieged synagogues and erected pagan statues in them. Claudius reinforces the Roman law about free practice of religion that had existed since Augustus and applies it to the Jews.

89–90. Most scholars understand the Jewish efforts "to seek more than what they formerly had" to refer to their gaining Alexandrian citizenship. But Kasher 322–23 has raised serious objections to this view, without proposing his own solution.

90–92. " . . . nor, as if they lived in two (separate) cities, to send two embassies in the future" (referring to the Jews). The two Jewish embassies to Claudius constitute the main historical problem of the letter. The least complicated explanation appears to be the one according to which Claudius accepted only one embassy, that of the Alexandrian Greeks, and denied the Jews the right to their own embassy. But against this there are serious considerations, including the existence of the Jewish embassy to Claudius's predecessor Gaius Caligula under Philo's leadership. The alternative is to reckon with the possibility of two Jewish embassies, which would understandably have irritated Claudius. The first embassy could have been the more "aristocratic" one under Philo, which in this case will have remained in Rome into the principate of Claudius. The second embassy would then have arrived in Rome shortly before the writing of Claudius's letter and could have represented a different, more radical Jewish milieu that presented the emperor with more drastic demands; cf. only the discussions in Bell, Tcherikover, and Kasher.

92–93. The difficulty of these lines lies in the fact that they present both a text-critical problem (ἐπι-σπαίρειν vs. ἐπ-εισ-παίειν) and a translational problem, which in turn affect the historical reconstruction: Were the Jews in Alexandria seeking to "force their way in to" (ἐπεισπαίειν) the gymnasium as a way of becoming citizens? Since the most accessible English translations by Hunt and Edgar, Tcherikover, and White all take the same side on this question, beginning students lack a standard translation on which they might base an alternative historical reconstruction, and we must resort to the specialist study of Kasher. The complicated scholarship on these two lines must therefore be surveyed (and simplified).

We begin with the textual criticism and lexicography. Bell's original reading of ἐπισπαίρειν at the end of *l.* 92, where he marked the three letters -ιρε- as uncertain (*Jews and Christians*, 25; cf. 37), has since been emended to ἐπισπαίειν, without the *rho* (and with the -ιε- still marked uncertain), then corrected for the frequent itacism of -ισ- for -εισ- in this papyrus to ἐπ-εισ-παίειν. So all our standard translators: Hunt and Edgar (2:86 n. 92), Tcherikover (2:53), and White (137 n. 92). Even Bell changed his mind about ἐπισπαίρειν within a year of his *Jews and Christians* (cf. *Journal of Egyptian Archeology* 11 [1925] 95 n. 2), and Tcherikover notes that the emendation to ἐπ(ε)ισπαίειν "has been adopted by nearly all scholars." According to this "received" emendation, Claudius tells the Jews not "to force their way into" (Hunt and Edgar; White), "intrude themselves into" (Tcherikover), or "thrust themselves into" (P. G. W. Glare, ed., *Greek-English Lexicon: Revised Supplement* [Oxford 1996], s.v. ἐπεισπαίω) the games presided over by the *gymnasiarchoi* and the *kosmetai* (normally open only to citizens or citizens-to-be) as a back-door to becoming *epheboi* (see above on *l.* 53) and receiving a gymnasium education along with citizen rights. However, Kasher 310–21 has shown that the popular notion of large numbers of Alexandrian Jews trying to "infiltrate" the Greek social institution of the gymnasium is highly unlikely.[14] This would have been conspicuous and therefore preventable, and the bad experience that the Alexandrian Jews had already had with the gymnasium and its leaders in 38 CE would have turned them against it rather than toward it (see below).

[14] Kasher published in 1985, too late to be noticed by White in 1986, but Tcherikover criticized Kasher's predecessors, including Amusin, so the matter is still not settled.

This brings us back to Bell's original text. Bell's ἐπισπαίρειν presents an extremely rare word that is attested only once in the ancient Greek literary corpus (prior to Nonnus in the fifth century CE), in Plutarch, *Mor.* 327c. Based on the state of lexicography in 1924, Bell claimed that the sense "to be in alarm" that he found in the eighth edition of the *Greek-English Lexicon* of Liddell and Scott ([8]1897) for the Plutarch passage did not exactly fit the context of Claudius's letter. Therefore he modified this sense to make Claudius say that the Jews are not "*to strive* in gymnasiarchic or cosmetic games" (29). (In the meantime Bell's sense of P.Lond. VI 1912.92 has been suggested for Plutarch as well: "*pant, struggle*" [LSJ s.v. ἐπισπαίω]; "Greece was still *gasping* over Philip's wars" [*Mor.* 327c, LCL 4:387].) But this then says as much as the "received" interpretation: Jews are prohibited from competing (striving) in the games, and therefore from infiltrating the gymnasium by this means (if that was their intention).

It is Kasher who, building on predecessors such as Amusin (*Journal of Juristic Papyrology* 9–10 [1955–1956] 176), turns the discussion on its head (315–21). Regarding the verb, Amusin demonstrated that if the emendation ἐπεισπαίειν had meant that the Jews should stop "thrusting themselves *into*" the gymnasium games, it should have been followed by the preposition εἰς ἀγῶνας, whereas we have only the dative ἀγῶσι, with no corroborating evidence of ἐπεισπαίειν with the dative. Positively, Amusin interprets Bell's original ἐπισπαίρειν to mean "to oppose something or someone," "to cause obstructions," or "to resist." Kasher then adds the historical and textual exegesis to situate this meaning. Even if it were a historical fact, the Jews' supposed forcing of themselves into the gymnasiarchic athletic contests according to the received interpretation of *ll.* 92–93 could not be paralleled with the infiltration of the *epheboi* and gymnasium by young men born of slave mothers in *ll.* 56–57. For the latter was an act of trickery—Claudius says the impostors "*secretly entered* among you" (ὑπῆλθον ὑμᾶς)—whereas the former would have been public. Kasher concludes that "Claudius did not warn the Jews against penetrating the ranks of the ephebes, but rather sought to dissuade them from 'harassing' (ἐπισπαίρειν) the public performances organized by the gymnasiarchs and cosmetes since such action could readily inflame temper and so cause another 'war'" (320), which is clearly Claudius's chief concern as early as *l.* 74.

These "public performances" were not "games limited to an exclusive circle such as the competitions of the ephebes" (317), for a riot that could be described as a "war" would hardly have broken out among the spectators there. Rather, Kasher interprets the ἀγῶνες of *l.* 93 as "public spectacles" before large crowds in the theater, where Jews were sometimes mocked and even executed. He points to Philo's use of ἀγῶνες in precisely such a context: During the celebration of Gaius Caligula's birthday in 38 CE, his prefect A. Avillius Flaccus put on a "show" (θέα) in the Alexandrian theater in that involved "Jews being scourged, hung up, bound to the wheel, brutally mauled and haled for their death march through the middle of the orchestra" (Philo, *Flacc.* 85). Since these events are followed by "other amusements of theatrical competitions" (ἄλλα σκηνικῶν ἀθύρματα ἀγώνων), the "competitions" or ἀγῶνες here are not typical sports contests. Moreover, two of the gymnasiarchs in 38 CE, Isodorus and Lampon, who were later executed, were known opponents of the Jews and King Agrippa (see our introduction to Claudius's letter above). Apparently, then, the Jews "renewed the conflict" (*l.* 78) in 41 CE by attacking the popular spectacles sponsored by the gymnasiarchs, whose predecessors had proved to be the Jew-haters (even if the more recent shows need not have mocked the Jews), perhaps in the same theater where their fellow Jews had been abused in 38 CE, since it was adjacent to the main Jewish quarter. Josephus mentions that the Alexandrian Jews took up arms after the death of Gaius Caligula (*Ant.* 19.278), but he does not mention the later public exhibitions sponsored by the *gymnasiarchoi* and *kosmetai*.

95. One is almost involuntarily inclined to interpret the "alien city" in which the Jews nevertheless have an abundance of good things as a reference to the Jews' lack of civic rights in Alexandria. Differently Kasher 325–26: "[Claudius's] statement that the Jews should 'enjoy what is their own' (τὰ οἰκῖα) is contrasted with 'a city which is not their own' simply to stress that Alexandria, like all of Egypt, was the private possession of the emperor, and they therefore could not do as they liked in it." Kasher concludes: "In short, the expression ἐν ἀλλοτρίᾳ πόλει has nothing to do with civic status."

96–97. "Nor are they to bring in or to admit Jews who are sailing down from Syria or Egypt." This is certainly one of the keys to the entire debate. The Alexandrian Jews had recruited fellow

Jews from elsewhere to be able to defend themselves more effectively. The emperor will by no means tolerate this, because it
threatens security. An immigration of Syrian Christians, sometimes mentioned in scholarship, is hardly in view here.

99–100. This almost sounds like the later saying about the
Jews by Tacitus: "toward every other people they feel only hate
and enmity" (*Hist.* 5.5). Yet Claudius's sharp threat about taking
vengeance against the Jews as though they were a plague on the
whole world seems to spring not from a hardened judgment
against them but from his displeasure with the current situation—
perhaps exacerbated by unrest among the Jews in Rome?

103–104. Claudius means to say that in return for the good
conduct of the Alexandrians as a whole, he will care for the city as
if its residents had long been members of the same family as the
Roman people, not to mention relatives of the imperial household.

105–108. The metaphor of family relationships in the preceding lines is followed by the language of friendship, even if this
immediately applies only to two members of the Alexandrian
embassy, Barbillus and Tiberius Claudius Archibios from *ll.* 16 and
19 (though the name "Archibios" has to be supplied in *l.* 19 as a conjecture). The letter thereby acquires overtones of a friendship letter.

Claudius's position in this letter can be described as neither philo-
Semitic nor anti-Semitic. His chief concern is with the political
interests of Rome, and he has no use for ethnic or religious disrup-
tions in pursuing this objective. Within these non-negotiable constraints he resorts to the mediatorial religious politics under
Augustus. Neither party in the conflict receives everything they
asked for; both have their wings clipped. With this compromise
decreed from above Claudius restores peace in Alexandria for the
time being, thus showing more statesmanlike conduct than the
older research was ready to grant him.

Exercises

14. In lines 52 and 66 of Claudius's letter to the Alexandrians a new paragraph is introduced in Greek by περὶ δέ, "Now concerning." Compare with this with the Greek of 1 Cor 7:1; 8:1; 12:1; 16:1, 12, where the same expression is found. What emerges from the comparison of these two texts?

15. We take our leave from the official letters of kings and emperors with a letter of an entirely different type, though coming from no less than Augustus. What is especially striking about the text, now that you know its author? Where would you place or categorize it? The glosses inserted in the translation represent the Greek expressions that Augustus has sprinkled in his Latin text. The text comes from Aulus Gellius, *Attic Nights*, 15.7.3–5 (LCL, trans. J. C. Rolfe, vol. 3 [1927] 79). For further letters of Augustus and the other Roman emperors, see the Answer Key.

Greeting, my dear Gaius, my dearest little donkey, whom, so help me! I constantly miss whenever you are away from me. But especially on such days as today my eyes are eager for my Gaius, and wherever you have been today, I hope you have celebrated my sixty-fourth birthday in health and happiness. For, as you see, I have passed the *climacteric* (κλιμακτῆρα, *critical point*) common to all old men, the sixty-third year. And I pray the gods that whatever time is left to me I may pass with you safe and well, with our country in a flourishing condition, *while you are playing the man and preparing to succeed to* (ἀνδραγαθούντων ὑμῶν καὶ διαδεχομένων) my position.

4

Poetry and Philosophy—Literary Letters

A. Overview of Sources

In the wake of Adolf Deissmann's trailblazing works, New Testament exegesis became duly impressed with the wealth of original non-literary letters preserved mostly on papyrus and applied itself to comparative work with these letters, admittedly with considerable success. However, research into the comparative use of literary letters fell somewhat behind as a result.[1] Yet these letters also offer an abundance of textual material, which on closer inspection divides into very different categories and exhibits numerous points of contact with the New Testament letters. The following presentation therefore begins with a selective inventory of the available materials which, while not aiming at completeness, nevertheless provides an initial orientation to a very broad field.

For convenience, authors are divided into Greek and Latin language groups and are ordered alphabetically, with dates given as well. Texts and translations are presented in the order of the most accessible first, particularly the diglot editions of the Loeb Classical Library and other English translations where available, followed by the French or German diglots such as the Budé or Tusculum-Bücherei (with the occasional Italian edition), then by the most recent critical text and, where different, by the often older edition that underlies the *Thesaurus Linguae Graecae* (TLG) electronic text in the case of Greek works. Selected modern studies, where mentioned, are confined to the most essential, as are the

---

[1] On this point one has to agree with K. Berger, "Hellenistische Gattungen" (Bib. 7) 1326–27, 1337–39.

brief comments following the bibliographic entries for each author. After this first pass through the material, we will investigate four authors or text groups—Epicurus, Cicero, Seneca, and the Cynic Epistles—in more detail in part B.

Our overview extends far into history, reaching the sixth century CE, which means that Christian authors are also included in the temporal scope. One might very well ask given this long span of time why the church fathers with their extensive correspondence are generally not included here. This ultimately rests only on practical considerations, for otherwise the presentation would grow beyond limits and stray too far into the area of patrology. As it is, the most one can say is that the Christian authors who nevertheless receive mention here (e.g., Procopius of Gaza; Ausonius; Sidonius Apollinaris) orient themselves more to the letter conventions and examples of non-Christian antiquity, and less to the Christian letter tradition influenced by the New Testament, and that real theological content is mostly lacking.

Although they hardly fit the foregoing description as "non-theological," we cannot fail to mention that twelve of the writings of the Apostolic Fathers are letters that reflect the impact of the New Testament letter tradition: Clement to the Corinthians (*1 Clement*), the seven letters of Ignatius (to *Polycarp* and to the *Ephesians, Magnesians, Smyrnaeans, Philadelphians, Romans,* and *Trallians*), Polycarp to the *Philippians*, the *Martyrdom of Polycarp*—an account in the form of a letter from the church of Smyrna to the church of Philomelium by a certain Marcion (not the well-known heretic) and his scribe Evaristus (cf. 20:1-2)—the *Epistle of Barnabas*, and the *Epistle to Diognetus*. These, too, can be analyzed in terms of Greco-Roman and Christian letter conventions, as may be illustrated by the letter openings.[2]

---

[2] While *Barnabas* begins with the standard greeting χαίρετε (1:1) and the unknown writer to *Diognetus* addresses him as κράτιστε Διόγνητε, "most excellent Diognetus" (1:1; cf. κράτιστε Θεόφιλε, Luke 1:3; Κλαύδιος Λυσίας τῷ κρατίστῳ ἡγεμόνι Φήλικι χαίρειν, Acts 23:26 [outside letters in Acts 24:3; 26:25], but also Ἀντονίῳ Ἀλεξάνδρῳ τῷ κρατίστῳ ἐπιστρατήγῳ χαίρειν, P.Oxy. VIII 1119.15 [254 CE]), Clement, Polycarp, and Marcion in the *Martyrdom of Polycarp* send the (Pauline) Christian greeting of grace (mercy) and peace from God the Father Almighty and Jesus Christ, using the optative of wish πληθυνθείη to ask that this grace (or mercy) and peace "be multiplied" to the addressees,

Not a few of the following letters and letter collections raise the question of authenticity. This is not treated here comprehensively, but is merely mentioned on a case by case basis.

Because we will encounter the debate over authenticity again in discussing the New Testament letters (see chap. 8, sec. B.3), we might add here a word about M. L. Stirewalt, Jr., "Forgery and Greek Epistolography," in idem, *Studies* (Bib. 2) 27–42. He holds the somewhat surprising thesis that forged or spurious letters are basically unknown or occur only very infrequently in antiquity. But he reaches this conclusion only by a type of semantic trick, by which he differentiates between "forgery" on the one hand and fiction, school exercises, or careless transmission on the other. Stirewalt is willing to speak of forgery only when the pseudonymous author has an intention to deceive in order to gain some material or other advantage. Such a moralizing approach does not allow questions of the authenticity or inauthenticity of ancient letters and letter collections to be worked through adequately.

Excursus: Ancient Women and Ancient Letters. As a final preliminary note, we might observe that although men are the authors of most of the letters and letter collections below—for the letters attributed to famous men by others writing pseudonymously in their name are still written by other men—there are also a few significant letters from and to women. These include the real letters from the Epicurean woman philosopher Batis most probably in P.Herc. 176 (see below, sec. B.1) and from the aristocratic Roman

exactly as in 1 Pet 1:2; 2 Pet 1:2; Jude 2; Dan 4:37c LXX and Dan 4:1; 6:26 Theodotion (see further below chap. 8, sec. C on 2 Peter). Ignatius uses the standard opening greeting πλεῖστα χαίρειν in all his letters except to Polycarp (where he uses more familiar ἀσπάζομαι), but he expands the opening far beyond the usual Greco-Roman formula especially in *Romans* and *Philadelphians* (cf. also *Ephesians*). English-speaking readers are well served by three diglot editions all sharing the title *The Apostolic Fathers*, by K. Lake, LCL, 2 vols. (1912–1913); B. D. Ehrman, offering a new translation, LCL, 2 vols. (2003); and M. W. Holmes, *The Apostolic Fathers: Greek Texts and English Translations*, updated ed. (Grand Rapids [2]1999), who revises the work of J. B. Lightfoot; a forthcoming edition of translations only is M. W. Holmes, *The Apostolic Fathers in English* (Grand Rapids [3]2006). For analysis of Ehrman's edition (with a side-glance at the others) see the review article by B. Cline and T. Thompson, "Ignatius Redux: Bart Ehrman on Ignatius and His Letters," *JR* 86.3 (2006).

Cornelia to her son Gaius Sempronius Gracchus (below, A.3), as well as the real letters from the Neoplatonist philosopher Porphyry to his wife Marcella (below, A.1), from Plutarch to his wife in his *Consolation to His Wife* (below, A.1), and from Epicurus to his mother as preserved in the Oinoanda inscription (below, B.1). There are not surprisingly many more fictive letters attributed to women by male writers. Sometimes these are written as if from relatively realistically portrayed women, as in the letter exchanges between the Pythagorian women (below, A.1), but more often the letters are written for female figures known from tradition, mythology, or the novelistic genre, including Byblis in Ovid's *Metamorphoses* (below, A.2.c), Penelope, Dido, and Helen in Ovid's *Heroides* (below, A.3), the courtesans in the letters of Alciphron (below, A.1), and the courtesan Phoenicium in the opening of Plautus's play *Pseudolus* (below, p. 134 and p. 191). Nevertheless, when it comes to letters by "real" women, it is much easier to find women authors of the documentary papyrus letters than of these so-called literary letters; the only freestanding letter just mentioned that has been passed on by literary means, by Cornelia, is not of entirely certain authenticity, and the letter perhaps from Batis in P.Herc. 176 is, as a papyrus document, closer to the—admittedly inadequately defined—category of the "documentary" letter.

In recent research, papyrus letters from women in Egypt have opened up new windows for understanding their lives in the Hellenistic, Roman, and early Byzantine periods. Raffaella Cribiore writes, "It is especially women's letters that are part of archives that illuminate a woman's place in family and society, her relationships with other women and with male relatives and subordinates, her upbringing, the level of education she had attained, and her familiarity with writing."[3] Fortunately, there is an important forthcoming work dedicated to women's letters among the papyri.[4]

Although our introduction to *Ancient Letters* is not a text collection as such, we may nevertheless provide a few references to

---

[3] R. Cribiore, *Gymnastics of the Mind: Greek Education in Hellenistic and Roman Egypt* (Princeton and Oxford 2001) 91, part of a rich chapter on "Women and Education," 74–101.

[4] R. S. Bagnall and R. Cribiore, *Women's Letters from Ancient Egypt, 300 BC–AD 800* (Ann Arbor: University of Michigan Press, forthcoming); see also E. C. Goldsmith, ed., *Writing the Female Voice: Essays on Epistolary Literature* (Boston 1998).

ancient documentary letters by women from the following
sources. The Vindolanda tablets mentioned in the introduction to
chapter 2 above include our earliest documentary evidence of letters written by women to women in Latin. Vindolanda tablet no.
II 291 contains the following letter from Claudia Severa, wife of
Aelius Broccus, to Sulpicia Lepidina, wife of Flavius Cerialis (both
men were military commanders) of around 101–102 CE. The note
in the author's own hand in lines 7–8, which differs clearly from
that of the scribe, is of particular interest:[5]

> *(hand of a scribe)*
>
> Claudia Severa to her Lepidina greetings. On 11 September,
> sister, for the day of the celebration of my birthday, I give
> you a warm invitation to make sure that you come to us, to
> make the day more enjoyable for me by your arrival, if you are
> present. Give my greetings to your Cerialis. My Aelius and my
> little son send him their greetings.
>
> *(second hand, probably of Claudia Severa)*
>
> I shall expect you, sister. Farewell, sister, my dearest soul,
> as I hope to prosper, and hail.
>
> *(back to first hand)*
>
> To Sulpicia Lepidina, wife of Cerialis, from Severa.

There are many papyrus letters (as well as other types of documents) written in Greek by women, and even a few by children or
adolescents (cf. P.Oxy. I 119, from Theon to this father Theon,
above chap. 1, Exercise 4). Following is a list from J. L. White's
Light from Ancient Letters (Bib. 1):

> No. 10 = P.Col. III 6: Simale, mother of Heropantos, to Zenon,
> March 257 BCE.
>
> No. 20 = P.Mich. I 29: Senchons ("sister of Chons") to Zenon, July
> 256 BCE.

---

[5] Text in A. Birley, *Garrison Life at Vindolanda: A Band of Brothers*
(Stroud and Charleston 2002) 136–37; also in M. Trapp, *Greek and Latin
Letters* (Bib. 1) 82–83 §22, 229–30 (commentary).

No. 30 = P.Mich. III 183: Eirene (a wealthy woman) to three contractors, 182 BCE.

No. 33 = P.Mich. III 193: Eirene (as above) to four contractors, 178 BCE.

No. 34 = P.Lond. I 42: Isias to (her husband) Hephaiston, 168 BCE.

No. 37 = P.Milligan 5: Petition by Thaues and Taous, two twin sisters, 163–162 BCE.

No. 60 (letters 2 and 3) = P.Oxy. VIII 1148, 1149: Oracular questions to Serapis from two women, an anonymous mother and Nike, 1st–2nd cent. CE.

Nos. 63–65 = BGU IV 1204, 1206, 1207: Isodora to (her brother) Asklepiades, 2 October to 5 November 28 BCE.

No. 66 = P.Princ. III 160: A letter by the "wife of Kolanos" (*verso*), late 1st cent. BCE.

No. 90 = P.Mert. 63: Herenna to her father Pompeius, 18 January 57 CE.

No. 91 = P.Oslo.Inv. 1475: Charitous to her brother Pompeius, mid 1st cent. CE.

No. 94 = P.Oxy. II 300: Indike to her lady Thaisous, late 1st cent. CE.

No. 116 = P.Oxy. I 115: Eirene to Taonnophris and Philo, 2nd cent. CE.

1. Greek Authors

Bibliography 18: A. R. Benner and **F. H. Fobes**, *The Letters of Alciphron, Aelian and Philostratus*, LCL (1949). – **A. Dihle**, *Greek and Latin Literature of the Roman Empire: From Augustus to Justinian*, trans. M. Malzahn (London and New York 1994). – **R. Hercher**, *Epistolographi graeci* (Bib. 1). – **N. Holzberg**, ed., *Der griechische Briefroman: Gattungstypologie und Textanalyse*, Classica Monacensia 8 (Tübingen 1994), esp. 1–52. – **H. Hunger**, *Die hochsprachliche profane Literatur der Byzantiner*, vol. 1: *Philosophie – Rhetorik – Epistolographie – Geschichtsschreibung – Geographie*, Byzantinisches Handbuch 5/1 (Munich 1978). – **B. Kytzler**, *Erotische Briefe der griechischen Antike: Aristainetos,*

Alkiphron, Ailianos, Philostratos, Theophylaktos Simokattes (Munich 1967).
– **A. Lesky**, *Geschichte der griechischen Literatur* (Bern and Munich ³1971).
– **C. D. N. Costa**, *Greek Fictional Letters* (Bib. 1). – **M. B. Trapp**,
"Letters, Greek," *OCD*³ (2003) 846–47. – **P. A. Rosenmeyer**, *Ancient
Epistolary Fictions* (Bib. 2). – eadem, *Ancient Greek Literary Letters* (Bib. 1).

Our overview of the Greek literary letters has yet another goal,
since the only larger text collection currently available, still constantly used and cited, is the old work *Epistolographi graeci* by
Rudolph Hercher (1873). (With double-column pages of Greek
texts with Latin translations, it resembles J. P. Migne's *Patrologia
graeca*.) The material collected in this 843-page volume is in
urgent need of a critical examination. Therefore while the pages
in Hercher are cited in each case (where available), further information on the current publication status of these texts is also provided. For reasons that will become clear as we proceed, it will be
necessary to single out a group of mostly shorter letters and letter
collections from Hercher and reserve them for separate treatment
in part A.2.a on Quoted Letters.

The continuing importance of Hercher is seen not least in the fact
that his text provides the TLG text in many of the cases below. All of
Hercher's material on the letters quoted by other authors in part A.2.a
below is included in the TLG, with the exception of Hercher p. 132 on
Archytas. Our list of the authors of freestanding letters or collections
immediately below contains 38 authors, of which 15 take their TLG text
from Hercher: Aelian, Anacharsis, Aristotle, Brutus, Chion of Heraclea,
Crates, Diogenes, Dionysius of Antioch, Euripides, Heraclitus, Phalaris,
Socrates and the Socratics, Synesius, Themistocles, and Xenophon. We
have indicated the TLG text in each instance, whether from Hercher or
other editors, with the parenthetical comment (TLG).

Aelian (Claudius Aelianus) (ca. 165/70–230/35 CE)

Hercher 17–23 (reprint of ed. Hercher, Teubner 1866 = **TLG**). – **A. R.
Benner** and **F. H. Fobes**, *The Letters of Alciphron, Aelian and Philostratus*,
LCL (1949) 343–83. – **C. D. N. Costa**, *Greek Fictional Letters* (Bib. 1)
4–9, 125–28. – **D. Domingo-Forasté**, *Claudii Aeliani Epistulae et frag-
menta*, Teubner (Stuttgart 1994). – **P. A. M. Leone**, *Epistulae rusticae*,
Testi e documenti per lo studio dell'antichità 43 (Milan 1974). – **P. A.
Rosenmeyer**, *Ancient Epistolary Fictions* (Bib. 2) 308–21.

Although born in the vicinity of Rome, Aelian writes *Rustic Letters* or *Farmer Letters* (ἐπιστολαὶ ἀγροικικαί) in Greek with erotic allusions, drawing material from comics and orators from the fourth century BCE. Influence from the letters of Alciphron may be detected.

Aeneas of Gaza (ca. 500 CE)

Hercher 24–32. – **L. Massa Positano**, *Enea di Gaza: Epistole*, CSG 19 (Naples ²1962) 39–53 (**TLG**).

Listed by Hercher as Aeneas Sophista, Aeneas was a teacher of rhetoric and philosophy who straddled the boundary between Neoplatonism and Christianity. Twenty-five of his letters to friends and students have been preserved.

Aeschines (ca. 397–322 BCE)

Hercher 33–43. – **V. Martin** and **G. de Budé**, *Eschine: Discours*, vol. 2: *Contre Ctésiphon, Lettres*, Budé (Paris ³1991) 119–43 (**TLG**). – **N. Holzberg**, ed., *Briefroman* (Bib. 18) 17–22.

Under the name of this famous Athenian orator, politician, and opponent of Demothenes, who also worked as a teacher of rhetoric on Rhodes, twelve unquestionably inauthentic letters have circulated. The tenth of these presents a seduction story of a novelistic type. Since this is not what the historical Aeschines was known for, the fictionalizing goes even beyond speech in character.

Alciphron (second century CE)

Hercher 44–97. – **A. R. Benner** and **F. H. Fobes**, *The Letters of Alciphron, Aelian and Philostratus*, LCL (1949) 1–341. – **C. D. N. Costa**, *Greek Fictional Letters* (Bib. 1) 10–49, 128–53. – **F. A. Wright, A. R. Benner**, and **F. H. Fobes**, *Letters of Fisherman, Farmers, Courtesans, and Parasites* (London 1958). – **A.-M. Ozanam**, *Lettres de pêcheurs, de paysans, de parasites et d'hétaïres* (Paris 1999). – **K. Treu**, *Alkiphron: Aus Glykeras Garten: Briefe von Fischern, Bauern, Parasiten, Hetären*, Reclams Universal-Bibliothek 55 (Leipzig ²1982). – **M. A. Schepers**, *Alciphronis rhetoris epistularum libri iv*, Teubner (Leipzig 1905) (**TLG**). – **G. Anderson**, "Alciphron's Miniatures," *ANRW* II.34.3 (Berlin 1997) 2188–2206. – **P. A. Rosenmeyer**, *Ancient Epistolary Fictions* (Bib. 2) 255–307.

The Letters of Alciphron constitute one of the most attractive products of the Second Sophistic. Alciphron composed 118 fictive letters in four books: Letters of Fishermen; Farmers; Parasites; Courtesans (*hetairai*). The letters, which are indebted to the New Comedy of Menander, are ostensibly written by Athenians of the fourth century BCE and purport to give us a sketch of the social life of the city at that time. A letter of the courtesan Lamia to King Demetrius Poliorcetes begins with a rhetorical flourish that presents the letter as a representation of the writer's "entire self": "mighty king that you are, who nevertheless permit even a courtesan to write letters to you and who think it no harm to hold converse with my letters as you do with my entire self" (4.16.1).

Anacharsis (sixth century BCE)

Hercher 102–5 (**TLG**). – **A. Malherbe**, *The Cynic Epistles* (Bib. 1), trans. by A. M. McGuire, 6–9, 35–51. – **F. H. Reuters**, *Die Briefe des Anacharsis*, SQAW 14 (Berlin 1963). – **G. Cremonini** and **G. Morel**, *Anacharsis: Lettere*, Città antica 7 (Palermo 1991). – **P. A. Rosenmeyer**, *Ancient Epistolary Fictions* (Bib. 2) 209–17.

The historical Anacharsis lived in the sixth century BCE and was a Scythian, that is, for Greeks a barbarian, even though he came from a princely line. Herodotus, our earliest source (4.76.1–4.77.2), tells us that Anacharsis's quest for wisdom and knowledge led him to study among the Greeks, but that when he returned, he was killed by his brothers for the same reason. Anacharsis was later styled as the "noble savage" and was sometimes included among the Seven Sages; he may also have had a novel or romance written about him. Of the ten certainly spurious letters transmitted under his name, the brief *Ep.* 10 to Croesus comes from Diogenes Laertius 1.105. The other nine represent an independent collection, presumably by a single author. The letters display a Cynic tendency, inasmuch as they seek to abolish the distinction between Greeks and barbarians, compare Anacharsis to a Spartan dog, and advocate reducing one's physical needs to a minimum. Here Letter 5 especially stands out, according to which Anacharsis's Scythian lifestyle exactly corresponds to the humble Cynic lifestyle: "For me, a Scythian cloak serves as my garment, the skin of my feet as my shoes, the whole earth as my resting place, milk, cheese and meat as my favorite meal, hunger as my main course. Therefore, since I am free from those things for which most people sacrifice their leisure. . . ." Cicero translates this letter in his *Tusculan Disputations* 5.90 (written in 45 BCE), which requires it to be dated no later than the early first century BCE. Reuters dates the entire collection of nine letters as far back as the third century BCE, which would make them the oldest Cynic letters (see below, sec. B.4).

Apollonius of Tyana (first century CE)

Hercher 110–30. – **F. C. Conybeare**, *Philostratus: The Life of Apollonius of Tyana Books VI–VIII, Epistles of Apollonius, Treatise of Eusebius*, LCL, vol. 2 (1912) 407–81. – New edition: **C. P. Jones**, *Philostratus: The Life of Apollonius of Tyana*, LCL, 3 vols., vols. 1–2: *Life* (2005), Books 1–4 and 5–8; vol. 3: *Letters of Apollonius; Ancient Testimonia; Eusebius's Reply to Hierocles* (2006) 2–79. – **C. L. Kayser**, *Flavii Philostrati opera*, vol. 1, Teubner (Leipzig 1870) 345–68 (**TLG**). – **R. J. Penella**, *The Letters of Apollonius of Tyana: A Critical Text with Prolegomena, Translation and Commentary*, Mnemosyne Sup. 56 (Leiden 1979).

There exists a corpus of 100 letters under the name of the Neopythagorean philosopher, wandering teacher, and miracle-working holy man Apollonius of Tyana. While most of these can hardly be authentic (cf. Penella), some, such as *Ep.* 56, 75, 75a, show such a detailed knowledge of the life of Apollonius's time that they are "unlikely to be forgeries" (Jones 3:6). What is clear is that some of them are addressed to the residents of cities, such as the Milesians (*Ep.* 68) or the Trallians (*Ep.* 69). On the whole these are not to be confused with the other letters that Flavius Philostratus mentions in his highly novelistic "biography" of Apollonius (e.g., 1.7, 23–24) and sometimes quotes verbatim (e.g., 1.32), although there are 14 letters that overlap between Penella's collection of letters and Philostratus's *Life of Apollonius*. Philostratus's protest in *Life* 7.35 (cf. also 7.1 for his claims to veracity) that he has made a large collection of Apollonius's letters and knows their language and style well enough to detect the forgeries of others makes one feel somewhat skeptical and rather points to Philostratus as the author of the embedded letters in the *Life*.

Aristaenetus (fifth century CE)

Hercher 133–71. – **J. R. Vieillefond**, *Aristénète: Lettres d'amour*, Budé (Paris 1992). – **A. Lesky**, *Aristainetos: Erotische Briefe*, BAW (Zürich 1951). – **O. Mazal**, *Aristaeneti epistularum libri II*, Teubner (Stuttgart 1971) (**TLG**).

As the author of two books of love letters with partly novelistic content, Aristaenetus is a later representative of this literary genre.

Aristotle (384–322 BCE)

Hercher 172–74 (**TLG**). – **M. Plezia**, *Aristotelis epistularum fragmenta cum testamento*, Academia Scientiarum Polona: Auctorum Graecorum et

Latinorum opuscula selecta 3 (Warsaw 1968). – **J. Bielawski** and **M. Plezia**, *Lettre d'Aristote à Alexandre sur la politique envers les cités*, Archiwum Filologiczne NS 25 (Wroclaw 1970).

Hercher includes three letters of Aristotle to Philip II of Macedon, two letters to Alexander the Great, and one letter to Theophrastus. Plezia provides a thorough orientation to the (indirect) transmission of Aristotle's letters, additional witnesses to his correspondence, and collections of his letters.

Brutus (85–42 BCE)

Hercher 177–91 (**TLG**). – **L. Torraca**, *Marco Giunio Bruto: Epistole greche*, CSG 31 (Naples 1959). – **J. Moles**, "Plutarch, Brutus and Brutus' Greek and Latin Letters," in J. Mossman, ed., *Plutarch and his Intellectual World: Essays on Plutarch* (London 1997) 141–68. – **J. Deininger**, "Brutus und die Bithyner: Bemerkungen zu den sogenannten griechischen Briefen des Brutus," *RMP* 109 (1966) 356–72. – **P. L. Meucci**, "Le lettere greche di Bruto," *Studia italiani di filologia classica* 19 (1942) 47–102. – **R. E. Smith**, "The Greek Letters of M. Junius Brutus," *CQ* 30 (1936) 194–203.

Brutus, infamous as the murderer of Caesar, is the attributed author of a spurious collection of letters that "King Mithridates" gathered and introduced for his nephew (his letter of dedication, Hercher 177–78, goes by the separate title *Mithridatis epistula* in the TLG). The collection consists of 70 letters and includes correspondence to and from the residents of Pergamum, Rhodes, Cos, Patara, etc., which the editor of the collection obviously composed himself. Latin letters of Brutus that are more probably authentic can be found for example in the collections of Cicero's letters. Plutarch, *Brutus* 2.6 also quotes three letters of Brutus in Greek.

Chion of Heraclea (fourth century BCE)

Hercher 194–206 (**TLG**). – **I. Düring**, *Chion of Heraclea: A Novel in Letters*, Acta Universitatis Gotoburgensis: Göteborgs Högskolas Årsskrift 57.5 (Göteborg 1951; repr. New York 1979). – **H. Morales**, ed., *Greek Fiction: Daphnis and Chloe by Longus, Callirhoe by Chariton, and Chion of Heraclea by Anon*, Penguin Classics, trans. P. Vasunia (Longus), R. Omitowoju (Chariton), and J. Penwill (Chion) (forthcoming 2008). – **P.-L. Malosse**, *Lettres de Chion d'Héraclée* (Salerno 2004). – **P. A. Rosenmeyer**, "The Epistolary Novel," in J. R. Morgan and R. Stoneman, eds., *Greek Fiction: The Greek Novel in Context* (London and New York

1994) 146–65. – **N. Holzberg**, ed., *Briefroman* (Bib. 18) 28–32. – **D. Konstan** and **P. Mitsis**, "Chion of Heraclea: A Philosophical Novel in Letters," in M. C. Nussbaum, ed., *The Poetics of Therapy: Hellenistic Rhetoric in Its Rhetorical and Literary Context*, Apeiron 23.4 (1990) 257–79.

The name over this collection of 17 fictitious letters, which together form a short epistolary novel, is borrowed from a young man who killed a tyrant in the fourth century BCE. Proposed dates for the work lie in the period from about 100 BCE to 100 CE. In these letters the figure of "Chion" allows the reader to experience along with him how his study of Platonic philosophy and his personal acquaintance with Xenophon and Plato finally move him to return to his city with the premeditated plan of killing the tyrant Clearchus at the cost of his own life. Letter 8 is a short, very formal letter of recommendation, while Letter 9 is a good-bye letter to Plato, formulated in the consciousness of Chion's impending death. Ingemar Düring, to whom we owe our edition of the text and translation, sees the motto of the work expressed in a sentence in 14.4 (see p. 69), which boils down to the following maxim: "a tyrant can inflict all kinds of evils on my body, but he can never subdue my soul" (Düring 17).

Crates of Thebes (fourth century BCE)

Hercher 208–17 (**TLG**).

See below under the Cynic Epistles (sec. B.4).

Demosthenes (384–322 BCE)

Hercher 219–34. – **N. W. DeWitt** and **N. J. DeWitt**, *Demosthenes: Funeral Speech, Erotic Essay, Exordia and Letters*, LCL, vol. 7 (1949) 195–269. – **R. Clavaud**, *Démosthène: Lettres et fragments*, Budé (Paris 1987). – **J. A. Goldstein**, *Letters* (Bib. 2). – **W. Rennie**, *Demosthenis orationes*, vol. 3 (Oxford 1931) 1462–92 (**TLG**).

The six letters of Demosthenes, with the exception of the fifth, which must in any case be considered spurious, are addressed to the people and the council of Athens. Letters 1–4 and 6 have been subject to various evaluations in scholarship. Clavaud has once again recently declared all five to be authentic and assigns each one a distinct place in the orator's political career. Goldstein's book contains an important long section on the *rhetorical analysis* of Letters 1–4, which he categorizes as deliberative self-defense (95–181). The first letter begins with a prayer.

Dio Cocceianus (of Prusa), also known as Dio Chrysostom
(ca. 40–112 CE)

Hercher 259 (**TLG**). – **H. L. Crosby**, *Dio Chrysostom*, LCL, vol. 5 (1951) 356–59.

Five letters of the famous orator, two of which are to Musonius Rufus, perhaps written by Dio himself.

Diogenes of Sinope (fourth century BCE)

Hercher 235–58 (**TLG**).

See below under the Cynic Epistles (sec. B.4).

Dionysius of Antioch (before the sixth century CE)

Hercher 260–74 (**TLG**). – **M. Minniti Colonna**, "Le Epistole di Dionigi Antiocheno," *Vichiana* NS 4 (1975) 60–80.

A collection of 85 short letters, some to various addressees, others without an address. To their author the sophist Aeneas of Gaza (see above) addresses his Letter 17, a letter of recommendation for one of his students.

Dionysius of Halicarnassus (taught in Rome, 30–8 BCE)

Lacking in **Hercher**. – **S. Usher**, *Dionysius of Halicarnassus: Critical Essays*, LCL, vol. 2 (1985) 301–433. – **W. R. Roberts**, *Dionysius of Halicarnassus: The Three Literary Letters* (Cambridge 1901). – **L. Radermacher** and **H. Usener**, *Dionysii Halicarnasei quae exstant*, vol. 5, Teubner (Leipzig 1899) 221–48 (to Pompeius), 257–79 (to Ammaeus about Demosthenes), 421–38 (to Ammaeus about Thucydides) (**TLG**). – **M. L. Stirewalt, Jr.**, "The Form and Function of the Greek Letter-Essay" (Bib. 36) 149–50.

The author of *Roman Antiquities* was also a stylistic critic, and he has recorded his knowledge of this area in the form of three "literary letters." In his first letter to Ammaeus he treats Demosthenes, in his second to Ammaeus he treats Thucydides, and in his letter to Pompeius he defends among other things his criticism of Plato; he writes in response to a letter of Pompeius that he describes as an ἐπιστολὴν εὐπαίδευτον, a "scholarly letter" (§1).

Epicurus (341–270 BCE)

Lacking in **Hercher**.

See below, section B.1.

Euripides (480–406 BCE)

Hercher 275–79 (**TLG**). – **H. U. Gösswein**, *Die Briefe des Euripides*, BKP 55 (Hain 1975). – **N. Holzberg**, ed., *Briefroman* (Bib. 18) 13–17.

Five spurious letters, including four to King Archelaus and one to Sophocles, that were produced in the Augustan period or later (a certain Sabidius Pollio has been named as a possible author). The goal was to exonerate the esteemed tragic playwright Euripides from the charge of being a friend of tyrants (Gösswein 23). Not meant here are the letters that the authentic Euripides mentions or has read in his dramas, cf. *Iphigenia at Aulis* 98–123; *Iphigenia among the Taurians* 725–97; *Hippolytus* 856–80 (cf. P. A. Rosenmeyer, *Ancient Epistolary Fictions* [Bib. 2] 61–97; G. Monaco, "L'epistola nel teatro antico" [Bib. 2]).

Heraclitus of Ephesus (ca. 500 BCE)

Hercher 280–88 (**TLG**) – **A. J. Malherbe**, *The Cynic Epistles* (Bib. 1), trans. by D. R. Worley, 185–215. – **R. Mondolfo** and **L. Tarán**, *Eraclito: Testimonianze e Imitazioni*, Biblioteca di studi superiori 59 (Florence 1972) 279–359 (textual basis for Worley in Malherbe). – **A.-M. Denis**, *Fragmenta pseudepigraphorum quae supersunt Graeca*, PVTG 3 (Leiden 1970) 157–60 (Pseudo-Heraclitus), prints Epistles 4 and 7, following mainly Hercher's text (**TLG**). – **H. W. Attridge**, *First Century Cynicism in the Epistles of Heraclitus*, HTS 29 (Missoula 1976).

Nine letters are attributed to this pre-Socratic philosopher in the manuscripts, two of them (Letters 1 and 3) addressed to the Persian king Darius. Although broadly classified by Malherbe as "Cynic Epistles," we adopt a more narrow definition of that corpus below (cf. sec. B.4). Diogenes Laertius 9.13–14 also knows of two of these letters, namely Letters 1 and 2. The nine letters can be further subdivided into groups and go back to two or more authors who were active in the first century CE. An older assumption of Jewish influence, still reflected in the printing of Letters 4 and 7 in a series on the Old Testament Pseudepigrapha (Denis), has not been substantiated (see Attridge for the refutation of this theory, which goes back to Freudenthal in the nineteenth century). The spiritual orientation is rather to be described as Cynic, as Letters 4 and 7 especially make clear.

Hippocrates (born ca. 460 BCE)

Hercher 289–318. – **W. D. Smith**, *Hippocrates: Pseudepigraphic Writings. Letters, Embassy, Speech from the Altar, Decree*, Studies in Ancient Medicine 2 (Leiden 1990). – **É. Littré**, *Oeuvres complètes d'Hippocrate*, vol. 9 (Paris 1861) 312–428 (**TLG**). – **T. Rütten**, *Demokrit, lachender Philosoph und sanguinischer Melancholiker: Eine pseudo-hippokratische Geschichte*, Mnemosyne Sup. 118 (Leiden 1992), for letters 10–23. – **F. Heinimann**, "Diokles von Karystos und der prophylaktische Brief an König Antigonos," *MH* 12 (1955) 158–72. – **N. Holzberg**, ed., *Briefroman* (Bib. 18) 22–28.

The name of the famous physician from the island of Cos provides the label for a large corpus of Hippocratic writings. Some of this can perhaps be traced back to Hippocrates himself, but the letters will certainly not belong to this oldest strand of material. In the sequence of the text identified by Rütten we are presented with a biographical novel about Democritus in letter form.

Isocrates (436–338 BCE)

Hercher 319–36. – **G. Norlan**, *Isocrates*, LCL, 3 vols., vol. 3 translated by L. van Hook, *Evagoras ... Letters* (1945) 365–485. – **T. L. Papillon**, *Isocrates II*, The Oratory of Classical Greece 7 (Austin 2004) 243–81. – **B. G. Mandilaras**, *Isocrates: Opera omnia*, vol. 3, Teubner (Munich and Leipzig 2003) 205–38. – **É. Brémond** and **G. Mathieu**, *Isocrate: Discours*, vol. 4, Budé (Paris 1962) 185–223 (**TLG**).

Nine letters of the orator to rulers and princes, including Philip II and Alexander, who was 14 years old at the time. Letter 4 is a recommendation letter, while Letter 8 is a letter of request. The authenticity of these letters is debated (discussion in van Hook, with lit.; cf. also Lesky 659: Letter 2 is certainly authentic; Letter 5 very doubtful).

Julian (331–363 CE)

Hercher 337–91. – **W. C. Wright**, *Julian*, LCL, vol. 2: *Orations 6–8. Letters to Themistius, To the Senate and People of Athens, To a Priest. The Caesars. Misopogon*; vol. 3: *Letters. Epigrams. Against the Galilaeans. Fragments* (1913, 1923) 2:203–339; 3:3–293. – **B. K. Weis**, *Julian: Briefe*,

TuscBü (Munich 1973). – **L. Goessler**, *Kaiser Julian der Abtrünnige: Die Briefe*, BAW (Zürich 1971). – **J. Bidez**, *L'empereur Julien: Oeuvres complètes*, Budé (Paris), vol. 1.1 (1932) 213–35 (To the Senate and People of Athens); vol. 1.2 (²1960) 12–23, 26, 51–77, 84–91, 133–200, 205–7; vol. 2.1 (1963) 12–30 (To Themistius) (**TLG**).

Julian "the Apostate," so called because he turned away from Christianity, was coregent from 355 CE and Roman emperor for a few years from 360/61. He wrote a series of letters, which partly reflect his literary and philosophical interests and partly serve his religious politics. For some items in this collection of 87 letters one must leave the question of authenticity open.

Libanius (ca. 314–393 CE)

Lacking in **Hercher**. – **A. F. Norman**, *Libanius: Autobiography and Selected Letters*, 2 vols., LCL (1992). – **S. Bradbury**, *Libanius: Selected Letters of Libanius: From the Age of Constantine and Julian* (Liverpool 2004). – **G. Fatouros** and **T. Krischer**, *Libanios: Briefe* (Selection), TuscBü (Munich 1980). – **R. Foerster**, *Libanii opera*, vols. 10–11, Teubner (Leipzig 1921–1922) 10:1–758; 11:1–571 (**TLG**).

Libanius was a successful teacher of rhetoric, with whom several famous church fathers studied, including John Chrysostom and Theodore of Mopsuestia, and an adherent and confidant of the emperor Julian. Some 1,600 of his letters have been preserved, which makes them both in terms of their number and their scope the largest surviving letter collection from Greek antiquity. The address list reads like a *Who's Who* of his time.

Lucian of Samosata (ca. 120–180 CE)

Hercher 392–98. – **A. M. Harmon**, *Lucian*, LCL, 8 vols. (1913–1967), vol. 6, trans. by K. Kilburn (1959) 88–139 (*Saturnalia*), esp. 114–39 (Saturnalian Letters) (**TLG**). – **C. M. Wieland**, *Lukian: Werke in drei Bänden*, Bibliothek der Antike (Berlin ²1981) 2:17–28.

After a dialogue and the establishment of the laws for the festival, Lucian includes as the third and last part of his work *Saturnalia* the four Saturnalian Letters (§§19–39), which begin with a satirical exchange between the author and the god Cronus and move on to an exchange between Cronus and the Rich: "I to Cronus, Greeting," "Cronus to his well-beloved me," "Cronus to the Rich," "The Rich to Cronus." Here one can see the problem with the collection of Hercher, for this purely literary creation, which we would do better to include under embedded letters (see below, A.3), has nothing to do with the authentic letters of the emperor Julian which immediately precede this in Hercher.

Lysias (450–380 BCE)

Lacking in **Hercher**. – **L. Gernet** and **M. Bizos**, *Lysias: Discours*, vol. 2, Budé (Paris ⁵1989) 282.

Lysias was a master of ancient oratory. Next to his speeches the ancient sources mention a work on rhetoric and seven letters, six of which are love letters. A judgment about their authenticity can hardly be reached, because we have just a few lines quoted in later collections.

Musonius (30–108 CE)

Hercher 401–4. – **C. E. Lutz**, *Musonius Rufus: "The Roman Socrates,"* Yale Classical Studies 10 (New Haven 1947). – **O. Hense**, *C. Musonii Rufi reliquiae*, Teubner (Leipzig 1905) 135–43 (**TLG**).

Musonius Rufus, a Roman Stoic who wrote Greek, was the philosophical teacher of Epictetus. Excerpts from his discourses have been preserved, and Hercher presents a longer letter, whose authenticity Hense doubts, and which earns only a single sentence in a footnote in Lutz (5 n. 5). In addition Hense prints the brief letter exchange between Musonius and Apollonius of Tyana from Philostratus's *Life of Apollonius* (4.46), which Hercher has included under the correspondence of Apollonius (127–28).

Phalaris (sixth century BCE)

Hercher 409–59 (**TLG**). – **M. Trapp**, *Greek and Latin Letters* (Bib. 1) 28–29, 66–69, 86–87, 102–5, 126–29, 142–45, 164–67, 213–15, 235–36, 256–57, 279–80, 293–95, 309–10. – **V. Hinz**, *Nunc Phalaris doctum protulit ecce caput: Antike Phalarislegende und Nachleben der Phalarisbriefe*, Beiträge zur Altertumskunde 48 (Munich and Leipzig 2001). – **S. Merkle** and **A. Beschorner**, "Der Tyrann und der Dichter: Handlungssequenzen in den Phalaris-Briefen," in N. Holzberg, ed., *Briefroman* (Bib. 18) 116–68. – **H. Görgemanns**, ed., *Die griechische Literatur in Text und Darstellung*, vol. 5: *Kaiserzeit*, Reclams Universal-Bibliothek 8065 (Stuttgart 1988) 372–77. – **D. A. Russell**, "The Ass in the Lion's Skin: Thoughts on the *Letters* of Phalaris," *JHS* 108 (1988) 94–106.

Phalaris of Acragas (Agrigento) was the first important Sicilian tyrant (ca. 570–549 BCE); the 148 letters under his name present him as a type of the raging tyrant. They are famous in the history of scholarship not least because in 1697–1699 Richard Bentley used them to prove for the first time that these and similar letter collections were created by other authors than their attributed authors, and at much later times.[6]

Philostratus (160/70–244/49 CE)

Hercher 468–89. – **A. R. Benner** and **F. H. Fobes**, *The Letters of Alciphron, Aelian and Philostratus*, LCL (1949) 385–588. – **C. D. N. Costa**, *Greek Fictional Letters* (Bib. 1) 50–59, 153–61. – **C. L. Kayser**, *Flavii Philostrati opera*, vol. 2, Teubner (Leipzig 1871) 225–60 (**TLG**). – **P. A. Rosenmeyer**, *Ancient Epistolary Fictions* (Bib. 2) 322–28. – **G. Anderson**, *Philostratus: Biography and Belles Lettres in the Third Century A.D.* (London 1986).

Of the four Philostrati it is the second, L. Flavius Philostratus, author of the *Life of Apollonius of Tyana* (and other works such as the *Heroikos*), to whom we owe 73 letters, the majority of which are not real letters but purely artificial products in the genre of love letters. These freestanding letters are to be strictly differentiated from the letters attributed to Apollonius of Tyana that the same Philostratus has interspersed in his *Life* of this Pythagorean wandering philosopher (see above under Apollonius).

Plato (427–347 BCE)

Hercher 492–532. – **R. G. Bury**, *Plato*, LCL, vol. 9 (1929) 383–627. – **G. R. Morrow**, *Plato's Epistles* (Indianapolis 1962). – **J. Harward**, *The Platonic Epistles* (Cambridge 1932). – **L. A. Post**, *Thirteen Epistles of Plato* (Oxford 1925). – **W. Neumann** and **J. Kerschensteiner**, *Platon: Briefe*, TuscBü (Munich 1967). – **E. H. Howald**, *Die echten Briefe Platons*, BAW (Zürich 1951). – **J. Burnet**, *Platonis opera*, vol. 5, OCT (Oxford 1907) Stephanus pp. III.309–63 (**TLG**); **J. Moore-Blunt**, *Platonis Epistulae*, Teubner (Leipzig 1985). – **L. Edelstein**, *Plato's Seventh Letter*, Philosophia antiqua 14 (Leiden 1966). – **N. Gulley**,

---

6 Cf. R. Bentley, *A Dissertation upon the Epistles of Phalaris, Themistocles, Socrates, Euripides, and Others, and the Fables of Aesop* (London 1697); idem, *A Dissertation upon the Epistles of Phalaris: With an Answer to the Objections of the Honourable Charles Boyle, Esquire* (London 1699), with the comments in W. Roberts, *History of Letter-Writing* (Bib. 2) 48–66.

"The Authenticity of the Platonic Epistles," in K. von Fritz, ed., *Pseudepigrapha* I (Bib. 61) 103–30. – **N. Holzberg**, *Briefroman* (Bib. 18) 8–13. – **V. Wohl**, "Plato avant la lettre: Authenticity in Plato's Epistles," *Ramus* 27 (1998) 60–93.

Of the thirteen letters attributed to Plato, those that might be authentic include Letters 6, 7, and 8. Letter 7 contains important biographical information about Plato's life and education by way of his recollection of his trip to Sicily. For a recent view that sees these letters as a self-contained novelistic composition, see Holzberg.

Plutarch (ca. 45–125 CE)

Lacking in **Hercher**. – **F. C. Babbitt**, et al., *Plutarch: Moralia*, LCL, 15 vols. (1927–1976), vol. 2 (1928) 108–211 (*Consolatio ad Apollonium*); 298–343 (*Conjugalia praecepta*) (**TLG**). – **C. Hubert**, et al., *Plutarchi moralia*, vol. 3, ed. by W. R. Paton, M. Pohlenz, and W. Sieveking, Teubner (Leipzig 1929) 533–42 (*Consolatio ad uxorem*) (**TLG**). – **B. Perrin**, *Plutarch: Lives*, LCL, 11 vols. (1914–1926). – **M. L. Stirewalt, Jr.**, *The Form and Function of the Greek Letter-Essay* (Bib. 36) 150–53.

In view of the fact that Plutarch provides us with the most extensive surviving literary *oeuvre* from antiquity, the search for letters in his works proves surprisingly unproductive, as witnessed by the fact that he is not included in Hercher at all. The extracts from letters of other writers that he intersperses in his parallel lives belong to another category of non-freestanding letters (see below, A.2). Two writings have an external letter frame: the *Consolation to His Wife* (*Consolatio ad uxorem*, *Moralia* 608A–612B) and the pseudepigraphical *Letter of Condolence to Apollonius* (101F–122A). An epistolary prescript is also prefixed to a few other tractates that deal with concrete occasions, such as marriage, for example Plutarch's *Advice to Bride and Groom* (138B–164A: *Conjugalia praecepta*). (See Stirewalt.)

Porphyry (ca. 234–301/5 CE)

Lacking in **Hercher**. – **K. O'Brien Wicker**, *Porphyry, the Philosopher, to Marcella: Text and Translation with Introduction and Notes*, SBLTT 28; Graeco-Roman Religion Series 10 (Atlanta 1987). – **A. Zimmern**, *Porphyry's Letter to his Wife Marcella: Concerning the Life of Philosphy and Ascent to the Gods* (Grand Rapids 1986). – **E. des Places**, *Porphyre: Vie de Pythagoras, Lettre à Marcella*, Budé (Paris 1982) 87–150. – **W. Pötscher**, *Porphyrios: Πρὸς Μαρκέλλαν*, Philosophia antiqua 15 (Leiden 1969) 6–38 (**TLG**). – **K. Alt**, "Glaube, Wahrheit, Liebe, Hoffnung bei Porphyrios," in D. Wyrwa, ed., *Die Weltlichkeit des Glaubens in der Alten Kirche*, FS U. Wichert, BZNW 85 (Berlin 1997) 25–43.

At an advanced age Porphyry the Neoplatonist married Marcella, a widow of a close friend who had seven children, and shortly thereafter he addressed to her this *Letter to Marcella*, a protreptic doctrinal treatise in letter form, intended for publication. His listing of faith, truthfulness, love (ἔρως, not ἀγάπη), and hope in §24 as the main elements of a pious life before God (Τέσσαρα στοιχεῖα μάλιστα κεκρατύνθω περὶ θεοῦ· πίστις, ἀλήθεια, ἔρως, ἐλπίς) invites comparison with 1 Corinthians 13 (cf. Alt). Another letter of Porphyry, to an Egyptian priest named Anebo, is known only in fragmentary form.

Procopius of Gaza (ca. 465–529 CE)

Hercher 533–98. – **A. Garzya** and **R. J. Loenertz**, *Procopii Gazaei epistulae et declamaciones*, Studia patristica et Byzantina 9 (Ettal 1963) 3–80 (**TLG**). – **L. G. Westerink**, "Ein unbekannter Brief des Prokopios von Gaza," *ByzZ* 60 (1967) 2.

Procopius, a Christian, was head of a rhetorical school in his hometown of Gaza. His letter collection contains some 166 letters to relatives, pupils, and contemporaries.

Pythagoras and the Pythagoreans

Hercher 601–8. – **A. J. Malherbe**, *Moral Exhortation: A Greco-Roman Sourcebook*, LEC 4 (Philadelphia 1986) 82–85. – **E. A. Judge**, "A Woman's Behavior," *NewDocs* 6 (1992) 18–23. – **A. Städele**, *Die Briefe des Pythagoras und der Pythagoreer*, BKP 115 (Meisenheim am Glan 1980). – **H. Thesleff**, *The Pythagorean Texts of the Hellenistic Period*, Acta Academiae Aboensis: Ser. A, Humaniora 30.1 (Åbo 1965) 185–86 (to Anaximenes; to Hieron) (**TLG**). – **W. Roberts**, *History of Letter-Writing* (Bib. 2) 67–83.

Of the 12 Pythagorean letters printed by Hercher, we can first filter out the letter to Anaximenes that Diogenes Laertius attributes to Pythagoras (8.49–50). But it is also difficult to sort out the remaining 11 texts. If we do not follow Thesleff, with his tendency to early dating, but rather Städele with his better founded results, the following picture emerges: Letter 1 from Pythagoras to Hieron belongs in the same general category as the letters of Phalaris (see above) and is to be dated with those letters no earlier than the fourth or fifth century CE, whereas Letter 2 from Lysis to Hipparchus, with a longer tradition history behind it, could have been edited in the second century CE. Closely related to one another are several letters between women, including Letter 3 from Melissa to Kleareta about the true adornment of a woman, Letter 4 from Myia to Phyllis about the choice of a wet-nurse and, despite the change from the Doric dialect into Attic, also Letter 5 from Theano to Euboule about the raising of children, Letter 6 from Theano to Nikostrate about foregoing counter-measures against an unfaithful husband, and Letter 7 from Theano to Kallisto about managing household slaves; for these letters an origin in the second century CE suggests itself. There remain four short letters of Theano that have been transmitted independently and may be assigned to the fifth century CE. It may come as a surprise that so many letters from women to women are available, and one could interpret this as a reflection of women's participation in the Pythagorean movement. Nevertheless, the picture of women in these letters is thoroughly conventional and agrees in this respect with the non-epistolary presentations of the Pythagorean women Periktione and Phintys. Probably the pseudepigraphy that is certainly present in all the Pythagorean letters was taken a step further in these letters between women; the real authors or "authoresses" could actually have been men who used these letters to propagate their own ideal of women devoted to modesty and domesticity: "The reader's pleasure is heightened by the fiction that it is women themselves who are giving the laws to femininity" (Städele 253, following F. Wilhelm).[7]

Socrates and the Socratics (including Speusippus)

Hercher 609–35 (**TLG**). Hercher's material is divided in the TLG into three text files under Socrates (Hercher, 609–16), the Socratics, i.e., *Socraticorum epistulae* (616–29, 34–35), and Speusippus (632–34). However, the letter of Speusippus to King Philip II (in Hercher 629 bottom to 632 top) is entered into the TLG not from Hercher, but from the edition of Bickermann and Sykutris, 7–12 (see below). – **A. J. Malherbe**, *The Cynic Epistles* (Bib. 1), trans. by S. Stowers (*Ep.* 1–25) and D. R. Worley (*Ep.* 26–35), 217–307. – **M. Trapp**, *Greek and Latin Letters* (Bib. 1) 29, 68–71, 215–17. – **C. D. N. Costa**, *Greek Fictional Letters* (Bib. 1) 80–83. – **A. F. Natoli**, *The Letter of Speusippus to Philip II: Introduction, Text, Translation, and Commentary*, Historia Einzelschrift 176 (Stuttgart 2004). – **J.-F. Borkowski**, *Socratis quae feruntur epistolae: Edition, Übersetzung, Kommentar*, Beiträge zur Altertumskunde 94 (Stuttgart and Leipzig

---

[7] The reference is to F. Wilhelm, "Die Oeconomica der Neupythagoreer Bryson, Kallikrates, Periktione, Phintys," *RMP* NF 70 (1915) 161–223.

1997), deals with *Ep.* 1–7. – **J. Sykutris**, *Die Briefe des Sokrates und der Sokratiker*, Studien zur Geschichte und Kultur des Altertums 18.2 (Paderborn 1933). – **L. Köhler**, *Die Briefe des Sokrates und der Sokratiker*, Philologus: Supplementband 20.2 (Leipzig 1928). – **E. Bickermann** and **J. Sykutris**, *Speusipps Brief an König Philipp*, Berichte über die Verhandlungen der Sächsischen Akademie der Wissenschaften zu Leipzig: Philologisch-Historische Klasse 80.3 (Leipzig 1928), esp. 7–12 (**TLG**). – **N. Holzberg**, ed., *Briefroman* (Bib. 18) 38–47, with bib. 188–89. – **P. A. Rosenmeyer**, *Ancient Epistolary Fictions* (Bib. 2) 201–2, 206–8. – **B. Fiore**, *The Function of Personal Example* (Bib. 43) 101–63.

Of the thirty-five letters in this corpus, the first seven are presented as written by Socrates himself; according to Sykutris they were produced in the first century CE by a single author, who wants to present Socrates as an ethical model and uses him to make hortatory speeches in disguise. The rest of the letters are from pupils of Socrates, addressed in part to other pupils of Socrates. Sykutris subdivides them as follows: Letters 8–27 and 29–34 have a common author, who wrote in the third century CE and approaches the style of an epistolary novel. Letter 29 goes together with the possibly authentic letter of Speusippus to King Philip II of Macedon (cf. Bickermann and Sykutris), while Letter 35 possibly belongs with the Pythagorean letters. The philosophical orientation leans in a mildly Cynic direction (see below, B.4).

Synesius of Cyrene (ca. 370–412 CE)

Hercher 638–739 (**TLG**). – **A. Garzya**, *Synesii Cyrenensis epistolae*, Scriptores Graeci et Latini (Rome 1979). – **S. Vollenweider**, *Neuplatonische und christliche Theologie bei Synesios von Kyrene*, Forschungen zur Kirchen- und Dogmengeschichte 35 (Göttingen 1985).

Synesius, a Neoplatonist from a pagan family who was later elected a Christian bishop against his will, has left behind 156 letters in addition to other writings.

Themistocles (ca. 524–459 BCE)

Hercher 741–62 (**TLG**). – **N. A. Doenges**, *The Letters of Themistokles*, Monographs in Classical Studies (New York 1981). – **N. Holzberg**, ed., *Briefroman* (Bib. 18) 33–38. – **P. A. Rosenmeyer**, *Ancient Epistolary Fictions* (Bib. 2) 201–2, 206–8, 231–33.

Themistocles was an Athenian politician and general at the time of the Persian War. The 21 letters that he is supposed to have written come from the late first or the early second century CE (Doenges 63). They were conceived by a single author as a completed whole in order to help readers draw near to the fate of Themistocles by means of a "historical novellette in epistolary form" (Doenges 40).

Theophylact Simocatta (sixth/seventh century CE)

Hercher 763–86. – **G. Zanetto**, *Theophylacti Simocatae epistulae*, Teubner (Leipzig 1985) 1–44 (**TLG**). – **P. A. Rosenmeyer**, *Ancient Epistolary Fictions* (Bib. 2) 201–2, 206–8.

As a later representative of this genre Theophylact, often regarded as the last ancient historian, also wrote 85 moral, farmer, and courtesan letters in his early years. Notably, Nicolaus Copernicus made a Latin translation of them in 1509.

Xenophon (ca. 430–355 BCE)

Hercher 788–91 (**TLG**).

As his last collection Hercher prints seven letters attributed to Xenophon that first originated in the Roman imperial period. They have been transmitted in two ways, in the context of the letters of the Socratics (see above), and in the anthology of excerpts of earlier writers by John Stobaeus in the fifth century CE.

Exercise

16. Attempt to sort this list, which essentially rests on Hercher, into groups or categories. Can various types of letters be differentiated from each other? How should Hercher's edition (which prints the letters alphabetically by author) be judged in the light of your findings?

---

2. Non-Freestanding Letters

As already hinted at in the introduction to the preceding section and in Exercise 16, we must still deal with some twenty-seven additional names of Greek letter writers and their generally shorter texts from Hercher's *Epistolographi graeci*, not primarily because we will thereby discover another weakness in Hercher's collection, but because we will gain access to an often overlooked category, namely (a) letters quoted by other authors than the original letter writer. Two further forms of existence of letters in ancient literature will also come into view, (b) letters mentioned and perhaps summarized but not quoted, and (c) embedded letters that form part of a larger composition.

a) Quoted Letters

The material below from Hercher is interspersed alphabetically with the authors of the freestanding letter collections surveyed above in A.1, but we have separated it out here. All this textual material is included in the TLG databases,[8] except for Hercher's entry for Archytas.

Alexander the Great (Hercher 98–99). Hercher provides letters from Alexander (356–323 BCE) to Aristotle his teacher, Darius, and exiles from Greece. See further below (c) on the *Alexander Romance*.

Amasis (Hercher 100). Pharaoh Amasis of Egypt (570–526 BCE) writes to Polycrates and to Bias, one of the Seven Sages (and is thus presented as a kind of sage himself). The source of these two letters is not mentioned by Hercher, but the first to Polycrates is found in Herodotus 3.40.1–4, with Polycrates' answer (which is only mentioned, not quoted) in 43.4.

Amelius (Hercher 101), a pupil of Plotinus in the third century CE, is represented by a single letter, whose source Hercher does not give.

Anaximenes (Hercher 106). These two letters from the pre-Socratic philosopher Anaximenes (fl. 546–535 BCE) to Pythagoras are taken from Diogenes Laertius 2.4–5.

---

[8] Users of the TLG database may note that it is possible to locate material in the database not only by the name of the ancient author and by the standard Latin work title, e.g., *Epistulae* (176 entries in TLG), *Epistula* (549 entries, including *epistulam, epistulae*, etc.), but also by the publication details of the modern text edition; a search for Hercher, *Epistolographi graeci*, quickly reveals the forty-four data files where his texts may be found.

Antigonus II (?) (Hercher 107). A letter from the king Antigonus, presumably Antigonus II (ca. 320–239 BCE), to Zeno, founder of the Stoa (see below), taken from Diogenes Laertius 7.7.

Antiochus (III) the Great (Hercher 108–9). Two letters of this Syrian king (ca. 242–187 BCE), from Josephus, *Ant.* 12.138–44, 148–53.

Archytas (Hercher 132; not in **TLG**). A Pythagorean from the fourth century BCE (fl. 400–350). Diogenes Laertius has him write a letter to Dionysius about Plato in 2.22 and a letter to Plato in 8.80 (for Plato's answer see 8.81).

Arcesilaus (Hercher 131). A representative of the Middle Academy (316/15–242/41 BCE). This letter to a relative with his last will comes from Diogenes Laertius 4.44.

Artaxerxes (Hercher 175). Two letters of the Persian king to his satraps from Josephus, *Ant.* 11.216–19, 273–83. Their content is also familiar from the book of Esther.

Calanus (Hercher 192). According to Philo, *That Every Good Person Is Free* 95–96 (the source of this text), the Indian gymnosophist Calanus objects, first orally and then by letter, to Alexander's plan to take him back to Greece to serve an example of wisdom among the barbarians. Philo quotes Calanus's letter to prove that "more durable than his spoken are his written words."

Chilon (Hercher 193). One of the Seven Sages (ca. 556 BCE). This short letter to Periander is from Diogenes Laertius 1.73.

Cleobulos (Hercher 207), ca. 600 BCE, writes to Solon in Diogenes Laertius 1.93.

Demetrius of Phaleron (Hercher 218), ca. 350–280 BCE, is connected with the legend of the origin of the Septuagint by means of a letter purportedly from him to Ptolemy II Philadelphus, sponsor of that project, found in Josephus, *Ant.* 12.36–39. For the legend see also the *Letter of Aristeas*.

Menecrates (Hercher 399), of Syracuse, physician, fourth century BCE. According to Aelian, *Varia historia* 12.51, "The doctor Menecrates became so arrogant that he called himself Zeus. One day he sent Philip of Macedonia a letter in the following terms: 'Menecrates Zeus greets Philip.'" There are various versions of this story; the text given by Hercher is from Athenaeus, *Deipnosophistae* 7 (289D). See further O. Weinreich, *Menekrates Zeus und Salmoneus: Religionsgeschichtliche Studien*

zur Psychopathologie des Gottmenschentums in Antike und Neuzeit, Tübinger
Beiträge zur Altertumswissenschaft 18 (Stuttgart 1933), esp. 19–24.

Menippus of Gadara (Hercher 400), third century BCE. A philosophical teacher with Cynic leanings, which are confirmed by the content of
this short letter, whose source Hercher does not name. Diogenes
Laertius 6.101 also lists among Menippus's works a collection of letters,
described as "Epistles artificially composed as if by the gods."

Nicias (ca. 470–413; **Hercher** 405–6). Out of fear that his messengers will
not tell the whole truth and his desire for the Athenians to hear his own
opinion about the progress of the war without distortion, this Athenian
general from the fifth century BCE writes a long letter to the Athenians,
which Thucydides reproduces in his *Peloponnesian War* 7.11.1–7.15.2.

Pausanias (Hercher 407). Pausanias, the Spartan general (fifth century
BCE), secretly sends a letter to King Xerxes of Persia (Thucydides
1.128.6–7), who is pleased with it and writes a letter of response which
begins: ὧδε λέγει βασιλεὺς Ξέρξης Παυσανίᾳ, "Thus says King Xerxes
to Pausanias" (129.1–3).

Peisistratus (Hercher 490), a letter from this Athenian tyrant of the
sixth century BCE to Solon; the source is not given by Hercher.

Periander (Hercher 408). Two letters from this tyrant of Corinth (ca.
627–587 BCE), who was included as one of the Seven Sages; the source
is Diogenes Laertius 1.99–100.

Pherecydes (Hercher 460). A pre-Socratic philosopher (ca. 540 BCE),
to whom Diogenes Laertius 1.122 attributes a letter to Thales.

Philip II of Macedonia (Hercher 461–67). Most of the letters attributed to Philip (382–336 BCE) come from Demosthenes, especially from
his *De corona, Oration* 18.39, 77–78, 157, 166, 167, and also from his
Oration 12, which consists entirely of a letter of Philip (preceded in *Or.*
11 by Demosthenes' answer to Philip's letter in the form of a speech to
the Athenians). These texts can hardly be considered authentic (for a different view of *Or.* 12 see M. Pohlenz, "Philipps Schreiben an Athen,"
Hermes 64 [1929] 41–62). For the question of authenticity it must generally be kept in mind that the speeches of Demosthenes are often interrupted for statements of witnesses, recitation of decrees and laws, and
reading of letters (*Or.* 34.8; 49.13; 50.62). Thus for example in *De falsa
legatione, Oration* 19, we are told in §§36, 44, 51–52 that letters of Philip
were read or mentioned to the audience, and in §§161, 187 gaps are left
for their reading, but the full text is never quoted. This is precisely the
place were insertions by a later hand were most likely to occur.

Pittacus of Mytilene (Hercher 491), one of the Seven Sages (ca. 650–570 BCE), addresses a few lines to Croesus, quoted by Diogenes Laertius 1.81.

Ptolemy II Philadelphus (Hercher 599–600). A letter of this Egyptian king to the Jewish high priest Eleazar on the occasion of the origin of the Septuagint, together with Eleazar's answer, in Josephus, *Ant.* 12.45–50, 51–56.

Solon (Hercher 636–37). These four letters of the Athenian lawgiver (seventh or sixth century BCE) are taken from Diogenes Laertius 1.64–67.

Thales (Hercher 740). Diogenes Laertius 1.43–42 in turn provides the two letters of the pre-Socratic natural philosopher Thales to Pherecydes and to Solon (see above).

Thrasybulus (Hercher 787). This Athenian general and strategist around 400 BCE answers a letter or messenger from Periander (see above) with a letter in Diogenes Laertius 1.100.

Zeno (Hercher 792). With this last letter in Hercher's collection the founder of Stoicism (335–263 BCE) answers the above mentioned letter of King Antigonus (cf. Hercher 107). The text is from Diogenes Laertius 7.8–9.

The contents of Hercher's collection have now been fully surveyed (except for the texts on epistolary theory on pp. 1–16, mentioned in the introduction to chapter 5 below). This second series of texts has a peculiarity over against the first that also explains their brevity: they all involve the quotation of letters of very dubious origin by other authors, especially Diogenes Laertius,[9] then also Thucydides, Flavius Josephus, and others, although Hercher also

---

[9] Diogenes Laertius could have taken his letters of the Seven Sages of Greece in part from an epistolary novel about them, according to B. Snell, *Leben und Meinungen der Sieben Weisen*, TuscBü (Munich [3]1952) 122–33. See now also N. C. Dührsen, "Die Briefe der Sieben Weisen bei Diogenes Laertios: Möglichkeiten und Grenzen der Rekonstruktion eines verlorenen griechischen Briefromans," in N. Holzberg, ed., *Briefroman* (Bib. 18) 84–115. In English see C. Cavarnos, *The Seven Sages of Ancient Greece: The Lives and Teachings of the Earliest Greek Philosophers, Thales, Pittacos, Bias, Solon, Cleobulos, Myson, Chilon* (Belmont, Mass. 1996).

overlooks a few things—for example, the letter of Epimenides (ca. 600 BCE) to Solon in Diogenes Laertius 1.113. The transmission history of these letters is of a completely different type from that of the other, more or less self-contained collections. We therefore refer to such texts as *quoted letters*. Their authenticity must be judged from case to case, but it can be verified only very rarely.

Such quotations of letters are also found to a more limited extent in Latin literature, which we may also briefly consider here. In his histories, which we possess only in fragments, Sallust includes in addition to diverse speeches also letters from Pompeius (frag. 4) and Mithridates (frag. 6).[10] Tacitus has a habit of not quoting letters directly but of summarizing their contents in indirect discourse, sometimes at length. Because he straddles the boundary between quoted letters and summarized letters, we return to him in the next section.

In principle we might deal with letters in historical works in the same way as speeches, by assuming that the historian has freely recast them or has created them himself. But that speeches predominate for such purposes in historical works is beyond question, and this is even more true in Latin than in Greek works. As H. Peter says: "The letter is not seen [sc. by the Latin writers] as equally effective as the speech; outside of Sallust it is never used for characterization or to create a pause or a review of important events" (*Der Brief in der römischen Litteratur* [Bib. 19] 170).

---

[10] Cf. E. Bikerman, "La lettre de Mithridate dans les 'Histoires' de Salluste," *Revue des études latines* 24 (1946) 131–51. Even in antiquity Fronto recognized this letter of Mithridates as the invention of a historian or annalist.

Exercise

17. To what letter types that are already well known or perhaps less well known to us can the above quoted letters be assigned? Can you isolate a particular group from among the named authors? What conclusions should we draw from this?

b) Summarized Letters

From the directly quoted letters reviewed above we must differentiate another category, the *summarized* or *reported* letters. This refers to cases in which a letter or a letter exchange is mentioned and its content implied or partly reported, but not quoted verbatim. The number of such letter reports in ancient literature is legion, but we should at least make ourselves familiar with the phenomenon by a few examples.

The oldest mention of a letter in Greek literature is found in the **Iliad** and ascribes the letter an ominous function: Proteus gives the hero Bellerophon "fatal tokens, scratching in a folded tablet signs many and deadly" (6.168–69)—significantly "the only passage in Homer which suggests knowledge of the art of writing" (LCL note). The parallel to King David's letter to his general Joab about Uriah the Hittite in 2 Samuel 11:14-15 is unmistakable (see below, chap. 6, sec. A.1.a). The reason for Proteus's ill will also has a biblical parallel, since Bellerophon has been unjustly accused of sexual advances by Proteus's wife, just as Joseph was by Potiphar's wife. But the parallel to Uriah is limited, for Bellerophon survives the ordeals that the letter unleashes.

Herodotus mentions among others a letter exchange between Harbagus, who slit open a hare's belly and hid a letter in it, and Cyrus (1.123.1–125.2). On another occasion letters were written in the name of Darius by one of his delegates and used first to test the loyalty of a group of soldiers and then to order them to kill Darius's opponent (3.128.1–5). Darius also writes a letter to one of his generals (5.14.1–2). Herodotus's tendency to novelistic embellishment is seen in the episode where certain traitors in sending their secret messages "would wrap [the letter] round the shaft of an arrow at the notches and put feathers to the letter, and shoot it to a place whereon they had agreed," although in this case the letter misses its mark and the plot is discovered (8.128.1–3).

Thucydides. In 4.50.2 the Athenians succeed in capturing a messenger of the Persian king to the Spartans and deciphering his letter written in Assyrian. Thucydides also reports about an exciting letter exchange in an intrigue centering on the Athenian general Alcibiades (8.50.2–51.3).

Xenophon is recruited by a letter to join the Greek mercenary army for Cyrus the Younger's campaign through Asia Minor to Persia (*Anabasis* 3.1.5). Later he is once again sent back to the army with a letter as his passport (7.2.8). A letter from the Greek generals to the senate and assembly of Athens is part of the evidence for which they must give an account in Xenophon's *Hellenica* 1.7.4. Xenophon also quotes an intercepted letter of truly laconic brevity which the Spartans sent back home: "The ships are gone. Mindarus is dead. The men are starving. We do not know what to do" (*Hell.* 1.1.23).

Diogenes Laertius in his many lists of the written works of the philosophers also mentions letter collections, for example for Carneades (4.65), Theophrastus (5.46), Strato (5.60), and Demetrius of Phaleron (5.81). He also says that Polycrates sent Pythagoras a letter of introduction to Pharaoh Amasis in Egypt (8.3).

Caesar. Without letters Caesar's campaigns would not have been a success. A militarily important letter exchange between him and Cicero has its perils: The messengers carrying Cicero's letters are cut off (*Bellum gallicum* 5.40.1), and it is a slave who, unsuspected "as a Gaul among Gauls," first breaks through to Caesar with news (45.3–4). Caesar responds immediately with messengers and letters (46.1–4). In one of his letters to Cicero, Caesar writes in Greek so that the enemy will not be able to understand it if it is intercepted. The messenger throws the letter with a spear into Cicero's camp, where it is not discovered until the third day, but then it is read to the assembled troops and causes great joy (48.3–9).

Tacitus knows how to weave letters into his presentation in a masterful way. The exact opposite of a friendship letter is mentioned by him in *Annals* 2.70.2: Germanicus writes a letter to terminate his friendship with Piso, whom he suspected of poisoning him. For his part Piso, in a letter forwarded to Tiberius, accuses the recently deceased Germanicus of luxury and arrogance (78.1). Tacitus reproduces in indirect discourse the gist of a letter from Sejanus, captain of the Praetorian Guard, to Tiberius, and also gives the gist of the emperor's letter of reply up to a certain point, after which he switches out of indirect discourse without comment and has Tiberius address Sejanus directly (4.39.1–40.7).

Exercise

18. Read and evaluate the following passage from Tacitus, *Hist.* 2.98.1–2 (trans. C. H. Moore, *Tacitus*, LCL, vol. 2 [1936] 319):

> At first the commander, Valerius Festus, loyally supported the wishes of the provincials. But presently he began to waver; in his public letters and documents he favoured Vitellius, but by secret messages he fostered Vespasian's interest and was ready to take whichever side prevailed. Some soldiers and centurions who had been dispatched through Raetia and the Gallic provinces were arrested with letters and proclamations of Vespasian on their persons, sent to Vitellius, and put to death. The majority of the messengers, however, escaped arrest, being concealed by faithful friends or escaping by their own wits.

c) Embedded Letters

By *embedded letters* we mean letters interspersed throughout a larger dramatic or narrative work. Occasionally the letters make up almost the whole work, which is then known as an epistolary novel (assuming the letters are fictional). In our overview under A.1 we have already mentioned the letters that Euripides has his dramatic characters read out loud in his tragedies about Iphigenia, as well as the Saturnalian letters of Lucian in his work on the festival of Saturnalia and the letters in Philostratus's *Life of Apollonius of Tyana* (see above under Apollonius; the love letters listed under Philostratus are a completely separate freestanding collection). These can all be considered embedded letters. We encounter such letters especially in ancient novels. Leading up to this development are on the one hand the novelistic embellishment of letter exchanges in Herodotus, and on the other hand the fictive letter collections of the type associated with the figure of Chion of Heraclea. The latter work already exhibits the connected thread of action that a novel requires; one thinks, for example, of the ability of letters to tell an entire story, as in Goethe's famous epistolary novel *Die Leiden des jungen Werthers* (1774; trans. *The Sorrows of*

Young Werther)—or in the best known English examples, Samuel Richardson's *Pamela* (1740) and *Clarissa* (1748), or the corresponding French one, Pierre Choderlos de Laclos's *Les Liaisons dangereuses* (1782; trans. *Dangerous Connections*, 1784, and *Dangerous Acquaintances*, 1924). The erotic letters of a writer like Alciphron are also related to much novelistic literature in terms of motif, for the erotic element is a driving force for the *erotici scriptores*, as the authors of ancient novels are sometimes called,[11] and the four modern examples just mentioned all involve either love or seduction. Moreover, the German word for a novel, *Roman*, is not accidentally related to our word "romance"; hence the work we refer to as the *Alexander Romance* is in German *Der Alexanderroman*, the Alexander "novel," though of course the romantic or novelistic genre is a much broader than the "erotic" per se.

As examples of this use of letters we must content ourselves with two representatives of the novel genre, the *Alexander Romance* just mentioned and Chariton's novel *Callirhoe*, followed by an excerpt from a verse epic, Ovid's *Metamorphoses*. But first we may slightly expand the range of genres to which embedded letters are well suited by noting that the Latin writer Plautus (ca. 254–184 BCE) also uses them in his comedies, in which he follows older Greek examples. Hence in Plautus's play *Pseudolus*, everything in the first 74 lines revolves around a letter that a courtesan has sent to her lover on wax tablets (see below, p. 191). Plautus also has a revealing comment on writing materials in his *Bacchides* 715: *stilum, ceram et tabellas, linum*, "a stylus, wax and tablets, some tape."

The Greek Alexander Romance (Pseudo-Callisthenes)

K. Dowden, trans., "Pseudo-Callisthenes, *The Alexander Romance*," in B. P. Reardon, ed., *Collected Ancient Greek Novels* (Berkeley 1989) 17–124; reprinted in W. Hansen, ed., *Anthology of Ancient Greek Popular Literature* (Bloomington, Ind. 1998) 163–248. - **R. Stoneman**, *The Greek Alexander Romance*, Penguin Classics (London 1991). - **H. van Thiel**, *Leben und Taten Alexanders von Makedonien: Der griechische Alexanderroman nach der Handschrift L*, Texte zur Forschung 13 (Darmstadt 1974). - **R. Merkelbach**, *Die Quellen des griechischen Alexanderromans*, Zetemata 9

---

[11] Once again Rudolph Hercher is one of the earlier editors of such literature, *Erotici scriptores graeci*, 2 vols. (Leipzig 1858–1859).

(Munich ²1977 [¹1954]) 48–72; "Alexandri epistolae," 230–52. – **W. W. Boer**, *Epistola Alexandri ad Aristotelem ad Codicum Fidem Edidit et Commentario Critico instruxit* [1953], BKP 50 (Meisenheim am Glan 1973). – **W. Kroll**, *Historia Alexandri Magni* (Berlin 1926) (**TLG**). – **P. A. Rosenmeyer**, *Ancient Epistolary Fictions* (Bib. 2) 169–92. – **T. Hägg**, *The Novel in Antiquity* (Oxford and Berkeley 1983) 125–40. – **E. M. Jeffreys**, **A. Cutler**, and **A. P. Kazhdan**, "Alexander Romance," in A. P. Kazhdan, ed., *The Oxford Dictionary of Byzantium*, 3 vols. (Oxford and New York 1991) 1:58–59. – **A. B. Bosworth**, "Pseudo-Callisthenes," *OCD*³ (2003) 1270.

In introducing this text, which sometimes goes by its generic Latin title *Historia Alexandri Magni* (cf. Kroll)[12] and is falsely attributed to Alexander's court historian Callisthenes, W. Hansen writes (163):

> The *Alexander Romance*, or more properly *The Life and Deeds of Alexander of Macedon*, has been called antiquity's most successful novel, and if the success of a work of fiction can be judged by the number of versions in which it eventually existed (eighty), the number of languages into which it was translated (twenty-four), the length of time it has appealed to readers (from its composition in antiquity well into the age of printing), and the number of literary works it inspired, this estimate is certainly true.

The many Greek versions of this work go back to a third century CE Greek original that is no longer extant, but which for its part goes further back to older source documents from the Hellenistic period. As one of its preliminary phases we can still make out the remains of an "epistolary novel," interspersed in the existing version, in which the course of Alexander's conquests is sketched through letters of the main characters, including the Persian king Darius III. In manuscript L,[13] which is the basis of H. van Thiel's

[12] Kroll is the source of the TLG text, which must be found not under Pseudo-Callisthenes as author, nor under *Historia Alexandri Magni* as title, but under this designation as *author* (TLG Canon author no. 1386).

[13] In the first complete English translation of these materials, Stoneman translates all of manuscript L and adds, where feasible, the extra material from the other recensions and manuscripts within brackets in the text. Material that does not fit conveniently in the text is found in an appendix (161–88).

edition and Dowden's translation, we find several series of mostly shorter letters preserved for example in 1.38.1–40.5 (five letters of Alexander, Darius, and his satraps), in 2.10.3–12.4 (eight letters), or in 3.25.1–26.7 (four letters exchanged between Alexander and the Amazons), which is immediately followed in 3.27–28 by a single longer letter from Alexander to his mother (see below). In these letters the author often seeks to imitate the style of Persian royal letters, though by his exaggerations he unwittingly caricatures it. In a letter of the Great King the identification of the sender runs as follows: "King of Kings, kinsman of the gods, I who rise to heaven with the Sun, a god myself, I Darius to my servant Alexander give these orders" (1.36.2).

Another group of longer letters can be designated as *fantastic letters* because they report marvelous experiences in far-away lands. One especially extensive piece (more than eight pages in Dowden's translation) begins in 2.23.1 with "King Alexander, to my much-beloved mother and to Aristotle, my most-esteemed teacher, greetings" and ends later in 2.41.13. In another letter to his mother (3.27–28) Alexander describes the City of the Sun: "There were twelve towers built of gold and emeralds, and the wall of that city was in the Indian style. In the middle was an altar built of gold and emerald, with sixty steps" (3.28.3). Although we have already mentioned Aristotle's inclusion in the address of a letter sent to Alexander's mother, there is a separate *Letter to Aristotle* that circulated independently of the manuscripts of the *Alexander Romance* and also exists in a Latin translation (cf. van Thiel 198–233).

Chariton's *Callirhoe*

G. P. Goold, *Chariton: Callirhoe*, LCL (1995). – B. P. Reardon, *De Callirhoe narrationes amatoriae*, Teubner (Munich 2004). – idem, trans., "Chariton, *Chaereas and Callirhoe*," in B. P. Reardon, ed., *Collected Ancient Greek Novels* (Berkeley 1989) 17–124. – H. Morales, ed., *Greek Fiction: Daphnis and Chloe by Longus, Callirhoe by Chariton, and Chion of Heraclea by Anon*, Penguin Classics, trans. P. Vasunia (Longus), R. Omitowoju (Chariton), and J. Penwill (Chion) (forthcoming 2008). – B. Kytzler, ed., *Im Reiche des Eros: Sämtliche Liebes- und Abenteuerromane der Antike*, Winkler Weltliteratur Dünndruckausgabe (Munich 1983) 513–672. – K. Plepelits, *Chariton von Aphrodisias: Kallirhoë*, Bibliothek der griechischen Literatur 6 (Stuttgart 1976). – G. Molinié, *Le roman de Chairéas et*

Callirhoé, Budé (Paris 1979). – **W. E. Blake**, *Charitonis Aphrodisiensis de Chaerea et Callirhoe amatoriarum narrationum libri octo* (Oxford 1938) 1–127 (**TLG**). – **F. Létoublon**, "La lettre dans le roman grec ou les liaisons dangereuses," in S. Panayotakis, M. Zimmerman, and W. Keulen, eds., *The Ancient Novel and Beyond*, Mnemosyne Sup. 241 (Leiden and Boston 2003) 271–88. – **P. A. Rosenmeyer**, *Ancient Epistolary Fictions* (Bib. 2) 133–68.

The name Callirhoe means "beautifully flowing," and this is the tale of her and her beloved Chaereas. Recent efforts at dating place it in the first century CE, if not in the first century BCE, although the story itself is set in the time of Artaxerxes II, king of Persia (404–358 BCE). Letters play an essential role in carrying forward the leitmotif in books 4 and 5. The satrap Mithridates, who himself has designs on Callirhoe, advises Chaereas to write a letter from a distance to Callirhoe, who thinks he is dead, for which Mithridates promises to find a carrier (4.4.5). Chaereas writes the letter in tears, and it is quoted verbatim (4.4.6–10). Mithridates then briefs his trusted servant Hyginus about the situation, including his love for Callirhoe, and gives him Chaereas's letter to her as well as one of his own. Hyginus sets out with three slaves to deliver the letters to Callirhoe, though to prevent suspicion the others are told that the letters are for her husband, the influential landowner Dionysius in Miletus.

Unfortunately, while Hyginus "was carrying out his orders, Fortune determined a sequel other than that intended" (4.5.3). At a certain point on the journey Hyginus leaves the slaves behind in Priene while he advances to scope out the situation in Miletus. Meanwhile, the letters come into the possession of the chief magistrate in Priene, who interrogates the slaves and learns what they thought to be the case, namely that the letters that we know to be addressed to Callirhoe were instead meant for Dionysius. Without opening the letters the magistrate therefore forwards them with a cover letter to Dionysius (4.5.5–7), who reads to his great dismay the opening words: "To Callirhoe from Chaereas: I am alive" (4.5.8). He collapses, but keeps a tight hold of the letters and rereads them in private (4.5.9–10). Because he too is convinced that Chaereas is dead, he suspects that the letter supposedly from Chaereas is actually a trick of Mithridates, and he accuses him before the governor Pharnaces—yet another man secretly in love with Callirhoe—of writing adulterous letters to his wife (4.6.1–2). The governor presents Dionysius's case in a confidential letter to King Artaxerxes (4.6.3–4), which counts as a fourth letter. With two further one-line letters to Mithridates and Pharnaces, the Great King summons Mithridates and his accuser Dionysius to trial in Babylon, along with Dionysius's beautiful wife Callirhoe, whom the king too wants to see (4.6.8). Naturally Dionysius brings "his" letters, those written by Chaereas and by

Mithridates, to the trial, and the letter of Pharnaces to Artaxerxes that initiated the trail together with Artaxerxes' letter of response are read first (5.4.7–8). In 5.6.7–10 the convoluted history of the other two letters, one of which, from Chaereas, was thought to have been written by Mithridates, is recapitulated in Dionysius's opening plea, and for this purpose Chaereas's letter is also read out loud ("From Chaereas: I am alive"), as in the speeches of the Athenian orator Demosthenes.

Although we cannot follow this thread further, we should note that later on Chaereas takes his leave of Artaxerxes by letter (8.4.2–3), as does Callirhoe from Dionysius (8.4.5–6); there is a mark of Callirhoe's own hand in §6, ταῦτά σοι γέγραφα τῇ ἐμῇ χειρί, "This I have written with my own hand," with which we may compare Dionysius's reaction when he receives it: "Recognizing Callirhoe's handwriting, he first kissed the letter, then opening it, clasped it to his heart as though it were Callirhoe in person" (8.5.13). Moreover, the ominous earlier letter from Chaereas stating he was alive is not neglected in the final summation, where it is mentioned in a speech of Chaereas (8.8.4–5). Without exaggeration we can say that letters influence the structure in the second half of the novel, for as J. G. Altman puts it, "In fact, the letter form seems tailored for the love plot, with its emphasis on separation and reunion" (*Epistolarity* [Bib. 8] 14).

Ovid's *Metamorphoses*

F. J. Miller, *Ovid: Metamorphoses*, 2 vols., LCL Ovid vols. 3–4, revised by G. P. Goold, vol. 1 (³1977); vol. 2 (²1984). – **C. Martin**, *Ovid: Metamorphoses* (New York 2004). – **D. Raeburn**, *Ovid: Metamorphoses*, Penguin Classics (London 2004). – **M. von Albrecht**, *P. Ovidius Naso: Metamorphosen*, Reclams Universal-Bibliothek 1360 (Stuttgart 1994). – **E. Rösch** and **N. Holzberg**, *Publius Ovidius Naso: Metamorphosen*, TuscBü (Munich and Zürich ¹²1990). – **C. J. Classen**, "Liebeskummer— eine Ovidinterpretation (Met. 9,450–665)," *AuA* 27 (1981) 163–78.

In the West, Ovid composed his *Metamorphoses* or "Transformations" between 2 CE and his exile in 8 CE. He drew his material, some 250 stories, from the numerous ancient sagas about divine and human beings undergoing a metamorphosis or supernatural change of shape. These he poured into hexameter and provided with a frame, intertextual connections, and architectonic structure. Despite their verse form, the *Metamorphoses* have a twofold relationship to prose according to M. von Albrecht: "On the one hand they stand close to the ancient novel, on the other hand the influence of rhetoric makes itself felt" (990). In the story of Byblis, who is smitten with the passion of an unlawful love for her twin brother Caunus (*Met.* 9.450–665), Ovid incorporates, in addition to soliloquies in the tragic style, a long love letter (9.530–63). Byblis wants to confess her love to her brother in writing and have him reciprocate it: "And she proceeds to set down with a trembling hand the words she has thought out. In her right hand she holds her pen, in her left an empty waxen tablet. She begins, then hesitates and stops; writes on and hates what she has written; writes and erases; changes, condemns, approves; by turns she lays her tablets down and takes them up again" (9.521–24). The tablet is quickly filled with words both timid and passionate, using up even the margins: "the last line coming to the very edge" (9.565). The servant delivers the sealed letter, the brother throws it to the ground only half-read in a sudden rage, and Byblis regrets having delivered such a personal message in writing rather than in person: "And yet I should have told him with my own lips, I should in person have confessed my passion, and not have trusted my inmost heart to waxen tablets!" (9.601–2). At the end of the episode Byblis is transformed into a fountain.

Exercise

19. Evaluate in the same manner as above the letter exchange in the fifth book of the ancient Greek novel by Achilles Tatius, *Leucippe and Clitophon*. Pursue your own investigation of the introductory questions of date, text and translations, etc.

---

d) Dedication Letters

As an appendix we might mention one more category related to, but not identical with, the embedded letters, namely *dedication letters*. That such letters accompany letter collections such as the ones we have reviewed for Greek authors and will encounter below for Latin authors is hardly surprising. Here, however, we are concerned with dedication letters prefixed to non-epistolary works of prose or poetry, which are also especially popular in scientific or technical works and which can be differentiated from a dedicatory address without epistolary features only with difficulty.

Pliny the Elder (23/24–79 CE) opens his already completed work of *Natural History* with a ten-page dedication letter to the emperor Titus (Vespasian), which begins: "Plinius Secundus to his dear Vespasian greeting. Most Gracious Highness . . . , I have resolved to recount to you, in a somewhat presumptuous letter, the offspring of my latest travail, my volumes of *Natural History*," etc. To this preface Pliny adds in his first book only a detailed table of contents, as he also announces to Titus at the end of the letter (trans. H. Rackham, *Pliny: Natural History*, LCL, vol. 1 [1938]):

> As it was my duty in the public interest to have consideration for the claims upon your time, I have appended to this letter a table of contents of the several books, and have taken very careful precautions to prevent your having to read them. You by these means will secure for others that they will not need to read right though them either, but only look for the particular point that each of them wants, and will know where to find it. (Preface 33)

Martial (ca. 40–104 CE) also uses this device in book 12 of his *Epigrams*. He prefaces this book with a prose dedication letter to his friend Priscus, in which he excuses himself for his long literary silence and blames it on his retirement to Spain, far from the inspirations of Rome (trans. D. R. Shackleton Bailey, *Martial: Epigrams*, LCL, vol. 3 [1993]):

> I miss the community to which I had grown accustomed. It is like pleading a case in a strange court. For if there is anything to please in my little books, the audience dictated it. The subtlety of judgments, the inspiration of the themes, the libraries, the theaters, the gatherings where pleasure is a student without realizing, to sum it all up, all those things which in my fastidiousness I forsook, I now regret as though they had deserted me. (Book 12, Preface 8–16)

3. Latin Authors

Bibliography 19: M. von Albrecht, *A History of Roman Literature: From Livius Andronicus to Boethius*, rev. by G. Schmeling, Mnemosyne Sup. 165 (Leiden 1997). – **P. Cugusi**, *Epistolographi Latini Minores*, 2 vols., Corpus scriptorum Latinorum Paravianum (Turin 1970–79). – **A. Dihle**, *Greek and Latin Literature of the Roman Empire* (Bib. 18). – **R. G. C. Levens, P. G. Fowler**, and **D. P. Fowler**, "Letters, Latin," *OCD³* (2003) 847–48. – **M. A. Marcos Casquero**, "Epistolografía romana," *Helmantica* 34 (1983) 377–406. – **H. Peter**, *Der Brief in der römischen Litteratur: Litterargeschichtliche Untersuchungen und Zusammenfassungen*, Abhandlungen der

Königl. Sächsischen Gesellschaft der Wissenschaften: Philologisch-historische Klasse 20.3 (Leipzig 1901; repr. Hildesheim 1965). – **M. Trapp**, *Greek and Latin Letters* (Bib. 1).

Our inclusion above of Sallust under the quoted letters, of Caesar and Tacitus under the summarized letters, of Ovid under the embedded letters, and of Pliny the Elder and Martial under the dedication letters has prepared the way for our transition to Latin literature. Here again our goal is to provide merely an overview that will convey a first impression of the most important letter collections and witnesses. Beyond this, a fundamental reference should be made to the comprehensive collection of Cugusi, which we cannot survey further here. This consists mainly of summarized letters and quoted letters—as distinct from the freestanding letters below—as they are found for example in Livy and Polybius (who, although he writes in Greek, includes Roman sources). The rich store of material collected by Cugusi in multiple volumes is still awaiting more detailed evaluation.

Ausonius (ca. 310–393/94 CE)

H. G. Evelyn-White, *Ausonius*, vol. 2, LCL (1921; repr. 1985) 2–153. – **R. P. H. Green**, *Decimi Magni Ausonii Opera*, OCT (Oxford 1999). – **H. Sivan**, *Ausonius of Bordeaux: Genesis of a Gallic Aristocracy* (London 1993).

Book 18 of Ausonius's poems consists of letters, most of which are composed in verse. From these letters we know that Ausonius was a Christian, nevertheless "his work belongs entirely to the cultivation of an educational tradition untouched by Christianity" (Dihle 580).

Cato (234–149 BCE)

O. Schönberger, *Marcus Porcius Cato: Vom Landbau, Fragmente*, TuscBü (Munich 1980) 274–85. – **P. L. Schmidt**, "Catos Epistula ad M. filium und die Anfänge der römischen Briefliteratur," *Hermes* 100 (1972) 568–76.

The remains of a letter of Marcus Cato to his son Marcus on the battlefield have been preserved in quotations of other writers (unfortunately, there is no easy-to-find English translation). The letter seems to have a tone of instruction, exhortation, and praise, and it looks like a tractate in letter form which, however, is adjusted to the military situation. To be differentiated from this (cf. Schmidt) is an encyclopedic letter of instruction addressed to Cato's son and dealing with the duties of a Roman *pater familias* and statesman.

Cicero (106–43 BCE)

See below, section B.2.

Cornelia (second century BCE)

E. S. Forster and **J. C. Rolfe**, *Lucius Annaeus Florus: Epitome of Roman History. Cornelius Nepos*, LCL (1929) 692–97 (frag. 1). – **A. E. Astin** and **E. Badian**, "Cornelia," *OCD³* (2003) 392. – **C. Bardt**, *Römische Charakterköpfe in Briefen* (Bib. 1) 3–10. – **M. Hofmann**, *Antike Briefe* (Bib. 1) 92–95. – **C. Horsfall**, *Cornelius Nepos: A Selection Including the Lives of Cato and Atticus* (Oxford 1989) 41–42. – **H. Rüdiger**, *Briefe des Altertums* (Bib. 1) 86–88.

This highly educated mother of the two famous tribunes Tiberius Sempronius Gracchus and Gaius Sempronius Gracchus warns her son Gaius in a letter from 124 BCE against applying for the office of tribune. The text is found as a fragment in manuscripts of the book of Cornelius Nepos on the Latin historians, and its authenticity is not entirely certain.

Dido

G. Showerman, *Ovid: Heroides and Amores*, rev. by G. P. Goold, LCL (²1977) 82–99. – **H. Isbell**, *Ovid: Heroides*, Penguin Classics (London 1990). – **D. Hine**, *Ovid's Heroines* (New Haven 1991) 108–15. – **P. E. Knox**, *Ovid: Heroides. Select Epistles*, CGLC (Cambridge 1995) 61–67, 201–33. – **G. Solimano**, *Epistula Didonis ad Aeneam*, Pubblicazione del Dipartimento di archeologia, filologia classica e loro tradizioni 114 (Geneva 1988). – **M. D. Reeve**, "Anthologia Latina," *OCD³* (2003) 101.

We enter the realm of the saga with this letter, which Dido, the legendary Queen of Carthage, addresses to her unfaithful would-be husband Aeneas, who has left her before their marriage. This letter from Dido to Aeneas stands as chapter 7 in Ovid's *Heroides* (see below), but a version of it has also found its way into the *Anthologia Latina* (cf. Solimano).

Fronto (second century CE)

C. R. Haines, *The Correspondence of Marcus Cornelius Fronto with Marcus Aurelius Antoninus, Lucius Verus, Antoninus Pius, and Various Friends*, LCL, 2 vols. (1919–1920). – **A. S. L. Farguharson** and **R. B. Rutherford**, *The Meditations of Marcus Aurelius: A Selection of the Letters of Marcus Aurelius and Fronto* (London 1989) 119–43, 184–91. – **M. Trapp**, *Greek and Latin Letters* (Bib. 1) 128–35, 282–86. – **S. K. Stowers**, *Letter Writing in Greco-Roman Antiquity* (Bib. 2) 81–82. – **M. P. J. van den Hout**, *M. Cornelii Frontonis Epistulae*, Teubner (Leipzig 1988). – idem, *A Commentary on the Letters of M. Cornelius Fronto*, Mnemosyne Sup. 190 (Leiden 1999).

Marcus Cornelius Fronto was a Latin orator, teacher of rhetoric, and tutor of the future emperors Marcus Aurelius and Lucius Verus, an appointment he received from the emperor Antoninus Pius. It was not until 1815 that someone discovered a palimpsest manuscript with parts of Fronto's correspondence with Antoninus Pius and his followers and with some of his friends. Some of the letters are written in Greek, and some of the Latin letters are tractates in letter form.

Horace (65–8 BCE)

H. R. Fairclough, *Horace: Satires, Epistles and Ars Poetica*, LCL (1929). – **N. Rudd**, *Horace: Satires and Epistles; Persius: Satires* (Hamondsworth [2]1979; repr. London 2005). – **R. Mayer**, *Horace: Epistles Book I*, CGLC (Cambridge 1994). – **N. Rudd**, *Horace: Epistles Book II and Epistle to the Pisones ("Ars Poetica")*, CGLC (Cambridge 1989). – **S. P. Bovie**, *The Satires and Epistles of Horace: A Modern English Verse Translation* (Chicago 1959; repr. 2002). – **H. Färber** and **W. Schöne**, *Horaz: Sämtliche Werke*, TuscBü (Munich and Zürich [10]1985) 418–537. – **B. Kytzler**, *Horaz: Epistulae, Briefe*, Reclams Universal-Bibliothek 432 (Stuttgart 1986). – **D. R. Shackleton Bailey**, *Q. Horati Flacci Opera*, Teubner (Stuttgart 1985). – **O. Schönberger**, *Horaz: Satiren und Episteln*, SQAW 33 (Berlin [2]1991). – **H. J. Hirth**, *Horaz, der Dichter der Briefe:* rurs *and* urbs—*die Valenz der Briefform am Beispiel der ersten Epistel an Maecenas*, Altertums-wissenschaftliche Texte und Studien 13 (Hildesheim 1985). – **O. A. W. Dilke**, "The Interpretation of Horace's 'Epistles,'" *ANRW* II.31.3 (1981) 1837–65 (with bib.). – **S. Harrison**, "Poetry, Philosophy, and Letter-Writing in Horace, *Epistles* I," in D. Innes, H. Hine, and C. Peeling, eds., *Ethics and Rhetoric: Classical Essays for Donald Russell on his Seventy-Fifth Birthday* (Oxford 1995) 47–61. – **M. Korenjak**, "Abschiedsbriefe: Horaz' und Ovids epistolographisches Spätwerk," *Mnemosyne* 58 (2005) 46–61, 218–34.

Horace can be seen as the creator of a new genre, the verse epistle or the epistolary poem, even if Lucilius was a forerunner with his satires in letter form. Horace wants to provide in his verse epistles what Seneca would later provide in his prose epistles: counsel on how to lead one's life. Although the poems are not real letters actually sent to their addressees, concrete historical persons are addressed in them: Maecenas, Horace's patron (1.1.3; 1.7.5; 1.19.1), or Caesar Augustus (2.1.1–4) in a type of open letter that satisfies the emperor's wish to be the addressee of one of Horace's poetic epistles (nevertheless, Horace did not accept the office of an *officium epistularium* or private secretary from Augustus). The last epistle (1.20) of book one functions as an epilogue to the completed work; the poet addresses his book as if it were a young and handsome slave eager to escape from his master's house and see the wider world through publication: "You seem, my book, to be looking wistfully toward Vertumnus and Janus [the booksellers' quarters in Rome], in order, forsooth, that you may go on sale, neatly polished with the pumice [used to smooth the ends of the papyrus roll] of the Socii [well-known booksellers]" (*ll.* 1–2).

Ovid (43 BCE–17/18 CE)

G. **Showerman**, *Ovid: Heroides and Amores*, rev. by G. P Goold, LCL (^{2}1977). – **H. Isbell**, *Ovid: Heroides*, Penguin Classics (London 1990). – **P. E. Knox**, *Ovid: Heroides. Select Epistles*, CGLC (Cambridge 1995) 61–67, 201–33. – **B. W. Häuptli**, *Ovid: Liebesbriefe / Heroides Epistulae*, TuscBü (Zürich 1995). – **W. Willige** and **N. Holzberg**, *Ovid: Briefe aus der Verbannung, Tristia, Epistulae ex Ponto*, TuscBü (Munich and Zürich 1990). – **H. Dörrie**, *Epistulae Heroidum*, Texte und Kommentare 6 (Berlin and New York 1971). – **S. E. Hinds**, "Ovid," *OCD*^{3} (2003) 1084–85. – **M. Beck**, *Die Epistulae Heroidum XVIII und XIX des Corpus Ovidianum: Echtheitskritische Untersuchungen*, Studien zur Geschichte und Kultur des Altertums 1/11 (Paderborn 1996). – **B. Chwalek**, *Die Verwandlung des Exils in die elegische Welt: Studien zu den Tristia und Epistulae ex Ponto Ovids*, SKP 96 (Frankfurt a.M. 1996). – **H. Dörrie**, *Der heroische Brief: Bestandsaufnahme, Geschichte, Kritik einer humanistisch-barocken Literaturgattung* (Berlin 1968). – **T. Heinze**, *Der XII. Heroidenbrief: Medea an Jason*, Mnemosyne Sup. 170 (Leiden 1997). – **J. Farrell**, "Reading and Writing the *Heroides*," *Harvard Studies in Classical Philology* 98 (1998) 307–38. – **S. H. Lindheim**, *Mail and Female: Epistolary Narrative and Desire in Ovid's Heroides* (Madison 2003). – **W. Lingenberg**, *Das erste Buch der Heroidenbriefe: Echtheitskritische Untersuchungen*, Studien zur Geschichte und Kultur des Altertums 1/20

(Paderborn 2003). – **L. Fulkerson**, *The Ovidian Heroine as Author: Reading, Writing, and Community in the Heroides* (Cambridge 2005).

Ovid further developed the genre of the poetic letter and moved it in the direction of elegiac poetry. His *Heroides* or "Heroines," for which there is a certain analogy in the letter of Arethusa inserted in Propertius, *Elegies* 4.3.1–72 (cf. LCL, ed. G. P. Goold [1990]), are fictive letters from female figures from the mythical tradition to their absent lovers or husbands (e.g., *Ep.* 1: Penelope to Ulysses; *Ep.* 7: Dido to Aeneas [see above]) which reveal their emotional state. In its first edition, the *Heroides* consisted of 14 letters; later Ovid added three other pairs of letters (e.g., Paris to Helen, with reply, etc.). Epistle 15, from Sappho to Phaon, is lacking from several important manuscripts of the *Heroides* and was probably not written by Ovid (cf. von Albrecht 793 with n. 1). In his works *Tristia* (8–12 CE, in five books, only partly in letter form) and the *Epistulae ex Ponto* (12–17 CE, in four books), Ovid works through the bitter experience of his exile, which caused him to end up on the coast of the Black Sea in 8 CE. In the reception history of the poetic epistle, the genre of the "hero's letter" dependent on Ovid's *Heroides* stands out with representatives well into the nineteenth century (cf. Dörrie).

Pliny the Younger (61/62–113 CE)

W. Melmoth, revised by **W. M. L. Hutchinson**, *Pliny: Letters*, LCL, 2 vols. (1915). – New edition: **B. Radice**, *Pliny: Letters and Panegyricus*, LCL, 2 vols. (1969). – eadem, *The Letters of Pliny the Younger*, Penguin Classics (Hammondsworth 1969). – **C. Greig**, *Pliny: A Selection of Letters* (Cambridge 1978). – **A. N. Sherwin-White**, *Fifty Letters of Pliny: Selected and Edited with Introduction and Notes* (Oxford ²1969) – **H. Kasten**, *Gaius Plinius Caecilius Secundus: Briefe*, TuscBü (Munich ³1976). – **H. Philips**, *Plinius: Epistulae, Buch 1–9*, Reclams Universal-Bibliothek 6979–87 (Stuttgart 1987–1995). – **M. Giebel**, *C. Plinius Secundus: Der Briefwechsel mit Kaiser Trajan: Das 10. Buch der Briefe*, Reclams Universal-Bibliothek 6988 (Stuttgart 1985). – **R. Morello** and **R. Gibson**, eds., "Re-Imagining Pliny the Younger," *Arethusa* 36.2 (2003) 109–262. – **S. E. Hofer**, *The Anxieties of Pliny the Younger*, American Classical Studies 43 (Atlanta, Ga. 1999). – **M. Ludolph**, *Epistolographie und Selbstdarstellung: Untersuchungen zu den "Paradebriefen" Plinius des Jüngeren*, Classica Monacensia 17 (Tübingen 1997). – **J. Radicke**, "Die Selbstdarstellung des Plinius in seinen Briefen," *Hermes* 125 (1997) 447–69. – **E. Aubrion**, "La 'Correspondance' de Pline le Jeune: Problèmes et orientations actuelles de la recherche," *ANRW* II.33.1 (1989) 304–74 (annotated bibliog. with over 700 entries). – **A. Weische**, "Plinius d.J. und Cicero: Untersuchungen zur römischen Epistolographie in Republik und Kaiserzeit," *ANRW* II.33.1 (1989) 375–86. – **R. Freudenberger**, *Das Verhalten der römischen Behörden gegen die Christen im 2. Jahrhundert, dargestellt am Briefe des Plinius an Trajan und den Reskripten Trajans und Hadrians*, Münchener Beiträge zur Papyrusforschung und antiken Rechtsgeschichte 52 (Munich 1967). – **A. N. Sherwin-White**, *The Letters of Pliny: A Historical and Social Commentary* (Oxford 1966).

Pliny himself edited the first nine books of his letters containing 247 texts from the years 97–100 CE, probably in individual groups. Most of these pieces were once private letters sent to a total of 105 real addressees, but they were stylistically reworked for this collection and represent only a selection of a still larger body of texts. Some of the pieces may also have been written specially for this collection. The shorter letters approach the style of the epigram, while the long presentation of the death of Pliny's uncle Pliny the Elder at the eruption of Mount Vesuvius addressed to Tacitus in 6.16 is reminiscent of history writing. Otherwise, the style of presentation can be called "essayistic," which corresponds with the variety of the treated themes, often from daily life. The correspondence of Pliny with the emperor Trajan from the time of Pliny's tenure as proconsul in Bithynia (ca. 112 CE) stands on its own. Here Pliny addresses official questions to the emperor, who answers them succinctly. These 121 letters were edited posthumously and were added to the collection in the Middle Ages as book 10. The letter in which Pliny asks for advice about how to deal with the Christians (10.96) together with Trajan's letter of reply (10.97) has become justly famous.

Sallust (86–34 BCE)

J. C. Rolfe, *Sallust*, LCL (1920). – **M. Trapp**, *Greek and Latin Letters* (Bib. 1) 74–75, 92–95, 128–29, 152–55, 221–22, 243–44, 281–82, 303–5. – **W. Eisenhut** and **J. Lindauer**, *Sallust: Werke*, TuscBü (Munich and Zürich 1985) 318–49. – **K. Büchner**, *Sallust: Zwei politische Briefe an Caesar*, Reclams Universal-Bibliothek 7436 (Stuttgart 1974; repr. 1991), both with copious bibliographic information. – **A. Kurfess**, *Sallusti in Ciceronem et invicem invectivae*, Teubner (Leipzig 1962).

Two letters or addresses to Julius Caesar with proposals for a political and moral reform of the state that were handed down anonymously have been attributed to Sallust since the Middle Ages. Their contents point respectively to the years 48 or 46 and 51 or 50 BCE, and their language clearly resembles that of Sallust, yet without the exaggerations that would necessarily betray an imitator. In the Loeb edition the former, chronologically later, document addressed to Caesar is called a "speech" (pp. 444–61) and the latter, chronologically earlier, a "letter" (pp. 462–91; cf. xvii–xix). If it is true that this second document, which presents itself as earlier, actually imitates and expands the first (so von Albrecht 459), then this would not only be an argument against the authenticity of at least this letter, but would also provide New Testament scholars with a nice analogy for the relationship between Ephesians and Colossians or between 2 Peter and Jude. Nevertheless, the question of authenticity still remains open. Both letters have their defenders; both are also ascribed by other scholars to a clever imitator.

Sidonius Apollinaris (430–ca. 486 CE)

W. B. Anderson, *Sidonius: Poems and Letters*, LCL, 2 vols. (1936–1965). – **A. Loyen**, *Sidoine Apollinaire: Poèmes et Lettres*, 3 vols., Budé (Paris 1960–1970). – **H. Köhler**, *C. Sollius Apollinaris Sidonius: Briefe Buch I*, BKAW NF 2/96 (Heidelberg 1995). – **J. Harries**, *Sidonius Apollinaris and the Fall of Rome, AD 407–485* (Oxford 1995).

Sidonius Apollinaris was the son-in-law of the emperor Avitus and was elected bishop of Averna in 469 CE. His extensive real letters from this period—next to nine artificially composed letters—contain some Christian elements but remain oriented to Pliny the Younger and Symmachus as models.

Symmachus (ca. 345–402 CE)

J. P. Callu, *Symmaque: Lettres*, 4 vols., Budé (Paris 1972–2002). – **S. Roda**, *Commento storico al Libro IX dell'Epistolario di Q. Aurelio Simmaco*, BSA 27 (Pisa 1981). – **A. Marcone,** *Commento storico al Libro VI dell'Epistolario di Q. Aurelio Simmaco*, BSA 37 (Pisa 1983). – idem, *Commento storico al Libro IV dell'Epistolario di Q. Aurelio Simmaco*, BSA 55 (Pisa 1987). – **A. Pellizarri**, *Commento storico al libro III dell'Epistolario di Q. Aurelio Simmaco*, BSA 81 (Pisa 1998). – **G. A. Cecconi**, *Commento storico al libro II dell'Epistolario di Q. Aurelio Simmaco*, BSA 86 (Pisa 2002). – **R. Klein**, *Symmachus: Eine tragische Gestalt des ausgehenden Heidentums*, Impulse der Forschung 2 (Darmstadt ²1986). – **K. Thraede**, "Sprachlich-stilistisches zu Briefen des Symmachus," *RMP* 111 (1968) 260–89. – **C. Sogno**, *Q. Aurelius Symmachus: A Political Biography* (Ann Arbor 2006).

Quintus Aurelius Symmachus (not to be confused with the Symmachus who produced a revision of the Greek Old Testament) was a great orator and a leader of the pagan faction of the senate against the Christian emperors. He left behind some 900 private letters in nine books, where the number nine follows the practice of Pliny the Younger. In *Ep.* 7.9, a letter to his son, Symmachus reflects on the difference between the rhetorical pomp of the public speech and the simplicity, brevity, and familiarity of the letter style. That Symmachus himself kept to this distinction is shown by a comparison between his letters and the remains of eight of his speeches. As in the collection of Pliny the Younger, a tenth book of Symmachus's letters contains his letters addressed to the emperor. These include the 49 *relationes* addressed to Valentinian II during Symmachus's tenure as urban prefect, which strike a more solemn tone.

Varro (116–27 BCE)

R. A. Kaster, "Varro (Marcus Terentius Varro)," *OCD*[3] (2003) 1582. – **P. Cugusi**, "Le epistole di Varrone," *Rivista di cultura classica e medioevale* 9 (1967) 78–85. – **H. Dahlmann**, "Bemerkungen zu den Resten der Briefe Varros," *MH* 7 (1950) 200–20.

Of Varro's gigantic literary *oeuvre*, which has been estimated at 75 different works totaling about 620 books, most has been lost, including seven or eight books of letters that an ancient list of his works knows as *Epistolicae quaestiones*. These will have included instructional writings, political pamphlets, and scholarly essays. There may also have been a collection of Varro's private letters.

Exercise

20. Which letter types already well known to us and which lesser known or new types are contained in the above overview of Latin letters?

B. Exegetical Case Studies

1. The Philosophical Doctrinal Letter: Epicurus

Bibliography 20: R. D. Hicks, *Diogenes Laertius: Lives of Eminent Philosophers*, LCL, vol. 2 (1925) 564–659. – **A. A. Long** and **D. N. Sedley**, *The Hellenistic Philosophers*, vol. 1: *Translations of the Principal Sources with Philosophical Commentary*; vol. 2: *Greek and Latin Texts with Notes and Bibliography* (Cambridge 1987). – **B. Inwood** and **L. P. Gerson**, *Hellenistic Philosophy: Introductory Readings* (Indianapolis and Cambridge ²1997) 5–31. – idem, *Epicurus Reader: Selected Writings and Testimonia* (Indianapolis 1994) 5–31. – **E. O'Connor**, *The Essential Epicurus: Letters, Principal Doctrines, Vatican Sayings, and Fragments* (Amherst, N.Y. 1993) 19–68. – **C. Bailey**, *Epicurus: The Extant Remains* (Oxford 1926; repr. Westport, Conn. 1979). – **H. Krautz**, *Epikur: Briefe, Sprüche, Werkfragmente*, Reclams Universal-Bibliothek 9984 (Stuttgart ²1985). – **O. Gigon**, *Epikur: Von der Überwindung der Furcht: Katechismus, Lehrbriefe, Spruchsammlung, Fragmente*, BAW (Zürich-Munich ³1983). – **A. Vogliano**, *Nuove lettere di Epicuro e dei suoi scolari: Edizione del Pap. Herc. 176*, Annali della Facoltà di Lettere della Regia Università di Cagliari (Bologna 1928). – **G. Arrighetti**, *Epicuro: Opere*, Biblioteca di cultura filosofica 41 (Turin ²1973) 35–117 (**TLG**). – **H. Usener**, *Epicurea*, Teubner (Leipzig 1887; repr. Stuttgart 1966).

A. Angeli, "Frammenti di lettere di Epicuro nei papiri d'Ercolano," *Cronache Ercolanesi* 23 (1993) 11–27 (with bib.). – **N. W. DeWitt**, *St. Paul and Epicurus* (Minneapolis 1954). – **P. Eckstein**, *Gemeinde, Brief und Heilsbotschaft: Ein phänomenologischer Vergleich zwischen Paulus und Epikur*, HBS 42 (Freiburg i.Br. 2004). – **M. Erler**, "Epikur, Die Schule Epikurs, Lukrez," in H. Flashar, ed., *Die Philosophie der Antike*, vol. 4 (Basel 1994) 29–490 (exhaustive bib.). – **K. H. Eller**, "Epikurs Lehrbrief an Menoikeus," in *Der Altsprachliche Unterricht* 32 (1989) 69–85. – **T. Gomperz**, "Ein Brief Epikurs an ein Kind," *Hermes* 5 (1871) 386–95. – **H. J. Klauck**, *Religious Context* (Bib. 7) 385–400 (with further lit.).

Born on the island of Samos in 341 BCE as the son of an Athenian schoolteacher who had emigrated there, Epicurus spent eventful years teaching and traveling before returning to Athens in 306 to settle down permanently. From then until his death in 270 he lived and worked there in a house with a garden, which led to the nickname "the Garden" (*kepos*) for his school of philosophy. Epicurus was a charismatic community founder and teacher whose followers projected onto him hopes of salvation and deliverance. His school led a life of intense, almost ascetic community based on the ideal of friendship. Friendship was the tie that bound master and disciple, and it also extended to the "therapy" that the members gave one another to heal the soul and spirit.

When friends are separated by distance, letters take the place of direct conversation. Epicurus too wrote letters to keep in contact with members of his rapidly growing school (which has led DeWitt to a premature comparison between Paul and Epicurus). Unfortunately only a very small portion remains of Epicurus's extensive written works. In his *Lives of Eminent Philosophers*, whose tenth book is devoted entirely to Epicurus, Diogenes Laertius (third century CE) can only begin to convey an impression of Epicurus's writings, which "amount to about three hundred rolls" (10.26); Diogenes lists 41 titles that he considers among the best (the first, *Of Nature*, on its own comprises 37 books). He then presents the full text of three of Epicurus's letters of philosophical instruction, to Herodotus, Pythocles, and Menoeceus, before concluding with Epicurus's forty "Principle Doctrines" (one of the 41 main writings).

Of these three instructional letters, the first, to Herodotus (10.35–83), draws up a terse, rather difficult outline of Epicurus's system of natural philosophy. The second, to Pythocles (10.84–116), is of disputed authenticity and deals with questions of astronomy and meteorology. Most accessible is the third, more ethical and practical letter to Menoeceus (10.122–35). This is conceived as a "protreptic" letter, i.e., a hortatory or doctrinal letter, and hence as an introduction to the basic ideas of Epicurean philosophy framed in letter form to attract new adherents. In this sense it follows the example of the lost *Protreptikos* of Aristotle (a work only partly reconstructable from the *Protreptikos* of Iamblichus and the papyrus fragment P.Oxy. IV 666). It is this letter to Menoeceus that is most relevant to the study of New Testament letters.

In this elementary course in philosophy, the letter's brief prescript, "Epicurus to Menoeceus, greeting," is immediately followed by an urgent call to "live philosophically" or "seek wisdom" (LCL), because only philosophy can lead to the greatest good of life, happiness or εὐδαιμονία (10.122–23, LCL [modified]):[14]

---

[14] A translation of Diogenes Laertius, *Lives of Eminent Philosophers* book 10 is available on the web at http://www.epicurus.net/en/lives.html.

122 Let no one be slow to seek wisdom when he is young nor weary in the search of it when he has grown old (Μήτε νέος τις ὢν μελλέτω φιλοσοφεῖν, μήτε γέρων ὑπάρχων κοπιάτω φιλοσοφῶν). For no age is too early or too late for the health of the soul. And to say that the season for studying philosophy has not yet come, or that it is past and gone, is like saying that the season for happiness (εὐδαιμονίαν) is not yet or that it is now no more. . . . . **123** Those things which without ceasing I have declared unto you, do them, and exercise yourself in them, holding them to be the elements of right life.

The last sentence shows that Menoeceus is no mere novice but is being called upon as a student to consistently practice and deepen what he has learned. But it remains noteworthy that this happens through presentation of the leading ideas, which contain as it were the paraenetic impulse to keep them. Hence the letter immediately follows with a paragraph about the Epicurean concept of God (123–24) before continuing with advice on how to think about the problem of death (124–27). Epicurus defines the sum and end of a blessed life as "health of body and tranquility of mind" (128). This in turn leads to his notorious pleasure principle, which was subject to various distortions even in antiquity and has been considered typically "Epicurean" ever since:

128 Wherefore we call pleasure the alpha and omega of a blessed life. **129** Pleasure is our first and kindred good. It is the starting-point of every choice and of every aversion, and to it we come back, inasmuch as we make feeling the rule by which to judge of every good thing.

In polemics against this doctrine of pleasure, which certainly has its limitations in that it inadequately accounts for the dynamics of various human drives, people often overlook the qualifications that Epicurus adds to this leading motif in the same breath. He immediately points out that people will often forgo certain pleasures when they believe they will do more harm than good in the long term. Even pains can be preferred to pleasures when submission to the pains for a long time results in an even greater pleasure at the end. Hence it is "by measuring one against another, and by looking at the conveniences and inconveniences, that all these matters

---

The translation relies on the Loeb edition by R. D. Hicks but slightly updates the English.

must be judged" (130). It is only for this reason that Epicurus can also plead for "independence of outward things" (αὐτάρκεια) as an ideal:

> **130** Again, we regard independence of outward things as a great good, not so as in all cases to use little, but so as to be contented with little if we have not much. . . . Plain fare gives as much pleasure as a costly diet, when once the pain of want has been removed, **131** while bread and water confer the highest possible pleasure when they are brought to hungry lips. To habituate one's self, therefore, to simple and inexpensive diet supplies all that is needful for health, and enables a man to meet the necessary requirements of life without shrinking, and it places us in a better condition when we approach at intervals a costly fare and renders us fearless of fortune.

Epicurus's strategies for maximalizing pleasure actually look very different from what one might expect based on the loaded term "pleasure." What emerges as an ideal is a sane and sober lifestyle that is scarcely distinguishable from a lightly disguised asceticism, even though moderate indulgences are allowed on occasion. A certain analogy between Paul and Epicurus is apparent in that both had to use letters to correct distorted presentations of their teaching by ill-willed opponents. An example of such clarification in Epicurus is the following:

> **131** When we say, then, that pleasure is the end and aim, we do not mean the pleasures of the prodigal or the pleasures of sensuality, as we are understood to do by some through ignorance, prejudice, or willful misrepresentation. By pleasure we mean the absence of pain in the body and of trouble in the soul. **132** It is not an unbroken succession of drinking-bouts and of revelry, not sexual lust, not the enjoyment of the fish and other delicacies of a luxurious table, which produce a pleasant life; it is sober reasoning, searching out the grounds of every choice and avoidance, and banishing those beliefs through which the greatest tumults take possession of the soul.

In his final appeal, which is formally directed to Menoeceus but implicitly addressed to all interested readers, Epicurus holds out the prospect of divine likeness to all who strive to live a philosophically sound life:

> **135** Exercise yourself in these and related precepts day and night, both by yourself and with one who is like-minded; then never, either in waking or in dream, will you be disturbed, but will live as a god

among men. For man loses all semblance of mortality by living in the midst of immortal blessings.

The three main doctrinal letters of Epicurus preserved by Diogenes Laertius are part of a larger correspondence with individuals and groups, as we can observe in some of the preserved fragments (for correspondence with groups, see the letter "To the Friends in Lampsakos," Usener frags. 108–9 or the letter "To the Philosophers in Mytilene," Arrighetti frags. 101–4). After the death of their master, Epicurus's pupils continued this practice of lively correspondence. Most of this has been preserved only fragmentarily (see frags. 95–216 Usener; frags. 40–133 Arrighetti; overview in Erler 103–19). In practice the process of recovering Epicurus's texts involves quotations in other ancient writers, papyrus finds, and even an inscription.

To begin with the inscription: An excerpt of a letter of Epicurus to his mother in which he warns her about superstitious ideas about God has been found as part of a monumental *Epicurean Inscription* of some 25,000 words on the wall of a colonnade in the city of Oinoanda in Asia Minor.[15] This was commissioned in the early second century CE by an Epicurean disciple named Diogenes. The inscription also contains fragments of two other letters attributed to Epicurus,[16] as well as several letters written by Diogenes himself.[17]

Further texts of Epicurean origin were brought to light by a chance find of a papyrus in Herculaneum, a city which like Pompeii

---

[15] For the *Letter to Mother* see frags. 125–26 (pp. 312–16) in the standard edition by M. F. Smith, *Diogenes of Oinoanda: The Epicurean Inscription*, La Scuola di Epicuro, Suppl. 1 (Naples 1993). Cf. also pp. 555–58 on the question of authenticity: "To sum up: the *Letter to Mother* is almost certainly addressed to Epicurus' mother; it is possible that the letter is spurious, but it is also possible that it is either a genuine letter, or an adaptation of a genuine letter, of Epicurus" (558). See now also the new edition by M. F. Smith, *The Philosophical Inscription of Diogenes of Oinoanda*, Denkschriften, Österreichische Akademie der Wissenschaften: Philosophisch-Historische Klasse 251 = Ergänzungsbände zu den Tituli Asiae Minoris 20 (Vienna 1996).

[16] See frags. 127 (letter to Hermarchos?) and 128 (letter to Dositheos) in Smith.

[17] See frags. 62–75, 120–22 in Smith.

was buried in lava and ash by the eruption of Mount Vesuvius in 79 CE. Numerous excerpts from letters of Epicurus and his immediate students are found in P.Herc. 176.[18] However, precise classification of these letters is often difficult because of their poor state of preservation. Such is the case for the following letter to a child, which has been attributed to Epicurus and cited as evidence of his affectionate kindness. As Gomperz puts it: "Who would wish to deny that the tender tone of the letter, the condescension to the language of the nursery, the banter with the little 'jester'—that all of this fully corresponds to the good-heartedness of the man [sc. Epicurus] which was so effusively praised?" (390). The letter runs in a literal translation (text in Vogliano frag. 23; Usener frag. 176; cf. also the alternative translation in Bailey 129):

> We have arrived at Lampsakos in good health—I and Pythikles and Hermarchos and Ktesippos. And there we have found Themisia and our other friends in good health. You do well, if you and your mama are in good health too and if you are obedient in all things to your papa and matron, as you were before. For you should know well, Napia,[19] that both I and all the others love you greatly, because you are obedient to them in all things. You will see me soon, for I will come quickly. . . .

Despite its earlier ascription to Epicurus, recent research has attributed this letter, which contains a modified health wish and concludes with a pleasant announcement of a visit, to Batis. As the sister of Metrodorus and the wife of Idomeneus, two of Epicurus's eminent disciples, Batis was an Epicurean of the first generation, and she addresses this letter to her niece Apia. Batis is also credited with other letter fragments in the relevant columns of P.Herc. 176 (cf. Erler 287).

[18] Cf. Vogliano; improved new edition by A. Angeli, "La scuola epicurea di Lampsaco nel PHerc. 176 (fr. 5 coll. I, IV, VIII–XXIII)," *Cronache Ercolanesi* 18 (1988) 27–51.

[19] Bailey 129 reads αἰτία following Gomperz, instead of ΝΑΠΙΑ with the papyrus. He thus loses the personal name and acquires a different sense: "Let me tell you that the *reason* that I and all the rest of us love you is that you are always obedient to them" (i.e., to the papa and matron).

Not to be overlooked as sources of Epicurean material, despite these more spectacular finds, are the embedded quotations in other authors. Once again Diogenes Laertius is primary. Not only is he the only author to have saved the three great doctrinal letters for posterity; he also quotes from other authentic letters in his biographical sketch of Epicurus's life. Among these are the moving farewell letter that Epicurus, conscious of his imminent death, addresses to his friend and pupil Idomeneus (10.22):

> On this blissful day, which is also the last of my life, I write this to you. My continual sufferings from strangury and dysentery are so great that nothing could increase them; but I set above them all the gladness of mind at the memory of our past conversations. But I would have you, as becomes your lifelong attitude to me and to philosophy, watch over the children of Metrodorus.

If we may trust this letter, Epicurus, although he faced death with considerable pain, still preserved the serenity that was the true goal of his philosophy of life, pictured in his letter to Menoeceus as the means of calming "the tempest of the soul" (10.128).

Exercise

21. The following text is also an excerpt from a letter of Epicurus embedded in the work of another ancient author, Plutarch. What is striking to you about the contents? Can you identify any motifs already mentioned above? (Plutarch, *Moralia* 1117B, *Reply to Colotes* §17, trans. B. Einarson and P. H. De Lacy, LCL 14 [1967] 249, 251 = Epicurus frag. 141, ed. Usener.)

> You (sc. Colotes), as one revering my remarks on that occasion, were seized with a desire, not accounted for on scientific lines, to embrace me by clasping my knees and lay hold of me to the whole extent of the contact that is customarily established in revering and supplicating certain personages. You therefore caused me to consecrate you in my turn and demonstrate my reverence. [. . .] Go about as one imperishable in my eyes, and think of me as imperishable too.

2. From Private Letter to Letter Corpus: Cicero's Letters

Bibliography 21: D. R. Shackleton Bailey, *Cicero: Letters to Atticus*, 4 vols., LCL Cicero vols. 22–24, 29 (1999); *Letters to Friends*, 3 vols., LCL Cicero vols. 25–27 (2001); *Letters to Quintus and Brutus; Letter Fragments; Letter to Octavian; Invectives; Handbook of Electioneering*, LCL Cicero vol. 28 (2002). – idem, *Cicero: Select Letters*, CGLC (Cambridge 1980). – idem, *M. Tulli Ciceronis Epistulae ad Quintum fratrem, Epistulae ad M. Brutum, Accedunt commentariolum petitionis, Fragmenta epistularum*, Teubner (Stuttgart 1988). – idem, *M. Tulli Ciceronis Epistulae ad familiares, libri I–XVI*, Teubner (Stuttgart 1988). – idem, *M. Tulli Ciceronis Epistulae ad Atticum*, Teubner (Stuttgart 1987). – **W. S. Watt**, *M. Tulli Ciceronis Epistulae*, OCT (London and New York 1982). – **H. Kasten**, *Marcus Tullius Cicero: Atticus-Briefe*, TuscBü (Munich and Zürich ⁴1990). – idem, *Marcus Tullius Cicero: An seine Freunde*, TuscBü (Munich and Zürich ⁴1989). – idem, *Marcus Tullius Cicero: An den Bruder Quintus, An Brutus, Über die Bewerbung*, TuscBü (Munich 1965). – **A. Salvatore**, *M. Tulli Ciceronis Epistulae ad Quintum fratrem* (Milan 1989).

K. Büchner, "M. Tullius Cicero, Briefe," in A. F. Pauly, ed., *Paulys Realencyclopädie der classischen Altertumswissenschaft*, new edition by G. Wissowa, second series, vol. VII/A1 (1948; repr. Stuttgart 1997) 1192–1235. – **J. Carcopino**, *Cicero: The Secrets of His Correspondence*, 2 vols. (London 1951; repr. New York 1969): use only with caution. – **P. Cugusi**, *Evoluzione* (Bib. 2) 159–76. – **A. Garcea**, *Cicerone in esilio: L'epistolario e le passioni*, Spudasmata 103 (Hildesheim 2005). – **G. O. Hutchinson**, *Cicero's Correspondence: A Literary Study* (New York 1998). – **W. Jäger**, *Briefanalysen: Zum Zusammenhang von Realitätserfahrung und Sprache in Briefen Ciceros*, SKP 26 (Frankfurt a.M. 1986). – **H. J. Klauck**, "Compilation of Letters in Cicero's Correspondence," in J. T. Fitzgerald, T. H. Olbricht, and L. Michael White, eds., *Early Christianity and Classical Culture: Comparative Studies in Honor of Abraham J. Malherbe*, NovTSup 110 (Leiden 2003) 131–55; also in idem, *Religion und Gesellschaft im frühen Christentum: Neutestamentliche Studien*, WUNT 152 (Tübingen 2003) 317–37. – **H. Koskenniemi** (see Bib. 14). – **J. Nicholson**, "The Delivery and Confidentiality of Cicero's Letters," *CJ* 90 (1994) 33–63. – idem, "The Survival of Cicero's Letters," in C. Deroux, ed., *Studies in Latin Literature and Roman History IX*, Collection Latomus 244 (Brussels 1998) 63–105. – **H. Peter**, *Der Brief in der römischen Litteratur* (Bib. 19). – **P. L. Schmidt**, "Cicero und die republikanische Kunstprosa," in M. Fuhrmann, ed., *Römische Literatur* (Frankfurt a.M. 1974) 147–79. – **T. Schmeller**, "Die Cicerobriefe und die Frage nach der Einheitlichkeit des 2. Korintherbriefs," *ZNW* 95 (2004) 181–208.

For the type and extent of his written legacy, the most important letter writer of antiquity was doubtless the Roman orator, statesman, littérateur, and philosopher Marcus Tullius Cicero (106–43 BCE). Why Cicero should be dealt with in a chapter on literary letters and not, for example, under private correspondence may be explained by an entry in a dictionary of literary studies, which claims that Cicero was the first to "make letter writing a potential literary genre, even if unwittingly and unwillingly" (Schmidt 152). Yet even apart from this judgment, it cannot be without significance that one of the greatest writers and orators of the Latin language was also a great letter writer. This is not to deny that the main value of most of his letters today is as unadulterated personal testimonies and first-class historical documents. But the very fact that people collected these letters from the beginning already points beyond their immediate occasion of writing. We therefore begin with an overview of the collections of Cicero's letters, which deserves our attention not least because of the analogous collection of Paul's letters.

We may pass over the purely instructional writings such as Cicero's *Orator*, *Topica*, and *De officiis*, which Cicero has given only a superficial letter form by adding a dedication to an individual. What remains are the four collections of Cicero's letters to his brother Quintus, Brutus, other Friends, and Atticus—*Ad Quintum fratrem* (in 3 books), *Ad Brutum* (now in 2 books, although these contain only the letters from book 9 of the original collection), *Ad familiares* (in 16 books), and *Ad Atticum* (in 16 books). Of the 864 numbered letters in these 36 or 37 books, 90 are addressed to Cicero and 774 are written by Cicero himself. Scholars therefore estimate that a little less than half of the letters have been preserved that belonged to the ancient collections of Cicero's letters in about 80 books.

About the original process of collecting the bulk of Cicero's letters scholarship is in no doubt. Immediately after the death of his master, Cicero's private secretary and confidant Marcus Tullius Tiro began not only to write his biography but also to put in order and publish his letters from the same feeling of piety and loyalty. Here Tiro could sometimes fall back on copies of important letters that Cicero had requested to be made and kept in his possession. In other cases Tiro asked for the originals to be returned by Cicero's correspondents or had them returned voluntarily. Tiro

first assembled Cicero's complete correspondences, each requiring
several books, with important personages such as Pompey, Caesar,
Octavian, Cato, Cornelius Nepos, and Cicero's son Marcus. The
well known letters to Cicero's brother Quintus and to Brutus
come from this collection. Over against this a supplemental collection, which only in the middle ages received the general title *Ad
familiares*, "To Friends, Clients, and Family Members," represents
the "gleanings" (Peter 84). This collection takes only marginal
account, if any, of the correspondents that had already been given
their own letter collection, and it dedicates no more than a single
book to any one of Cicero's other writing partners. The last book
of this collection contains, in passing, the letters of Cicero to Tiro
himself.[20]

Matters are once again different with Cicero's letters to his
slightly older best friend Titus Pomponius Atticus (whose sister
married Cicero's brother Quintus), who lived in Athens in 86–65
BC and owes his cognomen Atticus to his enthusiasm for Greece.
Cicero often corresponded with him daily or even several times a
day without having copies made for his personal use; this appeared
unnecessary because of the letters' very personal nature and too
time-consuming because of their volume. In this case it is Atticus
himself who collected the letters and deposited them in his family
archive, without yet publishing them. Publication did not follow
until a hundred years later, between 55 and 60 CE during the
reign of Nero, when people took "a new interest in the period of
the civil war and the beginning of the principate" (Büchner 1214).

At first, Cicero himself had no thoughts of either the wider
public or posterity as he composed his letters. But this "at first"
needs qualification, for Cicero sometimes wrote pieces that had
more the character of open letters, considered their possible
impact on the wider world, and envisaged with some reluctance
the probability of their publication. Hence Cicero's letter to
Lentulus of December 54 BCE (*Fam.* 1.9.1–26) contains a long
apology for his political career to date that was not meant just for
the immediate addressee. Cicero's first letter to his brother

---

[20] This overview also underscores the observations we made in chapter 2 about the postal system: "In sum, the sheer number and casualness
of Cicero's letters presuppose general ease, reliability, and economy of
delivery" (Nicholson 34).

Quintus (*Quint. fratr.* 1.1.1–46), written to him in 60 or 59 BCE when his brother was whiling away his time for yet a third year as proconsul of Asia (when the proconsulship normally lasted only one year), is presented as a general letter of advice about the proper discharge of one's public duties. (Whether Cicero in this letter is also replying to the work attributed to Quintus known as the *Commentariolum petitionis* or *Handbook of Electioneering*, a brotherly recommendation on correctly conducting a Roman election campaign, is a question that need not detain us here, since the truth of this attribution is contested.)

From this long first letter to Quintus we select just a few elements that illustrate typical letter functions. Cicero begins with an epistolary request meant to encourage Quintus in response to the unusual extension of his proconsulship: "Well, then, this is the first thing I ask of you: let there be no inner withdrawal or discouragement. Don't allow yourself to be submerged beneath a flood of a great responsibility. Stand up and face it, contend with business as it comes or even go out to meet it" (§4).[21] This is followed by a promise of what may happen if Quintus fulfills his duty in exemplary fashion: "As for the Greeks, when they look at you leading the life you do, they will think you are a character from history or a divine being come down from heaven into the province" (§7). The letter closing in §§45–46 once again brings to the fore typical features such as the letter as a substitute for direct conversation or as mediating one's personal presence, and the health wish:

> Now I do not wish it to appear as though my words were meant to wake a sleeper; rather, to spur a runner. . . . But when I read your letters I seem to hear you talk, and when I write to you it is as though I were talking to you. That is why the longer your letters the better I like them, and why I myself often write rather lengthily. This lastly I beg and urge of you: like good playwrights and hard-working actors, take your greatest pains in the final phase, the rounding off, of your appointed task. Let this third year of your term as governor

---

[21] All English translations of Cicero's letters in this section are taken from the Loeb editions by D. R. Shackleton Bailey. The editor has reordered and renumbered the letters so that they do not always follow the sequence of the standard "Vulgate" numbering system used here, but the Vulgate numbers are printed in Shackleton Bailey's running heads and can be found in the tables in his index.

be like the last act of a play: the most highly finished, best fitted-out of the three. This you will most easily accomplish if you imagine that I, whose single approval has always meant more to you than that of mankind at large, am ever with you, at your side in anything you say or do. It only remains for me to beg you to pay particular attention to your health, if you value mine and that of all your folk. (*Quint. fratr.* 1.1.45–46)

As to the potential wider audience of his letters, Cicero's cautionary request that his correspondents destroy letters written in the heat of the moment also makes no sense unless the public during and after his own lifetime is in view—"But please tear up sometime the letters in which I have written sharply about him (sc. Cicero's nephew Quintus, son of Quintus) for fear something may some day leak out" (*Att.* 10.12.3)—though in this case the time to tear up the letters never came. Cicero's most explicit statement about his anticipations and precautions regarding publication is found in a note in one of his letters to Atticus, even if this was originally said only with respect to the letters now collected in book 13 of *Ad familiares:* "There is no *recueil* (συναγωγή, collection)[22] of my letters, but Tiro has about seventy and I shall have to get some from you. I must examine and correct them. Then and only then will they be published" (*Att.* 16.5.5).

That a person who writes so many letters can also be expected to reflect now and then on their theory only stands to reason. Cicero does not do this in any formal way, but his thoughts appear occasionally in various letters, as in *Fam.* 2.4.1:

That there are many different categories of letters you are aware. But the most authentic, the purpose in fact for which letter-writing was invented, is to inform the absent of what it is desirable for them to know, whether in our interest or their own.

Cicero proceeds to distinguish between two categories of letters, "one familiar and jocular, the other serious and grave." His own best opportunity for familiar or incidental remarks came about in

---

[22] Cicero refers to the letter collection by the Greek term συναγωγή, just as we might speak in English of a writer's *oeuvre*, and accordingly the Loeb translator D. R. Shackleton Bailey inserts the French *recueil* in keeping with English patterns of educated speech.

his almost daily letter exchanges with Atticus, which were by no means meant only to convey content but which, by the briefest of texts, often served no purpose other than keeping open the lines of communication:

> You may wonder whether you have to expect a letter from me every day. The answer is "yes," provided I have people to take them. (*Att.* 9.9.1)

> I am sure you find daily letters a bore, especially as I give you no news and indeed can no longer think of any new theme to write about. (*Att.* 8.14.1)

> Since I have a chance of giving a letter to your people, I won't neglect it, though I have nothing to write about. (*Att.* 11.19.1)

> Although I have nothing to write to you, I write all the same because I feel that I am talking to you. (*Att.* 12.53.1)

> So I have received a letter from you (on the 10th) which had nothing in it for the good reason that you had nothing to communicate. Still I was not sorry to get what there was—I mean, to know, if nothing else, that you have no news. (*Att.* 12.42.1)

The above attitude is summarized neatly by another dictum of Cicero: "I prefer to write an empty letter than not to write at all" (*Fam.* 6.22.1). That friendship and longing to see one's friend is the real basis of an intimate and intensive letter exchange is said most clearly by Cicero in *Att.* 1.18.1–8:

> If between these lines you read much else which I leave unwritten, rejoin us at long last. The conditions here to which I am asking you to return are such that anyone might wish to run away from them, but I hope you value my affection enough to want to get back to *that*, even with all the accompanying disagreeables. (*Att.* 1.18.8)

Yet letters also enable one to raise issues that would be embarrassing to bring up in person, as when Cicero finally works up the nerve to ask his addressee Lucceius to write an epic about his own achievements, adding the telling expression *epistula enim non erubescit*, "a letter has no blushes" (*Fam.* 5.12.1). Cicero also knows that letters differ in style and tone from formal speeches (*Fam.* 9.21.1):

But tell me now, how do you find me as a letter writer? Don't I deal
with you in a colloquial style? The fact is that one's style has to vary.
A letter is one thing, a court of law or public meeting quite another.
Even for the courts we don't have just one style. In pleading civil
cases, unimportant ones, we put on no frills, whereas cases involving
status or reputation naturally get something more elaborate. As for
letters, we weave them out of the language of everyday.

Differences of style are to be found not only between letters and
speeches but also between different kinds of letters.[23] Letters to
opponents are most formal, those to friends most relaxed.
Generally Cicero strives to write his letters in a cultivated colloquial language that does not belie his background as a member of
the educated elite. He uses proverbs and riddles, weaves in quotations from literature and the letters of his correspondents, uses
code words and nicknames instead of proper names, and works
with ellipses and daring *ad hoc* constructions. The Greek expressions and phrases scattered throughout Cicero's letters can have
two functions: they refer back to common cultural material that he
and his addressees share, but they also occasionally conceal certain
content, at least from a letter carrier who knows no Greek.

Cicero often had to deal with problems of letter security, from
simple breaches of confidentiality to intentional espionage. He was
also aware of the danger of receiving spurious letters written in the
name of an important person such as Caesar: "[The letter] is mea-
grely written and arouses strong suspicion that he (sc. Caesar) did
not send it, as I think you will have observed" (*Att.* 11.16.1). There
was also the danger of others receiving forged letters as if from
him: "But if the letter was, as you say, not well expressed, you may
be sure I did not write it" (*Fam.* 3.11.5). The best counter-measure
is a letter in one's own inimitable handwriting, which is also a special sign of friendship. Cicero consistently wrote his letters to
Atticus in his own hand and excused himself when this was not possible because of eye problems, overwork, or travels:

> My eyes are even more troublesome than formerly, but I prefer to
> dictate this letter rather than not to give a line to our common and
> very good friend Fabius Gallus to take to you. (*Att.* 8.12.1)

---

[23] For the following see M. von Albrecht, "M. T. Cicero, Sprache
und Stil, Teil II A 3: in den Briefen," *Paulys Realencyclopädie der classischen
Altertumswissenschaft*, Suppl. 13 (1973) 1271–86.

> My clerk's hand will serve as an indication of my ophthalmia and likewise as an excuse for brevity, not that there is anything to say *now*. (*Att.* 8.13.1)

> I am dictating this letter as I sit in my carriage on my way to join the army, which is two days' journey away. In a few days' time I have got reliable persons to take letters, so I am reserving myself until then. (*Att.* 5.17.1)

> The very fact that this letter is in a secretary's hand will show you how busy I am. (*Att.* 4.16.1)

Cicero also wrote his brother Quintus in his own hand and only once remarked for example that his nephew came to eat in the meantime, during which Cicero dictated a paragraph to Tiro (*Quint. fratr.* 3.1.19). Yet even in such cases Cicero did not fail to add at least a postscript in his own hand, which sometimes contained particularly sensitive information:

> But here I go back to my own hand, for what follows is confidential. Even at this stage, do pray see about the will. (*Att.* 11.24.2)

> The following is in my own hand. (*Att.* 13.28.4: *Hoc manu mea*)

That we once again find ourselves in close proximity to the letters of Paul, which he dictated to a scribe and occasionally signed with a postscript in his own hand, goes without saying. It should however be noted in connection with 2 Corinthians 2:4 and its mention of Paul's "tearful letter" that Cicero too had to fight back tears while writing one of his letters to his family from exile: "When I write to you at home or read your letters I am so overcome with tears that I cannot bear it" (*Fam.* 14.4.1). The collection of Cicero's letters also offers potential parallels for the composite letters and pseudepigraphical letters that one may suspect to lie within the Pauline corpus. In Cicero's letter exchange with Brutus two letters of Cicero and one of Brutus may be shown to be redactional compositions in each case from two independent letters (*Ep. Brut.* 1.2.1, 3–6; 1.3.1–3, 4; 1.4.1–3, 3–6). An invective of Cicero's framed as a letter and addressed to Octavian a month before Cicero's death (see Shackleton Bailey, *Letters to Quintus and Brutus*, 342–57) is of doubtful authenticity according to recent scholarship; presumably we are dealing with a school exercise of a later time, which in turn brings us into the area of New Testament pseudepigraphy.

Finally it may be noted that a letter can be written over a longer period of time and that this process sometimes leaves traces in the text, as often assumed in the New Testament for the relationship of 2 Corinthians 1–9 and 2 Corinthians 10–13 or of 1 Corinthians 1–3 and 1 Corinthians 5–16. Our example for Cicero comes from one of the letters addressed to him by M. Caelius Rufus in book 8 of *Ad familiares*. In 8.6.5 Rufus refers to what he "wrote above" to Cicero and reports how the situation had changed in the meantime, saying of the maneuverings of a certain political figure, "He had not (yet) done this when I wrote the earlier part of this letter."

Exercise

22. Engagement with Cicero's correspondence requires considerable time and effort, and it is difficult to single out appropriate exercises from such a large letter collection. The selection here has been reproduced in excerpts from a rather long letter of Marcus Cicero to his brother Quintus. Analyze the contents to reconstruct the situation in which the two brothers find themselves, and record any other noteworthy features. (*Quint. fratr.* 1.3.1–10, trans. D. R. Shackleton Bailey, *Cicero: Letters to Quintus and Brutus*, LCL [2002] 64–75.)

   From Marcus to his brother Quintus greetings.
   My brother, my brother, my brother! Were you really afraid that I was angry with you for some reason and on that account sent boys to you without a letter, or even did not want to see you? I angry with you? How could I be? As though it was you who struck me down, your enemies, your unpopularity, and not I who have lamentably caused your downfall! That much-lauded Consulship of mine has robbed me of you, and my children, and my country, and my possessions; I only hope it has robbed you of nothing but myself. Sure it is that you have never given me cause for anything but pride and pleasure, whereas I have brought you sorrow for my calamity, fear of your own, loss, grief, loneliness. I not want to see you? No, it was rather that I did not want to be

seen by you! You would not have seen your brother, the man you left in Rome, the man you knew, the man who saw you off and said good-bye with mutual tears—you would not have seen any trace or shadow of him; only the likeness of a breathing corpse.

2 . . . As for the fact that my boys came to you without a letter, since you see that anger was not the reason, the reason was surely inertia and an endless stream of tears and grieving.

3 You can imagine how I weep as I write these lines, as I am sure you do as you read them. Can I put you out of my mind sometimes, or ever think of you without tears ? When I miss you, I do not miss you as a brother only, but as a delightful brother almost of my own age, a son in deference, a father in wisdom. What pleasure did I ever take apart from you or you apart from me ? . . .

4 However, I did write to you as best I could and gave the letter to your freedman Philogonus. I expect it was delivered to you later. In it I urge and ask of you, as in the verbal message brought you by my boys, to go straight on to Rome and make haste. . . .

5 Now if you can do what I, whom you always thought a strong man, am unable to do, then stand up and brace yourself for the struggle you may have to sustain. I should hope (if any hope of mine counts for anything) that your integrity, the affection in which you are held in the community, and in some degree also the pity felt for myself will bring you protection. . . .

10 My brother, I need not commend my daughter (and yours) and our Marcus to your care. On the contrary, I grieve to think that their orphaned state will bring you no less sorrow than me. But while you are safe, they will not be orphans. I swear that tears forbid me to write of other things—so may I be granted some salvation and the power to die in my country! Please look after Terentia too, and write back to me on all matters. Be as brave as the nature of the case permits.

Ides of June, Thessalonica.

3. Guidance for the Soul in Letter Form— Seneca to Lucilius

Bibliography 22: R. M. Gummere, *Seneca: Epistles (Ad Lucilium epistulae morales)*, LCL, 3 vols. (1917–1925). – **R. Campbell**, *Seneca: Letters from a Stoic (Epistulae Morales ad Lucilium)*, Penguin Classics (London 1969). – **M. Hadas**, *Stoic Philosophy of Seneca: Essays and Letters* (New York 1958). – **A. L. Motto**, *Seneca's Moral Epistles: Selected and Edited with Introduction, Notes, and Vocabulary* (Wauconda, Ill. 2001). – **C. D. N. Costa**, *Seneca: Dialogues and Letters*, Penguin Classics (London 1997) 87–104. – **M. Rosenbach**, *L. Annaeus Seneca: Philosophische Schriften*, vols. 3–4 (Darmstadt 1980, 1984). – **O. Apelt**, *Lucius Annaeus Seneca: Philosophische Schriften*, vols. 3–4: *Briefe an Lucilius*, Philosophische Bibliothek 189–90 (Leipzig 1924).

K. Abel, "Das Problem der Faktizität der Senecanischen Korrespondenz," *Hermes* 109 (1981) 472–99. – **H. Cancik-Lindemaier**, *Untersuchungen zu Senecas epistulae morales*, Spudasmata 18 (Hildesheim 1967). – eadem, "Seneca's Collection of Epistles: A Medium of Philosophical Communication," in A. Y. Collins, ed., *Ancient and Modern Perspectives on the Bible and Culture: Essays in Honor of Hans Dieter Betz*, Scholars Press Homage Series 22 (Altanta 1999) 88–109. – **P. Cugusi**, *Evoluzione* (Bib. 2) 195–206. – **P. Grimal**, *Seneca: Macht und Ohnmacht des Geistes*, Impulse der Forschung 24 (Darmstadt 1978) 155–64, 315–27. – **E. Hachmann**, *Die Führung des Lesers in Senecas Epistulae morales*, Orbis antiquus 34 (Münster 1995). – **I. Hadot**, *Seneca und die griechisch-römische Tradition der Seelenleitung*, Quellen und Studien zur Geschichte der Philosophie 13 (Berlin 1969). – **J. Henderson**, *Morals and Villas in Seneca's Letters: Places to Dwell* (Cambridge 2004). – **U. Knoche**, "Der Gedanke der Freundschaft in Senecas Briefen an Lucilius (1954)," in G. Maurach, ed., *Seneca als Philosoph*, Wege der Forschung 414 (Darmstadt 1975) 149–66. – **G. Maurach**, *Der Bau von Senecas Epistulae morales*, BKAW NF 2/30 (Heidelberg 1970). – **G. Mazzoli**, "Le 'Epistulae Morales ad Lucilium' di Seneca: Valore letterario e filosofico," *ANRW* II.36.3 (1989) 1823–77. – **W. Schindler**, "'speculum animi' oder Das absolute Gespräch," *Der Altsprachliche Unterricht* 32 (1989) 4–21. – **B. Schönegg**, *Senecas epistulae morales als philosophisches Kunstwerk*, Europäische Hochschulschriften: Reihe 20, Philosophie 578 (Bern 1999). – **A. Stückelberger**, *Senecas 88. Brief. Über Wert und Unwert der freien Künste*, BKAW NF 2/8 (Heidelberg 1965). – idem, "Seneca: Der Brief als Mittel der persönlichen Auseinandersetzung mit der Philosophie," *Didactica Classica Gandensia* 20 (1980) 133–48. – **M. Wacht**, "Angst und Angstbewältigung in Senecas Briefen," *Gymnasium* 105 (1998) 507–36.

The Roman philosopher and statesman Lucius Annaeus Seneca the Younger (ca. 4 BCE–65 CE)—not to be confused with his father Lucius Annaeus Seneca the Elder, also known as Seneca the Rhetorician (ca. 50 BCE–ca. 40 CE)—was born around the turn of the era in Cordoba, Spain. But he was sent for schooling at a young age to Rome, where he received an education in rhetoric and philosophy and chose a career in public service. After various ups and downs his fortunes led him to the be the tutor of the young Nero for five or six years at the peak of the Roman empire, before he increasingly withdrew from politics after 62 and, as a consequence of his involvement in the Pisonian conspiracy to murder Nero, was forced to commit suicide in 65 CE.

It is in these last years of his life that Seneca composed his most mature work, the *Moral Epistles to Lucilius* (*Epistulae morales ad Lucilium*), which has been described as "the most popular of Seneca's prose works at all times" (*OCD³*). A date between winter 62 (or 63?) and fall 64 CE for the composition of the letters may be arrived at from historical references in the text, for example to the fire at Lyons in the summer of 58 (or 64/65?) in *Ep.* 91.1–2, to the sham sea battle staged under Nero in 64 CE in *Ep.* 70.26, or simply to the month of December in *Ep.* 18.1 and to spring in *Ep.* 67.1. The publication of the letters followed in 64–65 CE, shortly before Seneca's death. The materials transmitted to us in various ways include 124 letters in twenty books, divided into *Epistles* 1–88 and 89–124. Nevertheless, a large lacuna is evident between books 11 and 13, and Aulus Gellius in his *Attic Nights* 12.2.3 quotes from a 22nd book, so that we must reckon with some loss of material, though not a very dramatic one.

Gaius Lucilius (Iunior), to whom the letters are addressed, is a historically attested person who was, moreover, not much younger than Seneca himself. This initially makes him a less than obvious candidate for Seneca's instruction, which seems to have been tailored for a younger man. But here the ideal of friendship, emphasized in several letters (e.g., *Ep.* 3; cf. Knoche; Cancik-Lindemaier 61–66), helps explain the relationship: it is the older friend Seneca who comes to the assistance of his younger friend in his striving for perfection, for nobody reaches this goal if left to themselves. After rising from poverty and obscurity to equestrian rank, Lucilius served as procurator in Cilicia in 63–64 CE; this would explain why Seneca had to communicate to him by letters but would also raise the question about possibilities for delivering them. Seneca also dedicated to Lucilius his late work *Naturales quaestiones* and had previously dedicated to him the dialogue *De providentia*. Yet the preface to the *Naturales quaestiones* does not in fact give the impression that Lucilius had any need of an introduction to Stoic philosophy, such as the letters provide. All the letters display the stereotypical letter frame, beginning with *Seneca Lucilio suo salutem*, "Greetings from Seneca to his friend Lucilius," and concluding with *vale*, "farewell." The letters reflect the act of letter communication in various ways, by taking up the objections of the writing partner, answering his questions, and fielding his complaints, or by discussing means for the conveyance of letters, without providing a direct reproduction of Lucilius's letters. The letter writer himself allows circumstances from his daily life or his friendship with his correspondent to flow into his letters, as the following examples show:

2.1 Judging by what you write me, and by what I hear, I am forming a good opinion regarding your future.

3.1 You have sent a letter to me through the hand of a "friend" of yours, as you call him. And in your very next sentence you warn me not to discuss with him all the matters that concern you, saying that even you yourself are not accustomed to do this; in other words, you have in the same letter affirmed and denied that he is your friend . . . (which leads Seneca into a discussion of true friendship).

19.1 I leap for joy whenever I receive letters from you.

38.1 You are right when you urge that we increase our mutual traffic in letters.

48.1 In answer to the letter which you wrote me while travelling—a letter as long as the journey itself—I shall reply later. I ought to go into retirement, and consider what sort of advice I should give you.

50.1 I received your letter many months after you had posted it; accordingly, I thought it useless to ask the carrier what you were busied with. He must have a particularly good memory if he can remember that!

72.1 The subject concerning which you question me was once clear to my mind, and required no thought, so thoroughly had I mastered it. But I have not tested my memory of it for some time, and therefore it does not readily come back to me.

86.1 I am resting at the country-house which once belonged to Scipio Africanus himself; and I write to you after doing reverence to his spirit and to an altar which I am inclined to think is the tomb of that great warrior.

106.1 My tardiness in answering your letter was not due to a press of business.

110.1 From my villa at Nomentum, I send you greeting and bid you keep a sound spirit within you (*te saluto et iubeo habare mentem bonam*).

The last letter opening illustrates how Seneca takes up and modifies typical letter components—in this case the health wish, which he also gives a philosophical twist in *Ep.* 15.1: not *si vales bene est*, "if you are well, it is well," but rather *si philosopharis, bene est*, "if you are studying philosophy, it is well." Something similar is done with the concluding greeting in *Ep.* 17.11, where Seneca says of Lucilius: "in your case I cannot say farewell (*valedicere*) without paying a price," i.e., without passing on some fitting words of wisdom. In expressions such as "I see you, my dear Lucilius, and at this very moment I hear you" (55.11) or "Whenever your letters arrive, I imagine that I am with you, and I have the feeling that I am about to speak my answer, instead of writing it" (67.2), the topos of the letter as a conversation despite the distance shines through.

In a subsequent letter Seneca draws consequences from this for the style of his letters. Lucilius had apparently complained that Seneca's letters to him were "rather carelessly written." In response Seneca writes: "I prefer that my letters should be just what my conversation would be if you and I were sitting in one another's company or taking walks together—spontaneous and easy; for my letters have nothing strained or artificial about them" (75.1). Nevertheless, this comment should not be allowed to deceive us about the considerable amount of literary artistry Seneca invested to achieve his letter style, which, while simple, was also very lively and enriched by short questions and numerous illustrations.[24]

[24] On Seneca's style see B. Kytzler, "Die nachklassische Prosa Roms," in M. Fuhrmann, *Römische Literatur*, Neues Handbuch der

Such observations bring us to an old, controversial question which has still not been finally resolved. If one takes all these components together—the real historical addressee of the letters, their meshing with contemporary history, the reflexes of a lively letter exchange, etc.—then one can easily understand how some scholars continue to claim that a letter exchange between Seneca and Lucilius actually took place and that its sequence can be reconstructed (cf. Grimal). But even from the perspective of this thesis it is often conceded that Seneca also had a later publication in view from the very beginning and that he extensively reworked the actual correspondence for publication (so Cugusi). Yet once this is admitted we are no longer very far from the other, more consistent—and to my mind more appropriate—position according to which Seneca never sent these letters to Lucilius but planned only a complete literary letter collection from the beginning (cf. esp. Abel). Lucilius is then more or less only the dedicatee. The incidents from daily life and the epistolary forms serve to advance the literary fiction, which by all accounts must be judged successful, as the ongoing discussion attests.

This last thesis, which takes the fictive character of the letter form seriously with no ifs, ands, or buts, is supported by observations from the individual letters. Seneca makes it clear enough in *Epistle* 8, which acquires programmatic significance not only for the introductory first book consisting of *Epistles* 1–12 but for the entire collection, that he is writing his literary-philosophical testament for posterity. The direct statements to the public—in this case by means of second person plural imperatives (*vitate, subsistite*)—which Seneca intersperses here and elsewhere no longer apply primarily to Lucilius, but immediately turn to a wider readership (*Ep.* 8.1–3):

Literaturwissenschaft 3 (Frankfurt a.M. 1974) 291–322, esp. 298: It is a "dynamic, lively, aroused and arousing style, which wants to attack, address, grab, and shake up the reader; the style of a missionary who is used to presenting his good news with the greatest possible emphasis." On Seneca's pictorial language see M. von Albrecht, *History* (Bib. 19) 1179: "Since an organic and continuous development of the addressee is a major concern of Seneca in the *Epistulae morales*, he shows a preference for imagery taken from the domain of natural growth, nutrition, and medicine."

8.1 My object in shutting myself up and locking the door is to be able to help a greater number. I never spend a day in idleness; I appropriate even a part of the night for study. . . . **2** I have withdrawn not only from men, but from affairs, especially from my own affairs; I am working for later generations, writing down some ideas that may be of assistance to them. There are certain wholesome counsels, which may be compared to prescriptions of useful drugs; these I am putting into writing; for I have found them helpful in ministering to my own sores, which, if not wholly cured, have at any rate ceased to spread. **3** I point other men to the right path, which I have found late in life, when wearied with wandering. I cry out to them: "Avoid (*vitate* [2nd plur. impv.]) whatever pleases the throng: avoid the gifts of Chance! Halt (*subsistite*) before every good which Chance brings to you, in a spirit of doubt and fear. . . ."

The thesis that the letters to Lucilius are a literary fiction receives further support from observations that are increasingly being made about the overall composition of the work (esp. by Cancik-Lindemaier, Maurach, and Hachmann). Recent research has exposed a very conscious planning of the work and a means of guiding the general reader (not Lucilius) through it that extends to both the smaller letter groups and the larger whole. Such a master plan would be hard to execute with authentic letters that reacted to questions of the correspondent. The outworking of such a plan with all its ramifications is naturally very complex. Let us single out the treatment of Epicurus (cf. Hachmann 220–37), who is in any case relevant to our concerns. In *Epistles* 2–29 Seneca quotes sayings of Epicurus repeatedly and with approval, yet just before his initial quotation ("Contented poverty is an honourable estate") in *Ep.* 2.6, he introduces a qualification to indicate that he does not regard himself as a convert to Epicureanism: "I am wont to cross over even into the enemy's camp—not as a deserter, but as a scout." In other words, he "culls from another man's Garden," the "Garden" of Epicurus (*Ep.* 4.10). In *Ep.* 33.3 Seneca admits the eclecticism of his own Stoicism:

> Such thoughts as one may extract here and there in the works of other philosophers run through the whole body of our (sc. Stoic) writings. Hence we have no 'show-window goods,' nor do we deceive the purchaser in such a way that, if he enters our shop, he will find nothing except that which is displayed in the window.

From this point onward Seneca no longer needs the help of Epicurus, whom he had used only for promotional purposes, but rather polemicizes against him where necessary (e.g., *Ep.* 90.35). His presentation becomes increasingly dominated by purely Stoic themes, which results in several very long letters in the later books that have the effect of minor treatises (e.g., *Ep.* 88, "On Liberal and Vocational Studies," or *Ep.* 95, "On the Usefulness of Basic Principles").

The only remaining question for our purposes is why Seneca took his leave from the genres of dialogue and tractate and turned to the letter form for his legacy. This is ultimately a matter of internal considerations. The letter is especially well suited to the dialogical and communicative manner in which Seneca does philosophy. In conversation, which the letter form imitates, philosophical truth as the foundation for life is transmitted not statically in one fell swoop but through a longer process of development. In the figure of Seneca's friend Lucilius, whiling away his time in a distant place, the role of the implied reader is already inscribed into the text. The author's devotion of his attention to his absent friend through the medium of the friendly letter, which was the ideal letter type in antiquity, creates an emotional bond between author and reader. The letter form also provides a suitable outlet for Seneca's penchant for working with examples. He justifies this in *Ep.* 6.5, "The way is long if one follows precepts, but short and helpful, if one follows patterns," and treats it ironically in *Ep.* 24.6, "'Oh,' say you, 'those stories have been droned to death in all the schools; pretty soon, when you reach the topic 'On Despising Death,' you will be telling me about Cato.'" To which Seneca replies, "But why should I not tell you about Cato?" and proceeds unperturbed with his examples.

Seneca himself sets us on a further trail that helps place his letters within the history of literature when he refers to Epicurus and Cicero in *Epistle* 21. Epicurus, in writing to the government minister Idomeneus, made him immortal (21.3–4), Cicero did the same for Atticus (21.4), and Seneca promises Lucilius: "I shall find favour with later generations; I can take with me names that will endure as long as mine" (21.5). Seneca knew the tradition of the philosophical doctrinal letter that reached its zenith with Epicurus (cf. also the allusion to Epicurus's farewell letter in *Ep.* 92.25). Perhaps he was also familiar with the corpora of doctrinal letters that had been assembled secondarily, such as those of Plato or the original letters of Crates. In the same way, Seneca knew of the collections of Cicero's letters (cf. also *Ep.* 118.2), which Pliny would later consciously take as his model. In addition one could suspect a possible influence of Horace, with his two complete books of verse epistles (Maurach 196–99; for Seneca's affinities to Horace see also Cancik-Lindemaier 54–58). Nevertheless, Seneca created from these antecedents something uniquely his own: a fictional letter collection, conceived as a corpus from the start, in which the individual letters form the sections and the various books the chapters of an entire work (cf. Maurach 197)—a philosophical letter-novel whose hero is the soul of the individual, which in its search for happiness must pass through numerous adventures and tests.

Exercise

23. Find comparable statements and passages from the New Testament for the following excerpts from Seneca's *Epistles*:

Ep. **50.3** Nobody understands that he is himself greedy, or that he is covetous. Yet the blind ask for a guide, while we wander without one.

Ep. **52.5** Suppose that two buildings have been erected, unlike as to their foundations, but equal in height and in grandeur. One is built on faultless ground, and the process of erection goes right ahead. In the other case, the foundations have exhausted the building materials, for they have been sunk into soft and shifting ground and much labour has been wasted in reaching the solid rock.

Ep. **53.8** Philosophy, however, is the only power that can stir us, the only power that can shake off our deep slumber. Devote yourself wholly to philosophy!

Ep. **78.16** What blows do athletes receive on their faces and all over their bodies! Nevertheless, through their desire for fame they endure every torture, and they undergo these things not only because they are fighting but in order to be able to fight. Their very training means torture. So let us also win the way to victory in all our struggles—for the reward is not a garland or a palm. . . .

> ***Ep.* 94.1** That department of philosophy which supplies precepts appropriate to the individual case, instead of framing them for mankind at large—which, for instance, advises how a husband should conduct himself towards his wife, or how a father should bring up his children, or how a master should rule his slaves—this department of philosophy, I say, is accepted by some as the only significant part. . . .

4. Personified Propaganda and Paraenesis— The Cynic Epistles

Bibliography 23: R. Hercher, *Epistolographi graeci* (Bib. 1), esp. 208–17 (Crates of Thebes), 235–58 (Diogenes of Sinope) (**TLG**). – **A. J. Malherbe**, *The Cynic Epistles* (Bib. 1). – **E. Müseler**, *Die Kynikerbriefe: 1. Die Überlieferung; 2. Kritische Ausgabe mit deutscher Übersetzung*, Studien zur Geschichte und Kultur des Altertums NF 1/6–7 (Paderborn 1994) for Diogenes and Crates.

M. Billerbeck, ed., *Die Kyniker in der modernen Forschung: Aufsätze mit Einführung und Bibliographie*, Bochumer Studien zur Philosophie 15 (Amsterdam 1991). – **L. R. Donelson**, *Pseudepigraphy and Ethical Argument in the Pastoral Epistles* (Bib. 43). – **F. G. Downing**, *Cynics and Christian Origins* (Edinburgh 1992). – idem, *Cynics, Paul, and the Pauline Churches* (London and New York 1998). – **O. Gigon**, "Kynikerbriefe," *LAW* 1658–59. – **M. O. Goulet-Cazé** and **R. Goulet**, eds., *Le cynisme ancien et ses prolongements (Actes du colloque international du CNRS. Paris, 22–25 Juillet 1991)* (Paris 1993). – **R. F. Hock** and **E. N. O'Neil**, *The Chreia in Ancient Rhetoric*, vol. 1: *The Progymnasmata*, SBLTT 27 (Atlanta 1986). – idem, *The Chreia and Ancient Rhetoric: Classroom Exercises*, SBL Writings from the Greco-Roman World 2 (Atlanta 2002). – **K. M. Schmidt**, *Mahnung und Erinnerung im Maskenspiel* (Bib. 48). – **M. L. Stirewalt**, *Studies in Ancient Greek Epistolography* (Bib. 2) 43–64. – **M. Sicherl**, "Bemerkungen zum Text der Kynikerbriefe," *Illinois Classical Studies* 18 (1993) 263–77. – **T. L. Wilder**, *Pseudonymity, the New Testament, and Deception* (Bib. 61) 82–100.

Ancient tradition traces the origins of the popular philosophical movement known as Cynicism back to Socrates's pupil Antisthenes (ca. 455–360 BCE), if not to Socrates himself. However, it is above all Diogenes of Sinope (ca. 350 BCE) who is known as the prototypical representative of this movement. It is he who bore the derisive nickname κύων, "dog," and whose grave marker at one of the city gates of Corinth is said to have been decorated with the figure of a dog, because he lived a "dog's life" and displayed the proverbial shamelessness of a dog. This less than flattering attribute may be the source of the designation "Cynic" or "Cynicism"; alternatively, it has been suggested that the name goes back to that of the Athenian gymnasium "Kynosarges," where Antisthenes taught. One of Diogenes' pupils was Crates of Thebes, who found in Hipparchia, a woman from a good family, a like-minded life partner. Crates was in turn a teacher of Zeno, founder of Stoicism. Cynics are distinguished by their nonconformity; they seek fulfillment in self-imposed marginalization, which requires Cynicism's strictest proponents to lead a wandering life that minimizes physical needs. A great number of anecdotes about Diogenes, Crates, Hipparchia, and other followers of Cynicism are collected in book 6 of Diogenes Laertius's *Lives of Eminent Philosophers* (already considered above in connection with Epicurus). There are close lines of influence between Cynicism and Stoicism, without the two movements being simply equated. Within Cynicism itself it is possible to distinguish between a radical "hard" Cynicism and a milder "soft" Cynicism. After a temporary plateau Cynicism experienced a reawakening in the early imperial period. As a representative we might mention the famous orator Dio Chrysostom (Dio Cocceianus) of Prusa in Bithynia, who was forced by external circumstances to live for a long time as a wandering Cynic philosopher during the reign of the Flavian emperors.

One instrument of literary propaganda that Cynicism used to spread its message was the pseudepigraphic Cynic epistle. In the wider sense this genre can include all writings in letter form that display Cynic content and tendencies. In this sense the designation applies to the letters of Anacharsis, Heraclitus, and Socrates and the Socratics surveyed in the first part of this chapter (see under A.1) and included in A. J. Malherbe's edition of *The Cynic Epistles*. But Cynic epistles in the narrower sense must also have a prominent proponent of Cynicism as their author—a definition supported, for example, by O. Gigon. By this definition only two authors remain: Diogenes and Crates (cf. Müseler). The standard text collections by Hercher, Malherbe, and Müseler ascribe fifty-two letters to Diogenes and thirty-six to Crates. The addressees of these pseudonymous letters vary widely but remain within the historical sphere of influence of these two Cynic teachers. Hence Diogenes writes repeatedly to the residents of his hometown of Sinope and to Antisthenes, Hipparchia, Crates, Alexander the Great, and Plato, while Crates writes to his wife Hipparchia, his students, Diogenes, the wealthy, the youths, and the Athenians. The letter form is reduced to the absolute minimum and is sometimes barely recognizable. The sender's name, assumed to be constant throughout each collection, is omitted, as is the opening greeting, which Hercher often supplies in the form εὖ πράττειν or χαίρειν, and the concluding farewell. Readers must therefore get by with the mere adscription "To Hipparchia" or "To the same" (Τῇ αὐτῇ) or "To His Students" or "To the same" (Τοῖς αὐτοῖς), and so on. Where the full letter prescript does exceptionally appear, it is not very flattering for the addressees (*Ep.* 28): "Diogenes the Dog to the so-called Greeks, a plague on you!" (Διογένης ὁ κύων τοῖς καλουμένοις Ἕλλησιν οἰμώζειν—with οἰμώζειν replacing χαίρειν).

Modern scholarship dates the origin of the Cynic Epistles between the first century BCE and the end of the second century CE. The interrelationships and dependencies between the individual epistles are very complex and can be correctly determined only with a combination of literary criticism and tradition history. Within the epistles of Diogenes one can make out three or more authors, so that epistles 30–40 for example clearly stand out from the rest because of their length and somewhat different character. The epistles of Crates likewise do not come from a single hand, and most of them appear to depend on the epistles of Diogenes. Thus *Epistle* 9 of Diogenes (to Crates) is obviously related to *Epistle* 8 of Crates (to Diogenes), the latter being a response to the former about the dramatic turning point in Crates' life:

> To Crates: I hear that you brought all your property to the assembly (ἐκκλησία), delivered it over to your fatherland, and, standing in the midst of the people, cried out, "Crates, son of Crates, sets Crates free." Thus the whole citizenry were pleased at the gift and wondered about me, the person who creates men of this sort. They, therefore, wished to send for me from Athens; but you, aware of my mind on the matter, prevented them. So I commend you for your good sense in this, and am delighted with your surrender of your property, since you became superior to popular opinion faster than I

expected. But do return quickly, for you still need training in other matters, and it is not safe to linger where there is no one like you. (Diogenes, *Epistle* 9)

To Diogenes: We are indeed already free from wealth, but fame has up to this point not yet released us from bondage to her, although, by Heracles, we have done everything to be set free from her. Anyway, I shall redeem myself also from this mistress and shall sail to Athens to offer myself to you as a gift which is superior to all possessions in return for the freedom for which your word has set us free. (Crates, *Epistle* 8)

This example is also well suited to illustrate how such letters may have come about, for the information about Crates' surrender of his property is also found the *Lives of Eminent Philosophers* by Diogenes Laertius, albeit in anecdotal rather than epistolary form: "So he (Crates) turned his property into money—for he belonged to a distinguished family—and having thus collected about 200 talents, distributed that sum among his fellow-citizens" (Diog. Laert. 6.87). Similar observations about the connections between the older anecdotal or apothegmatic tradition and the epistles can be made in the case of Diogenes. His famous answer to Alexander the Great, to whom he responded to the offer of a free wish, made when Alexander was blocking the sun, with the inimitable reply, "Stand out of my light" (Diog. Laert. 6.38), turns up again in a much less apothegmatic form in a letter of Diogenes, *Ep.* 33.1: "They say of the moon, that it disposes of the sun by getting in its way, and you have done the same thing by coming here and standing near me." (In *Ep.* 33.4 we find another remark of Alexander's from Diog. Laert. 6.32: "Had I not been Alexander, I should have liked to be Diogenes.")

In Diogenes Laertius 6.37 two anecdotal incidents are juxtaposed, from which two letters have been produced: (1) Diogenes observes a child drinking out of his hands, exclaims, "A child has beaten me in plainness of living," and throws away his drinking cup; this is the theme of Diogenes, *Epistle* 6. (2) Diogenes is said to have reasoned thus: "All things belong to the gods. The wise are friends of the gods, and friends hold things in common. Therefore, all things belong to the wise." This reasoning, which employs a fundamental topos of the ancient ethic of friendship to glorify the figure of the Cynic-Stoic sage, is transposed in Diogenes, *Epistle* 10 as follows:

> Socrates used to say that the sages do not beg but demand back, for
> everything belongs to them, just as it does to the gods. And this he
> tried to infer from the premises that the gods are masters of all, that
> the property of friends is held in common, and that the sage is a
> friend of gods.

These examples allow us to conclude that the shorter Cynic epistles in part simply clothe the apothegms of Cynic teachers, consisting of pointed sayings set in a rudimentary framework, or
anecdotes about them—both of which can be described as *chreiai*
(χρεῖαι; see Hock and O'Neil)—with a new mantel, for which the
simple transformation from "he" form to "I" form is often sufficient. The longer Cynic epistles have in part the character of a
dialogue (e.g., Diogenes, *Ep.* 31 and 36); they imitate the philosophical conversation and its literary realization since the time of
Plato. An occasion for the transformation of this content into letters may lie in the fact that Diogenes Laertius lists letters among
the works of the Cynic Diogenes (6.80; cf. 6.23) and also mentions
a work of Crates entitled *Epistles* (6.98). Later Cynics sought to imitate these non-extant collections.

Essential for understanding the *Sitz im Leben* of this literary
production is a knowledge of the ancient rhetorical technique
known as "prosopopoeia" (προσωποποιία), in Latin also *sermoci-
natio*, which was taught and practiced in the schools. Despite its
technical-sounding designation, this is nothing more than the
ancient art of literary personification, impersonation, or dramati-
zation, of putting speeches into the mouths of historical characters. It can therefore also be called "speech in character." Derived
from πρόσωπον, "countenance" or "person," and ποιεῖν, "to
make," *prosopopoeia* involves transporting oneself back into the life
of a well-known person in the past and formulating a speech or
saying that that person could have uttered in a particular situation.
(*Prosopopoeia* or "personification" is thus hard to distinguish from
ethopoeia, "characterization" or "character construction" [ἠθοποι-
ία].) To take just one situation from the Septuagint, what did the
Syrian king Antiochus IV Epiphanes say when he wanted to com-
pel the Jews to eat pork, and what was the aged priest Eleazar's
answer to him? Very little is said about this in the original story in
2 Maccabees 7, but this provided the "vacuum" that begged to be
filled with a great speech composed by prosopopoeia, which is
precisely what the author of 4 Maccabees did for Antiochus and

especially Eleazar in chapter 5. Ovid raises this technique of prosopopoeia in letters to a literary art form in his *Heroides* (see above under A.3) when he has Penelope write to Ulysses, Dido to Aeneas, and Medea to Jason in poetic verses. Naturally the writer of "speech in character" must always bring out what was characteristic of the personified individual in the tradition. Thus people could give their students or themselves as authors the assignment of composing letters such as a Diogenes or a Crates might have written in certain situations or to certain addressees. One was hardly at a loss for material, since one could freely plunder the rich store of anecdotes about these figures.

Nevertheless, the purpose of the Cynic epistles is not identical with their manner of invention. They are ultimately intended not as mere exercises for students and teachers, but rather (as already indicated) as means of propagating the ideal of the Cynic life, of gaining more followers, and of keeping the new adherents on the right track. Canvassing for converts is the one goal, while the second, exhortation to perseverance, is perhaps even stronger. To this end the example of Diogenes is repeatedly presented, because the writers not unreasonably assumed that personalized paraenesis is more effective than the mere moral appeal, and that one graphic example says more than many words (cf. Crates, *Ep.* 20: "since action teaches endurance more quickly than words"). As a Cynic self-portrait written to appeal to potential adherents, *Epistle* 30 of Diogenes, addressed to his father, is especially well suited:

30.1 I came to Athens, Father, and, when I heard that the companion of Socrates was teaching about happiness, I went to listen to him. Now he happened to be lecturing at the time about the two roads that lead to it. He said that they are two and not many: the one a short cut, and the other the long way. Consequently each person can proceed along whichever of the two he wishes. I remained silent at the time that I heard this, but when we returned to him on the next day, I urged him to speak to us about the two roads. He quite readily rose from his seat and led us to town and straight through it to the acropolis. **2** And when we were near, he pointed out to us a certain pair of roads leading upward: the one short, rising up against the hill and difficult; the other long, smooth and easy. And as soon as he had brought us down, he said, "Such are the roads leading to the acropolis, and the ones to happiness are like them. Each of you, choose the one you want and I will guide you." Then the others, fearstruck at the difficulty and steepness of the road, backed down and urged him to lead them along the long and smooth one. But since I was superior to the hardships, I chose the steep and rough road, for the person hurrying on toward happiness (εὐδαιμονία) must proceed even if it be through fire and sword. **3** And after I chose this road, he took off my mantle and tunic, put a double, coarse cloak around me, and hung a wallet from my shoulder, putting bread, drink, a cup, and a bowl into it. He attached an oil flask and a scraper on the outside of it, and gave me a staff too. Furnished with this equipment, I asked him why he put a double, coarse cloak on me. He explained, "So that I might assist you in your training for both eventualities: the burning heat of summer and the cold of winter."

"What?," I said. "Did not the single one do this?"

4 "Not at all," he replied. "It does bring relief during the summer, but in the winter it causes more bodily hardship than a person can put up with."

"But why did you put the wallet around me?"

"So that you might carry your house with you everywhere," he explained.

"And the cup and bowl, why did you throw them in?"

"Since you have to drink and use an appetizer," he said, "some other appetizer if you don't have mustard."

"The oil flask and scraper, why did you hang them alongside?"

"The one is useful for hard work," he said, "the other for oil and dirt."

"The staff, what is that for?" I asked.

"For security," he answered.

"How's that?"

"For what the gods use it, against the poets."

The letter begins with the picture of the two roads or ways (ὁδοί), which is already familiar to us from early Christian literature but which also has a long prehistory.[25] Here it is not simply chosen incidentally, for the figure of the two roads comes to its most famous expression in Prodicus's story about Heracles at the parting of the ways (in Xenophon, *Mem.* 2.1.21–34), and the labors of Heracles were a favorite paradigm for the Cynics of their own strivings and aspirations. The picture of two roads is appropriately used to define Cynicism as the shorter but harder road to moral perfection and happiness. By its radicalness Cynicism allows its

[25] Cf. the numerous ancient parallels in K. Niederwimmer, *The Didache*, trans. L. M. Maloney, Hermeneia (Minneapolis 1998) 59–63.

leading ideas to be realized more uncompromisingly than was possible in the related Stoic movement (cf. also Crates, *Ep*. 16: "To be a Cynic is to take a short cut in doing philosophy"). The letter also explains how the typical appearance of a Cynic philosopher came to be. A coarse woolen philosopher's cloak, which doubled as a blanket at night, a leather wallet for the daily portions of food received by begging, and a walking staff, which could also be used for protection, are the standard equipment of a Cynic. The final sentence gives the whole presentation an ironic twist: The Cynic needs protection not from highway robbers, but from the poets, who caricature him in their works.

Such a conclusion underscores once again that we are moving in the realm of the literary letter and not, for example, in that of the documentary letter. It is precisely as literary testimonies that the Cynic epistles help us achieve a nuanced definition of the phenomenon of pseudepigraphy, that is, the production of letters with "fake" or "forged" authors' names. Yet in our letters there can be no talk of forgery in the strict sense. The authors do not really intend to pull the wool over the eyes of their audience, nor would the readers have been so easily deceived. The authors and readers share a common knowledge of the traditional anecdotal material about the Cynics and of the rhetorical technique of prosopopoeia, which could be adapted to letters. One can therefore regard the production and reading of the Cynic epistles as a kind of serious game that was played with the full consent of all the players—serious to the extent that it aimed at finding a successful plan for life, which kept the game going.

Exercise

24. The overcoming of popular societal norms (see the letters of the Scythian Anacharsis [cf. Reuters]) that allowed the true Cynics to become committed cosmopolitans also found a partial counterpart in the overcoming of the gulf between the sexes. Seven of the letters of Crates are addressed to his wife Hipparchia, who under certain circumstances was accepted as a philosopher of equal status. "Diogenes" also considers her worthy of at least one letter (*Ep*. 3: see below) and mentions her in another to her home town of Maroneia, which had changed its name in her

honor (*Ep.* 43). In the following three texts dealing with
Hipparchia, verify the typical elements of the Cynic epistles already discussed and augment the picture with your
own insights:

Hipparchia too, sister of Metrocles, was captured by their doctrines. Both of them were born at Maroneia. She fell in love with
the discourses and the life of Crates, and would not pay attention
to any of her suitors, their wealth, their high birth, or their
beauty. But to her Crates was everything. She used even to
threaten her parents she would make away with herself, unless
she were given in marriage to him. . . . The girl chose and, adopt-
ing the same dress, went about with her husband and lived (i.e.,
slept; cf. LSJ συγγίγνομαι II.3) with him in public and went out
to dinners with him. (Diogenes Laertius 6.96–97)

To Hipparchia: I admire you for your eagerness in that, although
you are a woman, you yearned for philosophy and have become
one of our school, which has struck even men with awe for its
austerity. But be earnest to bring to a finish what you have begun.
And you will cap it off, I am sure, if you should not be outstripped
by Crates, your husband, and if you frequently write to me, your
benefactor in philosophy. For letters are worth a great deal and
are not inferior to conversation with people actually present.
(Diogenes, *Epistle* 3)

To Hipparchia: Some have come from you bringing a new tunic,
which, they say, you made so that I might have it for the winter.
Because you care for me, I approved of you, but because you are
still uneducated and not practicing the philosophy for which I
have tutored you, I censure you. Therefore, give up doing this
right now, if you really care, and do not pride yourself in this kind
of activity, but endeavor to do those things for which you wanted
to marry me. And leave the wool-spinning, which is of little benefit, to the other women, who have aspired to none of the things
you do. (Crates, *Epistle* 32)

5

Epistolary and Rhetorical Theory

In his text collection of the ancient Greek letter writers, *Epistolographi graeci* (Bib. 1), Rudolph Hercher prefaces the main body of his work with six texts on pp. 1–16 that bear the titles (in translation): "Demetrius of Phaleron's *Epistolary Types*," "Proclus the Platonist's *Epistolary Forms*," "From Demetrius's Work *On Style*," "From Philostratus," "From Gregory of Nazianzus's Letter to Nicobulus," and "A Letter of Photius to the Metropolitan Amphilochus of Cyzicus." The first two refer to the two ancient letter writing guides that circulated under the names of Demetrius and Proclus or Libanius. These are followed by an excerpt from a work of another Demetrius *On Style*. The sophist Philostratus of Lemnos (3rd cent. CE) wrote a short tractate about letter writing with a critical view to the letters of the imperial scribe Aspasius of Ravenna. Finally, Gregory of Nazianzus (in *Ep.* 51) and the later Byzantine scholar Photius (ca. 810–893) delve briefly into the question of letter composition. Although this does not quite exhaust the list of treatments of letter theory from antiquity, it mentions the most important ones, above all the two works having a "Demetrius" as their actual or attributed author. Since these are at the same time the oldest witnesses in the list, we turn our attention to them in our first two sections.

A. Letter Styles and Topoi

Bibliography 24: L. Radermacher, *Demetrii Phalerei qui dicitur de elocutione libellus*, Teubner (Leipzig 1901) 3–62 (**TLG**). – **W. Rhys Roberts**, *Demetrius: On Style*, in *Aristotle: The Poetics. "Longinus": On the Sublime. Demetrius: On Style*, LCL Aristotle, vol. 23 (1927; ²1932) 255–487. – New edition: **D. C. Innes**, *Demetrius: On Style*, in *Poetics: Aristotle;* ed. and trans. Stephen Halliwell. *On the Sublime: Longinus;* ed. and trans. W. H. Fyfe; rev. Donald Russell. *On Style: Demetrius;* ed. and trans. Doreen C. Innes; based on W. Rhys Roberts, LCL (1995) 309–525. – **P. Chiron**, *Démétrios: Du style*, Budé (Paris 1993). – **A. J. Malherbe**, *Theorists* (Bib. 2) 16–19. – **M. Trapp**, *Greek and Latin Letters* (Bib. 1) 42–44, 188–93 (text of Demetrius, *De elocutione* 223–35), 317–20 (notes).

   G. M. A. Grube, *A Greek Critic: Demetrius on Style*, Phoenix Sup. 4 (Toronto 1961). – **H. Koskenniemi**, *Studien* (Bib. 2) 18–53. – **K. Krautter**, "*Asci ore ad os* . . . Eine mittelalterliche Theorie des Briefes und ihr antiker Hintergrund," *AuA* 28 (1982) 155–68. – **W. G. Müller**, "Der Brief als Spiegel der Seele: Zur Geschichte eines Topos der Epistolartheorie von der Antike bis zu Samuel Richardson," *AuA* 26 (1980) 138–57. – **B. Sebaste**, *Lettere e Filosofia* (Bib. 2) 55–97. – **K. Thraede**, *Grundzüge* (Bib. 2) 17–25. – **D. M. Schenkeveld**, *Studies in Demetrius "On Style"* (Amsterdam 1964).

1. Theoretical Foundations: Demetrius, *On Style*

The Athenian philosopher and statesman Demetrius of Phaleron (Phalerum) from the school of Aristotle was active in the late fourth century BCE and wrote a treatise on rhetoric, among other subjects. Accordingly, part of the manuscript tradition of the work known as *On Style*, Περὶ ἑρμηνείας or *De elocutione*, claims Demetrius of Phaleron as its author, although the work must actually be attributed to an otherwise unknown Demetrius or regarded as anonymous. Περὶ ἑρμηνείας is about "the prose style" (ἡ ἑρμηνεία ἡ λογική, §1) as distinct from verse and more particularly about "the types of style" (οἱ χαρακτῆρες τῆς ἑρμηνείας, §35; cf. 114) within prose, of which there are four: ἰσχνός, μεγαλοπρεπής, γλαφυρός, δεινός, the "plain," the "grand," the "elegant," and the "forceful" (§36). The letter form is a particular expression of the plain style (see below).

   The tractate stands in the Peripatetic tradition. Unfortunately its dating remains uncertain. Serious consideration is given to dates between the beginning of the second century BCE and the end of the first century CE, with the mediating position, represented by Schenkeveld, holding that an author from the first century CE has incorporated Peripatetic materials from the third or second century BCE. As to other proposals, Rhys Roberts (271–77) identifies the author as Demetrius of Tarsus, known from

Plutarch, *Def. orac.* 2 (410A). This would lead to a date in the late first century, but has not been widely accepted. Chiron (p. xxxix) draws attention to a Demetrius in Cicero, *Brutus* 315 and Diogenes Laertius 5.84, whose dates he gives as ca. 140–80 BCE.

In his discussion of the plain style, Demetrius includes an excursus on letter writing (§§223–35) that we reproduce below in full as the oldest such reflection in ancient literature. The treatment of the plain style begins in §190, where Demetrius observes by way of introduction that "The diction throughout should be normal and familiar," not "unfamiliar and metaphorical," like the grand style. This is supported by many examples and details such as word choice and sentence structure before we reach the excursus on letters that forms the last part of the treatment of the plain style (trans. Innes in the revised LCL):

> **223** We will next discuss the style for letters (ὁ ἐπιστολικὸς χαρακτήρ), since that too should be plain (lit., of plainness, ἰσχνότητος).
>
> Artemon, the editor of Aristotle's *Letters*,[1] says that a letter should be written in the same manner as a dialogue; the letter, he says, is like one of the two sides to a dialogue. **224** There is perhaps some truth in what he says, but not the whole truth. The letter should be a little more formal than the dialogue, since the latter imitates improvised conversation, while the former is written and sent as a kind of gift (δῶρον).
>
> **225** Who would ever talk to a friend as Aristotle writes to Antipater on behalf of an old man in exile? "If he is a wanderer over all the world, an exile with no hope of being recalled home, it is clear that we cannot blame men like him if they wish to return home, to Hades."[2] A man who talked like that would seem to be making a speech (ἐπιδεικνύμενος), not chatting.
>
> **226** Yet a series of abrupt sentence breaks such as <sc. suits the dialogue> does not suit the letter. Abruptness in writing causes obscurity, and the imitation of conversation is less appropriate to writing than to real debate. Take the *Euthydemus*: "Who was it, Socrates, you were talking to yesterday in the Lyceum? There was certainly a large crowd standing round your group." And a little

[1] Our author Demetrius apparently had access to a collection of Aristotle's letters that is no longer extant.

[2] Aristotle, frag. 665 Rose (cf. V. Rose, *Aristotelis qui ferebantur librorum fragmenta*, Teubner [Leipzig 1886]). This example implies that Aristotle spoke pompously in his letters.

further on he adds: "I think he was a stranger, the man you were talking to. Who was he?"[3] All this sort of style in imitation of reality suits
oral delivery better (lit., suits an actor, ὑποκριτῇ πρέπει [so Rhys
Roberts]), it does not suit letters since they are written.

227 Like the dialogue, the letter should be strong in character-
isation (τὸ ἠθικόν). Everyone writes a letter in the virtual image of
his own soul. In every other form of speech it is possible to see the
writer's character, but in none so clearly as in the letter.

228 The length of a letter, no less than its range of style, should
be restricted. Those that are too long, not to mention too inflated in
style, are not in any true sense letters at all but treatises with the
heading, "Dear Sir" (τὸ χαίρειν). This is true of many of Plato's letters, and that one of Thucydides.[4]

229 The sentences should also be fairly loosely structured. It is
absurd to build up periods, as if you were writing not a letter but a
speech for the law courts (δίκη). Nor is it just absurd to be so formal
in letters, it is even contrary to friendship (οὐδὲ φιλικόν), which
demands the proverbial calling of "a spade a spade."

230 We should also be aware that there are epistolary topics
(πράγματά τινα ἐπιστολικά) as well as style. Certainly Aristotle is
thought to have been exceptionally successful in the genre of letters,
and he comments, "I am not writing to you on this, since it is not
suitable for a letter."[5] **231** If anyone should write in a letter about
problems of logic (σοφίσματα) or natural philosophy (φυσιολο-
γίας), he may indeed write, but he does not write a letter. A letter's
aim is to express friendship (φιλοφρόνησις) briefly (σύντομος), and
set out a simple subject in simple terms.

232 It has its own beauty, but only in expressions of warm
friendship (φιλικαὶ φιλοφρονήσεις) and the inclusion of numerous
proverbs. This should be its only permitted philosophy, permitted
since the proverb is ordinary, popular wisdom. But the man who
utters sententious maxims and exhortations seems to be no longer
chatting in a letter but preaching from the pulpit.[6]

---

[3] Plato, *Euthydemus* 1 (271A).

[4] Perhaps a reference to the letter of Nicias in Thucydides 7.11.1–
7.15.2.

[5] Aristotle, frag. 670 Rose.

[6] This may be an allusion to the *deus ex machina* or "god from the
machine" in the ancient theater, who was brought on stage by mechanical means and spoke in solemn words from an exalted vantage point (supported, e.g., by Innes 485 note "c," but doubted by Chiron 127).

233 Aristotle, however, sometimes even develops proofs, though in such a way that they suit the letter. For instance, wanting to prove that large and small cities have an equal claim on benefactors, he says: "The gods (θεοί) are equal in both; so, since the Graces (αἱ χάριτες) are gods (or rather goddesses, θεαί),[7] you will find grace stored up equally in both."[8] The point being proved suits a letter, and so does the proof itself.

234 Sometimes we write to cities and kings (βασιλεῦσιν):[9] such letters must be a little more elaborate, since we should consider the person to whom the letter is written, but it should not be so elaborate that the letter turns into a treatise, like those of Aristotle to Alexander or that of Plato to Dion's friends.[10]

235 In summary, in terms of style the letter should combine two of the styles, the elegant (or graceful, χαρίεις) and the plain (ἰσχνός),[11] and this concludes my account of the letter, and also of the plain style.

This discussion of letters and the plain style is followed by a few paragraphs about its "faulty counterpart," the "arid" (ξηρός) style. We may therefore summarize Demetrius's theory of the letter style. Demetrius takes up positively the comparison of the letter with one side of a dialogue that was already at home in the Peripatetic tradition, but he also relativizes and develops it. He furthermore points out that the letter leans to the written side of

---

[7] There is a wordplay on χάριτες, which as the plural of χάρις means "the gifts," but which also alludes to the three sister goddesses Aglaia, Euphrosyne, and Thalia known as "the Charities," the goddesses of grace personified, who were related to the muses.

[8] Aristotle, frag. 656 Rose.

[9] This passage permits some sociological conclusions about the intended audience. One could think of the holders of public office or secretaries in responsible positions with prominent people. A considerable amount of education is presupposed of the audience throughout the work.

[10] An allusion to Plato's famous *Epistle* 7.

[11] Compare what is said in §§36–37 about the possibilities and limits of combining the different styles. The "graceful" (χαρίεις) style is not mentioned in the list of the four styles in §36, but no doubt corresponds to the "elegant" (γλαφυρός) style in that passage, for this is further characterized as the style of grace in §§127–72 (e.g., §§127–28: "We will next discuss the elegant style, which is speech with charm and a graceful lightness"). The preference for the term χαρίεις here in §235 may go together with the use of χάριτες in §233.

communication and dialogue to the oral side, regardless of whether the dialogue is written or actually spoken: a written dialogue would still not be the same as a letter (§226). Another noteworthy distinction is that between the letter and the speech, which is illustrated by the genres of epideictic rhetoric (cf. ἐπιδεικνύμενος, §225) and forensic rhetoric in a law court (cf. δίκη, §229). Additional negative examples to be avoided in letters include the philosophical treatise (§§228, 231, 234) and the theater, represented by the speeches of an actor (cf. ὑποκριτής, §226) and the *deus ex machina* (§232). Plato's letters are mentioned in a disparaging tone as "treatises" (§228), which would presumably also apply to the doctrinal letters of Epicurus (see above chap. 4, sec. B.1). By contrast the letter shares with the dialogue the lighter tone of a chat, which can at most be enhanced by a touch of grace and charm. Only letters to cities and kings constitute a partial exception, because they tend to require slightly more elevated language (§234). Somewhat surprisingly, one finds that the letter form also allows for "the inclusion of numerous proverbs," which enhance its beauty (§232). Proverbs are chosen for their communicative potential to create a quick consensus based on popular wisdom.[12] With his picture of the letter as the "image of the soul" in §227 Demetrius has succeeded in framing an element of epistolary theory that has an important subsequent history (cf. Müller). Demetrius uses this to support his claim that letters should reveal the character of their authors. The central catchword in this regard is φιλοφρόνησις, "friendship" (§231; see on Koskenniemi in section 2 below) or its plural φιλοφρονήσεις, "expressions of friendship" (§232), here further qualified as φιλικός, "warm"; an overly formal style can also be contrary to what is friendly or φιλικόν (§229). This was already anticipated in the opening passage: A letter is a gift to a friend in written form (§224).

2. From Theory to Practice: Topoi and Phraseology

Bibliography 25: D. E. Aune, *Literary Environment* (Bib. 4) 172–74. – idem, *Dictionary* (Bib. 4), s.v. "Topos," 476. – **P. Cugusi,** *Evoluzione* (Bib.

---

[12] For illustrations see P. Cugusi, *Evoluzione* (Bib. 2) 96–98, who includes among other things examples of Greek and Latin proverbs in Cicero (above chap. 4, sec. B.2).

2) 73–104. – **H. Koskenniemi**, *Studien* (Bib. 2). – **G. Karlsson**, "Formel-haftes in den Paulusbriefen?" *Eranos* 54 (1956) 138–41. – **F.** Schnider and **W. Stenger**, *Studien zum neutestamentlichen Briefformular* (Bib. 4). – **H. A. Steen**, "Les clichés épistolaires dans les lettres sur papyrus grecques," *Classica et mediaevalia* 1 (1938) 119–76. – **K. Thraede**, *Grundzüge* (Bib. 2). – **J. L. White**, "Epistolary Formulas and Cliches in Greek Papyrus Letters," *SBLSP* 14 (1978) 289–319. – idem, *Light from Ancient Letters* (Bib. 1) 211–13. – **H. Zilliacus**, "Anredeformen," *JAC* 7 (1964) 167–82, esp. 171–72; "Grußformen," *RAC* 12 (1983) 1204–32, esp. 1214–15.

Based on Demetrius, *On Style* and other texts about epistolary theory, Heikki Koskenniemi has traced the ideological underpin-nings of the Greek letter back to the three concepts of *philo-phronesis, parousia*, and *homilia*, which are also central to the Latin letter tradition, according to Klaus Thraede. *Philophronesis* is the element brought out so prominently by Demetrius, the friendly disposition that undergirds the letter exchange. *Parousia* is closely connected with this and stresses that letters facilitate an exchange between friends separated by distance and circumstances, for the letter transforms bodily absence into spiritual presence. This is in turn connected with the dialogical character of letters, repre-sented by the term *homilia* in the sense of ὁμιλεῖν, "to converse with" or "associate with." The letter brings the correspondents together in conversation and creates "a basis for their common life" (Koskenniemi 45).

Koskenniemi's study is valuable above all because he succeeds in demonstrating how these basic ideas are realized in the actual formulas and expressions of the papyrus letters. Koskenniemi refers to this comprehensively in the title of his book as "phrase-ology" (cf. *Studien zur Idee und Phraseologie des griechischen Briefes*), as the linguistic expression of the previously discovered "ideolog-ical" concerns. Nevertheless, the relationship between theory and practice is not linear but dialectic: the theory is read off from the practice but also for its part informs the practice; the same holds true for the letter writing guide of Pseudo-Demetrius to be dis-cussed in the next section.

According to Koskenniemi, the fiction of a conversational sit-uation in and through the letter that epistolary theory designates as one half of a dialogue already begins with the standard letter model that we worked out in chapter 1 (part D). This imitates in its own way a personal encounter: the prescript corresponds to the greeting or mutual introduction; the letter body forms the actual conservation with the exchange of ideas and the transfer of information; in the letter closing the partners again take their leave of one another. It is important to recall that the prescript is already found on the inside of the letter in this period. The identification of the sender and addressee necessary for postal delivery was inscribed on the outside of the folded or rolled papyrus. As a mere delivery instruction, the repetition of the sender and addressee on the inside would fulfill no practical function, but it served another purpose by conveying the greeting χαίρειν, which remained indispensable (Koskenniemi 157–58).

Such observations can be extended to numerous other features of form and content in ancient letters that we have already encountered. These involve certain set expressions and typical constellations which are given a multitude of different names in scholarship. Thus we hear talk for example of letter conventions, typical phrases, topoi, formulas, and clichés without it being sufficiently clear—despite many attempts—what possibilities for differentiation exist in the midst of this convoluted terminology. Most easily clarified with the help of ancient rhetoric is the term topos (cf. Aune). A topos is literally a "place" where one finds themes and arguments, then also a "commonplace" that encapsulates a cluster of motifs and figures applicable to a certain situation. Formulas realize individual elements of the letter function, depending on their position within the letter prescript, the body opening, middle, or closing, or the letter closing, whereas clichés are used to qualify certain expressions, providing for example a circumlocution for a command or a more reserved formulation of a request (cf. White). Despite the still unresolved questions of definition, it is possible to identify additional common letter elements:

- Forms of address that characterize the relationship of the sender to the addressee, such as φίλτατος, "dearest" and τιμιώτατος, "most esteemed," which do not occur in family letters, or the more familiar γλυκύτατος, "sweetest" or "dearest" (cf. Zilliacus).
- The *formula valetudinis* or health wish.
- The *proskynema* formula, providing assurance of the sender's prayers for the addressee, and the mutual remembrance formula.

- The request for a letter together with reasons for that request, as well as the expression of joy over the receipt of a letter with its good news.

- The ἀφορμή formula (Koskenniemi 82), so called when an author writes a letter mainly because an ἀφορμή or "opportunity" for sending it has arisen, as stated in the letter itself.

- The disclosure formula in expressions such as "I want you to know" or "I do not want you to be unaware," and the corresponding request for information.

- The closing greetings in their various forms and the concluding wish, often consisting of ἐρρῶσθαι, "farewell," or similar expressions.

- Various clichés, including "if it seems good to you," "if possible," "you will do well to," "the gods willing," "but above all," and many others (cf. Steen, esp. 168–72 with a table of about 100 expressions).

Here we may investigate one more point somewhat more fully, namely the topos of epistolary "presence" or *parousia*, which Koskenniemi has developed. This topos is also frequent in Paul, especially in 1 Corinthians 5:3-4 (see also 1 Thess 2:17 and Col 2:5), which is another reason for our interest.

The idea of a mediated presence is surprisingly common not only in letters but in literature that mentions them. We may begin with the Roman comic poet Turpilius († 104 BCE), who is said by Jerome to have described letters as "the only means of making absent people present."[13] Even before this the comic playwright Plautus (ca. 254–184 BCE), author of the earliest Latin works to have survived complete, had already included this theme in his play *Pseudolus*. The star-struck lover Calidorus, pining away for his beloved Phoenicium after having received a letter from her on wax tablets, gives the letter to his father's slave Pseudolus, who, as he begins to read, tells Calidorus that he can see his girlfriend in the letter, "at full length on the tablets, lying in wax" (vv. 35–36). As Pseudolus reads on, Calidorus responds, "Yes, yes, for it makes me feel that I am talking with her. Read!" (vv. 63–64). Both these Roman authors may have been indebted at this point to Greek New Comedy and therefore to Greek epistolary theory.

---

[13] Frag. 215 Rychlewska, in Jerome, *Ep.* 8.1: *"sola," inquit, "res est, quae homines absentes praesentes faciat."*

The great letter writer Cicero defines a letter in one of his speeches as "the communion of friends in absence" (*Philippics* 2.4 §7: *amicorum conloquia absentium*). Similar thoughts appear in various places in his letters (cf. Thraede 39–47), for example in *Fam.* 15.16.1: "I don't know how it is, but when I write something to you, I seem to see you here in front of me. I am not speaking according to the doctrine of appearances of images, to use the terminology of your new friends" (which is then cleverly used to launch an attack against Epicurean epistemology), in *Fam.* 12.30.1, and especially clearly in *Fam.* 2.9.2: "It's hard to put it into words, but I saw you in imagination (*absentem*) and it was as though I was talking to you (*quasi coram tecum*)"—especially clearly, since the Latin expressions *absentem* and *quasi coram tecum* obviously evoke the corresponding Greek expressions ἀπών and ὡς παρών. We meet this pair of terms ἀπών and παρών in an often cited papyrus letter from the third century CE in which a father congratulates his son on his wedding, in which the father could not participate, though this need not exclude a later celebration (cf. the last two lines):[14]

> Herakleides to his son Heras: Greetings.
> Above all I greet you, rejoicing together (with you)
> about what has happened to you, i.e., a good, pious, and
> happy marriage, according to our common
> prayers and petitions, to which the gods,
> upon hearing them, granted fulfilment. And we by hearsay,
> being far away (ἀπόντες) but as being present (ὡς παρόντες) at the
>   occasion
> have rejoiced, wishing (you) well for the things to come and that we,
> having arrived at your home, may celebrate together
> a doubly luxuriant banquet. . . .

The poet Ovid (43 BCE–17 CE) answers the question why he is writing from exile by saying, "I am eager to be with you all in some fashion—no matter how" (*Trist.* 5.1.79–80). Elsewhere he further develops the topos of a letter writer's presence in spirit (e.g., *Ep. ex Pont.* 4.4.43–46; cf. Thraede 55–61). In his *Ars amatoria* Ovid advises the writer of a love letter to compose it "so that you seem

---

[14] BGU IV 1080.1–10; reprinted in J. Hengstl, *Griechische Papyri* (Bib. 1) 187–88.

to be speaking in her presence" (*Ars* 1.468). This reminds us that the writers of fictional erotic letters such as Alciphron as well as the writers of embedded letters in romantic novels knew very well how to employ this topos,[15] which brings us full circle back to Plautus.

We may transition to our next section on ancient letter writing handbooks with the help of one of these works, Pseudo-Libanius, *Epistolary Styles*, from late antiquity (ca. 4th–6th century CE). Before enumerating the many different types of letters, the author pauses for a brief theoretical reflection that is fully in the tradition of Demetrius, *On Style* (Pseudo-Libanius, *Epistolary Styles* 2):[16]

> A letter, then, is a kind of written conversation (ὁμιλία τις ἐγγράμ-ματος) of one absent person with another (ἀπόντος πρὸς ἀπόντα), and it fulfills a definite need. One will speak in it as though one were in the company of the absent person.

Exercises

25. Compare the following excerpt from Julius Victor, *Ars rhetorica* 27 (fourth century CE) with the excursus on letters in Demetrius, *On Style*, and identify similarities (trans. J. H. Neyrey in Malherbe, *Theorists* [Bib. 2] 63):

> The openings and conclusions of letters should conform with the degree of friendship (you share with the recipient) or with his rank, and should be written according to customary practice. One ought to answer letters by having at one's fingertips the very letters to which one would reply lest one forgot to what it was that he was replying. As a rule, the ancients wrote in their own hands to those closest to them, or at least frequently appended a postscript. . . . It is pleasant to add a Greek phrase or two in your letter, provided it is not ill-timed or too frequent. And it is very much in form to use a familiar proverb, a line of poetry, or a snatch of verse.

---

[15] For illustrative quotations from Alciphron and Chariton see above pp. 111 and 138; cf. Koskenniemi 180–84.

[16] Trans. Malherbe, *Theorists* (Bib. 2) 67 (modified); cf. also M. Trapp, *Greek and Latin Letters* (Bib. 1) 189.

26. Identify the elements of epistolary theory and the typical epistolary topics in the following quotation from Seneca's *Epistles* 40.1 (trans. R. M. Gummere, *Seneca: Epistles*, LCL, vol. 1 [1917] 263, 265):

> I thank you for writing to me so often; for you are revealing your real self to me in the only way you can. I never receive a letter from you without being in your company forthwith. If the pictures of our absent friends are pleasing to us, though they only refresh the memory and lighten our longing by a solace that is unreal and unsubstantial, how much more pleasant is a letter, which brings us real traces, real evidences, of an absent friend! For that which is sweetest when we meet face to face is afforded by the impress of a friend's hand upon his letter—recognition.

B. Letter Types and Letter Writing Guides

Bibliography 26: V. Weichert, *Demetrii et Libanii qui feruntur* τύποι ἐπιστολικοί *et* ἐπιστολιμαῖοι χαρακτῆρες, Teubner (Leipzig 1910) (**TLG**). – **R. Foerster**, *Libanii opera*, Teubner, vol. 9 (Leipzig 1927) 1–48, esp. 27–47: *Characteres epistolici*. – **A. J. Malherbe**, *Theorists* (Bib. 2) 30–81. – **M. Trapp**, *Greek and Latin Letters* (Bib. 1) 44–45, 188–93 (partial text of Pseudo-Libanius), 323–26 (notes). – **P.-L. Malosse**, *Lettres pour toutes circonstances: Les traités épistolaires du Pseudo-Libanios et du Pseudo-Démétrios de Phalère* (Paris 2004).

    D. E. Aune, *Dictionary* (Bib. 4), s.v. "Epistolography," 162–68, esp. 162–64 (with comparative table of Pseudo-Demetrius and Pseudo-Libanius). – **A. Brinkmann**, "Der älteste Briefsteller," *RMP* 64 (1909) 310–17. – **H. Koskenniemi**, *Studien* (Bib. 2) 54–63. – **R. M. G. Nickisch**, "Briefsteller," in G. Ueding, ed., *Historisches Wörterbuch der Rhetorik*, vol. 2 (Tübingen 1994) 76–86. – **H. Rabe**, "Aus Rhetoren-Handschriften. 9. Griechische Briefsteller," *RMP* 64 (1909) 284–309. – **W. Schmid**, "Ein epistolographisches Übungsstück unter den Pariser Papyri," *NJPP* 145 (1892) 692–99. – **S. K. Stowers**, *Letter Writing* (Bib. 2) 51–57.

Similarly attributed to Demetrius of Phaleron (cf. *On Style* in the previous section) is the oldest ancient letter writing guide, known as *Epistolary Types* (Τύποι ἐπιστολικοί or *Formae epistolicae*). Since neither author is identical with the well-known Demetrius of Phaleron, we actually have two "*Pseudo*-Demetrioi" in this respect, though both of the real authors may actually have been named Demetrius as well. Nevertheless, it is conventional to refer only to the author of *Epistolary Types* as "Pseudo-Demetrius" and to reserve the name "Demetrius" for the author of *On Style* for differentiation, as, for example, in Malherbe's *Ancient Epistolary Theorists*. This work of Pseudo-Demetrius presumably originated in Egypt (cf. the mention of Alexandria in §18), the home of almost all the papyrus letters, and it may have reached its final form there in the third century CE. However, some of the materials included in this work show signs of great antiquity, and the preliminary phases of its current version may reach as far back as the second century BCE. We start by quoting its brief introduction, which begins with a dedication to Heraclides and concludes with a type of table of contents listing 21 letter types.

The translation that follows is that of Malherbe (*Ancient Epistolary Theorists*, 30–41), except for the portions of the introduction labeled "Author and addressee" and "Old age (author) and youth (addressee)," i.e., lines 10–21 in Malherbe's Greek text. See below, n. 17.

Title and dedication	According to the theory that governs epistolary types (τῶν ἐπιστολικῶν τύπων), Heraclides, (letters) can be composed in a great number of styles (εἰδῶν), but are written in those which always fit the particular circumstance (to which they are addressed).
Ideal versus practice	While (letters) ought to be written as skillfully as possible, they are in fact composed indifferently by those who undertake such services for men in public office.
Inductive procedure and layout of the work	Since I see that you are eager in your love to learn, I have taken it upon myself, by means of certain styles (ἰδέων), to organize and set forth (for you) both the number of distinctions between them and what they are, and have sketched a sample, as it were, of the arrangement (τάξεως) of each kind (γένους), and have, in addition, individually set forth the rationale (λόγος) for each of them.

**Author and
addressee**

(In doing so) I partly assume that this is pleasing to you too, since you will know something more than the others (i.e., the other young men of your age), not grounding the splendidness of your life in banquets (like them), but in professional skills. I also partly believe that I will share in the praise due (to you).

**Old age (author)
and youth
(addressee)**

Not that I strove for some such kind (of glory), also not fitting for my age, when inventing a method (for treating the subject), especially since the circumstance (of age, esp. young age) can hinder the most gifted one with respect to these things. For an older person, having lavished most of his time on learning, will (nevertheless) not find such approval as the one who has fully used (καταχρησάμενος) his precarious and hazardous (young) age for the noblest of the sciences.[17] For perhaps time, sustaining them (i.e., the old persons), has become (for them) a tolerant teacher of these things that have mani-

---

[17] Greek: οὐ γὰρ οὕτως ἀποδοχῆς τεύξεται πρεσβύτερος ἀνὴρ πλεῖστον καταναλώσας χρόνον πρὸς μάθησιν, ὡς ὁ τὴν ἐπισφαλῆ καὶ παρακίνδυνον ἡλικίαν πρὸς τὰ κάλλιστα τῶν μαθημάτων καταχρησάμενος. In his Teubner edition Weichert (followed by Malherbe, p. 30 line 19) sets a question mark at the end of this sentence, leading the reader to suppose that it is the older person who "will find approval" (ἀποδοχῆς τεύξεται) for "having used" (καταχρησάμενος) his study time wisely, whereas our translation applies this to the younger person. By ignoring this question mark after καταχρησάμενος, the present translation arrives at more appropriate presentation of the *captatio benevolentiae*. In Malherbe's translation there is only an attenuated *captatio* at best, because the author mainly praises himself (and Heraclides?) for having "used" his old age in study: "For will not an older person, by following this course of action and lavishing most of his time on learning, meet with approval *as one who has fully used* (ὡς ὁ ... καταχρησάμενος) his precarious and hazardous [old] age in pursuing the noblest of the sciences?" This translation would seem to present Heraclides as an older student, or to lack a *captatio*. In our translation Pseudo-Demetrius instead praises his *younger* addressee for his devotion to study and thus "captures" the good will of his audience: καταχρησάμενος is predicated of a young Heraclides, not of Pseudo-Demetrius (nor of an older Heraclides), and the "precarious and hazardous age" is that of youth, not old age.

fold (means of) persuasion, whereas the favorable time of the youth is contracted, because it has so many vexations.

The current state of the question and provisional nature of the presentation

There are, then, twenty-one kinds (γένη) that we have come across. Perhaps time might produce more than these, since it is a highly gifted inventor of skills and theories. But as far as we are concerned, there is no other type (τύπος) that properly pertains to the epistolary mode (εἰς ἐπιστολικὸν τρόπον ἀνήκων). Each of them is named after the form of style (ἰδέας) to which it belongs, as follows:

Table of Contents

(1) friendly (φιλικός),
(2) commendatory (συστατικός),
(3) blaming (μεμπτικός),
(4) reproachful (ὀνειδιστικός),
(5) consoling (παραμυθητικός),
(6) censorious (ἐπιτιμητικός),
(7) admonishing (νουθετητικός),
(8) threatening (ἀπειλητικός),
(9) vituperative (ψεκτικός),
(10) praising (ἐπαινετικός),
(11) advisory (συμβουλευτικός),
(12) supplicatory (ἀξιωματικός),
(13) inquiring (ἐρωτηματικός),
(14) responding (ἀποφαντικός),
(15) allegorical (ἀλληγορικός),
(16) accounting (αἰτιολογικός),
(17) accusing (κατηγορικός),
(18) apologetic (ἀπολογητικός),
(19) congratulatory (συγχαρητικός),
(20) ironic (εἰρωνικός),
(21) thankful (ἀπευχαριστικός).

The address of the *Epistolary Styles* to an inquisitive and eager student, Heraclides, who is immediately contrasted in the second sentence with those who write letters for others in public office without sufficient care, can be placed into its socio-historical context: The target audience of Pseudo-Demetrius consisted of scribes, secretaries, and possibly also the officials themselves, i.e., "those in prominent positions" in §1 (see below), who often had to write letters in their profession and could use a refresher course.

One also senses in this introduction an effort to achieve a theoretically reflected terminology with the mention of types, styles, categories, kinds, rationales, and the stylistic situation, even though these individual terms are not developed because of the brevity of the text, which also explains the difficulty of English translation.

That the friendly letter takes pride of place in Demetrius's table of contents is telling and once again underscores the leading role of the concept of *philophronesis* in the ideology of letters (cf. above §A.2). Otherwise the long list contains a confusing array of terms that sometimes appear to have very little differentiation. Thus judging from the terms alone, it is hard to distinguish between (3) a blaming letter and (9) a vituperative letter, or between (6) a censorious letter and (7) an admonishing letter. Does the rest of the handbook bring any help? The body of the work presents the 21 types in order, each illustrated by a definition and a sample letter, as we have already seen in the case of the letter of recommendation in chapter 3 (sec. B). Let us take a closer look at a few examples, beginning with the friendly letter:

(1) Friendly letter
   – *Definition:*   The friendly type, then, is one that seems to be written by a friend to a friend. But it is by no means (only) friends who write (in this manner). For frequently those in prominent positions are expected by some to write in a friendly manner to their inferiors and to others who are their equals, for example, to military commanders, viceroys, and governors. There are times, indeed, when they write to them without knowing them (personally). They do so, not because they are close friends and have (only) one choice (of how to write), but because they think that nobody will refuse them when they write in a friendly manner, but will rather submit and heed what they are writing. Nevertheless, this type of letter is called friendly as though it were written to a friend. It is as follows:

   – *Example:*   Even though I have been separated from you for a long time, I suffer this in body only. For I can never forget you or the impeccable way we were raised together from childhood up.

Knowing that I myself am genuinely concerned about your affairs, and that I have worked unstintingly for what is most advantageous to you, I have assumed that you, too, have the same opinion of me, and will refuse me in nothing. You will do well, therefore, to give close attention to the members of my household lest they need anything, to assist them in whatever they might need, and to write us about whatever you should choose.

(5) Consoling letter

– Definition:

The consoling type is that written to people who are grieving because something unpleasant has happened (to them). It is as follows:

– Example:

When I heard of the terrible things that you met at the hands of thankless fate, I felt the deepest grief, considering that what had happened had not happened to you more than to me. When I saw all the things that assail life, all that day long I cried over them. But then I considered that such things are the common lot of all, with nature establishing neither a particular time or age in which one must suffer anything, but often confronting us secretly, awkwardly and undeservedly. Since I happened not to be present to comfort you, I decided to do so by letter. Bear, then, what has happened as lightly as you can, and exhort yourself just as you would exhort someone else. For you know that reason will make it easier for you to be relieved of your grief with the passage of time.

(10) Praising Letter

– Definition:

It is the praising type when we encourage someone and express our approval of what he has done or has proposed to do, in the following manner:

– Example:

I had earlier shared in your excellent character through the letters that you wrote; now I approve of what you have done and encourage you, for it will be profitable to us both.

(11) Advisory letter

– *Definition:*	It is the advisory type when, by offering our own judgment, we exhort (someone to) something or dissuade (him) from something. For example, in the following manner:
– *Example:*	I have briefly indicated to you those things for which I am held in high esteem by my subjects. I know, therefore, that you, too, by this course of action can gain the goodwill of your obedient subjects. Yet, while you cannot make many friends, you can be fair and humane to all. For if you are such a person, you will have a good reputation and your position will be secure among the masses.

(21) Thankful letter

– *Definition:*	The thankful type calls to mind the gratitude that is due (the reader). For example:
– *Example:*	I hasten to show in my actions how grateful I am to you for the kindness you showed me in your words. For I know that what I am doing for you is less than I should, for even if I gave my life for you, I should still not be giving adequate thanks for the benefits I have received. If you wish anything that is mine, do not write and request it, but demand a return. For I am in your debt.

Over against the paradigmatic example of the friendly letter, which displays a lifelong intimacy from childhood, the preceding definition aims to show that one can also use a "friendly" letter tactically to achieve certain objectives, since it most purely embodies the character of letter communication. The definition's mention of "those in prominent positions" (ἐν ὑπάρχοις κείμενοι) who need to write letters to equals and inferiors is not what we would generally expect of a friendly letter and therefore only underscores that the "ideal readers" of the work are high officials or the professional scribes who work for them. Therefore the other definitions, including those of the letter types not discussed here, can be formulated more briefly as written for the already initiated. The example of the praising letter is scarcely longer than the definition itself and basically reproduces it. The example of the advisory letter, which depicts one ruler advising another about how to secure his authority and obtain the goodwill of his subjects, once again reaches into the field of politics.

No attention is given in this handbook to the external factors of letter writing. The obligatory prescript and closing greeting are never mentioned, even though they would provide the opportunity for customized formulations. Knowledge of such forms and procedures is presupposed among the addressees, who obviously had to bring a considerable amount of education to this task. This also shows that the treatise was not primarily intended for school instruction.

The handbook's proximity to or distance from actual practice can be further tested by comparing the definitions and examples to real letters. Here the results are mixed. Pseudo-Demetrius's model letter of recommendation, his "commendatory" type, already quoted above in chapter 3 (sec. B), is certainly closer to actual practice than is his treatment of the friendly letter, with its striking discrepancy between definition and example. Similarly, Pseudo-Demetrius's example of the advisory letter from one ruler to another is much too specialized to cover the phenomenon of advice giving in letters: Who except for rulers has to deal with "obedient subjects"? On the other hand, the handbook's sample letters do contain many topoi and formulas found in real letters. These include not only the famous topos of the letter's ability to mediate presence despite physical absence, or the polite circumlocution for a direct request with the expression καλῶς οὖν ποιή-σεις, "you will do well" (§1), but also the giving of reasons for the delay of a visit in the "accounting" letter, which gives an account of why something did or did not happen (§16), and the topos of clarifying misunderstandings through personal conversation, as expressed by the apologetic letter or letter of self-defense (§18).

We can now summarize the results of our study of this writing manual. Pseudo-Demetrius's letter types represent an after-the-fact systemization of epistolary practice which only partially influenced that practice. For as Brinkmann has observed, "The diversity of human relationships and needs naturally means that these letters, which the writing guide splits into separate types, will manifest themselves as such only occasionally in the actual practice of life" (313). The letter types are therefore of only limited use in classifying letters. They shed more light on the social situations in which letters were exchanged and their reflection in the style and tone of letters. They compress into the briefest space the logic of possible argumentative patterns, in the light of the existing relationships between the corresponding parties. In other words, "The types in the handbooks give a sample, in barest outline, of form and language that is appropriate to the logic of the social code in a particular instance" (Stowers 56).[18]

After Pseudo-Demetrius the second handbook of this type has a different title but essentially the same topic. It is known not as *Epistolary Types* (Τύποι ἐπιστολικοί, *Formae epistolicae*) but as *Epistolary Styles* ('Επιστολιμαῖοι χαρακτῆρες, *Characteres epistolici*), and is considerably more recent than the former, dating from the fourth to sixth century CE. The *Epistolary Styles* is extant in two versions, attributed respectively to Proclus and to Libanius, both pseudonymously.[19] Which of the two versions is older—usu-

---

[18] Cf. also S. K. Stowers, "Social Typification and the Classification of Ancient Letters," in J. Neusner et al., eds., *The Social World of Formative Christianity and Judaism*, FS H. C. Kee (Philadelphia 1988) 78–90, esp. 87: "The handbooks . . . contain a sort of implicit sociology of letter writing."

[19] These can be regarded as two versions of the same work because they begin the same way ('Ο μὲν ἐπισταλτικὸς χαρακτὴρ ποικίλος τε καὶ πολυσχιδὴς ὑπάρχει) and show many verbal agreements. However, in the scholarly literature one meets with contrary characterizations of how much they differ. Compare the statement of Malherbe, "There are two manuscript traditions of this work [sc. the *Epistolimaioi Characteres*], one attributing it to Libanius, the other to Proclus. They do not depend on each other, but derive from a common archetype which was produced by neither author. *The traditions differ considerably, in title, text, and the arrangement of the contents*" (*Ancient Epistolary Theorists*, 5, italics added), with that of Trapp, "This late-antique text . . . survives in *two not widely differing versions*" (*Greek and Latin Letters*, 323, italics added). Both authors are partly correct, as we may observe by comparing Foerster's Teubner text of Pseudo-Libanius (used by both Malherbe and Trapp) with Hercher's text of Pseudo-Proclus in *Epistolographi graeci* 6–13, in the absence of a more recent critical edition (though see Hercher's text-critical notes, p. xii). Trapp is right to suggest that the wording of many sections is identical, while Malherbe is right that the arrangement is different. Hence the introduction and the initial list of 41 letter styles are identical (i.e., §§1–4 in Pseudo-Libanius = pp. 6–7 of Pseudo-Proclus in Hercher), as are most of the definitions, whereas the arrangement of the

ally this is claimed to be Pseudo-Libanius, but Pseudo-Proclus also finds his defenders—is difficult to determine, and whether the author had any direct knowledge of the handbook of Pseudo-Demetrius remains uncertain. In any case, what Pseudo-Demetrius suspected in his proem, namely that the time might come when more than twenty-one letter types would be recognized, has indeed come to pass: Pseudo-Libanius, to concentrate on him for the moment, names forty-one types, twelve of which overlap precisely with the archetypes in Pseudo-Demetrius.[20] For

---

definitions with examples is different: Pseudo-Proclus lists definitions and examples together, while Pseudo-Libanius separates them. Thus Pseudo-Proclus begins with the definition of the paraenetic letter (Hercher p. 8, §α΄): Καὶ παραινετικὴ μὲν οὖν ἐστι δι' ἧς παραινοῦμέν τινι, προτρέποντες αὐτὸν ἐπί τι ὁρμῆσαι ἢ καὶ ἀφέξεσθαί τινος, and follows uninterrupted with the example: Ἡ ἐπιστολή· Ζηλωτὴς ἀεί, βέλτιστε, γενοῦ τῶν ἐναρέτων ἀνδρῶν, etc. By contrast, Pseudo-Libanius places this example in §52 and the definition in §5, where the definition moreover extends beyond the single line in Pseudo-Proclus.

[20] Thus Pseudo-Libanius types 2, 4, 5, 6, 7, 9, 13, 16, 21, 26, 30, and 31, designated respectively as blaming, commending, ironic, thankful, friendly, threatening, reproaching, congratulatory, consoling, praising, censorious, and inquiring, correspond to the types numbered in Pseudo-Demetrius respectively as 3, 2, 20, 21, 1, 8, 4, 19, 5, 10, 6, and 13, thus giving twelve points of correspondence. There would be a thirteenth correspondence if Pseudo-Libanius's ἀποφαντικὴ προσηγορία or "declaratory type," no. 34 (= §§4, 38, 85) could be paralleled with Pseudo-Demetrius's ἀποφαντικὸς τύπος or "responding type," no. 14 (= §14), as suggested by Aune, *Dictionary*, s.v. "Epistolography," 164. Nevertheless, despite the lexically identical designation of these two types in Greek by ἀποφαντικός/-ή, both the definitions and the sample letters in the two handbooks at types 34 and 14 diverge widely. The definition and the example of Pseudo-Demetrius's type 14 run: "The responding (ἀποφαντικός) type responds (ἀποφαίνεσθαι) to the person making an inquiry. For example: You wrote me asking whether So-and-so was with us. He still is, and furthermore says that he expects to wait until you arrive" (§14). This is not comparable with the definition of Pseudo-Libanius's type 34 in his §38: "The declaratory (ἀποφαντική) style is that in which we render and carry out a hard judgment against someone," which is followed by a fitting example in §85: "I have decided to punish my domestic slave because of the plot he devised against me." In short, it is necessary to translate the single

the other types only the terms have changed. Hence the "enig-
matic" (αἰνιγματική) letter of Pseudo-Libanius is similar to the
"allegorical" (ἀλληγορικός) of Pseudo-Demetrius. Among the
new letter types in Pseudo-Libanius are the paraenetic, the didactic, and the erotic. It is noteworthy that the last style included,
number 41, is the "mixed" (μικτή) style, understood as "that
which we compose from many styles (χαρακτήρων)" (§45). The
sample letter for this style contains a mixture of praise and blame
(§92). Beyond this Pseudo-Libanius appends a remark about the
letter prescript in §51, recommending only the simplest form,
"So-and-so to So-and-so, greeting (χαίρειν)," and adds a few
more theoretical and topical elements (e.g., the topos of the letter
making an absent person present in §2).

That the letter types could themselves provide the focus for
style exercises has been demonstrated by two papyrus discoveries,
the first of which is of added interest because of its early date. In
P.Par. 63 (cf. also UPZ 144–45) from the second century BCE,
two letters are copied in the free space of a papyrus document, one
in a very angry tone, the other addressed to someone who had suffered misfortune. They were identified by Wilhelm Schmid
already in 1892 as an "epistolographical exercise." Another fascinating document, the bilingual Latin-Greek *Bologna Papyrus* 5
from the third or fourth century CE, contains parallel Latin and
Greek versions of the same letters,[21] including between 10 and 13
individual letters depending on how one counts. Some of these are
assigned to various letter types by means of titles in the original
manuscript. Particularly well represented are the letter of advice,
with two examples of advice on how one should deal with very
small inheritances (*P.Bon.* 5, col. 3.3–13, 14–25 Latin, parallel to
4.3–13, 14–25 Greek), and the congratulatory letter, with five
examples of congratulations on the receipt of large inheritances
(5.13–11.5 odd cols., par. 6.13–12.5 even cols.) and one example of
congratulations to a slave on the reception of freedom (13.3–28

Greek term ἀποφαντικός/-ή differently in these two handbooks, as
Malherbe has done, for identity of terminology here does not imply
identity of substance.

[21] O. Montevecchi, *Papyri Bononienses* (*P. Bon.*), vol. 1 (Milan 1953).
Text with English translation by B. Fiore in Malherbe, *Theorists* (Bib. 2)
44–57. Also in P. Cugusi, *Corpus epistularum Latinarum* (Bib. 1) 1:79–84.

par. 14.3–28). The linguistic level is considerably below that of the letter writing handbooks, and there are no definitions or theoretical reflections. We reproduce here in translation the Greek version of the first letter of advice (*P.Bon.* 5, col. 4.3–13):[22]

> *(Letters) of Advice about Very Small Legacies*
>
> I heard that
> Licinnius has died, a
> genuine friend of
> yours, but one who
> little remembered your allegiance.
> I am sorry, but I
> urge you to bear it calmly. For while
> people draw up wills
> for their final depo–
> sitions, the fates
> dispose of them.

Exercises

27. Among the few statements about epistolary theory from late antiquity are a short work *On Letters* by Philostratus of Lemnos (third century CE) and a section from *The Art of Rhetoric* by Julius Victor (fourth century CE) (texts and translations in A. J. Malherbe, *Ancient Epistolary Theorists*, 42–43, 62–65). Identify the particular letter types alluded to in the following excerpts:

Philostratus of Lemnos, *De epistulis*:

While clarity is a good guide for all discourse, it is especially so for a letter. Whether we grant something or make a petition, whether we agree or disagree, whether we attack someone or defend ourselves, or whether we state our love, we shall more easily prevail if we express ourselves with clarity of style.

---

[22] Trans. by B. Fiore in Malherbe, *Theorists*, 47. Text and translation also in M. Trapp, *Greek and Latin Letters* (Bib. 1) 124–25 §49.

Julius Victor, *Ars rhetorica* 27:

A letter written to a superior should not be droll; to an equal, not cold; to an inferior, not haughty. Let not a letter to a learned person be carelessly written, nor indifferently composed when going to a less learned person; let it not be negligently written if to a close friend, nor less cordial to a non-friend. Be profuse in congratulating someone on his success so as to heighten his joy, but console someone who is grieving with a few words, for a wound bleeds when touched by a heavy hand. . . .

Recommendations should be written truthfully or not at all. They are proper only when you willingly give them to a dear friend and if you make credible and realistic claims in them.

C. Ancient Rhetoric and Its Applications

1. Introduction

Bibliography 27: R. D. Anderson, Jr., *Ancient Rhetorical Theory* (Bib. 5). – **M. Camargo**, "Ars dictandi, dictaminis," in G. Ueding, ed., *Historisches Wörterbuch der Rhetorik*, vol. 1 (Tübingen 1992) 1040–46. – **J. Dubois**, et al., *Rhétorique générale* (Paris 1970) = *A General Rhetoric*, trans. by P. B. Burrell and E. M. Slotkin (Baltimore 1981) – **H. Hunger**, *Literatur der Byzantiner* (Bib. 18). – **B. M. W. Knox**, "Silent Reading in Antiquity," *GRBS* 9 (1968) 421–35. – **U. Kühne**, "Brieftheoretisches in mittelalterlichen Briefen," *Romanische Forschung* 109 (1997) 1–23. – **W. G. Müller**, "Brief," in G. Ueding, ed., *Historisches Wörterbuch der Rhetorik*, vol. 2 (Tübingen 1994) 60–76. – **C. Ottmers**, *Rhetorik* (Bib. 5) 35–39. – **C. Perelman** and **L. Olbrechts-Tyteca**, *Traité de l'argumentation: La nouvelle rhétorique*, 2 vols. (Paris 1958) = *The New Rhetoric: A Treatise on Argumentation*, trans. by J. Wilkenson and P. Weaver (Notre Dame 1969). – See also the rest of the literature in **Bibliography 5**.

We have already encountered rhetoric in various ways. Some of the Hellenistic royal letters have been described as "almost more of a speech than a letter" (see above, p. 78). The letters of the great Attic orator (!) Demosthenes may be regarded as a form of deliberative self-defense, replacing speeches that could not be delivered because of time constraints (see above, p. 114). The reading of letters as evidence in court speeches was a common practice, but because these letters were left out when the speeches were published, there was an opportunity for the speeches to be supplemented by later fictitious additions (see above, p. 128 in connection with the letters of Philip II of Macedonia in Demosthenes). Another Attic orator, Isocrates, writes in one of his authentic letters (see above, p. 117) that he wanted to avoid making a speech: "I fear my advice may be inopportune; for even now I have unawares gradually drifted beyond the due proportions of a letter and run into a lengthy discourse" (*Ep.* 2.13). Cicero, who unites many roles in one person—orator, politician, author of rhetorical handbooks (see Bib. 28), and letter writer—also differentiates between a letter and a speech: "The fact is that one's style has to vary. A letter is one thing, a court of law or a public meeting quite another" (*Fam.* 9.21.1). We have seen the origin of the Cynic epistles as rhetorical exercises in prosopopoeia, in which a student seeks to slip into the role of a philosopher from the past. But what was being taught in this case was not letter writing as such, since prosopopoeia in letters was only a variation on the favorite exercise of writing fictional speeches for important people. Demetrius, in his treatise *On Style*, considered complicated periods to be a mark of forensic speeches in the law courts and wanted letters to be free of them (*De elocutione* 229). The early rhetorical handbooks treat letters only very tangentially. Quintilian (ca. 35–95 CE) dedicates an aside to letters, noting that "formal speech is either bound and woven together, or of a looser texture, like that of dialogues and letters," which lack "any steady flow or coherence" (*Inst.* 9.4.19–20). Theon (1st–2nd cent. CE) mentions letters in his *Progymnasmata* as a possible variety of prosopopoeia.[23]

The letter writing guides of Pseudo-Demetrius (*Epistolary Types*) and Pseudo-Libanius (*Epistolary Styles*) employ their own, letter-specific categories rather than the typical categories of rhetoric, with which there is only a little overlap, as in Pseudo-Demetrius's advisory (συμβουλευτικός, §11) and apologetic (ἀπολογητικός, §18) letters. In the fourth century CE Julius Victor added a separate section on the letter, *De epistolis*, as one of

---

[23] In L. Spengel, *Rhetores graeci*, vol. 2 (Leipzig 1854) 59–130, here 115–22.

two appendices in his *Art of Rhetoric*,[24] thus creating what has been called "the best theoretical work on the letter that we possess from antiquity."[25] Yet even here we must note its relegation to an appendix and late date. Likewise in the fourth century the orator and speech teacher Libanius, author of an extensive letter collection, writes to his friend Demetrius to request a letter before the latter's personal visit, making a comparison between letters and rhetoric: "But before you show us yourself in person, my dear man, show us the rhetor in you, for this art is also exhibited in letters."[26]

Although the above observations have arisen unsystematically, they can be considered symptomatic of the relationship between rhetoric and epistolary theory. There are affinities, but also divergences, and the relationship changes with the passing of time, from a striking reservation of rhetoric with regard to epistolary theory to the beginnings of an integration of letters into rhetoric. Rhetoric inherently has as its object the public oral speech. Letters by contrast are conceived as written documents, and they programmatically exclude the wider public in their ideal type, the friendly letter. One cannot gloss over this difference either by pointing to the many speeches that existed from the beginning only in written form and were never delivered, or that were written down before or after delivery and reworked for publication, or by invoking the dialogical character of letters and the fact that they were read out loud like all other texts in antiquity. A dialogue, especially one whose other half is "fictional" and has to be constructed by the reader, is not a speech. Likewise the speech, even when it is imitated in other purely written genres, cannot deny its origins in public oratory. Finally, neither the secondary orality of the letter that is read aloud nor the fact that a letter could be dictated to a scribe cancels out its originally written character.

The reading out loud of ancient texts, including letters, was in any case not as universally practiced as has often been claimed. We

---

[24] New text edition: R. Giomini and M. S. Celentano, *C. Iulii Victoris ars rhetorica*, Teubner (Leipzig 1980), here 105–6.

[25] J. Sykutris, "Epistolographie" (Bib. 2) 190.

[26] Greek: ἀλλ᾽, ὦ δαιμόνιε, δεῖξον ἡμῖν πρὸ τοῦ σώματος τὸν ῥήτορα· δηλοῦται μὲν γὰρ ἡ τέχνη καὶ διὰ τῶν γραμμάτων. Unfortunately, of Libanius's 1544 epistles (ed. R. Foerster, *Libanii opera*, Teubner, vols. 10–11), this one, *Ep.* 528, is not included in the collection of A. F. Norman, *Libanius: Autobiography and Selected Letters*, LCL, 2 vols. (1992).

have nice examples of silent reading of letters in particular: Caesar silently reads a note on a tablet that was delivered to him in the Senate. As others protest because they suspect a secret message from the opposing party, Caesar passes the tablet to Cato, who is forced to discover that it was an indecent love letter to Caesar from his own sister Servilia.[27] The female poet Sappho of Lesbos even has a relevant riddle that is recorded by Antiphanes and preserved by Athenaeus:[28]

> There is a feminine being which keeps its babes safe beneath its bosom; they, though voiceless, raise a cry sonorous over the waves of the sea and across all the dry land, reaching what mortals they desire, and they may hear even when they are not there; but their sense of hearing is dull. (Athenaeus, *Deipnosophistae* 10.450e–f)

After rejecting several wrong answers, Sappho solves the riddle:

> The feminine being, then, is an epistle, the babes within her are the letters it carries round; they, though voiceless, talk to whom they desire when far away; yet if another happens to be standing near when it is read, he will not hear. (*Deipn.* 10.451a–b)

This example also carries a warning: the analysis of epistolary theory with the help of rhetoric must not fall subconsciously into the error of valuing speaking higher than writing, as some ancients did (e.g., Plato), or of regarding writing and the written material in a letter as a surrogate for speaking or as a makeshift solution. Its writtenness is part of the essence of the letter that deserves to be respected, not dissolved.

Nevertheless, one common thread remains intact despite this analysis: public speaking and letter writing are both forms of human communication though language, and as such they are bound to bear some similarities. Some rapprochement has also

---

[27] Plutarch, *Brutus* 5.3–4. Cf. Knox 431–32. See also W. Rösler in *Gnomon* 64 (1992) 1: "In fact both the ancient testimonies and general considerations require us to acknowledge the practice of silent reading"; further F. D. Gilliard, "More Silent Reading in Antiquity: *Non Omne Verbum Sonat*," *JBL* 112 (1993) 689–96 (both with further literature).

[28] Fragments of Antiphanes 196 (Kock 2.95) in Athenaeus, *Deipnosophistae* 10.450e–f, 451a–b; trans. C. B. Gulick, *Athenaeus: The Deipnosophists, Books VIII–X*, LCL, vol. 4 (1930) 453, 455. Cf. Knox 432–33, who also evaluates Euripides, *Hippolytus* 856–80.

been fostered by the fact that over the centuries rhetoric developed into a primary force in education and permeated all aspects of culture, resulting in an increasing rhetorization of diverse literary genres. But the converging lines of the oration and the letter did not actually cross in theoretical reflection until late antiquity. From then on, among the Byzantines (cf. Hunger 208–13), in the Latin Middle Ages,[29] and in humanism, instruction in letter writing was considered a self-evident part of rhetoric. In the letter writing handbooks of the Middle Ages the parts of a speech were, with minor modification, also applied to the letter, producing a five–part scheme consisting of *salutatio, captatio benevolentiae, narratio, petitio*, and *conclusio* (cf. Camargo). When Erasmus published his work on epistolary theory, *De conscribendis epistolis*, which saw multiple editions between 1498 and 1534, in order adequately to cover letters he included a fourth rhetorical genre, the *genus familiare* (Müller 62), in addition to the traditional three genres of judicial, deliberative, and demonstrative rhetoric (see below).

Ancient rhetoric is a broad field in its own right, especially when its temporal span and long-term influence are taken into account. The benefits of a rhetorically assisted analysis of letters depend not least on what one understands by rhetoric and what area within rhetoric one refers to. The situation is additionally complicated by the influence of the New Rhetoric, above all the work of Chaïm Perelman and Lucie Olbrechts-Tyteca, which deals with questions of argumentation and persuasion within formal logic in the tradition of Aristotle's rhetoric.[30] The tendency is in the direction of equating rhetoric with persuasive communication as such. That rhetoric can be applied at the same time to different types of texts, including letters, is obvious, and it is only logical when it enters, as it often does, into a close connection with linguistics, structuralism, communication theory, and the sociology of literature. But this broad, generalizing understanding of

[29] Ottmers 35: "The letter was not treated as a rhetorical genre in its own right until the Middle Ages."

[30] Other writers like Jacques Dubois and his "Groupe Mu" collaborators Francis Edeline, Jean-Marie Klinkenberg, and Philippe Minguet also understand their *General Rhetoric* (Baltimore 1981) as a contribution to the New Rhetoric, but they limit themselves to a new theory of rhetorical figures.

rhetoric runs the risk of obscuring particular historical constellations that are not so obvious and need clarification. For the sake of clarity we concentrate here on ancient rhetoric, and we must first introduce a few basic elements, since it is only against this background that the utility of rhetoric for dealing with letters can be appreciated.

2. The Basics of Ancient Rhetoric

Bibliography 28 (the most important sources): **J. H. Freese**, *Aristotle: The "Art" of Rhetoric*, LCL Aristotle, vol. 22 (1926). – **W. S. Hett**, *Aristotle: Problems*, 2 vols. (LCL Aristotle, vols. 15–16); vol. 2 includes **H. Rackham**, *Rhetorica ad Alexandrum* (1937) 257–449 (by Anaximenes of Lampascus). – **H. Caplan**, *[Cicero]: Ad C. Herennium de ratione dicendi: (Rhetorica ad Herennium)*, LCL Cicero, vol. 1 (1954). – **H. M. Hubbell**, *Cicero: De inventione. De optimo genere oratorum. Topica*, LCL Cicero, vol. 2 (1949). – **E. W. Sutton** and **H. Rackham**, *Cicero: De oratore, Books I–II*, LCL Cicero, vol. 3 (1942; ²1948). – **H. Rackham**, *Cicero: De oratore, Book III. De fato. Paradoxa stoicorum. De partitione oratoria*, LCL Cicero, vol. 4 (1942). – **G. L. Hendrickson**, *Cicero: Brutus* and **H. M. Hubbell**, *Cicero: Orator*, LCL Cicero, vol. 5 (1939). – **H. E. Butler**, *The Institutio Oratoria of Quintilian*, LCL, 4 vols. (1920–1922). – Revised edition: **D. A. Russell**, *Quintilian: The Orator's Education*, LCL, 5 vols. (2001). – **W. Peterson**, *Tacitus: Dialogus*, in *Dialogus. Agricola. Germania*, LCL Tacitus, vol. 1 (1914).

Bibliography 29: D. E. Aune, *Dictionary* (Bib. 4), s.v. "Aristotle's *Rhetorica*," 59–62; "Arrangement," 62–64 (table); "*Captatio benevolentiae*," 89; "Cicero, *Brutus*," 97; "Cicero, *De inventione*," 97–98; "Cicero, *De optimo genere oratorum*," 98; "Cicero, *De oratore*," 98; "Cicero, *Orator*," 98; "Deliberative rhetoric," 124; "Enthymeme," 150–57; "Epideictic rhetoric," 162; "Ethos," 169–73; "Exordium," 175–76; "Forensic rhetoric," 187; "*Inventio*/invention," 234; "Pathos," 339–42; "Peroration," 347; "Prooimion," 380; "Quintilian, *Instituto oratoria*," 394–95; "Rhetoric," 414–15; "Rhetoric, divisions of," 415; "*Rhetorica ad Alexandrum*," 415–16; "*Rhetorica ad Herennium*," 416; "Rhetorical genres," 418–20 (table); "Rhetorical handbooks," 420–22; "Stasis," 449; "Style, or stylistics," 451–52; "Trope," 478. – **T. Habinek**, *Ancient Rhetoric and Oratory* (Malden, Mass. 2005). – **H. Lausberg**, *Handbook* (Bib. 5). – **L. Pernot**, *La rhétorique de l'éloge dans le monde gréco-romain*, 2 vols., Collection des Études Augustiniennes, Série Antiquité 137–38 (Paris 1993). – **C. Ottmers**, *Rhetorik* (Bib. 5). – **J. Sprute**, *Die*

Enthymemtheorie der aristotelischen Rhetorik, Abhandlungen der Akademie der Wissenschaften in Göttingen, Philologisch-Historische Klasse 124 (Göttingen 1982). – **S. K. Stowers**, *Letter Writing* (Bib. 2) 51–57. – **M. H. Wörner**, *Das Ethische in der Rhetorik des Aristoteles*, Alber-Reihe Praktische Philosophie 33 (Freiburg i.Br. and Munich 1990). – See also the rest of the literature in Bibliography 5.

Rhetoric is at heart the doctrine of giving speeches. Through rhetorical instruction and the handbooks it produced, rhetoric seeks to equip the future orator for a successful career. Its more prescriptive than descriptive orientation is relativized by the fact that rhetoric can find its recipe for success only in actual speeches that were considered especially effective. Rhetoric can therefore be applied to the analysis of speeches, whether delivered orally or fixed in writing. Some, though not all, of its tools can also be applied to other kinds of linguistic expression. Nevertheless, one should not forget to test the rhetorical arsenal against *speeches* that have actually been delivered. Especially useful in our case will be the speeches of authors who were also outstanding letter writers (see below Exercise 28).[31]

a) The Three Rhetorical Genres

Since Aristotle at the latest, speeches have been divided into three main genres that indicate their different social locations. One differentiates between:

(1) γένος δικανικός, *genus iudiciale*, judicial or dicanic rhetoric, also known as forensic or apologetic;

(2) γένος συμβουλευτικόν, *genus deliberativum*, deliberative or symbouleutic rhetoric, also called a "demegoric" speech or λόγος δημηγορικός (e.g., Aristotle, *Rhet.* 2.20.7 [1394a *l.* 2]), because it was a speech "to the people" in a public assembly;

(3) γένος ἐπιδεικτικόν, *genus demonstrativum*, demonstrative or epideictic rhetoric.

---

[31] So correctly Anderson 252: "There is no substitute for a personal reading of the rhetorical theorists (in their own language), and the *reading and application of this theory to typical speeches of the time*. I believe this would have a salutary effect on rhetorical scholarship in general" (italics added).

A *judicial* or *forensic* speech, as its name suggests, is held before a law court for the purposes of prosecution or defense. Before the assembly in Athens or the council of judges in Rome, such speeches sought to convince the audience of the guilt or innocence of the accused or to contest the rights of the plaintiff. A *deliberative* or symbouleutic speech has its *Sitz im Leben* in the deliberations of a general or legislative assembly. It offers advice about an upcoming decision, favoring a particular option or warning against it. The *epideictic* or demonstrative speech (cf. the excellent treatment of Pernot) is at home at a festival gathering or other ceremonial occasion, where it seeks to entertain the audience. It distributes praise and blame by, for example, extolling a deceased person, honoring a benefactor, or singing the praises of a city, but as a vituperative speech it can intend precisely the opposite. Because of its practical value the greatest interest lay in the forensic speech before the court, which took pride of place in the rhetorical handbooks to such an extent that the other two genres often received only a few pages. Let us seek to get a sense of the original flavor of these categories from the *Rhetorica ad Herennium*, a work by an unknown Roman author, perhaps written between 86 and 82 BCE, that has traditionally been ascribed to Cicero (1.2.2; 2.1.1):

> There are three kinds of causes (*Tria sunt genera causarum*) which the speaker must treat: Epideictic, Deliberative, and Judicial (*demonstrativum, deliberativum, iudiciale*). The epideictic kind is devoted to the praise or censure of some particular person. The deliberative consists in the discussion of policy and embraces persuasion and dissuasion. The judicial is based on legal controversy, and comprises criminal prosecution or civil suit, and defence. . . . By far the most difficult is the judicial.

Aristotle took his systematization a step further by dividing the three genres temporally with respect to the three times—the past: the forensic speech—the present: the festival speech before spectators—and the future: the deliberative or advisory speech (*Rhet.* 1.3.1–4 [1358b 13–20]). Nevertheless, this definition is not entirely accurate, and there were always new attempts to broaden the triad. Classifying actual speeches in terms of the three genres is not always as smooth as one would like to think. One might spontaneously classify a political speech as the paradigmatic example of the deliberative genre, but where it no longer leads to making a decision but only serves to praise a decision already made or to disparage a political opponent, it bears a more epideictic character (Ottmers 23–24). In his oration *On the Peace*, essentially a deliberative speech before the popular assembly that had come to debate war and peace, the Athenian orator Isocrates concludes that a speaker before such an audience must at one and the same time accuse (κατηγορῆσαι), praise (ἐπαινέσαι), and advise (συμβουλεῦσαι)—thus uniting the three traditional genres (*Or.* 8.27 [LCL 2:25]; cf. Pernot 27–28). The least clearly defined genre, epideictic, intrudes into the other two and functions as a catch-all for much that cannot clearly be identified with speeches before the court or the general assembly. Quintilian exposes the inadequacies of the usual classification when he retains the traditional three genres but admits that others see more and proceeds to enumerate the different possible speech acts by means of questions (*Inst.* 3.4.1–4):

> Whether there are three or more of these [sc. "kinds of causes," *genera causarum*, in which rhetoric is employed] is disputed. Of course, almost all the writers who are most authoritative among the ancients followed Aristotle, who [holds to the three *causae* and] merely changes one name and says "demegoric" (δημηγορική, *contionalis*) instead of "deliberative" (συμβουλευτική, *deliberativa*), and were happy with this [threefold] division. However, even in those days some slight attempt was made among certain Greeks (and also in Cicero's *De oratore*), and an overwhelming argument has been advanced by the greatest authority of our own day,[32] to prove that there are not only more than three such kinds (*genera*), but that they are almost innumerable. Indeed, if we place the function of praise and blame in the third part, on what "kind" (*genus*) are we to think ourselves engaged when we complain, console, pacify, excite, frighten, encourage, instruct, explain obscurities, narrate, plead for mercy, give thanks, congratulate, reproach, abuse, describe, commend (*mandamus*),[33] renounce, wish, opine, and so on and so forth?

[32] Russell in the revised LCL of Quintilian notes (2:30 n. 3): "Presumably someone still living; otherwise Q. would have named him."

[33] Both Butler in the original and Russell in the revised LCL translate *mandamus* here as "command" rather than "commend," but the latter is a viable option according to E. A. Andrews, C. T. Lewis, and C. Short, *A Latin Dictionary* (Oxford 1879), s.v. *mando* II.A. Similarly, the

> Adhering to the old views as I do, I have therefore to ask for indulgence, and inquire what motive can have induced earlier writers to confine such a broad field within such narrow bounds.

Quintilian here finds himself on a trail that he himself does not pursue to the end but that ultimately leads us to the twenty-one or forty-one epistolary types in the letter writing handbooks. Consoling, instructing, thanking, congratulating, reproaching, abusing, and recommending are there envisaged as universal language activities. If a speech can belong to two or more different rhetorical genres at once or can incorporate elements from different genres, so can a letter. Most of the letter types of Pseudo-Demetrius and Pseudo-Libanius could be regarded as examples of epideictic rhetoric, assigning praise or blame, but this does not yet do justice to their special nuances. Most disruptive of any neat paralleling of epistolary and rhetorical theory is the fact that, whereas many of the letter types are oriented to exhortation and address the ethical conduct and life-crises of the recipients, there is a general consensus that such *exhortatio* was not envisaged as part of rhetorical theory, but was rather classified as paraenesis in the realm of moral philosophy (cf. Stowers). It is not by accident that Cicero complains that for many important language functions, including those of "*exhorting*, comforting, teaching, and warning" (*cohortationes*, *consolationes*, *praecepta*, *admonita*), the standard rhetorical systems had no special place (*De oratore* 2.64).

b) The Five Steps of Speech Preparation

The ideal process that an orator would go through in preparing and delivering a speech consisted of five steps or phases:

(1) εὕρεσις, *inventio*, invention or conception
(2) τάξις, *dispositio*, arrangement

German translation of Helmut Rahn, *Marcus Fabius Quintilianus: Ausbildung des Redners*, 2 vols., Texte zur Forschung 2–3 (Darmstadt ¹1972–1975; ³1995), reads "empfehlen," i.e., "recommend." The Latin dictionary by K. E. Georges, *Ausführliches lateinisch-deutsches Handwörterbuch*, 2 vols. (Leipzig 1869), s.v. II.2 even gives the specific epistolary meaning "benachrichtigen lassen," i.e., to "to have a notice written" about someone.

(3) λέξις, *elocutio*, style

(4) μνήμη, *memoria*, memory

(5) ὑπόκρισις, *actio* or *pronuntiatio*, delivery

Cicero provides an overview of these *officia oratoris* or "duties of the orator"[34] in his *De oratore* 1.142 (cf. also *De inventione* 1.9):

> And, since all the activity and ability of an orator falls into five divisions, I learned that he must first *hit upon* (i.e., "discover," *reperire*) what to say; then manage and marshal his discoveries, not merely in *orderly fashion* (*ordine*), but with a discriminating eye for the exact weight as it were of each argument; next go on to say them in the *adornments of style* (*ornare oratione*); after that keep them guarded in his *memory* (*memoria*); and in the end *deliver* (*agere*) them with effect and charm.

Because the performance steps of "memory" and "delivery" fall out for letters, we may content ourselves with a few remarks about the remaining three steps.

(1) In the phase known as *inventio*, the speaker would first "invent" or "discover" the right strategy for the speech and begin gathering and sifting material. For finding appropriate arguments the standard doctrine of the rhetorical topoi provided a rich store of ready-made or half-prepared building blocks. There is a functional equivalent here with the letter topoi (see above), even though the contents diverge. A further aid for lawcourt speeches was the doctrine of the στάσις or *status* (also *constititio*), the "issue" at stake, which developed with Hermagoras of Temnos in the second century BCE and became the most important principle for distinguishing the issues of a court proceeding according to the *Rhetorica ad Herennium*. In simplified form, there are four kinds of questions that can be raised to get at the four typical "issues" in a court case: the issue of facts: Did the accused commit the murder or not? (*status coniecturae*); the issue of definition: Was it murder or manslaughter? (*status finitionis*); the issue of the quality of the action: Was it just? Are there mitigating circumstances? (*status*

---

[34] But see Quintilian, *Inst.* 3.3.11: "A number of teachers have also been of the opinion that these are not parts of rhetoric but functions of the orator, on the ground that it is his business to invent, dispose, put into words, and so on. But if we accept this view, we shall leave nothing to art" (trans. D. A. Russell in LCL).

qualitatis); and the issue of judicial procedure: Does this court have jurisdiction? (*status translationis*).

(2) The transition from *inventio* to *dispositio* unfortunately poses a considerable problem. One would expect the division of the speech into different parts to be the special domain of the *dispositio* or τάξις, as in Aristotle and the later Cicero. However, the majority of our ancient authors place the speech's multipart structure already at the foundation in the *inventio* phase, and the modern handbooks have followed suit. H. Lausberg for example writes (§444):

> Although *dispositio* is listed as the second phase of treatment following *inventio* . . . , the temporal relationship between the phases is not such that they are clearly separated sequentially. Rather, *inventio* and *dispositio* are inseparably intertwined.

Lausberg devotes 90 pages to the *inventio* (§§260–442, pp. 119–208) in the light of the four-part speech model of *exordium*, *narratio*, *argumentatio*, and *peroratio* (see below), but reserves only six pages for the *dispositio* (§§443–53, pp. 209–14). The basic assumption behind this kind of presentation is that even the initial phase, the *inventio*, cannot be carried out except in a structured manner, because the individual parts of the speech require different procedures. The *dispositio* then only applies the macro structure already used for the *inventio* to the specific case (e.g., a court case) on which the speech is being prepared. One could also assign to the *dispositio* the task of *dissimulatio artis*, of erasing all traces of preliminary work, allowing the speech to appear as spontaneous and natural as possible—a considerable art. But none of these considerations speak against reserving the treatment of a speech's different parts for the *dispositio*. We therefore cover this in our next section.

(3) The doctrine of *elocutio* or "style" deals especially with what one might regard as the special adornments of an oration, including the tropes and all sorts of syntactic, semantic, or pragmatic figures of speech. This field, which forms a bridge to general stylistics, is well established in rhetoric. The *Rhetorica ad Herennium* dedicates by far its longest book to it (book 4), while Quintilian needs three books (books 8–10). In this terminologically complex area one meets not only with familiar concepts such as parallelism, antithesis, inclusio, chiasm, alliteration, metonymy,

metaphor, and comparison, but also with a whole range of obscure technical terms that even the expert is forced to look up. These include *systole*, "the shortening of what is really a long syllable (by shortening its long vowel)" (Lausberg §491); *gradatio*, a progressive elaboration of an anadiplosis, where an anadiplosis is repetition of the last member of a sequence of words at the beginning of the next (§623);[35] *parisosis* (also *isocolon*), "the coordinated juxtaposition of two or more colons . . . or commas," where the terms "colon" and "comma" refer to clauses and phrases, not punctuation marks (§719); *subiectio*, "a mock dialogue (and so a monologue) with question and answer" (§771); and *concilatio*, "a manner of argumentation . . . by which an argument of the opposing party is exploited for the benefit of one's own party" (§783).

c) The Four Parts of a Speech

In his *Rhetoric* 3.13–19 (see esp. 3.13.1–5), Aristotle stipulates that a forensic speech must always contain at least two main parts, a "statement of the case" (πρόθεσις), which later writers usually refer to as a "narrative" (διήγησις), and a "proof" (πίστις). These are often but not always framed by an introduction or "exordium" (προοίμιον) and a conclusion or "epilogue" (ἐπίλογος). From this there arose the canonical structure of the forensic speech, with possible variations such as dispensing with the exordium in the other genres. There are ideally four parts of an oration (*partes orationis*), whose standard Greek and Latin designations are below:

(1) προοίμιον, *exordium*, exordium or opening speech
(2) διήγησις, *narratio*, narrative or statement of the case
(3) πίστις, *argumentatio*, argument or proof
(4) ἐπίλογος, *peroratio*, peroration or effective conclusion

That a linguistic expression has a beginning and end—states its theme and then deals with it—is virtually self evident. This observation does not tell against the four-part rhetorical model but

---

[35] An example of anadiplosis in English: "Aboard my ship, excellent performance is standard. Standard performance is sub-standard. Substandard performance is not permitted to exist. That, I warn you." Delivered by Humphrey Bogart in the movie *The Canine Mutiny* (source: www.americanrhetoric.com).

rather helps explain its success. It is appropriate to its subject matter and also sufficiently flexible in its application.

The further potential parts of an oration mentioned by the ancient authors can be understood as an extension of the basic model rather than as a reason for abandoning it. The *argumentatio* can be further subdivided into a positive proof (*probatio, confirmatio*) and a refutation of opposing viewpoints (*confutatio, refutatio*). A *propositio* summarizes in thesis form the central thought of the *narratio* or sometimes also of the *exordium*, usually at the end of this larger section. A *divisio* or *partitio* outlines what will follow, in accordance with the issue already raised. The initial *exordium* can be formulated as a *captatio benevolentiae*, a fishing for goodwill among the listeners. A *digressio* (also *excessus*) is an excursus into another area. From these building blocks a five-part or even a seven- or eight-part model of a speech can be put together (cf. the tables in Lausberg 122–23; Aune, *Dictionary*, s.v. "Arrangement," 64). Quintilian decides in favor of five *partes* and leaves room for other possible combinations (*Inst.* 3.9.1):

> Most authorities give five "parts" of the [forensic] speech: Prooemium, Narrative, Proof, Refutatation, Epilogue (*prohoemium narratio probatio refutatio peroratio*). Some have added Partition, Proposition, Digression (*partitionem propositionem excessum*).

On the individual parts only the following remains to be said. Quintilian neatly explains the first element (*Inst.* 4.1.5):

> The reason for a Prooemium [or *exordium*] is simply to prepare the hearer to be more favourably inclined towards us for the rest of the proceedings. Most authors agree that there are three ways of doing this: by making him well disposed, attentive, and ready to learn (*benevolem attentum docilem*). . . . It is by means of this that we gain admission to the judge's mind.

The *narratio*, as its name suggests, has primarily the character of a narrative or report that arises naturally from the facts of a given case or incident.

In the *argumentatio* the speaker uses means of persuasion that can initially be divided into "natural" or "inartificial" (ἄτεχνοι) proofs that the speaker did not create but finds ready at his disposal, such as laws, witnesses, and contracts (cf. Aristotle, *Rhet.* 1.15), and "artificial" (ἔντεχνοι) proofs that the speaker must first invent through his own skills (cf. *Rhet.* 1.2). Among the "artificial" proofs, those which are rhetorical in the narrower sense, two deserve special mention, Aristotle's favorite "enthymeme" (ἐν-θύμημα) and his "example" (παράδειγμα). The enthymeme is a syllogism, sometimes a truncated one, in which one or more parts of the syllogism's formal three-part logic are left implied, so that the enthymeme is less exact and often works with the plausibilities of everyday life (cf. Sprute; Aune). Among the examples the historical ones are the most persuasive because people usually grant their truth. Nevertheless, this effect does not depend solely on the congruence of these examples with real events, but more on their familiarity through their fixed place in tradition and literature. In the areas of invented or non-historical examples, Aristotle mentions comparisons or fables, including those of Aesop (*Rhet.* 2.20.1–3, 5–8 [1393a 28–30; 1393b–1394a]). Finally, the division of proofs within the *argumentatio* into the three area of *ethos*, *pathos*, and *logos* also goes back to Aristotle: "Now the proofs furnished by the speech are of three kinds. The first depends on the moral character (ἤθος) of the speaker, the second upon putting the hearer into a certain frame of mind (διαθεῖναί πως), the third upon the speech itself (αὐτὸς ὁ λόγος), insofar as it proves or seems to prove" (*Rhet.* 1.2.3, cf. 4–6 [1356a]). *Ethos* refers to the trustworthy self-presentation established by the speaker or writer, and later also to the formulation of character sketches of the accused, the witnesses, and even the judge. *Pathos* is concerned with positively influencing the emotions of the audience: "The orator persuades by means of his hearers, when they are roused to emotion (πάθος) by his speech" (*Rhet.* 1.2.5). *Logos* involves the use of rational means (cf. Wörner 285–362).

Finally, the *peroratio* of an oration summarizes its main points one last time, with the aim of refreshing the memory and affecting the emotions. Hence Quintilian writes: "But here, if anywhere, we are allowed to release the whole flood of our eloquence" (*Inst.* 6.1.51).

Exercise

28. Analyze in terms of the four-part model of *exordium, narratio, argumentatio,* and *peroratio* the following two short speeches by famous orators whom we have also come to know as great letter writers, namely Demosthenes and Cicero: Demosthenes' oration *On the Peace (Or.* 5) and Cicero's oration for the poet Aulus Licinius Archias. Determine the rhetorical genre in each case. Texts may be found in J. H. Vince, *Demosthenes: Olynthiacs. Philippics. Minor Public Speeches. Speech against Leptines,* LCL, vol. 1 (1930) 101–19 and N. H. Watts, *Cicero, The Speeches: Pro Archia poeta. Post reditum in senatu. Post reditum ad quirites. De domo sua. De haruspicum responsis. Pro Planico,* LCL, vol. 11 (1923) 2–43.

3. Applications of Ancient Rhetoric in New Testament Scholarship

Bibliography 30: R. D. Anderson, Jr., *Ancient Rhetorical Theory* (Bib. 5). – **D. E. Aune,** *Dictionary* (Bib. 4), s.v. "Rhetorical criticism," 417–18 – **H. D. Betz,** "The Literary Composition and Function of Paul's Letter to the Galatians," *NTS* 21 (1975) 353–79. – idem, *Galatians* (Bib. 39). – **C. J. Classen,** "Paulus und die antike Rhetorik," *ZNW* 82 (1991) 1–32; revised and republished: "St Paul's Epistles and Ancient Greek and Roman Rhetoric," in S. E. Porter and T. H. Olbricht, *Rhetoric and the New Testament* (Bib. 5) 265–91. – **D. A. deSilva,** *4 Maccabees: Introduction and Commentary on the Greek Text in Codex Sinaiticus,* Septuagint Commentary Series 3 (Leiden 2006). – **D. Dormeyer,** *The New Testament* (Bib. 7) 205–13. – **G. A. Kennedy,** *New Testament Interpretation through Rhetorical Criticism* (Chapel Hill 1984). – **P. H. Kern,** *Rhetoric and Galatians: Assessing an Approach to Paul's Epistle,* SNTSMS 101 (Cambridge 1998). – **H. J. Klauck,** "4. Makkabäerbuch," in *Unterweisung in lehrhafter Form,* JSHRZ 3/6 (Gütersloh 1989) 645–763. – idem, "Zur rhetorischen Analyse der Johannesbriefe," *ZNW* 81 (1990) 204–24. – **B. W. Longenecker,** *Rhetoric at the Boundaries: The Art and Theology of the New Testament Chain-Link Transitions* (Waco, Tex. 2005). – **B. L. Mack,** *Rhetoric and the New Testament,* GBS (Minneapolis 1990). – **J. Murphy-O'Connor,** *Paul* (Bib. 4) 65–95. – **S. E. Porter,** "The Theoretical

Justification for Application of Rhetorical Categories to Pauline Epistolary Literature," in S. E. Porter and T. H. Olbricht, *Rhetoric and the New Testament* (Bib. 5) 100–122. – **J. T. Reed**, "Using Ancient Rhetorical Categories to Interpret Paul's Letters: A Question of Genre," ibid., 292–324. – **D. F. Watson**, "Rhetorical Criticism of the Pauline Epistles since 1975," *CurBS* 3 (1995) 219–48. – **D. F. Watson** and **A. J. Hauser**, *Bibliography* (Bib. 5). – **J. Weiss**, "Beiträge zur paulinischen Rhetorik," in C. R. Gregory, et al., *Theologische Studien*, FS B. Weiss (Göttingen 1897) 165–247. – **W. Wuellner**, "Der vorchristliche Paulus und die Rhetorik," in S. Lauer, *Tempelkult und Tempelzerstörung (70 n. Chr.)*, Judaica et Christiana 15 (Bern and New York 1994) 133–65. – Further literature in the surveys of the New Testament letters in chapter 7 and the detailed analyses in chapter 8.

The use of ancient rhetoric in New Testament exegesis reached an almost unprecedented low in the twentieth century. A disregard for rhetoric, also observable in other disciplines, and the dominance of other theological agendas help explain this. Where scholars still echoed a living tradition of "Pauline rhetoric" from the nineteenth century, as J. Weiss did in 1897, they usually had in mind stylistics, sentence structure, and rhetorical figures, especially parallelism and antithesis—in other words, *elocutio* and not rhetoric as a whole. This reduction of rhetoric to the area of stylistics and rhetorical flourishes has often been deplored in the meantime, but it is not so hard to understand: nowhere were such subjects more intensely discussed than in rhetoric. The application of *elocutio* to all kinds of texts is immediately enlightening and could hardly be an area for serious controversy. Therefore, the microanalysis of texts by rhetorical means will also remain a task for the future. The temptation here may be for scholars to describe every simple investigation of structure as "rhetorical" in order to give their work a glossy finish. One also suspects that rhetoric in this reduced sense may sometimes be used as an excuse for avoiding the demands of historical criticism.

Fortunately, the situation has changed fundamentally and radically over the last 30 years or so. This change was inspired in part by H. D. Betz's contributions on Galatians. Betz identifies the rhetorical genre of this letter as apologetic, which essentially means forensic, and discerns in its macrostructure the parts of a speech, reproduced in the framework of a letter: prescript (Gal 1:1-5), *exordium* (1:6-11), *narratio* (1:12–2:14), *propositio* (2:15-21), *probatio* (3:1–4:31), *exhortatio* (5:1–6:10), postscript (6:11-18). Even here the form of the letter already appears somewhat unwieldy, and therefore the criticism of Betz's proposal begins here and extends to the rhetorical genre, which other scholars have identified as deliberative or epideictic, and to the delimitation of the individual parts. The approach initiated by Betz has even become the topic of an entire dissertation (cf. Kern) that criticizes—probably too one-sidedly—the application of Greco-Roman "handbook rhetoric" to the New Testament letters.[36] But none of this changes the exciting character of Betz's advance. The detailed outline extending down to parts of individual verses,[37] which has sometimes been criticized as excessive formalism, I find to be definitely enlightening.

In the 1980s there followed, in addition to F. Siegert's application of the New Rhetoric of Perelman and Olbrechts-Tyteca to Romans 9–11,[38] a contribution by the American specialist in classical rhetoric G. A. Kennedy, *New Testament Interpretation through Rhetorical Criticism*. In this slender volume, of which one cannot demand too much in terms of methodological stringency (cf. Anderson 28–30), Kennedy develops a five-part model for the application of rhetorical criticism. This involves (1) delimitation of the rhetorical unit, (2) description of the rhetorical situation, (3) determination of the rhetorical genre, the problem, and the status, (4) analysis of *inventio, dispositio,* and *elocutio,* and (5) evaluation of the rhetoric: did it correspond to the task posed by the rhetorical situation, and was it successful or not? This method emphasizes working with the *inventio* and *dispositio.* The rhetorical unit for the analysis can be an entire letter or Gospel or only a section or chapter. But here lies one of the weaknesses that has yet to be adequately clarified: How can one justify applying a structural model developed from self-contained, complete speeches to individual chapters of a letter?

---

[36] For a balanced review of Kern's book that nevertheless warns against some of his overly categorical statements, see Fredrick J. Long, review of Philip H. Kern, *Rhetoric and Galatians: Assessing an Approach to Paul's Epistle,* in *Review of Biblical Literature* [http://www.bookreviews.org] (2000). See also (more critically) M. M. Mitchell in *JR* 80 (2000) 497–98.

[37] Cf. Betz, *Galatians,* 16–23.

[38] F. Siegert, *Argumentation* (Bib. 36).

In the meantime Kennedy's model, which leaves conspicuously little room for epistolographical considerations, has been applied in various ways to the New Testament letters, especially the shorter ones.[39] In the longer letters some of the parts have been subjected to a complete rhetorical analysis,[40] sometimes, though not always, with the aim of producing additional arguments for the composite letter hypothesis: when all the parts of a speech can be identified—for example, in 1 Corinthians 8–10[41] or 2 Corinthians 1–9[42]—there is a greater probability that these chapters represent an originally independent letter. But here some scholars have rightly urged caution (cf. Murphy-O'Connor 79–83), because the interchangeability of a speech and a letter is too self-evidently pre-supposed and the suspicion of circular reasoning cannot be easily dismissed.

The integration of rhetoric and epistolography continues to require considerable effort.[43] L. Thurén attempts to cut the Gordian knot.[44] He divides epistolographic and rhetorical analysis into two levels: epistolography concentrates on the "vehicle," the outward, formal constituents of letter writing. Rhetoric occupies the "higher" plane of persuasion. When Thurén goes so far as to compare the composition of a letter with the *pronuntiatio* or "delivery" of a speech, the violence this does to the letter form becomes apparent. This depreciation of epistolography is unacceptable, and the comparison of letter writing with the *pronuntiatio* does not even hold from the standpoint of rhetoric.[45]

---

[39] For details see the literature survey and bibliography of Watson; further chap. 7 and 8 below.

[40] Cf. Mack 56–66 on 1 Cor 15; 2 Cor 9; 1 Cor 9 and 1 Cor 13 or D. F. Watson, "Paul's Rhetorical Strategy in 1 Corinthians 15," in S. E. Porter and T. H. Olbricht, *Rhetoric and the New Testament* (Bib. 5) 231–49.

[41] Cf. H. Probst, *Paulus und der Brief* (Bib. 37).

[42] Cf. H. M. Wünsch, *Der paulinische Brief* (Bib. 38).

[43] On 1 Corinthians see the not entirely satisfying attempt of M. Bünker, *Briefformular* (Bib. 37); considerably better is M. M. Mitchell, *Paul* (Bib. 37).

[44] L. Thurén, *Rhetorical Strategy* (Bib. 48).

[45] Thurén also makes inaccurate statements elsewhere, e.g., 64 n. 97: "A. Malherbe (1977) has gathered illustrative texts to show how much ancient rhetoricians were occupied with letter writing theory"—almost exactly the opposite is true.

We cannot attempt to write the history of the last three decades of rhetorical analysis of letters here. But we can summarize our impressions so far: A practically mechanical application of the classical four-part speech model to letters and letter components is more likely to discredit rhetorical analysis than to promote it. Rhetorical analysis must not be pursued at the expense of the unique features of the letter genre that epistolography has helped us understand. Inflated use of the term "rhetoric" should be avoided and the scope of its applicability precisely determined and stated. The division of rhetoric into several subdisciplines should also be kept in mind. If these boundaries are respected, then obviously rhetoric can be of great value in illuminating the argumentative structure of letters—for example, by working through enthymemes and examples or by relating the letter elements to the classical means of persuasion by ethos, pathos, and logos. The rhetorical analysis of smaller linguistic units such as tropes and figures of speech can also be applied to letters.

B. W. Longenecker (*Rhetoric at the Boundaries*) has recently demonstrated how fruitful such study of the more intricate techniques can be by calling attention to a neglected rhetorical device that he calls the "chain-link interlock" and finds in Old Testament and extrabiblical Jewish literature as well as in the New Testament and rhetorical theory (e.g., Quintilian). The figure marks the transition between two themes by treating the first theme fully (A), anticipating the next theme briefly (b), recapitulating the first briefly (a), then treating the second theme fully (B), so that the A–a and b–B themes overlap at the point of transition: A–b/a–B. With the thematic boundary marked by the virgule (/), there is therefore a "b" in A's territory (where some interpreters might think it does not belong), and an "a" extending into B's territory. If ovals are drawn around the A–a and the b–B elements in the A–b/a–B figure, the result is a visual overlap that produces a "chain link."

Longenecker's convincing application of this figure to the relationship of Romans 7:14-25 and Romans 8:1-39 (pp. 88–93) may be studied as a rhetorical solution that also has significant theological implications. For it undercuts the traditional Augustinian and Reformed claim that the agonized "I" and the present-tense verbs of 7:14-25 represent Paul's own present experience as a Christian, as well as the experience he regards as normal for other Christians. On this reading, the more "optimistic" Romans 8 is only one side of Christian experience, the other side of which is the supposedly more "realistic" Romans 7. Such an interpretation of Romans 7 and 8 is possible only when Romans 7:25a, "Thanks be to God through Jesus Christ our Lord" (which answers to the question: "Who will rescue me from this body of death?" in 7:24), is taken thematically to belong to chapter 7, the "A" theme, and therefore to imply that the "I" there must already be a Christian. However, in Longenecker's view, Rom 7:25a is precisely the small "b" of the overlapped transition and therefore looks forward to chapter 8 rather than backward to chapter 7. It anticipates the large "B," the Spirit-led Christian life of Romans 8, while Rom 7:25b, "So then, with my mind I am a slave to the law of God, but with my flesh I am a slave to the law of sin," represents the small "a" that recapitulates the "A" theme of the "wretched man" (Rom 7:14-24). Small "a" also signals that the "A–a" theme is now concluded, which would be especially helpful to an audience listening to Paul's text being read. The text's A–b/a–B structure therefore consists of *7:14-24* (*7:25a*) / (*7:25b*) **8:1-39**, keeping 7:14-24 and 8:1-39 quite distinct. It is also notable that the "I" language is dropped in chapter 8 and that the original manuscript reading of the singular pronoun in 8:2 is probably not the first-person "me" (με), as in the RSV, but the second-person "you" (σε), as in the NRSV: "The law of the Spirit of life in Christ Jesus has set *you* (sg.) free from the law of sin and death." This addresses the "I" of Romans 7 more distantly as "you" to show the distinction between the new identity and the old.

One question that continues to be raised concerns the education level of our New Testament letter writers. Did Paul, the writer to the Hebrews, and the rest of the New Testament authors learn the rules of rhetoric in school, so that they will have applied them self-consciously in their writing? We can most nearly answer this question in the affirmative for the author of Hebrews, otherwise we must register our reservations. That Greco-Roman rhetoric was used in Diaspora Judaism is beyond doubt in the light of the indisputable examples of 4 Maccabees (cf. Klauck; deSilva) and Philo of Alexandria. But Paul and the authors of the Catholic Epistles lag somewhat behind this education level. Yet this does not make recourse to classical rhetoric useless. The New Testament letter writers could have taken over some of the rhetorical features of their letters more subconsciously by imitation, through their confronting texts and a culture bearing a rhetorical stamp, and with the purpose of arguing persuasively in their own rhetorical situation.[46]

---

[46] Cf. the comment of P. Bürgel, *Der Privatbrief* (Bib. 8) 285 n. 18: "The intentionality of both the 'letter' and of 'rhetoric' meet in the phe-

Moreover, the analytical instrument used for studying ancient writings need not have come from ancient times or have been known to the original producers of the texts, otherwise the use of the New Rhetoric would not be justified at all. Modern scholars only need to state this clearly enough as a premise.

The question of the importance and relevance of rhetoric must finally be decided by working with individual texts. We therefore return to this question in the discussion of New Testament texts in chapter 7 and especially in chapter 8.

Exercises

29. Use the relevant elements of the four-part speech model to structure the second letter of Demosthenes. Text and translation in N. W. and N. J. DeWitt, *Demosthenes: Funeral Speech (60). Erotic Essay (61). Exordia. Letters*, LCL, vol. 7 (1949) 208–25. Translation also available in J. A. Goldstein, *The Letters of Demosthenes* (Bib. 2) 195–200.

30. Perform a rhetorical analysis of 2 and 3 John. Determine their rhetorical genre, their structure according to the standard four-part speech model, and their figures of speech. As a study aid, you may use the two articles on "Rhetorical Analysis" by D. F. Watson in Bibliography 11.

---

nomenon of the *persuasio*. However, this must be thought of as a nonreflective, quasi-subconscious rhetoric, not as the kind of rhetoric that arises from consciously following learned rules."

6

Letters in Early Judaism

Outside a few cross-references we have so far passed over not only early Christianity but also Judaism. Christianity originated as a reform movement within Judaism, and its letter writers wrote against a Jewish background. Greek and Roman literary forms and thought patterns were mediated to the early Christian writers to a great extent through their reception in Judaism. Some peculiarities of early Christian letters can also be traced to Jewish roots. We must therefore turn our attention to the Jewish letter tradition.

The format of this chapter resembles that of chapter 4 on the Greek and Roman literary letters. We begin with a non-exhaustive overview of the relevant material and then proceed to analyze several case studies in more detail.

A. Overview

Bibliography 31: P. S. Alexander, "Epistolary Literature" (Bib. 3). – **D. E. Aune**, *Literary Environment* (Bib. 4) 174–80. – **G. Beer**, "Zur israelitisch-jüdischen Briefliteratur," in A. Alt et al., *Alttestamentliche Studien*, FS R. Kittel, BWANT 13 (Leipzig 1913) 20–41. – **K. Berger**, "Apostelbrief" (Bib. 4). – **P. E. Dion**, "Les types épistolaires hébréo-araméens jusqu'au temps de Bar-Kokhbah," *RB* 86 (1979) 544–79. – **J. A. Fitzmyer**, "Aramaic Epistolography" (Bib. 3). – **J.-D. Gauger**, *Authentizität* (Bib. 2) 103–6, 205–10. – **M. Karrer**, *Johannesoffenbarung* (Bib. 4) 48–83. – **J. M. Lindenberger**, *Ancient Aramaic and Hebrew Letters*, SBLWAW 4 (Atlanta ²2003). – **D. Pardee**, *Handbook* (Bib. 3). – **D. Schwiderski**, *Handbuch des nordwestsemitischen Briefformulars* (Bib. 3). – **I. Taatz**, *Frühjüdische Briefe* (Bib. 3). – **A. Wagner,** ed., *Bote und Brief: Sprachliche Systeme der Informationsübermittlung im Spannungsfeld von Mündlichkeit und Schriftlichkeit*, Nordostafrikanisch/Westasiatische

Studien 4 (Frankfurt a.M. 2003). – **M. F. Whitters**, "Some New Observations about Jewish Festal Letters," *JSJ* 32 (2001) 272–88.

1. The Septuagint

For the letters in the Old Testament we will follow the Greek version (including its sometimes divergent verse numbering), since it is closer to the New Testament both linguistically and chronologically. This also applies to the added documents (e.g., 1–3 Maccabees) and the expansions of canonical books (e.g., Esther) in the Septuagint that are not part of the Hebrew Bible. In the older narrative literature we find only letter fragments embedded within a literary framework that includes the sender and the addressee (i.e., references to letters or brief quotations). But the more recent documents increasingly incorporate the letters as a whole (embedded letters). The texts from Kings and Chronicles will also allow us to illustrate the transition from the oral messenger to the written letter. Where Flavius Josephus has mentioned Old Testament letters we will integrate his use of this material into our overview and highlight his interpretive accents.

a) Samuel, Kings, and Chronicles

2 Samuel (2 Kgdms LXX) 11:14-15. David's letter (βιβλίον) about Uriah the Hittite to his general Joab has become a byword. This letter effectively sent Uriah, who inconveniently happened to be the husband of Bathsheba, to the front lines to die in battle. As the height of irony, David has this death warrant delivered by Uriah himself. Obviously an oral message would not do in this situation, which required a sealed letter. David's seal is not mentioned in the Bible but is highlighted by Josephus (*Ant.* 7.135–37).

1 Kings 21:8-10 (3 Kgdms 20:8-10). In the course of the dispute between King Ahab and Naboth about Naboth's vineyard in Jezreel, which he refused to sell to the king, Ahab's wife Jezebel wrote a letter (βιβλίον sg. for Heb. pl. סְפָרִים) in the king's name to the elders of Jezreel, asking them to stir up false charges against Naboth and stone him to death, which they do. The equivalence of the written and oral message is brought out in the aftermath in vv. 14-15: after honoring the request of Jezebel's letter, the elders "sent" (sc. an oral messenger) back to her, "saying" that Naboth had been stoned according to plan, and Jezebel "heard" their message.

2 Kings (4 Kgdms) 5:5-7. The king of Syria gives his general Naaman the Syrian a letter (βιβλίον) to take along to Jehoram king of Israel in his search for a cure for his leprosy. (The king of Israel is upset by the letter's request of a cure because he cannot provide it, but Naaman is later healed by following the instructions of Elisha to dip seven times in the Jordan.)

2 Kings (4 Kgdms) 10:1-8. The extermination of Ahab's line as represented in his seventy sons is brought about by a first and a second letter (βιβλίον) from King Jehu to the leaders of Samaria, who were the guardians of these sons: they kill them after the second letter. While each letter is answered by an oral messenger to Jehu in the biblical account, in Josephus *Ant.* 9.125–27 the Samaritans write back to Jehu.

2 Kings (4 Kgdms) 19:9-14. The Assyrian king Sennacherib sends messengers with instructions to Hezekiah to surrender Jerusalem. Sennacherib's message, contained in vv. 10-13, is introduced in v. 10 with a typically oral emissary formula, "*Thus* shall you *speak* to King Hezekiah of Judah" (Heb. כֹּה תֹאמְרוּן; Gk. lacks the literal translation οὕτως ἐρεῖτε). Nevertheless, the apparent orality was also put into writing, for v. 14 says: "And Hezekiah took the *letter* (τὰ βιβλία) from the hand of the messengers and read it; and he went up to the house of the Lord, and Hezekiah spread it before the Lord." Cf. Josephus, *Ant.* 10.15-16.

2 Kings (4 Kgdms) 20:12. The king of Babylon is said to have sent letters (βιβλία) and a present to Hezekiah because he had heard that Hezekiah had been sick; the letters are not quoted or excerpted.

2 Chronicles 2:10-15 LXX (vv. 11-16 ET). In 2 Chron 2:2-9 we are told that Solomon "sent" (ἀπέστειλεν, v. 2) his request for timber and an artisan to help build the temple to King Hiram of Tyre, apparently through a messenger without a letter. But in response Hiram clearly answers Solomon in "in writing" (v. 10: ἐν γραφῇ, בִּכְתָב; cf. NJPS). Although this letter might appear to begin in v. 10b with Hiram's assurance to Solomon that God has made him king because God loves Israel, it probably begins in v. 11 with Hiram's eulogy: "Blessed be the Lord, the God of Israel." First Kings and Josephus have different presentations, and the three taken together illustrate the historical transition from oral to written messages. According to 1 Kings 5:15 LXX (ET 5:1), Hiram first "sent his servants" to Solomon with an oral message of congratulations on his accession to the throne.[1] Thereafter the two kings exchange a pair of messages through oral messengers, without any mention of letters (5:16-20 Solomon; 5:22-23 Hiram [ET 5:2-6, 8-9]). From this 2 Chronicles takes a step forward with Solomon asking orally and Hiram responding in writing. Josephus completes the development in *Ant.* 8.50–57 with both kings writing extended letters. Solomon initiates with his letter (§§51–52) and Hiram responds (53–54). Josephus then uses the fact of the written and archived nature of this correspondence to underscore the veracity of his report (*Ant.* 8.55–56; cf. also *Apion* 1.111):

> To this day there remain copies of these letters, preserved not only in our books but also by the Tyrians, so that if anyone wished to learn the exact truth, he would, by inquiring of the public officials in charge of the archive of the Tyrians (τῶν ἐπὶ τοῦ Τυρίων γραμματο-φυλακείου δημοσίων), find that their records are in agreement with what we have said. These things I have given in detail because I wish my readers to know that we have said nothing more than what is

---

[1] In 1 Kings 5:15 LXX Hiram's support for the new king is expressed in part through his servants' anointing of Solomon, a detail which is lacking in 2 Chronicles (but see 1 Chron 29:22) and which comes out differently in the Hebrew. The MT of 5:15 reads: "King Hiram of Tyre sent his officials to Solomon when he heard that *he had been anointed king* in place of his father" (NJPS). But in the LXX this anointing is performed not by the Israelites but by Hiram's servants: καὶ ἀπέστειλεν Χιραμ βασιλεὺς Τύρου τοὺς παῖδας αὐτοῦ χρῖσαι τὸν Σαλωμων, "And Hiram king of Tyre sents his servants to anoint Solomon." This is doubtless the original Old Greek reading, over against which the Origenic recension (siglum: *O*) is an obvious correction toward the Hebrew: καὶ ἀπέστειλεν Χιραμ βασιλεὺς Τύρου τοὺς παῖδας αὐτοὺς πρὸς Σαλωμων, ἤκουσεν γὰρ ὅτι αὐτὸν ἔχρισαν εἰς βασιλέα, where the subject of ἔχρισαν is once again the Israelites.

true, and have not, by inserting into the history various plausible and seductive passages meant to deceive and entertain, attempted to evade critical inquiry.

2 Chronicles 21:12-15. King Joram (Heb. Jehoram) receives a letter (ἐγγραφή: only here in the LXX) from the prophet Elijah with an announcement of judgment that does not conform to epistolary convention but begins in the style of a judgment oracle: "Thus says the Lord, the God of your father David." Cf. Josephus, *Ant.* 9.99–101 (in indirect instead of direct discourse).

2 Chronicles 30:1. Hezekiah sent messengers to Israel and Judah and wrote letters (ἐπιστολὰς ἔγραψεν)[2] especially to Ephraim and Manasseh with the invitation to come to Jerusalem for Passover (v. 1). Messengers are then said to have carried these and additional letters from the king and the rulers to all Israel and Judah, where they also delivered an oral summons to return to the Lord (vv. 6-9).

b) Ezra, Nehemiah, and 1 Esdras

J. **Becker**, *Esra; Nehemia*, NEchtB (Würzburg 1990). – **D. J. A. Clines**, "1 Esdras," in W. A. Meeks, ed., *The HarperCollins Study Bible* (New York 1993). – **J. M. Myers**, *Ezra. Nehemiah*, AB 14 (Garden City, N.Y. 1965). – idem, *I and II Esdras*, AB 42 (Garden City, N.Y. 1974); here *II Esdras* (Vulgate numbering) = *4 Ezra* (*OTP*): see n. 3 below. – **K. F. Pohlmann**, "3. Esra-Buch," in *Historische und legendarische Erzählungen*, JSHRZ 1/5 (Gütersloh 1980) 375–425. – **D. Schwiderski**, *Handbuch des nordwestsemitischen Briefformulars* (Bib. 3) 343–82.

Note on book names: In the LXX the canonical books of Ezra and Nehemiah are combined as 2 Esdras and are numbered consecutively: Ezra = 2 Esdras 1–10; Nehemiah = 2 Esdras 11–23. Distinct from this is the LXX book of 1 Esdras, also sometimes called 3 Esdras (e.g., Pohlmann), after its name in the Vulgate appendix. It is neither one of the Roman Catholic Deuterocanonical books nor one of the traditional

---

[2] In the Old Testament books of pre-exilic history (Samuel, Kings, Chronicles) our familiar term ἐπιστολή occurs only here (2 Chron 30:1, 6). However, it is more frequent in the canonical books of Ezra (4x) and Nehemiah (6x) (i.e., LXX 2 Esdras), in LXX 1 Esdras (6x), and in Esther with its Greek additions (7x).

pseudepigrapha (hence not included in *OTP*). But because it is in the Greek and Slavonic Bibles (and in the Vulgate appendix) it is included in the extended "canon" of the NRSV, under its Septuagintal name 1 Esdras.[3] The book largely consists of parallels to 2 Chronicles 35–36, canonical Ezra, and Nehemiah 7–8; the only extensive unparalleled material is 1 Esdras 3:1–5:6, a contest between three Jewish bodyguards of the Persian king Darius, one of whom is Zerubbabel. Some of the letters in Ezra and Nehemiah were originally written in Aramaic.

1 Esdras 2:15-25. A parallel to the canonical Ezra (2 Esdras) 4:6–24 that has been abbreviated at the beginning. See below.

1 Esdras 4:47-63. The Persian king Darius gives Zerubbabel the necessary letters (ἐπιστολάς) for the rebuilding of Jerusalem (v. 47). He similarly writes letters on behalf of all the Jews who are returning to Judea. The content of these letters is not quoted but summarized, principally through the infinitive of indirect discourse.[4]

1 Esdras 6:7-21 LXX (vv. 7-22 NRSV). A parallel tradition to Ezra 5:6-17 (2 Esdras in LXX), on which see further below. As Zerubbabel is restarting the work of rebuilding the temple during the reign of the Persian king Darius, he is opposed among others by Sisinnes (Ezra: Tattenai), the governor of Syria and Phoenicia

---

[3] Not to be confused with any of these versions or numberings of canonical Ezra and Nehemiah or with the biblically based compendium in 1 Esdras LXX is the sixteen-chapter NRSV book of *2 Esdras* = pseudepigraphical *4 Ezra* (so *OTP*). Unlike the Septuagintal 2 Esdras (Ezra–Nehemiah) and 1 Esdras, NRSV 2 Esdras is not a Septuagintal book at all but, for the most part (i.e., chapters 3–14), a Jewish apocalypse preserved in Latin. The name 2 Esdras derives from the first line of some Latin manuscripts, "The *second* book of the prophet Ezra" (so *OTP*; not in NRSV), but this strictly applies only to the first two chapters (also called *5 Ezra*), which are a Christian composition within this composite work. The sixteen-chapter work exists as such only in Latin, and the whole of it is sometimes called *4 Ezra* for convenience, though this properly applies only to the Jewish apocalypse, chapters 3–14. See further B. M. Metzger in *OTP* 1:516–59.

[4] See, e.g., the use of μὴ ἐπελεύσεσθαι (v. 49), ὑπάρξειν (vv. 50, 53), δοθῆναι (v. 51), and δοῦναι (vv. 55, 56). Similar content is also summarized in ἵνα clauses (e.g., vv. 47, 50).

(1 Esd 6:3-7). First Esdras 6:8-21 LXX (6:8-22 NRSV) preserves a copy of the letter (ἐπιστολή) that Sisinnes and his associates sent to Darius, mentioning the Jewish elders' claim about the edict of Cyrus, which ordered the rebuilding of the temple (cf. 1 Esd. 2:3-7), and asking Darius whether Cyrus's decree was in the royal archives. Interesting differences exist between this and the version in Ezra. Whereas 1 Esdras begins the letter in standard Greek fashion with Βασιλεῖ Δαρείῳ χαίρειν, "To King Darius, greetings" (1 Esd 6:8), the formulation in canonical Ezra is more Jewish, with the ancient Near Eastern peace wish that we later find in Paul: Δαρείῳ τῷ βασιλεῖ εἰρήνη πᾶσα, "To Darius the king, *all peace*" (Ezra 5:7). After receiving this letter, Darius finds the edict of Cyrus and writes a letter back to Sisinnes and his associates, ordering them to allow the building of the temple. This letter is found in 1 Esdras 6:27-30, 32-33, with v. 31 being in indirect discourse (vv. 28-31, 33-34 NRSV), and the parallel version is found in Ezra 6:6-12. It might at first appear that Ezra's version of Darius's letter starts abruptly in 6:6, with no transitional sentence to introduce it after the end of the quoted Cyrus edict in 6:5, whereas 1 Esdras 6:26 (6:27 NRSV) seems to prepare better for its version of the letter by means of a preface, stating indirectly that "Darius commanded Sisinnes the governor [and his associates] . . . to keep away from the place, and to permit Zerubbabel . . . and the elders of the Jews to build this house of the Lord on its site," followed by the letter with Darius's direct discourse, "And I command," etc. But this is only a formal difference, for all this content is already included within the letter itself in Ezra's version (cf. 6:6-7).[5]

Ezra MT (2 Esdras LXX) 4:6-24. Opponents of the Jewish return to Jerusalem write letters to the Persian kings Ahasuerus (i.e., Xerxes, 4:6) and Artaxerxes (cf. 4:7). The latter letter, contained in Ezra 4:11b-16, is written in Aramaic by Rehum, one of Artaxerxes' deputies west of the Euphrates, and by a scribe named

---

[5] A comparison of 1 Esdras 6:26 with Ezra 6:6-7 and of 1 Esdras 6:31 (6:32 NRSV) with Ezra 6:11 reveals that it is mainly the negative elements that are quoted directly in Ezra's version of Darius's letter but summarized indirectly in 1 Esdras: Darius's restraining order against Sisinnes (Ezra: Tattenai) and his associates, and his threat of death by impalement to any who hinder the rebuilding of the temple.

Shimshai. In a reversal of the standard Greek letter formula the recipient of this letter is named first (addressed with πρός), while the identification of the senders follows in the nominative: Πρὸς Αρθασασθα βασιλέα παῖδες σου ἄνδρες πέραν τοῦ ποταμοῦ, "To Artaxerxes the king: Your servants, the men (sc. of the province) Beyond the River" (v. 11b). The letter of the king's servants in vv. 11b-16 is answered by the king in vv. 17-22. In the Greek, Artaxerxes' answer is introduced summarily rather than in quotation: "Then the king sent to Rehum the commander and Shimshai the scribe and the rest of their fellow-servants who lived in Samaria and the rest (sc. in the province) Beyond the River (sc. his greeting of) *peace*, and he said," etc. But after this the Greek text departs significantly from the Aramaic, replacing the two occurrences of the Aramaic נִשְׁתְּוָן, "letter," in vv. 18 and 23 by the Greek φορολόγος, which can hardly refer to a letter in the context of the Greek. Yet this unusual word is not easy to define.

According to the Greek lexica, s.v. φορολόγος (LEH; LSJ; cf. Brenton's LXX translation), in contrast to the Aramaic "The *letter* that you sent to us has been read in translation before me" (v. 18), we should rather understand the Greek to mean, "The *tax-collector* (φορολόγος) whom you sent to us has been called before me" (ὁ φορολόγος ὃν ἀπεστείλατε πρὸς ἡμᾶς ἐκλήθη ἔμπροσθεν ἐμοῦ). If this translation is correct, then the φορολόγος will have "carried" (cf. φέρειν) both taxes and a letter to Artaxerxes. But since the collection of current taxes is not mentioned in the context (there is only a warning to Artaxerxes that the Jews will not pay taxes in the future if the temple is rebuilt [v. 13] and a historical note that powerful Israelite kings of old used to collect taxes [v. 20]), it is hard to know why a translator would consciously choose this meaning. If, however, the Jewish-Greek translator understood φορολόγος purely etymologically, then this would designate the emissary literally as a "word carrier" and therefore a "letter carrier," which better fits the context.[6]

---

[6] The above treatment corrects a small but regrettable linguistic error in the original German version of this book. It might be conceivable etymologically to understand a letter itself as a φορολόγος or "word carrier" (German: *Wortträger*), so that a letter would stand behind both terms נִשְׁתְּוָן and φορολόγος in Ezra 4:18, 23, as suggested in the German edition, *Die antike Briefliteratur und das Neue Testament* (Paderborn 1998) 184: "Die Briefe heißen in V. 18 und V. 23 φορολόγος, 'Wortträger.'" Yet while this *translation* of φορολόγος is acceptable, its *reference* is not, since it yields a

In any case two φορολόγοι or "letter carriers" are mentioned, one sent by Rehum and Shimshai to Artaxerxes, and Artaxerxes' own φορολόγος sent in return. Artaxerxes receives the former: "He has been called before me" (Ezra 4:18 LXX). The latter travels to Jerusalem and reads Artaxerxes' letter of response to the recipients: "Then the letter carrier (φορολόγος) of King Artaxerxes read (sc. the letter) before Rehum and Shimshai the scribe," etc. Cf. Josephus, *Ant.* 11.27-30.

Ezra (2 Esdras) 5:6-17. Tattenai (= Sisinnes in 1 Esdras), the governor of the Persian province Beyond the River, inquires of King Darius in writing whether the postexilic people of Jerusalem really have the permission they claim to have to rebuild the temple (cf. above on 1 Esdras 6:7-21). A complete copy of the "letter" (ἐπιστολή, v. 6, Aram. אִגְּרָה) or "report" (ῥῆσις, v. 7a) that Tattenai and other Persian officials sent to Darius is included in vv. 7b-17. The king's affirmative answer by letter in Ezra 6:6-12 follows the consultation of the royal archives in 6:1-5, where a copy of the edict of Cyrus for the rebuilding of the Jerusalem temple is found. Josephus transforms this edict and its parallels into a formal letter from Cyrus to his satraps in *Ant.* 11.12–18, incorporating first materials from the original edict in Ezra 1:1-4 addressing the Jewish people, then from the differently worded copy of the edict in Ezra 6:2-5 focusing on the temple dimensions, then also from the list of temple vessels in Ezra 1:9—or perhaps from the parallels in 1 Esdras of all these accounts (as evidenced, for example, by Josephus's use of the name Sisinnes rather than Tattenai). One consequence of this presentation is that in the later letters from the Samaritans to Darius, Darius to Sisinnes, and Darius to the Samaritans in *Ant.* 11.97–119, the material from the letter in *Ant.* 11.12–18 is sometimes expanded upon but partly also repeated.

---

plausible sense only if the proposed reference of φορολόγος to the two letters to and from Artaxerxes is transported back into the Aramaic sentences. It does not work in the Greek sentences, for it would be odd to speak in Ezra 4:18 of a letter being "called before" (ἐκλήθη ἔμπροσθεν) the king, and impossible to say that a letter or φορολόγος "read," ἀνέγνω (rather than "was read," ἀνεγνώσθη) the letter of Artaxerxes in Ezra 4:23.

Ezra (2 Esdras) 7:11-26. An ordinance or commandment (διά-ταγμα) of King Artaxerxes (Heb. has נִשְׁתְּוָן, "letter") in the form of a letter to Ezra, with an embedded decree (γνώμη) in vv. 21-26. Cf. Josephus, *Ant.* 11.122–30.

Nehemiah 2:7-10 (2 Esdras 12:7-10). At Nehemiah's request Artaxerxes gives him letters of safe passage to the governors of the province Beyond the River; one might think of letters of recommendation. Cf. Josephus, *Ant.* 11.166–68.

Nehemiah 6:1-19 (2 Esdras 16:1-19). After multiple journeys by his messengers produced no result, Sanballat, as representative of the Jews' enemies, finally sent one of his servants (on the fifth try according to the MT) with a letter. As Nehemiah reports: "Then Sanballat sent his servant to me with an open letter in his hand" (v. 5; cf. the letter in vv. 6-7). In vv. 17-19 the Jews' enemies led by Sanballat the Horonite and Tobiah the Ammonite exchange "many letters" with members of the Jewish nobility who were likewise opposed to Nehemiah (and from whom Tobiah could expect allegiance through marriage ties). Tobiah himself also sends intimidating letters to Nehemiah.

c) Esther

H. Bardtke, "Zusätze zu Esther," in *Historische und legendarische Erzählungen*, JSHRZ 1/1 (1973) 15–62. – **G. Gerlemann**, *Esther*, BKAT 21 (Neukirchen-Vluyn ²1982).

Note: The full text of Greek Esther is translated in the Apocrypha section of the NRSV.

Esther 3:13a-g LXX = 13:1-7 NRSV Greek Esther (cf. Esth 3:12-15 in MT and NRSV canonical Esther). Haman has a letter written in the name of King Artaxerxes containing instructions for the extermination of the Jews. The MT relates only the process of writing and sending the letter and gives a summary of its contents ("Letters were sent . . . giving orders to destroy, to kill, and to annihilate all Jews," etc. [3:13]), but no direct quotation. Therefore the Greek translator takes advantage of this gap to compose a text for the letter, consisting of seven verses. Traditionally called Addition B, this Greek letter is inserted between the canonical Esther 3:13 and 3:14 in both Rahlfs's

Septuaginta (added verse numbers: 3:13a-g) and the NRSV of Greek Esther (added verse numbers: 13:1-7). The prescript connects the sender ("The Great King, Artaxerxes") and the addressees ("to the governors and the officials under them," etc.) with a phrase patterned on that of an oral messenger, hence "thus *writes* Artaxerxes" (τάδε γράφει) instead of "thus *says* . . ." (τάδε λέγει)—an innovation retained in Josephus, *Ant.* 11.215–20.

Esther 8:7-12 + 12a–x LXX = 16:1-21 NRSV Greek Esther (Addition E). In Esther 8:7-12 Esther and Mordecai are invited to publish an edict of toleration for the Jews bearing the royal seal and to have it delivered by the famous Persian post (see above pp. 61–62). The text of the letter-edict, Greek Addition E, is numbered Esther 8:12a–x in the LXX and 16:1-21 in the NRSV (placed after 8:12). It includes the usual χαίρειν in the prescript. Cf. Josephus, *Ant.* 11.270–88.

Esther 9:20-32. The festival of Purim is introduced by a letter (ἐπιστολή, v. 26) or book (βιβλίον, v. 20, cf. NRSV, "in a book") by Mordecai that is sent to all the Jews of the Persian empire. The content of the letter is reported but not directly quoted (so also Josephus, *Ant.* 11.293–94). Esther also adds her own written confirmation (στερέωμα) of the letter about Purim (v. 29).

Esther 11:1. Addition F, which concludes Greek Esther, is numbered 10:4–11:1 in the NRSV and 10:3a–l in the LXX. In Esther 11:1 (10:3 *l*) *the entire book of Esther* is identified as a "Letter about Purim." The tradition of Jewish festival letters is beginning to emerge.

d) The Books of the Maccabees

What has already begun to emerge in Ezra-Nehemiah and Esther comes to full expression in the books of the Maccabees: Here the Jewish letters connect up with the tradition of Hellenistic royal letters (see chap. 3, sec. C) and particularly with the type in which epistolary edicts appear as attachments in historical and narrative works. There is obviously more opportunity for forgery of such documents in literary works than in the inscriptions. Therefore the question of authenticity is always in the background, and the various answers to it often reflect a deep underlying controversy.

First Maccabees

K. D. Schunk, "1. Makkabäerbuch," in *Historische und legendarische Erzählungen*, JSHRZ 1/4 (Gütersloh 1980) 287–373. – J. A. Goldstein, *I Maccabees*, AB 41 (New York 1976). – J.-D. Gauger, *Authentizität* (Bib. 2) 261f.

1 Maccabees 5:9-15. The Israelites in Gilead fled to a stronghold from the Gentiles who were trying to destroy them. From there they sent a letter calling for help (v. 10: ἀπέστειλαν γράμματα) to Judas Maccabeus and his brothers (vv. 10-13). While this letter is being read other messengers arrive from Galilee with a similar report (vv. 14-15). Cf. Josephus, *Ant.* 12.331–32.

1 Maccabees 8:22-32. Although this is a paper copy of the *treaty* (not a letter) detailing the alliance between the Roman senate and the Jewish people, originally written on bronze tablets, in v. 22 it is nevertheless called "a copy of the *letter*" (ἀντίγραφον τῆς ἐπιστολῆς).

1 Maccabees 9:60. Bacchides the Syrian "secretly sent letters to all his allies in Judea."

1 Maccabees 10:1-21. The Seleucid ruler Demetrius I Soter offers terms of peace to Jonathan the Hasmonean in a letter (v. 3). Jonathan reads it to the people of Jerusalem (v. 7). After this Demetrius's competitor for power, Alexander Balas, writes his own letter to Jonathan, whom he addresses as "brother" (cf. Goldstein 400: "a mere flattering form"), appointing Jonathan as high priest and giving him the title "the king's Friend" (vv. 17-20). On this letter see Josephus, *Ant.* 13.44-46.

1 Maccabees 10:25-45. Demetrius I renews his offer to the Jews in an extended letter. Cf. Josephus, *Ant.* 13.47-57.

1 Maccabees 11:29-37. Demetrius II Nicator writes Jonathan a letter (ἐπιστολάς in v. 29; the plural is often used in the sense of the singular, as here; cf., e.g., Josephus, *Ant.* 12.225). Following the prescript "King Demetrius to his brother Jonathan, greetings" (v. 30), Demetrius merely quotes a copy of a letter he had sent to one of his advisors, Lasthenes, called his "kinsman" and "father" in the text, but only honorifically (vv. 31-37). Cf. Josephus, *Ant.* 13.125–28.

1 Maccabees 11:57. A very brief message of the young Antiochus VI Epiphanes to Jonathan.

1 Maccabees 12:1-23. Jonathan sends envoys to Rome and letters to Sparta and other places in order to renew friendships. The text of the letter to Sparta, addressed from collective to collective— "The high priest Jonathan, the senate of the nation, the priests, and the rest of the Jewish people (δῆμος) to their brothers the Spartans, greetings"—is given in full (vv. 6-18). It immediately refers in vv. 7-8 to a letter from the Spartan king Arius to the high priest Onias I from the distant past (around 300 BCE), a copy of which is appended at the end (vv. 19-23). The Jewish people's remembrance (μιμνησκόμεθα) of the Spartans in prayer is particularly developed (v. 11). The appended letter from King Arius makes a surprising statement: the Spartans and the Jews are brothers, because they both are of the family of Abraham; this has been found "in writing" (v. 21). The letter of Arius to Onias is also copied in Josephus, *Ant.* 12.225–27, with the addition: "Demoteles, the courier, is bringing this letter to you. The writing is square (or: the letter is written on a square sheet). The seal is an Eagle holding fast a serpent"—all serving as security against forgery. Whereas 1 Maccabees first cites Jonathan's letter to the Spartans, immediately followed by the older Spartan letter of Arius to Onias (vv. 6-18, 19-23), Josephus reverses this order and places each letter in its historical context so that they are now separated by some 90 Greek pages in the Loeb edition (cf. Arius to Onias, *Ant.* 12.226–27; Jonathan to the Spartans, 13.165–70).

1 Maccabees 13:34-40. Simon the Hasmonean asks King Demetrius II for tax relief, and the king sends him a favorable reply.

1 Maccabees 14:16-23. When the Romans and Spartans hear of Jonathan's death, both peoples write Jonathan's brother and successor Simon on bronze tablets that are read before the assembly (ἐκκλησία) in Jerusalem (vv. 18-19). While the Roman letter is not quoted, the letter from "the rulers and the city of the Spartans" is given in full (vv. 20-23). It fittingly contains a copy of a resolution of the Spartan people once again welcoming the friendship and envoys of the Jewish people in vv. 22-23, since it was customary to renew alliances when the leadership changed (see v. 18 and above on 1 Macc 12:1-23).

1 Maccabees 15:1-9. The Seleucid king Antiochus VII Sidetes writes from the island of Rhodes to Simon and the Jewish people; the letter confirms previous privileges and promises further rewards.

1 Maccabees 15:15-24. Historically this letter belongs after 14:24, where Simon sent his envoys, headed by Numenius, to Rome to confirm their alliance (cf. Goldstein). Here Numenius and his companions have returned safely from Rome with letters from the Roman consul Lucius to the kings and countries surrounding Israel, reminding them of the ancient Roman alliance with the Jewish people and advising them not to make war or alliances against them. A typical letter is cited in full, addressed to King Ptolemy VIII Euergetes II (vv. 16-21), and then a list of more than twenty other kings and counties receiving similar letters is appended (vv. 22-23).

1 Maccabees 16:18-19. Ptolemy son of Abubus, Simon's son-in-law, kills him (v. 16), then writes a report to King Antiochus VII Sidetes and sends letters to the captains of John Hyrcanus to draw them over to his side, while sending troops to kill John. But John is warned by a messenger who outruns the letters and therefore kills those who came to kill him (vv. 21-22).

Second Maccabees

(See below B.1)

Third Maccabees

M. Hadas, *The Third and Fourth Books of Maccabees* (New York 1953). – **H. Anderson,** "3 Maccabees," *OTP* 2:509–29. – **N. Clayton Croy,** *3 Maccabees,* Septuagint Commentary Series (Leiden 2006).

3 Maccabees 3:11-30. The Egyptian king Ptolemy IV Philopator writes a letter against the Jews to his generals, using the usual tripartite Greek prescript with sender, addressees, and a greeting that also merges into the health wish: "greetings and good health: I myself and our government are faring well" (vv. 12-13a). The key instruction of the letter is that the Jews should be rounded up and killed (v. 25). The introductory framework in v. 11 calls the letter an ἐπιστολή, and the concluding frame in v. 30 looks back to this with its expression ὁ μὲν τῆς ἐπιστολῆς τύπος, "such was the form of the letter." In 4:1 the letter is referred to as a πρόσταγμα, "decree."

3 Maccabees 7:1-9. King Ptolemy Philopator writes again to his generals a letter vindicating the Jews and ordering their protection, framed by narrative notes in 6:41 and 7:10.

e) The Prophetic Books

Isaiah

Isaiah 37:9-14 corresponds to 2 Kings 19:9-14, already discussed above; similarly **Isaiah 39:1** parallels 2 Kings 20:12 (see above), except that Isaiah uses ἐπιστολάς instead of βιβλία. **Isaiah 18:2 LXX** displays an interesting change, for where the Hebrew says that Ethiopia "sends ambassadors by the Nile (or by the sea, בַּיָּם) in *papyrus vessels* on the waters," the Greek reads, "he sends messengers by the sea, and *papyrus letters* (ἐπιστολας βυβλίνας) on the water," which makes sense if a letter is a messenger.

Jeremiah

Jeremiah 29 (LXX 36):1-23, 24-32. Very influential in subsequent times is the letter in Jeremiah 29:4-23 that Jeremiah sends from Jerusalem to the exiles in Babylon, even though the letter begins like a divine address, "Thus says the Lord of hosts" (v. 4), and only the narrative framework in vv. 1-3 identifies it as a letter or a book roll, "These are the words of the letter (βίβλος; סֵפֶר) that the prophet Jeremiah sent," etc. This first letter contains a series of words of the Lord, not all of which fit the situation it presupposes. The letter motif continues to play a role, however different, in vv. 24-32, where a letter of the false prophet Shemaiah is summarized in vv. 26-28. Apparently Shemaiah, one of the exiles prophesying in Babylon, has written a letter back to Jerusalem complaining of the message of Jeremiah's letter that the exile will last a long time (v. 28) and falsely telling the priest Zephaniah that the Lord has made him priest so that he can put Jeremiah in the stocks (v. 26). In response the word of the Lord tells Jeremiah to say to Shemaiah (presumably through a letter) that Shemaiah has sent his letter only in his own name, not the Lord's (v. 25), while another word tells Jeremiah to "send (a letter) to all the exiles," exposing Shemaiah as a false prophet and prophesying his punishment (vv. 30-32). But the flow of events is not entirely clear.

The Letter of Jeremiah

J. Ziegler, *Ieremias, Baruch, Threni, Epistula Ieremiae*, Septuaginta: Vetus Testamentum Graecum 15 (Göttingen 1957). – **C. A. Moore**, "Epistle of Jeremiah," in idem, *Daniel, Esther, and Jeremiah: The Additions*, AB 44 (Garden City, N.Y. 1977) 317–58. – **A. H. J. Gunneweg**, "Der Brief Jeremias," in *Unterweisung in lehrhafter Form*, JSHRZ 3/2 (1975) 183–92. – **W. Naumann**, *Untersuchungen über den apokryphen Jeremiasbrief*, BZAW 25 (Berlin 1913).

The Letter (or Epistle) of Jeremiah is transmitted as a free-standing book in the LXX but is numbered Baruch 6:1-72 in the Vulgate. The book is generally thought to be a translation into Greek from a Hebrew or Aramaic original of the Hellenistic period, but nothing of this putative Semitic original remains and the small piece of the book (vv. 43-44) from the Qumran papyrus fragment 7Q2 is in Greek. The book as such is extant only in Greek and dependent versions. Once again "Jeremiah" writes to the exiles in Babylon, but, departing from the encouraging style of the letter in Jeremiah 29, this "letter" (which is actually more of a homily) contains mainly warnings about idolatry and polemic against the idols of the Gentiles.

Ezekiel

The scroll written on the front and on the back that Ezekiel is commanded to eat in Ezek 2:9–3:3 is not a letter but is called a κεφαλὶς βιβλίου or "scroll of a book" (2:9), an uncommon expression found elsewhere in the LXX only in Psalm 40 (LXX 39):8 (ET 40:7) and quoted in Hebrews 10:7; the subsequent three references in Ezekiel 3:1-3 call the scroll merely a κεφαλίς, a use found only here in the Septuagint. The ingested scroll functions as a metaphor for the message that Ezekiel is commissioned to deliver orally.

Daniel

Daniel 3:31–4:34 MT (Aramaic) = **Theodotion 4:1-37** (so also ET) = **LXX Daniel 4:4-5, 10-37** (plus additions **4:37a, b, c**). Nebuchadnezzar reports at length about his second dream and Daniel's interpretation, and how the events predicted in the interpretation came to pass in Nebuchadnezzar's temporary insanity and restoration to the throne. The introduction in MT Daniel 3:31-33 = Theodotion Daniel 4:1-3 gives the whole extended passage an epistolary form: "King Nebuchadnezzar to all peoples, tribes, and tongues who dwell in all the earth: Peace be multiplied to you (εἰρήνη ὑμῖν πληθυνθείη)" (cf. 1 Pet 1:2, χάρις ὑμῖν καὶ εἰρήνη πληθυνθείη). The Septuagint version includes what appear to be two more letters (or a somewhat disorganized single letter) in its distinctive additions in Daniel 4:37b and 4:37c, about which the editorial comment at the end of 4:37c remarks, "and he sent letters about all that had happened to him in his kingdom to all the nations that were under his kingdom." The first letter in 4:37b is described as a "circular letter" (ἐπιστολὴ ἐγκύκλιος) to all the nations; it begins without a prescript with a call to "Praise the God of heaven and bring him sacrifice and offering gloriously." A second letter in 4:37c begins with the sender, addressees, and a peace wish for a greeting: Ναβουχοδονοσορ βασιλεὺς πᾶσι τοῖς ἔθνεσι καὶ πάσαις ταῖς χώραις καὶ πᾶσι τοῖς οἰκοῦσιν ἐν αὐταῖς· εἰρήνη ὑμῖν πληθυνθείη ἐν παντὶ καιρῷ, "Nebuchadnezzar the king to all nations and all lands and all who dwell in them: Peace be multiplied to you at all times."

Daniel 6:26-28. After Daniel's rescue from the lion's den, King Darius writes a letter to the whole world confessing God's wondrous power.

2. Pseudepigrapha and Historical Works

The Letter of Aristeas (to Philocrates)

R. J. H. Shutt, "Letter of Aristeas," *OTP* 2:7–34. – **A. Pelletier**, *Lettre d'Aristée à Philocrate*, SC 89 (Paris 1962) (**TLG**). – **H. St. J. Thackeray**, "Appendix: The Letter of Aristeas," in H. B. Swete, *An Introduction to the Old Testament in Greek*, rev. by R. R. Ottley (Cambridge ²1914) 531–606

(Greek text with introduction). – **N. Meisner**, "Aristeasbrief," in *Unterweisung in erzählender Form*, JSHRZ 2/1 (1973) 35–87.

This work, which contains the legend of the origin of the Septuagint, presents itself as a trustworthy "narrative" or "account" (διήγησις) of the events that the Alexandrian Jew Aristeas writes to and for his brother Philocrates. Despite an eight-verse introductory address to Philocrates that might be thought of as a more complicated and stylized parallel to Luke's dedication to Theophilus in Luke 1:1-4, and despite a return to the addressee in the epilogue (322), the work as a whole lacks clear epistolary features. Nevertheless, several letter exchanges are embedded in the narrative, including the following:

§11. At the suggestion of the royal librarian Demetrius of Phalerum,[7] the Egyptian king Ptolemy II Philadelphus (285–247 BCE) orders a letter to be written to the high priest Eleazar in Jerusalem to secure the manuscripts and scholars needed for a Greek translation of "the lawbooks of the Jews" (v. 10).

§§28–33. A narrative introduction and copy of the "memorandum" or "report" (εἰσδοσις, vv. 29, 33) that Demetrius of Phalerum sends to the king concerning the translation of the Torah. For a parallel see Josephus, *Ant.* 12.35–39.

§§34–40. A copy of the letter of King Ptolemy to Eleazar the high priest; cf. Josephus, *Ant.* 12.40–51.

§§41–46. Eleazar answers the king in a letter of similar length; the letter is also found in Josephus, *Ant.* 12.51–57 (cf. 12.86, 118). In due course the narrative also mentions the delivery of Eleazar's letter to the king by Aristeas and others (v. 173) and, ultimately, the king's reading of the finished translation (v. 312), together with his open letter of invitation to the translators to return to Egypt at any time to enjoy his hospitality (v. 321), followed by a postscript from Aristeas to Philocrates (322).

2 Baruch (Syriac Apocalypse of Baruch)

(See below B.2)

---

[7] We have met Demetrius of Phalerum already in chapter 5 as the putative author of the works *On Style* and *Epistolary Types* (see chap. 5, sec. A.1 and B).

Eupolemos

A. M. Denis, *Fragmenta Pseudepigraphorum quae supersunt graeca*, PVTG 3 (Leiden 1970) 179–86. – **F. Fallon**, "Eupolemus," *OTP* 2:861–72. – **N. Walter**, "Fragmente jüdisch-hellenistischer Historiker," in *Historische und legendarische Erzählungen*, JSHRZ 1/2 (Gütersloh 1976) 93–108. – **C. R. Holladay**, *Fragments from Hellenistic Jewish Authors*, vol. 1: *Historians*, SBLTT 20 (Chico, Calif. 1983) 93–156. – **B. Z. Wacholder**, *Eupolemus: A Study of Judaeo-Greek Literature* (Cincinnati, Ohio 1974) – **K. Mras**, *Eusebius Werke*, vol. 8: *Die Praeparatio evangelica*, GCS 43.1, 43.2 (Berlin 1954, 1956) (**TLG**).

Fragment 2 = Eusebius, *Praeparatio evangelica* 9.30.1–34.18. This fragment of the work of the Jewish historian Eupolemos of the second century BCE, which probably bore the title *On the Kings of Judea*, quotes letter exchanges between Solomon and an Egyptian pharaoh with the otherwise unknown name of Vaphres (Walter 101: "simply invented"; but see Fallon 866 note m) and between Solomon and Souron king of Tyre (cf. 2 Chron 2:2-15). According to Holladay these letters "illustrate the practice among Hellenistic historians of composing letters and other archival documents to include in their works" (143).

1 Enoch (Ethiopic Apocalypse of Enoch)

E. Isaac, "1 (Ethiopic Apocalypse of) Enoch," *OTP* 1:5–89. – **S. Uhlig**, "Das Äthiopische Henochbuch," in *Apokalypsen*, JSHRZ 5/6 (Gütersloh 1984) 461–780. – **M. Black**, *Apocalypsis Henochi Graece*, PVTG 3 (Leiden 1970) 1–44 (**TLG**). – **M. Karrer**, *Johannesoffenbarung* (Bib. 4) 53–59. – **G. W. E. Nickelsburg**, "The Epistle of Enoch and the Qumran Literature," *JJS* 33 (1982) 333–48, repr. with addional discussion in J. Neusner and A. J. Avery-Peck, eds., *George W. E. Nickelsburg in Perspective: An Ongoing Dialogue of Learning*, JSJSup 80 (Leiden 2003) 105–37.

***1 Enoch* 100:6.** Where the Ethiopic version of *1 Enoch* 100:6 reads, "and the sons of the earth shall give heed to all the words of this *book*" (*OTP*), the Greek tradition reads: τοὺς λόγους τούτους τῆς ἐπιστολῆς ταύτης, "these words of this *letter*." Similarly, the Greek *subscriptio* after 107:3 reads: ἐπιστολὴ Ἐνώχ. It is debated whether the designation as a "letter" applies to the whole work or only to its fifth book, which runs from chap. 91 (or 92) to chap. 107 (cf. Uhlig 708; Karrer).

Paraleipomena Jeremiou (2 Baruch)

(See below B.3)

Testament of Solomon

C. C. McCown, *The Testament of Solomon*, UNT 9 (Leipzig 1922) (**TLG**). – **D. C. Duling**, "Testament of Solomon," *OTP* 1:935–87. – **P. Busch**, *Das Testament Salomons: Die älteste christliche Dämonologie, kommentiert und in deutscher Erstübersetzung*, TU 153 (Berlin 2006).

Textual history: McCown reconstructs an "original" Greek text of 26 chapters (pp. 5*–75*); this is translated by Duling. He also offers the full text of his recensions C (76*–87*) and E (102*–120*), for which Duling does not offer a complete translation.

T. Sol. **22:1-5**. Adarkes the king of Arabia writes a letter to Solomon, who, after reading it, folds it and gives it to his servant with instructions to remind him of it in seven days (22:6). The letter makes an urgent request to Solomon for help in subduing the Arabian wind demon, which he does by sending his servant to Arabia to entrap the demon in a leather flask (22:9-15).

T. Sol. **Recension C 13:11-12** (McCown, p. 87*). Solomon writes a short letter (γραμμάτιον) to Hezekiah, the future king. The letter has an archaic style, with ἀπέστειλά σοι τάδε, "Solomon . . . writes/sends to you thus," at the end of the following prescript: τῷ Ἐζεκίᾳ τῷ μέλλοντι βασιλεῖ· Σολομῶν βασιλεύς, υἱὸς Δαυείδ, ἀπέστειλά σοι τάδε.

T. Sol. **Recension E 7:1-2** (McCown, p. 112*). The king of Assyria sends Solomon a letter.

3. Papyri and Related Archeological Discoveries

The texts discussed so far have been handed down in manuscripts written after the date of original composition or through secondary citations in other works, in any case through a literary process. But fortuitous discoveries have also made available original letters for the study of ancient Judaism, written on papyrus, potsherds, or similar materials. Although for convenience the texts below are grouped together as being recent discoveries, they are in fact a diverse group covering a long span of time. We pass over the early ostraca in the Aramaic language from Arad (ca. 600 BCE; Pardee, *Handbook* [Bib. 3] 24–67) and Lachisch (ca. 589 BCE; Pardee 77–114), but still include the somewhat later Aramaic papyri from Elephantine.

a) Elephantine

A. Cowley, *Aramaic Papyri of the Fifth Century B.C.* (Oxford 1923; repr. Osnabrück 1967). – **B. Porten** and **A. Yardeni**, *Textbook of Aramaic Documents from Ancient Egypt*, vol. 1: *Letters* (Jerusalem and Winona Lake 1986). – **J. M. Lindenberger**, *Letters* (Bib. 31) 41–79. – **B. Porten**, "Elephantine Papyri," *ABD* 2 (1992) 445–55 (literature). – **I. Taatz**, *Frühjüdische Briefe* (Bib. 3) 91–99.

The island of Elephantine in the Nile river at modern Aswan was home to a Jewish military colony in the fifth century BCE. Excavations at Elephantine and the surrounding vicinity have uncovered about thirty-five papyrus letters in Aramaic. They follow the official Persian style of the time, right down to the use of the formulaic expression "the gods" in the plural. The stereotypical form of the epistolary opening in correspondence to addressees of equal or greater status names the recipient first: "To B, A, greeting." For example: "To my lady Selava, your servant Hosea greeting (שלם)" (Cowley no. 39). If a superior was writing, the formula was inverted: "From A to B." Letters 21 and 30 have attracted the most attention. The introduction of Letter 21, from 419 BCE, runs, "To my brethren, Yedoniah and his colleagues the Jewish garrison, your brother Hananiah. The welfare (שלם) of my brethren may the gods (אלהיא) seek." The letter deals with the organization of the festival of Passover (פסח) at Elephantine. Letter 30 (408 BCE) is a petition to Bigvai (Bagoas), governor of Judea, from Yedoniah, the leader of the Jewish community at Elephantine. Yedoniah requests permission to rebuild the community's temple of "Ya'u the God" (יהו אלהיא) on Elephantine. The evaluation of Taatz puts these letters in perspective (99): "These two letters show that the Jews in the late fifth century BCE used the letter as the means of communication in religious matters to deliver instructions in the interest of strengthening cultic unity.

They can therefore be seen as a precursor to the [Hanukkah] letters to Egypt in 2 Maccabees [1:1-9; 1:10–2:18]."

b) Qumran

E. Qimron and **J. Strugnell**, *Qumran Cave 4. V: Miqsat Ma'ase ha-Torah*, DJD 10 (Oxford 1994). – **F. García Martínez** and **E. J. C. Tigchelaar**, *The Dead Sea Scrolls Study Edition*, 2 vols. (Leiden and Grand Rapids 2000). – **J. Maier**, *Die Qumran-Essener: Die Texte vom Toten Meer*, vol. 2: *Die Texte der Höhle* 4, UTB 1863 (Munich 1995) 144–47, 361–76.

4Q394–399 = 4QMMT[a–f] (*DSSSE* 2:790–805). These document numbers represent the fragments of several leather scrolls and of one papyrus (4Q398) that have been pieced together to form a series of six so-called Halakhic Letters (numbered a–f). The whole group of fragments is often referred to by the title *Miqsat Ma'ase ha-Torah* or מקצת מעשי התורה, "some of the works of the Torah," a Hebrew phrase found in one of the fragments, 4Q398 = *4QHalakhic Letter*, frags. 14–17 col. II, line 3 (for the text see below). At first scholars thought of these fragments collectively as a "Letter of the Teacher of Righteousness," written in his own hand. However, while it would certainly be valuable to have such an original document from of one of the founding fathers of the Qumran community, scholarship has since retreated from this maximalist position. Against the supposition of an original document lies the fact that the existing fragments come from six different exemplars and therefore give evidence of copying. No epistolary frame is currently recognizable, and whether an original letter frame has simply gone missing is not known. Nevertheless, the document, which deals with questions of ritual and the law, is written in an epistolary style with direct address to the readers. The final preserved section of 4Q398 *Halakhic Letter* (4QMMT[e]), frags. 14–17 col. II, illustrates this nicely and seems to conclude with a kind of epilogue (trans. *DSSSE* 2:803):

> 1 Remember David, who was a man of the pious ones, [and] he, too,
> 2 [was] freed from many afflictions and was forgiven. And also we
> have written to you 3 some of the works of the Torah which we think
> are good for you and for your people, for we s[a]w 4 that you have
> intellect and knowledge of the Law. Reflect on all these matters and
> seek from him that he may support 5 your counsel and keep far from
> you the evil scheming{s} and the counsel of Belial, 6 so that at the

end of time, you may rejoice in finding that some of our words are true. **7** And it shall be reckoned to you as justice when you do what is upright and good before him, for your good **8** and that of Israel.

The original editors are very cautious about identifying the genre but conclude in the end that the text "should be classed with corporate or public letters sent from one group to another, or even with treatises, rather than with the private letter" (Qimron and Strugnell 114).

4Q203 (4QEnGiants[a] ar) *4QBook of Giants[a] ar* (*DSSSE* 1:408–11). The fragments from the Book of Giants belong to the Enoch tradition. Fragment 7 col. II speaks of "two tablets," of which "the second has not yet been read up till now," while frag. 8 begins: "Copy of the seco[n]d tablet of [the] le[tter . . .] by the hand of Enoch, the distinguished scribe [. . .] and holy (one), to Shemihazah and to all [his] com[panions . . .]." But it is not possible to extract very much from this fragmentary text.

c) Wadi Murabbaat, Nahal Hever

P. E. Dion, "Letters (Aramaic)," *ABD* 4 (1992) 285–90. – **Y. Yadin**, "The Excavation of Masada—1963/64: Preliminary Report," *IEJ* 15 (1965) 1–120, esp. 110–11. – **D. Schwiderski**, *Handbuch des nordwestsemitischen Briefformulars* (Bib. 3) 241–45.

Not only Qumran but also other locations in the Judean desert served as sites where excavators discovered ancient texts, including letters. These sites are Wadi Murabbaat, Nahal Hever, Nahal Seelim, and Masada. Of the approximately 28 letters, some of which are very fragmentary, most date from the Bar Kokhba period. We return to them below in section B.4.

d) Corpus Papyrorum Judaicarum

V. A. Tcherikover and **A. Fuks**, *Corpus Papyrorum Judaicarum*, 3 vols. (Cambridge, Mass. 1957–1964).

Somewhat less than half of the texts collected in *CPJ* are of Jewish origin, for the volumes also include papyrus texts in which non-Jews refer to Jewish persons and affairs. In the following we select from among these texts only those letters that with reasonable likelihood deserve to be called "Jewish" (sometimes based on the personal names).

CPJ **12**. A Jewish guard named Somoelis (Samuel) reports on some business he has conducted for the administrator Zenon (from the Zenon archive, 3rd c. BCE).

CPJ **13**. A "memorandum" (ὑπόμνημα) to Zenon from Alexander and Ismaelos (Ishmael).

CPJ **37**. An ἔντευξις or petition (see Exercise 11, with Answer Key) to King Ptolemy from three farmers, whose names, Theodotus, Gaddaios, and Phanias, may together suggest a Jewish identity; see *CPJ* 1:184 n. 1 (date: 222 BCE).

CPJ **43**. Petition of a peasant farmer who explicitly introduces himself as Jewish: "from Judas son of Dositheos, Jew" (2nd c. BCE).

CPJ **128** (218 BCE). A woman complains in a letter to King Ptolemy about her husband, a Jew. Whether she herself is Jewish remains open.

CPJ **141**. A letter from the first century BCE from a certain Herakles to Ptolemy assumes in lines 8–9 that the addressee knows of some local hatred of the Jews: οἶδας γὰρ ὅτι βδελύσ<σ>ονται Ἰουδαίους, "For you know that they loathe the Jews." The further circumstances of the writing are not clear.

CPJ **469** (3rd c. CE). A business letter from a certain Aphynchis, who might be Jewish in the light of the name Eissak (Isaac) in line 16, although as Tcherikover admits, "This letter might have been written by a gentile as well as by a Jew or a Christian" (*CPJ* 3:30). The same uncertainty attaches to more than a few of the other texts in the collection, e.g., *CPJ* 474.

CPJ **479** (3rd–4th c. CE). A certain Gerontios sends a business letter to his banker Josep (Joseph), who bears "one of the commonest Jewish names in the Roman period," according to the editors (*CPJ* 3:42). Nevertheless, the fact that Gerontios greets Josep familiarly as "brother" need not imply that Gerontios too is Jewish.

4. Philo and Josephus

a) Philo of Alexandria

F. H. Colson, *Philo*, LCL 10: *The Embassy to Gaius* (1962). – **E. M. Smallwood**, *Philonis Alexandrini Legatio ad Gaium* (Leiden ²1970). – **L. Cohn** and **S. Reiter**, *Philonis Alexandrini opera quae supersunt*, vol. 6. (Berlin 1915; repr. 1962) 155–223 (**TLG**).

The absence of a large number of letters in most of Philo's writings is due mainly to the focus of his work on detailed philosophical exegesis of the Bible. At one point he does cite a letter of the Indian philosopher Calanos to Alexander the Great (*That Every Good Person is Free* 96 [LCL 9:64–67]; see above p. 127). But on a larger scale he gets involved with letters only in the work that most nearly approximates historiography, Philo's *Legatio ad Gaium* or *Embassy to Gaius*, the Roman emperor, better known as Caligula. The letters are not directly quoted but, as with Tacitus, are only mentioned or summarized, with the primary exception of the letter of Agrippa I in *Embassy* 276–329, discussed below.

Embassy **199–203**. Philo mentions the letter of Capito, the Roman tax collector in Judea, to Gaius Caligula in which Capito gave "an exaggerated account" (so Philo) of the incident in which the Jews tore down an altar of the imperial cult in Jamnia, which Caligula subsequently held against them. This leads to Caligula's decision to replace the altar in Jamnia by a "colossal statue" in the Jerusalem temple (203). While the form of the statue is not immediately identified and §265 presents Caligula as saying, "I ordered a statue of *Zeus* to be set up in the temple," it is clear from the later context that this essentially means, "a statue of *myself* as Zeus or Jupiter."[8] Compare *Embassy* 346, "he was proceeding to convert and transmogrify (the Jerusalem temple) into a temple of his own to bear the name of Gaius, 'the new Zeus made manifest,'" and Josephus, *Ant.* 14.261, "to set up an image of Gaius in the temple of God."

Embassy **207**. Caligula sends a letter to Petronius, the Roman legate in Syria, with orders to erect the statue (see above) in the Jerusalem temple. For the ensuing events see Josephus, *Ant.* 18.261–309.

Embassy **254**. Petronius's letter of response to Caligula, which he ponders carefully and discusses with his advisors (248–54a) before sending it

---

[8] Caligula liked to play Jupiter, as we know from other sources.

by means of experienced travelers. The letter explains the reasons for the delay in the erecting of the statue, trying to avoid blaming the Jews, but it only infuriates the emperor.

Embassy **259–60.** Caligula instructs one of his secretaries to answer Petronius, and Philo embeds a summary of the letter's contents and motives. Agrippa I, who is living in Rome, visits Caligula "knowing absolutely nothing about the contents of the letter sent by Petronius or of those written earlier and later by Gaius (Caligula)" (261). But Agrippa senses Caligula's increasing displeasure with the Jews after the arrival of Petronius's letter and is struck by fear into a coma (266–67).

Embassy **276–329.** A very long letter from Agrippa I to pacify Caligula (fourteen Greek pages in the Loeb edition), quoted in full. In the course of this letter Agrippa speaks of edicts of Augustus favorable to the Jews as ἐπιστολαί (291), mentions letters to and from Tiberius (301, 303, 305), and includes a transcript of the letter of the proconsul Gaius Norbanus Flaccus to the magistrates of Ephesus during the reign of Augustus concerning toleration of the Jews (314–15).

Embassy **330–34.** Caligula reads Agrippa's letter and responds by calling off the installation of the statue in the Jerusalem temple, sending letters to this effect to Petronius. Or at least he calls it off temporarily, for shortly thereafter in §337, Caligula regrets his decision and orders "another bronze statue of colossal size covered with gold to be constructed in Rome" and shipped to Jerusalem.

b) Flavius Josephus

H. St. J. Thackeray, et al., *Josephus*, LCL, 10 vols. (1926–1965). – **B. Niese**, *Flavii Iosephi opera*, 7 vols. (Berlin 1887–1895; repr. 1955) **(TLG)**. – **K. H. Rengstorf**, et al., *A Complete Concordance to Flavius Josephus*, 4 vols. (Leiden 1973–1983), s.v. ἐπιστολή and γράμμα(τα). – **C. J. Bjerkelund**, *PARAKALÔ* (Bib. 4) 98–104. – **M. Pucci Ben Zeev**, "Who Wrote a Letter Concerning Delian Jews?" *RB* 103 (1996) 237–43 (on *Ant.* 19.213–16). – **J.-D. Gauger**, *Authentizität* (Bib. 2) 195–204.

With the letters and other documents that he intersperses in his works along with speeches, Josephus takes on the style of a Greco-Roman historian. That he includes materials that have parallels with the Old Testament and the wider canon of the Septuagint (e.g., 1 Maccabees) as well as with the *Letter of Aristeas* and Philo has already been noted under the individual passages above. His many mentions of letters can easily be accessed by Rengstorf's concordance. We begin with a few summary observations: Troops are engaged through letters and on the basis of letters (*War* 2.66; *Ant.* 20.91; *Life* 285–87), fatal intrigues are plotted with the help of letters (*Ant.* 15.168–75; 16.332–33), a last will is read from a letter (*War* 1.667 par. *Ant.* 17.194). Letters are read in public (*War* 4.616–17) and are supplemented by the oral messages of their carriers (*War* 4.228–29, 233). Letters can fall into the wrong hands (*War* 1.261) and can be forged or regarded as forgeries (*War* 1.528). Complaints and grievances are registered in letters (*War* 2.23), and potential successors of Herod the Great apply to the emperor for the kingdom through letters (*Ant.* 17.228–29). The qualification δι' ἐπιστολῶν can be a synonym for "in writing" (*War* 1.174, 230, 317). The semantic range of ἐπιστολή is broad. An indictment (*Ant.* 18.250) or a money order (*Ant.* 12.199, 203) can stand under this heading. Written commands of all sorts can be called ἐπιστολαί—hence the governors of a Jewish stronghold have orders to obey only ταῖς αὐτογράφοις ἐπιστολαῖς, "the instructions given in Aristobulus's own hand" (*War* 1.137), and the term ἐπιστολή also covers the commands of the emperor (*Ant.* 18.277) and his officers (*Ant.* 19.267). This broad range of the term in Josephus has led to the frequent exchange of ἐπιστολή and ἐντολή, "commandment" or "statute," in the manuscript tradition (e.g., *Ant.* 18.188, 262, 294). In the following only especially striking passages or those with complete letters are listed.

War **1.602–61**. In almost novelistic fashion, Josephus details the use and misuse of letters in a highly complicated intrigue concerning Antipater, a son of Herod the Great, and his eventual execution. Before we join the story, Antipater has already launched an unsuccessful plot from Rome to poison his father (592–601; cf. 637–40). While still in Rome, Antipater forges letters to his father to the detriment of his brothers Archelaus and Philip (also in Rome at the time) and bribes his Roman friends to write against them as well (602–3)—a practice he has already engaged in earlier in Judea (604–5). While Antipater is on his way back from Rome, Herod gets involved in the intrigue by sending letters feigning affection for him, which he receives in Cilicia (608–10). Back in Jerusalem Antipater is confronted with the fact of his recent conspiratorial letter exchange with his mother, who warns him not to appear before Herod unless he has support from Caesar Augustus (620), which he is able to produce in the form of letters from the emperor (633). Nevertheless, at a hearing before Herod and the Roman official Varus (1.620; cf. 1.20), Antipater is convicted of the poisoning plot (637–38). Varus writes a report on this to Caesar that he delivers personally, while Herod also dispatches his own messengers to Rome (640). Later, a servant arrives from Rome to deliver a cover letter to Herod introducing other, defamatory letters written in the name of Herod's sister Salome by a certain maidservant Acme, whom Antipater had bribed for the task (641–43). Antipater is convicted by Acme's letter to him detailing the forgery and asking for payment:

> As you desired, I have written to your father and forwarded those letters [forged in Salome's name], and feel sure that, when he has read them, he will not spare his sister. Be good enough (καλῶς δὲ ποιή-σεις), when all is over, to remember what you promised. (*War* 1.643)

Herod writes to Augustus again with the news of the Acme plot (645) and receives a letter saying that Acme has been executed and Antipater condemned to death (661). Herod has Antipater executed just five days before his own death (664–65). For a longer version of Acme's letter to Antipater above, as well as a letter from Acme to Herod framing Salome, together with other letters, see *Ant.* 17.134–41.

War 2.203. See above Exercise 9 (p. 66) and the parallel in *Ant.* 18.308–9; similarly *Ant.* 19.10.

War 7.353. In his speech about the immortality of the soul, Eleazar speaks of the Indians who give "letters" (ἐπιστολάς; LCL "commissions") addressed to their departed relatives to those who themselves are about to depart for the afterworld by voluntarily committing their bodies to the fire.

Ant. 12.138–44. Copy of a letter from the Seleucid ruler Antiochus III the Great to one of his governors named Ptolemy[9] on behalf of the Jews (cf. 134–35). On Antiochus's following letter to Zeuxis, another of his governors, in *Ant.* 12.147–53 see above p. 79.

Ant. 12.257–64. In the historical "gap" between 1 Maccabees 1 and 1 Maccabees 2, Josephus inserts a letter exchange between the Samaritans, who do not want to be included in punitive measures against the Jews, and Antiochus IV Epiphanes.

Ant. 13.62–71. The Jewish high priest Onias IV writes a letter to Ptolemy and Cleopatra requesting permission to purify an abandoned temple in Leontopolis and rebuild it as a temple to the Most High God.

---

[9] Probably Ptolemy, son of Thraseas, not a member of the Ptolemaic dynasty (cf. LCL 7:71–72 note "b" at *Ant.* 12.138).

In their letter of response the two rulers grant permission but absolve themselves of any responsibility for the project.

Ant. **14.131.** A letter of the Jewish high priest Hyrcanus makes an impression even on the Jews living in Egypt.

Ant. **14.185–267.** Many of the documents that Josephus collects in *Antiquities* book 14, chapter 10 (§§185–267) have letter form or are designated as letters in the redactional comments. See especially the following letters: Gaius Caligula the Roman emperor to the Sidonians (190–91) and to the people of Parium or Paros (211–16); Dolabella the governor of Syria to the cities of the province of Asia (224–27); the magistrates of Laodicea to the proconsul Gaius Rabilius (241–43); Galba the proconsul to Miletus (244–46); and a letter (ἐπιστολή) attached to or containing a decree (δόγμα) of the Senate (252, 254). Josephus concludes: "Now there are many other such decrees by the Senate and the Imperators of the Romans . . . in reply to letters on the subject of our rights" (265). Cf. Josephus, *Against Apion* 2.37.

Ant. **16.166–73.** Three more edicts of the Roman emperor Augustus and his proconsuls and two orders of Augustus's friend Marcus Vipsanius Agrippa that include epistolary prescripts.

Ant. **18.161–67.** A letter from the Herodian king Marcus Iulius Agrippa I procures a warm reception with the emperor Tiberius on the island of Capri, but another letter that arrives shortly thereafter reporting Agrippa's huge unpaid debt causes him to lose favor with Tiberius until he gets a loan from Antonia, the grandmother of the future emperor Gaius Caligula, and pays this back with another loan from a certain Samaritan man (167). Having later been imprisoned by Tiberius for treasonous remarks to Gaius (168–69, 187–91), Agrippa is not set free until Gaius sends a letter securing his release after Tiberius's death (234–35).

Ant. **20.10–14.** A letter of the emperor Claudius including an expanded *superscriptio* of Claudius's titles, the names of the four letter carriers, and the date.

Ant. **20.182–84.** Nero's former tutor Beryllus (or Burrus) has now been appointed by Nero to the position of "secretary of Greek correspondence" (183: τάξιν τὴν ἐπὶ τῶν Ἑλληνικῶν ἐπιστολῶν πεπιστευμένος), *ab epistulis graecis* in Latin, and knows how to make money from this profession. See also the parallel τάξις ἐπιστολῶν, "position of a letter writer," which Agrippa II gives to Justus of Tiberias in Josephus, *Life* 356.

Life **48–51.** Letter carriers live dangerously. The deliverers of unpopular messages are executed.

Life **216–36**. A letter exchange spiked with malice between Josephus and his Jewish opponents. Josephus subsequently sees to it that their letters are intercepted (*Life* 240–41, 245), so that he can use them against them (254–55, 260–61).

Life **364–66**. Josephus says that Agrippa II wrote him 62 letters full of praise for his *History* of the Jewish War, and he quotes two of them.

5. Rabbinic Judaism

D. Pardee, *Handbook* (Bib. 3) 183–211. – **P. S. Alexander**, "Epistolary Literature" (Bib. 3) 581–82, 592–93. – **J. Neusner**, *The Talmud of the Land of Israel*, 35 vols., Chicago Studies in the History of Judaism (Chicago 1982–1994), vol. 20: *Hagigah and Moed Qatan* (1986). – **G. Dalman**, *Aramäische Dialektproben* (Leipzig ²1927; repr. Darmstadt 1960) 3. – **I. Taatz**, *Frühjüdische Briefe* (Bib. 3) 82–90.

Only a few letters and letter fragments from the Tannaitic (early rabbinic) period have been preserved in the traditional Jewish literature of the Mishnah, Tosefta, Midrashim, and Talmuds. (Pardee 183 identifies only thirteen letters or fragments of letters and provides the texts of ten.) Moreover, the attributions of the letters in these sources to the earlier bearers of the rabbinic tradition might need to be viewed for the most part with skepticism. But whether the letters date from these earlier times or not, they still allow us to take away something of value concerning letter practices and formulas. Thus for example we can recognize letters of recommendation and the greeting in the form of the biblical *shalom*. From Jerusalem as the center of Judaism or from Galilee after Jerusalem's destruction, letters were sent out into the provinces to decide controversial questions of the festival calendar and problems of Jewish religious life, such as the proper tithe on agricultural crops. This practice is also presupposed when Paul makes his way to Damascus with letters from the Jerusalem authorities (Acts 9:2; cf. 22:5) and when the Jews in Rome say that they have received no negative letters about Paul from Judea (Acts 28:21).

The most convenient study resource for Tannaitic letters in the rabbinic literature is Pardee's *Handbook*, because in addition to a commentary on the epistolographic features and general interpretation, he presents where available the parallel rabbinic sources of a given letter.[10] This is especially true of the best preserved letter, from a certain Rabbi Gamaliel, found in *t. Sanhedrin* 2:6, but also in *y. Sanh.* 18d, *y. Ma'aser Sheni* 56c, and *b. Sanh.* 11a–b (see Pardee 189–96 and below Exercise 31).[11] Pardee identifies the author as Gamaliel the Elder (195), the teacher of the Apostle Paul (Acts 22:3; cf. 5:34), but others identify him as Gamaliel's grandson Gamaliel of Yavneh, who became a leader in religious matters after the crisis of 70 CE and gained the respect even of the Romans. The authenticity of this letter is often doubted. Among the letters of other well-known Jewish leaders we can also refer to a letter of Judah the Patriarch to the Roman emperor Antoninus Pius in *Genesis Rabbah* 75.5 below (cf. Alexander 582).

***Talmud Yerushalmi, Hagigah* 76c (par. *y. Nedarim* 42b)**. The text, which is associated with the name of a rabbi from the late second or early third century CE, attests the practice of writing recommendation letters for short-term assignments (trans. Neusner, vol. 20:35 at *y. Hag.* 1:8 [III.K]):

> R. Hiyya bar Ba came to R. Eleazar, saying to him, "Recommend me to R. Yudah the Patriarch, so that he will write a letter of recommendation for me as I go abroad to make a living." He recommended him, and [the patriarch] wrote the following letter for him: "Lo, we send you a great man. He is our messenger and stands in our stead until he comes back to us."

***Talmud Yerushalmi, Hagigah* 77d (par. *y. Sanh.* 23c; *b. Sanh.* 107b; *b. Sotah* 47a)**. (See Pardee 204–7.) Judah ben Tabbai is about to be appointed patriarch in Jerusalem. But he flees to Alexandria, and the inhabitants of Jerusalem write a letter that follows him there. The letter reveals the considerable difference of authority between the two cities and exploits the metaphor of marriage: "From Jerusalem the Great to Alexandria the Small. How long shall my betrothed remain with you while I remain

---

[10] Nevertheless, Pardee does not provide the text of *y. Haggigah* 76c below dealing with recommendation letters.

[11] For a similar piece of tradition, see the letter "from Simeon b. Gamaliel and from Yohana b. Zakkai to our brothers in the Upper and Lower South," etc. from the Midrash in Pardee 184–89 (here 186).

grieving over him?"[12] Other versions read: ". . . while I remain celibate" (Pardee 205–6).

Genesis Rabbah 75:5. Rabbi Judah the Patriarch's scribe begins a letter from him to the emperor with the words: "From Judah the Patriarch to our Lord King Antoninus." Because this sounds like a superior writing to an inferior, in part because Judah's name comes first (cf. Pardee 200), Judah tears up the draft and insists that his scribe write, "From Judah *your slave* to our Lord King Antoninus" (Pardee 199).[13]

Exercise

31. By adding quotation marks and adding or altering other punctuation (including capitalization) at the appropriate places in the following text, attempt to delimit the actual letter(s) that Rabbi Gamaliel (i.e., Gamaliel the Elder: see above) dictated to his scribe, and interpret the content. Pay particular attention to the problems of punctuation and capitalization surrounding the two inserted question marks: "Write (?) [T]o our brothers of Upper and Lower Galilee (?) [M]ay your well-being increase!" Text: Tosefta, *Sanhedrin* 2:6 (text in M. Zuckermandl, *Tosephta Based on the Erfurt and Vienna Codices* [Jerusalem 1963] 416–17; trans. Pardee 193, punctuation modified).

A case involving Rabban Gamaliel and the elders who were sitting on the steps on the temple mount, with that scribe Yohanan before them. He told him, Write (כתוב) (?) [T]o our brothers (לאחנא בני) of Upper and Lower Galilee (?) [M]ay your well-being increase! We inform you that removal time has arrived, remove the tithes from the olive clusters.

And: To our brothers of the Upper and Lower South. May your well-being increase! We inform you that removal time has arrived. Remove the tithes from the wheat sheaves.

---

[12] Translated also in Neusner, vol. 20:56 at *y. Hag.* 2:2 [IV.D].

[13] For another English translation see the Soncino edition of M. Freeman and M. Simon, *The Midrash Rabbah*, 13 vols. in 10 (London ²1951) 2:692.

And: To our brothers belonging to the Babylonian diaspora, and belonging to the Median diaspora and all the other Israelite diasporas. May your well-being increase! We inform you that since the pigeons are thin and the lambs are tender and the springtime has not yet arrived, it seemed fit to me and my colleagues that we add thirty days to this year.

B. Exegetical Examples

1. Temple Propaganda: Letters in 2 Maccabees

Bibliography 32: W. Kappler and **R. Hanhart**, *Maccabaeorum liber II*, Septuaginta IX/2 (Göttingen ²1976). – **S. von Dobbeler**, *Die Bücher 1/2 Makkabäer*, SKK.AT 11 (Stuttgart 1997). – **W. Dommershausen**, *1 Makkabäer / 2 Makkabäer*, NEchtB (Würzburg 1985). – **J. A. Goldstein**, *II Maccabees*, AB 41A (New York 1983). – **C. Habicht**, "2. Makkabäerbuch," in *Historische und legendarische Erzählungen*, JSHRZ 1/3 (Gütersloh 1976) 165–285.

F. M. Abel, "Les lettres préliminaires du second livre des Maccabées," *RB* 53 (1946) 513–33. – **E. Bickermann**, "Ein jüdischer Festbrief vom Jahre 124 BCE (II Macc. 1,1-9)," *ZNW* 32 (1993) 233–54, also in idem, *Studies in Jewish and Christian History*, vol. 2, AGJU 9/2 (Leiden 1980) 136–58. – **A. Büchler**, "Das Sendschreiben der Jerusalemer an die Juden in Aegypten in II. Makkab. 1,11–2,18," *MGWJ* 41 (1897) 481–500, 529–54. – **J. G. Bunge**, "Untersuchungen zum zweiten Makkabäerbuch: Quellenkritische, literarische, chronologische und historische Untersuchungen zum 2 Makk als Quelle syrisch-palästinensischer Geschichte im 2. Jahrhundert v.Chr." (Diss. phil., Bonn 1971). – **R. Doran**, *Temple Propaganda: The Purpose and Character of 2 Maccabees*, CBQMS 12 (Washington 1981), esp. 3–12. – **H. Grätz**, "Das Sendschreiben der Palästinenser an die ägyptisch-judäischen Gemeinden wegen der Feier der Tempelweihe," *MGWJ* 26 (1877) 1–16, 49–60. – **J. W. van Henten**, *The Maccabean Martyrs as Saviours of the Jewish People: A Study of 2 and 4 Maccabees*, JSJSup 57 (Leiden 1997) 37–50. – **T. Nisula**, "'Time has passed since you sent your letter': Letter Phraseology in 1 and 2 Maccabees," *JSP* 14 (2005) 201–22. – **I. Taatz**, *Frühjüdische Briefe* (Bib. 3) 18–45. – **C. C. Torrey**, "The Letters Prefixed to Second Maccabees," *JAOS* 60 (1940) 119–50. – **B. Z. Wacholder**, "The Letter from Judah Maccabee to Aristobulus: Is Maccabees 1:10b–2:18 Authentic?" *HUCA* 49 (1978) 89–133.

The book of 2 Maccabees does not actually begin until its stylized preface in 2:19-32, literally "that which goes before the history" retold in chapters 3–15 (τὸ μὲν πρὸ τῆς ἱστορίας, v. 32). It is here that the author states his procedure and aims. He has before him five books of the Jewish historian Jason of Cyrene about the heroic acts of Judas Maccabeus. From these he wants to make an abridgement or "epitome" (ἐπιτομή, vv. 26, 28; cf. ἐπιτεμνεῖν, v. 23), an adaptation or "paraphrase" (μετάφρασις, v. 31) that will make fewer demands on the reader than the unabridged work. The abridgement aims "to please those who wish to read, to make it easy for those who are inclined to memorize, and to profit all readers" (v. 25).

The underlying work of the Jason of Cyrene, who possessed a good knowledge of Seleucid institutions and reliable documents, was probably written not too long after the events it narrates, which fall between the years 175 and 160 BCE, before Jonathan's elevation to high priest in 152 BCE (so Habicht; differently Goldstein, who favors a late date of 86 BCE). For the epitome the date of the first festival letter that is prefixed to the actual book of 2 Maccabees in 2 Maccabees 1:1-9, namely 124 BCE, should be considered probable (differently Goldstein: between 78 and 63 BCE). If yet a third redactional layer is to be postulated (so Habicht), then in view of the document's consistent high estimation of the temple, the final edition must be dated before 70 CE, probably somewhat earlier.

In its concluding title or *subscriptio*, added by the later copyists (see the final footnote in Rahlfs's *Septuaginta*), the entire book of 2 Maccabees, which Codex Venetus fittingly characterizes as "an excerpt (ἐπιτομή) of the acts of the Judas Maccabeus," is designated in Codex Alexandrinus as "a letter (ἐπιστολή) about the acts of Judas Maccabeus." Analogously to our appraisal of Esther as a foundation legend for the festival of Purim to which the Greek colophon attaches the label "Letter about Purim" (see above on Esth 11:1 NRSV), 2 Maccabees is presented in its opening chapters as an addendum to the two festival letters that begin the document. Before the epitomizer himself begins to speak in 2:19, we encounter in 1:1–2:18 a longer piece of text with formal letter features. Although scholars formerly found only one or as many as three letters in this section, in the meantime it has been established that two letters are present: a shorter one in 1:1-9 (according to the numbering in the NRSV and Rahlfs; or 1:1-10a in Hanhart's Göttingen ed.), and a longer one in 1:10–2:18. We will treat the first of these in somewhat greater detail and then single out the epistolary features of the second, dealing only summarily with its legendary contents and the questions of dating before finally taking a look at the remaining letters in 2 Maccabees.

a) The First Festival Letter

The first letter in 2 Maccabees 1:1-9 runs as follows (NRSV modified; cf. NJB and RSV):

> **1:1** To their brothers, the Jews in Egypt, greetings (χαίρειν), their brothers, the Jews in Jerusalem and in the land of Judea—‹and› good peace (εἰρήνην ἀγαθήν).
>
> **2** May God do good to you, and may he remember his covenant with Abraham and Isaac and Jacob, his faithful servants. **3** May he give you all a heart to worship him and to do his will with a strong heart and a willing spirit. **4** May he open your heart to his law and his commandments, and may he bring peace. **5** May he hear your prayers and be reconciled to you, and may he not forsake you in time of evil (ἐν καιρῷ πονηρῷ). **6** We are now praying for you here.
>
> **7** In the reign of Demetrius, in the one hundred sixty-ninth year, we Jews wrote to you as follows: "In the critical distress that came upon us in those years after Jason and his company fell away from (NRSV: revolted from, ἀπέστη ἀπό) the holy land and the kingdom **8** and burned the gate and shed innocent blood, we prayed to the Lord and were heard, and we offered sacrifice and grain offering, and we lit the lamps and set out the loaves."
>
> **9** And now see that you keep the festival of booths (τὰς ἡμέρας τῆς σκηνοπηγίας) in the month of Chislev, in the one hundred eighty-eighth year.

Despite some uncertainty about the details, the overall epistolary analysis of this text from 2 Maccabees 1:1-9 is not very difficult: Verse 1 contains the prescript, followed in vv. 2-6 by an expansion of the salutation in the form of a long proem. Within the letter body an older document is referred to in vv. 7-8. Verse 9 states the actual purpose of the letter with its invitation or call to the Egyptian Jews to join in the celebration of a festival of Palestinian Judaism.

The year 188 in the Seleucid calendar, to begin with the terminal date, corresponds to the year 124 BCE on our calendar. This is the time of writing of the first festival letter. However, the month of Chislev is equivalent to our December, whereas the Feast of Booths or Tabernacles (Sukkot) falls in September-October. The call to celebrate a "Feast of Booths" in December makes no sense unless it refers to another festival. What is meant is the Festival of Lights or Hanukkah, which commemorates the purification of the profaned temple by Judas Maccabeus on 25 Chislev 164 BCE. What happened on that occasion, and how a new eight-day festival became established—for this took time—is explained within the body of the epitome in 2 Maccabees 10:1-8. See especially 2 Maccabees 10:6: "They celebrated it [sc. the new festival] for eight days with rejoicing, in the manner of the festival of booths"; 10:7: "Therefore they carried ivy-wreathed wands and beautiful branches and also fronds of palm" (which recalls the original Festival of Booths); 10:8: "They decreed . . . that the whole nation of the Jews should observe these days every year." One gets a sense here of the connecting lines that run from the first festival letter in 2 Maccabees 1:1-9 to the epitome. The message that the Jews of Egypt—finally?—ought to adopt this new custom, and perhaps also that they should not let themselves be prevented from doing so out of improper deference to the illegal temple in Leontopolis, is the actual message of the festival letter, including the older insertion in 1:7-8 and the longer "attachment," the epitome.

The embedded letter in 1:7-8 serves to reinforce this request, and possibly also to shame the Egyptian Jews for not having practiced the custom of Hanukkah before now. Its dating points to the time when Demetrius II exercised his one-year rule over Palestine, beginning in late autumn 143 BCE (Seleucid year 169). More difficult to interpret are the first few words of the older letter, because the "critical distress" mentioned there could refer to the time when the letter was written in 143 BCE. It would then have in view the events surrounding the murder of Jonathan and the attack on Jerusalem by his murderer, the Syrian pretender to the throne Trypho. But these first few words could also be the beginning of the backward reference to the time under Antiochus IV Epiphanes, which starts at the latest in the subordinate clause "in those years after Jason and his company fell away" or "revolted" in 1:7 and continues to the end of v. 8. Allusively referred to here are the reform movement of the high priest Jason (175–172 BCE; cf. 2 Macc 4:7–5:10), which is interpreted as a "falling away"; the turning point under Judas Maccabeus, which was an answer to prayer; and the reorganization of the temple service with sacrifices and grain offerings, with burning lamps and the bread of the Presence (cf. also 10:3), which again brings us to the temple rededication in 164 BCE. This means that scarcely 20 years prior to the current letter of 124 BCE, the Jews of Egypt had already been asked in another letter of 143 BCE to be more enthusiastic about the commemoration of the events which at that time already lay some 20 years in the past in 164 BCE. One can recapitulate the very complex temporal nesting on the basis of the "we" form: "we Jews" in v. 7 are the letter writers and the ones now praying in 124 BCE for the Egyptian Jews (cf. vv. 2-5 with v. 6). They are at the same time the ones responsible for the earlier letter of 143 BCE. The phrases "we prayed" and "we offered sacrifice" in v. 8 have in view the participants in the events of 164 BCE, some of whom could very well still be alive now 40 years later in 124 BCE.

The long proem in 2 Maccabees 1:2-6 supplies the theological introduction to this sequence of events. The senders' assurance of their prayers for the recipients in v. 6 is a typical letter component, while v. 2a is reminiscent of the health wish, with a theological twist. The remaining verses between these endpoints bring in the covenant and the patriarchs, wish the addressees God's strength for right worship and the fulfillment of his law, and allude to his covenant faithfulness. The "time of evil" in v. 5 reflects the conditions similar to civil war that prevailed in Egypt due to a long struggle for power between Cleopatra II and Ptolemy VII. The peace wish at the end of v. 4 forms a bridge back to the peace wish in the prescript. The Greek wording in v. 3, καρδίᾳ μεγάλῃ καὶ ψυχῇ βουλομένῃ, "with a strong heart and a willing soul," is not actually as close to Deuteronomy 30:6, "with all your heart and with all your soul" as C. Habicht's German translation of 2 Maccabees suggests. But whoever wrote the letter probably did intend the close parallel to 1 Chron 28:9, ἐν καρδίᾳ τελείᾳ καὶ ψυχῇ θελούσῃ, "with a perfect heart and willing soul," because this verse is found in the last instructions of David to his son Solomon concerning the building of the temple, which evokes a situation similar to 2 Maccabees.[14]

---

[14] The intentionality of this parallel to the Greek text of 1 Chronicles 28:9 can be understood in different ways, depending on the

The prescript in v. 1 follows a pattern well known from Aramaic epistolography. It does not run, "A to B, greetings," but rather: "To B, greetings, A." Nevertheless, the typical dative form for the addressees and the nominative for the senders are retained, as is the infinitive χαίρειν. Two collectives are contacting each other, the Jews from Jerusalem and Judea and the Jews in Egypt. The addition "good peace" (εἰρήνην ἀγαθήν) in the accusative at the end of v. 1 can hardly be construed syntactically, even with the help of the conjectural emendation ‹καί› (for a complicated explanation see Goldstein 140–41). The Jewish peace wish shines through,[15] and it is reasonably certain that this letter was translated into Greek from Hebrew or Aramaic, unlike the work of Jason of Cyrene and the epitome, whose original language is Greek. The letter's contents suggest its designation as a "festival letter," a term we have already been using. For this there are ready points of comparison, including the Purim letters in Esther (9:20-32), the Passover letters in 2 Chronicles 30:1-9 and Elephantine (see above, sec. A.3.a), the later letters from rabbinic times, which are especially interested in fixing the exact day of the festivals, and not least the Easter letters in the ancient church (also referred to by Bickermann). The authenticity of this first festival letter is hardly ever contested. As already suggested, the writing of an epitome of Jason of Cyrene's historical work commemorating among other things the origin of Hanukkah could stand in a causal relationship with the writing of this festival letter about Hanukkah,

---

authorship of the first festival letter. If the letter was attached to 2 Maccabees by the epitomizer, he had the text at hand and did not create it *de novo*. That he rewrote some phrases, such as "with a strong heart and a willing soul" in v. 3, in order to make an intertextual connection between the temple plans of David and Solomon and the temple rededication by the Jews under Judas Maccabeus (as recorded in the epitome) is a possibilty that cannot be excluded. But the letter's affinities with the body of 2 Maccabees could also be explained simply by assuming that the letter's original author lived through the same historical events preserved in the epitome. The letter's mention of the liberation of the temple and the institution of a new festival need not be derived from 2 Maccabees at all.

[15] Cf. Bickermann 245: "The prescript is therefore neither Greek nor purely Semitic in its formulation. It is best understood as a translator's attempt to reproduce the full content of the Jewish blessing formula in a Greek manner."

which would offer a simple explanation for the combination of the two texts in 2 Maccabees.

b) The Second Festival Letter

Although it is written in idiomatic Greek, the second festival letter is also a work of translation. This time the analysis of the structure takes more effort, and not only because of the letter's greater length. The letter begins in 2 Maccabees 1:10 with a prescript. There follows a proem framed by vv. 11-12 and 17, within which a first episode of divine intervention is reported. Verse 18 then returns to the reason for writing and introduces the long letter body:

> **1:10** The people of Jerusalem and of Judea and the senate and Judas, to Aristobulus, who is of the family of the anointed priests, teacher of King Ptolemy, and to the Jews in Egypt: Greetings and good health (χαίρειν καὶ ὑγιαίνειν).
> **11** Having been saved by God out of grave dangers we thank him greatly for taking our side against the king, **12** for he drove out those who fought against the holy city. **13** When the leader reached Persia. . . . **17** Blessed in every way be our God, who has brought judgment on those who have behaved impiously.
> **18** Since on the twenty-fifth day of Chislev we shall celebrate the purification of the temple, we thought it necessary to notify you, in order that you also may celebrate the festival of booths and the festival of the fire given when Nehemiah, who built the temple and the altar, offered sacrifices. **19** For when our fathers were being led captive to Persia. . . .

The prescript once again follows the Greek form "A to B, greetings." The identification of the senders gives pride of place to the residents of Jerusalem and Judea, also mentioning the senate (γερ-ουσία) and Judas Maccabeus. As to the addressees, before the Jews of Egypt are mentioned, Aristobulus is named as a person commanding special respect. He was a Jewish scholar from a priestly family with connections to Ptolemy VI Philometor (181–145 BCE) and is presumably identical with the Jewish author whose expositions of the law we still possess in fragments (cf. *OTP* 2:831–42). In the greeting χαίρειν is expanded by ὑγιαίνειν, but since we have already observed this doubling in the lead tablet of Mnesiergos from the fourth century BCE (see above p. 19), the fact that this twofold formula is otherwise attested in private letters only from 60 BCE onward loses its force.

The proem begins in v. 11 with an epistolary thanksgiving using εὐχαριστεῖν that speaks of God's saving intervention in the battle for Jerusalem and the temple. At the end of the proem in v. 17 there is a blessing of God modeled on the Old Testament *berakah*, with εὐλογητός as a predicate adjective. Its archetype was perhaps the *berakah* from Solomon's prayer of dedication of the temple in 1 Kings 8:56: "Blessed be the Lord, who has given rest to his people Israel according to all that he promised." In this connection a story is told in vv. 13-16 in which God's intervention is exemplarily illustrated. Antiochus IV wanted to stage a wedding with the Mesopotamian goddess Nanaia in Persia in order to take possession of her temple treasures. But her priests set a trap for him and killed both him and his men in the sanctuary by throwing down boulders from a secret door in the ceiling. This version of the story of Antiochus's death may very well offer reason for praise and thanksgiving, but it disagrees with the other version of his death in the epitome in 9:5-12, 28-29. Therefore the epitome and the second festival letter were originally unconnected writings.

The transition to the letter body in 2 Maccabees 1:18 once again takes up the December commemoration of the purification of the temple, which the addressees in Egypt should also celebrate. As a motivation the story is told of the reestablishment of the temple cult under Nehemiah after Israel's return from the Babylonian exile. In a departure from the rest of the tradition, Nehemiah is here presented not as the builder of the city wall but as builder of the temple and the altar (Goldstein thinks the names of Nehemiah and Zerubbabel have been confused). The separate mention of a "festival of fire" may be connected with the fact that during Hanukkah, the lights that one burns for eight days in memory of the rekindling of the temple lamps have special meaning.

The legendary traditions that follow v. 18 in the letter body are also concerned with the temple and with fire. We are told that before they were taken away to "Persia" (i.e., Babylon, part of the Persian empire by the time of Nehemiah and Zerubbabel), the temple priests took fire from the altar and hid it in a dry cistern. When the descendents of these priests returned to the cistern years later, they found only a thick liquid that turns out to be petroleum oil. After it is poured over the pile of wood on the altar, it begins to burn under the rays of the sun (1:19-22). During the sacrifice of the burnt offering a prayer is addressed to God for the gathering of all the scattered members of the people (1:23-29).

Chapter 2 has more to say about the theme of fire, altars, and other holy objects. In 2 Maccabees 2:1-8 the written records associated with the prophet Jeremiah make their contribution. Jeremiah's instructions to the deportees in v. 2 "not to forget the commandments of the Lord, or to be led astray in their thoughts on seeing the gold and silver statues and their adornment" could be an allusion to the Letter of Jeremiah (see above, sec. A.1.e). Moreover, we are told that Jeremiah hid the original tent of meeting, ark of the covenant, and incense altar in a secret cave, where he prophesied that they would remain until God gathers his people again and reveals the holy objects through the cloud of his presence. This in turn recalls the tabernacle of Moses and the temple of Solomon, both of whom prayed to God and were answered by fire from heaven that consumed their sacrifices (2:9-12). According to 2:13-15 Nehemiah founded a library in Jerusalem that also housed "letters of (pagan) kings about votive offerings (in the Jerusalem temple)." After the Maccabean revolt Judas Maccabeus sought to restore the books that had been lost on account of the war (cf. 1 Macc 1:56-57). The Egyptian Jews are invited to borrow books from this library by "interlibrary loan" (2:15). The letter closing follows in 2 Maccabees 2:16-18:

> **2:16** Since, therefore, we are about to celebrate the purification, we write to you. You will do well to keep these days. **17** It is God who has saved all his people, and has returned the inheritance to all, and the kingship and the priesthood and the consecration, **18** as he promised through the law. We have hope in God that he will soon have mercy on us and will gather us from everywhere under heaven into his holy place, for he has rescued us from great evils and has purified the place.

The mention of the "purification" in vv. 16 and 18 recapitulates the occasion for the entire letter, the celebration of the rededication of the temple. Verse 16 contains a typical epistolary reflection on the act of writing, as well as a polite circumlocution for a direct request that the Egyptian Jews should also join in the celebration of Hanukkah, expressed in the phrase καλῶς οὖν ποιήσατε ἄγοντες τὰς ἡμέρας, "You will do well to keep these days." The acclamation of God in 2:17-18 formally takes up the thanksgiving and the blessing of God from the start of the letter in 1:11 and 1:17 and also parallels parts of the letter concerning the gathering of Israel (cf. 2:18 with 1:27; 2:7) and the remembrance of past acts of deliverance in times of danger or evil (cf. 2:18 with 1:11; in the first letter also 1:5).

The second letter, which purports to be sent by Judas Maccabeus and therefore to be dated between 164 and 160 BCE, owes its length above all to the fact that the letter framework has become the depository for traditions of various origins and forms, including prayers, historical reminiscences, and prophetic and cultic legends. It has received very different appraisals in scholarship. E. Bickermann regards it as a forgery and dates it to the year 60 BCE at the earliest, while his student J. Goldstein agrees with the designation as a forgery but dates it somewhat earlier in 103–102 BCE. J. G. Bunge sees an authentic letter in the framing sections 1:10-18 and 2:16-18, whose parts simply need to be rearranged; the intervening 1:19–2:15 is then a long interpolation. C. Habicht seems singularly unimpressed: "not authentic" (202). B. Z. Wacholder, followed by I. Taatz, once again champions the authenticity of the whole letter and its dating to 164 BCE, but with weak arguments. One has to concede that the second festival letter is fictional, perhaps in dependence on the first and with the aim of making room for the legendary traditional material it includes. But its insertion between the first festival letter and the epitome can only have occurred at the third level of redaction to which we owe the final form of 2 Maccabees.

c) Four Letters with Political Content

Before leaving 2 Maccabees it is worth mentioning that within the epitome, 2 Maccabees 11:16-38 quotes four diplomatic letters from the year 165–164 BCE that are probably authentic, even though they were written in a different order than presented here; hence Habicht reorders them in the sequence 3, 1, 4, 2. In the first letter, 11:16-21, Lysias, the chancellor of Antiochus IV, writes to the Jews, concluding his letter with ἔρρωσθε, "Farewell," and the date (so also letter 3 in 11:33; letter 4 reads ὑγιαίνετε instead of ἔρρωσθε in 11:38, but the NRSV renders this identically as "Farewell"). In the second example, 11:22-26, a letter from

Antiochus V Eupator to Lysias is cited in which the young king reflects on the death of his father and allows the Jews to restore the temple and freely practice their religion. Addressed directly "to the senate of the Jews and to the other Jews" (followed by a reciprocal health wish) is the third letter in 11:27-33, an earlier document in which Antiochus IV offers amnesty to the Jews and concessions to the Jewish reform party concerning the corrupt high priest Menelaus (who among other things had ushered Antiochus into the temple, cf. 5:15). In the final letter in 11:34-38 the Roman envoys Quintus Memmius und Titus Manius (presumably a miswriting for Manilius) articulate the political interests of the Romans.

Exercise

32. Second Maccabees 9:1-29 offers a detailed report about the terrible end of the tyrannical ruler Antiochus IV Epiphanes. Within this passage the king is presented as writing a letter to the Jews, reproduced in vv. 19-27, which the introduction in v. 18 describes as ἱκετηρίας τάξιν ἔχουσαν, "having the form of a supplication." Identify its formal features and seek to make a judgment about its authenticity (NRSV; but see vv. 20-21a note*).

9:18 But when his sufferings did not in any way abate, for the judgment of God had justly come upon him, he gave up all hope for himself and wrote to the Jews the following letter, in the form of a supplication. This was its content:

19 "To his worthy Jewish citizens, Antiochus their king and general sends hearty greetings and good wishes for their health and prosperity (πολλὰ χαίρειν καὶ ὑγιαίνειν καὶ εὖ πράττειν). **20** If you and your children are well and your affairs are as you wish, (sc. I am glad). [The Greek lacks this last parenthetical comment of the NRSV, therefore εἰ ἔρρωσθε καὶ τὰ τέκνα καὶ τὰ ἴδια κατὰ γνώμην ἐστὶν ὑμῖν concludes the clause.]] As my hope is in heaven, **21** I remember with affection your esteem and goodwill. [Another text reads: "If you and your children are well and everything that belongs to you is as you would have it, I am most grateful to God. I myself have been ill, but I remember you with affection."]* On my way back from the region of Persia I suffered an annoying illness, and I have deemed it necessary to take thought for the general security of all. **22** I do not despair of my condition, for I have good hope of recovering from my illness, **23** but I observed that my father, on the occasions when he made expeditions into the upper country, appointed his successor, **24** so that, if anything unexpected happened or any unwelcome news came, the people throughout the realm would not be troubled, for they would know to whom the government was left. **25** Moreover, I understand how the princes along the borders and the neighbors of my kingdom keep watching for opportunities and waiting to see what will happen. So I have appointed my son Antiochus to be king, whom I have often entrusted and commended to most of you when I hurried off to the upper provinces; and I have written to him what is written here. **26** I therefore urge and beg you to remember the public and private services rendered to you and to maintain your present goodwill, each of you, toward me and my son. **27** For I am sure that he will follow my policy and will treat you with moderation and kindness."

* *Textual note:* "I am glad" (2 Macc 9:20 NRSV). The NRSV's phrase is not present in Rahlfs's text, based on Codices A and V, and needs to be supplied by the reader, for in Greek we have only: εἰ ἔρρωσθε καὶ τὰ τέκνα καὶ τὰ ἴδια κατὰ γνώμην ἐστὶν ὑμῖν· εἰς οὐρανὸν τὴν ἐλπίδα ἔχων, etc. The REB translates the first part without the NRSV's addition: "May you and your children flourish and your affairs progress as you wish." There is also a longer version of the Greek text, printed in the Göttingen Septuagint (Kappler and Hanhart), but some specialists, particularly J. A. Goldstein, judge that certain Old Latin and Vulgate manuscripts more nearly approximate the original reading, printed in double brackets above. The reasons why the Latin evidence may be more faithful than the Greek in this instance are complicated; see the Answer Key.

2. Testament and Legacy: The Letter in *2 Baruch* 77–87

Bibliography 33: A. F. J. Klijn, "2 (Syriac Apocalypse of) Baruch," *OTP* 1:615–52. – idem, "Die syrische Baruch-Apokalypse," in *Apokalypsen*, JSHRZ 5/2 (Gütersloh 1976) 103–91. – **P. Bogaert**, *Apocalypse de Baruch*, 2 vols., SC 144–45 (Paris 1969). – **B. Violet**, *Die Apokalypsen des Esra und* *des Baruch in deutscher Gestalt*, GCS 32 (Leipzig 1924). – **C. Andresen**, "Formular" (Bib. 4) 237–43. – **A. M. Denis**, *Fragmenta Pseudepigraphorum quae supersunt graeca*, PVTG 3 (Leiden 1970) 118–20 (**TLG**). – **M. Karrer**, *Johannesoffenbarung* (Bib. 4) 49–53. – **F. J. Murphy**, *The Structure and Meaning of Second Baruch*, SBLDS 78 (Atlanta 1985). – **I. Taatz**, *Frühjüdische Briefe* (Bib. 3) 59–76. – **M. F. Whitters**, *The Epistle of Second Baruch: A Study in Form and Message*, JSPSup 42 (Sheffield 2003). – **J. E. Wright**, *Baruch ben Neriah: From Biblical Scribe to Apocalyptic Seer* (Columbia, S.C. 2003).

Second Baruch is also known as the *Syriac Apocalypse of Baruch* because it has been preserved mainly in a Syriac translation, apart from two Greek fragments covering 12:1–13:2 and 13:11–14:3 in P.Oxy. III 403 (also in Denis). The Syriac was translated from a Greek original, as the heading of the manuscript says, but there are indications that this Greek version may also have been a translation from Hebrew or Aramaic, although this is not absolutely certain. As its alternative name "apocalypse" suggests, *2 Baruch* belongs to the genre of early Jewish apocalyptic literature, like *4 Ezra* or *1 Enoch*, in which a seer is chosen to receive insights into the heavenly world, often dealing with the events of the end time, which he then relates to his followers. Such apocalyptic writings were usually named after a great man of the past who is said to have received the revelations, in this case Baruch, the secretary of the prophet Jeremiah, mentioned for example in Jeremiah 36:32: "Then Jeremiah took another scroll and gave it to the secretary Baruch son of Neriah, who wrote on it at Jeremiah's dictation all the words of the scroll that King Jehoiakim of Judah had burned in the fire." The figure of Baruch became a point of crystallization for the later recording of religious traditions, beginning with the deuterocanonical book of Baruch in the Septuagint (the Letter of Jeremiah is a separate book in the LXX and the NRSV but is counted as Baruch chapter 6 in the Vulgate; see above, sec. A.1.e). Relative to this Septuagintal book, which is sometimes called 1 Baruch, the Syriac apocalypse is numbered *2 Baruch*, and there is also a Greek apocalypse numbered *3 Baruch* (cf. *OTP* 1:653–79).

Second Baruch first emerged after the destruction of the temple in 70 CE, more precisely in Palestine between 95 and 120 CE, even though its fictitious literary setting is Jerusalem in the time of Jeremiah. Its speaker Baruch reflects back on the destruction of Jerusalem in 587 BCE and on the period of the Babylonian exile, a catastrophe that struck the tribes of Israel that remained in the south of the country, that is, the two and a half tribes of Judah, Benjamin, and half Levi. Moreover, in the concluding section with which we are primarily concerned, Baruch also addresses himself to the exiles of the earlier Assyrian deportation of the nine and a half northern tribes who were thought to live beyond the Euphrates, though this was more a hope than a reality at the time of *2 Baruch*. These earlier disasters are presented and interpreted by an alleged eyewitness in such a way as to suggest something about the contemporary situation that had arisen for the Jews at the end of the first century CE.

The book can be subdivided into seven parts, the first six of which are punctuated by Baruch's repeated seven-day fasts (cf. 9:2; 12:5; 20:5; 43:3; 47:2). These sections include backward looks at the destruction of Jerusalem, statements about the future, a lamentation, a catechetical section with questions and answers, visions, and a long prayer. The seventh part, which stretches from chapters 77 to 87, consists mainly of a long letter of Baruch addressed to the nine and a half northern tribes in the Assyrian Dispersion east of the Euphrates, although the composition also shows concern for the other part of the Jewish Diaspora in Babylon (see below on *2 Bar.* 77:12, 17). This long letter also has a separate life of its own in the manuscript tradition. Whereas the complete apocalypse, including the letter, is preserved in only a single manuscript in Milan, there are 38 further copies of the letter on its own. For although the apocalypse is not canonical in any Christian tradition, the letter was taken up separately into the Syriac Bible,[16] where it is placed, for example, between the Letter of Jeremiah and the book of Baruch, thus further illustrating the development of a letter tradition of Jeremiah and Baruch.

The sixth main part, Baruch's vision of a cloud, concludes in *2 Baruch* 77:1-17 with Baruch's address to the few people who

---

[16] The letter from *2 Baruch* 78–87 in the Syriac Bible is not included in the NRSV, for its extended "canon" does not represent the entire tradition of the Eastern churches, but only those churches, and hence biblical canons, with larger representation in English-speaking countries, principally the Greek Orthodox Church (hence the inclusion of *4 Maccabees* in the NRSV) and the Russian Orthodox Church (i.e., the Slavonic Bible).

remain with him in Jerusalem after its destruction (cf. 80:5) and their reaction. In v. 12 they make a special request: "Write to our brothers in Babylon a letter of doctrine and a roll of hope so that you might strengthen them also before you go away from us." This letter is intended for the exiles in Babylon, and the prophet, as is already clear, is about to die. The letter is therefore Baruch's spiritual legacy, which approaches the genre of a literary testament. But the author's impulse for having Baruch write a letter in the first place probably comes from the letter that Jeremiah sent to the deportees in Babylon in Jeremiah 29.

In *2 Baruch* 77:17 Baruch responds affirmatively: "I shall write to your brothers in Babylon, as you have said to me, and I shall send it by means of men. Also I shall write to the nine and a half tribes, and send it by means of a bird." The last main part of *2 Baruch* then begins in 77:18-19. Baruch sits alone in the shadows of an oak and writes the two letters. The one he sends by three men, the other by an eagle—a messenger of an extraordinary type (cf. Bogaert 2:137). Before sending it on its way, Baruch speaks a final word of exhortation to the eagle (77:21-26), challenging it with the example of three birds from Israel's salvation history who successfully completed their missions: the dove of Noah, the ravens that fed Elijah (1 Kgs 17:6), and the legendary bird that Solomon sent as a messenger (cf. *Ecclesiastes Rabbah* 2:25). The eagle is designated as the messenger of Zeus in a Greek epigram from the first century CE: "As the eagle who circles on high, who alone among the birds is an inmate of heaven, was bearing a message from Zeus . . ." (*The Greek Anthology* 9.223.1–2 [LCL 3:117]). When the "king of the skies" carries a letter, it must be a very unusual document with special authority. Evidently only the eagle can track down the missing northern tribes in a far distant land. Moreover, such a heavenly postal delivery, which arrives with a punch as the eagle is commanded to "cast down to them this letter" (77:22), better fits the apocalyptic milieu than a delivery by human messengers. In Revelation 8:18 an eagle flying in midheaven cries out its message of woe to those on earth.

The letter to the nine and a half tribes is given verbatim beginning in 78:2, but there is no longer any mention of the first letter to the exiles in Babylon, even though this is precisely the letter that the remnant in Jerusalem had requested. Some scholars have wanted to identify this apparently lost letter with the Septuagintal book of Baruch, which is certainly wrong (cf. Bogaert 1:78). But it is worth asking whether the entire *Apocalypse of Baruch* might not fulfill this function of a letter to the exiles to Babylon,[17] or whether there is an indirect reference here to an already existing earlier letter (Bogaert 1:80). After an introductory heading in 78:1, the actual letter to the nine and a half tribes begins in *2 Baruch* 78:2 with an epistolary prescript vv. 2-3a and a proem in vv. 3b-7 (on vv. 6-7 see below) patterned on Jeremiah 29:1 (trans. Klijn in *OTP*):

> **78:1** These are the words of the letter which Baruch, the son of Neriah, sent to the nine and a half tribes which were across the river in which were written the following things:
>
> **2** Thus speaks Baruch, the son of Neriah, to the brothers who were carried away into captivity: **3** Grace and peace be with you. I remember, my brothers, the love of him who created me, who loved us from the beginning and who never hated us but, on the contrary, chastised us. **4** And truly I know: Are we not all, the twelve tribes, bound by one captivity as we also descend from one father? **5** Therefore, I have been the more diligent to leave you the words of this letter before I die so that you may be comforted regarding the evils which have befallen you, and you may also be grieved with regard to the evils which have befallen your brothers, and then further, so that you may consider the judgment of him who decreed it against you to be righteous, namely, that you should be carried away into captivity, for what you have suffered is smaller than what you have done, in order that you may be found worthy of your fathers in the last times.

With its introductory "thus speaks Baruch," the prescript is oriented to the self-presentation of the messenger in the older oral messenger formula, yet without presenting the content as a Yahweh speech, as in the actual prophetic messenger formula. The address of members of one's own tribe or people as "brothers" comes from the Deuteronomistic tradition and is maintained throughout the whole book. The greeting, which stands as a separate element of the sentence, builds on the peace wish and expands it into a double expression. Since the Syriac can be translated in two different

---

[17] A possibility mentioned by Violet LXXV, who then however finds another rationale for the missing letter to Babylon, "Therefore I would prefer to think of an intentional secretiveness that will pique the interest and curiosity of the reader."

ways—either "mercy and peace" or "grace and peace"—it is impossible to tell whether the original Greek read ἔλεος καὶ εἰρήνη (cf. 1 Tim 1:2) or χάρις καὶ εἰρήνη (cf. Rom 1:7).

The remembrance of God and his love in *2 Baruch* 78:3 suggests a formal association with the usual remembrance of other people in prayer in the letter formula, and this could be intentional, even though the content is not a remembrance of others but an attribute of God. Verse 3 therefore resembles a thanksgiving or rather an epistolary eulogy that has taken on an unfamiliar form. The common fate of the entire twelve-tribed people of Israel that will be fully gathered only in the end time is invoked in v. 4. The reference to Baruch's impending death at the beginning of the long v. 5 also nudges this second letter to the northern tribes in the direction of a literary testament (cf. 77:12). Verse 5 also states the letter's three themes, which are that the nine and a half tribes should be comforted about the disaster of their own deportation, be grieved to learn that the same has now happened to their brothers of the southern tribes exiled to Babylon, and acknowledge the justice of God's judgment in their own exile to Assyria. These three themes are treated in a different order in the body of the letter (cf. Taatz 64–65): first comes the disaster that struck the southern tribes in chapters 79–80 (the fall of Jerusalem), then the comfort to the letter addressees about all these tribulations in chapters 81–83, then the call to the addressees to accept God's judgment and internalize the consequences in chapters 84–85. The aim of consolation is stated directly as an imperative in 81:1: "But also hear the word of consolation," which compares closely with characterization of the Letter to the Hebrews as a λόγος τῆς παρακλήσεως or "word of consolation/exhortation" (Heb 13:22). In 78:6, not printed above, the author offers a brief preview of the final judgment, from which the addressees can be spared by their present sufferings, while v. 7 appeals to God's faithfulness to the patriarchs in order to shine a ray of hope: the future ingathering of all Israel from the Dispersion to be one people in one land. Therefore with its disguised eulogy at the beginning, its naming of the main themes of the following letter in the middle, and its eschatological prospect at the end, the proem in *2 Baruch* 78:3b-7 bears an extraordinary resemblance to the introductions to the New Testament letters—for example, the proem in 1 Corinthians 1:4-9.

The phrase "Therefore, my brothers, learn first" (*2 Bar.* 79:1) opens the letter body, which is also structured by additional disclosure formulas, including: "But also hear" (81:1); "But you ought to know" (82:2); "Now, I gave you knowledge" (84:1); "Further, know that" (85:1). See also 82:1, "My brothers, therefore I have written you," and various imperatives such as 84:2, "Remember that," which serve to keep the address to the readership alive. Here we can provide only a cursory overview of the contents. According to 79:1-3, the sins of the southern tribes were the reason for Nebuchadnezzar's attack on the Holy City. Even the angels of God helped Israel's enemies in their demolition work (80:1), but not before the angels had first removed the holy vessels from the temple and hidden them safely (80:2). The grieving prophet is taught the "mysteries of the times" (81:4) in visions resembling those in earlier parts of the book, which open up a hopeful prospect for the future: God will punish his enemies (82:20), judge all people according to their works (83:1), and reverse present circumstances, changing health into illness, might into weakness, youth into old age, beauty into ugliness, glory into shame, and so on (see the impressive list in 83:10-13). After this, the special character of this letter as a last testament of its author again comes to the fore (84:1-11):

> **84:1** Now, I gave you knowledge, while I still live. . . . And I shall set before you some of the commandments of his judgment before I die. . . . **7** Therefore, let this letter be a witness between me and you that you may remember the commandments of the Mighty One, and that it also may serve as my defense in the presence of him who has sent me. . . . **9** And give this letter and the traditions of the Law to your children after you as also your fathers handed down to you.

Baruch's protestation of his innocence in *2 Baruch* 84:7 has a fixed place in the genre of the literary testament (cf. Acts 20:19-20).[18] The call to hand down the tradition, which 84:9 says can be done with the help of this letter, is also a standard part of this repertoire, as are the looks into the past, the glimpses of the future, and the

---

[18] For a detailed study see M. Winter, *Das Vermächtnis Jesu und die Abschiedsworte der Väter: Gattungsgeschichtliche Untersuchung der Vermächtnisrede im Blick auf Joh 13–17*, FRLANT 161 (Göttingen 1994).

general hortatory, instructional, and consoling tone of the letter, which also fits the characteristics of the paraenetic letter. This final section of *2 Baruch* displays an extensive overlapping of testamentary and epistolary forms, which can also be observed in 2 Timothy, while the interweaving of letter and apocalypse has a New Testament parallel in Revelation. There is even a bridge to the festival letters in 2 Maccabees when we read in *2 Baruch* 84:8, "do not forget the festivals and the sabbaths."

In *2 Baruch* 85:6 Baruch's letter to the exiles in Babylon is suddenly brought up again: "We also have written to our brothers in Babylon so that I may attest to them these things also." With "these things" is meant especially the paraenesis about judgment that is prepared for in 85:1-5 and intensifies after 85:7: "Therefore, before his judgment extracts its own . . . , let us prepare ourselves" (85:9); "There will not be an opportunity to repent anymore, nor a limit to the times" (85:12). From the concluding note of the letter in 86:1, the call to have it read "in your assemblies" deserves special mention for its parallels to the New Testament (cf. 1 Thess 5:27; Col 4:16). The whole book ends in 87:1 with a brief report about the preparation of the letter that also recalls the letter's narrative introduction about Baruch commissioning the eagle in 77:18-26 and the letter's heading "The letter of Baruch, the son of Neriah" (78:1):

> **86:1** When you, therefore, receive the letter, read it carefully in your assemblies. And think about it, in particular, however, on the days of your fasts. And remember me by means of this letter in the same way as I remember you by means of this, and always.

> **87:1** And it happened when I had finished all the words of this letter and had written it carefully until the end, I folded it, sealed it cautiously, and bound it to the neck of the eagle. And I let it go and sent it away.
>
> The end of the letter of Baruch, the son of Neriah.

The call to meditate on the letter during days of fasting, which is a regular practice of Judaism in connection with the Day of Atonement (Yom Kippur), can once again be interpreted as a gentle pointer in the direction of the festival letter, but is not enough to support speculation about a liturgical use of the isolated letter on this occasion (contra Taatz 74). The mutual act of remembrance between sender and addressees that was missing in the proem, and particularly the request that the addressees remember the sender (cf. 1 Thess 5:25), is finally supplied in 86:1.

If one compares the contents of the letter with the other six sections of *2 Baruch*, one ascertains extensive convergence. The only difference is that before, visionary, esoteric knowledge was transmitted in apocalyptic pictorial language to a limited audience that needed to have it deciphered, whereas now the letter is ultimately directed to all Israel. The letter bursts the bounds of the apocalyptic genre, apparently on purpose. It transforms "secret revelation" into public exhortation and consolation (cf. Bogaert 76), providing the key to understanding the whole work after the fact (Bogaert 121). In many formal and material details, the letter in *2 Baruch* 78–86 stands closer to the New Testament epistolary literature than any other document we know—including the rest of the Jewish letters, as profitable as their comparative study continues to be.

Exercise

33. Make a synoptic comparison of the epistolary opening in *2 Baruch* 78:1-3 (see above) with the opening verses of Jeremiah's letter in Jeremiah 29:1-5. Pay special attention to the use of typical letter features.

---

3. To Babylon and Back: *The Paraleipomena Jeremiou* or *4 Baruch*

Bibliography 34: J. R. Harris, *The Rest of the Words of Baruch: A Christian Apocalypse of the Year 136 A.D.*, Haverford College Studies 2 (London 1889). – **R. A. Kraft** and **A. E. Purintun**, *Paraleipomena Jeremiou*, SBLTT 1 (Missoula 1972) (**TLG**). – **S. E. Robinson**, "4 Baruch," *OTP* 2:413–25. – **J. Herzer**, *4 Baruch (Paraleipomena Jeremiou)*, SBL Writings from the Greco-Roman World 22 (Atlanta 2005). – **B. Schaller**, "Paralipomena Jeremiou," in *Historische und legendarische Erzählungen*, JSHRZ 1/8 (1998) 661–777. – **J. Riaud**, *Les Paralipomènes du prophète Jérémie*, Cahiers du centre interdisciplinaire de recherches en histoire, lettres et langues 14 (Angers 1994).

P. Bogaert, *Apocalypse* (Bib. 33) 177–221. – **G. Delling**, *Jüdische Lehre und Frömmigkeit in den Paralipomena Jeremiae*, BZAW 100 (Berlin 1970). – **B. Heininger**, "Totenerweckung oder Weckruf (ParJer 7,12-20)? Gnostische Spurensuche in den Paralipomena Jeremiae," *SNTU* 23 (1998) 79–112. – **J. Herzer**, *Die Paralipomena Jeremiae: Studien zu Tradition und Redaktion einer Haggada des frühen Judentums*, TSAJ 43 (Tübingen 1994). – **C. Wolff**, "Irdisches und himmlisches Jerusalem— Die Heilshoffnung in den Paralipomena Jeremiae," *ZNW* 82 (1991) 147–58.

The Greek title of this writing, known as the *Paraleipomena Jeremiou* (Latin: *Paralipomena Jeremiae*), runs Τὰ Παραλειπόμενα Ἰερεμίου τοῦ Προφήτου. It thus parallels the title of the Old Testament books of Chronicles in the Septuagint, each of which is called a (sc. Βιβλίον) Παραλιπομένων (I and II). Kraft and Purintun, followed by Robinson, render the title *Paraleipomena Jeremiou tou Prophetou* as "Things Omitted from Jeremiah the Prophet" (Herzer, *4 Baruch:* "The Matters Omitted")—or rather from the biblical book by his name—which are here preserved as an addendum. Unfortunately, this document is sometimes difficult to locate by its Greek title in English-speaking scholarship, where it is now often presented under the title of its *Ethiopic* version, "The Rest of the Words of Baruch," and given the siglum *4 Baruch*. Yet this can cause confusion, because the same writing has also been numbered *2 Baruch* or *3 Baruch*. Oddly enough, Robinson in his translation in *OTP* begins the book with its Greek title, "Things Omitted from Jeremiah the Prophet" (with the Ethiopic title in a footnote), while the editor's table of contents and running heads call it *4 Baruch*, with no mention of Jeremiah; Baruch is also given the priority in Herzer's title, *4 Baruch (Paraleipomena Jeremiou)*. In fact, Jeremiah is no less prominent in the final form of the book than Baruch, since he ends up delivering to Baruch (cf. 9:29) the mysteries he had seen during the three days of his death, before his resurrection (cf. 9:7-14).

In keeping with our focus on Greek sources for the comparison with the New Testament, we will use the Greek designation *Paraleipomena Jeremiou (Par. Jer.)*. Since the versification differs significantly in the editions, we will follow that of Kraft and Purintun and of Robinson in *OTP* (the basis of our comments) as the most accessible English editions, with cross references to the versification of Harris, which is followed by Herzer, *4 Baruch* (Schaller in German prints both numbering systems).

As in the Syriac apocalypse *2 Baruch*, which *Paraleipomena Jeremiou* partly parallels, the destruction of Jerusalem in 587 BCE serves as the fictitious setting, but what is actually meant is the destruction of Jerusalem by the Romans in 70 CE. The points of contact with *2 Baruch* can be explained either by the use of *2 Baruch* by the author of *Par. Jer.* or by mutual dependence on common sources. Whether the Greek version of *Par. Jer.* goes back to a Semitic original is a question we can leave open here. The origins of *Par. Jer.* are to be found in the early second century CE. In its literary setting the book spans the years from the destruction of Jerusalem by the Babylonians to the awakening of Jeremiah's servant Abimelech the Ethiopian from his long sleep 66 years later (*Par. Jer.* 5:2). But if one reads this in the light of the destruction by the Romans in 70 CE and adds these 66 years, one comes to the year 136 CE, which could justify viewing this writing as part of the fresh wave of messianic hopes associated with the Bar Kokhba revolt (so Robinson). The concluding section about Jeremiah's death and resurrection in 9:14-22 (or 9:11-22) is a later Christian addition, which raises the question of Christian interpolations in the other chapters. But generally the tendency in scholarship is to regard the rest of *Par. Jer.* as a work of pure Jewish origin and not, as in the earlier research (see Harris), as a Jewish Christian writing. But the last word about this has not yet been spoken.

Our reason for discussing *Paraleipomena Jeremiou* is the fact that it contains two shorter letters, one from Baruch to Jeremiah, who followed the people into exile, in 6:19-25 (Harris 6:17-23), and another as Jeremiah's reply to Baruch in 7:24-34 (Harris 7:23-29). Neither displays similarity of content with the long letter in *2 Baruch* 78–86, but by means of the eagle motif there still remain points of contact in the narrative framework. Both letters are very closely interwoven with the overall story, which makes it necessary to survey at least the most important elements of the narrative.

God announces to Jeremiah in chapter 1 that the conquest of Jerusalem by its enemies is already a settled matter. At his behest Jeremiah and Baruch go up onto the city walls in the sixth hour of the night. They watch as the angels of God prepare to set it on fire. In response to his urgent plea Jeremiah receives a short reprieve—just enough time to hide the holy vessels of the temple.

He also manages to secure a special privilege for Abimelech the Ethiopian (Ebed-melech in Jeremiah), who had helped him on another occasion (cf. Jer 38:6-13). In order to spare him from witnessing the city's demise, Jeremiah is allowed to send Abimelech to the vineyard of Agrippa (I) outside the city to collect figs (cf. Jer 24:1-10) and bring them back to the sick among the people (*Par. Jer.* 3:12-14, 21).

The city is captured, Jeremiah goes along into exile, and Baruch sits down in a tomb in despair (chap. 4). In the meantime Abimelech takes a siesta in the midday heat, and when he wakes up, the figs in his basket are still fresh, even though sixty-six years have passed without his knowing it, and it takes him a while to figure this out (chap. 5). An angel of the Lord escorts him to Baruch, who is still sitting in the tomb, but Baruch gains new hope when he sees the fresh figs: just like the figs, the people too will be preserved, and the whole exile will seem like the sixty-six years that Abimelech experienced as no more than a short nap (cf. Ps 126:1).

These events ought to be reported to Jeremiah in Babylon as a promising sign for the exiles there—but how? An angel of the Lord solves the problem: Baruch should write a letter to Jeremiah, and an eagle will come and deliver it (6:12). The basic content of the letter, which concerns the need for the Jews who have assimilated during the exile to separate themselves from Babylon and its ways, is revealed by the angel as a writing assignment for Baruch in 6:16-17 (Harris 6:13-14):

> **6:16** Therefore, write in the letter, "Speak to the children of Israel, 'Let him among you who has become a foreigner be expelled, and let them spend fifteen days, and after these things I will lead you into your city,' says the Lord. **17** 'Whoever is not separated from Babylon, let him not come into the city, and I will punish them with not being taken back again by the Babylonians,' says the Lord." (*OTP* 2:421)

At the beginning of this assignment there is a striking doubling of the commands to "write" and "speak," which stems from the adaptation of the prophetic oral proclamation to the artificial letter form. Also embedded in the content of what Jeremiah is to say to the exiles is a twofold "thus says the Lord." Baruch arranges to have papyrus and ink purchased from the marketplace of the Gentiles (see above Exercise 6) and writes the following letter in *Par. Jer.* 6:19b-25 (Harris 6:17-23):

6:19b Baruch, the servant of god, writes to Jeremiah in the captivity of Babylon: **20** Rejoice (χαῖρε; also translated "greetings") and be glad (ἀγαλλιῶ)! For God has not left us to pass out of this body grieving over the city which was desolated and outraged. **21** For this reason the Lord has taken pity on our tears and has remembered the covenant that he established with our fathers Abraham, Isaac, and Jacob. **22** And he sent his angel to me and told me these words which I have sent to you.

23 Now, these are the words that the Lord God of Israel, who led us from the land of Egypt, out of the great furnace, spoke:

"Because you did not keep my commandments, but your heart was lifted up and you stiffened your neck before me, in wrath and anger I delivered you to the furnace in Babylon. **24** However, if you will listen to my voice," says the Lord, "from the mouth of Jeremiah my servant, whoever listens I will bring him back from Babylon, and whoever does not listen will become a stranger to Jerusalem and to Babylon. **25** And you will prove them with the water of the Jordan; whoever does not listen will become known; this is the sign of the great seal." (*OTP* 2:421–22)

This letter exhibits several unusual formal features. Although epistolary prescripts usually lack a finite verb, this one has the verb γράφει, "Baruch *writes*," inserted between the sender and the addressee. The greeting also experiences a unique transformation. There are indeed other letter prescripts with the imperative χαῖρε, "be greeted," as here, instead of the infinitive χαίρειν, even though they are comparatively few. But they usually place the χαῖρε at the beginning, followed by an address to the recipient in the vocative.[19] Here the order is the usual one of sender, addressee, greeting, but because the χαῖρε is immediately followed by the verb καὶ ἀγαλλιῶ, the unit must be translated as "*rejoice* and be glad," instead of, for example, "*greetings* and rejoice" (cf. Kraft and Purintun). (The phrase itself is a familiar Jewish one, also found in the Septuagint and New Testament.[20]) This greeting is directly integrated into the rest of v. 20, which with its echoes of the typical expression of joy and its thankful remembrance of the great deeds of God now takes over the function of a proem. Therefore

---

[19] Examples in F. X. J. Exler, *Ancient Greek Letter* (Bib. 2) 35–36; see also H. Koskenniemi, *Studien* (Bib. 2) 164–67.

[20] Cf. Tob 13:15; Matt 5:12; 1 Pet 4:13; Rev 19:7 and the parallelism in Psalm 96 (LXX 95):12 and John 8:56.

the author of *Paraleipomena Jeremiou* uses well-known letter components for his own purposes. The decisive factor in these variations is the close coordination of the letter with its narrative context, which as early as 6:6 includes a call to rejoice (εὐφραίνου καὶ ἀγγάλου) that Baruch addresses to himself.

Par. Jer. 6:22-23a signals that the twofold word of the Lord that the angel gave Baruch to transmit to Jeremiah above in vv. 16-17 is about to be delivered. In fact, a very different saying of the Lord follows in which the command for assimilated Jews to be expelled from among the rest of the people is not explicitly repeated. Nevertheless, it is implicitly present in God's complaint about the transgression of his commandments (v. 23b), which can be brought about for example by the intermarriage of Jews with non-Jews, and in the references to Jeremiah's message, which will divide the faithful from the unfaithful, and to his testing of the people in the waters of the Jordan. When the people finally return from Babylon and arrive at the Jordan, the word of the Lord again comes to Jeremiah and requires him to ask the Jewish men and women to leave their non-Jewish spouses behind; this is the condition for crossing the river and entering Jerusalem (8:2-3). This is also the explanatory context for the puzzling "sign of the great seal" at the end of v. 25. Rather than being a reference to Christian baptism, as Robinson suggests (422 note *g*), this could refer to circumcision and the resulting obligation to keep the law, which when faithfully followed will identify those worthy to return to Jerusalem. Through the motif of the two "furnaces" in Egypt and Babylon in v. 21, the return from the exile is paralleled with the exodus from Egypt.

The angel's assignment to Baruch to write a letter in *Par. Jer.* 6:16-17 and the actual letter written in 6:19-25 complement each other and are composed with a view to the later information in 8:2-3. All of this underscores that this letter cannot be extracted from its narrative context. Other peculiarities, such as the absence of an epistolary closing in 6:25, can be explained the same way. Neither the angel's assignment in 6:16-17 nor the letter in 6:19-23 go into Abimelech's miraculously preserved figs nor his strange sleep, which according to 6:11 was supposed to be the content of Baruch's joyous message to Jeremiah. Here too we receive further help only from the larger narrative framework, for some of the figs still find their way to Babylon (cf. 7:7 with 7:37).

When Baruch leaves the tomb in chapter 7 after writing the letter, the eagle is already waiting for him outside and speaks to him in a human voice. Baruch binds the letter and fifteen figs from Abimelech's basket around the eagle's neck, admonishing it to deliver the letter safely to Jeremiah by imitating not Noah's raven, which never returned, but his dove. Arriving in Babylon, the eagle lands outside the city and waits until Jeremiah comes along with a funeral procession. The eagle then tells him to gather the people so that all can hear the letter's good news. As authentication the eagle quickly brings the dead man back to life. The people are deeply affected by the letter and promise to do all it asks in order to be able to enter Jerusalem again. Jeremiah then writes a letter of response to Baruch in 7:24-34 (Harris 7:23-29):

> **7:24** My beloved son, do not be negligent in your prayers pleading with God in our behalf, that he might speed our journey until we leave the jurisdiction of this lawless king. **25** For you were found righteous before God, and he didn't allow you to come here, so you wouldn't see the oppression which has befallen the people at the hands of the Babylonians. **26** For (it is) just as (when) a father has an only son and he is handed over for punishment; those who see his father and (are) consoling him cover his face so he won't see how his son is being punished and be racked by grief (even) more. **27** For God similarly had mercy on you and didn't allow you to come into Babylon so you wouldn't see the oppression of the people. **28** For since we came here, grief has not left us (even) today (after) sixty-six years! **29** For I would often go out and find (some) of the people hung up by King Nebuchadnezzar weeping and saying, "Have mercy on us, God Zar!" **30** Hearing these things, I would grieve and would weep a double lamentation, not only because they were hung up, but because they were calling upon a foreign god, saying, "Have mercy on us." **31** And I would remember the feast days that we used to celebrate in Jerusalem before we were taken captive, and remembering, I would groan and return to my house distressed and weeping. **32** So pray now in the place where you are, you and Abimelech, for this people, that they may listen to my voice and to the decrees of my mouth,[21] so that we may depart from here. **33** For I say to you that

---

[21] This phrase, "that they may listen to my voice and to the decrees of my mouth" in *Par. Jer.* 7:32, is totally missing from Robinson's translation, apparently by accident; in any case there is no textual note. Attested in MS C and the Ethiopic version, the phrase is present in the

the whole time we have been here, they have oppressed us, saying, "Sing us a song from the songs of Zion, the song of your God." **34** And we say to them, "How can we sing to you, being in a foreign land?" (*OTP* 2:422–23)

This "letter," which the introductory sentence expressly identifies as such (ἐπιστολή in v. 24a), actually lacks all letter features, unless one counts the focus on a recipient and the direct address as sufficient. The address is more reminiscent of a fatherly speech. The request for prayer in *Par. Jer.* 7:24 could be connected with the remembrance in prayer and the intercession in the typical letter proem, and its recurrence in v. 32 creates an inclusio around the central section. The conclusion in vv. 33-34 consists of a citation from Psalm 137 (LXX 136):3-4 (Herzer, *Die Paralipomena Jeremiae*, 123–24, considers it an interpolation). The middle section has many connections with the narrative context. The parable about friends who cover a father's face to prevent him seeing his son punished and its application to Baruch in vv. 26-27 illustrate the privileged position that Baruch takes on right from the beginning of the story, when he is spared having to see the affliction of the people in exile, even though this means living in a tomb. The 66 years at the end of v. 28 have already been given as the duration of Abimelech's sleep. The prayer wish in v. 32 that the people might listen to Jeremiah's voice as a condition for returning to Jerusalem looks back to the word of the Lord in Baruch's letter in 6:24 and forward to the parting of the ways at the Jordan or at Jerusalem in 8:2-3 or 4-8. Chapter 6:25-26 inserts an independent episode about the futile calling upon the name of the god "Zar" by members of the Jewish people doomed to die. "Zar," which here has become a proper name, is the Hebrew word for "strange" or "foreign" (זָר) and therefore corresponds to the θεὸς ἀλλότριος or "foreign God" in v. 30. The entire misery of the exile and its threat to Israel's faith identity are captured in this snapshot. The stark contrast with the earlier festal celebrations in Jerusalem brings

---

Greek texts of Harris (at 7:28) and of Kraft and Purintun, which Robinson took as his base (414 n. 1), as well as in the new edition of Herzer and the translation of Schaller ("damit sie hören auf meine Stimme und auf die Anordnungen meines Mundes"). Nor has Robinson substituted the variant from MSS A and B, ὅπως εἰσακουσθῇ ἡ δέησις ὑμῶν, "that your prayer may be heard" (see Harris).

back memories for Jeremiah and a groan that silently expresses his wish to return there (v. 31). Jeremiah's letter does not explicitly mention returning to Jerusalem, but only leaving Babylon, even though it is responding to a letter from Baruch saying that a return to Jerusalem has already been granted.

Jeremiah also binds his letter around the eagle's neck and releases his feathered messenger with the peace wish: "Go in peace, and may the Lord watch over us both!" (*Par. Jer.* 7:35). Baruch reads the letter, kisses it, and breaks into tears over the dismal situation of the people (7:36). Jeremiah gives the fifteen figs (cf. the fifteen days in 6:16) to the "sick among the people," presumably a metaphor for the exiles as such. This apparently helps them, even though the text does not say so specifically. Jeremiah for his part continues to admonish the people to separate from the Gentiles in Babylon (7:37).

In chapter 8 the people leave Babylon and come to the Jordan. This is the scene of a test proposed by the new word of the Lord in 8:2-3. The condition for crossing the Jordan and entering Jerusalem is the dissolution of mixed marriages.[22] Whoever refuses to accept this condition is also prevented by the Babylonians from reentering Babylon after having left it secretly. But they can still settle in Samaria, which thereby offers an etiology for the special relationship between the residents of Judea and those of Samaria. While offering sacrifice in the temple as the high priest, Jeremiah gives up his "life" or ψυχή (cf. Mark 10:45) in *Par. Jer.* 9:7. His revivification or resurrection may already have been

---

[22] There is some ambiguity in the text as to whether the final parting of the ways happens at the Jordan (8:5; cf. 8:2-3) or before the gates of Jerusalem (8:6-8). The latter seems more likely if the disobedient half of the returnees who remained in mixed marriages are still thinking of Jerusalem when they say, "We will not leave our wives behind forever, but we will bring them with us back to *our city*" (8:5). Ancient scribes also had difficulty with this verse and substituted the reference to Babylon (so MSS A, B, Armenian), to which this group does eventually try to return, calling it "our place" (8:8). But the final decision to return apparently occurred at Jerusalem, which all the people approached if 8:6 is read inclusively: "So *they* crossed over the Jordan and came to Jerusalem." We see once again that the later narrative is needed to clarify the word of the Lord in 8:2-3, which suggests that Jeremiah should have stopped the disobedient faction already at the Jordan, which he in fact failed to do.

hinted at in the original Jewish document, but this then shades into the Christian concluding section beginning in 9:14 (resurrection "after three days," with explicit mention of Jesus Christ) or already in 9:11-12 (a voice saying, "Do not bury one still living").

Further intuitively sensed symbolic values associated with the eagle (cf. Exod 19:4: "I carried you on eagle's wings"), the figs with their healing and enlivening effects, Abimelech's sleep and awakening, Baruch's time in the tomb, Jerusalem as the earthly city and the "city above" (5:35), and other narrative motifs cannot be investigated here because of the narrow textual basis we have chosen. Nevertheless, for the letters, our thesis stated at the beginning has been confirmed, as expected, on a larger scale: namely, that they were created from the outset by a single author to be placed in their present narrative context. Their purely literary existence as embedded letters, for which the author made very free use of typical letter components and forms of prophetic speech, is the reason for their many formal peculiarities. Within the broad letter tradition of Jeremiah and Baruch in Judaism (and Jewish Christianity?), they are both an independent and an idiosyncratic witness.

4. Life in Time of War: The Bar Kokhba Letters

Bibliography 35: J. A. Fitzmyer and **D. J. Harrington**, *A Manual of Palestinian Aramaic Texts*, BibOr 34 (Rome 1978) 158–63, 214–17. – **D. Pardee**, *Handbook* (Bib. 3) 114–44. – **B. Lifshitz**, "Papyrus grecs du désert de Juda," *Aegyptus* 42 (1962) 240–58. – **K. Beyer**, *Die aramäischen Texte vom Toten Meer* (Göttingen 1984) 350–52; vol. 2: *Ergänzungsband* (Göttingen 1994) 213–22. – **N. Lewis**, **Y. Yadin**, and **J. C. Greenfield**, *The Documents from the Bar Kokhba Period in the Cave of Letters: Greek Papyri; Aramaic and Nabatean Signatures and Subscriptions*, JDS (Jerusalem 1989) (no letters!). – **J. T. Milik**, "Textes hébreux et araméens," in P. Benoît, J. T. Milik, R. de Vaux, *Les grottes de Murabbaʿât*, 2 vols. (vol. 1, Texts; vol. 2, Plates), DJD 2 (Oxford 1961), vol. 1:65–205, esp. 155–68 on nos. 42–48; vol. 2, plates xlv–xlvii (abbr. **Pap.Mur.**) – **Y. Yadin**, "Expedition D—The Cave of Letters," *IEJ* 11 (1961) 36–52.

S. Bergler, "Jesus, Bar Kochba und das messianische Laubhüttenfest," *JSJ* 29 (1998) 143–91. – **P. Carelli**, "L'epistola greca di Bar Kokhba e la questione del vernacolo judaico nel II secolo," in A. Vivian, ed., *Biblische und judaistische Studien*, FS P. Sacchi, Judentum und Umwelt 29 (Frankfurt a.M. 1990) 271–78. – **H. Lapin**, "Palm Fronds and Citrons:

Notes on Two Letters from Bar Kosiba's Administration," *HUCA* 64 (1993) 111–35. – **J. T. Milik**, "Une lettre de Siméon bar Kokheba," *RB* 60 (1953) 276–94. – **J. Murphy-O'Connor** and **J. M. O'Brien**, "Wadi Murabbaat," *ABD* 6 (1992) 863–64. – **G. W. Nebe**, "Die beiden griechischen Briefe des Jonatan Archios in Engedi aus dem zweiten jüdischen Aufstand 132–135 nach Chr.," *RevQ* 17 (1996) 275–89. – **D. Schwiderski**, *Handbuch des nordwestsemitischen Briefformulars* (Bib. 3) 241–67. – **M. O. Wise**, "Bar Kokhba Letters," *ABD* 1 (1992) 601–6. – **Y. Yadin**, *Bar-Kokhba: The Rediscovery of the Legendary Hero of the Second Jewish Revolt against Rome* (London 1971) 124–39.

The second Jewish war against the Romans occurred between ca. 132 and 135 CE, during the reign of the emperor Hadrian. At first Hadrian pursued a tolerant politics of peace, but then by prohibiting castration, which also included circumcision, and by refounding Jerusalem as a pagan Roman city by the name of *Aelia Capitolina*, he turned the Jewish population against him.[23] The resulting revolt is closely bound up with the name of the Jewish rebel leader Bar Kokhba. Lacking, as we do, a parallel eyewitness historian to Josephus for this second war, we are only poorly informed from the literary sources about the dramatic events of this period. Our main witness is the Roman historian Cassius Dio (third century CE), whose report however has come down to us only in the abbreviated version of a Christian monk from the eleventh century. The additional information that we owe to archeological finds therefore proves all the more valuable. Thus we know for example from the coins of the Bar Kokhba period that the center of the revolt was Judea, but that an independent Jewish administrative structure developed there very quickly. Coin legends such as "Year one of the liberation of Israel" or "For the freedom of Jerusalem" and coin faces with pictures of the front of the temple, palm branches, grapes, an oil flask, temple trumpets, and so on illustrate the national hopes that this revolt raised.

Although the name traditionally given to the rebel leader, "Bar Kokhba," has long been known from Christian and rabbinic sources, we did not learn his forename until it was found on a coin with the legend "Shimon, prince (*nasi*) of Israel." And only the discovery of the letters that we are about to discuss below enabled us

---

[23] For this section Georg Scheuermann kindly made available to me some of his preliminary work.

to reconstruct his real name. This energetic man, who was apparently as strong as a bear, was named "Shimon bar Kosiba." This is a simple patronym: "Shimon, son of Kosiba," with the father's name spelled with a *samek* in the middle (שמעון בר כוסבה). Unfortunately, we no longer know its precise meaning; even the correct vocalization of the Hebrew name *kwsbh* is known only from one of the Greek letters discovered along with those in Hebrew and Aramaic: Σίμων Χωσιβᾶ, "Simon [bar] Chosiba" (5/6HevEp 6; Lifshitz 248). But we do know that when spelled "Bar Kokhba," with a *kaf* in the middle, the name means "son of the star" in Aramaic. This appellation seems to have been given to Shimon by Rabbi Akiba as a messianic title based on Num 24:17: "A star shall come out of Jacob, and a scepter shall rise out of Israel; it shall crush the borderlands of Moab, and the territory of all the Shethites." The Talmudic sources prefer to speak of "Bar Koziba," with *zayin* in the middle, which means "son of a lie," in short, "liar." They reflect the bitter experience that the uprising ended in another catastrophic defeat. The Romans had to expend a considerable amount of military power to bring the situation under control, but eventually they managed to isolate the individual groups of rebels, drive them into their desert hideouts, and starve them out. Bar Kokhba himself fell in the battle at Bethar, one of his last fortresses.

It was such last refuges in the desert that also yielded up sensational collections of documents from the Bar Kokhba period, beginning in the early 1950s. These particular places of refuge were caves in the steep rock cliffs of the desert valleys that run westward as deep gashes from the Dead Sea and remain very inaccessible even today, miles away from the nearest road. As in Qumran the Bedouins were the actual discoverers, and the scholarly archeological expeditions followed in their tracks.

In 1952 one source of these textual finds was located in Wadi Murabbaat, between Qumran and En Gedi, followed in 1960–1961 by the exploration of Nahal Hever, which lies further to the south in between En Gedi and Masada. (If one begins from the northern end and visualizes En Gedi roughly halfway down the western shore of the Dead Sea, Wadi Murabbaat is about a third of the way down and Nahal Hever a little more than halfway

down.)[24] Besides textiles, tools, pottery, and coins, written documents were also unearthed, including about twenty-two letters (or
more; the fragments are sometimes too tiny to reach a confident
conclusion).[25] Two of these were in Greek, the others in Hebrew
or Aramaic, and while most are written on papyrus, there is one on
a wooden tablet (5/6 HevEp 1) and another on a potsherd. Of the
22 letters, 7 were found in Wadi Murabbaat, all written in Hebrew
on papyrus (hence Pap.Mur.) and published in a critical edition,[26]
whereas the 15 Nahal Hever letters (5/6HevEp) are a mixture of
Hebrew, Aramaic, and Greek and are available in scattered publications without a critical edition.[27]

The majority of the Bar Kokhba letters provide insights into
the administrative abilities of Bar Kokhba. Most were apparently
dictated to various scribes, but in one case Bar Kokhba himself
seems to have wielded the pen. We therefore begin our small

[24] For a map of the Dead Sea region showing the location of Wadi
Murabbaat and Nahal Haver, see, e.g., J. G. Campbell, *Deciphering the
Dead Sea Scrolls* (Oxford ²2002) 4.

[25] M. O. Wise conveniently lists the 22 most important bar Kokhba
letters in a table giving the addressee, sender, language, and general contents (*ABD* 1:602–3).

[26] *Editio princeps:* J. T. Milik in DJD 2, vol. 1:155–68, nos. 42–48,
with French translations. Pardee includes all seven letters with English
translation and commentary (114–20, 122–39). For a German translation
of nos. 42–46, see Beyer, *Ergänzungsband,* 216–22 (siglum: *hM).

[27] M. O. Wise, presumably writing around 1990 (for publication in
1992), states that "the fifteen letters from Nahal Hever have not been
published" (*ABD* 6:602). If this refers to a critical edition with photo-
graphs, then it is accurate, but otherwise it is misleading. The publications more or less divide the letters up by language groups. Of the fifteen
Nahal Hever letters Pardee presents the four that are in Hebrew, nos. 5,
7, 9, 12 (139–44). The two Greek letters, 5/6HevEp 3 and 6, are printed
in Lifshitz 241, 248. This leaves nine remaining letters, one of uncertain
language (no. 13) and eight in Aramaic: 5/6HevEp 1, 2, 4, 8, 10, 11, 14,
15. All are published in transcription. Beyer includes in his first volume
nos. 1, 4, 8, 11, 14, 15 under the siglum ySK (*Texte,* 350–52), with revised
transcriptions and translations in his supplementary volume of nos. 1, 4,
8, 11, 14, 15, and a new addition of no. 10 (*Ergänzungsband,* 213–16).
Fitzmyer and Harrington present all eight Aramaic letters (texts 158–63;
comments 214–17), based on the publication by Yadin, "Expedition D"
(1961).

selection of these texts with the Wadi Murabbaat Hebrew letter in Bar Kokhba's own hand, Pap.Mur. 43 (trans. Pardee 130 [modified]; cf. Beyer, *Ergänzungsband*, 219–20):

> From Shimon ben Kosiba to Yeshua
> ben Ga[l]gula and to the men of Ha-Baruk (הברך or הכרך)
>   (Pardee: "the men of your company"):
> Greetin[gs] (*shalom*). I swear by the heavens:
> Should harm co[me] to any one of the Galileans
> who are with you, I'll put your feet
> in fetters as I di[d]
> to ben Aflul.
> [Sh]imon be[n Kosiba, writer.]

The prescript is of the form "From A to B, greeting." The greeting is the biblical peace wish *shalom*. The addressees are a certain Yeshua, son of Galgula, and his men; we know Yeshua from another letter as the commander of a military camp (Pap.Mur. 42:2; Pardee 123–24). According to Milik, "Ha-Baruk" refers to a strategic location five km east of Hebron, but according to another reading it means "the men of your company" (Pardee) or "the men of the fortress." In line 3 a solemn oath formula (see Deut 4:26: "I call heaven and earth to witness against you today"; cf. 30:19; 31:28) introduces the letter body. Bar Kokhba issues a sharp warning against his subordinate commander and points to a precedent where he carried out his threat without the least squeamishness. But what are the circumstances of the Galileans for whom Bar Kokhba must intervene? Some scholars have thought of Jewish Christians from Galilee who did not want to take part in the revolt (Milik 1953, differently 1961). But since in this case Yeshua would presumably not be asked to treat them better but to stop sparing them, another reading and translation is needed to explain the type of situation that Yeshua would have to prevent in order to escape punishment, such as, "if any of the Galileans who are with you desert" (Beyer, *Texte*, 220). It is therefore simpler to assume that these are refugees from Galilee who now live in the south of Judea and have come into some minor conflict with the commander of the camp; Yeshua must forgo reprisal. The epistolary closing consists only of the signature, which is in the sender's own hand. Whether one sees the entire letter as written by the sender depends on whether one discerns differences in the handwriting (Pardee) or a uniform hand (Milik). A closing greeting is lacking.

This letter is part of a larger context of communication, in that the report about Yeshua's poor treatment of the Galileans must already have reached Bar Kokhba earlier, and he must have calculated the after-effects of his threatening letter. Moreover we have another letter of Bar Kokhba to the same addressee (Pap.Mur. 44; Pardee 132), in which Bar Kokhba asks Yeshua to be the middle-man for a shipment of wheat, to offer hospitality to the men he has sent for it, and to let them spend the sabbath with him. The precarious food supply is therefore just as evident as the effort to achieve a devout Jewish life in keeping with the law. This letter is more neutral in tone, and also contains the closing greeting הוא שלם, "Be at peace" (*l.* 8).

Of the fifteen letters found in Nahal Hever in the so-called "Cave of Letters," one certainly deserving of mention is the Aramaic letter written on wood, 5/6 HevEp 1, not only because of its unusual material, but also because its prescript runs similarly to a coin legend: "Simeon, son of Kosiba, the ruler (*nasi*) over Israel, to Jonathan and Masabbala, peace (*shalom*)!" (Fitzmyer and Harrington 158–59). The content of this letter includes orders for the arrest of a certain person identified by the name of Jesus, son of the Palmyrene.[28] Of the other Aramaic letters on papyrus, the well preserved Bar Kokhba letter 5/6HevEp 15 merits special attention because of its content (trans. M. O. Wise in *ABD* 1:604):[29]

> Shimon to Yehuda bar Menasseh, at Qiryat Arabaya. I have sent to you two donkeys that you should send with them two men to Yehonatan bar Ba'yan and Masabala. They are to load them with [palm] branches and citrons and send them to the camp, to you. As for you, send other men to bring to you myrtles and willows. Prepare them (= tithe them?) and send them to the camp (i.e., to Shimon) because the men comprising the forces are numerous. Be well (הוא שלם).

---

[28] So Fitzmyer and Harrington 159. However, Beyer, *Ergänzungsband*, 213–14 is able to decipher more of the Aramaic text, which adds instructions for receiving a certain amount of wheat in lines 3–8.

[29] For text and translation, see also Fitzmyer and Harrington 162–63; Beyer, *Texte* (1984) 352.

This time Bar Kokhba uses only his forename and dispenses with an introductory greeting (like 3 John). The addressee is his local commander Yehuda (Judah) bar Menasseh, who is to send two of his men to Yehonatan (Jonathan) and Masabala, to whom the wooden letter 5/6 HevEp 1 is also addressed. Yehuda the addressee lives in Qiryat Arabaya, which may mean "city of the willows." Request is made for the "four kinds," namely the palm branches, citrons, myrtle branches, and willow boughs needed for the celebration of the festival of booths in Bar Kokhba's camp, perhaps located in the Herodion or in Bethar. As Wise suggests in his text above, their "preparation" may involve the setting aside of the tithe (at least for the citrons) so that all the requirements of the law may be fulfilled. The request for the items needed for the celebration is necessary because of the great number of fighters with Bar Kokhba, and the fact that the Greek letter 5/6HevEp 3 (Lifshitz 241) also asks for citrons suggests that this may be a second request. This letter breathes a concern for details and a traditional piety that desires to celebrate the great pilgrimage festival in the proper manner even in the hardest circumstances. The images of palm branches and citrons on the Bar Kokhba coins reflect the same attitude. The function of the concluding Greek greeting ἔρρωσθε is accomplished in this Aramaic Bar Kokhba letter with the help of *shalom*, just as *shalom* is used in the salutation in other Bar Kokhba letters (see above on Pap.Mur. 43). The two Greek Bar Kokhba letters, 5/6HevEp 3 and 6, follow the expected pattern with χαίρειν in the prescript and ἔρρωσο as the closing greeting.

Two other letters from Nahal Hever show that the rebels apparently addressed each other as "brothers." In the Greek letter 5/6 HevEp 6 (Lifshitz 248) the addressee Jonathan is twice addressed as "brother," in the opening greeting and in the closing formula, presumably without being a physical brother of the sender Ananos. This sense is also clear in Bar Kokhba's sharp denouncement of the men of En Gedi in the Hebrew letter 5/6HevEp 12 (Pardee 142–43): "Well off you are—eating and drinking from the goods of Beth-Israel and not giving a thought to your brothers."

These original documents from the time of the Bar Kokhba revolt hardly contain the kind of information that would be useful in writing history; in this respect their value is rather modest. Nevertheless, they offer valuable illustrations of the internal life of a rebel army, including its strict organization, disciplinary problems, food shortages, and the keeping of sabbaths and festivals.

From an epistolographical standpoint the letters from the Bar Kokhba period are important because they help us trace letter practices and conventions in their historical development and relative constancy. In the identification of the sender there is a difference between the Hebrew Bar Kokhba letters, like Pap.Mur. 43, that read "From A to B," and the Aramaic letters, like 5/6HevEp 15, that keep the sender in the nominative. In the salutation of the Bar Kokhba letters the *shalom*, where present, simply seems to have replaced the Greek χαίρειν; the possibility of extending the greeting into a second independent sentence is hardly taken advantage of. In our second main example, 5/6HevEp 15, the further division into letter body and closing is preserved and a few other typical letter formulas are evident. The indication that our first example from Pap.Mur. 43 was written in Bar Kokhba's own hand should be separately noted in view of Paul's remark in Galatians 6:11. On the whole the Bar Kokhba letters document that "the convergence of letter-forms was towards Greek practice."[30]

---

[30] P. S. Alexander, "Epistolary Literature" (Bib. 3) 592.

Exercise

34. Against the background of our studies so far, analyze the following Hebrew document from Wadi Murabbaat and seek to place it in its context (Pap.Mur. 42; trans. Pardee 124):

> From the village managers of Beth-Mashko, from Yeshua and Elazar,
> to Yeshua son of Galgula, camp commander: Greetings. We (hereby) apprise
> you that the cow which Yehosef son of Ariston took from Yaaqov
> son of Yehuda, whose residence is in Beth-Mashko, is his (Yehosef's) . . .
> If the "Gentiles" were not so close to us, I would have gone up
> and declared you free of obligation on this account. For I don't want you to say that it is through neglect that
> I have not come up to see you. Best wishes to you and to all Beth-Israel.
> Yeshua son of Elazar, writer.
> Elazar son of Yehosef, writer.
> Yaaqov son of Yehuda, principal party.
> Shaul son of Elazar, witness.
> Yehosef son of Yehosef, witness.
> Yaaqov son of Yehosef, notary.

7

New Testament Letters I: Overview

When we open the New Testament and look at its Table of Contents, the first striking thing is how many letters are represented there: The Letter to the Romans, the First Letter to the Corinthians . . . , the Letter of James, the First Letter of Peter, etc. The different letters are organized into two corpora, the Pauline corpus with fourteen letters (including Hebrews; see below) and the Catholic Epistles with seven letters. We therefore have a total of twenty-one letters, which numerically accounts for the great majority of the twenty-seven writings of the New Testament canon. Whether these are all real letters in terms of their genre is another question, which we will address on a case to case basis. A somewhat different picture of the New Testament emerges when we count not the number of letters but their length. No letter even approaches the length of the Gospel of Luke or the book of Acts. But even according to length the letters still comprise about a third of the New Testament text. Moreover, there are other letters outside the letter corpora. Two are incorporated in Acts (15:23-29 and 23:26-30), and Revelation not only contains seven letters of a special type—the open letters to the churches of Asia in chapters 2–3—but also has its own overall letter frame.

Following our presentation of the Greek and Roman literary letters (chap. 4) and of the Old Testament and early Jewish letters (chap. 6), we here approach the New Testament letters in two stages. Before our more detailed analysis of 1–2 Thessalonians, 2 Peter, and the letters in Acts in chapter 8, we first take stock of the other letters in the present chapter. Each letter is briefly introduced with a summary of the present state of research, particularly regarding epistolary and rhetorical criticism,[1] and with select bibliographies, first listing the more recent commentaries and then some representative essays and monographs. Questions of authenticity, dating, and composition are addressed only in so far as they are important for epistolography. For the sake of clarity we follow the canonical order of the letters, since every other organization—for example, according to date or content—would involve exegetical decisions that would first need to be justified. At the end of the presentations of the Pauline and the Catholic Letters, the origins of these letter collections are also investigated.

A. The Pauline Letters

1. The Letter to the Romans

Bibliography 36: C. E. B. Cranfield, *A Critical and Exegetical Commentary on The Epistle to the Romans*, 2 vols., ICC (Edinburgh and New York 1975–1979; rev. ed. ⁶2001). – **J. D. G. Dunn**, *Romans*, 2 vols., WBC 38A, 38B (Dallas 1988). – **J. A. Fitzmyer**, *Romans*, AB 33 (New York 1993). – **R. Jewett**, *Romans: A Commentary*, Hermeneia (Minneapolis forthcoming). – **L. Keck**, *Romans*, ANTC (Nashville 2005). – **E. Lohse**, *Der Brief an die Römer*, KEK 4 (Göttingen 2003). – **D. J. Moo**, *The Epistle to the Romans*, NICNT (Grand Rapids 1996). – **W. Schmithals**, *Der Römerbrief: Ein Kommentar* (Gütersloh 1988). – **U. Wilckens**, *Der Brief an die Römer*, 3 vols., EKKNT 6 (Zürich and Neukirchen-Vluyn 1978–1982).

D. E. Aune, "Romans as a Logos Protreptikos in the Context of Ancient Religious and Philosophical Propaganda," in M. Hengel and U. Heckel, eds., *Paulus und das antike Judentum*, WUNT 58 (Tübingen 1991) 91–121; reprinted also in K. P. Donfried, ed., *The Romans Debate* (see below) 278–96. – **S. Byrskog**, "Epistolography, Rhetoric and Letter Prescript: Romans 1:1-7 as a Test Case," *JSNT* 65 (1997) 27–46. – **K. P. Donfried**, ed., *The Romans Debate* (revised and expanded edition; Peabody, Mass. 1991). – **A. B. du Toit**, "Persuasion in Romans 1:1-17,"

---

[1] Especially helpful on epistolary and rhetorical criticism are the articles on the individual New Testament letters in D. E. Aune's *Dictionary* (Bib. 4), as listed in this chapter. These provide a level of detail greater than what we have included in this chapter, but less than that of chapter 8. For a helpful a survey covering most of the issues considered in this chapter see also R. W. Wall, "Introduction to Epistolary Literature," *NIB* 10 (2002) 369–91.

BZ 33 (1989) 192–209. – **N. Elliott**, *The Rhetoric of Romans: Argumentative Constraint and Strategy and Paul's Dialogue with Judaism*, JSNTSup 45 (Sheffield 1990). – **H. J. Gamble**, *The Textual History of the Letter to the Romans: A Study in Textual and Literary Criticism*, SD 42 (Grand Rapids 1977). – **A. J. Guerra**, *Romans and the Apologetic Tradition: The Purpose, Genre and Audience of Paul's Letter*, SNTSMS 81 (Cambridge 1995). – **L. A. Jervis**, *The Purpose of Romans: A Comparative Letter Structure Investigation*, JSNTSup 55 (Sheffield 1991). – **R. Jewett**, "Romans as an Ambassadorial Letter," *Int* 36 (1982) 5–20. – **M. Müller**, *Vom Schluß zum Ganzen* (Bib. 4) 208–39. – **F. Siegert**, *Argumentation bei Paulus gezeigt an Römer 9–11*, WUNT 34 (Tübingen 1985). – **M. L. Stirewalt**, "The Form and Function of the Greek Letter-Essay," in K. P. Donfried, ed., *The Romans Debate* (see above) 147–71. – **M. Theobald**, *Der Römerbrief*, EdF 294 (Darmstadt 2000). – **R. M. Thorsteinsson**, *Paul's Interlocutor in Romans 2: Function and Identity in the Context of Ancient Epistolography*, ConBNT 40 (Stockholm 2003). – **T. H. Tobin**, *Paul's Rhetoric in Its Context: The Argument of Romans* (Peabody, Mass. 2004). – **W. Wuellner**, "Paul's Rhetoric of Argumentation in Romans," in K. P. Donfried, ed., *The Romans Debate* (see above) 128–46.

Paul wrote his Letter to the Romans in around 56–57 CE from Corinth, or rather, he dictated it there to a scribe named Tertius, who registers his presence in 16:22 with a concluding greeting— and no doubt also a sigh of relief that his time-consuming task was now coming to an end. The letter, which is probably the last Paul wrote (only Philippians might have been later among his authentic epistles), is addressed to several house churches in Rome that Paul had neither founded nor visited, a theme that he elaborates in the letter's framing sections (cf. 1:11-15; 15:22-24, etc.). Because Paul usually mentions his co-workers in his epistolary prescripts only when they are known to his addressees, his failure to mention any co-workers here may be explained against the same background.

Despite the letter's unusual length—it is the longest in the Pauline corpus (and one of the longest real letters from antiquity)[2]—its basic epistolary structure is not hard to detect. In the

---

[2] With about 7,111 words and 32 pages in the Nestle-Aland text (27th ed.), Romans is much longer than, for example, any of the letters of Cicero. And as argued above (chap. 4, sec. B.3), the *Moral Epistles* of Seneca, whose longer contributions are still only half or two-thirds the length of Romans (e.g., *Ep.* 88, with 15 Latin pages in the LCL; *Ep.* 95, with 23 pages), are not real letters to Lucilius in a specific situation.

prescript in Rom 1:1-7, again one of the longest in antiquity (cf. Aune, *Dictionary* [Bib. 4] 429), the superscription or indication of the sender is severely over-extended by the insertion of a christo-logical confession in 1:3-4. Furthermore, the direct second-person address of the audience with reference to "all the Gentiles . . . , among whom you also are" in 1:5-6 stands in tension with the more typical and neutral third-person address in 1:7, "To all God's beloved in Rome, who are called to be saints."

Paul composes a proem in 1:8-15, consisting of a thanksgiving in vv. 8-12 followed by a biographical retrospect and an epistolary self-recommendation in vv. 13-15. There follows a thesis state-ment in 1:16-17, which is developed in several successive treat-ments in the letter body. Here we may single out only Paul's development of his main theme of God's righteousness. This is presented over against the world's sinfulness (1:18–4:25) and in relationship to both the life of faith (5:1–8:39) and the destiny of God's people Israel (9:1–11:36), before the general (12:1–13:14) and special (14:1–15:13) exhortations that follow from it are intro-duced, along with a recapitulation of important catchwords in 15:7-13, which serves as the body closing.

The letter closing is fairly elaborate. It consists of travel plans (15:14-29), a prayer request and a peace wish (15:30-33), a recom-mendation of the deaconess Phoebe from Cenchrea near Paul's place of writing in Corinth, who may have delivered the letter (16:1-2), fifteen greetings using the greeting request form ἀσ-πάσασθε (16:3-15), a request for the recipients to "Greet one another with a holy kiss" (16:16a), and the forwarding of an ecu-menical greeting, "All the churches of Christ greet you" (16:16b)—before the flow is interrupted by a somewhat surprising final warning about agitators in 16:17-19 (where some scholars suspect an interpolation), which then transitions into a promise of deliverance by the God of peace and a concluding grace benedic-tion, which Paul may have written in his own hand (16:20).

Ideally, the letter ought to have ended here in Rom 16:20. However, in 16:21-23 Paul's added greetings from Timothy and from some of his other co-workers and hosts, as well as the direct greeting from Tertius already mentioned, form an appendix that makes for a somewhat abrupt second ending. Because of the abruptness of ending a letter with a list of greetings, rather than, for example, with a grace benediction as in 16:20, in the process of collecting and publishing the Pauline letters, two alternative endings arose that are attested in the manuscripts: a grace with an "Amen" in 16:24: "The grace of our Lord Jesus Christ be with all of you. Amen" (a verse lacking not only in the modern English versions but also in the KJV; see NRSV note), and a doxology that breathes a deutero-Pauline spirit in 16:25-27 (marked off by brackets in the Nestle-Aland text, but not in the English versions; see Exercise 35). Typical letter components and expressions also occur within the letter body, including direct addresses and disclosure formulas (cf., e.g., 7:1; 11:25). Other question-and-answer exchanges (e.g., 2:3-4; 6:1-4, etc.) are reminiscent of the style of the diatribe, the lively informal popular philosophical lecture (cf., e.g., Seneca's moral instruction in letter form in chap. 4, sec. B.3).[3]

In the area of rhetorical analysis, the correct identification of 1:16-17 as the *propositio* ought especially to be maintained. As the formulation of the main theme in thesis form, the *propositio* is usually placed at the end of the *narratio*, but in longer works it can also be attached to the *exordium*, as here. To classify next the entire body of Romans as a *probatio*, a proof concerning God's righteousness, might not be wrong but does not lead much further, which can basically be said for all other attempts to discern the *dispositio* or arrangement of Romans by rhetorical criticism.[4]

All three of the traditional Aristotelian rhetorical genres have already been claimed for Romans. Within a fundamentally epideictic rhetoric R. Jewett has classified Romans more narrowly as a diplomatic or "ambassadorial letter" (cf. the πρεσβευτική or "diplomatic" type of Pseudo-Libanius, *Epistolary Styles* 4, i.e., style no. 25), whereas the classification of Romans as a "letter-essay," with Stirewalt, or as a "Logos protreptikos," a speech meant to advise and lead to a particular viewpoint, following Aune (who casts a side-glance at Pseudo-Demetrius, *Epistolary Types* 11, the so-called συμβουλευτικός or "advisory" type of letter, which is also explained by the term προτρέπειν, to exhort or urge on), tends in the direction of deliberative rhetoric. In fact, in terms of

---

[3] Cf. T. Schmeller, *Paulus und die "Diatribe": Eine vergleichende Stilinterpretation*, NTA NF 19 (Münster 1987); S. K. Stowers, *The Diatribe and Paul's Letter to the Romans*, SBLDS 57 (Chico 1981).

[4] See the overview in D. F. Watson, *Rhetorical Criticism* (Bib. 30) 226–28 and the conclusion of Aune, "Romans."

its scope and its partly didactic style, Romans can be compared with the doctrinal letters of Epicurus or with the long pieces in the later books of Seneca's *Moral Epistles*. Yet over against these works Romans still remains much more anchored to a particular situation, which comes to expression especially in the epistolary framing sections, but also elsewhere.

The literary integrity of Romans has also been called into question. W. Schmithals, to name only the most obvious example, differentiates two letters, a longer Letter A, which essentially consists of chapters 1–11 with 15:8-13, and a more recent Letter B, to which most of chapters 12–15 and 16:21-23 belong. Within these sections there are also various interpolations (e.g., 13:1-7, 11-14) and glosses (e.g., 2:16; 8:1). Finally, 16:1-20 must also be separated out as an independent letter of recommendation C, which was given to Phoebe on her travels, but was addressed not to Rome but to Ephesus. Schmithals's literary-critical reconstruction is partly supported by arguments about letter types—for example, by reference to the letter of recommendation as distinctive genre—and would therefore be interesting for epistolographical questions. Nevertheless, the discussion of composition has led to the consensus that Romans as we have it in 1:1–16:23 should be seen as a self-contained whole from the hand of Paul.

Exercise

35. Using the critical edition of the New Testament, try to evaluate the evidence for Romans chapters 15–16 in the manuscript tradition. What versions of the letter were in circulation, and how are the textual variants to be explained?

2. The Corinthian Correspondence

a) The First Letter to the Corinthians

Bibliography 37: R. F. Collins, *First Corinthians*, SP 7 (Collegeville, Minn. 1999). – **H. Conzelmann**, *1 Corinthians: A Commentary on the First Epistle to the Corinthians*, Hermeneia (Philadelphia 1975). – **G. D.**

Fee, *The First Epistle to the Corinthians*, NICNT (Grand Rapids 1987). – **A. Lindemann**, *Der erste Korintherbrief*, HNT 9/1 (Tübingen 2000). – **H. Merklein** and **M. Gielen**, *Der erste Brief an die Korinther*, 3 vols., ÖTBK 7/1–3 (Gütersloh and Würzburg 1992–2005). – **W. Schrage**, *Der erste Brief an die Korinther*, 4 vols., EKKNT 7/1–4 (Solothurn and Neukirchen-Vluyn 1991–2001). – **A. C. Thiselton**, *The First Epistle to the Corinthians*, NIGTC (Grand Rapids 2000). – **B. Witherington**, *Conflict and Community: A Socio-Rhetorical Commentary on 1 and 2 Corinthians* (Grand Rapids 1994). – **C. Wolff**, *Der erste Brief des Paulus an die Korinther*, THKNT 7 (Berlin 1996).

D. E. Aune, *Dictionary* (Bib. 4), s.v. "Corinthians, First Letter to the," 113–15. – **L. L. Belleville**, "Continuity or Discontinuity: A Fresh Look at 1 Corinthians in the Light of First-Century Epistolary Forms and Conventions," *EvQ* 59 (1987) 15–37. – **M. C. de Boer**, "The Composition of 1 Corinthians," *NTS* 40 (1994) 229–45. – **M. Bünker**, *Briefformular und rhetorische Disposition im 1. Korintherbrief*, GTA 28 (Göttingen 1983). – **R. F. Collins**, "Reflections on 1 Corinthians as a Hellenistic Letter," in R. Bieringer, ed., *The Corinthian Correspondence* (Bib. 7) 39–61. – **A. Eriksson**, *Traditions as Rhetorical Proof: Pauline Argumentation in 1 Corinthians 15*, ConBNT 29 (Stockholm 1998). – **D. Lührmann**, "Freundschaftsbrief trotz Spannungen: Zu Gattung und Aufbau des Ersten Korintherbriefs," in W. Schrage, ed., *Studien zum Text und zur Ethik des Neuen Testaments*, FS H. Greeven, BZNW 47 (Berlin 1986) 298–314. – **M. M. Mitchell**, *Paul and the Rhetoric of Reconciliation: An Exegetical Investigation of the Language and Composition of 1 Corinthians*, HUT 28 (Tübingen 1991; repr. Louisville 1993). – **H. Probst**, *Paulus und der Brief: Die Rhetorik des antiken Briefes als Form der paulinischen Korintherkorrespondenz*, WUNT 2/45 (Tübingen 1991). – **G. Sellin**, "Hauptprobleme des Ersten Korintherbriefes," *ANRW* II.25.4 (1987) 2940–3044. – **J. F. M. Smit**, "Epideictic Rhetoric in Paul's First Letter to the Corinthians 1–4," *Biblica* 84 (2003) 184–201. – **A. Stewart-Sykes**, "Ancient Editors and Copyists and Modern Partition Theories: The Case of the Corinthian Correspondence," *JSNT* 61 (1996) 53–64. – **J. A. D. Weima**, *Neglected Endings* (Bib. 4) 201–8.

Paul carried on his extensive correspondence with "the church of God in Corinth" in 54–56 CE, not long before he wrote Romans and a couple years after the end of his long founding visit to the church in Corinth around 50–52 CE (cf. Acts 18:1-18). He wrote sometimes from Macedonia but mainly from Ephesus, where he stayed for a long time after his initial visit to Corinth (cf. Acts 19:1-22). Our canonical 1 Corinthians is therefore part of a larger correspondence. Paul had already sent a previous letter to Corinth

(1 Cor 5:9) and had received a letter with questions from the church (7:1), which he answers one by one in his letter of reply from Ephesus, namely 1 Corinthians (see Exercise 14). He also has further oral information from both named (e.g., Chloe's people, 1:11) and unnamed sources (5:1; 11:18). Visitors have also been underway in both directions, from Ephesus to Corinth (Timothy, 4:17) and from Corinth to Ephesus (Stephanas, Fortunatus, and Achaicus, 16:17).

Although 1 Corinthians does not display the formal well-roundedness of Romans, several of its epistolary features stand out. These include the prescript in 1:1-3, with its elaboration of the recipients in 1:2, and an extended thanksgiving that serves as the proem in 1:4-9. Likewise the longer epistolary closing in 16:13-24 includes five short imperatives as final exhortations (16:13-14), a recommendation of Stephanas and his household (16:15-16), Paul's expression of joy at their visit (16:17-18), three forwarded greetings from the churches of Asia, Aquila and Prisca, and "all the brothers" (16:19-20a), an instruction for the Corinthians to greet one another with a holy kiss (16:20b), a greeting in Paul's own hand (16:21), a curse formula for unbelievers (16:22), a concluding grace benediction (16:23), and the assurance of the abiding presence of love for those in Christ as an appendix (16:24).[5]

The body of 1 Corinthians can be outlined thematically. Party divisions within the church are dealt with in 1:10–4:21, a section so complete in itself that a letter could almost conclude at its end (causing M. de Boer, for example, to postulate that Paul received fresh reports about the local situation between his writing of chapters 1–4 and 5–16). Paul deals with the three scandals of a church member living with his father's wife, lawsuits among believers, and sexual immorality with prostitutes in chapters 5–6, with questions of marriage and celibacy in chapter 7, and with food offered to idols in chapters 8–10. The conduct of worship services stands center stage in chapters 11–14, while chapter 15 is dedicated to the resurrection of the dead, before the body closing in 16:1-12 covers the final topics, including the collection for the poor believers in Jerusalem and the travel and visitation plans of Paul, Timothy,

---

[5] O. Roller, *Formular* (Bib. 4) 167 asks whether 1 Cor 16:24 might not be a final greeting from the hand of Paul's co-sender Sosthenes (cf. 1 Cor 1:1), which would explain its character as an appendix.

and Apollos. Tellingly, Paul promises to provide the delegates carrying the collection to Jerusalem with *letters* (16:3), which suggests an individual letter of recommendation for each delegate to serve as an identification card or passport.

For the epistolary type of 1 Corinthians as a whole, we may suggest the paraenetic or exhorting style (cf. Pseudo-Libanius, *Epistolary Styles*, no. 1, §5) and also, with modifications, the friendly style, though this does not prevent features of other letter styles from being manifested in individual passages. A rhetorical outline of the letter as a whole (cf. Mitchell) identifies 1:10, concerning agreement instead of division, as the main thesis of the letter. First Corinthians 1:11-17 supplies the *narratio* or statement of facts, 1:18–15:57 the series of proofs, and 15:58 the rhetorical conclusion, after which the letter framework once again stakes over (chap. 16). Other scholars have preferred to subject individual passages of the letter to rhetorical analysis. These include 1 Corinthians 1–4;[6] 2:1-5;[7] 8:1-6;[8] 8–10;[9] 10:23–11:1;[10] 12–14;[11] 13;[12] 15;[13] etc. Yet such

---

[6] Bünker (Bib. 37); also D. Litfin, *St. Paul's Theology of Proclamation: 1 Corinthians 1-4 and Greco-Roman Rhetoric*, SNTSMS 79 (Cambridge 1994); S. M. Pogoloff, *Logos and Sophia: The Rhetorical Situation of 1 Corinthians*, SBLDS 134 (Atlanta 1992).

[7] M. A. Bullmore, *St. Paul's Theology of Rhetorical Style: An Examination of 1 Corinthians 2:1-5 in Light of First Century Greco-Roman Rhetorical Culture* (San Francisco 1995).

[8] J. F. M. Smit, "1 Cor 8,1-6: A Rhetorical *Partitio*. A Contribution to the Coherence of 1 Cor 8,1–11,1," in R. Bieringer, *Correspondence* (Bib. 7) 557–91.

[9] Probst (Bib. 37).

[10] D. F. Watson, "1 Corinthians 10:23–11:1 in the Light of Greco-Roman Rhetoric: The Role of Rhetorical Questions," *JBL* 108 (1989) 301–18.

[11] J. F. M. Smit, "Argument and Genre of 1 Corinthians 12–14," in S. E. Porter and T. H. Olbricht, *Rhetoric and the New Testament* (Bib. 5) 211–30.

[12] C. Focant, "1 Corinthiens 13: Analyse rhétorique et analyse de structures," in R. Bieringer, *Correspondence* (Bib. 7) 199–245.

[13] Bünker (Bib. 37); also I. Saw, *Paul's Rhetoric in 1 Corinthians 15: An Analysis Utilizing the Theories of Classical Rhetoric* (Lewiston 1995); D. F. Watson, "Paul's Rhetorical Strategy in 1 Corinthians 15," in S. E. Porter and T. H. Olbricht, *Rhetoric and the New Testament* (Bib. 5) 231–49; see above p. 224 n. 40.

a method is not without its problems, inasmuch as it deals with the rhetorical function of *dispositio* or arrangement, which an ancient orator usually worked out for an entire speech (see above p. 224).

The existence of a previous letter from Paul to the Corinthians has continued to raise the question of whether 1 Corinthians might not contain portions of this earlier letter, which an editor could have combined with Paul's response letter to form a unity. Possible incorporations from Paul's previous letter might include 1 Corinthians 5:1-8; 6:1-20; 9:24–10:22; 11:2-34 (Sellin). This kind of partition theory would still be feasible despite the technical challenges of an editor and a scribe working together with two or three scrolls (cf. Stewart-Sykes). The same cannot be said of the more complicated partition theories that in the extreme case seek to identify as many as nine different letter fragments in 1 Corinthians (see the overview in Sellin 2965–68). The instruction for women to be silent in the churches in 1 Corinthians 14:33b-35 should probably be viewed as a subsequent interpolation.

b) The Second Letter to the Corinthians

Bibliography 38: P. Barnett, *The Second Epistle to the Corinthians*, NICNT (Grand Rapids 1997). – **H. D. Betz**, *2 Corinthians 8 and 9: A Commentary on Two Administrative Letters of Paul*, Hermeneia (Philadelphia 1985). – **V. P. Furnish**, *II Corinthians: Translated with Introduction, Notes, and Commentary*, AB 32A (Garden City 1984). – **E. Grässer**, *Der zweite Brief an die Korinther*, 2 vols., ÖTBK 8/1–2 (Gütersloh and Würzburg 2002–2005). – **M. J. Harris**, T*he Second Epistle to the Corinthians*, NIGTC (Grand Rapids 2005). – **F. J. Matera**, *II Corinthians: A Commentary*, NTL (Louisville 2003). – **M. E. Thrall**, *A Critical and Exegetical Commentary on The Second Epistle to the Corinthians*, 2 vols., ICC (Edinburgh 1994–2000). – **C. Wolff**, *Der zweite Brief des Paulus an die Korinther*, THKNT 8 (Berlin 1989). – **F. Zeilinger**, *Krieg und Friede in Korinth: Kommentar zum 2 Korintherbrief des Apostels Paulus: Teil 1: Der Kampfbrief – Der Versöhnungsbrief – Der Bettelbrief; Teil 2: Die Apologie* (Wien 1992–1997).

J. D. H. Amador, "Revisiting Second Corinthians: Rhetoric and the Case for Unity," *NTS* 46 (2000) 92–111. – **D. E. Aune**, *Dictionary* (Bib. 4), s.v. "Corinthians, Second Letter to the," 115–17. – **E.-M. Becker**, *Schreiben und Verstehen: Paulinische Briefhermeneutik im Zweiten Korintherbrief*, Neutestamentliche Entwürfe zur Theologie 4 (Tübingen 2002); English trans. by H. S. Heron, *Letter Hermeneutics in 2 Corinthians: Studies in Literarkritik and Communication Theory*, JSNTSup

279 (London and New York 2004). – **L. L. Belleville**, "A Letter of Apologetic Self-Commendation: 2 Cor. 1:8–7:16," *NovT* 31 (1989) 142–63. – **R. Bieringer** and **J. Lambrecht**, *Studies on 2 Corinthians*, BETL 112 (Leuven 1994). – **B. Bosenius**, *Die Abwesenheit des Apostels als theologisches Programm: Der zweite Korintherbrief als Beispiel für die Brieflichkeit der paulinischen Theologie*, TANZ 11 (Tübingen 1994). – **L. Brink**, "A General's Exhortation to His Troops: Paul's Military Rhetoric in 2 Cor 10:1-11," *BZ* 49 (2005) 191–201; 50 (2006) 74–89. – **J. A. Crafton**, *The Agency of the Apostle: A Dramatistic Analysis of Paul's Responses to Conflict in 2 Corinthians*, JSNTSup 51 (Sheffield 1991). – **F. W. Danker**, "Paul's Debt to the *De Corona* of Demosthenes: A Study of Rhetorical Techniques in Second Corinthians," in D. F. Watson, ed., *Persuasive Artistry* (Bib. 5) 262–80. – **M. M. DiCicco**, *Paul's Use of Ethos, Pathos, and Logos in 2 Corinthians 10–13*, Mellen Biblical Press Series 31 (Lewiston 1995). – **J. T. Fitzgerald**, "Paul, the Ancient Epistolary Theorists, and 2 Corinthians 10–13: The Purpose and Literary Genre of a Pauline Letter," in D. L Balch, E. Ferguson, and W. A. Meeks, eds., *Greeks, Romans, and Christians: Essays in Honor of A. J. Malherbe* (Philadelphia 1990) 190–200. – **B. Kuschnerus**, *Die Gemeinde als Brief Christi: Die kommunikative Funktion der Metapher bei Paulus am Beispiel von 2 Kor 2–5*, FRLANT 197 (Göttingen 2002). – **B. K. Peterson**, *Eloquence and the Proclamation of the Gospel in Corinth*, SBLDS 163 (Atlanta 1998). – **N. H. Taylor**, "The Composition and Chronology of Second Corinthians," *JSNT* 44 (1991) 67–87. – **D. D. Walker**, *Paul's Offer of Leniency (2 Cor 10:1): Populist Ideology and Rhetoric in a Pauline Letter Fragment*, WUNT 2/152 (Tübingen 2002). – **H. M. Wünsch**, *Der paulinische Brief 2Kor 1–9 als kommunikative Handlung: Eine rhetorisch-literaturwissenschaftliche Untersuchung*, Theologie 4 (Münster 1996).

Second Corinthians reflects the history of a very conflicted relationship between Paul and his congregation. New opponents of Paul have gained a foothold in the church since his founding visit and departure. He has therefore made a second "painful visit" which went poorly (2 Cor 2:1) and has written a "tearful letter" from Ephesus in response (2 Cor 2:4: "I wrote you . . . with many tears"), on which he repeatedly reflects (e.g., 7:8, 12). This letter had been sent through Titus, who has since returned to Paul (7:6-8). Yet now Titus is once again underway to the Corinthians with two co-workers and recommendations from Paul (8:17-24).

All this makes the letter's structure less than completely transparent. In the short prescript in 1:1-2 the extension of the address to include "all the saints throughout Achaia" stands out. In the proem in 1:3-11, a eulogy of God with the catchword "comfort" in vv. 3-7 and a biographical retrospect in vv. 8-11 combine to function as a self-recommendation. Paul's travel plans and his memories of his painful visit and tearful letter are addressed in 1:12–2:13, a section that is not actually picked up and continued again until the conciliatory statements in 7:2-16. In between comes Paul's apology for his apostleship in 2:14–6:11, introduced by a thanksgiving (2:14). The analysis of this section is additionally complicated by the fact that the pericope about not being unequally yoked with unbelievers in 6:14–7:1 is often seen as a non-Pauline interpolation. With a slight shift of accent chapters 8 and 9 seek to promote and organize the collection for Jerusalem, before Paul takes his opponents sharply to task in chapters 10–13, of which the long "fool's speech" in 11:16–12:13 is the central element. Paul's visitation plans in 12:14–13:10 mark the body closing before the brief but multi-faceted letter closing in 13:11-13. This consists of final exhortations, encouragement, instructions about the holy kiss, greetings from all the saints, and a Trinitarian concluding grace.

The literary unity of 2 Corinthians is still sometimes defended today by scholars who view chapters 10–13 as an appendix to the original letter in Paul's own hand,[14] or who postulate a time delay allowing for the reception of additional news and a change of mood between chapters 1–9 and 10–13, which is not impossible in the light of the concrete example of this very thing in a letter from one of Cicero's friends (see above p. 164). Nevertheless, one does better to view chapters 1–9 and 10–13 as parts of two originally independent letters. The only question is whether chapters 10–13 were written later and sent off after chapters 1–9, or whether chapters 10–13 do not rather preserve parts of the older "tearful letter." Other literary critical approaches that produce up to six different letters in 2 Corinthians take, for example, the apology in 2:14–7:4 as an independent letter and recognize in chapters 8 and 9 two separate collection letters.

Rhetorical analysis of 2 Corinthians is correspondingly laborious because it must first determine which parts of the letter may safely be taken as complete rhetorical units. Hence in addition to the two collection letters (cf. Betz), there have also been efforts to

---

[14] See G. J. Bahr, *Subscriptions* (Bib. 4) 37–38.

use rhetorical criticism to prove the existence of a separate letter of reconciliation.[15] Chapters 10–13 attract special attention,[16] not least because of their bitter irony, which escalates into open sarcasm.[17]

As to the epistolary types, Pseudo-Demetrius's "ironic" letter (no. 20) fits 2 Corinthians very well. The "apologetic" letter (no. 18) is also relevant, as are the "blaming" type (no. 3) and the "accusing" type (no. 17). In view of the sharp counterattack Paul undertakes in chapters 10–13, one can also refer to the type that Pseudo-Libanius calls "counter-accusing" or ἀντεγκληματική (no. 18, explained in §22 and §69). As so often happens, 2 Corinthians presents us with a "mixed" letter type.

Exercise

36. Compare Plato's Epistle 7, esp. 330B–337B, with 2 Corinthians 2–7. Are there structural analogies? Text in R. G. Bury, *Plato*, LCL, vol. 9: *Timaeus. Critias. Cleitophon. Menexenus. Epistles* (1929) 463–565.

---

3. The Letter to the Galatians

Bibliography 39: H. D. Betz, *Galatians: A Commentary on Paul's Letter to the Churches in Galatia*, Hermeneia (Philadelphia 1979). – **J. D. G. Dunn**, *The Epistle to the Galatians*, BNTC (London 1993). – **R. B. Hays**, "The Letter to the Galatians," *NIB* 11 (2000) 181–348. – **R. N. Longenecker**, *Galatians*, WBC 41 (Dallas 1990). – **F. J. Matera**, *Galatians*, SP 9 (Collegeville 1992). – **J. L. Martyn**, *Galatians: A New*

---

[15] F. W. Hughes, "The Rhetoric of Reconciliation: 2 Corinthians 1:1–2.3 and 7:5–8:24," in D. F. Watson, *Persuasive Artistry* (Bib. 5) 246–61.

[16] Cf. J. P. Sampley, "Paul, His Opponents in 2 Corinthians 10–13, and the Rhetorical Handbooks," in J. Neusner, et al., eds., *The Social World of Formative Christianity and Judaism*, FS H. C. Kee (Philadelphia 1988) 162–77.

[17] Cf. G. S. Holland, "Speaking Like a Fool: Irony in 2 Corinthians 10–13," in S. E. Porter and T. H. Olbricht, *Rhetoric and the New Testament* (Bib. 5) 250–64.

Translation with Introduction and Commentary, AB 33A (New York 1997).
– **F. Mussner**, *Der Galaterbrief*, HTKNT 9 (Freiburg i.Br. ⁵1988).
– **S. K. Williams**, *Galatians*, ANTC (Nashville 1997).

D. E. Aune, *Dictionary* (Bib. 4), s.v. "Galatians, Paul's Letter to the"
191–94. – **M. Bachmann**, *Sünder oder Übertreter: Studien zur
Argumentation in Gal 2,15ff*, WUNT 59 (Tübingen 1992). – **J. M. G.
Barclay**, *Obeying the Truth: A Study of Paul's Ethics in Galatians*, SNTW
(Edinburgh 1988). – **R. Brucker**, "'Versuche ich denn jetzt, Menschen zu
überreden . . . ?'—Rhetorik und Exegese am Beispiel des Galaterbriefes,"
in S. Alkier and R. Brucker, eds., *Exegese und Methodendiskussion*, TANZ
23 (Tübingen 1998) 211–36. – **R. E. Ciampa**, *The Presence and Function of
Scripture in Galatians 1 and 2*, WUNT 2/102 (Tübingen 1998). – **S. A.
Cooper**, "Narratio and Exhortatio in Galatians according to Marius
Victorinus Rhetor," *ZNW* 91 (2000) 107–35. – **S. A. Cummins**, *Paul and
the Crucified Christ in Antioch: Maccabean Martyrdom and Galatians 1 and 2*,
SNTSMS 114 (Cambridge 2001). – **R. G. Hall**, "Historical Inference and
Rhetorical Effect: Another Look at Galatians 1 and 2," in D. F. Watson,
ed., *Persuasive Artistry* (Bib. 5) 308–20. – **G. W. Hansen**, *Abraham in
Galatians: Epistolary and Rhetorical Contexts*, JSNTSup 29 (Sheffield 1989).
– **J. D. Hester**, "Placing the Blame: The Presence of Epideictic in
Galatians 1 and 2," in D. F. Watson, ed., *Persuasive Artistry* (Bib. 5)
281–307. – **H. Hübner**, "Der Galaterbrief und das Verhältnis von antiker
Rhetorik und Epistolographie," *TLZ* 109 (1984) 241–50. – **P. H. Kern**,
Rhetoric and Galatians: Assessing an Approach to Paul's Epistle, SNTSMS 101
(Cambridge 1998). – **V. Jegher-Bucher**, *Der Galaterbrief auf dem
Hintergrund antiker Epistolographie und Rhetorik: Ein anderes Paulusbild*,
ATANT 78 (Zürich 1991). – **D. Kremdahl**, *Die Botschaft der Form: Zum
Verhältnis von antiker Epistolographie und Rhetorik im Galaterbrief*, NTOA
46 (Freiburg, Switzerland and Göttingen 2000). – **B. W. Longenecker**,
The Triumph of Abraham's God: The Transformation of Identity in Galatians
(Edinburgh and Nashville 1998). – **G. Lyons**, *Pauline Autobiography:
Toward a New Understanding*, SBLDS 73 (Atlanta 1985). – **D.
Mitternacht**, *Forum für Sprachlose: Eine kommunikationspsychologische und
epistolär-rhetorische Untersuchung des Galaterbriefs*, ConBNT 30
(Stockholm 1999). – **M. D. Nanos**, *The Irony of Galatians: Paul's Letter in
First-Century Context* (Minneapolis 2002). – idem, ed., *The Galatians
Debate: Contemporary Issues in Rhetorical and Historical Interpretation*
(Peabody, Mass. 2002). – **D. Sänger**, "Bekennendes Amen: Zur
rhetorischen und pragmatischen Funktion von Gal 6,18," in K.-M. Bull
and E. Reinmuth, eds., *Bekenntnis und Erinnerung*, FS H.-F. Weiss,
Rostocker Theologische Studien 10 (Münster 2004) 235–57. – **J.
Schoon-Janssen**, *Umstrittene "Apologien" in den Paulusbriefen* (Bib. 4)
66–113. – **J. F. M. Smit**, "The Letter of Paul to the Galatians: A
Deliberative Speech," *NTS* 35 (1989) 1–26. – **A. H. Wakefield**, *Where to*

Live: The Hermeneutical Significance of Paul's Citations from Scripture in Galatians 3:1-14, Academia Biblica 14 (Atlanta 2003). – **J. A. D. Weima**, *Neglected Endings* (Bib. 4) 157–74. – **T. Witulski**, *Die Adressaten des Galaterbriefes: Untersuchungen zur Gemeinde von Antiochia ad Pisidiam*, FRLANT 193 (Göttingen 2000).

Galatians is not, as sometimes assumed, the oldest or second oldest Pauline letter (after 1 Thessalonians), but rather belongs in the period between the completion of Paul's Corinthian correspondence and the writing of Romans, around 55–56 CE. Proponents of an earlier dating, either before or shortly after the Acts 15 Apostolic Council of 48 CE, generally identify the addressees of the letter, "the churches of Galatia," with those in the southern part of the Roman *province* of Galatia (on the southern destination, see most recently Witulski, though his case is more complicated because he divides Galatians into two letters, a move few have followed). According to this South Galatian or "provincial" hypothesis, Paul will have sent the letter to the churches of his first missionary journey, such as Lystra and Derbe, even though the majority of the residents there were only politically and not ethnically "Galatians" (cf. Gal 3:1). The later date usually goes together with a more northern destination of the letter in the ethnically Gallic "region (χώρα) of Galatia," near present-day Ancyra. It assumes that the churches where planted there on Paul's second missionary journey (although Acts is not explicit about this, cf. 16:6) and visited again on the third journey (Acts 18:23). Nevertheless, there is no necessary connection between the later date and the northern destination; Matera in his commentary dates the letter in the mid-50s but has it addressed to the South Galatian churches. The fact that Jewish communities are well attested in the South but not in the North of Galatia is also used to argue for a southern destination in the light of the letter's dominant Jewish concerns.

In the prescript in Galatians 1:1-5, Paul exceptionally names "all the brothers with me" (καὶ οἱ σὺν ἐμοὶ πάντες ἀδελφοί) as co-senders. The use of such first-person language as "with me" here and elsewhere in the Pauline prescripts (cf. Rom 1:5; Tit 1:3) defies the rule that the superscription or indication of the sender would normally use only the more distant third person. After the address, which includes several Galatian churches, Paul expands his grace greeting here, as nowhere else, with a traditional self-surrender formula ("who gave himself for our sins to set us free from the present evil age"), followed by a doxology. However, a thanksgiving or eulogy of the audience is lacking. Instead, the place of the epistolary proem is taken up by the sharp criticism in 1:6-10, for whose function and opening with θαυμάζω Hansen offers parallels from twelve papyrus letters. This criticism leads into an inverted self-recommendation in vv. 8-10: not even Paul would deserve to be recommended, but only cursed, if he preached a different gospel.

The letter body consists of three main parts. In Galatians 1:11–2:21 Paul explains the origin of his gospel proclamation by a series of biographical retrospects, compressing his overall theme of justification by faith into a kind of thematic statement in 2:15-21, which, however, is expressed in a diatribe style with statement and counter-statement. The section from 3:1 to 5:12 develops the content of the doctrine of justification (note Paul's desire to be personally present with the Galatians in 4:20, παρεῖναι), while the paraenetic section in 5:13–6:10 draws out the practical implications for daily life. (Hansen has a different outline, distinguishing a "rebuke section" in 1:6–4:11 and a "request section" in 4:12–6:10.)

The epistolary closing in 6:11-18 begins with a remark in Paul's own hand in v. 11. It then distances Paul once again from his opponents through a presentation of Paul's own position in vv. 12-15 and continues with a conditional peace wish for "those who follow this rule" in v. 16 and with an instruction for others to stop making trouble for Paul in v. 17 before finally concluding with a grace wish in v. 18. All forms of closing greeting are lacking, apparently on purpose.

With this analysis the pioneering and now famous rhetorical analysis of Galatians by H. D. Betz largely agrees. If we disregard the epistolary prescript (1:1-5), then we first encounter Betz's *exordium* in 1:6-11, which basically corresponds to our epistolary proem, then the *narratio* or statement of facts in 1:12–2:14, comparable with our autobiographical first main part. The thesis statement in 2:15-21 is singled out by Betz as the *propositio*, the proposition or main theme. There follow the *probatio* or proofs in 3:1–4:31, with six arguments and one digression (3:19-25), and the *exhortatio*, which is not strictly speaking part of rhetorical theory, in 5:1–6:10. One might only disagree about the beginning of the paraenetic section, which is rather to be placed at 5:13. The functions of a rhetorical *peroratio* are taken over by 6:12-17.[18]

Apologetic features are present only in the autobiographical first main part of the letter. Later on the deliberative motif dominates, while the criticism in 1:6-9, for example, rather belongs to epideictic rhetoric. In 4:12-20 numerous topoi of the friendly letter are discernible. The ambivalence of mood can be seen in the changing forms of address, which vary between "You foolish Galatians!" in 3:1 and "(dear) brothers" in 4:12, 28, 31, etc. The categories of the "magical letter" (see above p. 69) and the "heavenly letter" (see below pp. 352–53) that Betz has brought into play have not proved relevant for Galatians. R. N. Longenecker in his commentary analyzes Paul's argument in terms of the rhetorical functions of *ethos*, *pathos*, and *logos* (cxiv–cxix). However, the claim that Galatians is no more than an "oration in an envelope" (Jegher-Bucher 5, repeated 204) is by no means justified.

4. The Letter to the Ephesians

Bibliography 40: E. Best, *A Critical and Exegetical Commentary on Ephesians*, ICC (London 1998). – **H. W. Hoehner**, *Ephesians: An Exegetical Commentary*, BECNT (Grand Rapids 2002). – **A. T. Lincoln**, *Ephesians*, WBC 42 (Waco 1990). – **M. M. MacDonald**, *Colossians and Ephesians*, SP 17 (Collegeville, Minn. 2000). – **P. T. O'Brien**, *The Letter to the Ephesians*, Pillar New Testament Commentary (Grand Rapids 1999). – **P. Perkins**, *Ephesians*, ANTC (Nashville 1997). – **P. Pokorný**, *Der Brief des Paulus an die Epheser*, THKNT 10/2 (Berlin 1992). – **R. Schnackenburg**, *Der Brief an die Epheser*, EKKNT 10 (Zürich and Neukirchen-Vluyn 1982).

C. E. Arnold, *Ephesians: Power and Magic*, SNTSMS 63 (Cambridge 1989). – **D. E. Aune**, *Dictionary* (Bib. 4), s.v. "Ephesians, Paul's Letter to the," 158–62. – **N. A. Dahl**, "Adresse und Proömium des Epheserbriefes," *TZ* 7 (1951) 241–64. – **C. A. Kittredge**, *Community and Authority: The Rhetoric of Obedience in the Pauline Tradition*, HTS 45 (Harrisburg 1998). – **A. Lindemann**, "Bemerkungen zu den Adressaten und zum Anlaß des Epheserbriefes," *ZNW* 67 (1976) 235–51. – **T. Moritz**, *A Profound Mystery: The Use of the Old Testament in Ephesians*, NovTSup 85 (Leiden 1996). – **H. Merkel**, "Der Epheserbrief in der

---

[18] For a tabularic comparison of other rhetorical analyses of Galatians see Aune, *Dictionary*, 194.

neueren exegetischen Diskussion," *ANRW* II.25.4 (1987) 3156–3246.
– **R. Reuter**, *Synopse zu den Briefen des Neuen Testaments: Teil I: Kolosser-,
Epheser-, II. Thessalonicherbrief,* Arbeiten zur Religion und Geschichte des
Urchristentums 5 (Frankfurt a.M. 1997). – **E. Mouton**, "The
Communicative Power of the Epistle to the Ephesians," in S. E. Porter
and T. H. Olbricht, eds., *Rhetoric, Scripture and Theology* (Bib. 5) 280–307.
– **R. Schwindt**, *Das Weltbild des Epheserbriefes: Eine religionsgeschichtlich-
exegetische Studie*, WUNT 148 (Tübingen 2002).

Ephesians presents itself in the superscription as written by Paul
himself (1:1a), who was in prison at the time according to 3:1 and
4:1, which has led to the letter's traditional inclusion among Paul's
"prison epistles" (Ephesians, Philippians, Colossians, Philemon).
But in fact Ephesians originated in the Pauline school and may not
have been written until 80–90 CE. This is suggested, for example,
by its dependence on Colossians, which can be demonstrated in its
structure and in individual passages right down to the wording
(see Exercise 37).[19] Ephesians was intended for the Pauline
churches in Asia Minor, including the city of Ephesus, where it
may have originated. The local address "to the saints who are *in
Ephesus*" (1:1b) need not tell against the letter's origin in Ephesus
if a fictitious authorship is assumed. But this designation is lacking
in some of the oldest manuscripts, and it may have replaced an
older address, perhaps to Hierapolis and Laodicea.

The letter opening includes, after the prescript in 1:1-2, a long
eulogy in 1:3-14. This is followed in 1:15-23 by a thanksgiving
with its own unusual introduction and an assurance of intercession. Rather than allocating this thanksgiving report to the letter
opening, where it would duplicate the eulogy, one does better to
regard it as the body opening, whose first main part in 2:1–3:21
expands themes from the thanksgiving, partly in the language of
prayer. This section includes a self-recommendation in 3:1-13 and
concludes in 3:20-21 with a doxology. The second main part in
4:1–6:20 (possibly with the military metaphor in 6:10-20 as the
body closing) is reserved mainly for exhortations, which run from
the general to the specific. The letter is concluded by 6:21-24,

---

[19] However, Best in his commentary (p. 35) has suggested that while
the letters share some kind of literary relationship, the dependence of
Ephesians upon Colossians cannot be proved.

without greetings but with a report about the sending of Tychicus and a peace wish and final grace wish.

When one analyzes the letter in rhetorical terms, then with Lincoln one can present 1:1-23 as the *exordium*, 2:1–3:21 as the *narratio*, 4:1–6:9 as the *exhortatio*, and 6:10-24 as the *peroratio*. But since the long exhortation in 4:1–6:9 is not strictly part of the standard speech model, and because this outline dispenses with the *argumentatio*, the genre of the speech, even an epideictic one (where argument or proof may be thought less essential than in forensic rhetoric), has actually been left behind. Among the possible letter types Lincoln considers for the first main part the congratulatory letter, in which the writer rejoices with the recipient (Pseudo-Demetrius no. 19), and for the second main part the advisory or paraenetic letter (Pseudo-Demetrius no. 11 or Pseudo-Libanius no. 1). The rather general content, from which the letter's actual situational grounding—which it certainly had—is hard to reconstruct, has led to the classification of Ephesians variously as a homily, tractate, theological treatise, wisdom speech, or prayer letter.[20]

Exercise

37. Compare the household codes in Colossians 3:18–4:1 and Ephesians 5:21–6:9. Note structural analogies and try to evaluate possible dependency. Cf. also Colossians 4:7-8 with Ephesians 6:21-22.

---

5. The Letter to the Philippians

Bibliography 41: M. N. A. Bockmuehl, *The Epistle to the Philippians*, BNTC (London 1997; Peabody, Mass. 1998). – **G. D. Fee**, *Paul's Letter to the Philippians*, NICNT (Grand Rapids 1995). – **J. Gnilka**, *Der Philipperbrief*, HTKNT 10/3 (Freiburg i.Br. ³1980). – **M. D. Hooker**, "The Letter to the Philippians," in *NIB* 11 (Nashville 2000) 467–549. – **U. B. Müller**, *Der Brief des Paulus an die Philipper*, THKNT 11/1

---

[20] For detailed analysis see U. Schnelle, *The History and Theology of the New Testament Writings* (Bib. 7) 299–314, esp. 306.

(Leipzig 1993). – **C. Osiek**, *Philippians, Philemon*, ANTC (Nashville 2000). – **P. T. O'Brien**, *The Epistle to the Philippians*, NIGTC (Grand Rapids 1991). – **B. B. Thurston** and **J. M. Ryan**, *Philippians and Philemon*, SP 10 (Collegeville, Minn. 2005).

L. Alexander, "Hellenistic Letter-Forms and the Structure of Philippians," *JSNT* 37 (1989) 87–101. – **D. E. Aune**, *Dictionary* (Bib. 4), s.v. "Philippians, Letter to the," 356–59. – **L. G. Bloomquist**, *The Function of Suffering in Philippians*, JSNTSup 78 (Sheffield 1993). – **L. Bormann**, *Philippi: Stadt und Christengemeinde zur Zeit des Paulus*, NovTSup 78 (Leiden 1995). – **R. Brucker**, *"Christushymnen" oder "epideiktische Passagen"?: Studien zum Stilwechsel im Neuen Testament und seiner Umwelt*, FRLANT 176 (Göttingen 1997). – **J.-B. Édart**, *L'épître aux Philippiens, rhétorique et composition stylistique*, EBib 45 (Paris 2002). – **T. C. Geoffrion**, *The Rhetorical Purpose and the Political and Military Character of Philippians: A Call to Stand Firm* (Lewiston 1993). – **P. A. Holloway**, *Consolation in Philippians: Philosophical Sources and Rhetorical Strategy*, SNTSMS 112 (Cambridge 2001). – **S. R. Llewelyn**, "Sending Letters in the Ancient World: Paul and the Philippians," *TynBul* 46 (1995) 337–56. – **M. Müller**, *Vom Schluß zum Ganzen* (Bib. 4) 131–205. – **G. W. Peterman**, *Paul's Gift from Philippi: Conventions of Gift-Exchange and Christian Giving*, SNTSMS 92 (Cambridge 1997). – **E. A. C. Pretorius**, "New Trends in Reading Philippians: A Literature Review," *Neot* 29 (1995) 273–98. – **J. T. Reed**, *A Discourse Analysis of Philippians: Method and Rhetoric in the Debate over Literary Integrity*, JSNTSup 136 (Sheffield 1996). – **J. Reumann**, "Philippians, Especially Chapter 4, as a 'Letter of Friendship': Observations on a Checkered History of Scholarship," in J. T. Fitzgerald, ed., *Friendship, Flattery, and Frankness of Speech: Studies on Friendship in the New Testament World*, NovTSup 82 (Leiden 1996) 83–106. – **A. H. Snyman**, "Persuasion in Philippians 4:1-20," in S. E. Porter and T. H. Olbricht, eds., *Rhetoric and the New Testament* (Bib. 5) 325–37. – **D. F. Watson**, "A Rhetorical Analysis of Philippians and its Implications for the Unity Question," *NovT* 30 (1988) 57–88. – idem, "The Integration of Epistolary and Rhetorical Analysis of Philippians," in S. E. Porter and T. H. Olbricht, eds., *The Rhetorical Analysis of Scripture: Essays from the 1995 London Conference*, JSNTSup 146 (Sheffield 1997) 298–426. – idem, "A Reexamination of the Epistolary Analysis Underpinning the Arguments for the Composite Nature of Philippians," in J. T. Fitzgerald, T. H. Olbricht, and L. M. White, eds., *Early Christianity and Classical Culture: Comparative Studies in Honor of Abraham J. Malherbe*, NovTSup 110 (Leiden 2003) 157–77.

Paul wrote this letter to his favorite church in Philippi as a prisoner (cf. Phil 1:7, 13, 17). The possible places of his imprisonment include Caesarea (rather improbable), Ephesus, and Rome. If Paul wrote from prison in Ephesus, as might be surmised from indications in his letters and Acts, then Philippians originated in temporal proximity to Galatians. If, on the other hand, the letter was written while Paul was in Roman custody, it would come after Romans, around 60 CE.

The prescript in 1:1-2 with its unique mention in the authentic Pauline corpus of "bishops and deacons" in the adscription and the thanksgiving with a concluding intercession in 1:3-11 combine to form the letter opening. The self-recommendation in 1:12-26 provides the body opening, which introduces Paul as an example. Christ is then introduced as an example in 2:5-11, within the larger section of exhortations in 1:27–2:18, before Paul once again becomes the example in chapter 3. In 2:19-30 Paul commends the traveling messengers Timothy and Epaphroditus. The section from 3:1 (or 3:2) to 4:1 deals with the issue of false teachers, while the concluding exhortations in 4:4-9 function as the body closing. The belated thanksgiving for Paul's receipt of gifts sent through Epaphroditus in 4:10-20 should be regarded as part of the letter closing and serves as an appendix to the proem, where thanksgiving for gifts would normally be mentioned (unless gifts are already alluded to there by terms such as κοινωνία in 1:5 in the sense of financial "sharing" or "partnership" in the gospel; cf. Peterman).[21] Without this section the letter closing, which would consist only of the postscript with greetings and a concluding grace benediction in 4:21-23, would be rather meager.

Typical letter features are especially abundant in Philippians. The motif of *parousia* and *apousia* or personal presence and absence appears in various forms (cf. εἴτε ἐλθὼν . . . εἴτε ἀπών in 1:27

---

[21] Both Peterman and O'Brien—significantly for epistolography—think that Paul mentions the Philippians' remembrance of him in 1:3 rather than Paul's remembrance of them, making μνεία ὑμῶν in 1:3 a subjective rather than objective genitive. For Peterman this becomes one more allusion to the Philippians' financial gift to Paul already in the proem, alleviating some of the pressure on the so-called "thankless thanks" in 4:10-20: I thank God for your recent remembrance of me (sc. through your gift) (1:3). But since the papyrus letters virtually always mention the author's remembrance of the addressee rather than the other way around, this would be a very striking Pauline inversion, if it could be proved.

and παρουσία/ἀπουσία in 2:12), Paul's hopes of making a visit are repeatedly expressed (1:26; 2:24), messengers go to and fro, and last but not least, the expression of joy becomes the leitmotif of the letter (1:4, 18; 2:2, 29; 3:1; 4:4, 10). Especially conspicuous in 4:10-20 but also elsewhere is Paul's borrowing of the Hellenistic language of friendship. But he also uses family metaphors, so that among the letter types, none of which is ideally realized in Philippians, one can consider next to the friendly letter also the family letter, and perhaps even the administrative letter. As a rough outline in rhetorical terms the following has been proposed, among others (cf. Watson 1988; Geoffrion; other summaries in Aune): *exordium* in 1:3-26 (too long in my view), *narratio* with *propositio* in 1:27-30 (better Bloomquist: *narratio* with *partitio*, 1:12-18a), *probatio* in 2:1–3:21, and *peroratio* in 4:1-20.

The abrupt change in tone between 3:1 and 3:2 has inspired literary-critical investigations. According to these studies Philippians would consist of a Friendship Letter A (reconstructed by Gnilka for example as 1:1–3:1a; 4:2-7, 10-23) and a Conflict Letter B (3:1b–4:1, 8-9). Philippians 4:10-20 is sometimes further singled out as an independent Thanksgiving Letter C. Nevertheless, the arguments for the literary integrity of the letter carry greater weight.

6. The Letter to the Colossians

Bibliography 42: J. N. Aletti, *Saint Paul: Épître aux Colossiens*, EBib 20 (Paris 1993). – **J. M. G. Barclay**, *Colossians and Philemon*, NTG (Sheffield 2001). – **J. D. G. Dunn**, *The Epistles to the Colossians and to Philemon*, NIGTC (Grand Rapids 1996). – **D. M. Hay**, *Colossians*, ANTC (Nashville 1997). – **E. Lohse**, *A Commentary on the Epistles to the Colossians and to Philemon*, Hermeneia (Philadelphia 1971). – **P. T. O'Brien**, *Colossians, Philemon*, WBC 44 (Waco, Tex. 1982). – **P. Pokorný**, *Der Brief des Paulus an die Kolosser*, THKNT 10/1 (Berlin 1987). – **M. M. Thompson**, *Colossians and Philemon*, Two Horizons New Testament Commentary (Grand Rapids 2005). – **M. Wolter**, *Der Brief an die Kolosser, Der Brief an Philemon*, ÖTBK 12 (Gütersloh and Würzburg 1993).

C. E. Arnold, *The Colossian Syncretism: The Interface Between Christianity and Folk Belief at Colossae*, WUNT 2/77 (Tübingen 1995). – **D. A. Aune**, *Dictionary* (Bib. 4), s.v. "Colossians, Paul's Letter to the," 103–7. – **W. Bujard**, *Stilanalytische Untersuchungen zum Kolosserbrief als Beitrag zur Methodik von Sprachvergleichen*, SUNT 11 (Göttingen 1973).

– **R. Burnet**, *Épîtres* (Bib 4) 210–25. – **R. E. DeMaris**, *The Colossian Controversy: Wisdom in Dispute at Colossae*, JSNTSup 96 (Sheffield 1994). – **T. W. Martin**, *By Philosophy and Empty Deceit: Colossians as Response to a Cynic Critique*, JSNTSup 118 (Sheffield 1996). – **H. Merklein**, "Paulinische Theologie in der Rezeption des Kolosser- und des Epheserbriefes," in K. Kertelge, ed., *Paulus* (Bib. 7) 25–69. – **P. Müller**, *Anfänge der Paulusschule: Dargestellt am zweiten Thessalonicherbrief und am Kolosserbrief*, ATANT 74 (Zürich 1988). – **T. H. Olbricht**, "The Stoicheia and the Rhetoric of Colossians: Then and Now," in S. E. Porter and T. H. Olbricht, eds., *Rhetoric, Scripture and Theology* (Bib. 5) 308–28. – **A. Standhartinger**, *Studien zur Entstehungsgeschichte und Intention des Kolosserbriefs*, NovTSup 94 (Leiden 1999). – **C. Stettler**, *Der Kolosserhymnus: Untersuchungen zu Form, traditionsgeschtlichem Hintergrund und Aussage von Kol 1, 15-20*, WUNT 2/131 (Tübingen 2000). – **J. G. van der Watt**, "Colossians 1:3-12 Considered as an *Exordium*," *JTSA* 57 (1986) 32–42.

The church of Colossae, a city in the Lycus River valley in southwest Asia Minor near the cities of Hierapolis (Col 4:13) and Laodicea (2:1; 4:13, 15-16), was founded by Paul's co-worker Epaphras according to Colossians 1:7 (cf. 4:12-13). Paul himself had never visited this church, which gives a special relevance to the letter topos of his absence "in body" and presence "in spirit" (Col 2:5). This letter also gives the impression that its sender finds himself in prison (4:3, 10, 18). Nevertheless, it was probably not written by Paul, nor even by a personal secretary acting on Paul's instructions (e.g., Timothy). Rather, as the oldest deutero-Pauline letter, Colossians may have been written around 70 CE by another student of Paul, and both its origin and its intended sphere of influence are to be found in southwest Asia Minor.

Colossians has borrowed its structure from the older Pauline letters. Coupled with the brief prescript in Colossians 1:1-2 is a relatively long proem in 1:3-23, which in addition to a thanksgiving (1:3-8) and an intercessory prayer (1:9-14) also includes a Christ hymn (1:15-20) that is directly applied to the readers (1:21-23). The body opening can be found in the (fictitious) "self-recommendation" of the apostle in 1:24-2:5. In the middle stand the dispute with the false teachers in 2:6-23 and the exhortations in 3:5–4:1 (after the transition in 3:1-4), which include among other things lists of vices (3:5-8) and virtues (3:12) and a household code (3:18–4:1). The general exhortations to prayer and action in 4:2-6 provide the body closing. In the letter closing in 4:7-18, the frustrated attempts at a visit by the apostle are compensated for by a promised visit from his emissaries Tychicus and Onesimus (4:7-9). Forwarded greetings from Paul's friends and co-workers and instructions to convey Paul's own greetings to others follow in 4:10-17, before the greeting in Paul's own hand and the grace benediction in 4:18 signal the end of the letter. Colossians 4:16 deserves special attention: The present letter is to be read in the church of the Laodiceans, but another letter, sent to Laodicea but lost to posterity, is also to be received and read in the church in Colossae.

The epistolary proem consisting of 1:3-12 or preferably of 1:3-23 can also be designated in rhetorical terms as the *exordium*. The *partitio* stating the letter's themes has been identified alternatively as 1:21-23 (Aletti) or 2:6-8 (Wolter). The rest of the parts must be arranged accordingly. A consensus can most nearly be reached in the allocation of 2:6-23 to the *argumentatio* or *probatio* and *refutatio*. Otherwise the identifications of the *peroratio* as either 3:1-4 (Wolter) or 4:2-6 (Aletti) once again diverge and raise questions about the rhetorical arrangement of the paraenetic parts. A basic deliberative tenor has been implemented with the help of epideictic features—for example, in the Christ hymn—but also in the description of the church's possession of salvation.

Questions about the literary integrity of Colossians have not generally been raised. It has often been maintained, as in our treatment above, that the author of Ephesians, who is not identical with the author of Colossians, has freely used Colossians as his *Vorlage* (see also Exercise 37).

7. The Thessalonian Correspondence

a) The First Letter to the Thessalonians

See below, chap. 8, part A.

b) The Second Letter to the Thessalonians

See below, chap. 8, part B.

8. The Pastoral Letters

Bibliography 43: R. F. Collins, *1 & 2 Timothy and Titus: A Commentary*, NTL (Louisville, Ky. 2002). – **L. T. Johnson,** *The First and Second Letters* *to Timothy: A New Translation with Introduction and Commentary*, AB 35A (New York 2001). – **I. H. Marshall**, *A Critical and Exegetical Commentary on The Pastoral Epistles*, ICC (Edinburgh 1999). – **W. D. Mounce**, *Pastoral Epistles*, WBC 46 (Nashville 2000). – **L. Oberlinner**, *Die Pastoralbriefe*, 3 vols., HTKNT 11/2 (Freiburg i.Br. 1994–1996). – **J. D. Quinn**, *The Letter to Titus: A New Translation with Notes and Commentary and An Introduction to Titus, I and II Timothy, the Pastoral Epistles*, AB 35 (New York 1990). – **J. D. Quinn** and **W. C. Wacker**, *The First and Second Letters to Timothy: A New Translation with Notes and Commentary*, ECC (Grand Rapids 2000). – **J. Roloff**, *Der erste Brief an Timotheus*, EKKNT 15 (Zürich and Neukirchen-Vluyn 1988). – **A. Weiser**, *Der zweite Brief an Timotheus*, EKKNT 16/1 (Zürich and Neukirchen-Vluyn 2003).

D. E. Aune, *Dictionary* (Bib. 4), s.v. "Pastoral Letters," 338–39; "Pseudepigrapha, NT," 386–87; "Timothy, First Letter to," 473–74; "Timothy, Second Letter to," 474; "Titus, Letter to," 475–76. – **R. Burnet**, "La pseudépigraphie comme procède littéraire autonome: L'example des Pastorales," *Apocrypha* 11 (2000) 77–91. – **C. J. Classen**, "A Rhetorical Reading of the Epistle to Titus," in S. E. Porter and T. H. Olbricht, eds., *The Rhetorical Analysis of Scripture: Essays from the 1995 London Conference*, JSNTSup 146 (Sheffield 1997) 427–44. – **L. R. Donelson**, *Pseudepigraphy and Ethical Argument in the Pastoral Epistles*, HUT 22 (Tübingen 1986). – **B. Fiore**, *The Function of Personal Example in the Socratic and Pastoral Epistles*, AnBib 105 (Rome 1986). – **M. Frenschkowski**, "Pseudepigra-phie und Paulusschule: Gedanken zur Verfasserschaft der Deuteropauli-nen, insbesondere der Pastoralbriefe," in F. W. Horn, ed., *Das Ende des Paulus: Historische, theologische und literaturgeschichtliche Aspekte*, BZNW 106 (Berlin 2001) 239–72. – **G. Häfner**, *"Nützlich zur Belehrung" (2 Tim 3,16): Die Rolle der Schrift in den Pastoralbriefen im Rahmen der Paulusrezeption*, HBS 25 (Freiburg i.Br. 2000). – **M. Harding**, *Tradition and Rhetoric in the Pastoral Epistles*, Studies in Biblical Literature 3 (New York 1998). – **G. Lohfink**, "Paulinische Theologie in der Rezeption der Pastoralbriefe," in K. Kertelge ed., *Paulus* (Bib. 7) 70–121. – **A. Merz**, *Die fiktive Selbstauslegung des Paulus: Intertextuelle Studien zur Intention und Rezeption der Pastoralbriefe*, NTOA 52 (Göttingen and Fribourg 2004). – **M. M. Mitchell**, "Reading to Virtue," in A. Y. Collins, ed., *Ancient and Modern Perspectives on the Bible and Culture: Essays in Honor of Hans Dieter Betz*, Scholars Press Homage Series 22 (Altanta 1999) 110–21. – eadem, "PTebt 703 and the Genre of 1 Timothy: The Curious Career of a Ptolemaic Papyrus in Pauline Scholarship," *NovT* 44 (2002) 344–70. – **J. Murphy-O'Connor**, "2 Timothy Contrasted with 1 Timothy and Titus," *RB* 98 (1991) 403–18. – **R. I. Pervo**, "Romancing an Oft-neglected Stone: The Pastoral Epistles and the Epistolary Novel," *Journal of Higher Criticism* 1 (1994) 25–47. – **M. Prior**, *Paul the Letter-Writer and* *the Second Letter to Timothy*, JSNTSup 23 (Sheffield 1989). – **Y. Redalié**, *Paul après Paul: Le temps, le salut, la morale selon les épîtres à Timothée et à Tite*, MdB 31 (Geneva 1994). – **R. Reuter**, *Synopse zu den Briefen des Neuen Testaments: Teil II: Die Pastoralbriefe*, Arbeiten zur Religion und Geschichte des Urchristentums 6 (Frankfurt a.M. 1998). – **W. A. Richards**, *Difference and Distance in Post-Pauline Christianity: An Epistolary Analysis of the Pastorals*, Studies in Biblical Literature 44 (New York 2002). – **E. Schlarb**, *Die gesunde Lehre: Häresie und Wahrheit im Spiegel der Pastoralbriefe*, MThSt 28 (Marburg 1990). – **D. C. Verner**, *The Household of God: The Social World of the Pastoral Epistles*, SBLDS 71 (Chico 1983). – **M. Wolter**, *Die Pastoralbriefe als Paulustradition*, FRLANT 146 (Göttingen 1981).

The name "Pastoral Letters" (or "Epistles") was applied to 1 and 2 Timothy and Titus in German-language exegesis in the eighteenth century, because people found there instructions for the proper exercise of the "pastoral" office that were also relevant for their own times. The letters claim to have been written by Paul to his closest co-workers, but in fact they are "doubly pseudonymous" in that both the sender and the recipients are fictitious. Such a presentation picks up on topoi from the authentic Pauline letters and epistolary theory: The apostle is absent not only geographically but also temporally; he can no longer really come to the recipients (cf. 1 Tim 3:14). The same goes for the co-workers who represented Paul and his interests during his lifetime. What remains is the text of the letters, which allows the figure of the apostle and his students to appear again before the eyes of the readers decades after their death. As Aune notes, "The implied author 'Paul' and the implied recipients 'Timothy' and 'Titus' all function as typological constructs of ideal Christian ministers" (339).

The Pastoral Letters were written around 100 CE, and in comparison with the deutero-Pauline letters Ephesians, Colossians, and 2 Thessalonians, they may be designated as trito-Pauline. (There is also a later dating that has the Pastorals directed against Marcion around 140 CE.) Their author, whom scholars have attempted to identify as Luke or Polycarp of Smyrna, is unknown. As a place of origin the Pauline mission field in Asia Minor suggests itself, particularly Ephesus, yet scholars also mention Rome as a possibility. The Pastoral Letters were conceived as a complete collection by their author, who intentionally chose the number three for effect, and they were intended to be read in the order in which they are mentioned in the Muratorian Canon (see Exercise 39): Titus, 1 Timothy, and 2 Timothy (although Wolter, favored by Aune 338, argues for the order 1 Timothy, Titus, 2 Timothy). This original order has been upset by our current canonical order, which places the letters according to length (see below n. 24).

Picturesque details, such as Paul's request for his cloak and books (2 Tim 4:13), which some scholars eagerly cite as evidence of Pauline authorship, do not merely seek to authenticate this cleverly executed fiction. They also to a great extent carry the argument of the letters, which presents the ethos of Paul and his students in order to elicit the pathos of the audience. For as Pervo writes, "One cannot doubt that the reader is to be left in tears when the abandoned and shivering apostle has finished the enumeration of his woes" (42–43). Among the other rhetorical techniques the rich use of examples (Fiore) and deductive enthymemes (Donelson) deserve special mention. Because of its conception as a single whole, its occasional sprinkling of narrative material, and its surprisingly frequent mention of individual persons, the corpus of the Pastoral Letters can be compared to some extent with an epistolary novel such as the one attributed to Chion of Heraclea (see above pp. 113–14; cf. Pervo).

a) The First Letter to Timothy

According to the situation imagined in 1 Timothy, Paul writes from Macedonia to Timothy in Ephesus. The prescript in 1:1-2 includes in the salutation the triad "grace, mercy, and peace." The long *exordium* (or epistolary proem) in 1:3-20, which defines Timothy's task of refuting the false teachers, contains a very unusual thanksgiving in 1:12-17 in which Paul looks back at his pre-Christian life as the chief of sinners and a persecutor of the church (cf. Gal 1:13). The letter body in 2:1-6:2 is filled with instructions about church order and the proper duties of people in the different stations of life, as is typical for the Pastoral Letters. In the programmatic paragraph in 3:14-16, the fictionality of the setting in Paul's own lifetime is almost given away when "Paul" says that he hopes to come soon but is writing in case he is "delayed."[22] The concluding paraenesis in 6:3-19 runs partly

---

[22] The above comment assumes that the author's intention was to write full-scale prosopopoeia or speech in character in the name of Paul

parallel with 1:3-20, and in the epistolary postscript in 6:20-21, the closing grace benediction is expressed with a plural pronoun that betrays a wider audience than the individual Timothy: Ἡ χάρις μεθ᾿ ὑμῶν, "Grace be with *you* (plural)."

The analogies for the genre of 1 Timothy (and Titus) are to be found in cases where a figure of the highest authority addresses "instructions by letter to authorized officers and mandate bearers" (Wolter 196). In particular this includes the Hellenistic royal letters and the instructions in the letters of the Roman emperors. The letters of the emperor Trajan to his governor Pliny the Younger (cf. Book 10 of Pliny's letters) would be one example among many.

b) The Second Letter to Timothy

Written by "Paul" in (Roman?) custody (cf. 1:8, 16; 2:9), 2 Timothy involves a change of genre over against both 1 Timothy and Titus. This is seen, for example, in the fact that Paul's longing to see Timothy in 1:4 involves a topos of the friendly letter. But more importantly, the letter framework now also includes topoi that are familiar from the literary testament and the farewell speech. It is therefore no accident that 2 Timothy shares many motifs in common with Paul's farewell speech to the Ephesian elders in Miletus in Acts 20:17-35. This is most clear in Paul's consciousness of his imminent death in 2 Timothy 4:1-8, but Paul's warnings about false teachers, his giving of a final personal account, and his concern for Timothy as his successor are also all standard building blocks of testamentary literature.

After the epistolary prescript in 2 Timothy 1:1-2 we encounter in 1:3-5 a proem with a brief thanksgiving (introduced by χάριν

---

and therefore *not* to provide inadvertent hints (like this one) that the real Paul may not be on the scene. However, whether such "epistolary fictions" should even be spoken of as being "revealed" or "given away" depends on their initial degree of hiddenness, a question about which various views exist. Thus, for example, I. H. Marshall in his recent ICC commentary on the Pastorals (see Bib. 43) has created a category of authorship ("allonymity") which does not involve deception, but rather the writing of letters in which another author transparently claims apostolic authority by using Paul's name. See further below, pp. 402, 404.

ἔχω) and an assurance of prayers, followed by a self-recommendation in 1:6-14 as the body opening. The letter body, which
includes exhortations and warnings, concludes in 4:1-8 with the
apostle's final instructions before his death. The letter closing in
4:9-22 is especially full. In vv. 9-17 the apostle names seven persons (Demas, Crescens, Titus, Mark, Tychicus, Carpus, and
Alexander the coppersmith) and includes four instructions for
Timothy (come to me soon, bring Mark, bring the cloak and
books, and beware of Alexander). There follow a doxology (v. 18),
greetings from Paul (v. 19) and forwarded greetings from others (v.
21), final bits of information and instructions (vv. 20-21a), and as
a concluding signal the grace benediction in v. 22: "The Lord be
with your spirit. Grace be with *you*" (plur.).

This long closing already suggests that 2 Timothy was meant
to conclude the corpus of the three Pastoral Letters. The elements
of the genre of the literary testament also fit in with this theory
(the epistolary novel of Chion of Heraclea also concludes with a
farewell letter that speaks of the consciousness of impending
death). Therefore the peculiarities of 2 Timothy compared with 1
Timothy and Titus need not be made a reason for postulating a
special place for 2 Timothy, potentially as an authentic letter of
Paul (Prior). Instead they can be readily explained by the overar-
ching composition of the three-letter corpus and the conscious
imitation of the testamentary genre in 2 Timothy.

c) The Letter to Titus

In contrast to 2 Timothy, Titus is distinguished by an extensive
prescript in 1:1-4, whose expanded superscription in vv. 1-3 is
comparable with Romans 1:1-6. The prescript is so long because
it not only opens Titus, but also the mini-collection of the Pastoral
Letters. Perhaps this is also the reason why a true proem with a
thanksgiving and prayer is lacking. The letter immediately
launches into the body in 1:5-3:11, yet as a transition 1:5 nevertheless makes sure that the epistolary situation is clear: Paul is
writing to Titus, whom he has left behind in Crete with certain
tasks, and he does so from Nicopolis, as 3:12 subsequently informs
us. The letter closing in 3:12-15 is composed of personal notes
combined with travel plans, forwarded greetings from Paul's companions to Titus and a request for Titus to send Paul's greetings to
others, and a grace benediction.

Exercise

38. By close reading of the three Pastoral letters, try to reconstruct the position of the theological opponents of the
author (relevant not so much for the distant time of Paul,
but for the author's own present time). Pay special attention to possible quotations of or references to the teachings
of the opponents. Excurses in the major commentaries may
be of assistance.

---

9. The Letter to Philemon

Bibliography 44: P. Arzt-Grabner, *Philemon*, Papyrologische
Kommentare zum Neuen Testament 1 (Göttingen 2003). – **M. Barth**
and **H. Blanke**, *The Letter to Philemon: A New Translation with Notes and
Commentary*, ECC (Grand Rapids 2000). – **A. D. Callahan**, *Embassy of
Onesimus: The Letter of Paul to Philemon*, The New Testament in Context
(Valley Forge, Pa. 1997). – **J. A. Fitzmyer**, *The Letter to Philemon: A New
Translation with Introduction and Commentary*, AB 34C (New York 2000).
– **J. Gnilka**, *Der Philemonbrief*, HTKNT 10/4 (Freiburg i.Br. 1982). – **P.
Stuhlmacher**, *Der Brief an Philemon*, EKKNT 18 (Gütersloh and
Neukirchen-Vluyn ³1989). – The commentaries from Bibliographies
41–42.

    D. A. Aune, *Dictionary* (Bib. 4), s.v. "Philemon, Letter to," 354–56.
– **D. L. Allen**, "The Discourse Structure of Philemon: A Study in
Textlinguistics," in D. A. Black, ed., *Scribes and Scripture: New Testament
Essays in Honor of J. H. Greenlee* (Winona Lake, Ind. 1992) 77–96. – **A. D.
Callahan**, "Paul's Epistle to Philemon: Toward an Alternative
Argumentum," *HTR* 86 (1993) 357–76. – **F. F. Church**, "Rhetorical
Structure and Design in Paul's Letter to Philemon," *HTR* 71 (1978)
17–33. – **J. A. Harrill**, *Slaves in the New Testament: Literary, Social, and
Moral Dimensions* (Minneapolis 2006) 1–16. – **J. P. Heil**, "The Chiastic
Structure and Meaning of Paul's Letters to Philemon," *Biblica* 82 (2001)
178–206. – **C. Kumitz**, *Der Brief als Medium der agape: Eine Untersuchung
zur rhetorischen und epistolographischen Gestalt des Philemonbriefs*,
Europäische Hochschulschriften, Reihe 23, Theologie 787 (Frankfurt
a.M. 2004). – **C. J. Martin**, "The Rhetorical Function of Commercial
Language in Paul's Letter to Philemon (Verse 18)," in D. F. Watson, ed.,
Persuasive Artistry (Bib. 5) 321–37. – **N. P. Petersen**, *Rediscovering Paul:
Philemon and the Sociology of Paul's Narrative World* (Philadelphia 1985).

– **J. L. White**, "The Structural Analysis of Philemon: A Point of Departure in the Formal Analysis of the Pauline Letter," *SBLSP* 1 (1971) 1–47. – **A. Wilson**, "The Pragmatics of Politeness and Pauline Epistolography: A Case Study of the Letter to Philemon," *JSNT* 48 (1992) 107–19.

The circumstances of the authentically Pauline Letter to Philemon, which Paul writes as an "old man" (v. 9) from prison (vv. 1, 13), involve the same alternatives as for Philippians: either Philemon originated during an Ephesian imprisonment of the apostle, which would suggest a time around 53–55 CE, or it was written around 61 CE in Rome; but independent of the decision regarding Philippians, there is more in favor of Ephesus for Philemon. The addressee Philemon, to whom Paul is appealing in the matter of Philemon's slave Onesimus, is assumed to live in Colossae by most scholars because of the overlap of personal names between the Letter to Philemon and Colossians 4:4-17. But other cities such as Smyrna, Troas, Pergamum, and Laodicea have also been mentioned. It should be noted that Philemon is not a purely private letter, since the adscription also includes "Apphia our sister," "Archippus our fellow soldier," and the church in Philemon's house (cf. the prescript of the letter P.Lond. I 33b [161 BCE]: "Apollonios to Hippalos and Sarapion and Berenike and Pyrrhos and to all in their house, greetings").[23]

An epistolary analysis of Philemon has already been proposed in the solution to Exercise 5. As to the rhetorical analysis, one can classify vv. 4-7 (i.e., the epistolary proem with a thanksgiving and an assurance of prayer) as an *exordium* without further ado, because this section performs the function of a *captatio benevolentiae*. However, Church's identification of vv. 8-16 as a *probatio* and vv. 17-22 as a *peroratio* disagrees with the epistolary analysis and therefore requires correction. Yet this is not to deny that Paul here argues rhetorically, employing both ethos in his self-portrait and his character sketch of Onesimus, and pathos in his subtle (or not so subtle) play on the keyboard of his relationship with Philemon. Regarding the letter types, the letter of request dominates, with features of a recommendation letter for Onesimus based on a friendly relationship with Philemon mixed in. We may compare vv. 10b-13 and especially v. 17: "So if you (Philemon) consider me your *partner* (κοινωνός), welcome him (Onesimus) *as you would welcome me*" (cf. also the notion of κοινωνία or sharing in v. 6).

[23] Text also in S. Witkowski, *Epistulae* (Bib. 1) 74.

10. The Collection of the Pauline Letters

Bibliography 45: K. Aland, "Die Entstehung des Corpus Paulinum," in idem, *Neutestamentliche Entwürfe*, TB 63 (Munich 1979) 302–50. – **D. E. Aune**, *Dictionary* (Bib. 4), s.v. "Letter Collections," 267–68; "Pauline Letters," 344–46. – **H. Gamble**, "The Redaction of the Pauline Letters and the Formation of the Pauline Corpus," *JBL* 94 (1975) 403–18. – idem, *Books and Readers in the Early Church: A History of Early Christian Texts* (New Haven 1995). – **J. Knox**, *Philemon among the Letters of Paul* (New York 1935). – **C. L. Mitton**, *The Formation of the Pauline Corpus of Letters* (London 1955). – **J. Murphy-O'Connor**, *Paul* (Bib. 4) 114–30. – **S. E. Porter**, ed., *The Pauline Canon*, Pauline Studies (Leiden 2004). – **E. R. Richards**, "The Codex and the Early Collections of Paul's Letters," *BBR* 8 (1998) 151–66. – idem, *Paul* (Bib. 4), esp. 210–23: "Collecting Paul's Letters." – **A. Sand**, "Überlieferung und Sammlung der Paulusbriefe," in K. Kertelge, ed., *Paulus* (Bib. 7) 11–24. – **W. Schmithals**, "Der Hebräerbrief als Paulusbrief: Beobachtungen zur Kanonbildung," in D. Wyrwa, ed., *Die Weltlichkeit des Glaubens in der Alten Kirche*, FS U. Wilckert, BZNW 85 (Berlin 1997) 319–37. – **D. Trobisch**, *Die Entstehung der Paulusbriefsammlung: Studien zu den Anfängen christlicher Publizistik*, NTOA 10 (Freiburg [Switzerland] and Göttingen 1989). – idem, *Die Paulusbriefe und die Anfänge der christlichen Publizistik* (Gütersloh 1994). – idem, *Paul's Letter Collection: Tracing the Origins* (Minneapolis 1994) (English version by the author). – idem, *The First Edition of the New Testament* (Oxford 2000). – **P. Trummer**, "Corpus Paulinum-Corpus Pastorale: Zur Ortung der Paulustradition in den Pastoralbriefen," in K. Kertelge, ed., *Paulus* (Bib. 7) 122–45.

No single Pauline letter has been transmitted to us in isolation; each is found only in collections. To begin with we can differentiate two different end products of the collection process, a collection with fourteen and another with thirteen Pauline letters. The difference results from the different placement of Hebrews in the manuscripts. Hebrews is certainly not one of the letters of Paul, not even in the sense of pseudonymous or deutero- or trito-Pauline authorship. Nevertheless, the subsequently added title Πρὸς Ἑβραίους, "To the Hebrews," is patterned on the titles of the Pauline Letters, which name the addressee, rather than on those of the Catholic Letters, which name only the author in the title, e.g., Ἰακώβου, "(The Letter) of James." In our text editions we encounter Hebrews at the end of the series of Pauline Letters, and this is also its place in the great number of manuscripts representing the Byzantine text. Nevertheless, in older textual witnesses Hebrews stands between Paul's letters to the churches and those to individuals, i.e., between 2 Thessalonians and 1 Timothy, and in 𝔓⁴⁶ even between Romans and 1 Corinthians, or in another manuscript between Galatians and Ephesians. There are other codices of the Pauline corpus (F, G) that contain only thirteen Pauline letters, without Hebrews. The reason for increasing the number from thirteen to fourteen, in addition to the need to find a place for Hebrews, was probably the desire to arrive at the symbolic number seven (14 = 2 x 7).

The familiar order of the Pauline Letters in our Bibles is mainly determined by the length of the individual letters, with the longest, Romans at 7111 words, placed first and the shortest, Philemon at 335 words, placed last. A slight inaccuracy arises by this method of ordering for Galatians, which actually has slightly fewer Greek words than the following Letter to the Ephesians (2230 against 2422),[24] yet, for example, according to one ancient count of the number of *stichoi* or lines, Galatians has as many lines as Ephesians. There is a greater discrepancy of length between 2 Thessalonians (823 words) and the following letter of 1 Timothy, which is almost twice as long (1591 words), but here another principle comes into play: letters to the churches are placed before letters to individuals.

We have already indicated above that the three Pastoral Letters originated as a unit around 100 CE. We can now expand this theory by supposing that they were written in the course of a revision of an already existing collection of Pauline Letters, in order henceforth to become part of that collection (cf. Trummer). The Pastoral Letters were therefore preceded by a collection of ten Pauline Letters, and when we group together the letters that were addressed to a particular church or group of churches (in this

---

[24] Otherwise the principle of ordering by Greek word count works perfectly for the first nine Pauline letters, with respective word counts of 7111 (Romans), 6829 (1 Corinthians), 4477 (2 Corinthians), 2230 (Galatians), 2422 (Ephesians), 1629 (Philippians), 1582 (Colossians), 1481 (1 Thessalonians), and 823 (2 Thessalonians). After the order restarts with the letters to individuals, the same principle applies, with word counts of 1591 (1 Timothy), 1238 (2 Timothy), 659 (Titus), and 335 (Philemon).

respect Philemon goes with Colossians), we once again arrive at seven destinations: Romans, 1–2 Corinthians, Galatians, Ephesians, Philippians, Colossians, 1–2 Thessalonians.

The other endpoint of the development that eventually led to the Pauline corpus of thirteen or fourteen letters is set by the individual letters themselves. These were preserved in the churches to which they were sent and potentially also copied and distributed from there. It is also possible that copies of outgoing letters remained with Paul or with the churches where he wrote them. How matters played out between these two poles of the individual letter and the complete collection is difficult to say. As possible places for the necessary work of collecting and editing the letters scholars have mentioned Corinth and Ephesus, but also Rome. Any tendencies that may have been at work in this process must be deduced very carefully from the sparse indices in the texts themselves, from the divergent order of the Pauline Letters in the manuscripts, and from analogies to other ancient letter collections (such as those of Cicero and Pliny).

One theory holds, for example, that the slave Onesimus, known from the Letter to Philemon, produced the first letter collection when he later became bishop of Ephesus, adding "his" letter, which has been preserved only for this reason (cf. Knox). Onesimus then presumably composed Ephesians himself as a "cover letter" for the entire collection (cf. the presentation of Mitton). A different theory is proposed by D. Trobisch, who holds that Paul made his own author's recension of his letters. According to the simplified version of Trobisch's thesis in his more recent publication on *Paul's Letter Collection*, Paul himself supposedly had before him seven (!) letters to the Corinthians, Romans 1–15, and Galatians. He then revised and (in the case of the Corinthian correspondence) combined these letters, and published them with Romans 16 as a cover letter to Ephesus. This resulted in a core Pauline collection of 1–2 Corinthians, Romans, and Galatians—precisely the *Hauptbriefe* of modern scholarship. In his older work on this topic (1989), Trobisch additionally postulates a further "catholic" collection consisting of Romans, Hebrews, 1 Corinthians, and Ephesians. It is easy to see that such reconstructions work with far-reaching historical and literary critical hypotheses but only a weak basis in the texts. In fact, the development of the Pauline corpus may have worked in a more complex and multifaceted way, beginning with small local letter collections (cf. Aland). The order of the letters was also not nearly as constant as our overview perhaps suggests. Finally, the collection of the Pauline Letters has far-reaching consequences, since it was a decisive first step toward the formation of the canon of the New Testament.

Exercise

39. The "Muratorian Canon" is a Latin list of the writings of the New Testament from the 2nd or 3rd century CE. An excerpt of lines 39–67 follows that deals with the letters of Paul. What shape does the collection of Paul's letters have in this document? Do you have any especially notable observations? (Text in W. Schneemelcher, *New Testament Apocrypha*, 2 vols., rev. ed. [Cambridge and Louisville 1991–1992] 1:35–36):

> [39b] The epistles, however,
> of Paul themselves make clear to those who wish to know it
> which there are, from what place and for what cause they were
>   written.
> First of all to the Corinthians (to whom) he forbids the heresy
> of schism, then to the Galatians (to whom he forbids)
>   circumcision,
> then to the Romans (to whom) he explains that Christ
> is the rule of the scriptures and moreover their principle,
> he has written at considerable length. We must deal with these
> severally, since the blessed
> apostle Paul himself, following the rule of his predecessor
> John, writes by name only to seven
> churches in the following order: to the Corinthians
> the first (epistle), to the Ephesians the second, to the Philippians
> the third, to the Colossians the fourth, to the Galatians the
> fifth, to the Thessalonians the sixth, to the Romans
> the seventh. Although he wrote to the Corinthians and to the
> Thessalonians once more for their reproof,
> it is yet clearly recognisable that over the whole earth one church
> is spread. For John also in the
> Revelation writes indeed to seven churches,
> yet speaks to all. But to Philemon one,

> and to Titus one, and to Timothy two, (written) out of goodwill
> and love, are yet held sacred to the glory of the catholic Church
> for the ordering of ecclesiastical
> discipline. There is current also (an epistle) to
> the Laodiceans, another to the Alexandrians, forged in Paul's
> name for the sect of Marcion, and several others,
> which cannot be received in the catholic Church;
> for it will not do to mix gall with honey.

B. The Letter to the Hebrews

Bibliography 46: H. W. Attridge, *Hebrews: A Commentary on Hebrews*, Hermeneia (Philadelphia 1989). – **P. Ellingworth**, *The Epistle to the Hebrews*, NIGTC (Grand Rapids 1993). – **W. L. Lane**, *Hebrews*, 2 vols., WBC 47A, 47B (Dallas 1991). – **E. Grässer**, *An die Hebräer*, 3 vols., EKKNT 17/1–3 (Zürich and Neukirchen-Vluyn 1990–1997). – **C. R. Koester**, *Hebrews: A New Translation with Introduction and Commentary*, AB 36 (New York 2001). – **H. F. Weiss**, *Der Brief an die Hebräer*, KEK 13 (Göttingen [15/1]1991).

D. E. Aune, *Dictionary* (Bib. 4), s.v. "Hebrews, Letter to the," 211–13. – **K. Backhaus**, "Der Hebräerbrief und die Paulus-Schule," *BZ* 37 (1993) 183–208. – **M. R. Cosby**, *The Rhetorical Composition and Function of Hebrews 11: In Light of Example Lists in Antiquity* (Macon, Ga. 1988). – **D. A. deSilva**, *Despising Shame: Honor Discourse and Community Maintenance in the Epistle to the Hebrews*, SBLDS 152 (Atlanta 1995). – **J. Dunnill**, *Covenant and Sacrifice in the Letter to the Hebrews*, SNTSMS 75 (Cambridge 1992). – **W. Eisele**, *Ein unerschütterliches Reich: Die mittelplatonische Umformumg des Parusiegedankens im Hebräerbrief*, BZNW 116 (Berlin 2003). – **P. Garuti**, *Alle origini dell'omiletica cristiana: La lettera agli Ebrei: Note di analisi retorica*, Studium Biblicum Franciscanum 38 (Jerusalem 1995). – **H. J. Klauck**, "Moving in and Moving out: Ethics and Ethos in Hebrews" (forthcoming). – **C. R. Koester**, "The Epistle to the Hebrews in Recent Study," *CurBS* 2 (1994) 123–45. – idem, "Hebrews, Rhetoric, and the Future of Humanity," *CBQ* 64 (2002) 103–23. – **T. H. Olbricht**, "Hebrews as Amplification," in S. E. Porter and T. H. Olbricht, eds., *Rhetoric and the New Testament* (Bib. 5) 375–87. – **J. W. Thompson**, *The Beginnings of Christian Philosophy*, CBQMS 13 (Washington 1982). – **W. G. Übelacker**, *Der Hebräerbrief als Appell*: I. *Untersuchungen zu exordium, narratio und postscriptum (Hebr 1–2 und*

13,22–25), ConBNT 21 (Stockholm 1989). – **A. Vanhoye**, *Structure and Message of the Epistle to the Hebrews*, SubBi 12 (Rome 1989).

One should not treat Hebrews as an appendix to the Pauline corpus but should rather take seriously its special place in the New Testament, which it owes to its independent theology and refined language. Its unknown author writes the best Greek of the New Testament, and he obviously enjoyed a good rhetorical education. His work does not bear any unmistakable epistolary features until the end in 13:22-25 or 18-25 (see below). In 13:22 the work is characterized as a λόγος παρακλήσεως or "word of exhortation" (or "encouragement"), which reminds us of a speech, as do other expressions such as "we are speaking in this way" (6:9; cf. 2:5). Nevertheless, this "speech" was not first given as a sermon and only secondarily committed to writing. Rather, it was conceived as a written work from the beginning. In this sense it is analogous to *4 Maccabees*, which presents itself as an epideictic speech yet was never delivered as such, but rather was planned from the start as a literary showpiece.

Rhetorical techniques on the level of *elocutio* or "style" can be demonstrated in Hebrews at every turn (as detailed by Garuti). The proem or *exordium* in 1:1-4, to take only one example, is already very artfully executed, with a fivefold π-alliteration in the first verse that is also used elsewhere (**Π**ολυμερῶς καὶ **π**ολυτρόπως **π**άλαι ὁ θεὸς λαλήσας τοῖς **π**ατράσιν ἐν τοῖς **π**ροφήταις) and might remind us of the π-alliteration in the beginning verses of Homer's *Odyssey*, and also with antithesis, parallelism and inclusio, a series of relative clauses, and a type of connected end rhyme with feminine genitive endings (e.g., ἀπαύγασμα τῆς δόξης, χαρακτὴρ τῆς ὑποστάσεως, ῥήματι τῆς δυνάμεως, ἐν δεξιᾷ τῆς μεγαλωσύνης). For the outline of the body of the work, a three-part and a five-part model compete with one another. In the three-part model, which has something to be said for it, the main parts consist of 1:5–4:13, the church's attentive listening to God's word about his Son; 4:14 to 10:18 (or 10:31), Jesus Christ as the heavenly high priest; and 10:19 (or 10:32) to 13:17, the testing and proving of faith, including examples. As the body closing, the concluding paraenesis in 13:1-17 signals the end by its steady alternation of short christological and paraenetic statements, which have also been alternated in larger blocks throughout the body.

Since Hebrews is an oration developed in writing that belongs partly to deliberative and partly to epideictic rhetoric, it only stands to reason that with regard to the *dispositio* or "arrangement," the standard rhetorical terms will apply more closely here than elsewhere in the New Testament. After the *exordium* or opening speech in 1:1-4 one can identify the section from 1:5 to 2:18, or rather to 4:13, as the *narratio* or statement of the case, with either 2:17-18 about Jesus as the high priest who had to become like his brothers, or preferably 4:14-16 about the same theme, as the *propositio* or thesis for what follows. The *argumentatio* or proof can be marked out accordingly from 3:1, or preferably, from 4:17 to 10:18, followed by an extensive *peroratio* beginning in 10:19, with an impressive set of examples in chapter 11. This basically incorporates the three main parts of the rough outline sketched above. (Garuti finds the different parts of a speech to be repeated throughout the body and therefore concludes that Hebrews is a compilation.)

The epistolary-style conclusion, not used in the introduction, raises particular questions, and its extent is disputed. It certainly includes, to begin from the end, the grace benediction in 13:25 and the greetings in v. 24, but also the announcement of the author's impending visit and his personal note about "our brother Timothy" in v. 23, together with his plea in v. 22 for the indulgence of his audience in reading his preceding "word of exhortation." Beyond this the intercessory prayer with the peace motif and doxology in vv. 20-21 could also come from the arsenal of epistolary topoi, as could in a more distant sense the request for prayer in vv. 18-19. Scholars sometimes try to explain this epistolary conclusion as an appendix by another hand intended to transform this anonymous writing into a pseudepigraphical letter of Paul, which certainly is a possibility to be reckoned with. But if this was the aim, one wonders whether it would not have required a more consistent execution. Alternatively, the epistolary conclusion may signal what the written oration was intended to communicate, and in terms of epistolography, the philosophical doctrinal letters of Epicurus, for example, offer themselves as a partial parallel. The "Pauline" atmosphere can also be understood as arising from loose cross-connections between the author of Hebrews and the Pauline school, without making him a student or co-worker of Paul or supposing that he must have known the Pauline letters directly (cf. Backhaus).

Finally, it should be noted that the classical introductory questions about Hebrews are insoluble. Even the question of whether Hebrews was directed to Jewish Christians, as its secondary title "To the Hebrews" suggests, remains highly doubtful. Some scholars assume that Hebrews was addressed to a Roman house church, but Rome is also proposed as the place of writing, next to many other places. (The greeting that the author forwards from "those from Italy" in 13:24 is often thought to favor the idea that some expatriate Italians among his companions are sending greetings back to Rome, but unfortunately this is ambiguous.) In the light of internal statements about the past history of the Christian faith and the church, the date of writing should not be set too early, i.e., not before 80 CE. As authors, various figures including Apollos and Prisca have been proposed, but our author intentionally wanted to remain anonymous. If so, then the implication for interpretation is clear: "No one needs to know who wrote Hebrews in order to understand it" (Grässer 19).

C. The Catholic Letters

1. The Letter of James

Bibliography 47: R. J. Bauckham, *James*, NTR (London 1999). – **C. Burchard**, *Der Jakobusbrief*, HNT 15/1 (Tübingen 2000). – **M. Dibelius**, *James: A Commentary on the Epistle of James*, Hermeneia (revised by H. Greeven; translated by M. A. Williams; Philadelphia 1975). – **H. Frankemölle**, *Der Brief des Jakobus*, 2 vols., ÖTBK 17/1–2 (Gütersloh and Würzburg 1994). – **L. T. Johnson**, *The Letter of James: A New Translation with Introduction and Commentary*, AB 37A (New York 1995). – **S. Laws**, *The Epistle of James*, BNTC (Peabody, Mass. 1980). – **R. P. Martin**, *James*, WBC 48 (Waco, Tex. 1988). – **F. Mussner**, *Der Jakobusbrief: Auslegung*, HTKNT 13/1 (Freiburg i.Br. ⁵1987). – **W. Popkes**, *Der Brief des Jakobus*, THKNT 14 (Leipzig 2001).

D. C. Allison, "The Fiction of James and its Sitz im Leben," *RB* 108 (2001) 529–70. – **E. Baasland**, "Literarische Form, Thematik und geschichtliche Einordnung des Jakobusbriefes," *ANRW* II.25.5 (1988) 3646–84. – **D. E. Aune**, *Dictionary* (Bib. 4), s.v. "James, Letter of," 238–41. – **T. B. Cargal**, *Restoring the Diaspora: Discursive Structure and Purpose in the Epistle of James*, SBLDS 144 (Atlanta 1993). – **F. O. Francis**, "The Form and Function of the Opening and Closing Paragraphs of James and I John," *ZNW* 70 (1970) 110–26. – **M. A.**

Jackson-McCabe, "A Letter to the Twelve Tribes in the Diaspora: Wisdom and 'Apocalyptic' Eschatology in the Letter of James," *SBLSP* 35 (1996) 504–17. – **S. R. Llewelyn**, "The Prescript of James," *NovT* 39 (1997) 385–93. – **K. W. Niebuhr**, "Der Jakobusbrief im Licht frühjüdischer Diasporabriefe," *NTS* 44 (1998) 420–43. – **T. C. Penner**, *The Epistle of James and Eschatology: Re-reading an Ancient Christian Letter*, JSNTSup 121 (Sheffield 1996). – **W. Popkes**, *Adressaten, Situation und Form des Jakobusbriefes*, SBS 125/126 (Stuttgart 1986). – **M. Tsuji**, *Glaube zwischen Vollkommenheit und Verweltlichung: Eine Untersuchung zur literarischen Gestalt und zur inhaltlichen Kohärenz des Jakobusbriefes*, WUNT 2/63 (Tübingen 1997), esp. 5–50: "Der Jakobusbrief als christlicher Diasporabrief." – **D. F. Watson**, "James 2 in Light of Greco-Roman Schemes of Argumentation," *NTS* 39 (1993) 94–121. – idem, "The Rhetoric of James 3:1-12 and a Classic Pattern of Argumentation," *NovT* 35 (1993) 48–64. – **W. H. Wachob**, *The Voice of Jesus in the Social Rhetoric of James*, SNTSMS (Cambridge 2000). – **W. Wuellner**, "Der Jakobusbrief im Licht der Rhetorik und der Textpragmatik," *LB* 43 (1978) 5–66.

The Letter of James begins with a prescript in 1:1 that holds formally to the Hellenistic model: "James, a servant of God and of the Lord Jesus Christ, to the twelve tribes in the Dispersion: Greetings" (χαίρειν). The address can only be understood against a Jewish apocalyptic background, since it presupposes the restoration of the twelve-tribed people of Israel in the end times. The letter is directed to the Christians as the eschatological people of God that experiences its existence in the word as a sojourn on foreign soil in the Dispersion (cf. also 1 Pet 1:1). The author's name, James or Jacob (Ἰάκωβος), recalls Israel's patriarch Jacob from ancient times. The intention of the prescript is to establish James, the Lord's brother (cf. Gal 1:19; Acts 15:13, etc.), as a new "patriarch," who led the Jerusalem church until his violent death in 62 CE. But the claim that James the Lord's brother actually wrote James and that it must therefore be dated around 60 CE or even earlier (so once again Johnson) is disputed by the majority of scholarship. The indication of the author serves the purposes of a pseudepigraphical fiction, and one must look to a time around 90–100 CE for the date of composition. Nothing certain can be said about the place of origin; Palestine, Syria, Rome, and Alexandria have all been suggested.

As to the structure, the prescript in 1:1 is followed by a proem in 1:2-18 that echoes epistolary formalities with its call to joy and its address "my brothers." The proem presents the individual themes that will be developed in the body by a rhetorical *amplificatio* (cf. Frankemölle; Johnson has a different but related idea when he terms 1:2-27 an *epitome* or short version of what follows). The body of the letter in 1:19–5:6 is best divided into seven or eight thematic units consisting partly of sayings and parables and partly of short treatises. The letter, which closely follows the pattern of the book of Sirach, here takes on the character of a wisdom writing, whereas the orientation to the Parousia in 5:7 once again provides for a more apocalyptic framework. The opening proem is counterbalanced by a concluding epilogue in 5:7-20. The abrupt ending in 5:20 without any standard letter components would speak against the epistolary character of James if we took only private letters and Pauline letters as our standard, but matters already look somewhat different in literary and doctrinal letters. Moreover, there are motifs in James 5:7-20 that do show affinities to the typical topoi of epistolary closings, including the eschatological outlook, concern for the health of sick church members, mutual intercessory prayer, and with qualifications also the prohibition of swearing oaths (cf., e.g., Francis).

The author of James, who himself belongs to the class of teachers whom he exhorts (3:1), writes an elegant Greek that is nearer to the quality of Greek of Hebrews than that of Paul. He employs alliteration, such as the fourfold π in 1:2 (Πᾶσαν χαρὰν ἡγήσασθε . . . , ὅταν πειρασμοῖς περιπέσητε ποικίλοις), uses figures of speech, coins fine comparisons and metaphors, and strives for pregnant brevity to the point of intentional paradox. With his dialogical elements, including direct address, rhetorical questions, imaginary interlocutors, and the reproduction of possible reactions of his audience in direct discourse (e.g., 2:3), our author approaches the style of the diatribe (cf. Johnson 7–10).

2. The First Letter of Peter

Bibliography 48: P. J. Achtemeier, *1 Peter: A Commentary on First Peter*, Hermeneia (Minneapolis 1996). – **M. E. Boring**, *1 Peter*, ANTC (Nashville 2001). – **N. Brox**, *Der erste Petrusbrief*, EKKNT 21 (Einsiedeln and Neukirchen-Vluyn ⁴1993). – **P. H. Davids**, *The First Epistle of Peter*, NICNT (Grand Rapids 1990). – **J. H. Elliott**, *1 Peter: A New Translation with Commentary*, AB 37B (New York 2000). – **L. Goppelt**, *A Commentary on 1 Peter*, trans. J. E. Alsup (Grand Rapids 1993). – **J. R. Michaels**, *1*

Peter, WBC 49 (Waco 1988). – **D. P. Senior** and **D. J. Harrington**, *1 Peter, 2 Peter, Jude*, SP 15 (Collegeville, Minn. 2003).

    D. E. Aune, *Dictionary* (Bib. 4), s.v. "Peter, First Letter of," 350–52. – **D. L. Balch**, *Let Wives Be Submissive: The Domestic Code in 1 Peter*, SBLMS 26 (Chico 1981). – **J. H. Elliott**, *A Home for the Homeless: A Sociological Exegesis of 1 Peter, Its Situation and Strategy* (Philadelphia 1981). – **R. Feldmeier**, *Die Christen als Fremde: Die Metapher der Fremde in der antiken Welt, im Urchristentum und im 1. Petrusbrief*, WUNT 64 (Tübingen 1992). – **D. G. Horrell**, "The Product of a Petrine Circle? A Reassessment of the Origin and Character of 1 Peter," *JSNT* 86 (2002) 29–60. – **T. W. Martin**, *Metaphor and Composition in 1 Peter*, SBLDS 131 (Atlanta 1992). – **A. Reichert**, *Eine urchristliche praeparatio ad martyrium: Studien zur Komposition, Traditionsgeschichte und Theologie des 1. Petrusbriefes*, BBET 22 (Frankfurt a.M. 1989). – **K. M. Schmidt**, *Mahnung und Erinnerung im Maskenspiel: Epistolographie, Rhetorik und Narrativik der pseudepigraphen Petrusbriefe*, HBS 36 (Freiburg i.Br. 2003). – **W. L. Schutter**, *Hermeneutic and Composition in I Peter*, WUNT 2/30 (Tübingen 1989). – **L. Thurén**, *The Rhetorical Strategy of 1 Peter: With Special Regard to Ambiguous Expressions* (Åbo 1990). – idem, *Argument and Theology in 1 Peter: The Origins of Christian Paraenesis*, JSNTSup 114 (Sheffield 1995). – **P. L. Tite**, "The Composi-tional Function of the Petrine Prescript: A Look at 1 Pet 1:1-3," *JETS* 39 (1996) 47–56.

The First Letter of Peter, whose existence is already presupposed in 2 Peter 3:1 ("This is now, beloved, the second letter I am writing to you"), is best understood as an attempt by a Petrine school in Rome between 80 and 90 CE to cultivate the legacy of Simon Peter and connect it with the tradition of Paul and his circle. This program is partly carried out through the personal names in the letter, which connect the fictional author Peter in 1:1 with the equally fictitiously represented figures of Silvanus (= Silas in Acts) and Mark in 5:12-13, who were known as companions of Paul and who had contacts with the historical Peter through their Jerusalem origins. When Peter says in 5:13 that he wrote (ἔγραψα) the letter "through" Silvanus, in ancient terms this means that "Silvanus" delivered the letter as a messenger, not that he wrote it down as a scribe or composed it independently as a secretary. Composition of the letter in Rome is suggested at least internally by the greetings sent to the addressees from "your sister church in Babylon, chosen together with you" (5:13), since Babylon, especially in the eastern regions where this letter was sent, was current as a Jewish-

Christian code name for Rome. The letter is addressed to the eastern half of the Roman empire with special reference to the Anatolian provinces of Pontus, Galatia, Cappadocia, Asia, and Bithynia, because the Christians living there were increasingly being exposed to local persecutions, some of which were initiated by the Roman authorities.

Next to the prescript in 1:1-2 (see Exercise 40), the epistolary opening consists of a proem in the form of a eulogy in 1:3-12. This includes an eschatological prospect in 1:9 and a self-recommendation of the author as one of the preachers of the gospel in 1:12. At the other end, in the closing in 5:10-14, the praise of God in vv. 10-11 serves as an epilogue, taking up a structurally corresponding position to the proem. The postscript in 5:12-14 gives the author the opportunity to commend "Silvanus" as the implied deliverer of the letter and to characterize his own work as a brief word of exhortation (v. 12). He then forwards greetings from the church in "Babylon" and from Mark, whom he refers to as "my son" (v. 13), and instructs the addressees to greet one another with a "kiss of love" (instead of Paul's "holy kiss"), before closing with a peace wish (v. 14).

Older partition theories concerning 1 Peter do not seek to find multiple letter fragments but rather question whether the composition was framed as a letter in the first place, speculating that 1:3–4:11 may originally have been a baptismal address, for example, because of the doxology in 4:11. The letter frame and the update in 4:12-14 will then have been added secondarily. But this is hardly a convincing thesis.

Exercise

40. Analyze on your own the prescript in 1 Peter 1:1-2.

---

3. The Second Letter of Peter

See below, chap. 8, part C.

4. The Letters of John

a) The First Letter of John

Bibliography 49: J. Beutler, *Die Johanesbriefe*, RNT (Regensburg 2000). – **R. E. Brown**, *The Epistle of John: Translated with Introduction, Notes, and Commentary*, AB 30 (Garden City, N.Y. 1982). – **H. J. Klauck**, *Der erste Johannesbrief*, EKKNT 23/1 (Zürich and Neukirchen-Vluyn 1991). – **J. Painter**, *1, 2, and 3 John*, SP 18 (Collegeville, Minn. 2002). – **D. K. Rensberger**, *1, John, 2 John, 3 John*, ANTC (Nashville 1997). – **R. Schnackenburg**, *The Johannine Epistles: Introduction and Commentary*, trans. R. Fuller and I. Fuller (New York 1992). – **G. Strecker**, *The Johannine Letters: A Commentary on 1, 2, and 3 John*, trans. L. M. Maloney, Hermeneia (Minneapolis 1996). – **W. Vogler**, *Die Briefe des Johannes*, THKNT 17 (Leipzig 1993). – **F. Vouga**, *Die Johannesbriefe*, HNT 15/3 (Tübingen 1990).

D. E. Aune, *Dictionary* (Bib. 4), s.v. "John, First Letter of," 241–43; "John, the Letters of," 249–50. – **T. Griffiths**, *Keep Yourselves from Idols: A New Look at 1 John*, JSNTSup (Sheffield 2002); see the review by H. J. Klauck in *CBQ* 66 (2004) 320–21. – **G. Guirisato**, *Struttura e teologia della prima lettera di Giovanni: Analisi letteraria e retorica, contenuto teologico*, AnBib 138 (Rome 1998). – **K. L. Hansford**, "The Underlying Poetic Structure of 1 John," *Journal of Translation and Textlinguistics* 5 (1992) 126–74. – **J. V. Hills**, "A Genre for 1 John," in B. A. Pearson, ed., *The Future of Early Christianity: Essays in Honor of H. Koester* (Minneapolis 1991) 367–77. – **H. J. Klauck**, "Analyse" (Bib. 30). – idem, *Die Johannesbriefe*, EdF 276 (Darmstadt ²1995), there further lit. – **D. Neufeld**, *Reconceiving Texts As Speech Acts: An Analysis of I John*, Biblical Interpretation Series 7 (Leiden 1994). – **H. Schmidt**, *Gegner im 1. Johannesbrief? Zu Konstruktion und Selbstreferenz im johanneischen Sinnsystem*, BWANT 159 (Stuttgart 2002). – **D. F. Watson**, "1 John 2:12-14 as *Distributio, Conduplicatio*, and *Expolitio*: A Rhetorical Understanding," *JSNT* 35 (1989) 97–110. – idem, "An Epideictic Strategy for Increasing Adherence to Community Values: 1 John 1:1–2:27," *Proceedings of the Eastern Great Lakes Biblical Society* 11 (1991) 144–52.

Unlike a pseudonymous letter, which names a famous person as the author instead of the real author, the First Letter of John is an anonymous letter because it does not claim to have been written by the Apostle John, whom later church tradition claims as its author. First John also does without any indirect characterization of its author by the honorary title "elder" or "presbyter" (πρεσβύτερος), as in the superscription of 2 and 3 John (although this need not preclude all three being written by the same author). However, in thought and language 1 John shares a very close relationship with the Gospel of John that extends to their very structure:

	1 John	*Gospel of John*
Prologue:	1:1-4: "What was from the beginning . . ."	1:1-18: "In the beginning was . . ."
Body opening:	1:5: "And this is the message . . ."	1:19: "And this is the witness . . ."
Body closing:	5:13: "These things I have written to you . . ."	20:31: "But these are written . . ."
Appendix (second hand):	5:14-21	21:1-25

These parallels are most easily explained by assuming that the author of 1 John had access to the Gospel, but that the letter was formulated not by the Gospel's main author but by another member of the Johannine school, as a reader's guide to the correct understanding of the Gospel, whose Christology had faded into the twilight in the wake of a church split. This brings us temporally to the end of the first century CE (for another explanation see Strecker). First John's departures from the normal letter form (no prescript, no real epistolary closing) are also conditioned by its orientation to the Gospel. Nevertheless, the motif of joy in 1:4 (cf. the expression of joy as a standard component of an epistolary proem), the frequent reflection on the act of writing by γράφω (2:1, 7, etc.) and ἔγραψα (2:14, etc.), and the repeated direct address of the audience can all be considered indications of an epistolary act of communication.

A confusing array of outlines from two to ten parts has already been suggested for body of this writing in 1 John 1:5–5:12. But when one considers that the love commandment is spoken about three times in three increasingly intense treatments, one almost automatically arrives at the three main sections in 1:5–5:12 (cf. the love theme in 2:5, 10, 15); 2:18–3:24 (cf. 3:10, 14-24) and 4:1–5:12 (cf. 4:7–5:3). This also agrees with a preference for the number three already observable elsewhere (cf. only the three witnesses in 5:6-8).

In the area of rhetorical criticism, one examination of the *dispositio* or "arrangement" of 1 John, by F. Vouga, designates 1:5–2:17 as the *captatio benevolentiae* (too long!), 2:18-27 as the *narratio* or statement of the case, 2:28-29 as the *propositio* or thesis, 3:1-24 as the *probatio* or proof, 4:1-21 as the *exhortatio*—even though this was not a standard part of ancient rhetorical theory (as has frequently been noted since H. D. Betz introduced this category into his Galatians commentary in 1979)—and 5:1-12 as the *peroratio* or conclusion. Yet a competing rhetorical analysis by D. F. Watson designates 1:5–2:11 as the *probatio* and 2:12-14 as a *digressio*. This only illustrates the difficulty of applying rhetorical categories to 1 John (for discussion see Klauck, "Analyse").

Exercise

41. What might the following quotation from Seneca, *Epistles* 33.6–7 contribute to the analysis of 1 John? (trans. R. M. Gummere, *Seneca: Ad Lucilium epistulae morales*, LCL, vol. 1 [1917] 237):

For single maxims sink in more easily when they are marked off and bounded like a line of verse. That is why we give to children a proverb, or that which the Greeks call *Chreia*, to be learned by heart; that sort of thing can be comprehended by the young mind, which cannot as yet hold more.

---

b) The Second and Third Letters of John

See above, chap. 1, part C and Exercise 30 (with its Answer Key).

5. The Letter of Jude

Bibliography 50: R. J. Bauckham, *Jude, 2 Peter*, WBC 50 (Waco, Tex. 1983). – **P. H. Davids**, *The Letters of 2 Peter and Jude*, Pillar New

Testament Commentary (forthcoming). – **J. H. Neyrey**, *2 Peter, Jude: A New Translation with Introduction and Commentary*, AB 37C (New York 1993). – **H. Paulsen**, *Der zweite Petrusbrief und der Judasbrief*, KEK 12/2 (Göttingen 1992). – **A. Vögtle**, *Der Judasbrief, Der 2. Petrusbrief*, EKKNT 22 (Solothurn and Neukirchen-Vluyn 1994). – See also Bib. 63 on 2 Peter.

D. E. Aune, *Dictionary* (Bib. 4), s.v. "Jude, Letter of," 255–57. – **R. J. Bauckham**, *Jude and the Relatives of Jesus in the Early Church* (Edinburgh 1990). – **J. D. Charles**, "Literary Artifice in the Epistle of Jude," *ZNW* 82 (1991) 106–24. – idem, "Jude's Use of Pseudepigraphical Source-Material as Part of a Literary Strategy," *NTS* 37 (1991) 130–45. – **J. J. Gunther**, "The Alexandrian Epistle of Jude," *NTS* 30 (1984) 549–62. – **R. Heiligenthal**, *Zwischen Henoch und Paulus: Studien zum theologiegeschichtlichen Ort des Judasbriefes*, TANZ 6 (Tübingen 1992). – **S. Joubert**, "Facing the Past: Transtextual Relationships and Historical Understanding in the Letter of Jude," *BZ* 42 (1998) 56–70. – **J. Kahmann**, "The Second Letter of Peter and the Letter of Jude: Their Mutual Relationship," in J. M. Sevrin, ed., *The New Testament in Early Christianity: La réception des écrits néotestamentaire dans le christianisme primitif*, BETL 86 (Leuven 1989) 105–21. – **P. Müller**, "Der Judasbrief," *TRu* 63 (1998) 267–89. – **D. F. Watson**, *Invention, Arrangement, and Style: Rhetorical Criticism of Jude and 2 Peter*, SBLDS 104 (Atlanta 1988). – **T. R. Wolthuis**, "Jude and the Rhetorician: A Dialogue on the Rhetorical Nature of the Epistle of Jude," *CTJ* 24 (1989) 126-34 (an imaginative conversation between Cicero and "Jude").

In the first line of the prescript in vv. 1-2 the author identifies himself as "Jude (Greek: Judas), a servant of Jesus Christ and brother of James." According to its original intention, this can hardly be referred to anyone but the Lord's brother by the name of Jude or Judas (Mark 6:3; par. Matt 13:55), even though this once again involves intentional pseudepigraphy and presupposes a knowledge of the Letter of James. On the other hand, the Letter of Jude has served as a literary *Vorlage* for 2 Peter (see below, chap. 8, sec. C), so that we arrive at a time of composition between 90 and 100 CE. As to the place of writing, the panorama of proposals stretches from Alexandria through Palestine and Syria to Asia Minor and beyond.

The letter can helpfully be analyzed in both epistolary and rhetorical categories. The salutation "May mercy, peace, and love be yours in abundance (πληθυνθείη)" is distinguished by an unusual triad without the standard early Christian "grace" (e.g., "grace, mercy, and peace" [2 John 2]), supplied in the parallel in 2

Peter 1:2, and by the optative of wish πληθυνθείη, which Jude
shares with both 1 Peter 1:2 and 2 Peter 1:2. Verse 3 addresses the
readers as "beloved," calls attention to the act of writing ("while I
was eagerly preparing to write to you about the salvation we
share"), and states the purpose for writing ("to urge you to contend
for the faith that was once for all entrusted to the saints"), before
verse 4 follows with an inferential γάρ that introduces the false
teachers who are to be sharply attacked in what follows. Together
verses 3 and 4 take over the double function of an epistolary proem
and a body opening (which may explain why Watson designates v.
3 in rhetorical terms as the *exordium* and v. 4 as the *narratio*).

The body middle in vv. 5-16 (Watson's *probatio*, with three
proofs) presents negative examples in groups of three (e.g., the
wilderness generation, the fallen angels, and Sodom and
Gomorrah in vv. 5-7; Cain, Balaam, and Korah in v. 11), sometimes drawing from the Old Testament and sometimes from apocryphal or pseudepigraphical traditions (cf. the dispute between
Michael and the devil over the body of Moses in v. 9; the quotation of Enoch material in vv. 14-15 [cf. *1 Enoch* 18:15-16; 21:5-6]),
and interpreting the examples polemically against the opponents.

The direct address in vv. 17 and 20 divides the body closing in
vv. 17-23 into two parts, vv. 17-19 and vv. 20-23 (cf. Watson's *peroratio*, similarly divided into a *repetitio* in vv. 17-19 and an *adfectus*
in vv. 20-23). This then leads to the actual letter closing, for which
the doxology in vv. 24-25 is reserved. Structurally the first element
of the body closing, about scoffers who indulge their own lusts in
vv. 17-19, corresponds to the second element of the proem or
body opening about the intruders who promote licentiousness in
v. 4. By the same token the second element of the body closing,
which strengthens the addressees in the faith in vv. 17-23, corresponds more closely to the first element of the proem or opening
about the faith delivered once for all to the saints in v. 3. A certain
concentric structure is therefore evident, and the thesis about the
double function of vv. 3-4 as both proem and opening is confirmed
by vv. 17-23.

6. The Collection of the Catholic Letters

Bibliography 51: D. E. Aune, *Dictionary* (Bib. 4), s.v. "General
Epistles," 195–96. – **D. Lührmann**, "Gal 2,9 und die katholischen

Briefe: Bemerkungen zum Kanon und zur regula fidei," *ZNW* 72 (1981) 65–87. – **B. M. Metzger**, *The Canon of the New Testament* (Oxford 1987). – **E. Preuschen**, *Analecta: Kürzere Texte zur Geschichte der Alten Kirche und des Kanons, II. Zur Kanonsgeschichte*, SAQ 8/2 (Tübingen ²1910). – **J. Schlosser**, ed., *The Catholic Epistles and the Tradition*, BETL 176 (Leuven 2004). – **J. S. Siker**, "The Canonical Status of the Catholic Epistles in the Syriac New Testament," *JTS* 38 (1987) 311–29. – **F. Vouga**, "Apostolische Briefe als 'scriptura': Die Rezeption des Paulus in den katholischen Briefen," in H. H. Schmid and J. Mehlhausen, eds., *Sola Scriptura: Das reformatorische Schriftprinzip in der säkularen Welt* (Gütersloh 1991) 194–210.

The designation "catholic epistle" first seems to have been used for 1 John and was already known, also with reference to other letters, around 200 CE. Eusebius of Caesarea then uses the term more comprehensively around 300 CE, particularly in the context of James and Jude, when he writes, for example, in *Hist. eccl.* 2.23.24–25:

> Such is the story of James, whose is said to be the first of the Epistles called Catholic. It is to be observed that its authenticity is denied, since few of the ancients quote it, as is also the case with the Epistle called Jude's, which is itself one of the seven called Catholic; nevertheless we know that these letters have been used publicly with the rest in most churches.

The attribute "catholic" involves two ideas. The original idea was that such a letter was addressed not to an individual church but to all of Christianity and thus had a more general audience, which also leads to the English designation "General Epistles" (cf. Aune). Later "catholic" also essentially came to mean "canonical"; such a letter was accepted by the whole church. This was at first applied relatively unproblematically only to the longer letters of 1 Peter, 1 John, and with reservations also James. The expansion of this group by the addition of 2 Peter, 2 John, 3 John, and Jude results not accidentally in the number seven. With the 14 letters in the extended Pauline corpus (including Hebrews), one thereby arrives at 3 x 7 letters in the New Testament, which scores two important symbolic numbers at once. The artificiality of the entire construction is thereby only underlined. This is also shown by the fact that as products of the Johannine school, 1–3 John, together with the Gospel of John (and possibly Revelation), actually constitute the scriptural canon of the Johannine churches, and therefore the Johannine Letters belong with the Gospel in terms of content, rather than with the Catholic Letters.

The traditional internal sequence of the Catholic Letters in our Bibles was not the only one in antiquity but dominates in the majority of manuscripts. The principle of ordering was once again decreasing length, though strictly speaking 1 John (2141 words) would have to precede James (1742) and 1 Peter (1684), and the ordering by length is also interrupted by an effort to keep the letters attributed to a single author together (1–2 Peter; 1–3 John). It is therefore all the more interesting to note that the present, not strictly length-dependent order of the three major letters corresponds to the order of the three "pillars" of the Jerusalem church, "James and Cephas and John," in Galatians 2:9.

The Greek manuscripts do not place the Catholic Letters as a whole where our modern editions do, between Hebrews and Revelation, but rather between Acts and the Pauline corpus. The priority of the three pillar apostles before the Apostle Paul is thereby emphasized, but in the same breath this order also apparently seeks to present the agreement of the four great witnesses in essential matters of faith.

It is a little known fact that the boundaries of the church's canon are fuzzy when it comes to the minor Catholic Letters. The Syrian Orthodox churches hold until today to the canon of the Peshitta, the Old Syriac translation, into which only James, 1 Peter, and 1 John found acceptance, but not 2 Peter, 2–3 John, and Jude.

Exercise

42. Evaluate the list of canonical writings in the so-called Cheltenham Codex of around 360 CE. Text in B. M. Metzger, *The Canon of the New Testament* (Oxford 1987) 311–12:

    Four Gospels: Matthew, 2700 lines
          Mark, 1700 lines
          John, 1800 lines
          Luke, 3300 lines
      All the lines make 10,000 lines

Epistles of Paul, 13 in number
The Acts of the Apostles, 3600 lines
The Apocalypse, 1800 lines
Three Epistles of John, 350 lines
One only
Two Epistles of Peter, 300 lines
One only.

D. Letters in Acts and Revelation

1. The Acts of the Apostles

See below, chapter 8, part D.

2. The Revelation to John

Bibliography 52: D. E. Aune, *Revelation*, 3 vols., WBC 52A, 52B, 52C (Dallas and Nashville 1997–1998). – **G. K. Beale**, *The Book of Revelation: A Commentary on the Greek Text*, NIGTC (Grand Rapids 1998). – **H. Giesen**, *Die Offenbarung des Johannes*, RNT (Regensburg 1997). – **R. H. Mounce**, *The Book of Revelation*, NICNT (Grand Rapids 1997). – **U. B. Müller**, *Die Offenbarung des Johannes*, ÖTBK 19 (Gütersloh and Würzburg ²1995). – **J. Roloff**, *The Revelation of John: A Continental Commentary*, trans. by J. E. Alsup (Minneapolis 1993).

D. E. Aune, "The Form and Function of the Proclamation to the Seven Churches (Revelation 2–3)," *NTS* 36 (1990) 182–204. – **A. Deissmann**, *Light from the Ancient East* (Bib. 1) 244–45, 374–75. – **F. Hahn**, "Die Sendschreiben der Johannesapokalypse: Ein Beitrag zur Bestimmung prophetischer Redeformen," in G. Jeremias, H.-W. Kuhn, and H. Stegemann, eds., *Tradition und Glaube: Das frühe Christentum in seiner Umwelt*, FS K. G. Kuhn (Göttingen 1971) 357–94. – **C. J. Hemer**, *The Letters to the Seven Churches of Asia in Their Local Setting*, JSNTSup 11 (Sheffield 1986). – **M. Karrer**, *Johannesoffenbarung* (Bib. 4). – **J. T. Kirby**, "The Rhetorical Situation of Revelation 1–3," *NTS* 34 (1988) 197–207. – **F. Martin**, "Apocalypse: Les lettres aux sept Églises," in L. Panier, ed., *Les lettres dans la Bible* (Bib. 4) 195–206. – **T. Pippin**, *Death and Desire: The Rhetoric of Gender in the Apocalypse of John*, Literary Currents in Biblical Interpretation (Louisville 1992). – **A. Sand**, "Briefe als interpretierende Begleitschreiben: Die sieben Sendschreiben der Joh-

Apokalypse," in K. Bauckhaus and F. G. Untergassmair, eds., *Schrift und Tradition*, FS J. Ernst (Paderborn 1996) 373–86. – **H. Ulland**, *Die Vision als Radikalisierung der Wirklichkeit in der Apokalypse des Johannes: Das Verhältnis der sieben Sendschreiben zu Apokalypse 12–13*, TANZ 21 (Tübingen 1997).

a) The Epistolary Frame

The Revelation to John, which originated in the last years of the reign of the emperor Domitian in 90–95 CE, displays an even more intensive overlay of the apocalyptic and epistolary genres than *2 Baruch* (see chap. 6, sec. B.3). The entire book of Revelation has its own letter frame, for after an extensive heading or title for the book in Revelation 1:1-3 ("The revelation of Jesus Christ," etc.) and before the beginning of the vision report in 1:9, which is also preceded by a prophetic quotation in 1:7 and a divine self-identification in 1:8, there stands in 1:4-6 an epistolary prescript that to some extent conforms to the conventions of the Pauline and deutero-Pauline letters.

In the superscription the author introduces himself with his probably authentic, but not very revealing name "John" (which hardly helps us identify him historically), while the adscription designates the recipients as "the seven churches that are in Asia." Analogously to Galatians, the salutation or greeting, which begins in typically Pauline manner with "grace to you and peace," contains a significant expansion upon the senders of that grace and peace, which in this case come not "from God our Father and the Lord Jesus Christ, who gave himself for our sins" (Gal 1:3-4), but "from him who is and who was and who is to come, and from the seven spirits who are before his throne, and from Jesus Christ, the faithful witness, the firstborn of the dead, and the ruler of the kings of the earth" (Rev 1:4-5a). The salutation concludes with a doxology, here addressed not to God the Father (as in Galatians) but to Jesus Christ, "who loves us and freed us from our sins by his blood . . . , to whom be glory and dominion forever and ever. Amen" (Rev 1:5b-6).

At the beginning of the author's report of his visionary encounter with the "one like a son of man" in Revelation 1:9-20, he receives a command to "write" to the seven churches, which are listed by name as the those in Ephesus, Smyrna, Pergamum, Thyatira, Sardis, Philadelphia, and Laodicea (1:11). These are the

same churches addressed by letter in 2:1–3:22, which by their
mention here in 1:11 and also in 1:19-20 receive a fixed place in
the introduction to the book of Revelation. The conclusion of the
book in 22:6-21 ends in v. 21 with an epistolary grace wish, while
the request "Come, Lord Jesus" in v. 20 corresponds to the
"Maranatha" in 1 Corinthians 16:21.

Despite these undeniable letter features it remains questionable whether we should classify the entire book of Revelation as a
letter. What is clear is that the author exploits the communicative
potential of the letter form, especially that of the adapted and
developed Pauline letter form, to facilitate communication
between himself and his addressees, who live in former Pauline
congregations (cf. Ephesus at the head of the list)—thus bringing
his message home.

b) The Letters to the Seven Churches

The open letters in Revelation 2–3 are dictated by the risen
Christ to the seer John, who addresses them to the angels of the
seven churches, for whom the angels of the seventy (or seventy-
two) nations from Jewish apocalyptic tradition serve as background. Ephesus as the first church addressed is the city among
the seven that stands most nearly opposite the island of Patmos
where the author finds himself according to 1:9 (the city of
Miletus would have been even closer, but it is not mentioned;
perhaps the author is writing from there instead of from Patmos,
where he originally saw the vision; or there was no Christian
community yet in Miletus). If one connects the seven cities in the
order in which they are mentioned in Revelation by a line, one
comes up with a circular route (cf. the map in Roloff 35) that can
be interpreted as a postal route. This is not to say that one should
abstract any of the letters from the macro text and refer it only to
the individual church addressed. All the letters are meant to be
read by all the churches, and all were written by the author originally for this context.

Despite variations in detail there is a fixed structure for all
seven letters that incorporates the following parts:

- *adscription* "To the angel," etc., with the command to "write"
  (γράψον)
- *messenger formula* Τάδε λέγει, "Thus says," etc.

- *christological title,* e.g. "the one who holds the seven stars," "the first and the last," "the one who has the sharp two-edged sword," "the Son of God," "the one who has the seven spirits of God," "the holy one," "the faithful and true witness"
- *situational description* beginning with "I know," e.g., "I know your works," "I know your affliction," "I know where you live"
- *call to listen:* "Let anyone who has an ear listen to what the Spirit is saying to the churches" (sometimes placed after the final element below)
- *promise to the one who conquers or overcomes,* τῷ νικῶντι, ὁ νικῶν

These individual elements have little to do with the standard Greco-Roman letter model and its typical motifs but go back in part to prophetic modes of speech, which in turn sometimes influence ancient letters (hence τάδε λέγει is not only the prophetic messenger formula but also appears in archaic letter prescripts). There is therefore a certain justification for comparing the letters of Revelation with prophetic letters such as Jeremiah 29 (cf. vv. 4, 31, "Thus says the Lord," etc.) or 2 Chronicles 21:12-15.

A. Deissmann in his day wanted to solve the puzzle of the letters to the seven churches by categorizing them as "letters from heaven" (*Light from the Ancient East*, 244–45, 374–75). A letter from heaven, as its name suggests, falls from heaven to earth, sent from the gods to humans, and contains oracles, threats, and promises. Unfortunately there is little research on the prehistory of such letters and a general lack of standard preliminary works on them.[25] The letter from heaven apparently had its antecedents in Egypt, where we also find its counterpart, the letter from people to the gods, which probably developed from the letter to the dead.[26] In the Hellenistic cultural realm the letter from heaven appears, for example, in association with the healing god Asclepius. To one of his worshipers who was almost blind Asclepius sends a female poet "with a sealed writing tablet" that the afflicted is instructed to read, even though he is unable to do so. However, "because he hoped for a favorable sign from Asclepius, he removed the seal, looked at the wax tablet, and was healed" (Pausanias, *Description of Greece* 10.38.13; further examples in

---

[25] Scholars continue to depend on the monograph of R. Stübe, *Der Himmelsbrief: Ein Beitrag zur allgemeinen Religionsgeschichte* (Tübingen 1918).

[26] Cf. K. T. Zauzich, "Paläographische Herausforderungen I: Ein langer Brief an Götter," *Enchoria* 19–20 (1992–1993) 165–79.

Aelius Aristides, Flavius Philostratus, and the emperor Julian). Epicurus's work *Rule* or *Standard of Judgment*, which Cicero refers to as a *caeleste volumen* or "heavenly writing" (Cicero, *De natura deorum* 1.43; cf. *De finibus* 1.63: *quasi delapsa de caelo*), does not have an epistolary form. The Christian reception of the letter from heaven does not really seem to begin until the fourth or sixth century CE. But from then on, the letter from heaven or its counterpart, the letter from hell, plays a not insignificant role in the popular piety of the medieval and modern periods (for a modern parallel for letters between demons, rather than from hell, or heaven, to earth, see C. S. Lewis's *Screwtape Letters*).

We can leave aside the discussion of letters from heaven, because this genre does not shed any significant light on the letters in Revelation 2–3. Among other things, letters falling straight from heaven would underplay the intermediary role of the seer John. On the other hand, another of Deissmann's suggestions has stood the test of time (cf. *Light*, 375 with nn. 5–7). For the messenger formula in the letters from Christ in Revelation, Deissmann pointed to the use of *dicit* and τάδε λέγει in Roman imperial letters. With the qualification that this deals more particularly with imperial edicts (in contrast to decrees, prescripts, and mandates), D. E. Aune now also goes back to the royal and imperial edicts, whose form he claims has been combined in the letters to the seven churches with that of the prophetic paraenetic oracles of salvation and judgment.

Exercise

43. Identify the fixed structural elements in the letter to Pergamum in Revelation 2:12-17.

8

New Testament Letters II: Selected Texts

A. A Letter of Hope: First Thessalonians

Bibliography 53 (selected commentaries): **E. Best**, *The First and Second Epistles to the Thessalonians*, BNTC/HNTC (London and New York 1972). – **E. von Dobschütz**, *Die Thessalonicher-Briefe*, KEK 10 (Göttingen ⁷1909; repr. 1974). – **G. L. Green**, *The Letters to the Thessalonians*, Pillar New Testament Commentary (Grand Rapids 2002). – **T. Holtz**, *Der erste Brief an die Thessalonicher*, EKKNT 12 (Zürich and Neukirchen-Vluyn 1986). – **F. Laub**, *1. und 2. Thessalonicherbrief*, NEchtB 13 (Würzburg 1985). – **A. J. Malherbe**, *The Letters to the Thessalonians: A New Translation with Introduction and Commentary*, AB 32B (New York 2000). – **W. Marxsen**, *Der erste Brief an die Thessalonicher*, ZBK 11/1 (Zürich 1979). – **P. G. Müller**, *Der erste und zweite Brief an die Thessalonicher*, RNT (Regensburg 2001). – **E. J. Richard**, *First and Second Thessalonians*, SP 11 (Collegeville 1995). – **C. A. Wanamaker**, *The Epistles to the Thessalonians*, NIGTC (Grand Rapids 1990).

Bibliography 54 (monographs, anthologies, etc.): **J. Bickmann**, *Kommunikation gegen den Tod: Studien zur paulinischen Briefpragmatik am Beispiel des Ersten Thessalonicherbriefes*, FB 86 (Würzburg 1998). – **R. F. Collins**, *Studies on the First Letter to the Thessalonians*, BETL 66 (Leuven 1984). – idem, ed., *The Thessalonian Correspondence*, BETL 87 (Leuven 1990). – **R. Jewett**, *The Thessalonian Correspondence: Pauline Rhetoric and Millenarian Piety*, FF (Philadelphia 1986). – **B. C. Johanson**, *To All the Brethren: A Text-Linguistic and Rhetorical Approach to I Thessalonians*, ConBNT 16 (Stockholm 1987). – **A. J. Malherbe**, *Paul and the Thessalonians: The Philosophic Tradition of Pastoral Care* (Philadelphia 1987). – **M. M. Mitchell**, "1 and 2 Thessalonians," in J. D. G. Dunn, ed., *The Cambridge Companion to St. Paul* (Cambridge 2003) 51–63. – eadem, "Thessalonicherbriefe," in H. D. Betz, D. S. Browning, B. Janowski, and

E. Jüngel, eds., *Religion in Geschichte und Gegenwart*, 4th ed., vol. 8 (Tübingen 2005) 360–61; forthcoming English version in *Religion Past and Present* (Leiden). – **C. R. Nicholl**, *From Hope to Despair in Thessalonica: Situating 1 and 2 Thessalonians*, SNTSMS 126 (Cambridge 2004). – **T. D. Still**, *Conflict at Thessalonica: A Pauline Church and its Neighbours*, JSNTSup 183 (Sheffield 1999). – **S. Walton**, *Leadership and Lifestyle: The Portrait of Paul in the Miletus Speech and 1 Thessalonians*, SNTSMS 108 (Cambridge 2000). – **K. K. Yeo**, "The Rhetoric of Election and Calling Language in 1 Thessalonians," in S. E. Porter and D. L. Stamps, eds., *Rhetorical Criticism and the Bible*, JSNTSup 195 (Sheffield 2002) 526–47.

Paul arrived at Thessalonica (modern-day Thessaloniki or Salonica), a city of Macedonia on the main east-west Roman road through northern Greece, the Via Egnatia, around 49–50 CE on the great missionary journey that took him for the first time outside Asia Minor to Greece (the so-called "second" missionary journey according the chronology of Acts). He had just come from Philippi, where he had planted the first successful church on the European mainland, and after leaving Thessalonica he traveled on to Berea, Athens, and Corinth. The First Letter to the Thessalonians may have been written from Corinth around 50–51 CE. However, new proposals regarding Pauline chronology seek to push Paul's first mission trip to Greece back almost a decade to the early 40s, prior to the so-called Apostolic Council of Acts 15 (ca. 48 CE), so that we would have to subtract about 10 years from all the dates concerned with this trip. Nevertheless, the arguments for the early dating have not yet proved convincing. Much depends on how one evaluates the historical reliability of Acts. The author Luke reports about Paul's stay in Thessalonica only very briefly in Acts 17:1-9. His presentation gives the impression that Paul stayed there only three weekends and preached only in the synagogue. But this presentation needs correction in at least these points, for according to the impression one gets from 1 Thessalonians, Paul's initial stay must have been somewhat longer, and his mission success was achieved mainly with a pagan public (hence he writes that "you turned to God from idols, to serve a living and true God," 1:9), which could not have been fully reached by working only through the contacts of the Jewish community.

Fortunately, we need not probe more deeply here into these general introductory questions, because they bear only marginally on the literary aspects of the letter in which we are mainly interested. A few more insights into the letter's situation will result from our analysis of its structure and content, which we will examine by epistolography before turning to questions of literary and rhetorical criticism. In our first step we will purposely work with a very detailed outline that extends to the individual verses, because (a) this will help us grasp the content better, and because (b) such outlines are also offered by other scholars who undertake a rhetorical analysis of New Testament letters. These include H. D. Betz on Galatians (cf. above chap. 5, sec. C.3; chap. 7, sec. A.3), and on 1 Thessalonians R. Jewett (72–76) and F. W. Hughes ("Rhetoric" [Bib. 57] 109–16). We will furthermore proceed from the assumption that 1 Thessalonians is the oldest Pauline letter and therefore also the oldest document in the New Testament, which makes engagement with this text especially exciting. We will maintain this prevailing position against recent attempts to reclaim this pride of place for Galatians.

1. Structure and Content

Bibliography 55: D. E. Aune, *Dictionary* (Bib. 4), s.v. "Cosenders," 118. – **S. Byrskog**, "Co-Senders, Co-Authors and Paul's Use of the First Person Plural," *ZNW* 87 (1996) 230–50. – **G. Friedrich**, "Lohmeyers These über das paulinische Briefpräskript kritisch beleuchtet," *TLZ* 81 (1956) 343–46. – **R. W. Funk**, *Parables and Presence* (Bib. 4). – **J. Lambrecht**, "Thanksgivings in 1 Thessalonians 1–3," in R. F. Collins, ed., *The Thessalonian Correspondence* (Bib. 54) 183–205. – **G. Lyons**, *Pauline Autobiography* (Bib. 39) 177–221. – **A. J. Malherbe**, "Did the Thessalonians Write to Paul?" in R. T. Fortna and B. R. Gaventa, eds., *The Conversation Continues: Studies in Paul and John in Honor of J. L. Martyn* (Nashville 1990) 246–57. – **M. Müller**, *Vom Schluß zum Ganzen* (Bib. 4) 83–129. – **P. T. O'Brien**, *Introductory Thanksgivings* (Bib. 4) 141–66. – **E. J. Richard**, *1 and 2 Thessalonians* (Bib. 53). – **E. R. Richards**, *Paul* (Bib. 4). – **J. A. D. Weima**, *Neglected Endings* (Bib. 4) 174–86. – **G. P. Wiles**, *Paul's Intercessory Prayers* (Bib. 4) 45–71, 175–86.

    I.   Letter Opening (1:1-10)

          A. Prescript (1:1)
              1. *Superscriptio*
                 a) Paul
                 b) Co-senders: Silvanus and Timothy

2. *Adscriptio*
   a) Naming of the addressees
   b) Theological qualification
3. *Salutatio*

First Thessalonians contains the shortest prescript of all the Pauline letters. This also applies to each of the three parts of the prescript, for although the superscription here does contain three names, Paul, Silvanus, and Timothy, they are not expanded by any of the usual titles (see below). The three parts appear distinctly in 1 Thessalonians, but elsewhere in Paul they can be significantly expanded, as with the superscription in Romans, the address in 1 Corinthians, or the greeting in Galatians. The brevity in 1 Thessalonians may also be explained by the fact that Paul in his earliest writings was still in the process of discovering and developing the potential that lay in such prescripts (cf. Friedrich 346: "We see how Paul first had to feel his way before he found his final form"). Moreover, Paul's other prescripts often reflect the specific problems of the church situation to which the letter reacts, including challenges to Paul's apostleship, divisions in the church, infiltration by Paul's opponents, or the lack of a personal basis for communication that needs to be established. In other words, these prescripts are marked by both currency and conventionality, to borrow a phrase from E. Lohmeyer.[1] The more conventional prescript of 1 Thessalonians may therefore signal that although there were problems in Thessalonica, they were structured more simply and did not yet reach the complexity of later controversies.

Paul as the main sender is appropriately mentioned first, but here and in 2 Thessalonians alone in the Pauline corpus, his name lacks any of its usual qualifying titles, such as "an apostle of Jesus Christ" (1 Cor 1:1) or "a servant of Jesus Christ" (Rom 1:1); his co-senders Silvanus and Timothy are similarly referred to by name alone, without any further designation such as "servants" (cf. Phil 1:1 for Timothy). Silvanus is presumably identical with the Silas whom Paul takes along as his travel companion from Antioch on his second missionary journey in Acts 15:40, while Timothy, who appears as Paul's co-sender also in 2 Corinthians, Philippians, and Philemon (as well as in Colossians and, with Silvanus, in 2

---

[1] E. Lohmeyer, "Grußüberschriften" (Bib. 4) 9.

Thessalonians among the deutero-Paulines), joins the group in Derbe according to Acts 16:1-3. Both co-workers therefore participated in Paul's founding mission in Thessalonica. By including them in the line about the sender, Paul does not mean to say that all three participated in writing the letter to the same extent, nor does he name the others only as a formality to bolster the authority of a letter for which he alone bears responsibility. Rather, he wishes to indicate that he discussed the essential contents of the letter with his trusted co-workers.[2]

One question that has not yet been fully answered concerns how the "we" language in the body of 1 Thessalonians relates to the collective of three senders at the beginning (cf. Bryskog). This can vary from letter to letter, and different nuances must be taken into account even within the same letter. In 1 Thessalonians it is worth asking whether the "we" that immediately follows the pre-script in 1:2 ("We always give thanks to God for all of you," etc.) should be referred to Paul alone, as is commonly done by assuming a literary plural "we" instead of "I," or whether here at least Silvanus and Timothy could also be included. Later in 2:4 when it says that "God tests *our hearts*," the word "hearts" stands unexpectedly in the plural.

In examining all the "we" forms in the letter—which is what a full solution would require—we encounter several passages that call for further reflection. When Paul says in 3:1-2, "Therefore when we could bear it no longer, we decided to be left alone in Athens; and we sent Timothy, our brother and co-worker . . ., to strengthen and encourage you," the reference of the "we" need not be limited to Paul alone. Rather, after both Silas and Timothy had joined Paul in Athens (according to Acts 17:15), it is possible that when Timothy was sent back to Thessalonica, as indicated here, Silas remained with Paul (where Acts is silent), and is thus included in the "we": both Paul and Silas will have been "left behind" when Timothy departed. The NRSV's "left alone" may therefore be misleading if it is taken to imply only one person left

---

[2] To give Paul the priority as as the author but also to indicate that he speaks for his co-senders, Richard 37, 40 translates the expression Παῦλος καὶ Σιλουανὸς καὶ Τιμόθεος by "Paul, *also* Silvanus and Timothy" (italics added).

on his own.[3] On the other hand, readers might have trouble maintaining the plural reference of Paul's "we" in 1 Thess 2:7, where he writes, "we might have made demands *as apostles of Christ* (ὡς Χριστοῦ ἀπόστολοι)." Nevertheless, it is still possible that Paul used the title "apostle" here in its full theological sense, meaning more than just a "messenger" or "emissary" (cf. 2 Cor 8:23; Phil 2:25), and that he extended its application, if not to Timothy, then to Silas as his fellow apostle (the absence of the title "apostle" from the superscription makes this unclear). The "we" has another use in a statement such as 1 Thessalonians 5:10, "[Christ] died for us, so that whether we are awake or asleep we may live with him." Here Paul clearly includes himself together with all other Christians, so that his style can be called a communicative "we" form. In a few passages in 1 Thessalonians Paul expresses himself directly in the first person, as in 2:18, "For we wanted to come to you—certainly I, Paul, wanted to again and again—but Satan blocked our way" (cf. also 3:5; 5:27). But how far this first-person singular reference extends in the text is not so clear. In other, later letters like 2 Corinthians, where the "we" often acquires an exemplary character that makes Paul the model for the realization of general Christian values, matters once again look somewhat different.

Our small mission team addresses their letter "to the *ekklesia* of the Thessalonians." In and of itself this could designate, for example, the "assembly" in the theater of a city's free citizens who possess voting rights, as in Acts 19:32 "the assembly (ἐκκλησία) was in confusion" (with reference to Ephesus). That the term ἐκκλησία cannot mean this in 1 Thessalonians but rather refers to a small group of new Christians that could still meet in a household setting is made clear by the theological qualification, "To the *ekklesia* of the Thessalonians *in God the Father and the Lord Jesus Christ*." In slightly modified form this phrase then migrates to the salutation in other Pauline letters. In its brevity the opening greet-

---

[3] Some other translations of 1 Thessalonians 1:1 leave more room for both Paul and Silas to remain in Athens when Timothy leaves. Cf. the NJB, "When we could not bear it any longer, we decided it would be best to be left without a companion [i.e., Timothy; not plural 'without companions'] at Athens." More explicit is the NIV, which by its use of "ourselves" virtually requires Silas to be included with Paul: "So when we could stand it no longer, we thought it best to be left by *ourselves* in Athens."

ing "grace to you and peace" (χάρις ὑμῖν καὶ εἰρήνη) still recalls the χαίρειν of the standard Greek prescript, now replaced by χάρις. The twofold salutation by greetings and peace and its syntax as a verbless clause, which expects the reader to supply "peace *is* with you" or "peace *be* with you," has its precedent in Jewish letters of the Maccabean period at the latest, e.g. 2 Maccabees 1:1, "Greetings and true peace" (see above, chap. 6).

    B. Proem (1:2-10)
        1. Thanksgiving and its grounds (1:2-5)
            a) Thanksgiving (1:2a)
            b) Remembrance in prayer, μνείαν ποιούμενοι (1:2b), μνημονεύοντες (1:3a)
            c) Faith, love, hope (1:3)
            d) God's choice (1:4)
            e) Work of the mission team in Thessalonica (1:5)
        2. Reaction of the addressees (1:6-10)
            a) Imitation of Paul and his companions (1:6)
            b) Example to other believers in Greece (1:7)
            c) Spread of the church's reputation (1:8a–b)
            d) *Praeteritio* (1:8c-10)
                i) Introduction (1:8c)
                ii) The εἴσοδος or "entrance" of Paul and companions (1:9a)
                iii) Conversion of the Thessalonians (1:9b–c)
                iv) Eschatological prospect (1:10)

As is usually the case for Paul, the proem is formulated as a thanksgiving, or more precisely as a report about the thanksgiving that Paul had directed to God on other occasions as part of his frequent intercessory prayers for the church. He thanks God for the joyous inward and outward attitude of the Thessalonians, as depicted in v. 3 with the help of the triad of faith, love, and hope. In v. 4 at the latest, Paul, to speak only of him as the main author for simplicity, begins to allude to themes from the letter body. This involves a first retrospective look at the successful ministry of Paul and his companions in Thessalonica, which was accompanied by numerous demonstrations of the spiritual dynamic of the gospel proclamation. Where Paul speaks in only general terms of a gospel that came to the addressees "not in word only, but also in power and in the Holy Spirit" (1:5), we may perhaps think in terms of miracles of healing, speaking in tongues, and sensational individual conversions. The first Greek sentence ends here in 1:5 and thereby also the first train of thought.

Paul's reasons for thanksgiving also include what he reports about the reaction of the addressees in the second section of the proem in 1:6-10. By receiving the word that was preached to them despite all the external opposition and discomfort this could cause, they became imitators of the apostles and of the Lord Jesus and a paradigmatic example for all of Macedonia and Achaia, that is, for all of Greece (1:6-7). In v. 8 Paul records the spreading of the church's good reputation almost like a miracle story. In so doing he skillfully combines two themes: the ongoing proclamation of the word of the Lord and the ongoing success story in Thessalonica. All this naturally also plays the role of a *captatio benevolentiae*, by which an author tips his hat to his audience to gain favor. Paul hopes to secure the same welcome for his letter as he did for his initial preaching.

When Paul says at the end of 1:8 that he does not need to say any more about the growing reputation of the Thessalonian church, he makes use of the classical rhetorical figure of *praeteritio* or preterition, whereby one emphasizes something by pretending not to mention it. Hence vv. 9 and 10 go on to develop precisely what Paul says he need not say any more about. Once again he turns attention back to the successful "entrance" or "reception" (εἴσοδος, a keyword picked up again immediately in 2:1) that he and his companions enjoyed in Thessalonica. We learn almost in passing that the addressees first had to be converted from idols to the true God of Israel (v. 9) and that they were therefore mostly pagans, though perhaps with some god-fearing Gentiles among them who already knew something about the necessary prerequisites for this step from their previous contacts with Judaism. The conclusion of the proem in v. 10 already looks forward to the coming of Jesus, whom God raised from the dead, for the purposes of judgment, particularly for saving believers from the wrathful judgment of God. This prepares the way for the eschatological themes in chapters 4 and 5 of the letter body.

Even in his earliest epistolary proem, Paul takes advantage of the language of thanksgiving and intercessory prayer to lay a theological and spiritual foundation for the following letter and to draw his addressees into the exchange that the letter seeks to facilitate. He probably owes the idea for doing so to an inner-Jewish reception and development of the Greek letter model, as it becomes tangible, for example, in the proem of the second Hanukkah letter in 2 Maccabees 1:11-17.

II. Letter Body (2:1–5:11)
    A. Body Opening: Epistolary Self-Recommendation (2:1-12)
        1. First pass (2:1-8)
            a) Transition (2:1)
            b) Disaster in Philippi (2:2a–b)
            c) Preaching in Thessalonica (2:2c)
            d) Contrast I (2:2-4)
                i) Negative aspect (2:3)
                ii) Positive aspect (2:4)
            e) Contrast II (2:5-8)
                i) Negative aspect (2:5-7a)
                ii) Positive aspect (2:7b-8)
        2. Second pass (2:9-12)
            a) Refusing support and manual labor (2:9)
            b) Paul's "ethos" (2:10)
            c) Family metaphor (2:11-12c)
            d) Eschatological prospect (2:12d)

In the long body of 1 Thessalonians we must content ourselves with presenting the most important considerations concerning structure, because anything else would quickly develop into a full-scale exegesis of the text. It is advisable first to delimit the body opening, which runs from 2:1 to 2:12 and involves an epistolary self-recommendation of Paul. Striking features include the frequent appeals to the addressees' accurate knowledge of the facts under review: "You yourselves know, brothers" (v. 1a), "as you know" (v. 5b), "you remember our labor and toil, brothers" (v. 9a; the renewed address of the "brothers" marks a somewhat larger break, identified as a sub-paragraph in the Nestle-Aland text), "you are witnesses" (v. 10a), "as you know" (v. 11a). On top of this is the repeated appeal to God as witness (vv. 5, 10). Some scholars have concluded from this that Paul had to defend himself against massive accusations from opponents in the church, but that is not necessary in this case. It is enough to see this as a self-recommendation (rather than as a self-defense) and to attribute it to the author's obvious desire to prepare the ground as well as possible for his own purposes.

Several other details also deserve attention: the allusion to
Paul's past negative experience in Philippi (1 Thess 2:2), the double antithetical comparisons in vv. 3-4 and vv. 5-8 (where the
increasing number of elements from one to the next results from
the rhetorical technique of *augmentatio*), the contrasting family
metaphors of Paul as mother with the role of giving tender care (v.
7) and of Paul as father with the role of urging and encouraging (v.
11), and Paul's reference in v. 9 to his refusal to take financial support from the Thessalonians and his own manual labor that made
up for it (although Paul was later grateful when such support
reached him in Thessalonica from the Philippians, cf. Phil 4:15-
16). The conclusion of 2:12 may once again need to be interpreted
eschatologically, in keeping with 1:10: the "kingdom and glory"
into which God had called believers are future realities that cast
their light into the present and thus make possible a life or "walk"
(cf. περιπατεῖν) oriented to their claims.

B.   Body Middle I: Paul's Desire to Visit and His Sending of a
     Messenger (2:13–3:13)
     1.   Renewed thanksgiving (2:13-16)
          a)   Thanksgiving (2:13)
          b)   A new form of imitation (2:14)
          c)   A *vituperatio* (2:15-16)
               i)   Four incriminating behaviors (2:15-16c)
               ii) Two consequences (2:16d–e)
     2.   Desire to make a visit (2:17-20)
          a)   Separation (2:17a)
          b)   Prospect of meeting face to face (2:17b)
          c)   Hindrances (2:18)
          d)   Complement to the church with eschatological
               prospect (2:19-20)
               i)   Question (2:19a–b)
               ii) Mention of the Parousia (2:19c)
               iii) Answer (2:20)
     3.   Sending of Timothy (3:1-5)
          a)   Motive and consequence (3:1)
          b)   Person of the messenger (3:2a)
          c)   Clarification of purpose (3:2b-3)
          d)   Prophecy and fulfillment (3:4)
          e)   Repetition of motive, sending, and purpose (3:5a–c)
          f)   The tempter (3:5d–e)
     4.   Return of Timothy (3:6-10)
          a)   Report of the messenger (3:6)

The letter body divides in the middle into two thematic main parts, whose interconnection will be examined at the end of this survey. In the first part in 1 Thessalonians 2:13-3:13, Paul speaks in 2:17–3:13 mainly of his desire to visit the Thessalonians, even though he cannot realize this at the moment, and of his sending of Timothy. This is preceded in 2:13-16 by a renewed thanksgiving. That this is a conscious repetition can perhaps be inferred from the introduction of v. 13, "And for this reason we *also* give thanks" (Καὶ διὰ τοῦτο καὶ ἡμεῖς εὐχαριστοῦμεν, etc.). The thanksgiving is grounded in the fact that God's word has, so to speak, fallen on fertile soil in Thessalonica. To the local believers, who had to put up with social discrimination because of their faith and therefore needed to be strengthened in their still fragile new identity, Paul sends a word of consolation in v. 14. He reminds them that through their sufferings they have once again become imitators, now not just of the suffering apostle and his Lord, as in 1:6 (cf. 2:2), but also of the Christian churches in Judea that had been exposed to persecutions from their Jewish compatriots.

This mention of the persecution of Jewish Christians by other Jews in 2:14 leads in 2:15-16 to an incredibly sharp anti-Jewish polemic—sharp not least because at one point it uses an argument from the pagan anti-Judaism of Paul's Greco-Roman environment: the Jews are "hostile to all people" (πᾶσιν ἀνθρώποις ἐναντίων). One can also read this in Tacitus (*Hist.* 5.5: "toward every other people they feel only hate and enmity"; cf. also Philostratus, *Life of Apollonius* 5.33), and ironically the same accusations were later brought by pagan authors against Christians. Scholars sometimes try to ease the situation by making a non-Pauline interpolation responsible for vv. 15-16 or even all of vv. 13-16. But this does not help much, since the real problem is only pushed back one step, from Paul to the earliest Christian copyists who on this hypothesis will have influenced all subsequent manuscripts of 1 Thessalonians (there is no direct evidence of an interpolation in the textual tradition). If Paul did not write these verses, then the apparent contradiction would be resolved between this passage and his more positive statements in Romans 9–11 about the Jewish people, to whom he still unquestionably belonged, at least according to his own self-understanding. But we must be ready to assume that Paul expressed himself differently at different times and in different situations.

Some scholars have attempted to interpret the statement that God's wrath has come upon the Jewish people at the end of 2:16 as a later interpolation that refers to the destruction of Jerusalem by the Romans. But there were already enough unfortunate historical events for the Jews in the 40s that one could interpret as God's wrathful judgment of his people, assuming that Paul even had particular historical events in mind. From a literary standpoint Paul here makes use of an invective that corresponds to the rhetorical figure of the *vituperatio* or vituperative speech, but simply giving something an ancient name provides little comfort about its content. Nor is it particularly helpful for us to know that Paul is falling back on an inner-Jewish Deuteronomistic tradition, according to which Israel always persecuted and killed its prophets, which moreover is not strictly true.

The main reason why Paul suddenly becomes so aggressive can still be seen in the first part of v. 16: His main purpose is winning the Gentiles to faith in Christ, and this can only happen on a large scale when he does not have to worry too much about Jewish sensibilities. This allows some details of the passage to be reappraised: Paul's invective need not be interpreted as a timeless final judgment but can be read as a final call. Nevertheless, we would much prefer that Paul had never written these sentences, and there is no way around this judgment.

In 2:17 Paul finally gets around to assuring the Thessalonians that he constantly wanted to visit them but was continually hindered, which he attributes in v. 18 the activity of Satan, who threw stones in his way (cf. the parallel in 2 Cor 12:7, where Paul traces back his chronic illness, which repeatedly tormented him by acute attacks, to the activity of an angel of Satan). The family metaphor also takes on a new twist in v. 17: separated from the Thessalonians, Paul feels truly "orphaned" (ἀπορφανισθέντες, another hard-to-interpret plural), which makes him metaphorically the child rather than the mother or father. Another typical letter feature, which we learned about in the context of epistolary presence and absence (παρουσία, ἀπουσία), surfaces in v. 17: Paul is absent "in person" (προσώπῳ) but not "in heart" (καρδίᾳ); with his heart he is still in Thessalonica and has his letter there to represent him. The rhetorical questions and answers in vv. 19-20 once again amount to a compliment to the church. In the midst there stands in v. 19 a forward look to the παρουσία, the arrival of the Lord Jesus, which was already alluded to in 1:10 but here for the first time is designated by the technical Greek term, which was also known in the cities of Greece and Asia Minor from the ritual of a ruler's visit.

From the Parousia of Jesus Christ in 2:19 we quickly transition back to the "parousia" of his apostle Paul in chapter 3. Next to his personal presence and his mediated presence through his letter there is a third form of Paul's presence in the Thessalonian church, namely, his sending of a trustworthy messenger from his inner circle (cf. Funk). Paul has taken advantage of this means of representation by sending off Timothy. He wants the Thessalonians to interpret his depriving himself of Timothy's company as a proof of his own love and care for them. Paul correctly realizes that the Thessalonians need a new impulse or some support to firmly establish their still developing church life, and a visit from at least one of the three founding missionaries should provide such a stabilizing factor.

Timothy is once again with Paul by the time Paul is writing this letter; he has returned from his special mission and has good news to report (for this news Paul uses the term εὐαγγελισαμένου in 3:6, elsewhere associated with the gospel message). The mutual longing for a personal visit between Paul and the church remains undiminished on both sides, but Paul draws strength and comfort from Timothy's encouraging information (vv. 7-8). In 3:9 Paul begins a third thanksgiving, this time with the circumlocution εὐ-χαριστίαν ἀνταποδοῦναι, "to render thanks." The prayer, which we know from the proem (where, however, the prayer's content is not actually stated in the form "we pray *that* . . ."), is here focused on the possibility of an actual face-to-face meeting, which would also allow Paul to address certain weak points in the Thessalonians' faith. However, one need not understand this "restoring whatever is lacking in your faith" in 3:10 as a rebuke of the church, but rather as an indication that a deepening of faith and growth in faith belong to the essence of faith itself.

The themes of the first main part are recapitulated in the form of a prayer in 3:11-13, which also prepares readers for the second main part in 4:1–5:11. The first petition in 3:11 is devoted to the idea of God directing one's steps or making straight one's path (cf. Prov 3:6; 16:9; Jer 10:23): God and Jesus are asked to direct Paul's ways so that his steps lead him back to Thessalonica. The second petition is devoted to the Thessalonians and their growth in love. The purpose of this second request is given in 3:13: as they grow in love God will also strengthen the Thessalonians' hearts in holiness so that they will be ready for the coming Parousia of Jesus "with all his *holy ones*." Against the NRSV translation "all his *saints*," this presumably refers to the throng of angels, who will accompany the Son of Man when he comes for judgment according to apocalyptic pictures of the end times. The subliminal eschatological theme is thereby focused on the Parousia in the first main part, in such a way as to anticipate a resolution in the second main part. At the same time the idea of God establishing the Thessalonians in holiness raises questions of Christian lifestyle that are further developed in the paraenesis of part two.

C. Body Middle II: Living before the End (4:1–5:11)
    1. A God-pleasing life (4:1-12)
        a) Epistolary request, ἐρωτῶμεν καὶ παρακαλοῦμεν (4:1-8)
            i) Multi-part introduction (4:1-2)
            ii) God's will: sanctification (4:3a)
            iii) Sexual behavior (4:3b-5)
            iv) Business integrity (?) (4:6)
            v) Grounds: God's call to holiness (4:7)
            vi) Warning against rejecting the gift of the Spirit (4:8)
        b) Change of theme, continuing the foregoing request (4:9-12)
            i) *Praeteritio:* brotherly love in practice (4:9-10a)
            ii) Renewed *paraclesis,* παρακαλοῦμεν (4:10b-12)
    2. On the sleeping and the living (4:13-18)
        a) Future of "those who have fallen asleep" (4:13-14)
            i) Disclosure formula (4:13a)
            ii) Contrast with "those who have no hope" (4:13b-c)

      iii) Faith formula: the death and resurrection of Jesus
           (4:14a-c)
      iv) Consequence: God's dealings with those who have
           already died (4:14d)
   b) A "word of the Lord" (4:15-18)
      i)   Formal qualification (4:15a)
      ii)   Those living at the Parousia (4:15b–c)
      iii) Stages of the end-time events (4:16-17)
      iv) Refrain: Mutual encouragement, παρακαλεῖτε
           ἀλλήλους (4:18)
3. Correct approach to the eschatological future (5:1-11)
   a) Times and seasons (5:1-3)
      i)   *Praeteritio* (5:1)
      ii)   Like a thief in the night (5:2)
      iii) Sudden labor pains (5:3)
   b) Darkness of night and light of day (5:4-5)
   c) Sleeping and wakefulness (5:6-7)
   d) Christian armor (5:8)
   e) God's purpose: Salvation and life (5:9-10)
   f) Refrain: Mutual encouragement, παρακαλεῖτε
      ἀλλήλους (5:11)

The second main part of the body of 1 Thessalonians in 4:1–5:11 focuses on the last two points that have come up in 3:13: a life in keeping with the demands of holiness and expectations or fears associated with the Parousia. The first section in 4:1-12 sketches the foundations of a God-pleasing lifestyle, first generally, then with special reference to sexual behavior (from v. 3b through at least v. 5) and perhaps business dealings (v. 6), although it is disputed whether this might not be a continuation of the theme of sexual behavior, as assumed by almost all the English translations, which tend to interpret the article in the expression ἐν τῷ πράγματι as anaphoric: "[God's will is] that no one wrong or exploit a brother or sister in *this* matter [sc. of sexual relations]" (NRSV).[4] In epistolographical terms it is clear that this part of the

---

[4] Even those translators who interpret 1 Thessalonians 1:6 in terms of "issues of justice rather than sexuality" (Richard 188) do not necessarily place all of the weight on the translation of πράγμα, which can be rather general, but instead include the sense of justice that arises from the designation of the Lord as ἔκδικος: it is God's will "that none transgress or defraud against their brother or sister *in their activity* (ἐν τῷ πράγματι),

text, with its introduction by ἐρωτῶμεν followed by παρακαλοῦμεν, is formulated as an epistolary request. That Paul by
introducing his next theme of brotherly and sisterly love
(φιλαδελφία) in 4:9 with the expression, "Now concerning," Περὶ
δέ (cf. 4:13; 5:1), might wish to indicate, as he does 1 Corinthians,
that he is responding to questions from the church is a possibility
that deserves to be mentioned. However, if this is the case, then
the questions from Thessalonica would presumably be oral and
not written (but see also the discussion in Malherbe). By introducing this new theme of brotherly or sisterly love once again by the
rhetorical figure of *praeteritio*, by which he first says that he need
not write to them about love but then does so anyway, Paul only
underscores the naturalness with which the members of the
Thessalonian congregation practiced mutual love, even beyond
their own church with the brothers and sisters throughout
Macedonia. The renewed paraclesis beginning in 4:10b (παρακαλοῦμεν) does not just call the readers to perfect their practice of
love but also introduces other ideals, including living a quiet life of
meeting one's own needs by working, so as to make a good impression on outsiders and gain self-sufficiency.

However we interpret the formula περὶ δέ, whether as a simple transition or as a reference to particular questions from the
church, in any case there was a controversial point in Thessalonica
that Paul takes up in 4:13-18 (περὶ τῶν κοιμωμένων) and treats
in more depth in 5:1-11 (περὶ δὲ τῶν χρόνων καὶ τῶν καιρῶν).
Apparently his initial preaching was not sufficiently clear about
the resurrection of the dead, the relationship of this event to the
Parousia, and the fate of those living at the Parousia. There was
enough room for misunderstandings and uncertainties. With the
disclosure formula "we do not want you to be uninformed," Paul
turns his attention in 4:13 to the subject of "those who have fallen
asleep," a euphemism for the dead, and grounds their future fellowship with God and the Lord Jesus in the resurrection of Jesus
(4:14).

In the next segment in 4:15-18, Paul goes back to a "word of
the Lord," although we cannot delimit its extent with certainty in
the following text, nor do we know whether Paul had in mind a

---

because the Lord is an *executor of justice* (ἔκδικος) in all these things"
(ibid. 186, italics and glosses added).

word of the earthy Jesus or a prophetically mediated word of the risen Lord. The main concern of this section is the fate of those who remain, who are still alive at the time of the Parousia, among whom Paul clearly includes himself when we speaks of "we who are alive." In sufficient detail for this short letter, but in relative brevity compared with other apocalyptic pictures of the end, Paul develops the individual stages of the future events in vv. 16-17: a cry of command goes out from the Lord Jesus, the archangel's call is heard, God's trumpet sounds, the Lord Jesus descends from heaven, the dead in Christ rise, and the resurrected dead together with the remaining believers who were left alive are caught up in the air to meet the Lord, after which both groups stand in fellowship with him, probably in heaven rather than on a renewed earth. A call to the believers to comfort one another (παρακαλεῖτε ἀλλήλους) with this confidence rounds off this picture of the Parousia in 4:18.

In 5:1-11 further topics associated with the apocalyptic expectation of the imminent end appear, but they are freshly arranged with a more warning undertone. The leading question is what consequences an orientation to the Parousia has for life in the present. This gains urgency from the fact that nobody knows the exact time of the end any more than one knows about a thief in the night or the onset of labor pains (vv. 2-3). Therefore Paul does not need to write about times and seasons according to v. 1 (once again a *praeteritio*). Partly interlocking metaphors then follow: the contrast of the darkness of night and the light of day in vv. 4-5, the call to be sober and awake instead of asleep in v. 6 (where "sleeping" is now understood differently from before, as a metaphor for moral slumber rather than death), with an aphoristic justification in v. 7. In 5:8 faith, love, and hope from the proem are transposed into the armor that the Christian uses to survive the battle in the remaining time. According to vv. 9-11 God's purposes with believers center around their salvation and future life with him, whether they are awake or already asleep. As in 4:18 a call to the believers to encourage one another (again παρακαλεῖτε) follows as a refrain in 5:11, supplemented by a call to build one another up, together with the assurance that all this is already happening.

D. Body Closing: Individual Exhortations (5:12-22)
    1. Request for respect of the proto office-bearers (5:12-13)

     a)   Request formula, ἐρωτῶμεν (5:12a)
     b)   Identification of the group for whom the request is made (5:12b–d)
     c)   Attitude toward them (5:13a–b)
     d)   Peace on all sides (5:13c)
  2.   Exhortation to mutual discipline (5:14-15)
     a)   Exhortation formula, παρακαλοῦμεν (5:14a)
     b)   Four imperatives (5:14b–f)
     c)   Prohibition of retaliation (5:15)
  3.   A series of imperatives (5:16-22)
     a)   Rejoice (5:16)
     b)   Pray (5:17)
     c)   Give thanks (5:18)
     d)   Do not quench the Spirit (5:19)
     e)   Do not despise prophecies (5:20)
     f)   Test everything (5:21)
     g)   Abstain from evil (5:22)

The body closing is found in the paraenetic section in 5:12-22, which is dominated by imperative forms from v. 14. The request in vv. 12-13 is introduced by ἐρωτῶμεν, the exhortations in vv. 14-15 by παρακαλοῦμεν. The former section shows that there are already certain members in the church who are taking on special tasks, committing themselves, and bearing responsibility; in other words, the processes are already underway that will eventually lead to the crystallization of particular offices in the churches. Paul has not in fact installed office holders in Thessalonica, but he recommends that his readers acknowledge such developments as necessary and honor special commitment with special respect. The imperatives in v. 14 aim at a type of *correctio fraterna*, or brotherly or sisterly correction of, but also care for, those described as idle, fainthearted, and weak. Verse 15 begins with the language of retribution or payback but inverts it: Evil should not be paid back by evil, but by good. Finally the thought branches out in 5:16-22 into a series of very short sentences with imperatives that are more closely related in only a few instances.

  III. Letter Closing (5:23-28)
     A. Epilogue: Intercessory Prayer (5:23-24)
       1. Sanctification (5:23a)
       2. Preservation of the whole person at the Parousia (5:23b)
       3. Faithfulness of God's call (5:24)

B. Postscript (5:25-28)
   1. Request for prayer (5:25)
   2. Instruction to convey greetings (5:26)
   3. Solemn command to have the letter read (5:27)
   4. Concluding grace wish (5:28)

Like the body closing, the letter closing in 5:23-28 is rather loosely structured out of various elements, among which only the intercessory prayer in 5:23-24 stands out as a longer component and a counterpart to the thanksgiving in the proem. It closes with a saying about God's faithfulness and repeats prior to this for one last time the great theme of the whole letter, the Parousia of the Lord Jesus. In the following postscript Paul asks for the prayers of the church (v. 25) and instructs the readers to greet all the brothers (and sisters) for him, which they may do by a "holy kiss" (v. 26). The kiss was a common greeting, and the adjective "holy" brings it into the special atmosphere of an assembly of the believing community. Paul lays great stress on his injunction, introduced by ἐνορκίζω, that the letter should be read to all the members of the church, as the translations bring out: "I adjure you by the Lord" (RSV); "I charge you" (NIV); "I solemnly command you" (NRSV). He may be thinking that the letter will be read in different house churches (rather less probable for Thessalonica) or that it might need to be read on different occasions, because not all can attend the meeting at the same time (cf. also the parallel instructions to a small group of readers in Plato, *Epistle* 6 [323C]: "All you three must read this letter, all together if possible, or if not by twos; and as often as you possibly can read it in common, and use it as a form of covenant and a binding law, as is right"). A blessing or grace wish, which picks up the term χάρις from the salutation, concludes the letter.

One aspect of 1 Thessalonians that continues to engage the minds of exegetes is the relationship of the first and second main parts of the letter body. One possibility that appears more hidden in the background suggests itself: The first main part of the letter is concerned in effect with the "parousia" or presence of the apostle, which can be conveyed by a visit, a letter, or a messenger. The second main part brings out a question more fully that was already hinted at earlier and that now concerns the circumstances surrounding the Parousia of Jesus Christ. It looks as though Paul wants cautiously to create a connection: The Lord's visit to his church still awaits the future, but there are also advance heralds of this, including the apostle, his messenger, and his letter. From the one apostolic "parousia," which is not referred to by this precise term in the letter but which could be so identified in ancient epistolary theory, the addressees should make a connection to the other Parousia and thereby be strengthened in their hope in the coming of the Lord.

2. Literary Criticism: Partition Theories?

Bibliography 56: C. J. Bjerkelund, *PARAKALÔ* (Bib. 4) 125–40. – **C. Demke**, "Theologie und Literarkritik im 1. Thessalonicherbrief: Ein Diskussionsbeitrag," in G. Ebeling, E. Jüngel, G. Schunack, eds., FS Ernst Fuchs (Tübingen 1973) 103–24. – **R. Pesch**, *Die Entdeckung des ältesten Paulus-Briefes*, Herderbücherei 1167 (Freiburg i.Br. 1984). – **E. J. Richard**, *1 and 2 Thessalonians* (Bib. 53). – **W. Schmithals**, "Die Thessalonicherbriefe als Briefkompositionen," in E. Dinkler, ed., *Zeit und Geschichte: Dankesgabe an R. Bultmann* (Tübingen 1964) 296–315; revised as "Die historische Situation der Thessalonicher-briefe," in idem, *Paulus und die Gnostiker: Untersuchungen zu den kleinen Paulusbriefen*, Theologische Forschung 35 (Hamburg 1965) 89–157. – **P. Schubert**, *Form and Function of the Pauline Thanksgivings* (Bib. 4) 16–27.

One striking formal feature of 1 Thessalonians is the duplication or triplication of the thanksgiving in 1:2; 2:13 and 3:9. Several scholars therefore identify the thanksgiving section as running from 1:2 all the way to 3:13 (e.g., Malherbe), while some go further and declare thanksgiving to be the main content of the letter, to which two paraenetic calls are merely appended in chapters 4 and 5 (so Schubert; on the discussion see Bjerkelund; Malherbe sees the paraenetic sections as more integral to the letter and classifies the whole of it as "pastoral paraenesis" in both form and function [pp. 81–86]; cf. also Pseudo-Libanius's paraenetic letter no. 1). But designating the entire first half of the letter as thanksgiving is hardly a very satisfying explanation of the phenomenon of repeated thanksgivings, for it nullifies all attempts at determining the form of other individual parts in these chapters. Moreover, these are not the only real or apparent repetitions in the letter. There is a resemblance, for example, between the intercessory prayer in 3:11-13, at the end of the first main part of the letter body according to our outline, and the one in 5:23-24, where not only the second main part but the entire letter is concluded.

Repetitions and duplications are also a classic criterion of literary criticism and integrity, and therefore the literary critical hypotheses also begin here (cf. Schmithals). Such analyses typically discover in 1 Thessalonians two originally independent letters of Paul to Thessalonica, an earlier one and a later one, which a later editor supposedly combined to form a single letter. A procedure that in itself is possible, and in the case of 2 Corinthians also very plausible, is thereby claimed for 1 Thessalonians. Despite their intermittent popularity (cf. Pesch) developments in this direction had quieted down in the meantime, so that it almost seemed as though partition theories for 1 Thessalonians had been filed away in the archives. But this impression was misleading, for in his commentary E. J. Richard has once again decisively made a partition model the foundation for his exegesis. We therefore forgo discussion of the other individual reconstructions that share certain emphases and review as an example Richard's recent effort.

Richard does not divide 1 Thessalonians simply in half, but takes out its middle and makes an additional epistle out of its ends. He thus finds an "early missive" in 2:13–4:2 relatively intact (except for its prescript, which is missing, and for 2:14-16, which Richard regards as a later interpolation), leaving a "later missive" completely intact, consisting of 1:1–2:12 + 4:3–5:28. The former letter has the following structure, which we present in a slightly modified form from that of Richard (p. 13) in order to facilitate comparison with our own outline above:

I. Epistolary Opening
   A. Prescript [not preserved, but identical or nearly so to 1 Thessalonians 1:1]
   B. Thanksgiving (2:13)
     [The Jews and Divine Retribution: 2:14-16—interpolation]
II. Letter Body (2:17–3:13)
   A. Body Opening: Reason for Concern and Frustration (2:17-20)
   B. Body Middle:
     1. Timothy's Mission to Thessalonica (3:1-5)
     2. Timothy's Return and Report (3:6-8)
   C. Body Closing: Paul's Joy and Prayer (3:9-13)

III. Epistolary Closing
  A. Final Exhortation (4:1-2)
  B. Greetings, etc. [edited and partially preserved in 5:25-28]

Whether it is very useful to combine Paul's thanksgiving and prayer in 3:9-10 into a single unit of "Joy and Prayer" with the next section in 3:11-13, which we have labeled "Recapitulation and Transition," is a question that one might spontaneously ask about this model. Assuming that this earlier letter existed as a separate document, Paul will have written it in Athens shortly after his departure from Thessalonica. According to Richard, "the document's focus is on apostolic presence: the desire to be there, the pain at being separated in trying circumstances, and the sending of an emissary and letter because of the missionaries' absence" (14). Paul writes with affection and concern for the continued success of a promising beginning.

The remaining portions of our 1 Thessalonians, namely 1:1–2:12 and 4:3–5:28, make up Richard's "later missive." Presented in standard letter format, it looks as follows (cf. Richard 16, slightly modified):

I. Epistolary Opening
  A. Prescript (1:1)
  B. Thanksgiving (1:2-10)
II. Letter Body
  A. Body Opening: Missionary Behavior as a Paraenetic Model (2:1-12)
  B. Body Middle
    1. Initial Exhortation on Holiness (4:3-8)
    2. On Love of Others (4:9-12)
    3. On the Faithful Departed and the Parousia (4:13-18)
    4. On Being Ready for the Lord's Return (5:1-11)
  C. Body Closing: Final Exhortation on Community Life (5:12-22)
III. Epistolary Closing
  A. Final Prayer (5:23-24)
  B. Postscript (5:25-28)

In this letter Paul reacts partly to oral reports from Thessalonica (esp. in 2:1-12) and partly to written questions that have reached him, a procedure that recalls Paul's later letter of 1 Corinthians.

Paul wrote this letter of response from Corinth. Enough time has now passed for the reputation of the church of the Thessalonians to have spread as recorded in 1:6-9 and, no less importantly, for the first deaths among church members to have occurred. This somewhat more extensive second letter was preserved completely intact and was used as the frame into which a redactor fitted the earlier letter, omitting only its prescript and epistolary closing. The result is the 1 Thessalonians we know as part of the New Testament canon.

This most recent literary critical reconstruction has its merits: it works with epistolary observations, arguments, and models, and therefore has potential for shedding light on the origin of the text as a letter, even if one does not ultimately follow its approach to the partitioning of 1 Thessalonians. But Richard also leaves several important questions unanswered. The motives that moved the final redactor to exactly this and no other procedure with his materials remain unclear: were there not other ways to preserve the two original letters? This is doubtless a weakness of this project. But even more decisive is the question of whether Richard's observations about the text really carry enough weight to force us to postulate two letters with two different situations, and this we will have to answer in the negative. Canonical 1 Thessalonians also appears as a letter whose structure is sufficiently transparent and coherent in its present form. The multiple—not only double!—thanksgiving and the multiple prayers contribute to the special character of this letter, which appears to have originated in a still largely untroubled atmosphere. In any case nothing can be detected in 1 Thessalonians of the later battles over Paul's apostleship and gospel message.

3. Rhetorical Analysis

Bibliography 57: D. E. Aune, *Dictionary* (Bib. 4), s.v. "Thessalonians, First Letter to the," 460–63, esp. 461; "Rhetorical analysis," 462 (table). – **J. Bickmann**, *Kommunikation gegen den Tod* (Bib. 54). – **J. Chapa**, "Is First Thessalonians a Letter of Consolation?" *NTS* 40 (1994) 150–60. – idem, "Consolatory Patterns? 1 Thes. 4:13-18; 5:11," in R. F. Collins, ed., *The Thessalonian Correspondence* (Bib. 54) 220–28. – **J. D. Hester**, "The Invention of 1 Thessalonians: A Proposal," in S. E. Porter and T. H. Olbricht, eds., *Rhetoric, Scripture, and Theology* (Bib. 5) 251–79. – **R. Hoppe**, "Der erste Thessalonicherbrief und die antike Rhetorik: Eine

Problemskizze," *BZ* 41 (1997) 229–37. – **F. W. Hughes**, "The Rhetoric of 1 Thessalonians," in R. F. Collins, ed., *The Thessalonian Correspondence* (Bib. 54) 94–116. – **R. Jewett**, *The Thessalonian Correspondence* (Bib. 54). – **B. C. Johanson**, *To All the Brethren* (Bib. 54). – **T. H. Olbricht**, "An Aristotelian Rhetorical Analysis of 1 Thessalonians," in D. L. Balch, E. Ferguson, and W. A. Meeks, eds., *Greeks, Romans, and Christians: Essays in Honor of A. J. Malherbe* (Philadelphia 1990) 216–36. – **J. Schoon-Janssen**, *Umstrittene "Apologien" in den Paulusbriefen* (Bib. 4) 39–65. – **A. Smith**, *Comfort One Another: Reconstructing the Rhetoric and Audience of 1 Thessalonians*, Literary Currents in Biblical Interpretation (Louisville 1995). – **S. Walton**, "What Has Aristotle To Do with Paul? Rhetorical Criticism and 1 Thessalonians," *TynBul* 46 (1995) 229–50. – **C. A. Wanamaker**, *The Epistles to the Thessalonians* (Bib. 53). – **W. Wuellner**, "The Argumentative Structure of 1 Thessalonians as Paradoxical Encomium," in R. F. Collins, ed., *The Thessalonian Correspondence* (Bib. 54) 117–36.

In our own work on the structure and content of 1 Thessalonians we have already used various rhetorical terms such as *praeteritio* and *vituperatio*, which mostly belong to the area of *elocutio* or individual elements of style. The fact that we have designated our outline point II.A.2.b as "Paul's Ethos" can also be traced back to rhetoric, for the argument from the speaker's or writer's ethos or character is regarded as one of the means of persuasion within the *argumentatio* or proofs, as we have already seen (above p. 220). A completely different task associated with rhetoric is to find motifs in popular philosophical speeches, especially figures of speech that provide the grounds for moral appeal, that can be compared with the means of persuasion that Paul uses. This would satisfy our objective raised in our treatment of rhetoric in chapter 5 of incorporating more actual speeches into exegetical work. Therefore this is also addressed in the following exercise.

Exercise

44. Read the following excerpt (*Oration* 32.7–12) from a long speech that Dio Chrysostom delivered as an exhortation to the Alexandrians (translated by J. W. Cohoon and H. L. Crosby, *Dio Chrysostom*, LCL, vol. 3 [1940]). With what passages from 1 Thessalonians can we relate this passage, whether positively or negatively?

32.7 But you have no such critic, neither chorus nor poet (like the Athenians) nor anyone else, to reprove you in all friendliness and to reveal the weaknesses of your city. . . . **8** And perhaps this situation is not of your making, but you will show whether it is or not if you bear with me today; the fault may lie rather at the door of those who wear the name of philosopher. For some among that company do not appear in public at all and prefer not to make the venture, possibly because they despair of being able to improve the masses; others exercise their voices in what we call lecture-halls, having secured as hearers men who are in league with them and tractable. **9** And as for the Cynics, as they are called, it is true that the city contains no small number of that sect, and that, like any other thing, this too has had its crop—persons whose tenets, to be sure, comprise practically nothing spurious or ignoble, yet who must make a living—still these Cynics, posting themselves at street-corners, in alley-ways, and at temple-gates, pass round the hat and play upon the credulity of lads and sailors and crowds of that sort, stringing together rough jokes and much tittle-tattle and that low badinage that smacks of the market-place. Accordingly they achieve no good at all, but rather the worst possible harm. . . . **10** Those, however, who do come before you as men of culture either declaim speeches intended for display, and stupid ones to boot, or else chant verses of their own composition, as if they had detected in you a weakness for poetry—To be sure, if they themselves are really poets or orators, perhaps there is nothing so shocking in that, but if in the guise of philosophers they do these things with a view to their own profit and reputation, and not to improve you, that indeed is shocking—For it is as if a physician when visiting patients should disregard their treatment and their restoration to health, and should bring them flowers and courtesans and perfume. **11** But there are only a few who have displayed frankness in your presence, and that but sparingly, not in such a way as to fill your ears therewith nor for any length of time; nay, they merely utter a phrase or two, and then, after berating rather than enlightening you, they make a hurried exit, anxious lest before they have finished you may raise an outcry and send them packing, behaving in very truth quite like men who in winter muster up courage for a brief and hurried voyage out to sea. But to find a man who in plain terms and without guile speaks his mind with frankness, and neither for the sake of reputation nor for gain makes false pretensions, but out of good will and concern for his fellow-men stands ready, if need be, to submit to ridicule and to the disorder and the uproar of the mob—to find such a man as that is not easy, but rather the good fortune of a very lucky city, so great is the dearth of noble, independent souls and such the abundance of toadies, mountebanks, and sophists. **12** In my own case, for instance, I feel that, I have chosen that role, not of my own volition, but by the will of some deity. For when divine providence is at work for men, the gods provide, not only good counselors who need no urging, but also words that are appropriate and profitable to the listener. . . .

Although we have been advocating a broader approach to ancient rhetoric and the New Testament, what previous scholars have presented under the heading of rhetorical analysis of the New Testament letters, and 1 Thessalonians in particular, has often had a more specific focus. This concerns above all the structure of the letter, which is seen in analogy to a speech, and the determination of its rhetorical genre, which broadens to the question of genre as such. We will pursue both topics below.

a) The Rhetorical Structure of 1 Thessalonians

Since the early 1980s a whole series of outlines have been proposed for 1 Thessalonians that have chosen rhetorical terms for the main outline points of the letter in an effort to grasp its argumentative structure. Some models are very similar to each other and differ mainly in the amount of detail they go into, while others involve greater disagreement. Regarding the ideal types it is possible to make out two main approaches, which differ mainly in the delimitation of the *argumentatio* or proof. Each of these basic models is presented with two selected examples.

In the first model scholars assume a relatively long *narratio* or statement of facts and begin the *argumentatio*, sometimes identified by different terms (such as *probatio*), in 1 Thessalonians 4:1. R. Jewett limits himself to the essential parts of a forensic speech, while his student F. W. Hughes basically fits within this scheme but partly fills it out:

R. Jewett (1986)	F. W. Hughes (1990)
exordium 1:1-5	*exordium* 1:1–10
narratio 1:6–3:13	*narratio* 2:1–3:10
	partitio 3:11-13
probatio 4:1–5:22	*probatio* 4:1–5:5
	peroratio 5:4-11
	exhortatio 5:12-22
peroratio 5:23-28	*conclusio* 5:23-28

Because the *argumentatio* here involves only a positive proof, it is called a *probatio* by both authors. The *exordium* is certainly better identified by Hughes as 1:1-10 than by Jewett as 1:1-5; it corresponds to our letter opening consisting of prescript and proem (1:1-10). To designate Paul's prayer in 3:11-13 as a *partitio* with Hughes and thereby to wish to find in 3:12-13 three outline points that anticipate respectively the three proofs in 4:9-12; 4:1-8 and 4:13–5:3,[5] despite the fact that the first two are out of order, certainly does not commend itself. Preferable is the characterization of all of 3:11-13 as a *transitus* or transition between two main parts, which Jewett includes as a subordinate point in his outline ("Transitus in benedictory style," 74).[6] Hughes admittedly tries to

---

[5] So Hughes, "Rhetoric," 104: "The phrase 'increase in love' (3,12) in the *partitio* relates to the second proof (4,9-12) which is introduced by the formula, 'concerning brotherly love', in 4,9. The phrase 'to establish your hearts blameless in holiness before our God and Father' (3,13) similarly relates to the first proof (4,1-8) concerning right behavior which is introduced by the phrase 'how it is necessary to walk and to please God' (4,1). The phrase 'at the coming of our Lord Jesus Christ with all his saints' (3,13) also relates to a third proof (4,13–5,3) which is introduced by 'concerning those who have fallen asleep' in 4,13."

[6] Hughes 103 with n. 38 also refers to the *transitio* but applies it only to 3:11, with 3:12-13 assigned the *partitio* functions in the preceding note.

do justice to the exhortations in the concluding chapters by singling out the pericope 5:12-22 as an *exhortatio*. But he thereby not only bursts the bounds of rhetorical theory, which knows no standard part of an oration termed the *exhortatio*, but also has to deal with the fact that the *peroratio* definitely comes too early in this scheme. Finally, Hughes introduces as a pure invention a *conclusio*. The two outlines agree—and this is the decisive point—in presenting Paul's backward look at his ministry in Thessalonica, his desire to make another visit, and his sending of Timothy as his delegate as the *narratio*.

It is precisely this point that turns out differently in the alternative proposal, where the *narratio* is either drastically reduced or left out entirely:

D. Dormeyer (1993)	T. A. Olbricht (1990)
prescript 1:1	prescript 1:1
exordium 1:2-12	*exordium* 1:2-3
	narratio 1:4-10
argumentatio 2:1–3:13	*argumentatio* 2:1–5:11
exhortatio 4:1–5:22	
	epilogue 5:12-25
postscript/*salutatio* 5:23-28	postscript 5:25-28

Olbricht does not speak exactly of *narratio* and *argumentatio* but of "statement" and "proof," though it is clear that he means the same thing. It is questionable whether one should try to abstract from the *exordium* a short *narratio*, as Olbricht does. It may be recalled that the *narratio* or statement of the case is required only in forensic rhetoric, but not in deliberative or epideictic rhetoric. Therefore, this decision about the *narratio* also paves the way for the determination of the rhetorical genre. In this sense Dormeyer is more consistent when he does without a *narratio* entirely. A striking agreement is that both authors have the *argumentatio* or proof beginning in 2:1. Whereas in the course of the letter Olbricht does not take the exhortation into account or subordinates it self-evidently to the proof, this element takes up almost two chapters for Dormeyer as the *exhortatio*.

That the application of supposedly "scientific" rhetorical categories nevertheless leads to such divergent results could provide an occasion for skepticism about the entire rhetorical approach. But then it also needs to be admitted that analyses with the help of epistolography typically fail to produce any noticeably greater consensus. If one is forced to choose between the two basic types of rhetorical model for 1 Thessalonians, then the one that dispenses with the *narratio* should be preferred. There are points of convergence between the rhetorical model and the typical letter model, not only between the *exordium* and the epistolary proem (see above) but also partly between the *peroratio* (cf. Jewett) and the epistolary closing. But beyond this the remaining designation of the letter body as a proof (*argumentatio* or *probatio*) does not actually accomplish very much. In order to be really helpful the rhetorical rough outline needs to be complemented by a more extensive fine outline, as undertaken for example by Hughes and extended to the level of individual verses. When this is done, then there are many more points of contact between rhetorical analyses and our own analysis of content by means of epistolography presented above than the disagreements about terminology at the highest level of the respective outlines would suggest.

Exercise

45. Study for yourself the following two outlines of 1 Thessalonians, and then compare them to the models discussed above:

C. A. Wanamaker (1990)	W. Wuellner (1990)
prescript 1:1	
exordium 1:2-10	*exordium* 1:1-10
	(with *propositio* 1:8-10)

	argumentatio
narratio 2:1–3:10	I = 2:1–3:13
transitus 3:11-13	
probatio 4:1–5:22	II = 4:1–5:22
peroratio/epistolary closing 5:23-28 *peroratio* 5:23-28	

b) The Rhetorical Genre of 1 Thessalonians

Among the three rhetorical genres the *genus iudiciale* or judicial speech does not really come into consideration for 1 Thessalonians. Even if the passage about Paul's exemplary ministry among the Thessalonians in 2:1-12 bore a purely apologetic character and was intended mainly as a self-defense against attacks from opponents, this would still not carry enough weight to justify seeing the entire letter as apologetic and therefore as forensic. Because this is probably not an accurate view of 2:1-12 in any case, the last support for this view slips away.

There remain the symbouleutic or deliberative and the epideictic or demonstrative genres, both of which have been claimed for 1 Thessalonians. Much depends on how one evaluates the paraenesis in 1 Thessalonians and its relationship to the rhetorical genres. One can admit that much of 1 Thessalonians is marked by direct and indirect paraenesis without declaring paraenesis the only theme of the letter. There is a tendency among scholars to equate paraenetic with deliberative, but this is not necessary. Deliberative rhetoric is intended to urge the addressees to make a decision for a certain behavior in the future. But paraenesis can also aim at praising a behavior in the present and encouraging its continued practice in the future. In this case it would no longer be strictly deliberative, but epideictic.

Most authors favor a predominately epideictic rhetoric in 1 Thessalonians (though a mixture of other elements cannot be excluded according to rhetorical theory). This is in keeping with the praise that Paul speaks to the church, the thanksgiving that he repeatedly expresses, and the joy that he manifests. Above all 1 Thessalonians is a thanksgiving to and praise of God for the great things he has done in the church of Thessalonica. First Thessalonians provides an example worth taking to heart that epideictic can be used to exhort men and women more effectively than constant criticism or mere scolding.

W. Wuellner has classified 1 Thessalonians as a subset of the epideictic genre known as the "paradoxical encomium"—paradoxical because the letter calls its readers to joy amidst suffering and quiet confidence while waiting for the Parousia. A further, perhaps more important sub-genre of epideictic rhetoric is the funeral oration (ἐπιτάφιος), which not only praises those who have fallen in battle, but also contains elements of consolation for those left behind that can also be expanded into a proper speech of consolation.

This immediately sets us on a further track that leads back to the epistolary types, for here too there is a category for a consoling letter (παραμυθητικός), number 5 in Pseudo-Demetrius (for the text see above p. 199). But let us first ask which epistolary types the scholars appeal to and which offer themselves for comparison. That scholars should think of the paraenetic letter (cf. Pseudo-Libanius no. 1) is understandable in the light of the paraenetic portions of 1 Thessalonians, but the thankful letter (Pseudo-Demetrius no. 21) is also appealed to (by Jewett). Yet what should probably come before both of these is the friendly letter (Pseudo-Demetrius no. 1), which expresses the essence of epistolary communication in an especially pure form. First Thessalonians is dominated by an atmosphere that can rightly be called "philophronetic" (cf. Koskenniemi's concept of *philophronesis* or friendship as the basic ideal of the Greek letter, also found as φιλοφρόνησις in Demetrius, *On Style* 231–32; cf. above, pp. 188–89). Paul's assurance of his love and his continuing presence with the Thessalonians "in heart" (2:17), his desire to see them again, his fervent concern, his thankful joy, his fond recollections of their time together—all this and more contributes to the creation of a friendly atmosphere that allows us to see the ideal of *philophronesis* realized in 1 Thessalonians and to identify many of its features as those of the friendly letter. The family metaphor that Paul uses in various ways can also very easily be fitted in here.

Nevertheless, the ideal of friendship does not yet capture what is typical about 1 Thessalonians, for Philippians, for example, is also a friendly letter (combined with a somewhat indirect letter of thanks for a financial gift). The particular emphasis of 1 Thessalonians is to be found in its motif of consolation, to which we now return. The addressees' need of consolation results in the first instance from the unexpected deaths in the congregation and from the related uncertainty about the Parousia. Yet it does not tell at all against the consoling function of the letter when Paul calls his addressees in a repeated refrain to comfort one another (παρακαλεῖτε ἀλλήλους) and thereby does not seek to do it all himself (cf. 4:18; 5:11 and below Exercise 46). The theme of consolation goes beyond comfort about departed church members or the topic of the Parousia to include comfort about the absence of the apostle and the Thessalonians' experience of marginalization and discrimination because of their new faith (cf. Smith with further examples). A family or friendship connection is also presupposed in the pagan examples of acts of consolation, so that the philophronetic character of 1 Thessalonians is entirely in keeping with this.

This brings us finally to the connection between 1 Thessalonians and ancient consolation literature, which comes in various forms, including speeches, essays, dialogues, and letters (on the last see only Plutarch's letter of consolation to his wife, *Consolatio ad uxorem*), and which treats other themes besides death, including exile and separation. To be sure, 1 Thessalonians does not include all the features of the consolation genre and offers some things that go beyond it, and is therefore not described exhaustively by its designation as a consolation letter (cf. Chapa, but also, with different tendencies, Bickmann). Nevertheless, the consolation letter may prove to be the one common denominator that covers more and integrates more than any other single term. Paul the letter writer slips into the role that the people of Israel offer to the prophet Baruch, not only to write "a letter of doctrine and a roll of hope" (*2 Bar.* 77:12) but also to speak "a word of consolation" (*2 Bar.* 81:1).

Exercise

46. Compare the following private papyrus letter P.Oxy. I 115
    from the second century CE (text and translation in White,
    Light from Ancient Letters [Bib. 1] 185) with Pseudo-
    Demetrius's example of a consoling letter (no. 5; above p.
    199) and with 1 Thessalonians:

P.Oxy. I 115
Eirene to Taonnophris and Philo,
   be of good courage (εὐψυχεῖν).
I was grieved and wept for the
departed one (εὔμοιρος) as much as I wept for Didymas.
And everything that was fit-
ting I have done, as well as my entire
household, Epaphrodeitos and Thermou-
thion and Philion and Apollonius
and Plantas. But, notwithstanding,
one is unable to do anything against such things.
Therefore, comfort one another (παρηγορεῖτε ἑαυτούς).
   May you fare well (εὖ πράττετε). Hathyr 1 (i.e., October 28)

B. A Necessary Correction: Second Thessalonians

Bibliography 58 (select commentaries): **E. Best**, *The First and Second Epistles to the Thessalonians* (Bib. 53). – **F. Laub**, *1. und 2. Thessalonicherbrief* (Bib. 53). – **G. L. Green**, *The Letters to the Thessalonians* (Bib. 53). – **A. J. Malherbe**, *The Letters to the Thessalonians* (Bib. 53). – **W. Marxsen**, *Der zweite Thessalonicherbrief*, ZBK 11/2 (Zürich 1982). – **M. J. J. Menken**, *2 Thessalonians*, NTR (London and New York 1994). – **P. G. Müller**, *Der Erste und Zweite Brief an die Thessalonicher* (Bib. 53). – **E. J. Richard**, *1 and 2 Thessalonians* (Bib. 53). – **W. Trilling**, *Der zweite Brief an die Thessalonicher*, EKKNT 14 (Zürich and Neukirchen-Vluyn 1980). – **C. A. Wanamaker**, *The Epistles to the Thessalonians* (Bib. 53).

Even if one wishes to concentrate only on its epistolary features, it is not possible to pass over the usual introductory questions of author and date when discussing 2 Thessalonians. For even from an epistolographical standpoint the close parallels between 2

Thessalonians and 1 Thessalonians call for further clarification and ultimately raise the question of authenticity. Nevertheless, in our first pass through the material we will focus exclusively on the structure and content of 2 Thessalonians before going into the comparison and its consequences.

Exercise

47. As preparation for the next phase of work, undertake an independent formal analysis of 2 Thessalonians with the means at your disposal, including epistolary and rhetorical analysis, and also thematic analysis.

---

1. Structure and Content

Bibliography 59: G. S. Holland, *The Tradition That You Have Received from Us: 2 Thessalonians in the Pauline Tradition*, HUT 24 (Tübingen 1988) 8–33. – **F. W. Hughes**, *Early Christian Rhetoric and 2 Thessalonians*, JSNTSup 30 (Sheffield 1989). – **R. Jewett**, *The Thessalonian Correspondence* (Bib. 54). – **M. J. J. Menken**, "The Structure of 2 Thessalonians," in R. F. Collins, ed., *The Thessalonian Correspondence* (Bib. 54) 373–82. – **P. T. O'Brien**, *Introductory Thanksgivings in the Letters of Paul* (Bib. 4) 167–96.

a) Epistolary Analysis

    I.   Letter Opening (1:1-12)
        A. Prescript (1:1-2)
            1. Senders (1:1a)
            2. Addressees (1:1b)
            3. Grace wish as greeting (1:2)
        B. Proem (1:3-12)
            1. Thanksgiving with grounds (1:3-4)
               a) Obligation to give thanks (1:3a)
               b) Grounds: growth of faith and love (1:3b)
               c) Boasting (1:4a)
               d) Grounds: steadfastness during persecution (1:4b)
            2. *Digressio:* eschatological perspective on persecution (1:5-10)

  a) Reward at the judgment of God (1:5)
  b) Two-sided payback (1:6-7a)
  c) Revelation of the Lord Jesus and its consequences
   (1:7b-9)
  d) Experience of salvation on the day of his coming
   (1:10)
 3. Assurance of continual intercessory prayer (1:11-12)
  a) Constancy of prayer (1:11a)
  b) Content of prayer (1:11b)
  c) Goal: mutual glorification of the Lord and his
   people (1:12a)
  d) Means: grace (1:12b)

In the letter opening the prescript (1:1-2) with its indication of the senders, recipients, and greeting presents no special problems. However, since the named senders are again Paul, Silvanus, and Timothy (for comparison with 1 Thess 1:1 see below), we once again face the question of who is primarily speaking in the document's dominant first person plural verbs, in the light of the fact that as in 1 Thessalonians (cf. 2:18; 3:5; 5:27), Paul does speak a couple times in the first person singular (2 Thess 2:5; 3:17).

  The proem in 1:3-12 is relatively long because of the inclusion of both a thanksgiving in 1:3-4 and an intercessory prayer in 1:11-12, coupled with the eschatological excursus in 1:5-10. One might wonder whether the prayer in vv. 11-12 might not rather be allocated to the body opening than the proem, but against this speaks the close connection of the prayer in vv. 11-12 to the thanksgiving in vv. 3-4 or also to the grace greeting in v. 2, by means of the phrase "according to the grace of our God and the Lord Jesus Christ" in v. 12, which forms an *inclusio*. With its forward look to the time "when the Lord Jesus is revealed from heaven with his mighty angels in flaming fire" (1:7-8) and his coming "on that day" (v. 10), the middle section in 1:5-10 prepares the way for the apocalyptic theme of the first main part of the letter body. Important for the communicative situation is the mention of "our testimony to you" that "was believed" in 1:10, because this refers to the initial missionary preaching.

 II. Letter Body (2:1–3:13)
  A. Body Opening: The Theme and Its Implications (2:1-2)
   1. Coming of the Lord and our meeting with him (2:1)
   2. Effect of false information from dubious sources (2:2)

B. First Main Part: Refutation of the Erroneous Thesis by a
    Sketch of the End-Time Events (2:3-12)
    1. The eschatological adversary: the "man of lawlessness"
        (2:3-4)
        a) Introductory warning (2:3a)
        b) Revelation of the opposing power (2:3b)
        c) His blasphemous behavior (2:4)
    2. Reminder of past teaching: I told you so! (2:5)
    3. A restraining factor (2:6-8a)
        a) That which now restrains (2:6)
        b) The restrainer and the consequences of his
            removal (2:7-8a)
    4. The double Parousia (2:8b-10)
        a) Parousia of Jesus to destroy the "lawless one"
            (2:8b)
        b) Preceding "parousia" of the "lawless one" (2:9a)
        c) His powers of deception (2:10)
    5. God's judgment on false belief (2:11-12)
C. Second Main Part: Thanksgiving, Exhortation, Prayer
    (2:13–3:5)
    1. Second thanksgiving (2:13-14)
        a) Thanksgiving and grounds (2:13)
        b) God's call and its eschatological goal (2:14)
    2. Call to stand firm and encouragement in the form of a
        prayer (2:15-17)
        a) Call to stand firm (2:15)
        b) Assurance of God's love and care (2:16)
        c) Wishes for the future (2:17)
    3. Mutual intercessory prayer (3:1-5)
        a) Prayer request for Paul and his mission (3:1-2)
        b) Promise of the Lord's faithfulness (3:3)
        c) Expression of confidence (3:4)
        d) Author's prayer for the addressees (3:5)
D. Body Closing: Individual Exhortations and Self-
    Recommendation (3:6-13)
    1. Keep away from the "idle" or "unruly" brothers (3:6)
    2. Paul as example (3:7-10)
        a) Obligation of imitation (3:7a)
        b) Paul's forgoing of financial support and his manual
            labor (3:7b-8)
        c) Purpose: to set a worthy example (3:9)
        d) Reminder of an old rule (3:10)

3. Call to get to work (3:11-12)
    a) Information about those unwilling to work (3:11)
    b) Command to them (3:12)
4. General exhortation to do good (3:13)

In the body opening in 2:1-2, which starts with an epistolary request (ἐρωτῶμεν, another plural), the catchword "Parousia" is immediately mentioned at the beginning in 2:1, while the catch phrase "the day of the Lord" stands at the end of 2:2. This forms the main theme of the letter: there existed among the addressees the erroneous view that the return of the Lord Jesus stood immediately at hand or had indeed already taken place, ἐνέστηκεν (perfect tense): "the day of the Lord has come" (RSV), "the day of the Lord is already here" (NRSV). Especially illuminating for us are the ways in which Paul imagines this opinion might have spread: "either by spirit or by word or by letter, as though from us" (2:2), that is, through a prophetic oracle, through a likewise oral sermon or teaching, or through a letter that claimed to be from Paul, or from Paul, Silvanus, and Timothy (like both 1 and 2 Thessalonians). If the text is to be believed, such a "forged" letter of Paul in fact seems to have been known among the addressees.

The portrait of the eschatological adversary in 2 Thessalonians 2:3-12, best known by his Johannine title "the Antichrist" (1 John 2:18, 22; 4:3; 2 John 7), but here designated variously as "the man of lawlessness," "the lawless one," "the son of destruction," and "the one who opposes and exalts himself above every so-called god" and "declares himself to be God," is not developed as an end in itself but rather serves to refute the false theology that had been spread: Before the Lord can come, various other events must play themselves out that are already on the horizon but still require more time for their ultimate realization. The author appeals to eschatological secret knowledge that he and his addressees share according to v. 6 ("And you know"), and in a side-remark in v. 5, he declares the present and future events he describes to be a fulfillment of the prophetic predictions he made during his founding visit to the church.

The loosely organized next section in 2:13–3:5 is structured internally by the direct address of the "brothers" in 2:13; 2:15 and 3:1, which are in turn bracketed externally by the use of "brothers" in 2:1 and 3:6 and, as a final *inclusio*, the phrase "And as for you, brothers" (Ὑμεῖς δέ, ἀδελφοί) in 3:13. The second thanksgiving in 2:13-14 has matched its first phrase (Ἡμεῖς δὲ ὀφείλομεν εὐχαριστεῖν τῷ θεῷ πάντοτε περὶ ὑμῶν, ἀδελφοί) almost exactly with that of the first thanksgiving in 1:3 (Εὐχαριστεῖν ὀφείλομεν, etc.), and like the proem in 1:3-12, but more quickly, it leads immediately to an eschatological climax in 2:14. In 2:15 Paul refers the church to "the traditions that you were taught (by us), either by (our) word of mouth or by our letter." One can argue whether the teaching that came through the letter here refers to an earlier letter of the apostle, which is more likely in view of the backward-looking reference and the coupling with an earlier oral proclamation, or whether the present letter instead is meant. From 3:1-5 we may highlight the "rapid spreading," literally the "running" (cf. τρέχω) of the word of the Lord among the addressees that Paul wants to see duplicated elsewhere according to v. 1, and his confidence in their continued obedience in v. 4.

The body closing in 3:6-13 combines situation-specific exhortations with the elements of an epistolary self-recommendation, here about the apostle who works for his living, which we might otherwise expect to find earlier in a typical letter. The exhortations combat the negative consequences of certain people's fixation on the imminent end, which has led them to the abandonment of all work and a rapturous living for today as if there were no tomorrow. In his counter-offensive Paul again appeals to values and experiences from the church's past: an "idle" or "disorderly" brother is not living according to the tradition that the church received from Paul (v. 6). Paul's going without financial support from the Thessalonians and his hard work for his own bread are brought into play, and he recalls a maxim that he first coined: "Whoever will not work should not eat" (v. 10). Finally, we have already noted that the direct address of the "brothers" in the final call in 3:13 does more than simply hark back to the most recent use of "brothers" in 3:6. Rather, by going all the way back to the initial epistolary request in 2:1 that begins with the same form of address, it brackets by *inclusio* the entire letter body from 2:1 to 3:13.

III. Letter Closing (3:14-18)
    A. Epilogue: Reception of the Letter (3:14-16)
        1. How to deal with unruly brothers (3:14-15)
        2. Peace wish and "the Lord be with you" (3:16)

B. Postscript (3:17-18)
   1. Greeting in Paul's own hand (3:17)
   2. Closing grace wish (3:18)

In the letter closing the foregoing letter finally and unambiguously comes to its action point in the epilogue in 3:14, when Paul reckons with the possibility that there may be some in the congregation who are unimpressed by his written remarks. Here he recommends social exclusion and shaming as hard therapy, but with the goal of *correctio fraterna* or fraternal correction, so that the church as a whole will experience the peace promised by the peace wish in v. 16, augmented by the phrase "the Lord be with you all." In the postscript, prior to the closing grace wish in v. 18, the closing greeting in Paul's hand in v. 17a, "I, Paul, write this greeting with my own hand," is supplemented by an elaborate certification that must be seen as a peculiarity and that looks somewhat suspicious: "This is the mark in every letter of mine; it is the way I write" (v. 17b).

b) Rhetorical Analysis

After the preliminary work that we have already done in the area of rhetorical analysis we can here content ourselves with summarizing three previous models of the rhetorical *dispositio* or arrangement of 2 Thessalonians and adding a few evaluative comments (for the titles of the three works see above in Bib. 59):

	Jewett	Holland	Hughes
exordium	1:1-12	1:3-4	1:1-12
narratio	—	1:5-12	—
partitio	2:1-2	—	2:1-2
probatio	2:3–3:5	2:1-17	2:3-15
peroratio	—	—	2:16-17
exhortatio	3:6-15	3:1-13	3:1-15
peroratio	3:16-18	3:14-16	—

To the extent that the prescript in 1:1-2 is left out of the rhetorical outline of Holland, just as the postscript in 3:16-18 or 3:17-18 is left out by both Holland and Hughes, they are set apart from rhetorical analysis as purely epistolary features. Once again there is a series of agreements between the rhetorical analysis and our structure obtained by epistolary analysis, but also several problems. There is no special difficulty in regarding 1:1-12 or preferably 1:3-12 as the *exordium*. Since a *narratio* or statement of the case is not necessarily required in deliberative rhetoric, it is better left out (against Holland). The designation of our body opening in 2:1-2 as a *partitio* (Jewett, Hughes) rightly recognizes that this brief section mentions the main themes for all that follows, namely the Parousia and the incorrect understanding of the day of the Lord. The *probatio* or section of proofs is subdivided by Jewett into the two proofs of 2:3-12 and 2:13–3:5, which agrees with our view of the two main parts of the letter body. Hughes's *peroratio* in 2:16-17 is placed much too early and also lacks the right content. The paraenetic section that we have identified as the body closing in 3:6-13 is identified in these rhetorical analyses as an *exhortatio* with slightly different boundaries (3:6-15; 3:1-13; 3:1-15), but in any case correctly as an independent unit. Yet once again the attempt to derive the *exhortatio* in a letter from actual orations is a bit forced (the first letter of Demosthenes that Hughes analyzes with reference to Goldstein [Bib. 2] cannot bear the weight put on it). Whether we can find a true rhetorical *peroratio* in 3:14-16 (Holland) or 3:16-18 (Jewett) remains doubtful.

Exercise

48. Before turning to the next section, search on your own for parallels in structure and wording between 2 Thessalonians and 1 Thessalonians. Pay special attention to the letter openings and closings and to prominent transitions. How would you evaluate and explain the similarities that come to your attention?

2. The Question of Authenticity

Bibliography 60: J. A. Bailey, "Who Wrote II Thessalonians?" *NTS* 25 (1979) 131–45. – **R. F. Collins**, *Letters That Paul Did Not Write: The Epistle to the Hebrews and the Pauline Pseudepigrapha*, GNS 28 (Wilmington 1988) 209–41. – **H. Holtzmann**, "Zum zweiten Thessalonicherbrief," *ZNW* 2 (1901) 97–108. – **F. Laub**, "Paulinische Autorität in nachpaulinischer Zeit (2 Thes)," in R. F. Collins, ed., *The Thessalonian Correspondence* (Bib. 54) 403–17 (pp. 373–515 contain twelve contributions to 2 Thess). – **A. Lindemann**, "Zum Abfassungszweck des zweiten Thessalonicherbriefs," *ZNW* 68 (1977) 35–47. – **P. Müller**, *Anfänge der Paulusschule* (Bib. 42). – **W. Schmithals**, *Die Briefe des Paulus in ihrer ursprünglichen Form*, Zürcher Werkkommentare zur Bibel (Zürich 1984) 111–22. – **W. Trilling**, *Untersuchungen zum zweiten Thessalonicherbrief*, ETS 27 (Leipzig 1972). – **A. G. van Aard**e, "The Second Letter to the Thessalonians Re-read as Pseudepigraph," *HvTSt* 56 (2000) 105–36. – **W. Wrede**, *Die Echtheit des zweiten Thessalonicherbriefes*, TU 24/2 (Leipzig 1903).

In our overview of the New Testament letters in chapter 7 we spoke repeatedly of pseudonymous or pseudepigraphal letters that originate not from the author named in the *superscriptio* but from another contemporary or later writer who is for some reason using his name.[7] We cannot avoid treating the phenomenon of pseudepigraphy in its own right, which we will do in section 3 below. As a concrete occasion for this discussion we have chosen 2 Thessalonians. The authenticity of this document has increasingly been called into question since the first critical voices were heard at the turn of the 18th to the 19th century, yet among the disputed Pauline epistles its authenticity is still more frequently defended today by critical scholars than that of any of the other disputed Paulines (e.g., Colossians). Why the question arises at all will first have to be explained, and for this we need to make a comparison of 2 Thessalonians with 1 Thessalonians.

[7] Even to speak of a pseudonymous author "writing in his name" already involves interpretation by suggesting that the actual author is motivated by a desire to represent the named author and his interests, which may or may not be the case.

a) Parallels of 2 Thessalonians to 1 Thessalonians

Second Thessalonians displays close points of contact with 1 Thessalonians involving both the overall structure and the wording of individual passages. The structural parallels go beyond what one could attribute to accidental agreements resulting from the use of a common letter model. Especially striking is the second thanksgiving included in both 1 Thessalonians and 2 Thessalonians, though the fact that this is numbered 2:13 in both letters is of course an accident arising from the later introduction of chapter and verse numbers. Several of the agreements that are simultaneously both verbal and structural are summarized in the following table, which treats in order the prescript, the first and second thanksgivings, a few transitions in the paraenetic sections, and the letter closing:

1 Thessalonians	2 Thessalonians
1:1 *Prescript* Paul, Silvanus, and Timothy, To the church of the Thessalonians in God [our] Father and the Lord Jesus Christ: Grace to you and peace.	1:1-2 *Prescript* Paul, Silvanus, and Timothy, To the church of the Thessalonians in God our Father and the Lord Jesus Christ: Grace to you and peace from God [our] Father and the Lord Jesus Christ.
1:2, 4 *First thanksgiving* We always give thanks to God for all of you ... brothers beloved by God	1:3 *First thanksgiving* We must always give thanks to God for you, brothers
2:13 *Second thanksgiving* And for this reason we also constantly give thanks to God	2:13 *Second thanksgiving* But we must always give thanks to God for you, brothers beloved by the Lord
3:11, 13 *Transition* Now may our God and Father himself and our Lord Jesus. . . . And may he strengthen your hearts	2:16-17 *Transition* Now may our Lord Jesus Christ himself and God our Father . . . comfort your hearts and strengthen them

4:1; 5:14 *Transitions*
Finally, brothers,
we ask and urge you in the Lord
Jesus. . . .
And we urge you, brothers, to
admonish the idlers

3:1, 6 *Transitions*
Finally, brothers. . . .
Now we command you, brothers, in
the name of [our] Lord Jesus Christ,
to keep away from every brother
who is living in idleness

5:23, 26, 28 *Letter closing*
Now may the God of peace himself
sanctify you. . . .
Greet all the brothers with a holy
kiss.
The grace of our Lord Jesus Christ
be with you.

3:16, 17, 18 *Letter closing*
Now may the Lord of peace himself
give you peace. . . .
I, Paul, write this greeting with
my own hand.
The grace of our Lord Jesus Christ
be with all of you.

Verbal agreements can also be observed in passages that are not structural parallels but are rather located in different parts of the respective letters. As already noted, Paul's appeal to his working for his own living as his self-recommendation comes rather late in 2 Thessalonians in the body closing, whereas in 1 Thessalonians it is placed in a more usual position in the body opening. But the two passages nevertheless agree closely in wording: compare 1 Thessalonians 2:9, "You remember our labor and toil, brothers; we worked night and day, so that we might not burden any of you" with 2 Thessalonians 3:8, "but with toil and labor we worked night and day, so that we might not burden any of you." Moreover, the prayers, prayer wishes, and prayer reports that unfold in rapid succession in 2 Thessalonians almost always have a counterpart in 1 Thessalonians.

Other areas show more disagreement between the letters. An underlying theme throughout both is the coming of the Lord, referred to by the Greek technical term "Parousia," which comes clearly to the surface in 1 Thessalonians 4:13-5:11 and in 2 Thessalonians 2:1-12. Nevertheless, these two passages are not only differently placed in their respective letters—in the body middle II in 1 Thessalonians and in the body opening and first main part in 2 Thessalonians—but also have different contents, insofar as 1 Thessalonians does not mention any intermediate events that must still take place before the Parousia, and certainly not an eschatological opponent or Antichrist. Differences have also been sought in the areas of vocabulary, syntax, and style (see the commentaries).

But these have never dominated the discussion of the relationship between 1 and 2 Thessalonians, and most authors who question the authenticity of 2 Thessalonians (see below) nevertheless agree that its author has faithfully imitated Paul in language and generally in style, as an effective writer of speech in character.

b) Proposed Explanations

These findings, with their intertwining of similarities and differences, require an explanation even on the assumption that Paul himself wrote both letters. Scholars sometimes assume for example that Paul sent off 2 Thessalonians only a few weeks after 1 Thessalonians, when the wording of his first letter was still etched in his mind. This thesis can escalate all the way up to the ingenious proposal that Paul kept a draft of 1 Thessalonians and referred to it while writing 2 Thessalonians. Sometimes the canonical order of the letters is also reversed, so that 2 Thessalonians is identified as the first letter, before 1 Thessalonians (cf. most recently Wanamaker). Others reckon with different groups of recipients in the church, postulate the help of a secretary, or make a later redactor responsible for the present form of the Thessalonian correspondence, which supposedly originally comprised four or five letters (Schmithals).

The situation immediately becomes more manageable when one admits that 2 Thessalonians does not come from Paul, but rather that an unknown author, separated from Paul by some time, self-consciously patterned his letter on the copy of 1 Thessalonians that he had before him, probably as his only Pauline letter. His aim was to attack at its root an erroneous imminent expectation of the Parousia, which could perhaps appeal to 1 Thessalonians. Was he so radical in this that he wanted to degrade 1 Thessalonians to the status of a forged Pauline letter by his comment about "a letter, as though from us" in 2 Thessalonians 2:2 and to replace it by his own "authentic" letter (so, e.g., Lindemann)? This is a possibility worth mentioning, but it is open to the objection that the post-Pauline author would thereby rob himself of the basis that supposedly authorized his new letter. In any case the unique closing remark, "This is the mark in every letter of mine; it is the way I write" (3:17) is not well suited to dispel doubts about Pauline authorship. It rather raises the suspicion of trying to prove too much.

It is almost impossible to locate the post-Pauline author of 2 Thessalonians in time and space. He need not have written in Thessalonica, nor for Thessalonica. It is enough to assume that 1 Thessalonians was known in his circles. As to the time of composition little more can be said than that it must have been before the end of the first century CE, for from that point forward we have to reckon with the existence of Pauline letter collections in which 2 Thessalonians was included. If one places the author in a Pauline school, then one must immediately add that this school had various "classes," for our author shares hardly any points in common with the Pauline students responsible for Colossians and Ephesians.

3. The Phenomenon of Pseudepigraphy

Bibliography 61: A. Baum, *Pseudepigraphie und literarische Fälschung im frühen Christentum: Mit ausgewählten Quellentexten samt deutscher Übersetzung*, WUNT 2/138 (Tübingen 2001). – **R. J. Bauckham**, "Pseudo-Apostolic Letters," *JBL* 107 (1988) 469–94. – **N. Brox**, *Falsche Verfasserangaben: Zur Erklärung der frühchristlichen Pseudepigraphie*, SBS 79 (Stuttgart 1975). – idem, ed., *Pseudepigraphie in der heidnischen und jüdisch-christlichen Antike*, WdF 484 (Darmstadt 1977); collection with important older works. – **L. R. Donelson**, *Pseudepigraphy and Ethical Argument* (Bib. 43). – **J. N. Duff**, "A Reconsideration of Pseudepigraphy in Early Christianity," D.Phil. Diss., Oxford 1998. – **M. Frenschkowski**, "Pseudepigraphie und Paulusschule" (Bib. 43). – **K. von Fritz**, ed., *Pseudepigrapha* I: *Pseudopythagorica, Lettres de Platon, Littérature pseudépigraphique juive*, Entretiens sur l'antiquité classique 18 (Geneva 1972). – **P. Gerlitz**, "Pseudonymität I: Religionsgeschichtlich," *TRE* 27 (1997) 659–62. – **M. Janssen**, *Unter falschem Namen: Eine kritische Forschungsbilanz frühchristlicher Pseudepigraphie*, Arbeiten zur Religion und Geschichte des Urchristentums 14 (Frankfurt 2003). – **D. G. Meade**, *Pseudonymity and Canon: An Investigation into the Relationship of Authorship and Authority in Jewish and Earliest Christian Tradition*, WUNT 39 (Tübingen 1986). – **A. Merz**, *Die fiktive Selbstauslegung des Paulus* (Bib. 43). – **B. Metzger**, "Literary Forgeries and Canonical Pseudepigrapha," *JBL* 91 (1972) 3–24. – **Karlheinz Müller**, "'Die Propheten sind schlafen gegangen' (syrBar 85,3): Nachbemerkungen zur überlieferungsgeschichtlichen Reputation der Pseudepigraphie im Schrifttum der frühjüdischen Apokalyptik," *BZ* 26 (1982) 179–207. – **P. Müller**, *Anfänge der Paulusschule* (Bib. 42). – **P. Pokorný**, "Pseudepigraphie I: Altes und Neues Testament," *TRE* 27 (1997) 645–55. – **W. Speyer**, *Die literarische Fälschung im heidnischen und christlichen Altertum: Ein Versuch ihrer*

Deutung, Handbuch der Altertumswissenschaft 1/2 (Munich 1971). – **A. Standhartinger**, *Studien zur Entstehungsgeschichte und Intention des Kolosserbriefs* (Bib. 42) 29–59. – **G. Stemberger**, "Pseudepigraphie II: Judentum," *TRE* 27 (1997) 656–59. – **T. L. Wilder**, *Pseudonymity, the New Testament, and Deception: An Inquiry into Intention and Reception* (Lanham, Md. 2004). – **M. Wolter**, "Die anonymen Schriften des Neuen Testaments: Annäherungsversuch an ein literarisches Phänomen," *ZNW* 79 (1988) 1–16. – idem, "Pseudonymität II: Kirchengeschichtlich," *TRE* 27 (1997) 662–70.

a) Definition of Terms

In discussing the subject generically known as "pseudepigraphy," we must first introduce a series of sometimes alien and artificial sounding terms, which are nevertheless used to impose some order on a very complex field and to prepare the way for a proper understanding of the question of authorship in the New Testament writings, particularly in the epistolary literature. It will therefore be useful to distinguish the following terms and concepts:

Anonymity (from ἀν- "without" + ὄνομα "name"). When written documents fail to carry any indication of the author on their own, they are said to be anonymous. In the New Testament this applies to all four Gospels and Acts, and among the letters to Hebrews and 1 John (though 2 and 3 John represent a special case, since while the author is not in fact named by his personal name, he does bear the honorary title "the elder," which allows him to be half-identified). How the secondary attributions to famous authors of these anonymous New Testament documents came to be added in the first place and whether these attributions are also grounded in the texts themselves (as can be argued, for example, for Luke as the author of Luke-Acts) is a separate question in its own right; but if these later attributions prove unfounded, they too cross over into the territory of pseudonymity.

Orthonymity. This is an artificial word coined on the analogy of "pseudonymity" (see below) and composed of the two components ὀρθός, "correct," and ὄνομα, "name." As such it forms a counterpart both to anonymous writings, which bear no name, and to pseudonymous writings, which bear a false name: here we have the true name. Examples of orthonymous writings include all the authentic letters of Paul.

Homonymity (from ὁμός "same" + ὄνομα "name"), not to be confused with homonymy in lexical semantics, deals with the phenomenon of an actual writer bearing the "same name" as another more famous person. This often leads later readers to misattribute the text to the more famous person, which the real author may or may not have intended. Hence when the author of the Revelation to John calls himself "John" in Revelation 1:1, he apparently does so without wanting to signal, for example, that he was identical with John the son of Zebedee from the circle of the Twelve, as later church tradition assumed.

Pseudonymity (from ψευδο- "false" + ὄνομα "name") is a more familiar English term covering various phenomena of writing or publication under a "false name." But it is also used somewhat differently in biblical studies than in mainstream literary criticism. When we speak of an author writing under a "pseudonym" or "pen name" today, we usually mean that an author uses a made-up name for their publications, yet without claiming the identity of any other figure by that name. Jane Austen's essentially anonymous pseudonym "A Lady" for her first novel *Sense and Sensibility* obviously makes no false claim to fame, while Mary Ann Evans with her more enduring pseudonym George Eliot was not "falsely" claiming to be an otherwise famous George Eliot, but only to be a man; both authors needed these pseudonyms to increase their own chances of publication, but not to infringe on the rights of others.[8] It is a different matter when a little known or unknown author borrows the name and therefore the authority of a famous author for their own purposes, as for example when somebody publishes his or her own poems under Goethe's name after Goethe's death. The spectrum of pseudonymity thus runs from "harmless" publication under a made-up pen name like George Eliot to the opposite extreme of conscious forgery with the intent to deceive and usually also to gain an advantage. Biblical and extrabiblical Jewish or Christian pseudepigrapha attributed to figures such as Enoch, the sons of Jacob, Daniel, or Peter always use known names, though not necessarily famous ones, since Daniel, for example, would be a minor biblical figure without the biblical book by his

---

[8] The pen name of male writer Samuel Clemens as Mark Twain is a somewhat different phenomenon in that it does not involve a gender change. While the complete origin of the pseudonym is unknown and various historical origins have been suggested, including by Twain himself, his more attractive pen name parallels the practice of modern actors choosing "stage names," e.g., Alan Alda (Alphonso Joseph D'Abruzzo), Woody Allen (Allen Stewart Konigsberg), Marilyn Monroe (Norma Jean Mortenson).

name. In any case the real names of the writers of such pseudepigrapha are never known.

Deuteronymity is a new word coined on the analogy of "deutero-
Pauline" in order to characterize the especially close teacher-student
relationship that the authors of Colossians, Ephesians, and perhaps
also 2 Thessalonians are thought to have had to the historical Paul
(cf. P. Müller 318–21). It is therefore a special type of pseudonymity
that applies to only a few New Testament letters.

Allonymity refers to writing in the name of "another" (ἄλλος) so as to
claim their authority without actually claiming to be that person.
The term therefore seeks to remove the usual "pseud-" from
"pseudepigraphy," according to I. H. Marshall, who is responsible
for introducing the term into the English-language discussion.[9] The
real author avoids close imitation of the style of the ascribed author
in an effort to prevent potential readers from being deceived about
the letter's true origin; the nature of the composition was thus transparent to the initial readers. The facts of the letter's origin were, nevertheless, often forgotten by later readers who erroneously identified
the actual author with the inscribed author.

The kind of pseudonymity that does not just invent a name (e.g.,
George Eliot) but that self-consciously takes on a famous name is
the kind that occurs in the New Testament (although the name of
Jude the brother of James was not especially famous). For this we
will use the expression "pseudepigraphy," which one can paraphrase more judgmentally as a "false" or "forged" indication of the
author or more neutrally as a "borrowed" name of an author. This
pseudepigraphy must now be more carefully defined and set
within the wider context of pseudepigraphy in ancient literature.

b) Wider Context

It would be too much to claim that pseudepigraphy was a widespread and accepted practice in the ancient world to which nobody

---

[9] Cf. Marshall, *Pastoral Epistles* (Bib. 43) 83–92, esp. 84: "Since the
nuance of deceit seems to be inseparable from the use of the terms 'pseudonymity' and 'pseudepigraphy' and gives them a pejorative sense, we
need another term that will refer more positively to the activity of writing in another's name without intent to deceive: perhaps 'allonymity' and
'allegraphy' may be suggested as suitable alternatives."

ever objected. On the contrary, people had a feel for what we would today call "originality" and "intellectual property," and also for intentional forgery. Readers were most inclined to accept pseudonymous publication within an established corpus of traditional literature when later members of a school wrote in the name of the founder of their school, such as the schools of the philosophers and the physicians. The pseudo-Pythagorean philosophical and scientific writings (see above pp. 122–23) and the Hippocratic medical corpus may serve as examples. Whether there was an additional category of religious pseudepigraphy that was considered legitimate because the spirit or the deity himself was thought to speak through the unknown author remains contested (despite Speyer). Nevertheless, with this idea of a traditional literature we are already approaching the Old Testament-Jewish tradition, whose apocalyptic and wisdom strands stayed alive by gaining a new hearing for the authoritative voice of the earlier masters through the medium of pseudepigraphical texts.

A further consideration for our study is that epistolary literature was precisely the place in antiquity for pseudepigraphy in all its forms. It began with simple rhetorical school exercises in pseudonymous writing or prosopopoeia that would fool nobody (cf. above chap. 4, sec. B.4 on the Cynic Epistles and their origin) and continued on to planned forgery (Cicero suspected that he had had forged letters foisted upon him, see above chap. 4, sec. B.2). From our survey of literary letters in chapter 4 it emerges that many of the great personalities of literary and intellectual history had to lend their names to pseudepigraphical letter production, including Aeschines, Apollonius, Brutus, Chion, Democritus, Demosthenes (in part), Euripides, Heraclitus, Hippocrates, Isocrates (in part), Phalaris, Plato (in part), Pythagoras, Socrates, Themistocles, Xenophon, and perhaps Sallust, to name but a few. On the early Jewish side (see chap. 6) we may recall for example the pseudepigraphical letters from the Jeremiah-Baruch tradition, the fact that *1 Enoch* 91–105 is a letter, and the partly inauthentic embedded letters in the books of the Maccabees.

Why letters so frequently became the object of pseudepigraphical writing has various explanations. It begins with the more external fact that the *superscriptio* of a letter usually contains a personal name that can be especially easily exchanged or "forged" (a historical work for example is not required by the conventions of the genre to name its author to the same degree). Letters are also especially well suited by their communicative function to the transmission of content that the writer considers important. Finally, the very ideology of letters was conducive to pseudepigraphical use, which brings us to the situation of the New Testament letters. The epistolary "parousia," the mediated presence of one who is absent, is a leading idea of letter writing that Paul knew how to take full advantage of when he allowed himself to be represented in his churches by his letters and also by his co-workers, who often carried and delivered, helped to prepare, and commented on his letters. The idea therefore eventually suggested itself of transforming a former geographical distance between an author and his addressees into a temporal one. Paul and other authority figures of the first Christian generation could then remain present even after their death through letters, preferably those written by former co-workers. Through freshly written letters, these associates could then have the apostles speak to pressing problems that first came up after their death. This fits well with the temporal distribution of New Testament pseudepigraphy, which we encounter in the years from about 70 to 110 CE, when the goal was to preserve the legacy of the founding period for a new phase after the passing of the founding fathers.

The degree of pseudepigraphy and the manner in which it is realized varies among the relevant New Testament writings, as the coinage of a new term such as "deuteronymity" for just one subgroup of these writings seeks to capture. One must also draw careful distinctions with respect to another question, concerning how far the epistolary fiction of pseudepigraphy was transparent to the addressees and how far it was taken at face value. That the author planned his pseudepigraphy to be transparent to his addressees is easier to imagine for the Pastorals than for Colossians and Ephesians and for 2 Peter than for 1 Peter. This too has led to the coining of a new term, "allonymity," precisely for the Pastorals as documents presumably written or at least edited and published by "another" person than Paul, yet with a complete transparency that was also recognized by the first readers, aided perhaps by their knowledge of the real author.[10]

[10] Marshall, *Pastoral Epistles* (Bib. 43) 82 n. 100 refers to his general theory of allonymity as "the view which says that writings were produced

Against these various "transparency" theories of pseudonymous or allonymous writing one could in principle object that by announcing his literary artifice, the real author would have undercut the very basis of authority that he was trying to create, contrary to the principles of effective prosopopoeia. We may therefore need to make here a seldom considered distinction: Perhaps the real author, let us say of the Pastoral Epistles, reckoned on there being different groups among his addressees. Some groups will have shared the same education level as he and therefore will have seen through the prosopopoeia or literary personification involved in his pseudonymous writing. Other groups may have been content to accept what was in fact a borrowed authoritative name without further question. The former group would presumably do well not to try to "illuminate" the latter group with the fine points of the actual composition.

That there is something objectionable to our sensibilities about this split in the audience and the complicity or even duplicity of the writers cannot be denied, especially in our more transparent and egalitarian Western culture. Yet even with all our apologetic skills we will not be able to remove all offense from early Christian pseudepigraphy (although some scholars continue to try). Moreover, later in church history the orthodox church fathers record prominent examples where some potentially explosive insights were reserved for a knowledgeable elite of the true "Gnostics," both orthodox and heterodox, who could handle them, but were kept away from the "simple" church folks who

---

under false names but without any attempt to deceive, *since the readers knew perfectly well who the real author was*" (italics added). Yet this is more a theoretical than a historical construct (though see 91 n. 120 for Marshall's view that the identities of the writers of the technically "anonymous" canonical Gospels were also known to the first readers), since in his treatment of the allonymity of the Pastorals on pp. 83–92, Marshall makes very little use of the idea that the readers of the Pastorals knew the real author. Marshall also has difficulty, along with other scholars, in suggesting any actual author who would be different from Timothy and Titus yet would compile or edit documents (including some genuine Pauline fragments) intended to support the ministry of these still living persons. Against this, traditional theories of pseudepigraphy usually assume that not only Paul but also Timothy and Titus have died and were in no way involved in the production of these letters.

supposedly could not.[11] Therefore the church fathers not only attacked the Gnostics because of their elitism, but also sometimes favored among themselves the concept of a double truth, for the truly educated on the one hand and the broad masses on the other.

Modern scholarship also produces "knowledge" about the Bible that not everybody shares; whether this produces elitism varies from case to case. Yet many would contend that it is possible for one person to belong to multiple communities of knowledge (cf. the somewhat stereotyped distinction of "church" and "academy") and to speak different languages in different settings without necessarily being duplicitous. Research into the pseudonymous character of ancient documents has its primary *Sitz im Leben* in university settings. While these settings have an integrity in their own right that need not always be judged by the criterion of their "translatability" elsewhere, communication in appropriate terms to a wider audience remains essential to the research task.

It is only fitting that we have chosen below as our final example of a free-standing New Testament letter the Second Letter of Peter. For this is the only New Testament document that is almost unanimously seen a pseudepigraphical writing, even by otherwise very conservative researchers.[12] It also qualifies as the latest writing in the New Testament.

[11] Cf. the references in N. Brox, *Erleuchtung und Wiedergeburt: Aktualität der Gnosis* (Munich 1989) 53–59.

[12] Although the most conservative writers continue to support the authenticity of 2 Peter, they too acknowledge that "for no other letter in the New Testament is there a greater consensus that the person who is named as the author could not, in fact, be the author" (D. A. Carson and D. J. Moo, *An Introduction to the New Testament* [Grand Rapids ²2005] 659).

Exercises

49. In his ninth letter, the priest and monk Salvian of Marseille (400–480 CE) defends before his bishop Salonius a writing with an epistolary frame that he had previously published under the title "The Four Books of Timothy to the Church" (see O'Sullivan 269–371), without mentioning his own name as author. In his apologetic letter to the bishop, he also does not identify himself explicitly as the author. Evaluate the following passages of his argument (trans. J. F. O'Sullivan, *The Writings of Salvian, the Presbyter*, FC 3 [Washington 1947; repr. 1977] 256–62):

[p. 256] You ask me, my dear Salonius, why the name of Timothy was signed to the little treatise *To the Church*, done recently by a certain author of our day. In addition, you add that unless I add a clear reason for using the name, while the surname of Timothy is affixed to the treatise, the books may perhaps be reckoned among the apocrypha. . . .

. . . [By way of answer] I have already pointed out that the books deal with issues of today and that they were written by a man of our own day in his zeal and love for things divine. This alone could suffice for removing completely any suspicion of apocryphal composition. Those [p. 257] treatises which are recognized as not being Timothy's are not suspected as apocryphal. . . .

. . . In every volume, profit is sought more from reading the book than from the name of the author. Therefore, if there is profit in reading, and each author, no matter who he is, possesses the wherewithal to teach his readers, what matters to him a word which cannot help those who are seeking knowledge? . . . Since there is no profit in a name, he who finds profit in writings unnecessarily seeks the name of the writer. . . .

. . . [T]here are three things which can be asked. Why did the author address his book *To the Church*? Did he use a borrowed name or his own? If not his own, why a borrowed name? If a borrowed name, why in particular did he choose Timothy as the name to be written? . . .

[p. 260] . . . Now I speak about the second question: why the books are not titled with the author's name. . . . First, there is that reason which derives from the mandate of God, by whom we are ordered to avoid the vanity of worldly glory in all things, lest, while we seek a little breath of human praise, we lose a heavenly reward. . . .

[p. 261] . . . There remains an explanation of why the name Timothy was chosen. . . . [p. 262] . . . For, as love [of God] is expressed by the word Theophilus [cf. Luke 1:3], so is honor of the divinity expressed by the word Timothy.[13] Thus, when you read that Timothy wrote *To the Church*, you must understand thereby that it was written to the Church for the honor of God. . . . For this reason, therefore, the name of Timothy is inscribed in the titles of the books. Indeed, the writer thought it fitting that, since he was writing the books for the honor of God, he would consecrate the title to the very honor of the Divinity.

50. As preparation for the next section, compare Jude and 2 Peter and try to determine their relationship. Prepare a chart with the parallels in wording and content. Suggest possible ways of explaining this interdependence.

C. A "Latecomer": Second Peter

Bibliography 62: R. J. Bauckham, *Jude, 2 Peter* (Bib. 50). – **H. Frankemölle**, *1. und 2. Petrusbrief, Judasbrief*, NEchtB 18/20 (Würzburg ²1990). – **O. Knoch**, *Der erste und zweite Petrusbrief: Der Judasbrief*, RNT (Regensburg 1990). – **J. H. Neyrey**, *2 Peter, Jude* (Bib. 50). – **H. Paulsen**, *Der zweite Petrusbrief und der Judasbrief* (Bib. 50). – **K. H. Schelkle**, *Die Petrusbriefe, Der Judasbrief*, HTKNT 13/2. (Freiburg i.Br. ⁵1980). – **A. Vögtle**, *Der Judasbrief, Der 2. Petrusbrief* (Bib. 50). – See also Bib. 48 on 1 Peter and Bib. 50 on Jude.

Bibliography 63: R. J. Bauckham, "2 Peter: An Account of Research," *ANRW* II.25.5 (1988) 3713–52. – **K. Berger**, "Streit um Gottes Vorsehung: Zur Position der Gegner im 2. Petrusbrief," in J. W. van Henten, ed., *Tradition and Re-interpretation in Jewish and Early Christian Literature: Essays in Honour of Jürgen C. H. Lebram*, StPB 36 (Leiden 1986) 121–35. – **F. W. Danker**, "2 Peter 1: A Solemn Decree," *CBQ* 40 (1978) 64–82. – **A. Deissmann**, "A Note to the Literary History of

---

[13] "Timotheos" can be understood as composed of τιμή, "honor," and θεός, "God."

Second Peter," in idem, *Bible Studies* (Bib. 1) 360–68. – **P. Dschulnigg**, "Der theologische Ort des Zweiten Petrusbriefes," *BZ* 33 (1989) 161–77. – **T. Fornberg**, *An Early Church in a Pluralistic Society: A Study of 2 Peter*, ConBNT 9 (Lund 1977). – **A. Gerdmar**, *Rethinking the Judaism-Hellenism Dichotomy: A Historiographical Case Study of Second Peter and Jude*, ConBNT 36 (Stockholm 2001). – **T. Kraus**, *Sprache, Stil und theologischer Ort des zweiten Petrusbriefes*, WUNT 2/136 (Tübingen 2001). – **P. Müller**, "Der 2. Petrusbrief," *TRu* 66 (2001) 310–37. – **J. H. Neyrey**, "The Form and Background of the Polemic in 2 Peter," *JBL* 99 (1980) 407–31. – **J. Schlosser**, ed., *Catholic Epistles* (Bib. 51) 409–83. – **K. M. Schmidt**, *Mahnung und Erinnerung im Maskenspiel* (Bib. 48). – **L. Thurén**, "Style Never Goes out of Fashion: 2 Peter Re-Evaluated," in S. E. Porter and T. H. Olbricht, eds., *Rhetoric, Scripture and Theology* (Bib. 5) 329–47. – **D. F. Watson**, *Invention, Arrangement, and Style* (Bib. 50).

1. Structure and Content

Stylistically and formally, the Second Letter of Peter is a very peculiar writing. Its style departs from the plain style or at most the medium register recommended for letters for something grand and exalted. To outline the letter, especially in its central section, is not easy. But its opening section stands out clearly enough:

I. Letter Opening (1:1-11)
    A. Prescript (1:1-2)
        1. Sender (1:1a)
        2. Addressees (1:1b)
        3. Greeting (1:2)
    B. Proem (1:3-11)
        1. The saving deeds of God's divine power (1:3-4)
        2. The proper response (1:5-9)
            a) A series of virtues (1:5-7)
            b) Two opposite ways of life (1:8-9)
        3. Summary appeal with eschatological climax (1:10-11)

Differently than in 1 Peter 1:1, the superscription in 2 Peter 1:1 chooses the Hebraized, archaic, and therefore authoritative sounding double name Simeon Peter (cf. Acts 15:14). The address includes very generally "those who have received a faith as precious as ours," while the salutation in 1:2 is construed with the optative of wish πληθυνθείη, "*May* grace and peace *be yours in abundance*," as 1 Peter 1:2 and Jude 2. The salutation with grace and peace has already been mentioned above in connection with letters from the Jewish Diaspora such as 2 Maccabees 1:1, and for the particular form here we may also compare Daniel 4:37c LXX and Daniel 6:26 Theodotion, εἰρήνη ὑμῖν πληθυνθείη (cf. E. Peterson, "Praescriptum" [Bib. 4] 131–32).

The proem contains neither a thanksgiving nor a eulogy, even though grounds for thanksgiving are given in 1:3-4. Verse 11 with its mention of "entry into the eternal kingdom of our Lord and Savior Jesus Christ" displays the usual eschatological climax, which then also forms a ring composition with the prescript, where Jesus Christ is called Savior in v. 1 and Lord in v. 2. Verses 5-7 present a virtue catalogue in the form of a sorites (a chain of terms which build upon one another), while verses 8-9 distantly echo the doctrine of the two ways. A connection to the language of the Hellenistic "solemn decree" was already discovered in its rudiments by Deissmann and was demonstrated in detail by Danker; royal letters are also marked by the same style.

The "testament of the apostle" (see the outline below) in 2 Peter 1:12-15 is better allocated to the body opening than to the proem, even if the admission that the addressees already possess the requisite knowledge of the truth in v. 12b—which nevertheless does not make it superfluous for the "apostle" to remind them of it in vv. 12a and 13—fulfills the function of a *captatio benevolentiae*, which might otherwise come in the proem. In a stylized statement in 1:14-15 (e.g., "knowing that the laying aside of my tent is imminent," v. 14), the author suggests that he is facing death in the near future. This gives his further remarks the character of a literary testament, whose features include, for example, the nearness of the hour of death, giving of a personal final account, instructions for the future, warning about the onset of hard times, and an overall concern for the welfare of those who remain behind. One can also detect here the traces of an epistolary self-recommendation. In any case the next section in 1:16-18 certainly serves this purpose, where the writer makes himself an eyewitness of the transfiguration of Jesus in dependence on the Jesus tradition of the Gospels, in order to underscore his authority to confirm the prophetic word of Scripture and to tell his readers how to interpret it (1:19-20). Two thematic main parts with further subdivisions remain for the body middle in 2:1-22 and 3:1-13:

II. Letter Body (1:12–3:16)
    A. Body Opening: Epistolary Self-Recommendation (1:12-21)
        1. Testament of the apostle (1:12-15)
            a) The addressee's knowledge and the apostle's reminder (1:12-13)
            b) Stylized presentation of the apostle's impending death (1:14-15)
        2. The apostle as eyewitness (1:16-18)
            a) Negative example not followed (1:16)
            b) Allusion to transfiguration story (1:17)
            c) Personal certification (1:18)
        3. The prophetic word (1:19-21)
            a) Its reliability (1:19)
            b) Its origin and proper interpretation (1:20-21)
    B. Body Middle, First Main Part: The False Teachers (2:1-22)
        1. Announcement of their appearance (2:1-3)
        2. Judgment against them, with examples (2:4-10a)
            a) Angels that sinned (2:4)
            b) Noah and the flood (2:5)
            c) Sodom and Gomorrah (2:6)
            d) Lot's suffering and rescue (2:7-8)
            e) Application (2:9-10a)
        3. Invective: Disparagement of the opponents (2:10b-22)
            a) Point of departure: more daring than angels (2:10b-11)
            b) Comparison to animals and vice catalogue (2:12-14)
            c) Balaam as a warning example (2:15-16)
            d) Comparison to natural phenomena and list of errors (2:17-19)
            e) A miserable end (2:20-21)
            f) Two proverbs (2:22)
    C. Body Middle, Second Main Part: The Certainty of the Return of Christ (3:1-13)
        1. Renewed prediction (3:1-4)
            a) Communicative side-remark: this is the second letter (3:1-2)
            b) Scoffers of the last days (3:3-4)
        2. Destruction of the world through water and fire (3:5-7)
            a) Past flood (3:5-6)
            b) Future fire (3:7)
         3. God's timetable (3:8-9)

    4.   From the day of the Lord to the new creation (3:10-13)
        a)   Word picture: day of the Lord like a thief (3:10a)
        b)   Final catastrophe (3:10b)
        c)   Consequences for the readers' own lives (3:11-12)
        d)   New heavens and a new earth (3:13)
  D. Body Closing: Paraenesis Motivated by the Legacy of Paul
      (3:14-16)
    1.   The appeal (3:14-15a)
    2.   Confirmation through the letters of Paul (3:15b-16a)
    3.   Difficulties of understanding and misinterpretations
        (3:16b)

From the massive and colorful polemic against the false teachers in the first main part of the body middle, where there are many rhetorical subtleties that we could marvel at, let us focus only on the conclusion of the invective by two proverbs in 2:22. Even though these are two rather drastic proverbs, "The dog turns back to its own vomit" (Prov 26:11) and "The sow is washed only to wallow in the mud" (an ancient oriental proverb), the author is nevertheless following the advice of Demetrius, *On Style* 232, to adorn one's letters with proverbs, even if Demetrius presumably had more flattering or attractive proverbs in mind (see above pp. 186, 188).

The second main part of the letter body about the return of Christ in 3:1-13 goes together with the first about the false teachers in 2:1-22 by affirming what they deny: the certainty of the Parousia despite all the delays that people think they are experiencing (the slogan of the scoffers in 3:4, "the fathers have fallen asleep," would ironically have to include the historical apostle Simon Peter). The designation of the present letter as Peter's "second letter" in the transition in 3:1 (cf. P.Mich. III 209.6–9 [II CE]: "this is the second letter that I have sent you since I got home") raises the question of where the first letter is. This can only be 1 Peter, which the author presupposes his readers know as such, though not necessarily in its detailed contents, and which he refers to in order to authorize his own pseudepigraphical construction. Moreover, the author apparently also already knows of a collection of Paul's letters, which he refers to in the body closing in 3:15-16. But the extent of this collection can no longer be determined. His mention of "our beloved brother Paul" and his special wisdom may indeed be understood as a sign of respect and need not be ironic. But some things from his works, especially eschatological passages, are heavy going for the author, and the opposing side that he attacks apparently draws support from the Pauline traditions, illegitimately in his view.

The letter comes quickly to a close in 3:17-18 with final exhortations, expressed both negatively and positively, and with a doxology, which concludes with the mention of "our Lord and Savior Jesus Christ," forming an *inclusio* with titles already used in the prescript in 1:1-2 (cf. 1:11). The responsorial "Amen" seems to be secondary from a text-critical standpoint.

III. Letter Closing (3:17-18)
    A. Closing exhortation (3:17-18a)
       1. Negative (3:17)
       2. Positive (3:18a)
    B. Doxology (3:18b)

Exercise

51. D. F. Watson (*Invention, Arrangement, and Style*, 141–42) has produced a detailed rhetorical outline of 2 Peter, reproduced below in full. Study this outline yourself, isolate unknown technical terms, compare this model to our above thematic and epistolographical analysis, note similarities and differences, and make an evaluation.

A Rhetorical Outline of 2 Peter

I.   Epistolary Prescript (Quasi-*Exordium*): 1:1-2
II. *Exordium*: 1:3-15
    A. Miniature homily in the form of a complex enthymeme: 1:3-11
    B. Personal data: 1:12-15
III. *Probatio*: 1:16–3:13
    A. First Accusation and Refutation: 1:16-19
       1. Accusation: "The apostolic proclamation of the parousia is a cleverly devised myth." 1:16a
       2. Refutation: 1:16b-19
          a. Inartificial proof based on eyewitness testimony: "The apostles witnessed the precursor of the parousia, the Transfiguration." 1:16b-18

        b.   Inartificial proof based on a document: "The apostolic preaching of the parousia is dependable because it is based on OT prophecy." 1:19. Secondarily, an artificial proof based on the ethos of Peter.

B. Second Accusation and Refutation: 1:20-21

    1. Accusation: "The OT prophecy upon which the apostles base their teaching of the parousia are matters of the prophet's own interpretation and impulse, not that of the Holy Spirit." 1:20b-21a

    2. Refutation: Artificial Proof of enthymeme: 1:20-21

        a.   Conclusion: "Prophecy is not a matter of a prophet's own interpretation." 1:20

        b.   Premise: "Prophets are inspired by the Holy Spirit." 1:21

C. Counter-accusation: "The teachers within the congregation are false teachers, immoral, corrupting, and destined for destruction." 2:1-3a

D. Third Accusation and Refutation: 2:3b-10a

    1. Accusation: "Divine judgment is 'idle' and 'asleep.'" 2:3b (cf. 3:9)

    2. Refutation: Artificial proof based on historical examples: "If the wicked were punished and the righteous saved in history, then the same will occur at the future parousia and the judgment." 2:3b-10a

E. *Digressio*: denunciation serving to destroy the ethos of the opponents. 2:10b-22.

F. *Transitio* or "Secondary Exordium": 3:1-2

G. Fourth Accusation and Refutation: 3:3-13

    1. Accusation: "The apostolic preaching of an imminent parousia is to be denied on the basis of the death of the first generation of Christians who were prophesied would experience it, and on the basis of the lack of divine intervention in history." 3:3-4

    2. Refutation: 3:5-13

        a.   Artificial Proof of enthymeme: 3:5-7

            1. Premise 1: "By God's word water was stored for world judgment at the Flood and it occurred." 3:5-6

            2. Premise 2: "By God's word fire is stored for world judgment at the parousia." 3:7

            3. Implied conclusion: "Therefore God has and will act in judgment in history."

        b.   Inartificial Proof based on a document: "The seeming delay of the parousia is an illusion because divine and human time perspectives vary." 3:8

        c.   Artificial Proof of enthymeme: 3:9
           1.   Premise: "The Lord forbears waiting for repentance." 3:9b
           2.   Conclusion: "The Lord is not slow about his promises." 3:9a

        d.   Artificial Proof drawn from ethos: 3:10-13. Secondarily, an artificial proof based on example of the type of a judgment or popular belief and saying.
           1.   Affirmation of the reality of the parousia using gospel tradition. 3:10
           2.   *Epiphonema*: 3:11-12

        e.   Artificial Proof of pathos: 3:13

IV. *Peroratio*: 3:14-18
    A. *Repetitio*: 3:14-16
    B. *Adfectus*: 3:17-18
        1. *indignatio*: 3:17
        2. *conquestio*: 3:18

2. Comparison with the Letter of Jude

A comparison with the Letter of Jude is indispensable to the study of 2 Peter. In the following overview we take Jude as the basis of comparison and order the references to 2 Peter accordingly, but this involves a departure from the normal verse order of 2 Peter in only two places: first where we must refer to 2 Peter 1:12 at the beginning, although all the other parallels are from 2 Peter 2–3, and again when 2 Peter 2:15 must be placed before 2:13. The verbal points of contact in the Greek are highlighted by *italics*, with underlining for verbal parallels in English that reflect synonyms in Greek (cf. Jude 6, 10, 18 with 2 Pet 2:4, 12; 3:3), and **boldface** to call attention to a word play on ἀγάπαις, "love-feasts" and ἀπάταις, "dissipations" that does not translate into English (cf. Jude 12 with 2 Pet 2:13). But the parallels in content go far beyond this, as one can easily convince oneself by a parallel reading. Of course, what is left out from Jude or added in 2 Peter is also important. In the table below this can only be seen in the passages with a common substratum, otherwise it must be deduced from the gaps in the verse numbering and verified in the texts themselves. (The NRSV translation in the table has occasionally been modified to preserve verbal parallels and literal renderings.)

Jude	2 Peter
4 . . . who *deny* (ἀρνούμενοι) our only *Master* (δεσπότην) and Lord, Jesus Christ.	2:1 They will even *deny* (ἀρνούμενοι) the *Master* (δεσπότην) who bought them.
5 Now I desire *to remind you* (ὑπομνῆσαι ὑμᾶς), *though you know* (εἰδότας) all things.	1:12 Therefore I intend to keep on *reminding you* (ὑμᾶς ὑπομιμνῄσκειν) of these things, *though you know* (εἰδότας) them already.
6 And the *angels* (ἀγγέλους) who did not keep their own position, but left their proper dwelling, he has *kept* (τετήρηκεν) in eternal <u>chains</u> (δεσμοῖς) in *darkness* (ζόφον) *for the judgment* (εἰς κρίσιν) of the great Day.	2:4 For if God did not spare the *angels* (ἀγγέλων) when they sinned, but cast them into hell and committed them to <u>chains</u> (σειραῖς) of *darkness* (ζόφου) to be *kept* (τηρουμένους) *for the judgment* (εἰς κρίσιν).
7 Likewise, *Sodom and Gomorrah* and the surrounding *cities* (πόλεις), which, in the same manner as they, indulged in sexual immorality and went after strange *flesh* (see below), serve as an *example* (δεῖγμα) by undergoing a punishment of eternal fire.	2:6 and if by turning the *cities* (πόλεις) of *Sodom and Gomorrah* to ashes he condemned them to extinction and made them an *example* (ὑπόδειγμα) of what is coming to the ungodly.
8 Yet in the same way these dreamers also *defile* (μιαίνουσιν) the *flesh* (σάρκα), reject *authority* (κυριότητα), and *slander the glorious ones* (i.e., the angels, δόξας βλασφημοῦσιν). 9 But when the *archangel* (ἀρχάγγελος) Michael contended with the devil and disputed about the body of Moses,	2:10 —especially those who indulge their *flesh* (σαρκός) in the lust of *defilement* (μιασμοῦ), and who despise *authority* (κυριότητος). *Daring* (τολμηταί) and willful, they are not afraid to *slander the glorious ones* (i.e., the angels, δόξας βλασφημοῦντες), 2:11 whereas *angels* (ἄγγελοι), though greater in

he did not *dare* (ἐτόλμησεν) to bring a *judgment of slander* (κρίσιν βλασφημίας) against him, but said, "The *Lord* (κύριος) rebuke you!"

10 *But these people* (οὗτοι δὲ) *slander* (βλασφημοῦσιν) whatever they do not understand (οὐκ οἴδασιν), and they are *destroyed* (φθείρονται) by those things that, *like* the *irrational animals* (ὡς τὰ ἄλογα ζῷα), they know by *instinct* (φυσικῶς).

11 Woe to them! For they go *the way* (τῇ ὁδῷ) of Cain, and abandon themselves to *the error* (τῇ πλάνῃ) *of Balaam* for the sake of *reward* (μισθοῦ), and perish in Korah's rebellion.

12 These are *stains* (σπιλάδες) on your **love-feasts** (ἀγάπαις), while they *feast with* you (συνευωχούμενοι) without fear, feeding themselves. They are waterless (ἄνυδροι, see below) clouds carried along by the winds; autumn trees without fruit, twice dead, uprooted;

13 wild waves of the sea, casting up the foam of their own shame; wandering stars, *for whom the deepest darkness has been reserved* forever (οἷς ὁ ζόφος τοῦ σκότους εἰς αἰῶνα τετήρηται).

16 These are grumblers and malcontents; they indulge their own lusts; they are bombastic in speech, flattering people to their own advantage.

might and power, do not bring against them a *slanderous judgment* (βλάσφημον κρίσιν) from the *Lord* (κυρίου).

2:12 *But these people* (οὗτοι δὲ) are *like irrational animals* (ὡς ἄλογα ζῷα), mere creatures of *instinct* (φυσικά), born to be caught and killed. They *slander* (βλασφημοῦντες) what they do not understand (ἀγνοοῦσιν), and when those creatures are destroyed, they also will be *destroyed* (φθαρήσονται).

2:15 They have left the straight way and have *erred* (ἐπλανήθησαν), following *the way* (τῇ ὁδῷ) *of Balaam* son of Bosor, who loved the *reward* (μισθόν) of doing wrong.

2:13 suffering the penalty for doing wrong. They count it a pleasure to revel in the daytime. They are *stains* (σπίλοι) and blemishes, reveling in their **dissipations** (ἀπάταις) while they *feast with* you (συνευωχούμενοι ὑμῖν).

2:17 These are waterless (ἄνυδροι, see above) springs and mists driven by a storm, *for whom the deepest darkness has been reserved* (οἷς ὁ ζόφος τοῦ σκότους τετήρηται).

2:18 For they speak bombastic nonsense, and with licentious desires of the flesh they entice people who have just escaped from those who live in error.

17 But you, *beloved* (ἀγαπητοί), *remember the words* that were *spoken beforehand* (μνήσθητε τῶν ῥημάτων τῶν προειρημένων) by the *apostles* (ἀποστόλων) of our *Lord* (κυρίου) Jesus Christ;

3:1 This is now, *beloved* (ἀγαπητοί), the second letter . . . 3:2 you should *remember the words spoken beforehand* (μνησθῆναι τῶν προειρημένων ῥημάτων) by the holy prophets, and the commandment of the *Lord* (κυρίου) and Savior (spoken) by your *apostles* (ἀποστόλων).

18 for they said to you, "In the *last* (ἐσχάτου) time there will be *scoffers* (ἐμπαῖκται), *following after their* <u>own</u> ungodly *lusts*" (κατὰ τὰς ἑαυτῶν ἐπιθυμίας πορευόμενοι τῶν ἀσεβειῶν).

3:3 First of all you must understand this, that in the *last* (ἐσχάτων) days *scoffers* (ἐμπαῖκται) will come, scoffing and *following after their* <u>own</u> *lusts* (κατὰ τὰς ἰδίας ἐπιθυμίας αὐτῶν πορευόμενοι).

The main contents of Jude outside its framing sections have points of correspondence in 2 Peter, concentrated in the dispute with the opponents in 2 Peter 2:1–3:3. But this also means that the overall themes of each letter have little to do with each other, for in 2 Peter everything is oriented to reassuring the readers in view of the Parousia and the end of the world, in which Jude shows no interest. The close agreements show that the in itself conceivable idea that the two authors might have used a common source or tradition is no longer plausible; literary dependence is involved. That Jude presents a short version of 2 Peter is already very improbable in view of the change of theme as well as other reasons. Everything speaks in favor of the majority view of scholarship: Second Peter, as the later writing, is oriented to Jude, which it uses freely in an almost midrashic way, and it also does not shy away from omitting or reworking tricky passages, such as the dispute between Michael and Satan about the body of Moses in Jude 9 and the quotation from the book of Enoch in Jude 14–15. The reminiscence of the exodus in Jude 5 is lacking in 2 Peter because it comes in the "wrong" place, before the mention of the fall of the angels from Genesis 6 in Jude 6 and the cities of Sodom and Gomorrah from Genesis 19 in Jude 7.

However, this relationship of literary dependence (convincingly established by Fornberg) also has consequences for the placement of 2 Peter, quite apart from the confirmation of its pseudepigraphical character. Second Peter must have originated a considerable time after Jude. It presupposes the beginning of the collection of the Pauline letters, and its instruction to "wait for and hasten the coming of the day of God" in 3:12 reflects a much more distant expectation of the Parousia than the imminent expectation of the time of the apostles. We will have to postulate a time of origin in the early second century CE, perhaps between 110 and 120. Hence in our narrow selection of texts in this chapter we have at least dealt in the case of 1 Thessalonians and 2 Peter with the earliest and the latest letter in the New Testament. About the author's geographical location—Rome? Asia Minor? Egypt? Alexandria?— we can only speculate, and the same goes for the addressees. That 2 Peter's acceptance into the New Testament canon was especially contested and took an especially long time (the Muratorian Canon in Exercise 39 does not include 2 Peter, but then again neither does it include 1 Peter) should not be surprising given these circumstances of its origin.

D. Two Letters in Acts

Bibliography 64 (selected commentaries and monographs): **C. K. Barrett**, *A Critical and Exegetical Commentary on the Acts of the Apostles*, 2 vols., ICC (Edinburgh 1994–1998). – **J. A. Fitzmyer**, *The Acts of the Apostles*, AB 31 (New York 1997). – **E. Haenchen**, *Die Apostelgeschichte*, KEK 3 (Göttingen [16]1977); ET of the fourteenth German edition by B. Noble and G. Shinn; trans. rev. and brought up to date by R. McL. Wilson, *Acts of the Apostles: A Commentary* (Philadelphia 1971). – **L. T. Johnson**, *The Acts of the Apostles*, SP 5 (Collegeville 1992). – **G. Lüdemann**, *Das frühe Christentum nach den Traditionen der Apostelgeschichte: Ein Kommentar* (Göttingen 1987); ET by idem with the assistance of T. Hall, *The Acts of the Apostles: What Really Happened in the Earliest Days of the Church* (Amherst, N.Y. 2005). – **D. Marguerat**, *The First Christian Historian: Writing the "Acts of the Apostles,"* SNTSMS 121 (Cambridge 2002). – **R. I. Pervo**, *Profit with Delight: The Literary Genre of Acts of the Apostles* (Philadelphia 1987). – **E. Plümacher**, *Lukas als hellenistischer Schriftsteller: Studien zur Apostelgeschichte*, SUNT 9 (Göttingen 1972). – **R. C. Tannehill**, *The Narrative Unity of Luke-Acts*, vol. 2: *The Acts of the Apostles* (Minneapolis 1990). – **C. Talbert**, *Reading Luke-Acts in Its Mediterranean Milieu*, NovTSup 107 (Leiden 2003). – **A. Weiser**, *Die Apostelgeschichte*, 2 vols., ÖTBK 5/1–2 (Gütersloh and Würzburg 1981–1985). – **B. Witherington III**, *The Acts of the Apostles: A Socio-Rhetorical Commentary* (Grand Rapids 1998).

Texts with an epistolary character are also found in the New Testament outside the two great corpora of the Pauline Letters and Catholic Letters. Next to Revelation, with its overall letter frame and its special open letters to the seven churches, this also applies to Acts, into which the author, whom we shall call Luke, has inserted two short letters in Acts 15:23-29 and 23:26-30. Acts has the genre of a historical monograph with some novelistic features. Even on the basis of this genre classification it stands to reason that Luke has probably proceeded similarly to his fellow ancient historians. Next to speeches, to which they paid the greatest attention, ancient historians also wove other texts into their presentations such as records, statements of witnesses, foundation charters, and not least letters, and when necessary they composed such documents for their own historical-novelistic purposes. Examples can be found, as we have already seen, in writers including Thucydides, Flavius Josephus, Sallust and Tacitus, and—not to be forgotten—the books of the Maccabees. Embedded letters are also used to good effect in ancient novels—for example, in the Alexander novel or in Achilles Tatius (cf. Exercise 19). Letters also carry the leitmotif in books 4 and 5 of Chariton's story *Callirhoe* (see above pp. 136–38).

1. An Apostolic Decree: Acts 15:23-29

Bibliography 65: C. Andresen, "Zum Formular frühchristlicher Gemeindebriefe" (Bib. 4). – **F. W. Danker**, "Reciprocity in the Ancient World and in Acts 15:23-29," in R. J. Cassidy and P. J. Scharper, eds., *Political Issues in Luke-Acts* (Maryknoll, N.Y. 1983) 49–58. – **B. Jürgens**, *Zweierlei Anfang: Kommunikative Konstruktionen heidenchristlicher Identität in Gal 2 und Apg 15*, BBB 120 (Berlin 1999). – **Klaus Müller**, *Tora für die Völker: Die noachidischen Gebote und Ansätze zu ihrer Rezeption im Christentum*, Studien zu Kirche und Israel 15 (Berlin 1994). – **R. Neuberth**, *Demokratie im Volk Gottes: Untersuchungen zur Apostelgeschichte*, SBB 46 (Stuttgart 2001) 147–235. – **W. H. Shepherd, Jr.**, *The Narrative Function of the Holy Spirit as a Character in Luke-Acts*, SBLDS 147 (Atlanta, Ga. 1994) 218–19. – **A. J. M. Wedderburn**, "The 'Apostolic Decree': Tradition and Redaction," *NovT* 35 (1993) 362–89. – **J. Wehnert**, *Die Reinheit des "christlichen Gottesvolkes" aus Juden und Heiden: Studien zum historischen und theologischen Hintergrund des sogenannten Aposteldekrets*, FRLANT 173 (Göttingen 1997). – See also Bib. 64.

According to the Lukan presentation in Acts 15, emissaries from Judea arrive in the Christian church of Antioch demanding circumcision of the Gentle Christians as necessary for salvation (15:1). The dispute that breaks out over this cannot be settled at the local level. As the main opponents of the newcomers, Paul and Barnabas with a few others are sent by the church to Jerusalem to discuss the controversial question with the apostles and the elders (15:2-4). There a group that Luke associates with the party of the Pharisees makes the same demand: "The Gentiles must be circumcised and required to obey the law of Moses" (15:5).

As the first recorded speaker in the ensuing debate, Peter begins with his plea for the Gentile Christians, on whose behalf God himself has already testified "by giving them the Holy Spirit, just as he did to us" (15:8). He is looking back in particular to the events that he witnessed in connection with the conversion and baptism of the Gentile centurion Cornelius in Caesarea (cf. esp. Acts 10:44-48; 11:15-17). Peter alludes to circumcision indirectly as a "yoke" that should not be laid on the new disciples (15:9). Barnabas and Paul are then allowed to speak of their first miraculous missions successes among the Gentiles (15:12). Finally, James the Lord's brother speaks up and also declares himself indirectly in favor of dispensing with circumcision for the Gentiles: "we should not trouble those Gentiles who are turning to God" (15:19). Nevertheless, near the end of his speech he also formulates what has sometimes been called the "James clause": Gentile Christians should nevertheless still abstain "from things polluted by idols and from fornication and from whatever has been strangled and from blood" (15:20). These clauses also go by another name, namely the "apostolic decree." This rests on the fact that the requirements formulated by James are immediately framed in a letter. The apostles and the elders and the whole church choose two respected men as messengers, Judas called Barsabbas and Silas (the Silvanus of the Pauline letters), and they send them away with Barnabas and Paul to Antioch (15:22) carrying a letter that in a literal translation runs as follows (Acts 15:23b-29):

23b   The apostles and the elders, (your) brothers,
   c   to the brothers in Antioch and Syria and Cilicia who are from
        the Gentiles,
   d   greetings (χαίρειν).

24a   Since we have heard

  b   that some [+ MSS: who went out] from us have disturbed you with words,

  c   unsettling your souls,

  d   to whom we gave no instructions,

25a   **it seemed (good) to us,**

  b   having become of one mind

  c   (and) having selected men,

  d   to send (them) to you with our beloved Barnabas and Paul,

26a   persons

  b   who have risked their lives for the name of our Lord Jesus Christ.

27a   Therefore we have sent Judas and Silas,

  b   who themselves will also report the same things by (their) word,

28a   (namely that): **"It seemed (good) to the Holy Spirit and to us**

  b   to lay upon you no greater burden

  c   than these essentials:

29a   that you abstain from   things sacrificed to idols
                             and blood
                             and things strangled
                             and fornication;

  b   if you keep yourselves free from such things,

  c   you will do well (εὖ πράξετε).

  d   Farewell (ἔρρωσθε).

The epistolary prescript is true to the form of the Greek letter model. The apostles and the elders of the Jerusalem church appear as the collective senders. Although there is no longer any mention of the whole church as in the narrative in 15:22, the apostles and the elders still designate themselves as the "brothers" of the addressees. The letter thus uses family metaphors to express the feeling of togetherness among the Christian groups, analogously to the Jewish letters from the periods of the Maccabees and the Bar Kokhba revolt. As is to be expected from the preceding narrative, the addressees include the Gentile Christians of the city of Antioch, but also those in the provinces of Syria and Cilicia where the new regulation is likewise be put into effect. In fact only a little later on his second missionary journey Paul, accompanied by Silas, travels not only through Syria and Cilicia (15:41), where he presumably delivers the letter to these additional addressees just as he had done together with Barnabas, Judas, and Silas in Antioch (cf. 15:30), but also through the cities of the first missionary journey such as Lystra and Derbe, where he is said to have delivered the "decrees" (δόγματα) of the letter as well (16:4), even though these cities will have lain in the southern part of the province of Galatia, to which the letter was not formally addressed.[14]

The body of the letter then reveals two main contents, marked by the repetition of the phrase ἔδοξεν, "it seemed good," in vv. 25a and 28a. Acts 15:24 first recapitulates in all brevity the prehistory and makes it clear that whoever created the confusion in Antioch by demanding circumcision was not authorized by the Jerusalem authorities. The following formula ἔδοξεν ὑμῖν, "it seemed (sc. good) to us," "we have resolved," justifies our describing this as a resolution or decree. For sentences such as "it seemed good to the people and to the city council" occur constantly in the resolutions of magistrates and cities recorded in inscriptions or letters (cf. only the introduction to a decree of honor in Diogenes Laertius 2.142: ἔδοξε τῇ βουλῇ καὶ τῷ δήμῳ, etc.). Moreover, the essential content of 15:25-27, including the resolution formula, is already anticipated in the preceding narrative in 15:22, which begins with, "then it seemed good (ἔδοξε) to the apostles and the elders, with the whole church" (the ἔδοξε is obscured in the NRSV). Striking is finally also the parallel in sentence structure (complex period) and word choice with Luke's prologue in Luke 1:1-4: compare Acts 15:24-25, ἐπειδὴ ἠκούσαμεν . . . ἔδοξεν ἡμῖν with Luke 1:1-3, ἐπειδήπερ . . . ἔδοξε κἀμοί.

The topic of the first resolution is the choice and sending of two emissaries from Jerusalem, which was unanimous according to Acts 15:25b. Barnabas and Paul, who are called "beloved" in v. 25d, are provided for their journey back to Antioch with the two escorts, Judas and Silas (for the idea of four messengers see Chariton, *Callirhoe* 3.4.17: "two envoys from the assembly and two from the council will be sufficient"). A short word of praise or encomium is then spoken about Barnabas and Paul in v. 26: "persons who have risked their lives for the name of our Lord Jesus Christ." The expression "we have sent (ἀπεστάλκαμεν) Judas and Silas" in v. 27a uses an epistolary perfect (similar to an epistolary aorist), which looks back from the perspective of the letter's recipients at the past events of choosing and sending the emissaries, which happened roughly contemporaneously with the writing of

---

[14] What Luke means by Galatia or rather the "Phrygian and Galatian region" is disputed, cf. Acts 16:6; 18:23.

the letter (so that the writers could also have said, "we are send-ing," in the present tense). Also typical of epistolary communica-tion is the additional assignment for these messengers not only to deliver the letter together with Barnabas and Paul, but also to con-firm and clarify "by word of mouth" what is set down in writing.

The second resolution containing the actual decree once again gains a new quality from the fact that the active subject working alongside and behind the apostles and elders in this resolution is the Holy Spirit, according to Acts 15:28 (cf. v. 25): "It seemed good to the Holy Spirit and to us" (cf. the letter of Caesar Augustus in Josephus, *Ant.* 16.163, ἔδοξέ μοι καὶ τῷ ἐμῷ συμ-βουλίῳ, "It seemed good to me and my council," preceded in §162 with a reason introduced by ἐπειδή, as here in Acts 15:24). One could understand this as implying that the authority of the Holy Spirit has been formally usurped by the church leadership, as though they were claiming the Spirit and the authority to speak in his name for themselves alone. But this would certainly be an over-interpretation of the expression in its context, since both the pas-sage and the book as a whole give a somewhat different sense (cf. Shepherd). The Spirit has already made his will known in the book of Acts, and God has worked through him by intervening in his-torical events. The Spirit led the evangelist Philip to the Ethiopian eunuch and transported him away again after his baptism (Acts 8:29, 39). The Spirit led Simon Peter to the Gentile household of Cornelius (Acts 10:19-20; 11:12) and gave himself to Cornelius and the entire group assembled in his house (Acts 10:44-46; 11:15). Who would want to oppose something that was so clearly the pre-rogative of the Spirit (10:47-48)? Likewise the first missionary journey of Paul and Barnabas, in which they began their preaching in Pisidian Antioch in the synagogue but left the city having mainly reached the Gentiles (cf. Acts 13:13-52), was also inspired by the Holy Spirit, who even says so literally in Acts 13:2: "Set apart for me Barnabas and Saul for the work to which I have called them." A Spirit that speaks can also make resolutions and write letters. In Acts 15:28 the apostles and elders are therefore only picking up what Peter had already laid down as the foundation in 15:7-11 by recalling his visit in the house of Cornelius, when God gave the Holy Spirit to the Gentiles. The letter writers thereby confirm that they can recognize the work of the Spirit in the signs of the times and that they are making his decisions their own.

Because the decree focuses on the special conditions in Acts 15:29, the actually more important preceding statement in v. 28b recedes somewhat into the background. Expressed positively, this statement says that no "burden" (βάρος) is to be placed on the former Gentiles. In other words, in their case one can do without circumcision and keeping of the law. What still remains for the Gentiles to do is actually no burden at all, or only a relatively "unburdensome" one (cf. 1 John 5:3, βαρεῖαι οὐκ εἰσίν, "his commandments are not burdensome") that proves to be practically necessary from a certain standpoint (v. 28c). There follows in Acts 15:29a the second of a total of three statements in Acts containing the four clauses of the decree, the first of which has already appeared at the end of James's speech in 15:20 (see above). The third version follows in Acts 21:25, where it is presented as the conclusion of the speech that James and the Jerusalem elders address to Paul during his last Jerusalem visit, "But as for the Gentiles who have become believers, we have sent a letter with our judgment that they should abstain from what has been sacrificed to idols and from blood and from what is strangled and from fornication."

The three versions of the decree, whose text-critical variants need not detain us here (see Exercise 53), differ from one another in details of formulation and sequence. The oldest version may be the one found in the letter in Acts 15:29, because this is also the place where the congruence of the apostolic decree with the law about foreigners in Leviticus 17–18, which forms the background, becomes most evident. For aliens or foreigners who want to live in the land of Israel, Leviticus 17–18 establishes a few minimal regulations. These include, in order, ceasing to offer sacrifices to any demons or powers other than the Lord (Lev 17:7-9), abstaining from eating blood, from which the laws about slaughtering animals are derived (Lev 17:10-14), not eating the cadavers of dead animals (Lev 17:15-16), which relates to the "things strangled" in the apostolic decree, and finally keeping the law about marriage in Leviticus 18. This forbids sexual intercourse within certain degrees of kinship, but it also specifies other sexual sins and applies to aliens as well as native Israelites (cf. Lev 18:26). Because these regulations from Leviticus 17–18 were long since known also to Gentiles who sympathized with Judaism, the final sentence of James's speech in 15:21 has such regulations in view when it says: "For in every city, for generations past, Moses has had those who proclaim him, for he has been read aloud every sabbath in the synagogues."

The laws concerning resident aliens in Leviticus 17–18 have a ritual orientation, which still hovers in the background with the catchword "contamination" or "pollution" (ἀλίσγημα) in James's first mention of the four conditions in Acts 15:20. Contrary to popular opinion, this series of Levitical laws does not yet have anything to do with the so-called seven Noahide laws or commandments. These were first formulated in rabbinic Judaism in the second century CE, and strictly speaking they closely parallel the four provisions of our apostolic decree only in the prohibition of sexual immorality (broadly understood). But the idolatry prohibited in the Noahide commandments is not limited to the eating of meat offered to idols, as in the decree, and abstaining from "blood" in the commandments is understood as abstaining from bloodshed, that is, murder, and not from blood eating (cf. Klaus Müller).

Whereas the Noahide commandments seek to formulate a type of universal ethic for humanity from Jewish roots, the laws for resident aliens in Leviticus 17–18 aim at a peaceful coexistence of a minority of foreigners with the Jewish majority in Israel. However, the challenge facing the apostolic decree goes a great deal beyond both of these and is much more difficult to fulfill. Keeping a minimal set of ritual rules in the areas of meat eating and sexual behavior is supposed to guarantee that Jewish Christians and Gentile Christians can live together in one church and especially that they can have table fellowship with one another. Such a combination lies outside the horizon of Jewish analogies or precedents, and measured by this great task one can still regard these four clauses as relatively liberal. But it should also not be forgotten that the fronts quickly shifted into a situation where a Jewish Christian minority had to use these clauses to fight for their living space and for respect for their traditional religious culture in the midst of an increasingly Gentile Christian majority church. This ultimately proved futile, as we know, even though the decree was originally meant to respect Jewish sensitivities rather than to abandon them (cf. Andresen 234: "Gentile Christians take additional obligations upon themselves so that Jewish Christians could have dealings with them in everyday life without religious disputes").

There is a broad consensus in scholarship that the James clauses of the apostolic decree were not in fact the result of the

Jerusalem apostolic council, which rather met to give approval to the circumcision-free Gentile mission than to debate the particulars of Jewish food sensibilities. That Paul followed these clauses—or rather programmatically decided not to follow them— is improbable. In his arguments about eating meat sacrificed to idols in 1 Corinthians 8–10, he never mentions the apostolic decree, and in Galatians 2:6, 10 he insists emphatically that nothing was laid upon him at the apostolic council other than the collection for the poor in Jerusalem. The James clauses could rather have originated in the wake of the Antioch incident reported in Galatians 2:11-14, which is generally thought to have occurred after the Acts 15 council.[15] This incident shows that dropping the requirement of Gentile circumcision by no means answered all the questions about the coexistence of Jews and Gentiles in mixed Christian congregations. People needed further instructions, such as the apostolic decree. But it is Luke who, in view of this need,

---

15 If, on the other hand, the James clauses in Acts 15:20, 29 that require a relative Gentile purity in matters of food are taken to be historical, then this can be used as an argument for dating the Antioch incident about Jewish and Gentile table fellowship in Galatians 2:11-14, and with it the Letter to the Galatians, before the apostolic council of Acts 15. In this case the council will have met to deal with both of the issues raised in Galatians 2, namely circumcision and dietary laws, as the text of Acts suggests (see also Gal 2:12, where the issues of table fellowship and circumcision go together). This solution harmonizes Galatians with Acts in certain respects. But it also forces Paul's second recorded post-conversion visit to Jerusalem in Galatians 2:1-10 (cf. Gal 1:18-20 with Acts 9:26-30 for the first visit) to be identified with his famine relief visit of Acts 11:27-30, even though its description is too brief to offer many parallels to Galatians 2; this option is chosen mainly to settle issues of chronology (both passages would represent Paul's second post-conversion Jerusalem visit). Most scholars prefer to identify Galatians 2:1-10 with Acts 15 and to deal with Acts 11:27-30 in a number of different ways that need not concern us here. The pre-council date of Galatians also requires the rift caused by the Galatians 2 Antioch incident between Paul on the one hand and Peter and Barnabas on the other to be patched up very quickly to account for their unanimity at the council. Most scholars therefore place this rift after the council and see the superficial split between Paul and Barnabas over the issue of John Mark in Acts 15:36-41 as Luke's reflection of what Paul saw as a deeper and more theological disgreement about Barnabas's "hypocrisy" in Galatians 2:13.

first brought the James clauses into his very cleverly composed story about the apostolic council.

This has consequences not only for the evaluation of James's speech, but also for the explanation of the epistolary form of the decree. But let us stay with the text for now. After the listing of the four clauses in 15:29a, there follows in v. 29b–c the promise that if they keep themselves free from such practices, the addressees will "do well," which is probably the best translation of the Greek phrase εὖ πράξετε. One might also translate it alternatively as "it will go well with you," since in the epistolary prescript in 2 Maccabees 9:19, the phrase εὖ πράττειν is almost synonymous with the health wish ὑγιαίνειν that immediately precedes it (see also the εὖ πράττετε, "may you fare well," in the closing greeting of the letter of consolation in P.Oxy. I 115 in Exercise 46). Nevertheless, for Luke we will perhaps do better to favor the former perspective about "doing well" or "doing what is right," since he is apparently leaning here on an epistolary formulation of the type εὖ ποιεῖτε. The apostolic letter's closing with ἔρρωσθε, "farewell," forms that short wish which Latin speakers translate by *valete*.

In Acts 15:30-35[16] the narrative takes us back again to the starting point, namely Antioch. There the double embassy consisting of Paul and Barnabas on the one hand and Judas and Silas on the other delivers the letter. We learn that Judas and Silas had prophetic abilities and therefore could also have acted as charismatic interpreters of the letter, thus fulfilling their obligation, anchored in the letter itself, to be messengers who would also supplement the letter with oral information. As a result a general mood of joy settles over the church—joy about the possibility of the continued progress of the circumcision-free Gentile mission, and about the new foundation for the common life of the various people groups in the one Christian body.

That the apostolic decree with its four clauses for the Gentiles is older than Luke's book of Acts, that it was meant to be put into practice, and that Luke took it over from church tradition and did not invent it himself is all to be admitted. But as long as one has

---

[16] Acts 15:34, "But it seemed good to Silas to remain there," i.e. in Antioch (rather than to return to Jerusalem), is to be excluded as a text-critically secondary reading that was added to keep Silas in Antioch until the beginning of Paul's second missionary journey, cf. Acts 15:40.

even a modest ability to appreciate the literary techniques that the narrator Luke uses and is also able to fit them into the spectrum of what was usual at his time, one will consider it pointless to look for an older source or foundation for the apostolic letter in Acts 15:23-29. The clothing of the special clauses for the Gentiles in the form of a speech by James and a letter by the apostles and elders is Luke's own work, for which he needed nothing more than a knowledge of the contemporary letter form and the typical language of official documents.

Exercises

52. Compile a synopsis of the three versions of the apostolic decree in Acts 15:20, 29, and 21:25.

53. Attempt to find and evaluate the most important manuscript variants of the apostolic decree in the textual apparatus.

---

2. A Roman Official Letter: Acts 23:26-30

Bibliography 66: R. J. Cassidy, *Society and Politics in the Acts of the Apostles* (Maryknoll, N.Y. 1987) 96–100. – idem, *Paul in Chains: Roman Imprisonment and the Letters of St. Paul* (New York 2001) 211–34. – **O. Eger**, *Rechtsgeschichtliches zum Neuen Testament*, Rektoratsprogramm der Universität Basel für das Jahr 1918 (Basel 1919) 9–11. – **B. Rapske**, *The Book of Acts and Paul in Roman Custody*, The Book of Acts in Its First Century Setting 3 (Grand Rapids 1994) 135–58. – **A. N. Sherwin-White**, *Roman Society and Roman Law in the New Testament* (Oxford 1963; repr. 1969), 48–70, 144–71. – **P. W. Walaskay**, *"And So We Came to Rome": The Political Perspective of St. Luke*, SNTSMS 49 (Cambridge 1983) 52–54. – See also Bib. 64.

To an even greater extent than the letter containing the apostolic decree in Acts 15:23-29, the second letter in Acts 23:26-30 is woven into a larger narrative, here concerning Paul's Roman custody and trial, so that we must go further afield to place it in its context. We begin in Acts 21:27-30—in other words, immediately after James's last quotation of the conditions of the apostolic decree in Acts 21:25, because this is the point (cf. also 24:19) where Jews from the province of Asia (Ephesus?) stir up the crowd in the temple against Paul, thereby unleashing the following chain of events. The ensuing uproar alarmed the Roman troops together with their χιλι- ´αρχος or tribune, literally the leader of a thousand soldiers, but in practice the commander of a cohort (σπεῖρα, Latin *cohors*) of about 600 men (cf. BDAG). The tribune apparently saw Paul as the instigator of the disturbance. In any case he ordered him to be bound with two chains, and because the crowd was threatening his life, the tribune intended to have Paul immediately brought back to the barracks by his soldiers (Acts 21:31-36). But on the temple steps Paul addresses the tribune in the Greek language, which surprises him because he thought Paul was the "the Egyptian who recently stirred up a revolt and led the four thousand assassins (σικάριοι) out into the wilderness" (21:38). Paul asks for permission to speak to the assembled crowd, which he then does in Hebrew or rather Aramaic (22:3-21). But this speech only stirs up the crowd more. At this point Paul is really brought into the barracks, where the tribune wants him examined by flogging to find out why the crowd and was so angry with him (22:24). But at the last moment Paul asks the centurion (ἑκατοντάρχης) who was standing by whether it was legal to flog a Roman citizen who had not been condemned (22:25). Here Paul's Roman citizenship comes to light, and when the tribune hears of it, he is not only astonished but afraid because he has barely escaped overreaching his authority, which could have had disciplinary consequences for him (22:29). He cancels the planned flogging and has Paul released, but not until the next day, when he brings him to stand before the chief priests and the entire Sanhedrin (22:30–23:9). This intermediate measure also proves futile as Paul takes advantage of the famous split between the Pharisees and the Sadducees over the resurrection, and once again the barracks provide his place of refuge (23:10).

We have now sketched most of the situation behind the second letter in Acts, but there is one more step. More than forty Jewish extremists bind themselves by an oath, with which the chief priests and elders secretly conspire, that they will neither eat nor drink until they have killed Paul. Paul is to be led into a trap: the chief priests and the elders are to ask the tribune for another meeting with Paul so that they can reexamine his case, and while Paul is being transported from the barracks to the meeting place, the extremists are to kill the prisoner as the crowd is milling about (23:12-15). As chance would have it, one of Paul's sisters is married in Jerusalem and her son, Paul's nephew, gets wind of the plot and immediately makes it known to his uncle in the Roman barracks (23:16). Paul calls for the young man to be taken by one of the centurions to the tribune, who receives him kindly by taking him by the hand (cf. Haenchen [Bib. 64] 618, following Loisy: "never was a tribune so amiable") and speaks to him in private so as to preserve his anonymity. In his speech the nephew reproduces almost verbatim what we have previously learned from the mouths of the conspirators and the narrative context, and the tribune orders him to strict silence (23:20-22).

The situation seems so perilous to the tribune that he develops a detailed plan to save Paul, which Pervo dubs "Operation Paul" (32). He summons two of his centurions and instructs them to get ready to depart the same night "with two hundred soldiers, seventy horsemen, and two hundred spearmen," as well as with mounts for Paul to ride, in order to bring him safely to the Roman governor (ἡγεμών) Felix in Caesarea on the seacoast (23:23-24). He also writes a cover letter. In introducing it Luke comments: γράψας ἐπιστολὴν ἔχουσαν τὸν τύπον τοῦτον, "He wrote a letter having this *form*" (Acts 23:25). By his use of the word τύπος, "type" or "form," Luke unwittingly reminds us of the *Epistolary Types* (Τύποι Ἐπιστολικοί) of Pseudo-Demetrius (see above chap. 5, part B). Yet the anti-Jewish letter of the Egyptian king Ptolemy Philopater in 3 Maccabees 3:12-29 is also characterized at the end in the same way in which our letter in Acts is introduced: "The letter was written in the above *form* (τύπος)" (3 Macc 3:30), where the "form" can refer to the vocabulary, wording, or general character of the letter. Comparison can also be made with the *Letter of Aristeas*, where a letter of the Egyptian king Ptolemy II Philadelphus is introduced similarly: "The letter of the king was of the following *pattern* (τύπος)" (*Ep. Arist.* 34). (Instead of τύπος, the term τρόπος can be used to similar effect, as in 1 Maccabees 11:29; 15:2 and Josephus, *Ant.* 11.215.)

The first thing we learn from the letter itself in Acts 23:26-30 is the name of the tribune:

26a   Claudius Lysias,
   b   to the most excellent (κρατίστῳ) governor Felix,
   c   greetings (χαίρειν).
27a   This man
   b   was seized by the Jews

c   and was about to be killed by them,
d   but coming with the guard
e   I rescued (him from them),
f   having learned
g   that he was a Roman.
28a   And wanting to know the charge
b   for which they were accusing him,
c   I brought (him) down to their council (συνέδριον).
29a   I found him to be
b   accused concerning questions of their law,
c   but having no accusation deserving death or imprisonment.
30 a   And a plot having been reported to me
b   (as) about to take place against the man,
c   I sent (ἔπεμψα) (him) to you at once,
d   ordering his accusers also
e   to state their charges against him before you.

The conclusion of this episode is quickly narrated in Acts 23:31-35. The soldiers, who with their approximately 470 men make up roughly half of the Roman cohort in Jerusalem, escort Paul in a forced night march to Antipatris, a military post which lay about 60 km from Jerusalem and 40 km from Caesarea on the road between the two cities. From this point the horsemen who are traveling on with Paul are enough, and the foot soldiers return to their barracks in Jerusalem. In Caesarea the troops deliver the letter to the governor Felix and also present Paul before him. Felix asks Paul only what province he belongs to, in order to determine whether he even had jurisdiction over this case, which he appears to have had. Yet he delays the hearing until Paul's accusers have arrived, as announced in the letter of Claudius Lysias. Until then Paul remains under guard in Herod's former headquarters (πραιτώριον), which the governor has since taken over. Later, when the judicial proceedings before Felix have again bogged down, Felix will once again bring "Lysias the tribune" into the picture and delay the matter until he comes down to Caesarea to make a personal statement (24:22).

The letter, which a few manuscripts have augmented by supplying the lacking closing greeting ἔρρωσο, shows itself on closer examination to be a masterpiece of the psychological narrative art. The honorary address of the governor with κράτιστε as "the *most excellent* governor Felix" or "his Excellency" corresponds to the Latin expression *egregie* or *optime*. (The same form is used in the prologue to Luke's Gospel to address the dedicatee as *"most excellent* Theophilus" [Luke 1:3]). Claudius Lysias not only presents the past course of events in abbreviated form; he also reveals a pronounced tendency to color the picture positively when it comes to his own behavior. That Paul was a Roman citizen is something that Claudius Lysias first learned only later; it was not, as Acts 23:27 suggests, his initial reason for sending in the troops to rescue Paul. Strictly speaking he also did not want to rescue Paul from any danger, but rather to take him into custody because he regarded him as the main ringleader of the uprising. He is discreetly silent about the fact that he just barely escaped subjecting Paul to flogging and left him languishing in chains for too long, because he wants to avoid exposing himself to punishment for abuse of power against a Roman citizen. Moreover, in his dealings with the Sanhedrin, Claudius Lysias by no means proceeded in such a deliberate and well-planned manner as it appears in vv. 28-29. It is also almost a miracle that he gained the impression from the Sanhedrin's clamorous discussion in Hebrew that the debate concerned only inner-Jewish controversies about the interpretation of the law, but not the questions of public safety and order for which alone he was responsible as a Roman official. His reaction as recorded in the letter is nevertheless similar to that of Gallio who, as Roman proconsul of Achaia, told Paul's Jewish accusers that he did not want to get involved in inner-Jewish disputes because he was not responsible for such matters as a Roman judge (Acts 18:14-15). Yet in the same breath Claudius Lysias gives an official declaration of innocence for Paul in v. 29b, just as Herod and Pilate do for Jesus in the passion story of Luke's Gospel (Luke 23:4, 13, 15, 22). When the tribune says in his letter that Paul was charged with "nothing deserving death or imprisonment" (v. 29b), he goes strictly beyond the results of his preliminary investigation and anticipates a possible later judgment which he did not in fact reach.

Without naming his informant, Claudius Lysias briefly but correctly summarizes the plot against Paul and his reaction of sending Paul to Caesarea in Acts 23:30. The verb ἔπεμψα, "I sent," in v. 30c is itself an epistolary aorist, and as such it already represents the time perspective of the reader rather than that of the sender. But the verb tenses begin to blur even more in v. 30d, where the aorist participle παραγγείλας (here translated by the English present participle *"ordering* his accusers also"), which is dependent on ἔπεμψα, suggests that Claudius Lysias told Paul's accusers to go to Caesarea with their complaints no later than the time when he sent Paul there with this letter, thus acting with foresight once again. In fact this is the last thing he would have done, since the night transport of Paul was arranged "immediately" (ἐξαυτῆς) precisely to keep it a secret from these accusers. He thus presents as already accomplished something that he must have done only later, after Paul arrived in Caesarea. But the narrative does not go into these details, and in v. 35 the governor takes the letter at face value by promising Paul a hearing only after his accusers arrive, which in fact they do five days later, when the high priest Ananias, some of the elders, and the attorney Tertullus arrive to bring their charges against Paul. The letter thus serves to advance the story and to supply a key that was missing in narrative presentation.

The letter casts a slight shadow on the otherwise largely positive character sketch that the narrative develops of the Roman tribune Claudius Lysias, and the positive light in which the Roman authorities usually appear in Luke because of their correct response to Jewish-Christian controversies proves somewhat deceptive. Obviously, the narrator wants us to understand, the Roman side was thoroughly pursuing its own interests, and it was most important for it to save face outwardly. A person caught up in these events such as Paul could speak of luck when there was a more or less accidental congruence between what was best for him and the interests of the representatives of Roman power. The unusually fine tuning between the letter and the narrative context makes it hopeless to try to discern any authentic *libellus* of Claudius Lysias in the background. No one wrote this letter other than the author of Acts, and it never existed in any other form than as a part of this larger narrative. Or as Pervo puts it, "The letter of Claudius to Felix is likewise an invention, based upon neither data nor probability but wish" (77).[17]

---

[17] This is not to deny that Paul was ever transferred from one prison to another or that Roman official letters could have accompanied him on such occasions. But it is to deny that the author of Acts had access to them.

Epilogue

Bibliography 67 (texts and translations of the Apostolic Fathers): **J. B. Lightfoot**, *The Apostolic Fathers*, 2 parts in 5 vols. (London and New York, ²1890, ²1889). Part I: *S. Clement of Rome. A Revised Text with Introductions, Notes, Dissertations, and Translations*, 2 vols. (²1890). Part II: *S. Ignatius. S. Polycarp. Revised Texts with Introductions, Notes, Dissertations, and Translations*, 3 vols. (²1889). – **K. Lake**, *The Apostolic Fathers*, LCL, 2 vols. (1912–1913). – New edition: **B. D. Ehrman**, *The Apostolic Fathers*, LCL, 2 vols. (2003). – **M. W. Holmes**, *The Apostolic Fathers: Greek Texts and English Translations*, updated ed. (Grand Rapids ²1999). – idem, *The Apostolic Fathers in English* (Grand Rapids ³2006) (translations only). – **A. Lindemann** and **H. Paulsen**, eds., *Die Apostolischen Väter: Griechisch-deutsche Parallelausgabe* (Tübingen 1992). – **G. Schneider**, *Clemens von Rom: Epistola ad Corinthios = Brief an die Korinther*, Fontes Christiani 15 (Freiburg i.Br. 1994). – **TLG texts:** *1 Clement:* **A. Jaubert**, *Clément de Rome: Épître aux Corinthiens*, SC 167 (Paris 1971) 98–204. – *2 Clement:* **K. Bihlmeyer**, *Die apostolischen Väter: Neubearbeitung der Funkschen Ausgabe* (Tübingen ³1970 [= repr. of ²1956]) 71–81. – Ignatius, the seven authentic letters: **P. T. Camelot**, *Ignace d'Antioche, Polycarpe de Smyrne: Lettres. Martyre de Polycarpe*, SC 10 (Paris ⁴1969) 56–154. – Ignatius, six inauthentic letters (*Epistulae interpolatae et epistulae suppositiciae*): **F. Diekamp** and **F. X. Funk**, *Patres apostolici*, vol. 2 (Tübingen ³1913) 83–268. – Polycarp, *Philippians:* **K. Bihlmeyer**, *Die apostolischen Väter* (as above) 114–20. – *Martyrdom of Polycarp:* **H. A. Musurillo**, *The Acts of the Christian Martyrs* (Oxford 1972) 2–20. – *Epistle of Barnabas:* **R. A. Kraft**, *Épître de Barnabé*, SC 172 (Paris 1971) 72–218. – *Epistle to Diognetus:* **H.-I. Màrrou**, *À Diognète*, SC 33 bis (Paris ²1965) 52–84.

Bibliography 68: **J. G. Altman**, *Epistolarity: Approaches to a Form* (Bib. 8) 137–38, 189–90. – **A. Brent**, *Ignatius of Antioch and the Second Sophistic: A Study of an Early Christian Transformation of Pagan Culture*, Studien und

Texte zu Antike und Christentum 36 (Tübingen 2006). – **W. G. Doty**, *Letters in Primitive Christianity* (Bib. 4) 71–81. – **D. A. Hagner**, *The Use of the Old and New Testaments in Clement of Rome*, NovTSup 34 (Leiden 1973). – **C. E. Hill**, *From the Lost Teaching of Polycarp Identifying Irenaeus' Apostolic Presbyter and the Author of "Ad Diognetum,"* WUNT 186 (Tübingen 2006). – **M. Isaacson**, *To Each Their Own Letter: Structures, Themes, and Rhetorical Strategies in the Letters of Ignatius of Antioch*, ConBNT 42 (Stockholm 2004). – **C. N. Jefford**, *The Apostolic Fathers: An Essential Guide* (Nashville 2005). – **A. Lindemann**, *Die Clemensbriefe*, Apostolischen Väter 1; HNT 17 (Tübingen 1992). – **H. E. Lona**, *Der erste Clemensbrief*, Kommentar zu den Apostolischen Vätern 2 (Göttingen 1998). – **A. J. Malherbe**, *"'Seneca' on Paul as Letter Writer,"* in B. A. Pearson, ed., *The Future of Early Christianity: Essays in Honor of H. Koester* (Minneapolis 1991) 414–21. – **J. Michl**, *"Briefe, apokryphe,"* *Lexikon für Theologie und Kirche*[2] 2 (1958) 688–93. – **P. Müller**, *"Der Glaube aus dem Hören über das gesprochene und das geschriebene Wort bei Paulus,"* in L. Bormann, K. Del Tredici, and A. Standhartinger, eds., *Religious Propaganda and Missionary Competition in the New Testament World: Essays in Honor of Dieter Georgi*, NovTSup 74 (Leiden 1994) 405–42. – **R. Reck**, *Kommunikation und Gemeindeaufbau* (Bib. 7) 162–64, 199–217. – **J. M. Robinson**, ed., *The Nag Hammadi Library in English* (Leiden [4]1996). – **W. Schneemelcher**, ed., *New Testament Apocrypha*, 2 vols., vol. 2: *Writings Relating to the Apostles. Apocalypses and Related Literature*, trans. R. McL. Wilson (Louisville [2]1992). – **W. R. Schoedel**, *Ignatius of Antioch: A Commentary on the Letters of Ignatius of Antioch*, Hermeneia (Philadelphia 1985). – **H. J. Sieben**, *"Die Ignatianen als Briefe: Einige formkritische Bemerkungen,"* *Vigiliae christianae* 32 (1978) 1–18. – **H. Weder**, *Neutestamentliche Hermeneutik*, Zürcher Grundrisse zur Bibel (Zürich [2]1989) 314–25.

The body of our work on *Ancient Letters and the New Testament* concludes with the canonical letters of the New Testament. But this is precisely the point where the interesting history of other early Christian letter literature begins. There is even some chronological overlap, for the pseudepigraphical letter of 2 Peter is to be dated in the early second century, after the letter of church at Rome to the Corinthians known as *1 Clement*, which is usually dated in the last decade of the first century. This letter is in turn the earliest document and the first listed in modern collections of the Apostolic Fathers. As we have already seen in the introduction to chapter 4, most of the documents in this collection are letters: *1 Clement* is immediately followed by another "letter" known as *2 Clement*, which is actually more of a homily (like Hebrews), then by the seven letters of Ignatius, Polycarp's *Letter to the Philippians*, the *Epistle of Barnabas* attributed to the well-known companion of Paul, and the particularly puzzling *Epistle to Diognetus*, an apologetic document that is the latest in the collection (late second century).

The extent to which the documents of the Apostolic Fathers incorporate formal letter features and topoi beyond the prescript (on which see above, pp. 104–5 n. 2) and postscript must be judged from case to case. Even the classification of a document as a letter (or otherwise) can be partly a matter of custom or convention. Hence the *Epistle to Diognetus* is classified as a letter because of its traditional title and its dedicatory address to Diognetus, whereas another document of the Apostolic Fathers not listed as letter above in the light of its English title, the *Martyrdom of Polycarp*, is recognized as a letter by its Latin title, *Epistula ecclesiae Smyrnensis de martyrio sancti Polycarpi* (TLG). It is framed as a letter from the church of Smyrna to the church of Philomelium (see Exercise 52).

The critical issues in the letters of the Apostolic Fathers are not dissimilar to the issues we have encountered elsewhere in this book. In chapter 4 we saw that letters that have been passed down by literary means often stand in letter collections which, once formed, are also open to expansion by spurious additions. It is no different here. Collections of the letters of Ignatius, for example, have included, in addition to the seven authentic letters (to *Polycarp* and to the *Ephesians, Magnesians, Smyrnaeans, Philadelphians, Romans,* and *Trallians*) also the following six spurious letters: *Mary to Ignatius, Ignatius to Mary, Tarsians, Philippians, Antiochenes,* and *Hero.*[1] The question of the authenticity of the standard seven Ignatian letters has also come up for renewed discussion.[2]

---

[1] Texts in Diekamp and Funk, *Patres apostolici*, 2:83–268; translations in Lightfoot, *Apostolic Fathers*, part II/3, pp. 125–273 (interspersed with translations of the authentic letters).

[2] Particularly in the *Zeitschrift für Antikes Christentum* (*ZAC*). The first fascicle of this periodical saw the publication of R. M. Hübner, "Thesen zur Echtheit und Datierung der sieben Briefe des Ignatius von Antiochien," *ZAC* 1.1 (1997) 44–72. Reactions to Hübner in the same periodical over the next two years came from A. Lindemann, "Antwort auf die 'Thesen zur Echtheit und Datierung der sieben Briefe des Ignatius von Antiochien,'" *ZAC* 1.2 (1997) 185–94; G. Schöllgen, "Die Ignatianen als pseudepigraphisches Briefcorpus: Anmerkung zu den

In the writings known as the New Testament Apocrypha (cf. Schneemelcher), the letter genre recedes somewhat into the background as compared with the Apostolic Fathers. The writers of this literature rather took their lead from the characteristic larger genres of the New Testament: the Gospels, Acts, and the Apocalypse. Nevertheless, we still find here an *Epistle to the Laodiceans* attributed to Paul, a fictive letter exchange between Paul and Seneca (cf. Malherbe),[3] another between Abgar of Edessa and Jesus, a letter attributed to Titus (Pseudo-Titus), a *Third Letter of Paul to the Corinthians* as part of the *Acts of Paul* (Schneemelcher 2:255–56), a letter of Pilate to the emperor Claudius in the *Acts of Peter and Paul* (note the anachronism), and letters of Peter and Clement to James in the introductory matter to the Pseudo-Clementine literature—not to mention the other scattered epistolary elements such as letter in the Hymn of the Pearl in the *Acts of Thomas* (108–13) that first receives wings and becomes an eagle, then is transformed into a speech upon reaching its recipient,[4] and finally leads him home by its light. A Marcionite letter of Paul to the Alexandrians, mentioned only in the Muratorian Canon (*l.* 64; see above Exercise 39), is not extant, and the *Epistula Apostolorum* or *Epistle of the Apostles* is, despite its name, not a letter of the twelve apostles at all, but the designation for an alleged revelation of Jesus to his apostles in dialogue form.

Thesen von Reinhard M. Hübner," *ZAC* 2.1 (1998) 16–25; M. J. Edwards, "Ignatius and the Second Century: An Answer to R. Hübner," *ZAC* 2.2 (1998) 214–26; H. J. Vogt, "Bemerkungen zur Echtheit der Ignatiusbriefe," *ZAC* 3.1 (1999) 50–63. See further B. Cline and T. Thompson, "Ignatius Redux: Bart Ehrman on Ignatius and His Letters," *JR* 86.3 (2006).

[3] Cf. also I. Ramelli, "L'epistolario apocrifo Seneca-san Paolo: alcune osservazioni," *Vetera Christiana* 34 (1997) 299–310; G. G. Gamba, "Il carteggio tra Seneca e San Paolo. Il 'problema' della sua autenticità," *Salesianum* 60 (1998) 209–50; A. Fürst, "Pseudepigraphie und Apostolizität im apokryphen Briefwechsel zwischen Seneca und Paulus," *JAC* 41 (1999) 41–67; P. Berry, *Correspondence between Paul and Seneca*, Ancient Near Eastern Texts and Studies 12 (Lewiston, N.Y. 1999).

[4] *Acts of Thomas* 111 (Hymn of the Pearl, lines 51–52): "It flew in the form of an eagle, The king of <all> birds, It flew and alighted beside me And became all speech" (Schneemelcher 2:382).

Several tractates of the gnostic Coptic Nag Hammadi Codices (NHC) discovered at Nag Hammadi in Upper Egypt (cf. Robinson) display letter features or are designated as letters. Hence we encounter an *Epistola Jacobi apocrypha* or *Apocryphon of James* with an epistolary opening (NHC I/2),[5] a *Treatise on the Resurrection* addressed to a certain Rheginus (NHC I/4), a tractate known as *Eugnostos the Blessed* with an epistolary opening (NHC III/3),[6] and a *Letter of Peter to Philip* (NHC VIII/2).[7]

This brings us to the church fathers, including, for example, the three Cappadocians[8] Basil the Great,[9] Gregory Nazianzus,[10] and Gregory of Nyssa,[11] John Chrysostom,[12] and the Latin writers

[5] Epistolary opening: "James writes to [. . .]: Peace be with you from Peace, love from Love, grace from Grace, faith from Faith, life from Holy Life!"

[6] "Eugnostos, the Blessed, to those who are his. Rejoice in this, that you know. Greetings!"

[7] Title: "The Letter of Peter which he sent to Philip." Opening: "Peter, the apostle of Jesus Christ, to Philip, our beloved brother and our fellow apostle, and (to) the brethren who are with you: greetings!" There is no epistolary closing.

[8] G. A. Barrois, *The Fathers Speak: St Basil the Great, St Gregory of Nazianzus, St Gregory of Nyssa. Selected Letters and Life-Records* (Crestwood, N.Y. 1986).

[9] R. J. Defarrari, *Saint Basil: The Letters*, LCL, 4 vols. (1926–1934); Y. Courtonne, *Saint Basile: Lettres*, 3 vols. (Paris 1957–1966), with 366 letters (TLG).

[10] P. Gallay, *Saint Grégoire de Nazianze: Lettres*, 2 vols. (Paris 1964, 1967), with 249 letters and idem, *Grégoire de Nazianze: Lettres théologiques*, SC 208 (Paris 1974), with three letters (101–3) (both TLG). *St. Gregory of Nazianzus: On God and Christ. The Five Theological Orations and Two Letters to Cledonius* (Crestwood, N.Y. 2002), with the letters to Cledonius (Letters 101–2) translated by L. Wickham.

[11] P. Maraval, *Grégoire de Nysse: Lettres*, SC 363 (Paris 1990); R. Criscuolo, *Gregorio di Nissa: Epistole*, Quaderni di Koinonia 6 (Naples 1981); G. Pasquali, *Gregorii Nysseni opera*, vol. 8.2 (Leiden ²1959) 3–95, with 31 letters (TLG); Migne, PG 46:1101–8, letter to Evagrius the monk; p. 1112, to Philip the monk (TLG); Migne, PG 45:221–36, *Epistula canonica ad Letoium* (TLG).

[12] *NPNF*¹, vol. 9: *St. Chrysostom: On the Priesthood; Ascetic Treatises; Select Homilies and Letters; Homilies on the Statutes;* W. Mayer with B. Neil, *St. John Chrysostom: The Cult of the Saints: Select Homilies and Letters*

Augustine[13] and Jerome,[14] who also exchanged letters with each other.[15] All these ministered to others not least through their extensive correspondence, as the substantial volumes of letters in their collected works testify.[16] But it is an earlier church father to whom we wish to draw attention here. This is Dionysius of Alexandria, who served as bishop of Corinth at the end of the second century. Eusebius reports (*Hist. eccl.* 4.23.1–13) that he used his position to send "general epistles" (καθολικαὶ ἐπιστολαί) to churches all over the Mediterranean world. He addressed one to the Lacedemonians as "an instruction in orthodoxy on the subject of peace and unity," one to the Athenians as "a call to faith and to life according to the gospel," one to the Nicomedians "in which he

---

(Crestwood, N.Y. 2006); Migne, PG 52:623–748, letters 18–242 (TLG); J. Dumortier, *Jean Chrysostome: A Théodore*, SC 117 (Paris 1966) 46–78, 80–218 (TLG); A.-M. Malingrey, *Jean Chrysostome: Lettres à Olympias*, SC 13 (Paris 1968) 106–388 (TLG); P. G. Nicolopoulos, "Τοῦ ἐν ἁγίοις πατρὸς ἡμῶν Ἰωάννου τοῦ Χρυσοστόμου ἐπιστολὴ πρὸς μοναχούς," Αἱ εἰς τὸν Ἰωάννην τὸν Χρυσόστομον ἐσφαλμένως ἀποδιδόμεναι ἐπιστολαί (Athens 1973) 481–93 (TLG).

[13] W. Parsons, *Saint Augustine: Letters*, 6 vols., FC 12, 18, 20, 30, 32, 81 (New York and Washinton, D.C. 1951–1989); *NPNF*[1], vol. 1: *The Confessions and Letters of St. Augustin*; D. D. Doyle, *The Bishop as Disciplinarian in the Letters of St. Augustine*, Patristic Studies 4 (New York 2002).

[14] *NPNF*[2], vol. 6: *St. Jerome: Letters and Select Works* (1893); L. Schade, *Des heiligen Kirchenvaters Eusebius Hieronymus ausgewählte Briefe*, 2 vols., Bibliothek der Kirchenväter 2/16, 18 (Munich 1936–1937; repr. 1968).

[15] A. Fürst, *Augustinus-Hieronymus Epistulae mutuae = Briefwechsel*, Fontes Christiani (Turnhout 2002); idem, *Augustins Briefwechsel mit Hieronymus*, JAC, Ergänzungsband 29 (Münster 1999); R. Hennings, *Der Briefwechsel zwischen Augustinus und Hieronymus und ihr Streit um den Kanon des Alten Testaments und die Auslegung von Gal. 2,11-14*, Vigiliae christianae Sup. 21 (Leiden 1994); B. Conring, *Hieronymus als Briefschreiber: Ein Beitrag zur spätantiken Epistolographie*, Studien und Texte zu Antike und Christentum 8 (Tübingen 2001). See also S. Mratschek, *Der Briefwechsel des Paulinus von Nola: Kommunikation und soziale Kontakte zwischen christlichen Intellektuellen*, Hypomnemata 134 (Göttingen 2002).

[16] The *NPNF*[2] series also includes selected letters of Athansius (vol. 4) and Ambrose (vol. 10).

combats the heresy of Marcion," and one to the Cretan dioceses, with special praise for their bishop Philip. In his letter to the church of Cnossus, Dionysius exhorts the local bishop Pinytos "not to put on the brethren a heavy compulsory burden concerning chastity," while in his letter to the Romans he confirms that the letter of their former bishop Clement (i.e., *1 Clement*) is still being read by the Corinthian church. There is also a negative result of his letter-writing ministry that Dionysius laments, namely the falsification of his own letters and outright forgeries: "the apostles of the devil have filled them [sc. my letters] with tares, by leaving out some things and putting in others" (§12). On the whole we do not know how the communities that Dionysius addressed responded to his friendly advice and exhortations. Perhaps they saw the letters as meddling in their own internal affairs. But we do have at least one clear example of a response. Bishop Pinytos of Cnossus is happy to receive letters and advice from Dionysius, but he also offers his own advice in return: "he exhorted him in turn to provide at some time more solid food, and to nourish the people under him with a more advanced letter, so that they might not be fed continually on milky words" (§8).

The dominance of the letter genre in early Christianity and—to return to our theme—in the New Testament requires an explanation. From one perspective we can interpret it purely pragmatically. Early Christianity made use of this tried and tested means to keep the lines of communication between the traveling missionaries and the communities they founded from being severed, to establish links between widely scattered churches, and to work through problems and questions as they came up in order finally to spread the Christian message even further. Letter writing was placed in the service of the gospel and its proclamation, and also in the service of the development and establishment of gospel-oriented ways of life.

In serving this role, however, the letter also participates in the two-sidedness of the gospel as a proclaimed and proclaiming entity: The gospel is communicative in its very nature and has a communication-initiating effect (cf. Reck). It is communicative by nature because even in terms of lexical semantics, it has the fundamental structure of a message, with "gospel" meaning nothing other than "good news" or, in the profane language of antiquity, the news about a victory finally won. Such a message expects to be shared and passed on. The gospel has the effect of initiating communication because its content possesses an enormous internal dynamic which, when released, provides the initial spark, setting off the chain reaction that leads to the formation of new relationships. That an ancient means of communication par excellence was used in the process is only too understandable. The sense that there might be "an inner affinity between the gospel itself and the form of epistolary proclamation" (Weder 314) is therefore fully justified.

We can also take this a step further and draw in the literary form of the Gospels. The letter, as we have repeatedly observed, counts as half of a dialogue and as a form of the presence of one who is absent. Yet neither of these statements can be taken entirely literally, and each must be placed in the half-fictional realm. The true dialogue depends on immediate feedback; the letter imitates such a dialogue situation only in written form. Sometimes a letter allows its addressee to come to expression through quotations or paraphrases of his or her remarks so that it incorporates multiple voices, but its ability to transfer this dialogue back to the reader is limited, and feedback effects are only partially possible and require time. The absence of one's correspondent is not only overcome by the letter but is also made conscious and reflected upon. The spatial distance is overlaid and intensified by the typical epistolary phase delay, by the temporal distance between writing and reception. This also creates the necessary presupposition, as we have seen, for the apostles to come to expression after their death through pseudepigraphal letters, which in their own way make the distance conscious and seek to overcome it. But both these factors are also encountered in varied form the Gospels, understood as literary entitles and as results of a traditioning process: they carry on a dialogue with a certain addressee group in a particular situation, a dialogue that can be reflected only very indirectly and brokenly in a narrative text. By the way they allow Jesus to be presented as the earthly and the risen one, the Gospels reflect the dialectic of presence and absence, of the presence of the Lord experienced in spirit and of the painfully felt temporal distance from him.

It is not by accident that the most influential letter writer of antiquity, despite Cicero's impressive correspondence, was an early Christian author, the Apostle Paul. In dealing with a particular issue, namely his change of travel plans, Paul also expresses more fundamentally the hope that he attaches to all his letters but that also stands under an eschatological reservation:

> For we write you nothing other than what you can read (ἀναγινώσκετε) and also understand (ἐπιγινώσκετε); I hope you will understand (ἐπιγνώσεσθε) until the end—as you have already understood (ἐπέγνωτε) us in part—that on the day of the Lord Jesus we are your boast even as you are our boast. (2 Cor 1:13-14)

Letters articulate relationships. This means that understanding letters aims at a mutual understanding of persons and hearts, even if this can only be approximated under present conditions and complete understanding will remain reserved for the future time of consummation.

Exercise

54. Determine the epistolary features of the *Martyrdom of Polycarp* using one of the texts or translations listed in Bibliography 67, e.g., Ehrman, *The Apostolic Fathers*, vol. 1:366–401.

Answer Key

Exercise 1

Words for letters in English and German. It is not immediately obvious from the German word for a letter, *Brief*, that such a document should also be "brief" in the English sense (or *kurz* in the German), but in fact both words go back to the Latin *brevis (libellus)*, "a brief (writing)." There are many ways of filling out the phrases "letter of ____" or "____ letter." While some English letter types can only be designated by the latter format, e.g. "cover letter," others are more often attested in the former word order, hence "letter of agreement" and "letter of inquiry" are more common than "agreement letter" and "inquiry letter." Other common expressions for letter types include the acceptance letter, apology letter, application letter, business letter, complaint letter, congratulation letter, friendly letter, invitation letter, love letter, newsletter, prayer letter, recommendation letter, and rejection letter.

Exercise 2

The fate of letter writing today. According to H. Belke, *Literarische Gebrauchsformen*, 156 n. 21 (with reference to G. Jappe, "Vom Briefwechsel zum Schriftwechsel," *Merkur* 23 [1969] 351–62), the perfecting of the postal service has contributed to the decline of the letter, because during previous times of less frequent postal delivery, people knew how use this precious medium with greater care. Belke adds that the letter remained "a highly respected literary form governed by rhetorical and stylistic norms and rules well into the eighteenth century. Letter writing was considered an art, like poetry and oratory. . . . The increasing subjectivity of literary expression associated with the general retreat of normative poetics, especially in the romantic period, was naturally destined to have a great effect on the letter as the most personal form of communication." Finally the many new possibilities for communication also played their role in the decline of the letter. The quotation in Exercise 2 comes from T. W. Adorno in W. Benjamin, ed., *Deutsche Menschen: Eine Folge von Briefen ausgewählt und eingeleitet* (Frankfurt a.M. 1962) 128 (see Belke 156–57 for all these materials).

Exercise 3

Sample Letter: Determination of Context. This is in fact the last letter of Dietrich Bonhoeffer, which he wrote to his parents from prison on January 17, 1945, not long before his execution on April 9, 1945. The text may be found in D. Bonhoeffer, *Widerstand und Ergebung: Briefe und Aufzeichnungen aus der Haft*, ed. E. Bethge (Munich 1955) 276; the translation is from Bonhoeffer, *Letters and Papers from Prison*, rev. ed., ed. E. Bethge, trans. R. Fuller (London and New York ³1967) 222. The character of letters as a substitute for conversation is forcefully expressed in this context: "I read my letters here till I know them by heart." Some of Bonhoeffer's expressions have been the common stock of letters since ancient times, e.g., "I am getting on all right" and "Do keep well" (see below). Also distressing in the prison context is Bonhoeffer's reminder about the matches, wash cloths, and towel and his request for toothpaste, coffee beans, and books. As a comparison from the New Testament 2 Tim 4:13 immediately comes to mind, where "Paul" writes to his pupil: "When you come, bring the cloak that I left with Carpus at Troas, also the books, and above all the parchments."

Exercise 4

Theon to Theon, Greetings (P.Oxy. I 119). The translation is from P. A. Rosenmeyer, *Ancient Epistolary Fictions* (Bib. 2) 33; for the text and further commentary see, e.g., A. Deissmann, *Light from the Ancient East* (Bib. 1) 201–4. The father Theon has not taken his little son Theon along with him on his river journey from Oxyrhynchus to the great city of Alexandria, and he has furthermore sought to disguise his departure as representing a less extensive trip—all of which his son, who has since caught on to the deception, now protests vociferously and with broken grammar in this letter (as the notes to the text of the exercise show). Yet as Rosenmeyer notes, "even in this basic message, a piece of epistolary blackmail, the young Theon shows a startling familiarity with epistolary convention" (34). Thus he knows the letter formula with a formal prescript (*l.* 1) and a closing wish for well-being (*l.* 16), which here stands in place of the concluding greetings and is also followed by the date. The expression καλῶς ἐποίησας, "you did a fine thing," used ironically in *ll.* 2 and 11, is also a typical epistolary formula (see below on 3 John 6). Furthermore recognizable is the epistolary request by means of παρακαλῶ in *ll.* 13-14, which together with the accompanying threat in *ll.* 14-15 forms the body closing. A discreet proem is not so easy to discern, but we could possibly point to Theon's refusal to extend to his father a health wish in *l.* 5. Also noteworthy is the massive threat of a total cutoff of communication in *ll.* 4-7 and the reference to the affected third parties, the boy's mother and brother, in *ll.* 9-10. The gifts that the father has sent in the meantime to appease the boy are only treated with contempt in *ll.* 11-12. Here we also find in *l.* 17 the indication of the date that we have so far missed in the Apion letters and our other examples.

Exercise 5

Philemon: Epistolary Analysis. The letter opening in Philemon 1-7 includes the prescript and the proem. The prescript in vv. 1-3 with the sender, addressee, and greeting is constructed somewhat differently from the other prescripts we have encountered so far and is also more extensive (but see 2 John 1–3). In v. 7 the thanksgiving and expression of joy represent motifs that are at home in the letter proem.

The letter closing is more difficult to determine. Several considerations favor limiting it to vv. 21-25. Paul's expression of his confidence in Philemon's cooperation in the matter of Onesimus in v. 21 (combined with a reflection on the act of writing) and his additional request that Philemon prepare a guest room for his planned visit in v. 22 correspond to the proem and can therefore be designated as an epilogue. The postscript of vv. 23-25, analogous to the prescript, offers greetings from Paul's co-workers in vv. 23-24 and a concluding grace benediction in v. 25 (cf. Gal 6:10; Phil 4:23).

Verses 8-20 remain for the letter body, which is organized around an epistolary request. This is first prepared for by the self-recommendation in vv. 8-9, which functions as the body opening, and is then introduced in v. 10 with παρακαλῶ. The body closing is found in vv. 17-20 with its intensified repetition of the request that Philemon should allow Onesimus to return to Paul. This involves Paul in formulaic judicial language that obligates him to make financial restitution for Onesimus's debts if necessary according to vv. 18-19. From this point Paul appears to have continued the letter in his own hand. See further the literature in Bibliography 44 on Philemon.

Exercise 6

Paraleipomena Jeremiou *6:19-20 in the* OTP *(or 6:16-17 in the numbering of Harris and Herzer).* The book with the title *Paraleipomena Jeremiou,* i.e., "Things Omitted from Jeremiah," also referred to as *4 Baruch,* is one of the Jewish writings from the postbiblical Greco-Roman period. Its origin is to be placed in the period between the first and second Jewish revolts against Rome, i.e., roughly between 70 and 136 CE. The writing contains a legend about the prophet Jeremiah and his scribe Baruch in the wake of the first destruction of Jerusalem and the Babylonian exile. For the moment we may simply note that Baruch's procurement of paper and ink from the marketplace serves the purpose of writing a letter to Jeremiah in the Babylonian captivity. But we may also observe Baruch's epistolary prescript with the imperative χαῖρε, "Hail" or "Be greeted" instead of the usual infinitive χαίρειν. Although the existing editions of the Greek text with translation were out of print when the German edition of this work was published in 1998, we are now in a much better position with the recent publication by J. Herzer, *4 Baruch (Paraleipomena Jeremiou)*, SBL Writings from the Greco-Roman World 22 (Atlanta 2005). The translation used in the text of this exercise is that of S. E. Robinson in *OTP* 2:413–25, here 421. See further chap. 6, sec. B.3 with Bibliography 34.

Exercise 7

Aspects of Paul's letter writing practice in Romans, Galatians, and 1 Corinthians. According to Rom 16:22, Paul dictated Romans to a scribe named Tertius, who takes the opportunity to add a greeting of his own (of the first person type). The letter may have been written in Corinth, since the name "Gaius" given to a host of Paul in Romans 16:23 is also found in 1 Corinthians 1:14. That Paul should have dictated the long letter to the Romans syllable by syllable is hard to imagine. Perhaps Tertius was a skilled tachygrapher or shorthand writer, and maybe the fact that these skills were at Paul's disposal is one of the reasons why Romans became such a long letter (cf. Richards, *Secretary* [Bib. 4] 171).

Galatians too has obviously been dictated by Paul. He grabs the pen himself only for a postscript beginning in 6:11 (cf. 1 Cor 16:21; Philm 19; Col 4:18; 2 Thess 3:17). This note that he is writing in his own hand probably extends to the end of the letter in Galatians 6:11-18. That he writes with "large letters" should probably not be taken as a proof of an eye disease of Paul, as is occasionally done in exegesis.

On purely formal grounds, Sosthenes is introduced as a co-sender of 1 Corinthians in 1 Corinthians 1:1. Does this mean that he was also a co-author of the letter in the strict sense? And what about the other letters in which Paul names a co-sender? The question about a co-sender as co-author is usually answered in the negative, but it certainly deserves further consideration; cf. the full treatment in J. Murphy-O'Connor, *Paul* (Bib. 4) 16–34.

Exercise 8

Ancient dinner invitations in P.Köln 57 (Exercise 8) and in P.Oxy. I 110 and 111 (Introduction). These notes of invitation all lack a prescript with address and greeting. Most probably the messenger who delivered them greeted each guest orally and then read the invitation. In P.Köln 57 we have a peculiarity. This time it is the god himself (represented by a priest) who invites his guests in writing to a meal in his temple. Cf. C. H. Kim, "The Papyrus Invitation," *JBL* 94 (1975) 391–402.

Exercise 9

Letter from Gaius to Petronius (Josephus, War 2.203). Gaius is the emperor Caligula, Petronius the Roman legate of Syria. Petronius has delayed the execution of Caligula's command to erect a huge statue of himself in the Jerusalem temple, because he knew what this would mean for his Jewish subjects and how they would react. Therefore the emperor is angry, and he sends Petronius a death warrant or the order to commit suicide. But while this letter is underway, Caligula falls victim to an assassination in 41 CE. Petronius is on the lucky side. The news of Caligula's death arrives earlier than the other menacing letter.

Exercise 10

"Do we need letters of recommendation?" (2 Cor 3:1-3). Opponents of Paul have gained access to the Corinthian community by means of letters of recommendation that were issued by other local churches. Paul rejects this practice; he does not need this kind of help. Paul uses multi-layered imagery to give expression to his thoughts. On a first level, he expands on the concept of letter writing. On a second level, he contrasts "tablets of stone" and "human hearts" as writing materials, using fragments of Old Testament topics. The existence of a Christian community in Corinth is his strongest means of self-recommendation. This "letter" is inscribed on his heart, and he carries it to all the places he is visiting. So the Corinthians become a pointer to the activity of God in this world. This message is addressed to all human beings and can no longer be ignored by them. Paul himself is not the author of this letter; this honor belongs to Christ alone (NRSV): "you are a letter of Christ (NIV: *'from Christ'* [subjective or source genitive]), prepared by us (διακονηθεῖσα ὑφ' ἡμῶν)." Paul's role is only that of a scribal slave—or better, of a letter carrier, who is responsible for the circulation of the letter; hence other translations render διακονηθεῖσα ὑφ' ἡμῶν as "entrusted to our care" (NJB) or even as "delivered by us" (*NET Bible: New English Translation*, 1st ed. [Spokane, Wa. 2006]; available online at www.bible.org). The antitheses of "ink" and "Spirit" and of "tablets of stone" and "human hearts" leads in a subtle way to the next argument that compares Moses' activity at Mount Sinai with the task of the apostle Paul (2 Cor 3:4-18). Cf. in more detail B. Kuschnerus, *Die Gemeinde als Brief Christi* (Bib. 38), and A. de Oliveira, "'Ihr seid ein Brief Christi' (2Kor 3,3)," in R. Kampling, ed., *Ekklesiologie des Neuen Testaments*, FS K. Kertelge (Freiburg 1996) 356–77.

Exercise 11

To King Ptolemy from Apollodotus (P.Enteuxis 87). This text of 222 BCE is found in O. Guéraud, *ΕΝΤΕΥΞΕΙΣ: Requêtes et plaints addressées au Roi d'Égypt au IIIe siècle avant J.-C.*, Publications de la Société Fouad I de papyrologie. Textes et documents 1 (Cairo 1931), and in J. Hengstl, *Griechische Papyri* (Bib. 1) 83–85. This type of letter is called an "enteuxis," which means a "petition" or "intercession" (LSJ, s.v. ἔντευξις 4) and is derived from ἐντυγχάνω, "to petition, appeal to" (LSJ, s.v. ἐν-τυγχάνω II.3; cf. Acts 25:24); in our text see *l.* 7, τετυχώς (perf. act. ptc. of τυγχάνω), here translated as "I will be *one who has attained* justice" (ἔσομαι . . . τοῦ δικαίου τετυχώς) (cf. LSJ, s.v. τυγχάνω II.2, "*attain, obtain* a thing, c. gen.*"). Although an enteuxis is a non-literary document, it is also not a completely private one, but is rather an official piece of correspondence that was nominally addressed to the Egyptian king, as here King Ptolemy (the year 222 BCE marks the transition from the reign of Ptolemy III Euergetes to that of Ptolemy IV Philopator). In reality the letter was obviously dealt with at lower levels of the bureau-cracy, as represented in our document by titles like "administrator," "governor," and "overseer" (in Greek *oikonomos, strategos,* and *epistatês*). The prescript has a specific form. The king or civil servant comes first as addressee in the dative. This is followed by the usual greeting χαίρειν, and only at the end is the petitioner mentioned as sender in the geni-tive—hence: βασιλεῖ Πτολεμαίωι χαίρειν Ἀπολλόδοτος. Main topics in the body are the description of the case, the petition proper, and the expression of the hope of justice. The closing is formed by the farewell wish εὐτύχει. More formal matters are added by a second hand.

Exercise 12

Letter of recommendation about a freedman (Pliny the Younger, Ep. 9.21). Pliny the Younger (A) writes to "you," i.e., Sabinianus (B). The unnamed recommendee (C) is a freedman of Sabinianus. This implies that in con-trast to other letters of recommendation, the relation between B and C already exists and does not need to be established by the letter itself. But this existing relationship has suffered heavily. Pliny by his intervention intends to restore it. The request of Pliny addressed to Sabinianus strengthens the petition made by the freedman himself. Both invest strong emotional values. A comparison to Paul's letter to Philemon is an obvious next move.

Exercise 13

King Attalus to the council and people of Pergamum (Welles no. 67). The sender of this letter is Attalus III (138–33 BCE). Queen Stratonice is only his "honorary" mother, i.e., in reality an elder female relative. The style of an official decree is evident throughout (cf. Welles xliii). It begins with ἐπεί, "since," in *l.* 1 that introduces a very long and complex subordinate clause. We move on to the two main clauses beginning in *ll.* 9 and 12, but logically they are still part of the subordinate listing of reasons for establishing the cult of Zeus Sabazius. The real main clause starts only in *l.* 15 with κρίνομεν διὰ ταῦτα, "we decided," followed by a final clause that reveals the aim of the whole project: "that the ordinances written by us be entered in your sacred laws." Sabazius, a god of Asia Minor often identified with Zeus, is to be honored with his own cult, and a prominent position as hereditary priests is to be granted to Athenaeus and his descendants. Some overstatements are part of the game. Sabazius is enshrined with Athena as her companion in her temple, located outside the city gates. This is alluded to in *l.* 11. King Attalus seems to trust more in his own edict than in the sacred laws of the city of Pergamum. Therefore he orders in *ll.* 15–16 that his ordinances should become part of the laws of the city (cf. Welles 271). "Dius" in *l.* 17 is the first month of the Macedonian year. The function of Lytus in *l.* 17, who is said to have delivered "from Pergamum" this letter to Pergamum, is not completely clear (cf. Welles 269). He cannot have delivered a royal letter from Pergamum back to the sender, and there is no trace yet of any answer of the city of Pergamum to King Attalus that he could have conveyed. Perhaps he is a local authority who is in the end responsible for the correct handling of royal correspondence, a kind of public scribe or archivist.

Exercise 14

Περὶ δέ in Claudius's letter to the Alexandrians (P.Lond. 1912) and 1 Corinthians. In 1 Corinthians 7:1, περὶ δέ explicitly refers to an earlier letter from the Corinthians: "now concerning (περὶ δέ) the matters about which you wrote." The topic of chapter 7 is marriage, celibacy, and virginity. 1 Corinthians 8:1 introduces the dispute over idol meat, 12:1 the discussion of spiritual gifts, 16:1 Paul's recommendations about the collection for Jerusalem, and 16:12 the plans of a visit from Apollos, all using περὶ δέ. That in each case a new major topic is evoked and introduced, as in the parallel uses of περὶ δέ in the letter of Claudius to the Alexandrians, is obvious. But in the letter of Claudius it is also quite clear that the themes are not freely chosen by the emperor, but rather laid before him by the Alexandrians or their representatives, in oral and perhaps also written form. Although this is disputed, I still feel sympathy with the thesis that in all five cases in 1 Corinthians, not only in 7:1, Paul is answering questions put to him by the Corinthians in their letter.

Exercise 15

Letter from Augustus to Gaius (Aullus Gellius, Attic Nights 15.7.3–5). This letter was written by Augustus on September 23 in the year 1 CE to a certain grandson Gaius (not the future emperor Gaius Caligula) who was fighting the Parthians in the East. Although composed by the emperor himself, it looks more like a simple private or family letter, fascinating and even endearing in its warmth. We also feel that Augustus is truly concerned about Gaius's personal well-being and health. Towards the end, however, political considerations win the day. Augustus must still survive a little while longer in the best interest of the state. A grandson is a potential successor to the throne. Official correspondence of Augustus, written in Greek and fixed on inscriptions, is found in R. K. Sherk, *Documents* (Bib. 16) from p. 294. More letters are mentioned and sometimes also quoted in Suetonius, *Divus Augustus* 71.2–4, and other passages. For more material on the letters of the Roman emperors up to Hadrian see H. Bardon, *Les empereurs et les lettres latines d'Auguste à Hadrien*, Collection d'études anciennes (Paris ²1968), esp. 34–46 on Augustus; cf. also P. Cugusi, *Evoluzione* (Bib. 2) 265–70.

Exercise 16

Categorization of Greek literary letters (chap. 4, sec. A.1). It is possible to group these many texts according to different points of view:

(a) A prominent place is taken by the authentic correspondence that was actually written by the authors who give their name to it. This is the case with Aeneas of Gaza, Dionysius of Antioch, the emperor Julian, Libanius, Procopius of Gaza, and Synesius of Cyrene.

(b) This has to be distinguished from the purely fictitious letters that were intended as a literary composition from the beginning and show a certain tendency toward the epistolary novel. Here we might list Alciphron, Aristaenetus, Chion of Heracleia, Lucian of Samosata, Philostratus, and Theophylact Simocatta.

(c) We may also single out those letters that are certainly pseudepigraphic. This means that letters composed at some later time were intentionally attributed by their author to a much older authority. This is relevant in the case of "Aeschines," "Anacharsis," "Crates of Thebes," "Diogenes," "Euripides," "Heraclitus of Ephesus," "Hippocrates," "Phalaris," "Pythagoras," "Socrates," "Themistocles," and "Xenophon." But in some cases this is difficult to say, and judgment has to be suspended, as with Aristotle, Apollonius of Tyana, Dio of Prusa (Dio Chrysostom), Isocrates, and Plato.

(d) We also have in our collection didactic letters that are not fictitious, cf. Porphyry and perhaps Musonius.

One problem with Hercher's collection is that it simply places side by side these very divergent types of letters, without giving any explanation. The user gets the impression that all these texts are basically similar with regard to provenance, authorship, authenticity, literary character, and so on. Once we have dealt with the quoted letters in the next exercise, we will have to reinforce this criticism of Hercher.

Exercise 17

Analysis of quoted letters from Rudolph Hercher's Epistolographi graeci *(chap. 4, sec. A.2.a).* We may first note that we find here a whole series of letters of kings and generals, written in an official manner, cf. the letters by Antiochus III the Great, Artaxerxes, Nicias, Pausanias, Philip II of Macedonia (and by Pompeius and Mithridates in the Latin writings of Sallust). On the other hand, there are also rulers who address philosophers in a more personal mood—so Alexander the Great, Amasis in his letter to Bias, Antigonus, and Ptolemy II Philadelphus to Eleazar. Another major block of these texts might be classified as philosophical letters. Their authors belong to different philosophical schools. It is surprising that we find so many representatives of the pre-Socratic philosophy and more generally of early Greek philosophy. This is still more astonishing if we consider that most of these letters are taken from Diogenes Laertius, who writes at the end of the third century CE. This leads to the conclusion that there was "a rich production, especially from the first century BC onwards, comprising fictonal letters from almost all the great personalities of the past, from Hippocrates to Alexander" (A. Dihle, *Literature* [Bib. 18] 81).

Exercise 18

Setting and analysis of Tacitus, Hist. *2.98.1–2.* We find ourselves in the turbulent year of three or rather four Roman emperors, i.e., in 69 CE. There is a constant flow of letters sent around by parties that favor one or the other of the fellow competitors for the emperor's throne (cf., e.g., also Tacitus, *Hist.* 2.86.4). The chief commanders of the individual parts of the army cannot avoid opting for one of them. The commander Festus nevertheless succeeds in trimming his sails to the wind by cleverly using different forms and levels of communication. We also see that to be a carrier of letters could be a very risky task in times of war. We knew this already from Caesar, and now it is again confirmed. We should also take note of the varying terminology that Tacitus has at his disposal for characterizing letters as "public letters," "documents," "secret messages," and "proclamations."

Exercise 19

Letters in Achilles Tatius, Leucippe and Clitophon, *Book 5.* Achilles Tatius is now usually dated to the second century CE. A convenient bilingual edition is produced by S. Gaselee, *Achilles Tatius*, LCL (1969). On the story line: The lovers are as usual separated by adverse strokes of fate. First Leucippe recognizes her Clitophon and writes him a letter. He is able to identify its sender because of the handwriting. Its reproachful content is quoted in 5.18.3–6. Clitophon repeats the letter word by word; he sees Leucippe herself standing before him, represented by the letter (5.19.5). He answers with a letter of his own (5.20.5). Some further developments, e.g., that the letters fall into the wrong hands (5.24.1–3), are stereotypical or programmatic, as we have already seen with the letters in Chariton's *Callirhoe*.

Exercise 20

Categorization of Latin literary letters (chap. 4, sec. A.3). The poetic letter is new. Horace and Ovid, later followed by Ausonius, are its main proponents. Several times the didactic letter or the treatise in epistolary form is mentioned, with which we have not yet dealt so far. Better known are the genres of official and private correspondence, which are increasingly transformed into literature in Pliny the Younger and later authors.

Exercise 21

Epicurus, Reply to Colotes 17 (Plutarch, Moralia 1117B). Epicurus has addressed this letter to Colotes, a former disciple who remained in Lampsacus (Lampsakos) when Epicurus moved on. Epicurus evokes a memorable scene: During one of his talks, Colotes out of pure enthusiasm made obeisance before him. This is normally not the behavior of a philosopher, but Epicurus reproaches it only very lightly. He is impressed by the inner disposition that is expressed by this act. We find here an early example of the nearly religious reverence that was addressed to Epicurus already during his lifetime. The reciprocal gesture of Epicurus ("You therefore caused me to consecrate you in my turn and demonstrate my reverence") also demonstrates that philosophical life was valued as a kind of divine existence in the Epicurean school. We know this attitude already from the final paragraph of the letter to Menoeceus.

Exercise 22

Cicero to Quintus (Quint. fratr. 1.3.1–10). We first have to learn about the historical context of this letter. By the instigation of his archenemy Clodius, Cicero has been outlawed and exiled. On his flight he comes to Greece. At the same time, his brother Quintus leaves his province of Asia after his proconsulate there and travels by Athens to Rome. The two brothers did not succeed in meeting en route, which is discussed at the very beginning of the letter. Cicero fears that his own misfortune has also doomed his brother and his whole family. But he also has the hope that his brother might be able to achieve some improvement in Rome. The letter is composed in a very emotional and affective style (cf. W. Jäger, *Briefanalysen* [Bib. 21] 86–90). Also interesting are the allusions to other written and oral messages to his brother. The original date, which usually was eliminated by the collectors and editors of Cicero's letters, has been preserved in this case. With its mention of tears, its laments, but also its very guarded confidence, this letter recalls several passages of Paul's Second Letter to the Corinthians.

Exercise 23

Seneca, Ep. *50.3; 52.5; 53.8; 78.16; 94.1: Determination of New Testament parallels.* The metaphor of the blind asking for a guide in *Ep.* 50.3 reminds us of Luke 6:39 and Romans 2:19. – For *Ep.* 52.5 about the two buildings and their foundations see the concluding parable of the Sermon on the Mount, Matthew 7:24-27. – The appeal to be stirred from slumber by philosophy in *Ep.* 53.8 may be compared with the fragment of an early Christian hymn in Ephesians 5:14: "Sleeper, awake! Rise from the dead, and Christ will shine on you." – The agonistic metaphor of the boxer and the blows he receives in *Ep.* 78.16 has a direct parallel in Paul in 1 Corinthians 9:24-27. – The listing of groups in a household (husband and wife, children and father, slaves and master) gives the bare outline of a household code; cf., e.g., Col 3:18–4:1. – More parallels of varying importance are available in the indices in G. Strecker and U. Schnelle, eds., *Neuer Wettstein: Texte zum Neuen Testament aus Griechentum und Hellenismus*, vol. 2: *Texte zur Briefliteratur* (Berlin 1996) 1818–19.

Exercise 24

Cynic epistles and stories involving Hipparchia: Diogenes Laertius 6.96–97; Diognetus, Ep. *3; Crates,* Ep. *32.* The biographical note of Diogenes Laertius on Hipparchia forms the material basis for the composition of these two letters and gives an example of the often maligned Cynic indecency (Hipparchia used to sleep with her husband in public). – The letter of Diogenes underlines the fact that Hipparchia is the big exception among women and does something not at all typical of them by practicing philosophy. The main point of the letter is the exhortation to carry on. The exchange of letters with her mentor Diogenes should advance and serve that project (note the comparison of correspondence and conversation, typical for letter theory). This insistence on endurance can be seen as a main function of all the Cynic epistles. – In the letter of Crates, Hipparchia is reproached because she has not yet fully put her philosophy into practice. For example, she still cares too much about the material well being of her husband, just like ordinary housewives do. She demonstrates this by her wool-spinning, which is valued in the Pythagorean letters (cf. above chap. 4, sec. A.1) as a characteristic of the ideal wife. A Cynic woman should behave differently. She should care about her husband's philosophy, and nothing else.

Exercise 25

Comparison of Julius Victor, Ars rhetorica 27 with Demetrius, On Style. The common ground between Julius Victor, *Ars rhetorica* 27 (written in Latin) and the excursus on letters in Demetrius, *On Style* consists especially of the importance accorded to friendship and the advice to use proverbs in letters. We have seen the use of Greek phrases in Latin letters (as recommended by Julius Victor) also in Cicero and in the letter of Augustus to his grandson Gaius (see Exercise 15). On the highly valued writing in one's own hand, be it only a postscript, cf. also the following exercise.

Exercise 26

Epistolary topoi in Seneca, Ep. 40.1. The *parousia* topic is quite evident: A letter makes possible, nearly literarily, a discourse among friends, who are together despite the geographical distance between them. The letter is of even higher value than a portrait. The pictorial representation creates an illusion of closeness, but is in reality only a void promise. An important role is given to writing in one's own hand (cf. "the impress of a friend's hand upon his letter"). The identification of a friend's handwriting is compared to recognition in a personal encounter. That the letter form in Seneca is only fictitious (cf. above chap. 4, sec. B.3) does not have any real impact on the value of these observations. Basically, it only helps to emphasize the unbroken relationship of the letter form and key topics like *parousia, homilia,* and *philophronesis*.

Exercise 27

Letter Types in Philostratus of Lemnos, De epistulis *and Julius Victor,* Ars rhetorica 27. In Philostratus of Lemnos, we immediately identify the letter of request or supplicatory letter (making a petition), the apologetic letter (defending ourselves), and the erotic letter (stating our love). In Julius Victor we find the friendly letter, the congratulatory letter, the consoling letter, and the letter of recommendation. Both reflect further situations which might or might not be covered by one of the about fifty types offered by the guidebooks. The complexity and multiplicity of possible acts of communication cannot be strictly systematized. But the gaps left by these two authors also help us to define more precisely the function of letter types. They are devised for coping with such tasks as are given here.

Exercise 28

Rhetorical Analysis of Demosthenes, On the Peace (Or. 5) *and Cicero,* Pro Archia poeta. The speech of Demosthenes of the year 346 BCE belongs to the deliberative genre (cf. §2: "While deliberation is naturally a vexatious and difficult task . . ."). It may be structured in the following way:

§§1–3 *exordium*
§§4–10 *narratio* (returning to speeches formerly delivered, past tense)
§§11–23 *argumentatio* (new pieces of advice)
§§24–25 *peroratio* (introduced by an interjection of the listeners)

Cicero delivers in 62 BCE a forensic speech to save the status of the poet Archias of Antioch as a Roman citizen. It is composed of:

§§1–4 *exordium* (with *propositio* at the end)
§§4–7 *narratio* (life story of Archias)
§§8–30 *argumentatio*, subdivided into the argument proper concerning legal status in §§8–11, an excursus on the importance of education in §§12–16, and a secondary proof taken from Archias's importance as a poet in §§17–30 (strongly epideictic)
§§31–32 *peroratio* ("Save therefore, you judges, a man . . . !").

Exercise 29

Rhetorical analysis of Demosthenes, Ep. 2. Following J. A. Goldstein, *Letters* (Bib. 2) 157–73, §§1–2 form the proem and §3 contains the *propositio*. A *confirmatio* runs from §3 to §20 with three sub-paragraphs (§§3–6; 7–12; 13–20). The epilogue is found in §§21–26. A distinct *narratio* is missing, even though retrospectives in narrative form are scattered throughout the other passages. Goldstein takes this as a main argument for classifying the letter not as forensic (despite its apologetic tendency) but as deliberative.

Exercise 30

Rhetorical analysis of 2 and 3 John. Watson classifies the genre of 2 John as deliberative, of 3 John as epideictic and sees the issue in each case as involving the *status qualitatis*, i.e., the "quality" of Christology in 2 John and of hospitality in 3 John. His structuring of the two letters with the help of rhetorical tools is shown in the following synopsis:

	2 John	**3 John**
(1) *exordium*	v. 4	vv. 2-4
(2) *narratio*	v. 5	vv. 5-6
(3) *argumentatio*	vv. 6-11	vv. 7-12
(4) *peroratio*	v. 12	vv. 13-14

The prescript and final greetings are to be added before the *exordium* and after the *peroratio* (in other words, they do not really fit into the rhetorical arrangement). There are also many stylistic features in both texts.

Thus in the two *exordia* we find, e.g., *traductio* (a seemingly identical word with different meanings), *conduplicatio* (augmentation by repetition of words), *expositio* (interpretation by a slight change of linguistic expression), metaphor, and paronomasia. For a discussion, cf. H. J. Klauck, "Analyse" (Bib. 30).

Exercise 31

Letter of Rabbi Gamaliel in Tosefta, Sanhedrin *2:6.* There are different possibilities of punctuation of the words "Write (?) [T]o our brothers of Upper and Lower Galilee (?) [M]ay your well-being increase!," etc. that determine where the letter actually begins. One possibility is:

> He told him, "Write to our brothers of Upper and Lower Galilee: 'May your well-being increase! We inform you that removal time has arrived. . . .'"

In this case the letter proper begins only with the peace or well-being wish. The sender and addressees are then mentioned only in the narrative frame, since the prepositional phrase "to our brothers" is understood as the indirect object of the command to "write" and is therefore allocated to the narrative rather than to the letter itself. In the following two letters we would therefore have to supply this same verb at the beginning: "*Write also* to our brothers. . . ." The other possibility is the following one:

> He told him, "Write: 'To our brothers of Upper and Lower Galilee, may your well-being increase! We inform you that removal time has arrived. . . .'"

Here the brothers are integrated into the letter form as addressees; only the sender has to be supplied from the narrative frame. This second option is therefore the preferable one. An additional argument in its favor is that in the original, the language changes from Hebrew to Aramaic after the command to "write" (כתוב). This indicates that from there onward an older Aramaic document is quoted. The content confirms the thesis we proposed in our text above (chap. 6, sec. A.5): the Jewish authorities in Judea are addressing the Jewish population in the Diaspora and in the Eastern provinces of the Roman empire to negotiate matters of the festival calendar and, connected to it, the paying of the tithe. The letter from the midrash to Deuteronomy mentioned in chap. 6 n. 11, which has similar content, begins with both the senders and the addressees: "Write: 'From Simeon b. Gamaliel and from Yohanan b. Zakkai to our brothers in the Upper and Lower South, to Shahlil and to the seven southern toparchies: Well-being!'" (Pardee, *Handbook* [Bib. 3] 186).

Exercise 32

Letter of Antiochus IV Epiphanes in 2 Maccabees *9:19-27.* Compared to our standard Greco-Roman letter model, we notice a different sequence in the prescript (in Greek): "To B, greetings, A" = "To his worthy Jewish citizens, greetings, Antiochus." The salutation is expanded by "and good wishes for their health and prosperity." The health wish or *formula valetudinis* in v. 20 contains an allusion to an epistolary thanksgiving of biblical format, though the biblical terms εὐχαριστεῖν and εὐλογεῖν have been avoided, perhaps intentionally. However, this judgment also depends on which version of the text we regard as original, a problem already noted in the text of the exercise.

As noted above, in 2 Maccabees 9:20 the expected sender's side of the *formula valetudinis* or mutual health and well-being formula (see above chap. 1, sec. B.1.b), supplied by the NRSV's addition "I am glad," is lacking in the shorter version of the Greek text printed in Rahlfs (based on Codices A and V), which the REB translates as a complete sentence despite its beginning with εἰ: "May you and your children flourish and your affairs progress as you wish" (εἰ ἔρρωσθε καὶ τὰ τέκνα καὶ τὰ ἴδια κατὰ γνώμην ἐστὶν ὑμῖν·). This shorter, uncial-based Greek text could be original, but only if the sender's half of the formula in v. 20 was so well understood by literary convention at the time of the composition of the epitome portion of 2 Maccabees in the second or first century BCE that it could be left implicit in this context; the formula is sometimes written defectively elsewhere. Clearly, under the circumstances of his illness, Antiochus could hardly have responded ἔρρωμαι or ὑγιαίνω δὲ καὶ ἐγώ. Nevertheless, sensing the absence of some sort of counterbalance to the first half of the sentence, later scribes working in Greek, where the *formula valetudinis* had already passed out of style by 90 BCE (Goldstein 364), produced a longer version, preserved only in the minuscules, that Kappler and Hanhart include in their eclectic text: εἰ ἔρρωσθε . . ., εὔχομαι μὲν τῷ θεῷ τὴν μεγίστην χάριν, "If you are well . . ., I offer to God the greatest thanks" (*Maccabaeorum liber II*, 87). J. A. Goldstein (*II Maccabees*, AB 41A) has a more sophisticated argument, which essentially holds that since the *formula valetudinis* survived longer in Latin letters than in Greek letters, it was the Latin scribes who more readily recognized and preserved it. His solution, based on Latin manuscripts of both the Old Latin and the Vulgate traditions (La^LV), involves both vv. 20 and 21a, which he translates: "If you and your children are well and everything that belongs to you is as you would have it, I am most grateful to God. (21) I myself have been ill, but I remember you with affection" (344; cf. 364–67).

In 2 Maccabees 9:22-25 we find a very complicated sentence structure; after the anticipatory participles οὐκ ἀπογινώσκων, ἔχων, θεωρῶν, and κατανοῶν, the main verb ἀναδέδειχα ("I *have appointed* my son to be king") is finally placed at the end. This still reflects the style of the Hellenistic chancelleries. The end of v. 25 alludes to an attached document, which is no longer presented in the current version. If we recall how Antiochus IV is otherwise presented in 2 Maccabees as a typical tyrant, it seems almost cynical when the king now remembers with affection the esteem and goodwill of the Jews toward him (v. 21) or reminds them of the benefits which he granted to them (v. 26). In its literary context, this may find a somewhat fragile explanation if understood along with the prayer of the king that is reported in indirect speech in vv. 13-17. There the king even promises to become Jewish himself (v. 17). This serves as an example of the repentance of the former adversary of God that comes too late and of his complete emotional collapse. But if we omit vv. 19-20, nothing in the rest of the letter implies that it has been addressed to the Jewish people. The letter still sounds rather pompous when we think of other subjects in the heart of the Syrian empire as addressees, but it is not completely unheard of and ties in with diplomatic conventions. That the dying king must be interested in directing the succession in favor of his son seems plausible a priori. What are the results then for the question of the authenticity or inauthenticity of this letter? In its present context it must be regarded as a fiction, and not even a very successful one. But the author might have used materials from a royal edict that dealt with the problem of succession and was addressed perhaps to the army.

Exercise 33

Comparison of letters in 2 Baruch *78:1-3 and* Jeremiah *29:1-5.* A synopsis of the two texts clearly shows correspondences and differences:

2 Baruch 78:1-3	Jeremiah 29:1-5
1 These are the words of the letter which Baruch, son of Neria, sent to the nine and a half tribes	1 These are the words of the letter that the prophet Jeremiah sent from Jerusalem to the remaining elders
which were across the river	among the exiles, and to the priests, the prophets, and all the people, whom Nebuchadnezzar had taken into exile from Jerusalem to Babylon.
in which were written the following things: 2 "Thus speaks Baruch, the son of Neria, to the brothers who were carried away in captivity:	3 . . . It said: 4 "Thus says the Lord of hosts, the God of Israel, to all the exiles whom I have sent into exile from Jerusalem to Babylon:

Grace and peace be with you.	5 Build houses and live in them;
3 I remember, my brothers, the	plant gardens and eat what they
love of him who created me . . .	produce . . .

The narrative frame is more extended in Jeremiah 29:1-3, but the basic structure is identical. In contrast to *2 Baruch*, where "Thus speaks" represents only Baruch himself, the formula "Thus says" in the prescript in Jeremiah 29:4 is still derived from the prophetic messenger formula: Israel's God himself speaks through the mouth of his prophet. The greeting is missing in Jeremiah, and he also does not continue with a proem, as in *2 Baruch* 78.3. The imperatives of Jeremiah 21:5 and the following verses immediately get to the heart of the matter.

Exercise 34

Hebrew Bar Kokhba document from Wadi Murabbaat (Pap.Mur. 42). We know the addressee Yeshua son of Galgula, camp commander, from Bar Kokhba's letter in Pap.Mur. 43, perhaps written in his own hand. Times of war are invoked in *l.* 5 by the closeness of the "Gentiles," i.e., Romans. Nevertheless there is time for everyday business. The disputed selling and buying and perhaps even military confiscation of a cow has to be settled (we do not have to worry here about the precise implications of this transaction; they are not completely clear, mainly because of philological problems with the reading of the text). The feeling of solidarity among the insurgents is expressed by the final greeting to the house of Israel ("Beth-Israel"). The letter functions at the same time as a record or receipt of the deal about the cow. Therefore we find a list with six names appended at the end, including the two senders or authors of the letter (the form "I" used in the body notwithstanding), the principal affected party (i.e., the former owner of the cow), two witnesses, and a notary. Several individual names are used more than once in this short letter (Yeshua, Elazar, Yehosef, Yaaqov). This shows that the range of personal names was very limited and why patronymics were so important. All signatures seem to have been made by those signing in their own hand.

Exercise 35

Textual criticism of Romans 15–16. What stands out most is the fact that the final doxology in Romans 16:25-27 is moved around quite a bit. In the oldest codices, where 16:24 is completely missing, the doxology is found after 16:23. The majority text of Byzantine times places it between 14:23 and 15:1–16:24. $\mathfrak{P}^{46}$ inserts it between 15:33 and 16:1-23. The effect is that in $\mathfrak{P}^{46}$, Romans 16:23 indeed forms the conclusion of Romans. According to Origen, Marcion used a copy of Romans that consisted only of 1:1–14:23; it did not contain chapters 15–16 at all. This may be taken as evidence of the existence of short versions of Romans covering only chapters 1–14 and perhaps also, in a different tradition, chapters 1–15. The secondary character of 16:24 and 16:25-27 seems to be evident too. But beyond this we have to be rather careful with hypotheses concerning the oldest form of Romans, because the abridged versions are better seen as the result of a later intervention, e.g., an "amputation" of the long version Romans 1–16 by Marcion. On this very complex issue, cf. K. Aland, "Der Schluß und die ursprüngliche Gestalt des Römerbriefes," in idem, *Neutestamentliche Entwürfe*, TB 63 (Munich 1979) 284-301; H. J. Gamble, *Textual History* (Bib. 36).

Exercise 36

Comparison of Plato, Ep. 7 *with 2 Corinthians 2–7*. The apology in 2 Corinthians 2:14–7:4 interrupts the closely connected travelogues in 2:12-13 and 7:5-6. But this is also the case in Plato, in a similar way. He ends the narrative of his first (or second) journey to Sicily in 330B and starts the report of his second (or third) journey in 337E. In between he inserts a long deliberative part. It is interesting that in classical studies this has provoked the suspicion that Plato's seventh letter represents a secondary composition of uneven material—if indeed the letter is not thought to be a forgery from the outset, as it is by some scholars.

Exercise 37

Household codes in Colossians 3:18–4:1 and Ephesians 5:21–6:9. The shorter household code in Colossians and the longer one in Ephesians agree in structure. Wives and husbands, children and parents or fathers, slaves and masters are addressed in turn, exactly in this sequence and always in pairs. There is a surplus of material in Ephesians, most notably in 5:25-33 following the advice on marriage. This is best explained as expansion made in Ephesians on the basis of the text of Colossians. The parallel recommendations of Tychicus in the two letter closings correspond too closely, almost verbatim, as is shown in the following synopsis. This strongly suggests literary dependence. Colossians, with its more elaborate personal notes in 4:7-18, served as model for Ephesians.

Colossians 4:7-8	Ephesians 6:21-22
Tychicus will tell you	Tychicus will tell you
all the news about me;	everything.
he is a beloved brother,	He is a dear brother
a faithful minister,	and a faithful minister
and a fellow servant in the Lord.	in the Lord.
I have sent him to you	I am sending him to you
for this very purpose,	for this very purpose,
so that you may know	to let you know
how we are	how we are,
and that he may encourage your hearts.	and to encourage your hearts.

Exercise 38

Theological opponents in the Pastoral Epistles. The opponents reject marriage (1 Tim 4:3) and require abstinence from certain foods. Two of their leaders maintain, according to 2 Timothy 2:18, "that the resurrection has already taken place." They are accused of an unhealthy interest in "Jewish myths" (Tit 1:14). They are associated several times with "knowing" (Tit 1:16) and "knowledge" (1 Tim 6:20: γνῶσις). All this indicates an early form of Christian Gnosticism with Jewish components, cf. H. J. Klauck, *Religious Context* (Bib. 7) 434–35.

Exercise 39

Muratorian Canon, ll. 39–67: The Letters of Paul. The Muratorian Canon probably reflects the sequence of the letters of Paul that its scribe knew from a New Testament manuscript at his disposal. Hebrews is missing. The order runs: 1 Corinthians, Ephesians, Philippians, Colossians, Galatians, 1 Thessalonians, Romans. This brings us to the number seven, a fact that is emphasized in the text and is correlated to the letters to the seven churches in Revelation 2–3. Second Corinthians and 2 Thessalonians are also known as authentic letters for the "reproof" of these churches. Paul's "private" letters follow in the canon list, but Philemon is placed before Titus and 1 and 2 Timothy (note also the leading position of Titus). Letters to the Laodiceans and the Alexandrians are seen as forgeries of the Marcionites (cf. 2 Thess 2:2).

Exercise 40

Analysis of the epistolary prescript in 1 Peter 1:1-2. The structure is similar to that of the Pauline prescripts. The theological expansion of the address in 1:2a, just before the salutation ("who have been chosen and destined by God the Father and sanctified by the Spirit to be obedient to Jesus Christ and to be sprinkled with his blood"), may be compared with 1 Corinthians 1:2. The mention of the "elect exiles of the Diaspora" in 1:1 reminds us forcefully of James 1:1. At the same time, a leading metaphor—or rather, a cluster of leading metaphors of the whole writing—is introduced. In the salutation we find in Greek, surprisingly, a finite verb ("may it [sc. grace and peace] be in abundance," πληθυνθείη) instead of an infinitive. This has a formal and semantic parallel in a letter of Rabbi Gamaliel to the brothers in the Jewish Diaspora: "May your well-being increase" (in Tosefta, *Sanhedrin* 2:6; see Exercise 31). Like James, 1 Peter is rather close to the category of Jewish letters to the Diaspora. Cf. P. L. Tite, "Function" (Bib. 48).

Exercise 41

Implications of Seneca, Ep. 33.6–7 for 1 John. Seneca says that proverbs or maxims are especially well suited to communication with children. The author of 1 John addresses his audience several times as "(little) children" (2:1, 12, 18, etc.). He confronts them with concise maxims that are summaries of the kerygma in proverbial form. In scholarship this peculiarity has produced source theories; a collection of sentences has been said to form the oldest literary stratum of 1 John (details in H. J. Klauck, *Johannesbriefe* [Bib. 49] 51–56). But this is no longer necessary once the rhetorical strategy behind this feature has been correctly identified.

Exercise 42

Canon list in the Cheltenham Codex. There are thirteen Pauline letters; this means that Hebrews is missing. Of the Catholic epistles, we miss James and Jude. The indignant interjection "One only!" reflects the protest of a scribe, who found three letters of John and two of Peter in his *Vorlage* of this document, but was prepared to accept only 1 John and 1 Peter.

Exercise 43

Formal analysis of the letter to Pergamum in Revelation 2:12-17. Using Revelation 2:12-17 as an example, the structural pattern of the messages to the seven churches can be illuminated in the following way:

adscription and command to write:	And to the angel of the church in Pergamum write:
messenger formula and title of Christ:	These are the words of him who has the sharp two-edged sword:
description of the status quo:	I know where you are living, where Satan's throne is. . . .
call to listen:	Let anyone who has an ear listen to what the Spirit is saying to the churches.
promise-to-the-victor formula:	To everyone who conquers I will give some of the hidden manna, and I will give a white stone, and on the white stone is written a new name that no one knows except the one who receives it.

Exercise 44

Comparison of Dio Chrysostom, Or. 32.7–12 with 1 Thessalonians. In the proem of his speech, Dio constructs a positive portrait of his own character ("ethos"). He emphasizes this by insisting on his pure intentions in §12 and by contrasting himself implicitly with the negative examples that he lists in §11. Paul proceeds in a similar way in 1 Thessalonians 2:1-12 when he highlights his sincerity and his renunciation of financial gain and fame. Cf. A. J. Malherbe, "'Gentle as a Nurse': The Cynic Background to 1 Thessalonians 2," *NovT* 12 (1970) 203–17; also in *Paul and the Popular Philosophers* (Minneapolis 1989) 35–48.

Exercise 45

Comparison of rhetorical outlines of 1 Thessalonians by C. A. Wanamaker and W. Wuellner with other proposals. Wanamaker's model is very close to Jewett's, including an *exordium, narratio, probatio,* and *peroratio.* Only the *transitus,* which is also found in Jewett (but as a subordinate point), is now promoted to the status of a major part of the letter, and the epistolary frame is taken into account in its own right with the inclusion of the pre-script and epistolary closing. Wuellner on the other hand clearly favors the second model that does without a *narratio.* His *exordium* corresponds to our body opening, his *peroratio* to our letter closing. His division of the remaining argument, i.e., the main body of the text, into two large sections (I = 2:1–3:13 and II = 4:1–5:22) pretty much corresponds to our two main topics of the letter body, as explained above. But by introducing the categories of body opening and body closing, we have found additional instruments for the analysis.

Exercise 46

Comparison of the letter of Eirene to Taonnophris and Philo (P.Oxy. I 115) with Pseudo-Demetrius's consoling letter (Epistolary Types 5) and with 1 Thessalonians. Eirene's laconic maxim "one is unable to do anything against such things" in *l.* 10 has a parallel in the model letter in Pseudo-Demetrius (no. 5). Both Eirene and the model letter show that they have shared their readers' pain by their own weeping, while Pseudo-Demetrius also includes a deeper expression of identification ("I felt the deepest grief, considering that what had happened had not happened to you more than to me"). Both texts also advise their readers to console themselves (Pseudo-Demetrius: "exhort yourself just as you would exhort someone else"). Eirene's euphemistic description of the status of the "departed one" as a "fortunate one" (εὔμοιρος)[1] and her exhortation to comfort one another both remind us of 1 Thessalonians, with its description of the dead as οἱ κοιμηθέντες, "those who have fallen asleep" (4:13) and its repeated call to mutual comfort (4:18; 5:11). However, Paul does not participate in the fatalism shown by both texts, P.Oxy. 115 and Pseudo-Demetrius, but rather attributes this attitude to the "others who have no hope" (1 Thess 4:13). His Christian addressees will trust in Israel's God,

---

[1] White, *Light from Ancient Letters* [Bib. 1] 184–85 points to a similarity between Eirene's letter in P.Oxy. I 115 and the model letter of consolation in Pseudo-Proclus, *Epistolary Styles,* type 21, where the deceased person is referred to euphemistically as ὁ μακάριος, "the blessed one" (text of Pseudo-Proclus in Hercher, *Epistolographi graeci* [Bib. 1] 10). However, the parallel to Pseudo-Proclus's consoling letter that one expects to find in Pseudo-Libanius, *Epistolary Styles,* type 21 at §72 (cf. §§4, 25) is lacking due to a lacuna in the text (see Malherbe, *Ancient Epistolary Theorists* [Bib. 2] 79).

who is Lord also of death. On P.Oxy. 115, a real-life example of the genre
of the "consoling letter," cf. in more detail A. Deissmann, *Light from the
Ancient East* (Bib. 1) 176–78.

Exercise 47

Independent epistolary and rhetorical analysis of 2 Thessalonians. Possible
solutions are discussed in the following sections of our main text (chap.
8, sec. B.1.a–b). But you may also compare in advance some of the very
detailed outlines in the secondary literature cited in Bib. 59, e.g., Holland
8–33; Hughes 68–73; Jewett 82–85 (with a chart covering additional
models on 223–25). For an overview see also Aune, *Dictionary* (Bib. 4),
s.v. "Thessalonians, Second Letter to the," 463–65.

Exercise 48

Independent comparison of 2 Thessalonians with 1 Thessalonians. The answer
to this question is the content of the next section (chap. 8, sec. B.2). For
quick information, you may also compare U. Schnelle, *Introduction* (Bib.
7) 320–22.

Exercise 49

*Salvian of Marseille, Ep. 9: Defense of his publishing a treatise under the name
of "Timothy."* The author defends himself very ably, even craftily, without
really showing his hand. He claims to have withheld his own name only
out of humility. He also says that he did not have Paul's disciple in mind
when he used the name of "Timothy," fraught with meaning, to indicate
authorship. This then would not even be real pseudepigraphy, but more
pseudonymity in the modern sense, where a "telling" and transparent
name, in this case "honor to God" (Τιμό-θεος), is used. But this is precisely the heart of the problem. Despite his defense, one suspects that
Salvian really did like the specific association of his writing with the
Timothy known from the Pauline letters, and not just the general depic-
tion of himself as one who naturally gives the honor to God as an
unnamed author (as he claims). In addition to the translation by J. F.
O'Sullivan quoted in the exercise, see the Latin text in G. Lagarrigue,
Salvien de Marseille, SC 176 (Paris 1971) and the translation in A. E.
Haefner, "A Unique Source for the Study of Ancient Pseudonymity,"
Anglican Theological Review 16 (1934) 8–15.

Exercise 50

Independent comparison of Jude and 2 Peter. This task is discussed in detail
below in chap. 8, sec. C.2 (cf. esp. the synoptic table). But it is helpful to
construct a synopsis of your own, which may then be compared with
existing charts in the commentaries on these two letters (in Bib. 62) or in
D. F. Watson, *Invention* (Bib. 50) 164–69.

Exercise 51

Comparison of Watson's rhetorical outline of 2 Peter with our epistolary analysis. D. F. Watson in his rhetorical outline (*Invention, Arrangement, and Style*, 141–42) has an *exordium* in two parts (1:3-11, 12-15), skipping the prescript (1:1-2) and covering the same ground as our proem (1:3-11) and the first part of our body opening (part II.A.1: Testament of the Apostle, 1:12-15). Here one may debate which solution is better. We have already talked (cf. p. 220) about the enthymeme (an abbreviated syllogism, not fulfilling the strict norms of formal logic), and about the inartificial proofs (documents, testimony of eyewitnesses) and artificial proofs (parables, examples, enthymemes) that are mentioned in Watson's outline. The classification of the polemic against opponents in 2:10b-22 as a *digressio* is acceptable, as is the qualification of 3:1-2 as a *transitio*. There is no *narratio*, which is indeed not required in the deliberative genre. The rather long *probatio* (1:16–3:13) is divided into four very different arguments—an only partly convincing procedure. We are again on firmer ground with Watson's mention of the ethos of the author (cf. on 3:10-13) that is first constructed by the text and then used in an argumentative way, as well as the pathos (cf. on 3:13) that wants to elicit an emotional response from the audience. 2 Peter 3:11-12 may indeed be an *epiphonema* or stylized exclamation that sums up or concludes the discourse. Watson defines 3:14-18 as the *peroratio* and subdivides it. However, to characterize 3:14-16 as nothing more than a repetition (*repetitio*) of the basic thoughts of the whole writing (with Watson) means to ignore unduly the first early Christian mention here of Paul's letters outside the Pauline corpus. This feature deserves more attention also on a structural level. By using *adfectus* (or *affectus*, "affect," a state or disposition of mind produced by some influence) as the heading for 3:17-18, Watson alludes to the fact that according to rhetorical theory, it is here in the *peroratio*, "if anywhere," that "we are allowed to release the whole flood of our eloquence" (Quintilian, *Inst.* 6.1.51). Under this heading *indignatio* at 3:17 means "the inflaming of the audience's emotions in order to bring them to take sides against the opposing party," and *conquestio* at 3:18 conversely "the winning of the judges' (audience's) sympathy for one's own party by awakening sympathy for the injustice or misfortune which has befallen or is threatening one's own party" (H. Lausberg, *Handbook* [Bib. 5] §§438–39). But one may certainly imagine conclusions of letters that contain more emotions and arouse more affects than 2 Peter 3:17-18. This leads us again to the key question, namely whether this excessive use of rhetorical terminology really brings any commensurate increase in our understanding of the text.

Exercise 52

Synoptic comparison of the three versions of the apostolic decree: Acts 15:20, 29 and 21:25. A synopsis of the three versions of the apostolic decree in Acts looks as follows:

15:20	15:29	21:25
τοῦ ἀπέχεσθαι	ἀπέχεσθαι	φυλάσσεσθαι αὐτοὺς
τῶν ἀλισγημάτων		
τῶν εἰδώλων	εἰδωλοθύτων	τό τε εἰδωλόθυτον
καὶ τῆς πορνείας	καὶ αἵματος	καὶ αἷμα
καὶ τοῦ πνικτοῦ	καὶ πνικτῶν	καὶ πνικτὸν
καὶ τοῦ αἵματος.	καὶ πορνείας.	καὶ πορνείαν.

. . . to abstain	. . . to abstain	. . . that they should guard themselves with respect to
from the pollutions of idols	from idol meat (pl.)	idol meat (sg.)
and of fornication	and from blood	and blood
and of what is strangled (sg.)	and from what is strangled (pl.)	and what is strangled (sg.)
and of blood.	and from fornication.	and fornication.

Acts 15:29 and 21:25 are more closely related in terms of the order of the items. However, there is still a difference here in grammatical case—the list in 15:29 has the genitive following ἀπέχεσθαι (as in 15:20), the list in 21:25 the accusative of respect following φυλάσσεσθαι αὐτοὺς—and in 21:25 we also have two singulars for "idol meat" and "what is strangled" against the plurals in 15:29. Nevertheless, there is a greater difference between 15:29 and 15:20, because in 15:20 the whole list depends, strictly speaking, on ἀλισγημάτων + genitive = "pollutions of." We also do not find any "idol meat" in 15:20, but simply "idols," and "fornication" and "blood" have traded places in the second and fourth positions.

Exercise 53

Textual criticism of the Apostolic Decree. The most important variant is found in 15:20; the quotations in 15:29 and 21:25 have been partly assimilated to it by omission of one of the four categories. According to Codex D at 15:20, James suggests that the apostles should write to the Gentiles "to abstain from the pollutions of idols and of fornication and of blood, and that whatever they do not want to happen to them, they should not do to others." The formula has been divested of its ritual component by the deletion of "and from what is strangled." It may now be read in a strictly moral sense, dealing only with idolatry, fornication, and murder (i.e., bloodshed). The conclusion by the golden rule in its negative form ties in with this reading. The classification of idolatry, fornication, and murder as the three cardinal vices in later Christian tradition is inaugurated here. Also in early Judaism these three vices were brought together as the main prohibitions of the Torah; this happened no later than the first century CE and may be seen as a preparation for the formation of the so-called seven Noachide commandments.

Exercise 54

Epistolary analysis of the Martyrdom of Polycarp. (For the translation see B. D. Ehrman, *The Apostolic Fathers*, LCL, vol. 1 [2003].) It is not especially difficult to identify the prescript in the document's prologue (sender / recipients / greeting): "The church of God that temporarily resides (παροικοῦσα) in Smyrna / to the church of God that temporarily resides (παροικούσῃ) in Philomelium, and to all congregations of temporary residents everywhere, who belong to the holy and universal church. / May the mercy, peace, and love of God the Father and of our Lord Jesus Christ be multiplied (πληθυνθείη)." By πληθυνθείη (cf. 2 Pet 1:2; Jude 2, etc.) and also by παροικοῦσα (cf. *1 Clement* preface), the author continues the Jewish tradition of letters to the Diaspora. The next verse in 1:1 opens with an epistolary aorist: "We *are writing* you (ἐγράψαμεν), brothers, about those who were martyred, along with the blessed Polycarp. . . ." Typical of letters is also the request in 20:1b: "When you have learned these things, send our letter to the brothers who are further afield. . . ." A doxology in 20:2a is followed by a request to convey greetings and forwarded greetings from others: "Greet all the saints. Those who are with us greet you, as does Evaristus, the one who is writing the letter, with his entire household" (cf. Rom 16:22). In a postscript in 22:1 the author says farewell by using nearly the same words that we found in the two letters of Apion with which we began: Ἐρρῶσθαι ὑμᾶς εὐχόμεθα, ἀδελφοί, etc.

Index of Ancient Sources

NEW TESTAMENT

APOCRYPHA AND PSEUDEPIGRAPHA

EARLY CHRISTIAN LITERATURE

Index of Authors

Index of Subjects